U0876136

Transportation Planning

Wang Yuanqing　Ma Shuhong
王元庆　马书红　编著

人民交通出版社股份有限公司
China Communications Press Co.,Ltd.

图书在版编目(CIP)数据

交通规划 = Transportation Planning:英文 / 王元庆,马书红编著. — 北京:人民交通出版社股份有限公司, 2018.4

ISBN 978-7-114-14594-0

Ⅰ.①交… Ⅱ.①王… ②马… Ⅲ.①交通规划—高等学校—教材—英文 Ⅳ.①U491.1

中国版本图书馆 CIP 数据核字(2018)第 056352 号

书　　名:**Transportation Planning**
著 作 者:王元庆　马书红
责任编辑:李　晴
责任校对:张　贺
责任印制:张　凯
出版发行:人民交通出版社股份有限公司
地　　址:(100011)北京市朝阳区安定门外外馆斜街 3 号
网　　址:http://www.ccpress.com.cn
销售电话:(010)59757973
总 经 销:人民交通出版社股份有限公司发行部
经　　销:各地新华书店
印　　刷:北京印匠彩色印刷有限公司
开　　本:787 × 1092　1/16
印　　张:29.5
字　　数:690 千
版　　次:2018 年 4 月　第 1 版
印　　次:2018 年 4 月　第 1 次印刷
书　　号:ISBN 978-7-114-14594-0
定　　价:58.00 元
(有印刷、装订质量问题的图书由本公司负责调换)

Preamble

For new transportation planners who have ever taken transportation planning courses, they typically realize that the challenges in practice are much more complex than what they met in learning transportation planning textbooks: unable to clearly understand the unsustainability of the dependence of human on cars and do not know the standard of a good planning, leading to more traffic congestions and more serious urban traffic pollution; know few about the computer programming needed in transportation modeling thus feel hard to get started to develop transportation models; unable to effectively evaluate the reliability of the output from planning models thus hard to know the future traffic trends and identify core problems in planning areas; fail to select reasonable indices that can be used to evaluate the effect of problem-solving for different planning scenarios; and unable to appropriately integrate new and old planning techniques in planning design.

To the above challenges in transportation planning classes, the authors have been devoting to the improvements of contents and modes in transportation planning class teaching since 1990. In addition, the authors have actively participated in high-level research and consulting activities with multiple objectives and multiple levels in the field of transportation planning, and have finished many research projects at national level, such as projects from Ministry of Education, Ministry of Transport, and National Natural Science Foundation of China. The authors have also worked on many research and consulting projects funded by international agencies, including the World Bank, the Asian Development Bank, the American Energy Foundation, the Reason Foundation, and the Australian Research Foundation.

What is more, the authors have conducted multi-modal transportation planning for many regions, including the provinces of Shaanxi, Liaoning, Zhejiang, Guangdong, Hebei and the cities of Xi'an, Ningbo, Guangzhou; their proposed plans have been highly evaluated and well implemented in these regions.

After 20 years of continuous efforts, the transportation planning course has obtained fruitful achievements. The authors have worked with more than 200 graduate students and nearly 1000 undergraduate students to explore how to efficiently learn the key knowledge and skills needed in transportation planning, at the same time, to help establish a solid and diversified knowledge and methodology system for students to work in different areas in the future, such as research, consulting, decision-making, management, technology development, large-data mining and investment evaluation.

The course has been supported by the Ministry of Education, Education Department of Shaanxi Provincial Government, and Chang'an University in China. It has been granted the National Bilingual Teaching Demonstration Course, the Shaanxi Province Excellent Course and the Shaanxi Province Excellent Resources Sharing Class (http://jiaotongguihua.chd.edu.cn/). It has received a large number of reading online from various sectors of society and won the Second Prize of Teaching Achievement in Shaanxi Province, the First Prize of Transportation Education Science Excellent Achievement Award of China Transportation Education Research Association and the Third Prize of the Seventh Higher Education Scientific Research Achievement Award in Shaanxi Province. This course collaborated with the iCourse in 2017, which allows readers to learn the course online (http://www.icourses.cn/home/).

Compared with other transportation planning textbooks, this textbook strengthens the contents on transportation system and its characteristics, regional transportation models, model calibration and renewal, development of planning scenarios, index system of scenario evaluation and whole life-cycle cost analysis, which are in great demand but used to be overlooked. In addition, this textbook chooses the Cube software, which has a strong structure and is easy to apply multi-iteration molding, as a practical transportation model platform during the tutorial. The Cube's modeling idea, calculation parameters and data flow organization can also be used as reference for other transportation planning software packages. To improve students' thinking and application skills, the textbook adds a large number of practical examples based on the authors' practice, including many examples of practical applications. In view of an increasing importance of movement analysis (OD or PA analysis) in recent years in urban or regional planning, rail roads, public transit, urban design and large data calculation, the authors applied the "0 basis" concept in the book writing to make it easy for readers to learn.

The completion of the book gained support and help from many predecessors and friends in transportation field. Thanks to Prof. Wang Binggang (Chang'an University), Mr. Zhou Wei (Ministry of Transport), Ms. Sun Xiaoduan (University of Louisiana), Mr. Sam Zimmermans (World Bank) and Mr. Wang Quanlu (Argonne National Laboratory in the United States) for providing directions to the authors of this book. Thanks to Prof. Wang Wei (Southeast University) Prof. Yang Xiaoguang (Tongji University) Prof. Liu Xiaoming (Ministry of Transport), Prof. Lu Huapu (Tsinghua University) Prof. Shao Chunfu (Beijing Jiaotong University), Prof. Chen Yinsan (Chang'an University) and Prof. Wu Qiongqi (Chang'an University) for enlightening the authors from the beginning of their carrier.

Thanks to Mr. Ali Mekky (University of Ryerson, Canada) for the permission of using his reputable teaching materials in the book. Thanks to Prof. Pei Yulong (Northeast Forestry University), Prof. Pan Haixiao (Tongji University), Prof. Kuan Hongzhi (Beijing University of Technology), Mr. Kong Lingbin (China Regulatory Institute), Mr. Chi Qiuzhi (Transportation Department), Mr. Cheng Lihong and Mr. Chiao Guoan (American Citilabs Corporation in Asia), Mr. Ong Wichang and

Ms. Rowe (MVA Transportation Consulting Co., Ltd.), Prof. Han Sunsheng (University of Melbourne), Prof. Li Zongzhi (Illinois Polytechnic University), Mr. Ho Dongquan (Energy Foundation), and Ms. Jiang Yulin (Ministry of Transport to the Department), Mr. Zhang Xuekong (Taiwan university) and Mr. Xu Kangming (3E Traffic Consulting Company) for many years of guidance and help. Thanks to Mr. White at WSP for providing insights on Transportation modeling.

Thanks to the graduated students in my research group, including Zhang Fuyong, Feng Liguang, Zhang Zhimin, Zheng Yubin, Liu Zhije, Li Lei, Wang Zhicheng, Wang Li, Wang Mei and Jiang Shan, Ji Shujuan, Xu Zhiman, for their contributions to the book, and also thanks to the Office of Teaching Affairs of Chang'an University, School of Highway and the Colleagues of the Transportation Research Institute for their support.

Preface

Transportation Planning is a compulsory course of transportation engineering. It is one of the professional skills that a transportation planner needs to master. It has its own basic theory, also is integrated with a variety of basic curriculum knowledge, mainly including transportation engineering, civil engineering (roads, bridges, construction), economics, mathematics, systems engineering and computer applications. It is a comprehensive subject which integrates theory and practice; and the areas of learners engaging are diversified.

This book has 12 chapters, the contents in each chapter are presented as follows:

Chapter 1 introduces the background, development, and basic concepts of transportation planning, and discusses the location, composition and characteristics of transportation system.

Chapter 2 describes the types of transportation data, collection methods, commonly-used analytical methods and software packages, and some new data collection and processing methods.

Chapter 3 discusses the concept, structure, and classification of transportation model. It focuses on the basic principles of the Four-stage model and some typical transportation models.

Chapters 4 to 7 introduce the Four-stage model, namely tip generation, trip distribution, model split, and trip assignment. This is the core and key part of transportation planning theory. Each chapter narrates the basic principle and operation method of one step.

Chapter 8 talks about the contents of model calibration and validation.

Chapter 9 introduces the process and layout method of public transportation network planning, and the basic contents of public transportation facilities planning, which involve public transportation model modeling and public transportation service index calculation.

Chapter 10 presents several common methods of the generation of planning scheme from the aspects of regional network arrangement, urban center road network layout and urban new area planning.

Chapter 11 systematically introduces the whole life-cycle calculation method for planning project construction, including the basic methods and related cases of whole life analysis and evaluation, and also explains the basic principles and steps of game theory and Monte Carlo simulation to provide a reference for planning scheme choose.

Chapter 12 discusses the common indexes of different transportation planning schemes and the common methods of multi-index comparison. Readers can expand reading on the basis of the introduction of this chapter and study the transportation evaluation technology deeply.

In addition to basic theories, this book also provides a large number of planning practice examples from the author's planning practice and academic research to make the book easier for readers to understand.

Wang Yuanqing Ma Shuhong

Qctober, 2017

Author Introduction

Wang Yuanqing

Prof. Wang is a Level-Ⅱ Professor in the School of Highway at Chang'an University. He is the Director of Transportation Research Institute and the BRT Research Center of School of Highway. He has finished several teaching reform projects, such as the Shaanxi Province Innovation Experiment Area of Transportation Engineering Personnel Training Mode and the National Bilingual Teaching Demonstration Course of Transportation Planning. He has won the award of New Century Talents of Ministry of Education and Young Teacher Program of Huo Yingdong, as well as more than a dozen awards from the China Highway and Transportation Society, Shaanxi Province, Guangdong Province and Zhejiang Province. Focusing on transportation behavior research and theoretical research on quantitative analysis technology, Prof. Wang has successfully applied his research in transportation planning, public transport improvement, low-carbon transportation, transportation design optimization and intellectualization. He has completed more than 100 research projects, and published more than 160 academic papers and books, including 12 SCI-indexed papers, 36 EI-indexed papers, and 5 books.

Ma Shuhong

Ms. Ma is an associate professor in the School of Highway at Chang'an University.

In recent years, she has taught several transportation courses, including "Transportation Engineering" "Parking Planning and Designing" "Transport Hub and Static Transportation Facilities Design", and "Transportation Planning Principle". Since 2002, she has been engaged in research work on transportation planning, transportation economy, and transportation safety. She has published more than 30 SCI-indexed, EI-indexed, CSSCI-indexed or CSCD-indexed papers, and completed more than 10 research projects. Her research areas include highway network planning and evaluation, transportation economy, and policy research.

Authors: Wang Yuanqing, Ma Shuhong

Teachers who have assisted book writing:

Deng Yajuan, Ma Chaoqun, Han Rongliang, Yu Qian, Bai Qiang

Graduate students who have assisted book writing:

Chapter 1: Jiang Shan, Yuan Bo

Chapter 2: Liu Yuanyuan, Yang Ye, Ji Shujuan, Zhang Zihe

Chapter 3: Liu Yuanyuan, Hu Tengfei

Chapter 4: Gao Yanan, Ma Jinlei, Wang Zhen

Chapter 5: Gao Yanan, Zhang Jiaojiao, Wu Rui

Chapter 6: Gao Yanan, Yu Zhoulin, Li Di, Zhu Liang

Chapter 7: Gao Yanan, Yang Xiangyi

Chapter 8: Ding Ji, Zhang Junjie

Chapter 9: Liu Yuanyuan, Fu Xing, Liu Xiaojie

Chapter 10: Cao Hui, Xu Zhiman

Chapter 11: Liu Yuanyuan, Feng Shuo, Huang Yan, Zhou Rong

Chapter 12: Liu Yuanyuan, Feng Shuo

Contents

Chapter 1

Introduction

1.1 Overview

1.1.1 Transportation System is a Complex System

A complex system is a system composed of many components which may interact with each other to achieve a certain purpose through mutual restraint. It is an approach to study how the changes of system components lead to the variation of the whole system, and how the system interacts with its environment. The studying approach of a complex system provides reference for transportation planning which is concerned with the multi-factor interaction and developed rapidly since 1960.

There are three aspects of modern complex system research: a. How the interaction causes a change in the mode of behavior; b. The possibility of changes; c. The formation and evolution of complex systems. There are five characteristics of transportation systems:

· Adaptive/self-organizing. The system is composed of various components which have the ability of self-adaptation, self-learning and self-organization. The components can adjust their behavior and structure through self-learning to adapt to external and internal changes. The traffic participants will organize themselves to adapt to the system changes when the traffic capacity is insufficient.

· Uncertainty. Uncertainty is related to randomness and chaos. Randomness means irregular, unpredictable behavior and Chaos is the internal disorder. For example, the occurrence of traffic accidents are usually random or cannot be determined, and the impact of the accident may be non-significant or may lead to large-scale traffic system paralysis. When the road traffic system is almost saturated, the travel time of people changes with the congestion.

· Emergence. Emergence is the continuous interaction between the various parts of the system, resulting in system behavior constantly changing with time. After a period of time, it will evolve some new characters and modes. The emergence is similar to qualitative change. From the beginning of the system interaction, the parts of system can self-organize, self-coordinate, enlarge and develop, then qualitative change happened.

· Pre-determination. It decides the development trend of complex systems. It compares the expected state of future and the actual state of the system.

· Open. It refers to the exchange of material, information and energy between the system and the external environment and the subsystems. The complexity of the systems includes not only the system itself, but also the complexity of the exchange with the external environment.

Transportation system is a complex system. The system consists of transportation facilities, participants and vehicles. Transportation facilities include traffic network subsystem, traffic terminal subsystem, control subsystem, data and information collection, distribution, transmission subsystem. Transportation system participants, known as stakeholders, include not only travelers, but also operators, government officials, other decision makers, the land owners, practitioners, and so on. There are a large number of participants in the transportation system, leading to a variety of requirements, so it is more complex than other systems to coordinate and compromise the interests of all parties.

Some urban policymakers are concerned about whether the road is funky, bustling, how to reduce operating and maintenance costs, and rarely consider the potential costs of the economy and the environment caused by the later congestion; the developers of the road and the service providers care about their construction progress and profitability, they believe that government should take other ways to solve the traffic congestion caused by the development of facilities; track and bus operators expect transit priority, but the corridor traffic management impact is limited; vehicle manufacturers, new energy transport facilities providers, information technology providers concerned about their market share of the traffic corridor car (people) flow, however, the environmental effects are often not elaborate. Whether the traffic corridor will be congested, is the root causes of China's years of urban congestion and the reasons for the continued expansion of environmental impacts.

Source: *Author observation.*

The transportation system is a multi-level subsystem shared by regional economy, environment, culture and social system (Fig. 1-1). As a subordinate subsystem, the transportation system should consider the impact of its own development on environmental systems, economic systems, cultural systems, social systems, etc.. If the impact does not meet the requirements of superior system, the transportation system has to adjust itself to meet the development needs of the superior system. Transportation development relies on superior systems' support, for example, when the transportation system is difficult to achieve self-finance, the traffic development is often considered through the regional development to make up for transportation investment, or we will use other income to make up for transportation construction, operation, maintenance costs, in order to achieve the sustainable development of the whole region. Fig. 1-1 shows the composition of the transportation system and its internal relationship, and the relationship between the transportation system and the external system. It can be seen that the transportation system is a hierarchical system composed of various subsystems, components and their interrelations, including facilities, participants, transportation development goals, countermeasures and performance of four interrelated parts along with their influence and feedback with the external system. The internal subsystems' feedback and impact reflect the complexity of the transportation system, and the feedback of external environment, these interactions may change over time, and may produce mutations, that is, the relationship may be non-linear.

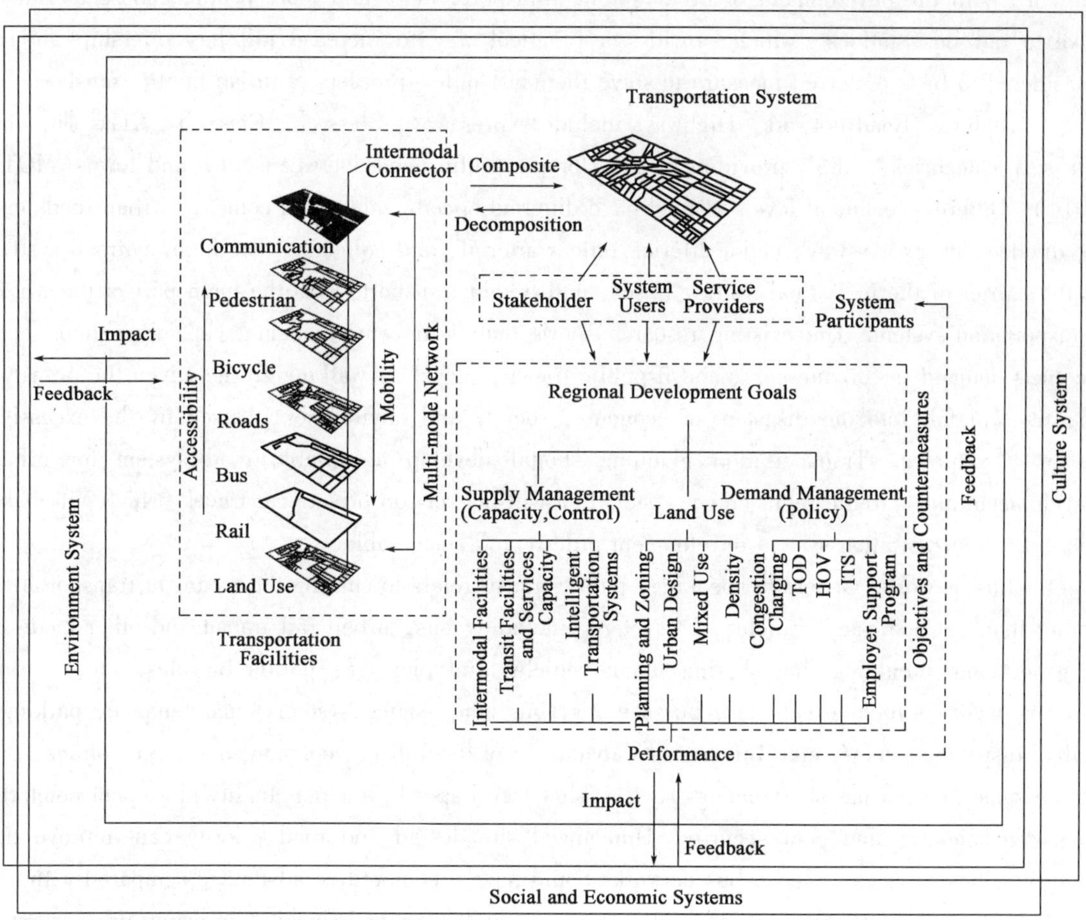

Figure 1-1 Components and relationship of transportation system

(1) Transportation facilities

The transportation facilities consist of subsystems of different transportation modes, terminals of different modes, and information/communication subsystems.

· Pedestrian (Walking) network. Walking is the best choice for people to travel in a short distance. It is an essential and complementary part for any other travel mode. The walking system is an important component of a city's business and tourism industry. According to the function of regional pedestrian system, it can be divided into walking area or channel, public transport or multi-mode traffic transfer area, and the multi-purpose road with pedestrian traffic function. The optimization of the walking system helps to improve the satisfaction of the transport service.

· Bicycle network. Bicycle has the advantages of convenience, flexibility, low cost, environmental-friendly and strong adaptability. The bike is also durable and easy to maintain. In addition, it has less noise, vibration, exhaust gas. Its shortcomings are slow speed, poor safety, and uncomfortableness. Bicycle network can be divided into bicycle road, bicycle channel with the isolation facilities, bicycle roads of the community, multi-purpose road with bicycle traffic function. In the 1-3km range, the bicycle has a travel advantage, but there is a competitive relationship with the car. With the development of urban public transport, more and more people choose to ride a bike to rail/bus stations, which provides a practical way to increase rail/bus ridership and is considered to be a preferred measure to solve the "last mile" problem of urban public transport.

· Highway/Road network. Highways include expressway, Class Ⅰ, Class Ⅱ, Class Ⅲ, and Class Ⅳ categories, mainly providing service for the traffic needs between cities and towns (MOT, 2014). Different technical levels of road have different speed, safety and comfort. Urban roads can be divided into expressway, major arterial, minor arterial, and collector. The highway/road system is the carrier of the individual traffic, buses, and freight transport; it is the main part of the whole transportation system. The existing research shows that if the environmental capacity cannot meet people's demand for private cars, and if public transit, bicycles, walking are not given the priority, the city will fall into the disasters of economy, society and environment caused by the excessive usage of vehicles. Transportation planning should develop a suitable road system for urban development and a traffic replacement system that will not rely on private car travel, which will make the entire transportation system development orderly and sustainable.

· Bus network. Generally speaking, public transit refers to sharing the means of transportation rather than the dedicated vehicles of travelers, including bus, urban rail transit and other mode of transportation (including time-sharing rental vehicles and bicycles, public bicycles, etc.). Bus network facilities include vehicles, bus stations, bus lane, signal systems, maintenance, parking, hubs, dispatch systems, etc. Bus has the advantages of flexibility, economy, and large volume, but at the same time, it has shortcomings such as slow travel speed, low punctuality rate, poor comfort, poor convenience, and poor security. Humanized site design and road priority can improve the quality of bus services. A good bus network should have a competitive advantage compared with car traffic in terms of service coverage, travel speed, and carrying capacity in major urban areas. Moreover, financial subsidies and construction costs should be affordable for government. Bus stations, hubs, corridors, and sites need a certain range of land. Therefore, urban planning should focus on and prioritize the public transit resources. Transit Oriented Development(TOD) pattern is often applied internationally, integrating public transit planning with the surrounding commercial, business and residential development, applying the Parking and Ride (P&R) mode, with the integrated parking and large-volume transit hub facilities, providing convenience for the suburban inhabitants to transfer, it can better meet the residents travel needs.

· Rail transit network. The rail transit network is a multi-level network system, including subway, light rail, tram, and external links of high-speed rail, ordinary railway, and suburban railway. Rail transit is an important part of the urban transportation system development. It is also an important part of the public transit subsystem. It has the advantages of fast speed, large volume, environmental protection, and safety, and also has the disadvantages of high cost and limited accessibility. The rail transit is not only the main support of the urban passenger corridor, but also the important channel between the city clusters. The intercity railway can play a role in the internal channel which is densely populated or needs timeliness. The transfer efficiency between rail transit and other modes of transportation has a very important role in its development.

· Information/Communication network. The information network is an important means to link the various subsystems of the whole transportation system. It is also an important link between the transportation operators, the public, and the managers. Information network functions the communication between systems by the information interaction. In recent years, the technology has developed rapidly, which includes integrated and automated data collection, remote transmission and e-commerce, traffic information inquiry and arrangement which combined with the communication technology, real-time traffic identification and route selection, service notice and real-time modification, electronic ticket purchase. It has brought great help to travelers, and should be considered synchronously in transportation planning of traffic facilities.

· Hub subsystem. In terms of passenger transport, the task of the hub subsystem is to accomplish the transfer between bicycle, rail transit, bus, walk, private car and other transportation modes. The mobility and accessibility between bicycles, rail transit, bus, and other subsystems are different; there are different advantages among the different traffic modes. Only when the transfer between the transportation modes is smooth and convenient, the high-quality transport services can be provided. This requires the transportation planning to be done with network planning and its connection to meet the needs of users of the system. For freight transportation, the task of hub subsystem is to complete cargo transshipment between aviation, rail transit, and highway, which requires the hub to possess the functions of warehousing and separation. Hubs occupy a large area and are crowded or cargo-intensive, so these features should be taken into account when we choose the location. At the same time, the hub can be designed combining business and office to achieve transit-oriented development based on these characteristics.

(2) System participants

Transportation system participants include not only travelers, but also operators, governments, landowners and practitioners, and businesses associated with the transportation.

· System users. In addition to every subsystem network, the transportation system includes the users of each network, i. e. pedestrian flow and traffic stream. The users and vehicles are the main body of the whole network; and their behavior affects the operation of the whole system. By inducing and managing the user behavior of the system, the operation of the whole transportation system can be effectively improved, such as management of the purchase or restriction of cars by policy, at the same time, improving the service quality of public transit to induce residents to use public transit.

· Stakeholders. The construction of the transportation system involves many parties, such as government, operators, regional residents, landowners, planners, etc. All stakeholders have their own considerations. For example, the government needs a smoother traffic, better landscape to increase government support rates. Operators want to use the least investment to obtain greater benefits. And residents hope to travel smoothly, economically, conveniently, safely and comfortably. So it is necessary to coordinate the interests of all parties in the construction of the whole transportation system to realize the sustainable development.

Ban the motorcycles and electric bicycle, multi-party game

In order to rectify the traffic order, the ban on motorcycles and electric bicycle policy was put forward. The policy affected the express industry greatly. The cause of this embarrassing situation is quite complex, on the surface, it is a simple "one size fits all" law enforcement, in fact, it is the result of multiple interests of the game. Now, Beijing and Shenzhen are implementing this policy, especially in Shenzhen, under a series of government "joint meeting", the city administration, traffic police, and even special police team unified action. Data show that in the first round of rectification operations, 17975 *of electric bicycles were seized,* 19 *people of Express Enterprises were detained.*

As early as 2009, *China's electric bicycle industry try to implement the policy, but it was opposed by the electric car business unanimously. The main reason for many enterprises to oppose is the interests of the game.*

Source: *Democracy and Law Times*, 2016.

· Facility service provider. Another important participant in the transportation system is the facility service provider. Traffic facilities are the basis of the transportation system, the system supply depends mainly on the basis of traffic construction. The large hubs, can not only provide traffic facilities for travelers, but also enable the transport operators to gain profits.

(3) Goals and objectives

Transportation system is a multi-target system. The basic goal of the system is to provide mobility and accessibility to society, people and goods. Mobility refers to the ability to move freely and conveniently; accessibility means the availability of transport services. Mobility and accessibility are relative concepts. Closed, dedicated, access control will achieve a higher mobility. However people must spend more time to get this service, which has a lower accessibility. The layout and control of transportation system must be based on the demand characteristics of people and economic constraints to balance the mobility and accessibility.

Transportation, life, work and recreation together constitute the four functions of the city, the layout of different functional sites of the city. Commercial development needs to consider the development of its traffic conditions. Traffic is the organizer of urban space, which requires the transportation system was planned from the perspective of service and organization of urban and rural development. With the globalization of the market, the rise of internet shopping, the rapid and economic development of transportation and industrial or regional economy is becoming more and more important. Convenient and economical transportation network is becoming the precondition of the high level of regional economy.

In addition, the existing research also found that transportation construction is an important condition to drive regional development. In addition to the construction period investment which led to the increase of local income, road construction can promote the exchange of technology, experience, resources, and then improve the conditions of areas. The highway as the core, supporting the improvement of both sides greening, landscape, improves the rural infrastructure and development of tourism resources to promote the beautiful countryside, urban and rural integration.

Transportation planning is aimed at sustainable development within the planning area. So that people travel more economical, convenient, safe, comfortable, the economy is more prosperous, the society is more harmonious and the environment is cleaner have become the goals of transportation planning. The complexity of the transportation system is created by the human complexity and the multi-objective of the system. So the balance of the system is relatively stable after the game. Transportation planning must be based on the characteristics of the system to achieve a better balance of transportation system through the layout planning, control and policy.

(4) Countermeasure subsystem

There are multi-objectives of transportation system, such as, improving the system's mobility, accessibility, stimulating economic growth, reducing environmental pollution, increasing social security and stability, improving the sense of belonging. There must be contradictions among goals, such as higher accessibility must correspond to lower mobility, the pursuit of rapid economic development may lead to pollution. In order to coordinate the non-linear relationship between the objectives and avoid the low traffic performance, the transportation planning needs to consider how to balance the system's internal and external relationship. Existing research suggests that good balance should be people-oriented, that is the movement of people and goods should be safe, convenient, comfortable and economical. Sustainability, that is the operation and maintenance of facilities, finance and traffic environment of its impact should be sustainable. So it is necessary to choose appropriate measures from the three aspects of supply management, demand management and land use management in transportation planning to control the development direction of the whole transportation system.

· Supply management. Supply management is to improve system performance by choosing to add new facilities or change the operation of existing facilities, such as the construction of new roads, the improvement of traffic signals, changing the congestion area to a single line, and the addition or alteration of existing lane to increase bus lanes. Intelligent Transportation Systems (ITS) technology is developing rapidly, and it can coordinate the traffic behaviors of participants with better information, in order to improve the safety, effectiveness and service capability of the transportation system.

The method of increasing traffic facilities is an effective way to alleviate traffic congestion in the short term, which can meet the demand by increasing supply. However, in the case of long-term development, the mere expansion of supply is likely to stimulate the increase in the number of vehicles, causing more serious congestion. The existing practice found that in cities, simply increasing lanes to satisfy car travel always lag behind the growth rate of the car. Transportation construction should consider the development of man, vehicle and road from the perspective of long-term equilibrium, so it can relieve congestion effectively. Therefore, it is very important for the transportation planner to provide a supply management strategy that meets the requirements of sustainable development, which based on the short-term and reasonable forecast results, not just the current traffic conditions.

Supply management is mainly to seek traffic counter measures from the traffic capacity and system control direction. At present, the supply management of the system can be studying from the following aspects: ITS management of the supply, the use of the Internet, intelligent information management of the transportation system; improving facilities and service quality, increasing the capacity; improving the transfer and connect facilities to improve travel efficiency; improving the energy use and promoting low-carbon travel.

· Demand management. Demand management is to adjust the traffic system operation state to a more affordable and sustainable equilibrium state, by limiting the city's excessive car travel and optimizing the operation of the whole traffic system, which includes bus priority. That is public transit travelers get better travel services to enhance the advantages of bus travel by adding or adjusting the use of facilities, which will increase the number and the proportion of bus trips, and can make the whole transportation system works better. Non-motorized traffic priority can providing a good walk, bike travel environment to improve the service of "the last mile". High occupancy lane (HOV) is adjusting the most efficient intermediate lane in each direction of the road in city's congested area to a lane that multiple people can use and encourage people to commute to work then reduce excessive commuting car traffic. Transit Oriented Development (TOD) is giving the priority construction of transit system in the early stages of urban development, then to do the construction of business, office and residence around the hub or transit site. It will attract people to choose public transit, and reduce vehicle travel. Parking demand management is to construct the Parking and Rider system around large-volume public transit site in the city edges. Then to restrict the parking time of the city center and reduce the number of parking spaces in congested areas, increase fees or limit allowable hours to reduce or inhibit excessive vehicle travel in the city center.

Demand management is mainly conducted from the policy aspect. Commonly used methods are: ITS management of the demand, that is, to provide road information for travelers through intelligent information technology, then to guide travelers to the right road; congestion pricing and other policies to reduce total travel demand during peak periods to ease traffic congestion; implement public transport priority policy, to encourage companies to implement employee travel support plan, such as, commuter car provision and bus subsidy system.

· Land use management. Land use is associated with urban traffic. Simply speaking, travel generation mode, travel volume and travel distribution form are the major basis for spatial distribution and land use. In the long term, land use and spatial distribution have an impact on travel mode, and in turn, the accessibility and mobility have an impact on land use. Therefore, in order to avoid traffic problems, we should pay attention to the coordination of land planning, transport services and local overall strategies, such as, in high-density development of congested urban centers, increasing the proportion of parking spaces will increase the number of parking and traffic then resulting in congestion strength, expansion of congestion time. Urban construction should take into account the impact of urban traffic, urban transport demand then urban transport supply capacity can be adapted.

(5) Performance

The measure index of the operation state of transportation system, such as, delay time, cost of tickets, travel economy and so on, can be called performance measures. From the perspective of the investment, performance can be measured by the Financial Net Present Value (FNPV), the Economic and social Benefit Cost Ratio (EBCR), the yield rate (EIRR), and so on. Traffic is people-oriented, therefore these performance indicators are gradually paid attention. The driver usually consider time efficiency to decide which travel mode to choose, buses or cars travel; the big city citizens are like to travel in an hour of time to select work, living and shopping place, so people focus on the first arrival, hour lap, bike lane width and continuity and other performance indicators, these details will be introduced in the relevant chapters in this book gradually.

(6) Impact and feedback

Transportation system is a hierarchical system composed of various subsystems, components and their interrelations, but it is not isolated, there are internal hierarchy and interacts with other external systems, such as environmental system, economic system, social system. There are mutual influence and interdependence between the systems, and the internal and external systems of the transportation system are connected at any time.

· Impact Range. Traffic impact can be divided into internal and external impacts according to the scope of influence. The internal impact of the system can be divided into global influence, regional influence, city cluster and urban area influence. The transportation network should achieve the balance of supply and demand overall, it is concerned about the balance between the entrance, the mode, the line and the transfer ability. There are some hierarchical structures within the transportation system. The road network is the skeleton expressway, including main trunk arterial road, collector, national road, provincial road and county road. The public transport includes the rail network, the Bus Rapid Transit, the general line, the distributing line and the distributing public bicycle. There must be mutual influence between the different traffic routes, so the planners need to pay attention to the mode transformation and the association influence scope.

· Impact. There are several impacts of transportation system, including the influence on transportation, economy, environment and society. The following is the example of Crown Town, Shaanxi Province.

The traffic, economy and society development of Crown Town

Crown Town is located in the northern of Ningxia province, 75 kilometers from the county, total cultivated area of which is 2635.3 acres, woodland area is 980000 acres, relying on forestry, arable land as the main source of the economy. But with social development, this economic model is increasingly unacceptable, the construction of Beijing-Kun Expressway provides a new development direction for Crown Town.

Crown Town forest covers up to 96% of the total area. Ecological resources and tourism resources are abundant, sunshine, forest, air, and water is the town's largest advantage resources. In addition, Jingkun Expressway passes through the Crown Town. An interchange is arranged near the market town, which is only one hour away from Xi'an. It has obvious advantages of traffic location and reliable tourist market. Crown Town builds a tourist boutique project combining immigrant relocation and town tourism. They choose a new area building with good location and high commercial value to build a house for farmers, each household a house, a layer of a commercial shop, second floor living room, so that the problem of living housing and operating room of peasants was solved.

From the example of Crown Town, the development of traffic has an impact on the region's economy, environment, society and culture. On the economic front, the construction of the Jingkun Expressway and the Xunhuang Road Interchange has improved the accessibility and convenience of the Crown Village, and the natural conditions and resources of the town contributed to the development of the tourism industry, thus stimulating the economic growth of the region. For environmental aspects, the development of tourism will inevitably increase the floating population in the region. Tourism vehicles will inevitably bring land, air, noise and other environmental problems; For social aspects, because of the desire to make full use of the advantages of JingKun Expressway to develop tourism, the town leader decides that the whole town moved from the original location to a more suitable location, and the direction of urbanization is developing, the job category of residents of the town is diverted from agriculture and forestry to commercial and tourism, so that the occupation of the local residents has changed; For culture aspects, the whole economic and social development changes, so that the lifestyle of residents changes, open towns bring the exterior culture into Crown Town and mixed with the local culture.

From the example of Crown Town(Fig. 1-2), *it can be seen that the development of traffic has a certain influence on the economy, society and culture of the region.*

· Feedback. System feedback includes internal feedback and external feedback on the transportation system. The feedback of the system is shown as the system participant to regulate the behavior according to the system performance, so that the system running state conforms to the participant's willingness. For example, after traffic congestion, the participant can choose to transfer to public transit; the government can also choose to create new roads and adjust the use of road rights to improve the efficiency of the road. The feedback in the urban transportation planning is to link the implementation of traffic strategy and the impact of community vision, objectives and the operating characteristics of the system itself, according to the model test, adjust the planning program to achieve better traffic development. In the operation of the transportation system, the performance of the transportation system can be improved by monitoring and evaluating the system function. The transportation system should fully utilize the market feedback mechanism, which can be regarded as commodities, by adjusting the price of commodities to increase or decrease demand, to regulate the demand and supply equilibrium of transportation service, and to maintain good performance and performance. One of the typical applications of the traffic area is to regulate traffic volume by adjusting the fares to direct more people to use public transport or expressway trips.

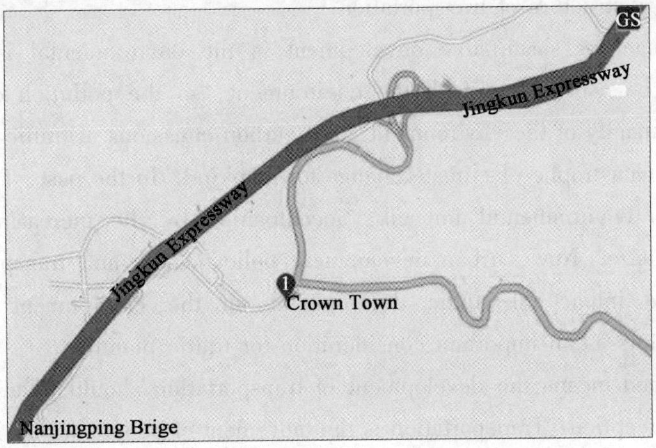

Figure 1-2 The location of Crown town

Source: *Adapted from relevant information.*

1.1.2 Objectives and Concepts

(1) Objectives

· To improve the sustainable, people-oriented development of transportation system. Transportation system is a multi-objective system, the adverse effects of achieving the goal should be avoided, such as pollution, congestion, excessive financial investment. There are two core concerns: one is sustainable and the other is people-centered.

a. Sustainable development of transportation systems. Considering the capacity of transport facilities, it is also necessary to consider whether the environment can be accommodated, whether energy can be supported, whether the financial viability and the use of land is reasonable. Traffic construction is a highly resource-consuming behavior; the most important resource consumed is the land. The infrastructure of railways, highways, buses and bicycles requires a large amount of land, not only the land for driving facilities, but also a large number of parking facilities. For the city center, the road that consumes a lot of land, however, it cannot solve the congestion problem (Dawns law). This is an important issue of transportation planning.

In addition to consuming a lot of land, traffic also consumes a lot of energy, mainly for diesel, gasoline and electricity. China's petrochemical energy import rate is very high, in recent years, energy prices fluctuate, indicating that the fragility of the current traffic energy in China is illustrated. The structure of good transportation energy is also a concern in transportation planning.

The countries of the world have adopted corresponding countermeasures against the problems of their own transportation energy. For example, in Japan, transportation development attaches great importance to the construction of electric energy-based rail system, and attaches great importance to the development of urban public transport to diversify the transportation energy and the structure. The current situation of China's transportation energy structure needs to be developed. High-speed rail and urban rail system and the use of pure electric vehicles should be promoted, and the government should encourage people to travel more by buses, walk, and bike to achieve the improvement of energy structure of transportation.

Another challenge for sustainable development is the environmental issues. Transportation development should be coordinated with the environment, so the pollution caused by the traffic cannot exceed the capacity of the environment, and carbon emissions of traffic should be reduced to reduce the potential catastrophe of climate change for mankind. In the past, Traffic planners do not attach importance to environmental impacts, accompanied by the increasing severity of global warming and urban haze. Now, urban development policymakers and transportation planners are concerned about the impact of traffic development on the environment and begin to take environmental indicators as an important consideration for traffic planning.

b. People-oriented means the development of transportation should follow the development of human needs and perception. Transportation is the movement of people or objects from the ground to the ground. In the whole process of transportation, if we blindly pursue the speed, then the resulting noise, congestion, accidents, excessive occupation of land, energy and financial difficulties will seriously affect the normal life and living environment of the residents and pedestrians. A large number of urban traffic statistics show that the vehicle real load rate is very low on the crowded road on the peak period, which will lead to a waste of road resources, resulting in no road for buses, bicycles, and pedestrians. This is the typical car-based transportation. Therefore, we should improve the transportation system, not only to consider the road congestion caused by the increase in demand for motor vehicle, but also to focus on the efficiency of transportation system. People-centered means balancing the relationship between cars, buses, bicycles, pedestrians and all travelers, so that transportation users can enjoy the comfortable, convenient, safe and economical urban traffic. Transportation planning should pay attention to the needs of driving trips and the construction of a good level of road system, then to guide people not only to rely on driving, but also to guide people to choose a reasonable mode to travel.

· To solve issues and optimize solutions of the existing transportation system. Transportation planning is to solve the problems of transportation development. It is to seek a solution which reconcile short-term and long-term objectives and choose the optimal way (or satisfactory, environmental, economic) for transportation development to solve problem, by various alternatives, such as construction, management and policy transport programs cannot be done only focus on the current interests, but also to consider long-term interests.

There are many studies should be conducted in our current transportation system. For example, how to adjust and change the system to ease traffic congestion, how to improve mobility and accessibility, enhance the transfer facility, and consider the transport infrastructure construction budget. Then we should study whether the traffic emergency rescue is appropriate and how to reduce the traffic collision, casualties, and fatal accidents. Different regions, different stages of development of the traffic situation is different, this requires planners to focus on planning research to find the main traffic problems, then analyze the causes and evolution characteristics of the problem, to conceive the optimal, comprehensive planning options. For example, there are many ways to solve traffic jams, such as increasing road capacity, setting up bus lanes, encouraging the high-occupancy vehicle (HOV) lane, inducing motorists to avoid congestion through information services, reducing the demand for travel, changing the lane to tidal lanes, prohibiting roadside parking, altering the intensity of land use, improving the way commuters travel, and connecting shopping malls and subway stations to reduce the number of trips, etc. So we should evaluate the alternatives and choose the most suitable scheme for the region, when discussing how to alleviate the congestion.

· To analysis transportation developing experience using professional and logical methods for the transport development action. In the process of transportation planning, we need to learn from the experience of predecessors. Before doing the plan, planner should gather relevant information, avoid risk and optimize the program, do not waste money in unnecessary places. Professional methods combine the theory of capacity, traffic flow, management and control, to design the planning scheme. Logical analysis process should be based on axiom and principle to obtain the solution concept, model algorithm, parameters and countermeasures adapted to the transportation development problem. A good solution of transportation problem cannot be dogmatic, cannot rely on brainstorm, but need to be boldly conceived with rigorous argumentation.

Planners should co-ordinate overall and comprehensive analysis. Because different people have different views on traffic, which is related to the economic conditions, life concerns and attributes of each person. Different people focus on the different issues, so the proposed development program will be different. Planners rely on their own experience to draw conclusions, may only focus on local transportation problems, cannot meet the wishes of all of people, so this requires us to find a way to solve the common problems of society based on reasonable survey samples and logical analysis. At present, the mainstream approach is to study the planning scope, investigate the large number of public data and the operation parameters of transportation facilities, then establish a professional model to complete the index calculation, introduce the public participation options, finally form a suitable development plan.

· To give useful, enough, correct information to decision makers. Transportation planning decisions need to be recognized by professionals, government leaders and other departments. These decision makers often do not understand the complexity of traffic development, and often rely on driving travel, so it is easy to make a choice from the angle of supply then only to construct some road, parking facilities. As a result, the city will suffer increasingly congested situation. This requires planners to focus on communication with leaders and the public, and to provide sufficient, useful, adequate and accurate information to decision makers. In planning, we should pay attention to collecting or analyzing the changes of various indexes, focusing on the accuracy of the parameters.

Then it can help the decision makers to identify the differences between planning programmes and enable the adoption of the right planning programme.

(2) Concept

The concept of transportation planning changes with time. Braybrooke and Lindblom argued in the Chicago Transportation Study (CATS, 1960) and the Detroit Transport Study (1961) that transportation planning was an objective law based on a stable link between human activities and their traffic needs. Mathematical models were used to quantify this link and calibrate it. Boulding (1974) proposed a decision-oriented view of transportation planning: a. The future of the world is the result of decision-making (or lack of decision-making), rather than planning. b. Planning decisions include the assessment of future scenarios and the choice of the best solution. c. The assessment and decision-making process is influenced by the uncertainty and is associated with the desires of planning. d. Planning results should increase the possibility to make wise decision. e. The results of the planning should be seen as communication with policy makers. Meyer and Miller (1984) emphasized that the planning and design of the transportation system is a political process and a technical process. They pointed that the planning process should be carried out with the interested public rather than for the public; Wachs (1985) believed that the planning method should provide a systematic, non-personal, decision-supporting information and transportation planning method has to make decision makers to identify traffic problems. Banister (1994) pointed out that traffic planning is part of a whole process of extensive decision making. In the past, traffic problems were often regarded as mere traffic. In fact, transportation planning must be part of land use planning and land development, which requires a comprehensive and clear perspective to analyze the cities and communities. we expect to live in. Domestic traffic planning also have their own thinking. Shao (2004) pointed out that the transportation planning is a series of actions to guide the traffic in a planned way, that is, how the planners put forward various objectives and how to put the proposed objectives into practice. Wang (2007) argued that it is based on the current situation and characteristics of the specific transportation system to use scientific methods to predict the development trend of transportation system demand and the demand of transportation supply then the construction task, construction scale, management mode and control method of traffic supply can be determined, in specific period. We should balance the transportation system demand and supply then make sure the transportation system is safe, unblocked, energy saving and environmental-protected.

To sum up, the concept of transportation planning can be summarized as: the process of a series of programmes provide to decision-makers to improved time, place, method, and associated effect to achieve predetermined goals. Transportation planning needs a realistic goal, such as relieving congestion, sustainable development, construction of clean and pleasant traffic, increasing bus sharing rate. Transportation planning should provide decision-makers with a specific solution to achieve the goal, that is, when and where to do what, then evaluate the performance of the program. The program also should take into account the constraints of the budget, the laws and policies.

There are five ways to determine the plan: a. Rational optimal method, that is, analyzing the problem rationally and proposing the optimum scheme. This method usually lists all the alternatives. We can select the program through a series of evaluation indicators, then adjust the plain accordance with the public, and ultimately get the best solution; b. Satisfaction method. Based on a reasonable choice of ideas to propose and select a solution that meets the minimum acceptable improvement, the scheme should bring some benefit and achieve the goals easily, and meet the requirement of public satisfaction; c. Progressive improvement method. In order to solve the more difficult problems, the planners should choose the existing problems to solve, test the "results-measures" "measures-results" adjustment process, the program to adjust several times to alleviate the serious problems, and gradually get the optimal; d. Organizational process method. That is to promote the decision-making by providing appropriate information with the consideration about the influence of decision organization system and related standards and norms, fully consider the preferences and problems of various organizations, and; e. Political consultation method. The planning programs can be decided through the political consultation process. The differences in the values, desires and interests of different decision makers lead to decision-making conflicts, so there is a need for consultation between decision-makers and the acceptable programmes of all parties; technically, the final result is not the best solution, it is a compromise after negotiation of decision makers, and many problems are temporarily ignored for future resolution.

1.1.3 Values

The transportation system is a system for people to travel. The provision of transportation system should be based on the kind of people. And the differences in the concept of decision-makers may lead to negative effects on the society. The planner should have the correct concept, and guide the community to configure the transportation facilities rationally, and then make the wise transportation management policies to achieve high levels of traffic management. In order to obtain a huge investment in transportation construction projects to complete the goal of regional economic growth, foreign countries experienced blind investment on the traffic facilities construction, the consequences are losing huge amounts of money and there were fewer transportation facilities users or traffic congestion cannot be relieved. Paying for traffic construction huge debt is difficult. Large number of social resources cannot be used efficiently, which lead to the decline in purchasing power of money and rise of goods prices. The current large-scale construction will lead to a large number costs of future transport infrastructure maintenance. Lack of transportation costs, facilities and high damage rate lead to difficulties to achieve basic good state. Rail and airport may be disorder. Bridge may be collapsed. Therefore, the concept of traffic performance is important in the development of traffic planning. In this way, the inefficient and unsustainable development of the entire country, region or city can be avoided.

Foreign experience can be concluded, if the traffic planning cannot reasonably deal with public transport, bicycles, pedestrians and other modes of transport, the dependence on cars will increase, traffic will be deteriorated and there are negative impacts on the life of some low-income travelers. Then there will be anti-social, anti-human vicious events. This requires that the planners must have the correct values.

Values are unified as a factor accepted by the community. It is defined as an abstract concept, such as freedom, equality. In view of the close relationship between transportation and people's production and life, the transportation planning should implement the social values to meet the people-oriented requirements in the transportation decision-making, then to meet the needs of traffic participants, but the planning cannot just meet the interests of some people and bring damage to the interests of another part of the people and let the vulnerable groups be treated unfairly. For example, the construction of is incomplete of the road for the blind. The relationships between the different modes of transport should be fair. Motor vehicles occupied sidewalks and bike paths, so that bicycles, pedestrians have no rights of roads, which is unfair. Planners and decision makers are committed to sustainable development in a fair and equitable direction in accordance with people-centered values.

In the process of implementing values, the transportation planning follows a set of standard procedures that the abstract social goals reflected in the social values can be defined as specific measurable indicators that can be accepted and appropriate. Goals and quantitative objectives, criteria and standards, two pairs of concepts are used internationally. But in Chinese it is difficult to identify the distinction between these concepts. They are used for logical reasoning of planning estimation.

The goal is a qualitative concept that is the direction of the consensus of society, which forms the basis of the computational effort validity and usually does not change over time and space, such as increasing accessibility, reducing accidents, reducing the use of cars. Quantitative objectives measure both goals and resources, which is more specific than the target, and related with time and space. For example, the number of accidents is reduced by 50 percent over 2001. The criterion is a measure to find whether we reach the goals. For example, the accessibility of the bus can be measured by the percentage of the population who is close to the bus station. The standard is the minimum acceptable level of the criteria. For example, the time to travel to the transport hub can not exceed 15 minutes.

It is important to establish quantifiable and quantitative targets. For example, the car indicators of travelled miles and the population be serviced and other accessibility indicators. It is important to compare several different alternatives with the same quantitative goals and criteria. According to multiple objectives, affected groups and multiple levels of decision-making and the use of measurable normative approaches can lead to difficulties in comparing different planning options and have difficult in persuading.

1.2 The Development and Evolution of Transportation Planning

According to the international and domestic transportation planning related events and significant progress, the evolution process of transportation planning can be summarized from three aspects, the international events, domestic important events, and traffic model.

1.2.1 The Important Events and Evolution Trend of International Transportation Planning

Modern transportation planning is the science category which is to reveal how facilities configuration, management and policy can coordinated with travel law by quantitative analysis and system analysis. The origin and evolution of modern transportation planning is closely related to the United States that hope to benefit and lead the development of the country by modern science and technology.

(1) The United States transportation legislation

In the past, people should travel for a long distance and consume long time. People require patience to travel and also need equipment, spare parts, emergency food and fuel. The dust float in the sunshine day on the road and, the road became muddy after raining. So according to the original proposal of American Association of State Highway Officials (AASHO), President Woodrow Wilson signed the Federal Aid Road Act in order to maintain the happiness, comfort and prosperous life of the country and the development of the city. After five years of signing this Act, the federal funded 75 million dollars to rebuild highways. For federal funds, rural roads must be free of charge. AASHO should consider the geography, population and the condition of existing roads, and require the applicant to submit the files which include project planning, survey and technical standard. The Bill continued to be effective. President Dwight Eisenhower in 1956 adjusted the scope and strength of the support in a large scale and proposed to invest $32.9 billion to build the interstate highway system, the total length of which was 66000 kilometers, covering more than 90% of urban areas and more than 50000 people. It is the largest public works project in American history. The law is also called the National Interstate and Defense Highways Act. The matched Highway Revenue Act of 1956 adopted increasing the tax on fuel, tire consumption and increasing commercial vehicle sales tax to raise the project funds, and put these tax in the Highway Trust Fund. With the support of the interstate highway construction funds, the federal government paid 90% and the state paid 10%. But local governments do not need to pay. This policy has been continued. Then the federal ministry of transport mainly focuses on the construction of American national interstate highway system. By 2005, the total length of the United States highway is 6.46 million kilometers, including the 75400 kilometers interstate highway.

In 1964 the United States issued the Urban Mass Transportation Act and it admitted to provide up to the two-thirds of the total investment for the rail transit project. Then Urban Mass Transportation Assistance Act of 1970 provided long-term federal financial commitments for public transportation project. The Act financed the city to develop private bus service and update the buses to enhance the basis of construction. From 1965 to 1974, the number increased from 58 to 308, of the public transport systems that the act supported.

In the critical moment when the interstate highway is basically completed, how to adjust the federal transport investment should be considered, "Surface Transport and Efficiency Act" (also known as the Ice Tea Act: Intermodal Surface Transportation Efficiency Act, ISTEA, 1991) issued as the US Department of Transportation's leading policy. Based on the extensive opinions, the act proposes to increase efficiency through multi-modal transport and propose the federal government should contribute 80% to extend and maintain15.5 million miles of national highway then support the public transport management, the work of metropolis planning organization (MPO), and the new technology of transportation such as Intelligent Transportation System (ITS). The bus research centers in five universities were established to strengthen the traffic safety, statistics, environmental protection work or management. The bill has a significant impact on the direction of transport planning and transport investment decisions. In the existing metropolis planning organization (MPO), the core work of the decision-making has expanded to include the provision of transport service equipment and manufacturers. During the implementation of the planning, the participation at all levels of government (state, city and county) has increased significantly. In planning the land use of the metropolitan area, the consideration of traffic was enhanced. And improving air quality is already one of the priorities of high-level coordination between state and city planning agencies.

In 1998, the United States issued the Transportation Equity Act for the 21st Century, also known as the new ISTEA. It proposed the budget category for new roads and public transportation. The state promised to return 90.5% of its tax revenue to the road trust fund. The new policy for application of the federal funds began at this time; The fund for the intelligent transportation system should be developed; In the metropolitan planning organization requirements, long-term comprehensive planning should be provided. There are seven parts should be considered in the early stages of planning: keeping energetic (including global competitiveness, productivity and efficiency), safety, mobility and flexibility of passengers and cargoes, environmental protection, the integration of transportation systems, connectivity and the efficiency of system management and operations, and the preservation of existing transport systems. "Streamlined" project planning and environmental review procedures should be started, independent investment research was no longer be conducted; The following considerations were added to federal public transport funds project evaluation process: the cost of unplanned expansion, the maintenance costs of the infrastructure due to the conservation of land use, the population density and the existing public transport modes of the traffic corridor and the technical capacity of the authorized person to undertake the project.

(2) The main event of transportation planning

The revolutionary event of urban transportation planning took place in 1960, Chicago, with "Chicago Transportation Study" and "Detroit Transportation Study" published in 1961. Chicago Transportation Study put forward that transportation planning is to compute the traffic intensity of people on the land, according to the intensity to equip with traffic facilities and these facilities associated the original and terminal point of human activities. In 1961, Detroit also did a similar study, the core work is the high-speed road planning. In the absence of data, planning is the subject of qualitative research. After understanding the scale and characteristics of the social activities, the appropriate transport system can be equipped. Rather than building road blindly, this is the origin of urban transportation planning. In 1962, the United States developed a new federal highway law that urban traffic planning must be done when more than 50000 people live in the city to get the federal government's financial subsidies. We can see the government's emphasis on urban transport planning.

In 1962, Hershey, Pennsylvania (PA) meeting suggested that traffic was not isolated, we should give full consideration to the conflict between the highway, the residential area and the land use target, and figure out how to use these goals comprehensively to make transportation planning better. Not only the transport of people and goods should be considered, but also whether these plans can be profitable, whether it is easy for people to transfer and other issues. So how to integrate the multi modes should be considered by planner. When we consider these issues, we also should pay attention to public participation, and traffic should be people-oriented. Public participation is a very necessary part. The public satisfaction is considered as an indication of good traffic planning (Mt. Pocono, PA, 1971). Meyer and Miller published "Urban transportation Planning: A decision-oriented Approach" in 1962. They call for an approach which focuses on the process of planning with the techniques. They realized that planning is a political and technical process and put forward problems at first then make plan and decisions, including schedule, budget, development, implementation and operation monitoring. After 1994, Maryland Department of Transportation (DOT) put forward Multimodal Transportation Planning based on Meyer's research in 1993. They began to establish Multimodal Transportation Planning which including parking fee, transportation system management, traffic improvement, public transport and highway capacity expansion, vehicle processing, non-motorized traffic, growth management and activity center land use strategy.

The intelligent research of the US transportation system began in the late 1960s, when it was called Electronic Route Guidance System. In March 1995, the US Department of Transportation published "the National Intelligent Transportation Project Plan". In the same year, the United States began to develop a unified National Architecture for ITS and published the first edition in 1997. After one year of trial and maintenance, the revised second edition was published. According to the news released by ITS America, the US National ITS Development Strategic Plan has been completed. The theme is "the use of intelligent transportation system to save lives, save time and money".

Although the emergence of intelligent transportation reduces the economic pressure to a certain extent, the new problem is that the cost of building road is low but with high conservation costs, so the road construction period and conservation period are taken into account. The application of economic analysis technology should be used to make the whole construction costs the lowest, which is the whole life. At the same time, traffic has a great impact on the environment. In order to solve the problem of increasing environmental pollution, greenhouse gas emissions should be reduced and the dependence on imported oil should be decreased. Countries have strengthened the research and development of alternative transportation fuels and advanced automobile technology. So life-cycle CO_2 emissions is very important.

In 1996, the United States Argonne National Laboratory (ANL) developed a GREET 1.7 life cycle traffic carbon emission measurement model for more accurate calculation of energy consumption and emissions with various types of fuel and automotive technology from the vehicle operation, fuel production process and vehicle production process.

In 2008, Chester and Horvath fully measured the energy consumption and carbon emissions of US public transport, light rail, heavy rail and airplanes in the construction of passenger transport in stations and railways, vehicle and fuel production, operation phase and maintenance and repair stage. In addition to life-cycle CO_2 emissions, the American Society of Civil Engineers focused on life-cycle engineering decision. In 2006, Todd Litman of Canada proposed to use economic analysis technology of cost utility and benefit cost analysis to compare the cost of alternative transportation scheme options and evaluate different traffic demand management schemes. In 2014, Jonas Wennstrom found that road-to-collision roads were more economical in full-life investments than ordinary roads. In the traffic system, there are a lot of measure indicators can be achieved with computer data analysis technology. As the New York Times wrote in a column published in February 2012, "big data" era has arrived (Fig. 1-3).

For the railway network, the United States established the Federal Railway Administration in 1966, with the main responsibility to ensure the implementation of the Railway Safety Regulations, to provide a railway management assistance program to support the improvement of national rail and rail transport safety research and development. The Federal Railways Authority attaches importance to integrity, excellence in value, transparency and accountability, innovation, stakeholder engagement and employee safety, forming a complete system of service values. Until today, the Federal Railways Authority continues to serve the society with this value. Since 1971, the railway company separate passenger and cargo management in America and now they are always divided into two categories, passenger railways and cargo rail companies. The National Passenger Railroad Company, Amtrak was founded in 1970 and it is the only intercity passenger railroad company in the United States. The speed of 60% of the train in Amtrak Railway Passenger Company is higher than 145km/h, covering 46 states in the United States and three provinces in Canada, operating mileage up to about 33920km. In recent years, with the rapid development of high-speed railway in the world, the US government's investment in high-speed railway development and research also increased significantly, which actively promote the state, the relevant agencies and private companies to participate in high-speed railway research and construction. In April 2009, based on the Passenger Railway Investment and Transformation Act in 2008, the US Economic Recovery and Reinvestment Act clearly stated that the United States would vigorously develop inter-city high-speed railways with an investment of 8 billion dollars and construct high-speed passenger rail network between major economic cities with the dense population. In order to achieve this goal, the Federal Railways Authority (FRA) set up the project in terms of the Inter-city High Speed Rail Project (HSIPR) in June 2009 and encouraged state governments and related agencies and companies to rely on existing railway passenger lines, transport equipment and a variety of transfer mode to research the US high-speed passenger dedicated line planning and construction objectives. The US government released the first six-year high-speed railway development plan in February 9th, 2011. They plan to invest 53 billion dollars for the new high-speed railway corridor and upgrade the existing lines to high-speed railway lines. In order to avoid relying on over-reliance on oil-fueled

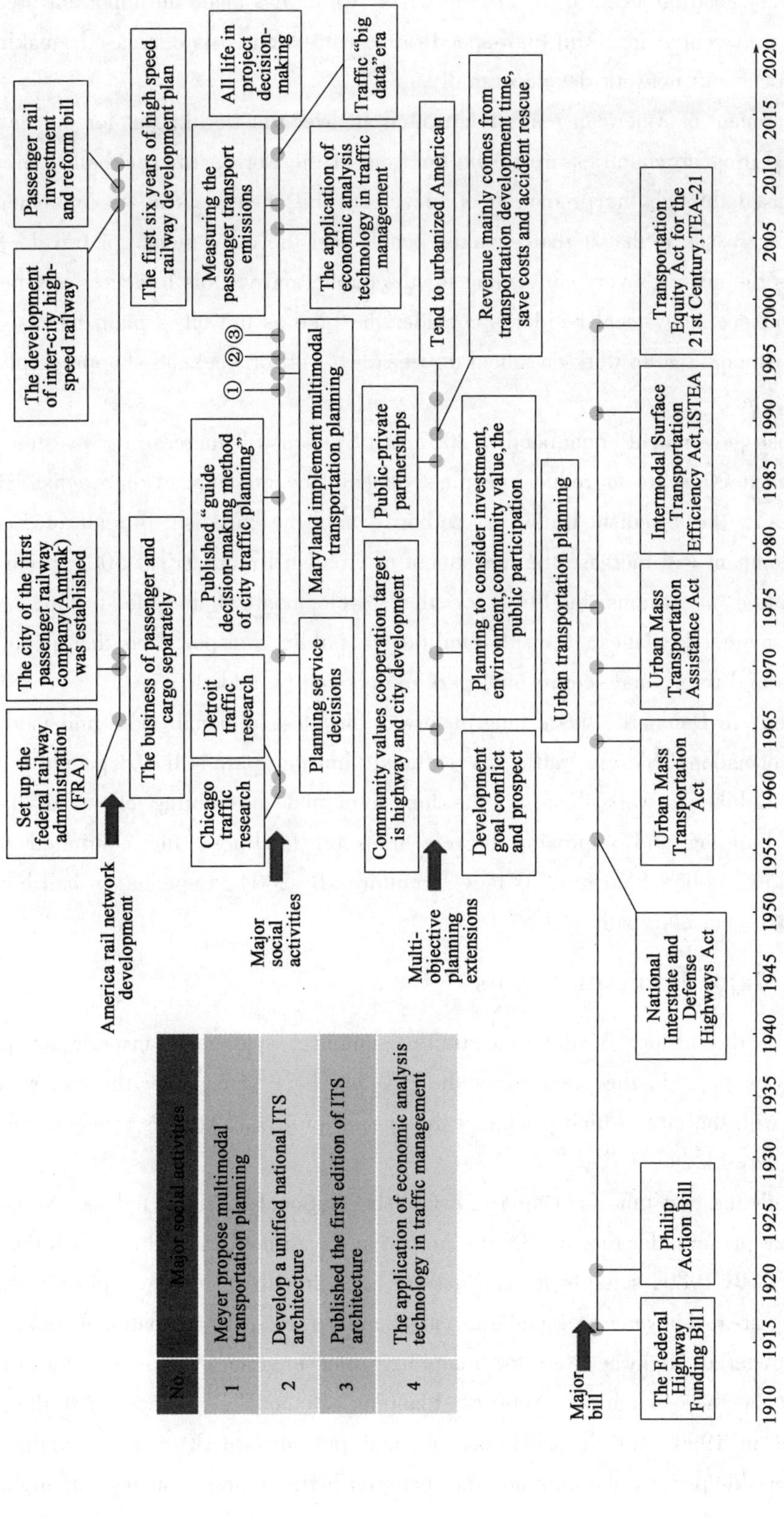

No.	Major social activities
1	Meyer propose multimodal transportation planning
2	Develop a unified national ITS architecture
3	Published the first edition of ITS architecture
4	The application of economic analysis technology in traffic management

Figure 1-3 Traffic planning major event

cars, France, Japan and other countries are committed to the development of high-speed railway, and there are very good projects. In recent ten years, China has made an important breakthrough in the high-speed rail technology. And high-speed rail construction costs decreased, making the entire national high-speed rail network develop rapidly.

The development of American roads is advance all over the world. But for the development of bicycles, some European countries are in the forefront of the world. In Stockholm, Sweden, traffic pressure was eased through the promotion of bicycles. This measure can be implemented quickly because the main reason is that it really makes people feel the convenience of travel. Rental bikes shop was across the city, it's very convenient for the public and visitors to access any network in the city. Every summer, many local residents consider the bike as the city's main means of transport, whether it is for them to go to work or school on weekdays, or for weekend shopping, picnic. People enjoy this cozy life.

The Swedish government announced in 2007 that Sweden will increase its investment in bicycle traffic for the next 20 years to reduce people's dependence on cars. The Swedish Highway and Transport Bureau, the Swedish Railways Authority and the Swedish Bureau of Economic and Regional Development will increase the investment of Swedish Krona (SEK) 500 million per year for the implementation of various facilities for the development of bicycle traffic, such as the construction of more bike lanes, transfer facilities of public transport. So that people can carry bicycles by bus and train, and secure bike parking lots can be added.

Copenhagen, in Denmark, has a long history of bicycles, although more and more Danes own cars, the ratio of national bicycle traffic has declined, but there are still 1/3 people in Copenhagen choose to ride a bike to work. Due to the long-term and unremitting efforts of the municipal government in building and improving bicycle transport facilities, the continued prosperity of Copenhagen bikes has benefited from its bicycle culture. By 2004, Copenhagen had built a 345 km bike way and a 14 km bike path.

1.2.2 Major Domestic Events

In terms of the history of domestic traffic planning, regional transportation planning are developing step by step. In the planning of the city, we have to consider the city people around, how to contact with the city, which produced the special project of various transport modes.

(1) Road network

In 1964, it's the first time for China to establish "National Arterial Highway Network Planning Draft" and make planning for the first 85000 km national road network and establish the backbone of China's highway. By 1980, some local road network planning also began to explore and try, such as Henan Xinxiang area, Luoyang area and Jiangsu Zhenjiang area. In the national traffic conference, the "National Arterial Highway Network Planning (pilot program)" was put forward. The real normative plan is the "Highway Network Planning Method" developed by the Ministry of Communications in 1990. And in 1991 the national put forward 30 years planning for arterial highway. During this period, the contradiction between highway and economy was highlighted, and the importance of highway network planning was realized at the national and local area. The plan was revised in 2007. But the planning for the arterial road network still provides limited support and the guidance of rural road network planning. In order to speed up the construction of roads in rural areas and promote the socio-economic development of rural areas, the Ministry of Communications in 2005 issued a "Rural Road Construction Planning". In the same year the State Council also promulgated the "National Highway Network Planning" referred to as "7918" network. This is the first "ultimate" highway skeleton layout planning in Chinese history and the highest level of highway access in the Chinese road network. On June 20, 2014, China's Ministry of Transport announced the "National Highway Network Planning (2013—2030)", which proposed that China's general national highway will reach 265000 km in the total scale and the national highway mileage would be up 118000 km by 2030. For this investment of about 4.7 trillion yuan, about 250 million is expected to invest to highway, rational layout, functional, wide range, safe and reliable national arterial highway network will be completed by 2030 to achieve that the national Capital was connected with provincial capital. Then provincial multi-line connectivity, high-speed access to the city and national road coverage can be provided.

(2) Railway network

Compared to the development of highways, the early development of the railway is slower. In 2004, "long-term railway network planning" was approved by the State Council's first industry planning and China's railway construction blueprint by 2020. Its development goals are the national railway operating mileage will be up to 100000 km by 2020. The system is mainly busy with the passenger and freight sub-line. The rate of electricity reached 50%. Transport capacity can meet the need of national economic and social developments. The main technical equipment reach or close to the international advanced level. At the end of 2008, China's railway operating mileage can reached 79000 km. The completion of passenger traffic reach 1.45 billion passengers and the cargo volume is 3.31 billion tons. The railway mileage ranked the third in the world after the United States, Russia. Railway passenger volume and freight volume rank the first in the world. In order to make passenger travel more efficient, the national high-speed rail network was put forward.

(3) Aviation network

In addition to the development of roads, railways and other modes of transport, it's essential to construct a large integrated transport hub for city to develop the air transport. In 2006, China promulgated the "11th Five-Year Plan for Civil Aviation Development" to clarify the development goals of China's civil aviation during the 11th Five-Year Plan period. The goal was rapid growth of air transport and improvement of quality; general aviation gross increased. The structure needs to be optimized; the infrastructure construction has been strengthened to ensure a significant increase in capacity; and the legal system is basically perfect for the basic formation of industry culture. To the end of the "11th Five-Year" period, the comprehensive strength of the aviation industry was enhanced. The overall role in the national integrated traffic is more prominent, the impact of the world's civil aviation can be further expanded and can adapt to the needs of national economic and social development basically. In 2008, the State Council issued the "National Civil Airport Layout Plan" and held the National Civil Aviation Working Conference at the same year, the China Civil Aviation Administration Group put forward a comprehensive plan to promote the construction of civil aviation and established the goal: to establish a global well-known brands of airlines among the world's top five by 2030; to establish air cargo companies with international competitiveness which can rank the world's top five. To build more than three international hub airports, more than 10 national and regional air hub airport; the number and layout of the airport will meet needs of more than 95% of the county-level administrative regions, more than 95% of population transport. The domestic production value of the serviced area reach 98% of the national total values. We should ensure a safe and reliable, efficient operation, with advanced technology, to adapt to the development of low cost service and achieve innovative ability to support the technical system. In addition, the formation of rational layout, the appropriate size of the airport and commuter airport structure should be ensured. Establish a full-featured, standardized service of the general aviation service system, covering all county-level administrative units. In 2011, the "12th Five-Year Plan for Civil Aviation Development" was promulgated. The plan revolved around the strategy of building a strong civil aviation strategy, recalling the rapid growth of the aviation business during the 11th Five-Year Plan period. By 2010, the total turnover of transport would be 53.8 billion ton, passenger traffic capacity reach 268 million, cargo and mail traffic volume reach 5.63 million ton and a substantial increase in infrastructure capacity, a total investment in five years reach 250 billion yuan, equal to the first 25 years of civil aviation construction funds. By 2010, the number of airport reached 175, covering 91% of the national economy, 76% of the population and 70% of the county-level administrative unit. And it also put forward the situation in the "12th Five-Year Plan" period the development of ideas and the main objectives were clarified to determine the key tasks. Planning was made to guide the market main body, to guide the behavior of the government, which is significant and is the development of industry programmatic documents. In 2013, the Ministry of Industry and Information Technology issued the "Medium and Long Term Development Plan for Civil Aviation Industry(2013—2020)", which proposed that the domestic market share of domestic trunk aircraft would reach more than 5% by 2020, and regional and general aircraft domestic market share increased significantly, civil aircraft industry annual operating income should be more than 100 billion yuan.

(4) Non-motorized transportation priority development

In 2001, Shanghai published the "Shanghai Urban Transport White Paper" for traffic jam and support the concept for the first time that is we should develop non-motorized traffic rapidly and make it easy for everyone to transfer to walk, bike and bus. In 2008, Hangzhou City launched the concept of public bicycles, proposed the design of a subway, buses, rental cars, water buses. And public bicycles formed a modular public transport network plan. In 2009, Beijing promulgated the "Green Beijing" Action Plan(2010—2012), proposed the construction of slow transport facilities, set up a bike lane on both sides of the road, in the main road, installed the fence and re-painted on the line to support slow traffic development.

(5) Bus priority and urban road network

In 2004, the Ministry of Construction included the "public transport priority" in the long-term strategic planning of urban traffic and issued "The Opinions on Prioritizing the Development of Urban Public Transport". The main objective was to establish the main status of public transport in the city and speed up compile the special planning of urban public transport. Beijing is one of the first cities in China to implement the "bus priority" strategy. In 2005, the "Beijing Transportation Development Program" was promulgated, which would give priority to the development of public transport strategy as a cure for urban traffic congestion. It was proposed the comprehensive public transport system which makes trail transit and large capacity rapid transit as the backbone, the ground bus as the main body, taxi as supplement. In April 2011, Ministry of Communications put forward the "second five" period will be selected in the country 30 cities to carry out "bus city" construction demonstration project. The first batch of "bus city" in 2012 was born. In 2013, the second batch of "bus city" have been born. At present, the third batch of bus city is being applied.

In 2014, the Ministry of Transport issued the Guidelines for the Compilation of Urban Public Transport, which regard as urban public transport include urban bus trams, urban rail transit and urban ferry and so on and the aim is to promote the establishment of urban public transport and guide the planning mode of urban development, to achieve the optimal allocation of urban public transport resources and to enhance the city public transport service capabilities and service levels, the maximum capacity to protect the basic needs of the public travel. In 2015, Ministry of Housing and Urban and Rural Development issued "on the further strengthening of urban planning and construction of a number of opinions", put forward "narrow road, dense road network, open neighborhood" urban road layout concept, and requested that no longer need to build a closed residential area in principle. Residential quarters and units of the compound which has been completed to be opened gradually to achieve internal road public, promote traffic problems easy to solve the layout of the road network to promote land conservation.

(6) Environmental assessment

In 2003, the Ministry of Environmental Protection issued the "Technical Guidelines for Planning Environmental Impact Assessment (Trial)" to promote the scientific and standardized planning of environmental impact assessment. In 2009, the State Council promulgated the Regulations on Planning Environmental Impact Assessment, and proposed to prevent environmental pollution and ecological damage from the source and promote the comprehensive, coordinated and sustainable development of economy, society and environment. In 2013, National Environmental Protection Department adopted the "National Highway Network Planning Environmental Impact Report" to solve the planning program uncertainty, environmental assessment technical requirements of higher complex issues, the practice of ecological civilization construction concept, and promote the green development of transport. In 2014, the Ministry of Environmental Protection issued the "Technical Guidelines for Planning Environmental Impact Assessment", which revised the technical guidelines for 2003, revised the contents, methods and requirements of environmental impact forecasting and evaluation, and increased the strength of planning and development, more comprehensive provisions of the planning of environmental impact assessment of the general principles, content, working procedures, methods and requirements.

With the economy and society of China, more and more complex, integrated transport system and foreign developed countries and the city has been comparable, and the need for the existing sub-rules established on the basis of a large framework, more comprehensive and streamline. The modes of transport are mutually reinforcing and mutually restrictive. The birth of high-speed rail network makes the passenger flow volume of short-range air transport traffic down. High-speed rail corridor faster than the car, so a lot of road transport companies need to transport from the trunk transport for the distribution of transport to survive. Similarly, the opening of the subway also affected the car, because the subway can ensure that people arrive at the destination more accurate and fast. The country promotes bus lanes, bicycle lanes and the "bus city" construction in recent years and green travel in order to reduce the pressure of urban roads. These ideas are not finished currently. Such as in the subway and public bicycles, airports, railway stations and buses, taxi connections, etc., to facilitate people to transfer, the establishment of a comprehensive urban integrated transport hub is causing widespread concern around. Learning transportation planning need to understand the overall situation of traffic in the whole country, learn to assess and analyze the current situation of traffic, and grasp the future direction of China's transportation development, scientific planning of China's integrated transport system is essential(Fig. 1-4).

1.2.3 Development of Traffic Model

In the transportation planning, the model played a crucial role in 1944, and the United States conducted the first time for the traffic travel home visits to study what people need, how should traffic for people. Subsequently in Japan in 1950 in Tokyo conducted a motor vehicle travel OD survey. In the year 1952, Wardrop proposed the first and second principles of network balance distribution, namely User Equilibrium(UE) and System Optimization(SO). People began to use the system analysis method and the balance analysis method to study the traffic flow distribution when traffic congestion, but how to solve Wardrop balance has become the most important research topic. In 1965, Beckmann et al. proposed a mathematical programming model that described the distribution of balanced traffic flow. In 1975, the algorithm of Beckmann model was designed by LeBlanc and other scholars, namely Frank-Wolfe algorithm. The subsequent four-stage approach was an important milestone, marked by the Chicago Area Transportation Study, published in Chicago in 1962, when transportation planning theory and methods were born. Traffic forecasts at the time were only about. In the late 1960s, the transportation planning of the Hiroshima metropolitan area in Japan proposed for the first time the new forecasting of different modes of transportation, and proposed a single person or family as a research unit to analyze, get more information on the disaggregate model(Disaggregate Model). By the 1970s, economist Daniel L. McFadden proposed the Logit model of the Random Utility Model(RUM), introduced by Moshe Ben-Akiva into the field of traffic demand forecasting, and the study of the disaggregate model to the practical stage.

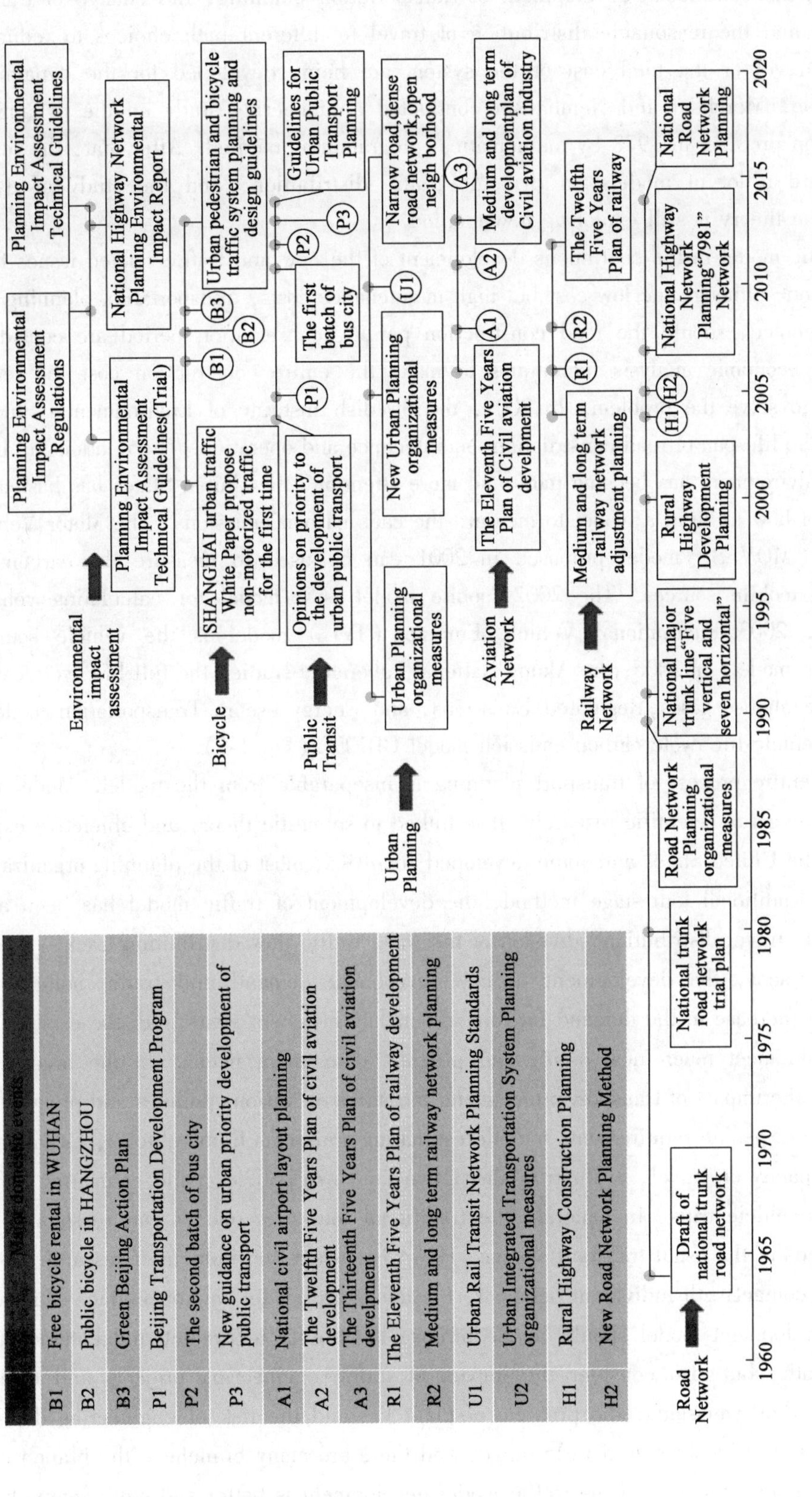

Figure 1-4 Typical events of traffic planning development in China

With the continuous development of transportation planning, the change of traffic conditions with time and the reasonable distribution of travel to different path choices to reduce the cost of personal travel or the total cost of the system are being developed for the dynamic traffic flow distribution. Merchant and Nemhauser conducted a pioneering study on the dynamic traffic flow distribution problem in 1978 by mathematical programming method. After that, the researchers also put forward a lot of models on dynamic traffic distribution, and the study of dynamic traffic distribution theory is still exploring new method.

Traffic model in the continuous development of the new and traffic-related issues followed: road construction, although the low cost but high maintenance costs, transportation planning should not be the first choice, should the road construction period, conservation period are considered and use legitimate economic analysis techniques to make the entire construction cost the least developed countries to solve the problem. In 2001, the Swedish Institute of Environmental Studies began to evaluate the lifespan of road construction, maintenance and operation. The relationship between traffic and the environment has become more and more attention, the United States has basically solved the problem of how to build a model to measure the car's carbon emissions. The Motor Vehicle Emission Simulator (MOVES) model proposed in 2001 can be used to measure the carbon emissions of integrated mobile sources. The 2002 mobile model is a model for calculating vehicle pollutant emissions. 2003 International Vehicle Emission (IVE) model is the vehicle source emissions calculation model. In 2006, the Akang National Laboratory studied the full life cycle carbon emission model Greenhouse gases, Regulated Emissions, and Energy use in Transportation model (GREET1) and the vehicle life cycle carbon emission model GREET2 (Fig. 1-5).

The entire process of transport planning is inseparable from the model. Model method is an effective means of scientific research. It is linked to scientific theory and objefctive existence of the bridge. The United States and some developed countries, most of the planning organization has been using the traditional four-stage method, the development of traffic model has been along the trip generation, travel distribution, division of the way, traffic flow distribution track.

At present, the development of new investment demand and traffic policy has led to a significant increase in the demand for forecast models in recent years, but the existing model is not sufficient to meet much new policy and program assessment needs. In the process of transport planning, the impact of transport projects and measures on various policies and programs needs to be considered. Specific requirements include estimating emissions from vehicles, estimating the impact of new capacity on travel, evaluating alternative land use policies, and estimating cargo flows and non-motor vehicle trips. In general, the traditional four-stage model can reasonably estimate the traffic needs of the usual transport system. However, when the problem of research is more detailed and more contact with individual behavior, the four-stage model cannot produce satisfactory results, so the development model should be to improve the ability to predict and enhance the ability to analyze both, but also consider the impact of traffic engineering projects and measures on air quality, carbon emissions, the problem of plant life and the risk of engineering decision-making. Traffic problems involved in a wide range, and there are many branches, the branch of the model, more and more refined, and the traffic model development is better and more comprehensive.

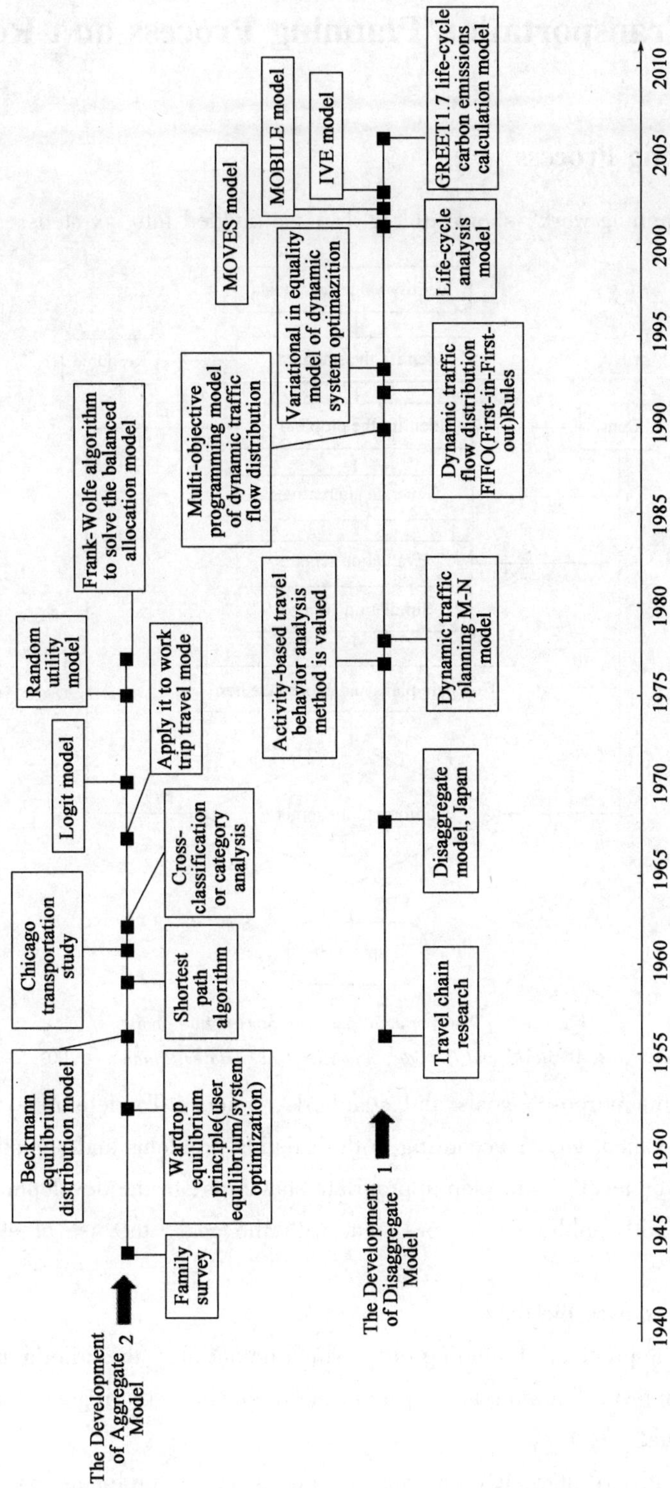

Figure 1-5 Development history of traffic planning model

1.3 Transportation Planning Process and Results

1.3.1 Planning Process

Transportation planning work, shown in Fig. 1-6, is divided into six steps.

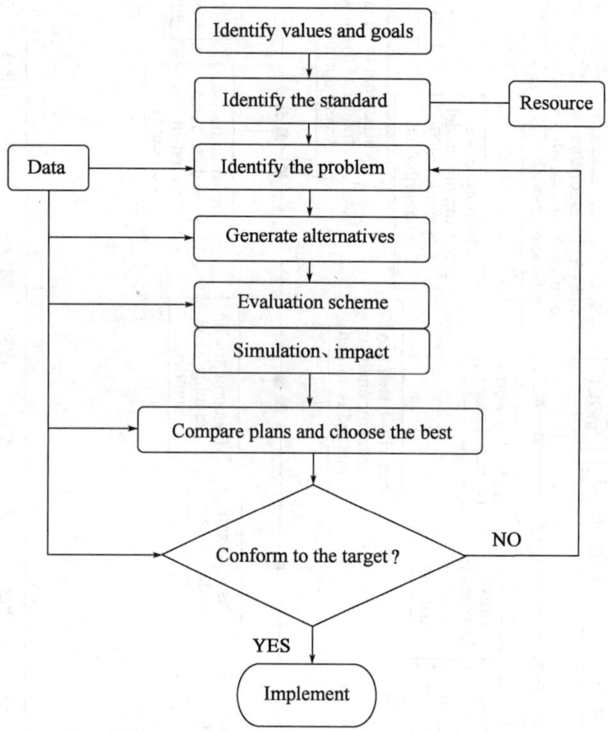

Figure1-6 Transportation planning process flow chart

Source: *Dr. Ali Mekky and P. Eng*, *Analytics Transportation Planning*, 2001.

· To determine the purpose, goals and standards, values. To determine the quality of the entire plan, the development goals; according to the existing problems and objectives, to determine the system to achieve the level, to develop appropriate standards; in the development of development programs, to comply with public views consistent with the goal, the use of effective resources, Experience.

· To collect and analyze the data.

· To determine the problem. Including those which do not meet the criteria and which meet the criteria but need to improve. Planning to determine the problems of the region, for the design of the problem, to collect data.

· Produce alternatives (alternative solutions). Focus on the problems existing in the system model, the development of reform and implementation of the program.

· Evaluation options. Including the simulation and evaluation of the impact of each option on users and non-users. Simulation of traffic flow, usually with simulation software to achieve. The impact is the assessment of the impact of the implementation of the plan, including the social impact of traffic, economic impact and environmental impact assessment, such as vehicle emissions of pollutants on the environment.

· To select the best one or more alternatives. After the evaluation of the program, it is necessary to compare the multiple schemes, compare all the schemes, compare the calculated results with the intended targets, and select the optimal plan. However, if the target requirements are not reached, it is necessary to re-examine whether the problem is correct, whether the target is appropriate, the program is accurate, and then re-program comparison, until the program is in line with the intended target can be implemented.

For a certain area of transportation planning, we must first according to the scope of the study, the target set, do the overall transportation planning and design, and then do four parts: a. research urban planning, industrial planning, economic development planning, observe the future of the above indicators. b. conduct the investigation of the current situation in the area, establish the traffic model according to the survey results, simulate the observation traffic flow, bus flow, travel time and discharge pollution equivalent, if the simulation found that there are planning objectives or standards cannot be reached and other issues, improve options until the program performance or performance meets the criteria. c. forecast the land use in the coming year. According to the industrial planning and forecasting of each department, the paper analyzes the nature and situation of land use in the planning area of the next year. d. issues raised and resolved. Through the status quo survey of a series of problems, analyze the direction of the problem and develop solutions based on the problem. On the basis of this, the preliminary scheme of forecasting the future traffic network is forecasted. The land use, demographic change and vehicle change are calculated into the model, and the problem is identified, that is, the key solution is needed. After the problem is solved, you can also fine-tune the program, analyze the results, and come to multi-angle optimization program.

1.3.2 Planning Results

Traffic planning design need to refer to the relevant norms and standards, as well as evaluation of the implementation. Such as urban road transport facilities design specifications, urban road traffic signal control mode applicable norms, urban rail along the planning and design guidelines, bus lane design specifications, garage design specifications, urban parking facilities design guidelines, etc., traffic planning involves many aspects. Different aspects of the standard specifications are different. Different levels of planning requirements of the planning results are also different, including the overall planning text, planning Atlas, planning research reports, special investigation reports and basic information compilation and so on. In addition, according to actual needs, the preparation of planning simple, planning and professional reports and other reports is needed.

(1) Text

The text is the planning and construction of the guidance book, provided to the implementation of the unit, requiring easy understanding, easy to implement, to provide the basis for the implementation of the latter part of the program. The mandatory content of the plan should be clearly stated in the planning text. The text expresses the planning conclusion in a textual manner, with clear and concise, instructive and operable. Take the planning of public transport as an example, the planning text includes 11 parts: a. General rule. Including the basis for the preparation, guiding ideology, planning principles, planning and so on. b. Transportation development status. Including the development of the situation, the status quo evaluation conclusions and summary of the problem. c. Traffic development strategy. Including the development of environmental analysis conclusions, functional positioning, strategic tasks, and development model selection. d. Traffic development goals. Including overall development goals, stage objectives, infrastructure development objectives and structure, and development objectives of transport services and support systems. e. Traffic network planning. Including a variety of modes of transport network planning and scale structure. f. Traffic hub, station layout. Including hubs, parking lots, maintenance sites, transportation sites and refueling (gas) and charging station layout programs. g. Operating organization. Including enterprise organization mode, line operation organization, capacity allocation and development, as well as hub, station operation organization mode. h. Traffic support system construction. Including intelligence, security emergency, priority traffic and human resources protection. i. Planning implementation arrangements. Including key tasks, planning the implementation of sequence arrangements and funding needs estimates. j. Plan the expected effect assessment. Including the expected level of service, technical level, and economic impact, social impact and environmental impact of the development of the planning program. k. Plan the implementation of safeguards. Including the implementation of the organization and protection, financial security, land security, technology support, fares and subsidies, green tourism and other aspects of cultural construction measures.

(2) Planning atlas

Planning atlas is the summary of the development of transportation and the relevant planning of the plan. Planning the contents and requirements of the atlas should be consistent with the planning text, and mark the map name, scale, legend, drawing time. Planning atlas mainly includes the current situation map, plan, and special map. Such as bike lane design, parking lot design, bus network design, track network design. Planning pre-atlas is mainly used for review. During implementation stage, atlas is used by the government to implement the planning program of the certificate, used to guide the planning and construction. The contents of the planning drawings should be clear and accurate, consistent with the contents of the planning text. The presentations, plans and analysis diagrams should respectively indicate that the legend should be consistent.

(3) Research report

The research report is used to carry out specific research, research, analysis and evaluation of the feasibility of the project, the effectiveness of the project and the proposed constructive suggestions. Planning research report should be in accordance with the preparation of the contents of the requirements, a detailed description of the technical methods used and analysis process, is the support of the planning text.

The general composition of the transportation planning report includes overview, status analysis and evaluation, demand forecast analysis, planning, program evaluation, conclusions, questions and suggestions. This paper mainly introduces the purpose and significance of planning, analyzes and evaluates the present situation, including the analysis and evaluation of the accessibility, mobility and safety of the system, and the existing problems of the system. Demand forecast analysis is the forecast of the next year development trends and status, and according to the needs of the next year to assess the planning program, if the standard requirements to determine the program; after the program to determine the program proposal to sum up.

The transportation planning report is classified according to different classification:

Master plan: transportation system planning, integrated transportation planning.

Stage planning: strategic planning, special planning, construction planning.

Special planning: road network planning, parking facilities planning, public transport planning, rail transit network planning.

Planning scope classification: national, provincial, city, county, urban level planning.

Medium view, micro-planning: such as area planning, intersection planning.

(4) Compilation of information

The planning process often involves a wide range of information, after the implementation of the program, the information compiled, can be used for late use. The compilation of basic information shall include relevant policy documents, relevant basic materials, reference materials and documents involved in the preparation of the plan.

(5) Special investigation and analysis report

This section may be used as an integral part of the planning study and may be prepared separately. Usually the special investigation and analysis report should be detailed description of the survey method, the investigation process, and the survey data to sort out and preliminary analysis, including the residents travel investigation and traffic conditions survey.

Take the bus special investigation report as an example, the general content may include: a. Overview, including the background, purpose, scope, content, sampling method, organization and implementation, and main conclusions of the survey. b. Basic information survey, including personal and family composition, income levels, place of residence, motor vehicle retention and so on. c. Traffic travel characteristics survey, including the travel volume, travel frequency, travel time and space characteristics, travel mode selection, travel destination, traffic OD (from the point of traffic between traffic) and so on. d. Network survey, including the urban public transport network function hierarchy, network layout, line length, network density, line repetition coefficient, non-linear coefficient, coverage, network accessibility and so on. e. City traffic capacity survey, including the total capacity of the capacity, capacity structure, capacity allocation, as well as the vehicle's vehicle age and intact rate. f. Passenger flow investigation, including the city public transport passengers travel starting point, travel time, and the overall distribution of passenger characteristics. g. Passenger satisfaction survey, including the passenger on the fares, travel information services, running punctuality, operating speed, waiting time, transfer convenience, ride comfort and other aspects of the evaluation. h. Other surveys, including traffic inspection line survey, speed survey, urban public transport site demolition survey. i. Accessories, including summary of all types of survey data.

1.4 Typical Planning Issues of Transportation Planning

Transportation planning often faces a wide variety of problems. In general, they can be attributed to three aspects: facilities to build layout and program selection issues, transportation management to solve the problem and policy formulation and optimization issues.

1.4.1 The Layout of Facilities Building and Program Options

The problem of building layout of facilities is mainly to solve what kind of facilities should be built, what kind of management system should be applied, what kind of norms, laws and requirements should be complied with. Once the program identified, multi-choice should be conducted in the final recommendation. After the program is determined, it will be discussed with the stakeholders as a basis for final implementation.

Melbourne's urban central activity area, known as the CBD area, provides the city's citizens with the soundest infrastructure, the finest business, office, business, culture and education functions. It is made by surveyor Robert Hoddle who planned urban road grid system in 1837. *In the planning of this road network system, the total population of Melbourne only was less than* 4000, *and then Governor Burke does not agree with Hoddle proposal that the main road should be built with a* 30-*meter-width. Hoddle advocated the main road should be* 20 *meters wide*(1 *chain*), *and the main road between the blocks should be* 10 *meters*(1/2 *chain*). *The achievements of these people on the scale of the streets and street buildings constitute a unique urban space, and gradually evolved into Melbourne. Now it is the most unique street*(*laneway*), *and gave birth to a unique street culture.*

Hodder Road, the main road width of 1. 5 *chain*(*Note: Chains, inch length unit.* 1 *chain is* 66 *feet, about* 20 *meters*; 1. 5 *chain is* 30 *meters*), *two-way traffic*; *four east-west road between the width of* 0. 5 *chain, about* 10 *meters, one-way traffic. Hodder Road is* 1 *mile long*(*about* 1. 6 km) *long and* 0. 5 *miles north-south*(*about* 0. 8 km), *and the long side is basically parallel to the Yarra River. The road network will be divided into* 32 *urban and rural areas are* 10 *long and* 20 *square meters that is* 201 *meters square blocks, and each block has been divided into* 20 *covers an area of about* 1920 *square meters of small plots, of which the street blocks were square, other plots for the long rectangle* (Fig. 1-7).

Melbourne CBD is so highly mixed with city features and features of the streets that attract people all over the world to live, work, study and live. Melbourne CBD is only 2. 4 *square kilometers, there are underground ring railway and five railway stations for service. Its underground ring railway started construction in* 1974, *open operation in* 1982, *is the metropolitan area of Melbourne and Victoria, the core of the regional railway network, the railway line around the CBD laying its uniform distribution of the five stations basically cover the CBD most of the Region; and the Melbourne municipal government and the planning department is like textbooks to practice the concept of TOD, the CBD within the scope of most of the high-intensity development focused on the railway site* 400 *meters radius of the service area and the surrounding area. In addition to the city rail network, Melbourne's most famous means of transport than tram. Melbourne has the world's largest tram network, the line mileage of* 250 km, *a total of* 25 *lines,* 1763 *stations, more than Berlin, Vienna, St. Petersburg and other European cities. Melbourne trams delivered more than* 180 *million passengers, effectively connecting the CBD and suburban areas, and metropolitan railways formed an effective complement.*

Source: *Zhang Naige, Surging news special draft*, 2016.

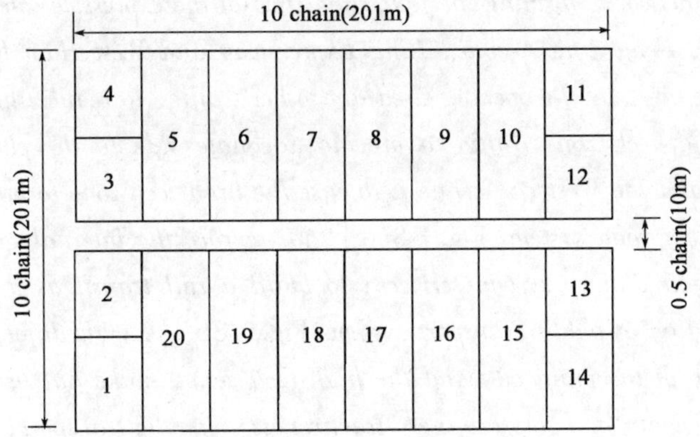

Figure 1-7 The block of Hodder proposed

Source: *Wiki pedia, authors hand painted.*

1.4.2 Transportation Management Upgrade

The improvement of transportation management is an effective way to improve the recent problem of local traffic problems. It is through as little as possible civil construction, more facilities deployment, change the way traffic facilities use the way to improve traffic. Traffic management mainly has the following ideas: a. facilities (as little as possible), b. management to enhance the way (microcirculation), c. bus improvement, d. bike improvement, e. parking induced, f. signal control adjustment, g. restrictions on vehicles and so on.

Xi'an High-tech Industrial Development Zone is the strongest economic growth pole and opening window in Shaanxi Province. It is located in the southwest development axis of the city. It is the southwest gateway of the main city, close to the central city, near the airport and Xi'an South Railway Station and other important transportation hub.

In order to cope with the traffic problems such as traffic congestion, insufficient traffic capacity, slow operation and slow environment, combined with the comprehensive system planning of Xi'an, the principle of bus priority is to change the independent state of each traffic system and construct the modern synthesis traffic system. By changing the traffic model, improve the efficiency of urban space utilization, ease the rigid relationship with the central city of a large number of demand and high-tech zones to the city center gradually narrowing the spatial contradictions, through a reasonable diversion of traffic flow, the use of urban renewal, large block development model led to the unreasonable network structure, slip network density and loss of branch network microcirculation problem. Through a clear bus network function classification, expand the coverage area and increase the bus station, to solve the bus problem. To improve the chronic status and to build a sound network and facilities, to completely change the slow line without attention, sidewalks for the motor vehicle lane is occupied, the conflict of people and vehicles to solve the problem of the supply and demand.

The overall traffic planning of the high-tech zone is guided by the layout of the high-tech zone space and industry, taking into account the road system of external traffic and internal service, adjusting the fast road network, forming the four-ring, two-of the expressway network structure, which the Second Ring Road, Feng Jing Avenue, Ring Expressway and West Ham large ring composed of four mitigation into the city, by the opening area and other traffic, to reduce the traffic pressure in the center city, for the high-tech zone traffic to provide adequate side to the channel, two horizontal technology eight road and the Western Avenue is to ease the high-tech zone to provide a new fast traffic channel. To build a clear road system[Fig. 1-8a)], *to improve the internal group contact, play the characteristics of micro-circulatory system services; to build a rail transit as a skeleton of the multi-level, efficient coordination of public transport system*[Fig. 1-8b)], *with different functional levels of public transport network in the main city and the high-tech zone, make full use of the hub function, improve the transfer efficiency and improve the attractiveness of public transport; build a comprehensive transport hub to meet the urban and external transport needs* [Fig. 1-8c)]; *to establish a comprehensive green road with Tang Yan Road and perfect non-motor vehicles and pedestrian network, to protect the chronic network* [Fig. 1-8d)]; *in accordance with the traffic characteristics of the implementation of parking control, the high-tech area is divided into parking control area and control areas to address the problem of parking gap; to avoid interference with urban transport, rational distribution of urban freight channels, distribution areas and traffic Mode and management measures to make the region logistics, freight distribution fast, safe and reliable.*

Traffic system upgrades by a number of subsystems to enhance the composition: a. Parking guidance system to guide the owners of orderly parking; b. Bus lane system, make full use of road conditions, optimize the bus route to speed the bus; c. Public bike network layout, in the small area, increase the system line layout, promote the use of public bicycles, to facilitate residents travel. For the original road connectivity is poor, the road grid is too large, in fact, can be opened up through the means of engineering to improve road connectivity; d. Open microcirculation bus, change part of the area bus ride unchanged; e. Signal linkage, by connecting the lights; f. Cargo system, the freight network layout in the periphery of the city, choose the right place to establish freight hub, to avoid the impact of goods through the city residents daily life and urban traffic, while paying attention to the layout of the distribution points to meet the residents to buy large home requirements.

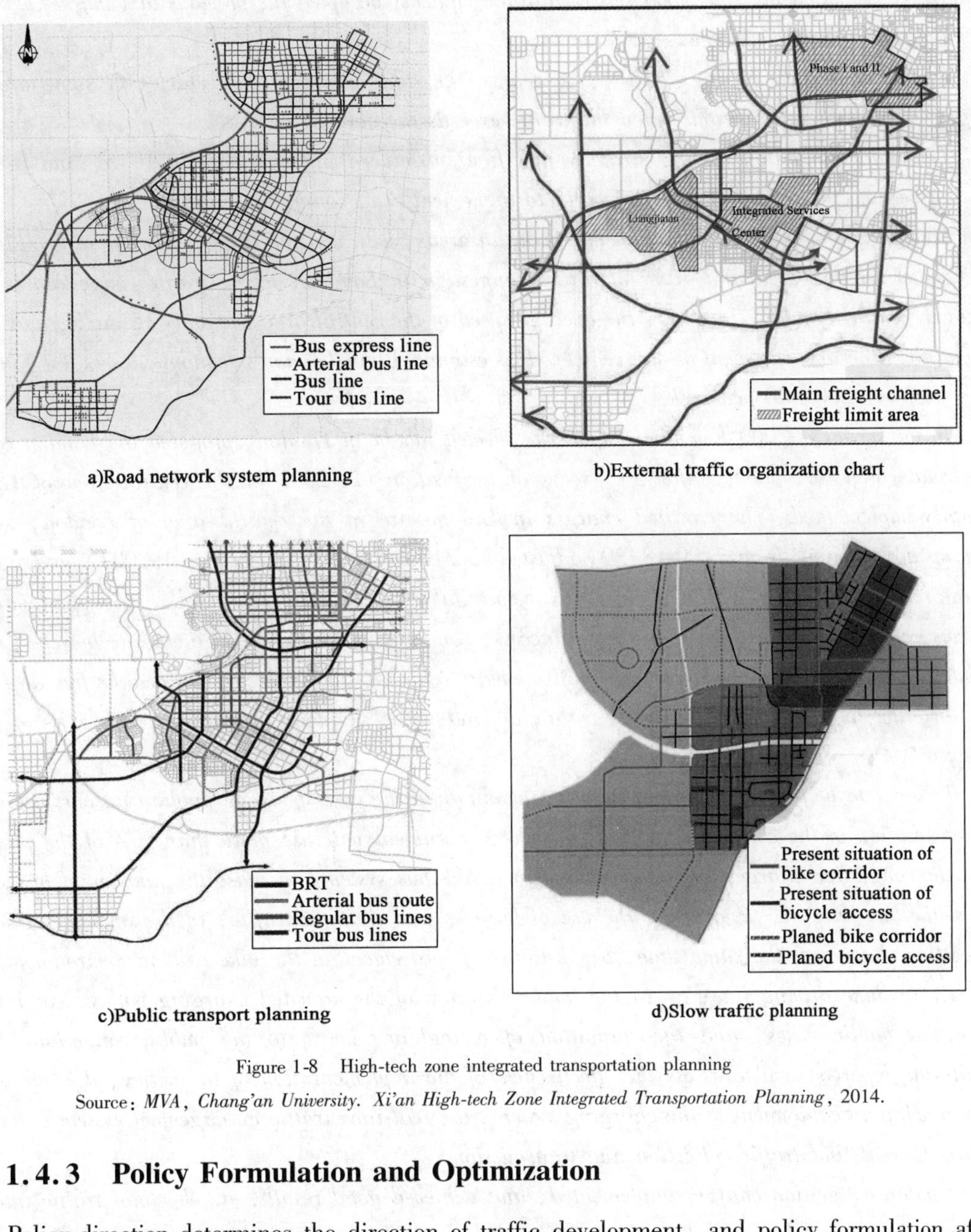

a)Road network system planning

b)External traffic organization chart

c)Public transport planning

d)Slow traffic planning

Figure 1-8 High-tech zone integrated transportation planning

Source: *MVA*, *Chang'an University. Xi'an High-tech Zone Integrated Transportation Planning*, 2014.

1.4.3 Policy Formulation and Optimization

Policy direction determines the direction of traffic development, and policy formulation affect the development of traffic planning and the formulation of the program. Followed by a network of cars and taxis, London congestion charges can be an example to illustrate.

Online booked car

With the progress of science and technology, the rise of the Internet plus, the taxi industry is facing great challenges. The emergence of the online booked car about the traditional taxi caused a huge impact. Due to the low level of traditional taxi services, traveler views, coupled with the emergence of the "Internet +" concept, network bus came into being. Network bus because of its convenient, fast, comfortable, economical, and good service attitude, quickly occupied the previous taxi market.

London crowded charges

Road Congestion Pricing (RCP): to reduce the additional cost of vehicles in some areas at congested roads or peak periods when the traffic exceeds the optimal level.

The road congestion pricing strategy was first introduced in Singapore in 1975, *and in* 2003 *London became the second city in the world to implement road congestion charges.*

London is one of Europe's largest metropolitan areas, with a population of more than 7 *million in the Greater London area and* 40% *of traffic congestion in London, where traffic congestion is more severe in central London. In* 2000, *the average speed of the central area was only* 15km/h, *and about half of the itinerary was spent on the vehicle. It is estimated that London's economic losses due to traffic congestion are* 200-400 *per week.*

In the spring of 2000 *Ken Livingstone was elected mayor of London, proposed the London central area road congestion policy, after two years of verification, in* 2003 *in the central area of London formally implemented. The crowded charges in London are in the central area of London, with a working day starting from* 7:00-18:30 *(adjusted to* 7:00-18: 00 *on February* 192007) *and a basic charge rate of* 8 *per day GBP (*£5 *per day before July* 4, 2005). *In the toll area, public welfare vehicles, disabled vehicles, taxis can be free access; London City to encourage the use of bicycles, motor vehicles, motorcycles and the use of alternative energy vehicles, these vehicles can also be free access.*

In order to take care of residents within the toll area, residents in the toll area enjoy a 90% *reduction.*

In order to be fair, the London government improved the corresponding public transport before the implementation of the congestion policy. a. The Government will use more than 2/3 *of the proceeds from the congestion charges for the improvement of the bus system, increase the number of buses and adjust the bus lines; b. Encourage the use of bicycles and walking traffic, in the implementation of congestion charges at the same time, a substantial improvement in the bike driving environment, the new* 72 km *bike driving line; c. In the implementation of the crowded charging policy, continue to investigate public views, and the formation of a regular release to the public congestion policy monitoring report system to assess the effectiveness of the implementation of the policy; d. Due to the high timeliness requirement of the charging system, the real-time traffic management system is built to realize the real-time traffic collection and transmission.*

London congestion charges implemented, and achieved good results. a. the total traffic into the urban area has not changed, but about 50% *of the car travel into public transport; b. the area of nitrogen oxides, carbon dioxide, suspended particulate matter have declined, the traffic accident rate is reduced about* 40%-70% *every year; c. although the implementation of the congestion charges, but the city center business has no significant impact;*

Source: *Adapted from Xue Meigen, Cheng Jie. London Road congestion policy*, 2007.

As can be seen from the above two cases, the formulation of policies can affect the development of traffic. Therefore, the policy formulation and optimization of transportation planning must be concerned about and planning alternative measures.

1.5 Technical Composition of Transportation Planning

1.5.1 Typical Method

Typical methods in transportation planning include logical analysis, program testing and comparison, and public participation.

(1) Logical analysis

Logical analysis is the study of the nature and development laws of research objects. Commonly used concepts, judgments, reasoning and other forms of thinking completed by covering the phenomenon, with the theory of the usual form of the general to reveal the essence.

Design of a good planning program need rigorous logic, clear concept, and is based on the concept of correct analysis of reasoning. This method requires the planner to understand and use the basic knowledge, with the ability of imagination, language ability and mapping ability, and then the planner can apply the deductive, induction and analogical reasoning method to get the optimal scheme.

(2) Program test and comparison method

The comparison of the program can be done by measuring the benefits, costs, satisfaction, reliability, risk and other indicators. There are number of different solutions for a region's transportation planning, each of which has its pros and cons. Thus it requires planners to compare and choose program according to the purpose and willingness of the traffic participant. Commonly used indicators are income-cost indicators, satisfaction, expectations, reliability and risk.

The evaluation of a project is often affected by many factors. There are certain mathematical models that can be used to find the interaction of the evaluation indicators for comprehensive study. Commonly used methods are analytic hierarchy process, Delphi method (expert opinion method), fuzzy comprehensive evaluation method, neural network method, barrel theory, benchmarking method, game theory and Monte Carlo method.

(3) Public participation method

Public participation method is to avoid limited personal logic analysis by the dialogue, and make the masses determine the program. The determination of the target, the list of projects, project evaluation and the program optimization, all of these need public participation to make sure analysis is comprehensive. On the other hand, public participation can avoid distorting project performance and the benefit for some people, so acceptance of public participation ensures that the results are more reasonable.

1.5.2 Data Analysis Technology

With of the development of big data concepts, the transportation industry is facing a major change. Transportation planning involves a big number of multi-source data, such as subway card data, bus credit card data, taxi time and space data, online ticket information, and mobile phone GPS information. Big data, a large number of data can be systematically analyzed, and then we can use these data to get a lot of travel related information, so it laid a good foundation for more scientific transportation reform.

Data acquisition and analysis techniques, such as mining, screening, interrogation techniques, data distribution, correlation and trend determination, can be applied to the transportation sector. From a large number of data mining, travel characteristics can be found, which is so-called data mining. For the existing data characteristics, screening out the reliable, useful data is the screening technology. In the process of data analysis, there are still many applicable technologies, including judging its mathematical distribution, studying the development trend of data, judging the correlation between the influencing factors, computer analysis of road network conditions, traffic flow evolution and evaluation of performance of the network model, according to the end point and road network conditions to select the shortest path based on shortest path algorithm.

1.5.3 Commonly Used Software

Transportation planning is a process of forecasting and planning alternative testing. Some data analyses, simulation software, transportation planning software were often used. The application was shown in Table 1-1.

Table 1-1 Transportation planning commonly used software

Software	Application
Excel/FOXBASE/ORACLE	Data storage/transmission/processing
AUTOCAD	Drawing software
ARCGIS/MAPINFO	Special map production/geographic data import/export/geographic information statistics
SPSS/LINGO	Statistical Analysis
CUBE/TransCAD/EMME/Visum/TranStar	Traffic demand forecast/estimate OD matrix/land use forecast/traffic signal timing optimization/traffic demand forecasting model: four-stage model/rapid response model/disaggregate model
Vissim/PARAMICS/Synchro/AIMSUM	Signal timing simulation/bus lane simulation/environmental impact analysis/intelligent traffic assessment

· Data storage analysis software: This type of software is mainly used for planning the early processing of traffic data and storage. Commonly used software is Excel, FOXBASE, SQL, ORACLE.

· Data statistical analysis software: This kind of software is mainly used for data entry, collation and analysis. The functions include data management, statistical analysis and chart analysis. Commonly used software are SPSS and LINGO.

· Drawing software: AUTOCAD can be used for two-dimensional drawing, detailed drawing, design documents and basic three-dimensional design. To describe the planning options, geographic/traffic software can identify information from this software.

· Geographic information software: This kind of software can describe, collect, deal with, store, manage and analyze the integration of geospatial information with the integrated software. ArcGIS and Mapinfo were commonly-used.

· Macro simulation software①Cube ②TransCAD ③EMME/3 ④VISUM ⑤TranStar. Traffic service levels and traffic-related performance parameters of the network traffic can be analyzed by these software.

· Micro-simulation software①VISSIM ②PARAMICS ③Synchro ④AIMSUM ⑤TransModeler. Traffic service level and traffic-related performance parameters can be analyzed for intersections, squares and other traffic flow.

1.6 The Contents of this Book

This book is composed of twelve chapters. The first chapter introduces the transportation planning system, planning concept and-commonly-used technical methods. Chapter 2 introduces the data in transportation planning and its application. Chapter 3 introduces the traffic model. Chapters 4-7 explain the specific modeling principles, implementation methods and methods of practical work of the four-stage model in detail. Chapter 8 describes the test and evaluation of the model. Chapter 9 introduces the bus planning. Chapter 10 describes the planning alternatives, and chapters 11 and 12 describe life-cycle and related methods. The specific examples of transportation planning are attached at the end of each chapter. The transportation planning and modeling common problems and examples of transportation planning application software were also introduced.

1.7 The Knowledge System Involved in Transportation Planning

Transportation planning is a comprehensive subject with its basic theory and the need for a wide range of other basic knowledge. The learner should master a variety of knowledge and can use the knowledge to balance the relationship between transportation and people, the transportation system and other system relationships. The various aspects of planning are shown Table 1-2.

Table 1-2 The knowledge system involved in transportation planning

Involving knowledge content	Application
Civil engineering(roads, bridges, buildings, etc.)	Planning basis
Intelligent Transportation Technology	
Management and policy knowledge	
Traffic model (UTPS correlation analysis, trend analysis, statistical model simulation model, decision model)	Fundament
Project cost calculation, life efficiency and cost estimation	Performance
Capacity, accessibility, service level	
Economy, environment, energy assessment technology	Planning programming
Public opinion collection	

1.8 Learning Methods for this Book

It is recommended that after completing studying the first chapter, understanding the background of the transportation planning, development trends and basic concepts, it is necessary to explore the transportation and think deeply. The second chapter is to learn the type of traffic data, acquisition methods, commonly-used analysis methods and software. At first we should read the content then we can be familiar with the above content by studying the cases further. In the third chapter, after understanding the basic concept and classification of the model, we should focus on the structure of the model and its principles and some typical model application methods. The Fourth, the fifth, the sixth and the seventh chapter are classic four-stage models of learning. When studying these chapters, we should pay attention to the logic, and the content coherence then we can be proficient in a variety of methods. We should understand and master the traffic model evaluation method and analysis process after studying Chapter 8. In the ninth chapter, according to the particularity of public transportation analysis, the basic contents of public transportation facilities planning and bus service planning is summarized. Chapter 10 describes how the transportation performance measurement is based on the cost and the impact of the whole life measurement method, which provides a reference for selecting the planning scheme. Chapter 11 introduces the method of calculating for transportation planning. This chapter can help future-oriented transportation planners to avoid only emphasizing on investment without considering the environment. Chapter 12 describes the different transportation planning program and analyze the pros and cons of common indicators and makes multi-index comparison. There are large numbers of cases behind each chapter, from the domestic and international planning practice report and summary or the author's planning practice based on planning practice of academic research. The actual value of the parameters of the situation is suitable for national conditions and domestic statistical analysis. The differences between commonly-used parameters and methods were also introduced. The purpose of this book is to help the reader understand the actual situation, learn to improve the understanding of transportation planning, experience and understand the characteristics of transportation planning. Some appendices will be easier to read which are useful to deepen the reader's understanding of the content to explore the interest are and the inspiration in transportation phenomenon, there are some content forth reader to enrich their knowledge.

Exercises

1. What is the relationship between America's transportation development history and laws?

What is the difference between America and China?

2. What aspects of the transport system to practice the socialist core values? Please briefly describe.

3. Why transportation planning need models?

4. According to the characteristics of complex systems, explain why do transportation system is a complex system?

5. With your understanding of the transportation planning, talk about the definition of transportation planning, objectives and guidelines.

References

[1] Shao Chunfu. Principles of Transportation Planning[M]. Beijing: China Railway Publishing House, 2004.

[2] Wang Wei. Traffic Planning[M]. Beijing: China Communications Press, 2007.

[3] Lu Huapu. Frontier of Transportation Planning Theory Research [M]. Beijing: Tsinghua University Press, 2007.

[4] Li Wei. Copenhagen Bicycle Traffic Policy (2002—2016) [J]. Beijing Planning and Construction, 2004,2:46-51.

[5] Michael D. Meyer, Eric J. Miller. Urban Transportation Planning: A Decision-oriented Approach[M]. USA, 2008.

[6] Ali Mekky, P. Eng. Analytics Transportation Planning[M]. America,2001.

[7] Weingroff, Richard F. Federal-Aid Highway Act of 1956:Creating the Interstate System[J]. Public Roads ,1996,60 (1).

[8] Lowr, Sam. A Brief Portrait of Multimodal Transportation Planning in Oregon and the Path to Achieving It, 1890—1974 [R]. Portland : Oregon Transportation Research and Education Consortium(OTREC), 2010.

[9] Vukan RVuchic. Transportation for Livable Cities [M]. USA: Center for Urban Policy Research, 1999.

[10] Research and Innovative Technology Administration, Bureau of Transportation Statistics. Public Road Length, Miles by Functional System:2005 [EB/OL]. http://www. bts. gov/publications state_transPortation_statistics/state_transportation_statistics_2006/html/table_01_01. html.

[11] Jones David W. Urban Transit Policy: An Economic and Political History [M]. Englewood Cliffs, NJ: Prentice Hall, 1985.

[12] Kirby, R. F. Public transportation [M]. Englewood Cliffs, NJ: Prentice Hall, 1992.

[13] FRA overview [EB/OL]. http://www. fra. dot. gov/Page/P0002.

[14] FRA High-speed intercity passenger rail (HSIPR) program [EB/OL]. (2010-12-09)[2011-03]. http://www. fra. dot. gov/rpd/passenger/2325. shtml.

[15] UIC. US to invest $53 billion into high speed rail network over six years [EB/OL]. (2011-03-24)[2011-03-24]. http://uic. org/.

[16] FRA. High-Speed Intercity Passenger Rail Program [EB/OL]. (2011-06-20)[2011-07]. http://www. fra. dot. gov/rpd/passenger/2243. shtml.

[17] City of Copenhagent. Cycle Policy 2002-2012[R]. Denmark, 2002.

[18] Efficient Transportation Equity Act [S]. USA, 1998.

[19] Moving Ahead for Progress in the 21st Century Act,MAP-21 [S]. USA, 2012.

[20] Fixing America's Surface Transportation Act[S]. USA, 2015.

[21] David EBoyce, Huw CWL. Williams. Forecasting Urban Travel:Past, Present and Future [M]. UK:Edward Elgar Publishing Limited, 2016.

[22] Ministry of Transport. Guidelines for Urban Public Transport Planning[S]. 2014.
[23] Xue Meigen, Cheng Jie. Road congestion charging policy in London[J]. Urban Transport, 2007,(06):14-18.
[24] Downs. The Lows of Peak-Hour-Express Way Congestion[J]. Traffic,1962,33(3):347-362.

Chapter 2

Transportation Planning Data

2.1 Introduction

Prior to the 1950s, transportation planning studies focused on the future traffic volumes of different transportation facilities in order to supply for transport facilities. And the annual traffic volume is estimated based on the current traffic volume and growth factors, so the main data required for the research was the flow and growth rates of various transport modes. Later, people recognized the relationship between transportation and land use, so the demand of data types and the amount of data significantly increased and it needs comprehensive travel survey when making traffic forecast. In recent years, with the rapid development of Internet of things, automatic detection, various traffic monitoring data and mobile phone data, it is the problem that how to forecast human behavior characteristics, land use intensity characteristics in transportation condition and travel behavior, transport planning are integrated into the new information age. Some of the methods of obtaining data through surveys may be replaced by new technologies, and some are difficult to be replaced. However, it could be a new tendency that these data can be collected by the new technology, and scope of data source is corresponded with the population and facilities that the planning is related to.

This chapter focuses on the transportation planning data and its requirements.

2.1.1 Data Requirements

Transportation planning is based on the information of temporal and spatial characteristics of travel, performance characteristics of traffic facilities, the degree of traffic impact and the evolution of time-related changes in the performance characteristics of different travel programs. To make a logical description of these aspects, estimation and planning alternatives, it needs to be based on data consistent with definition, format, and the same scope of the transport disciplines. These data includes the one that can describe the condition of transportation systems, the circumstances which traffic is in-land use and development of social economic(e. g. population of urban planning and the rate of economic growth). In this regard, the data of transportation planning is divers and enormous. Then the relative data includes:

· Data on transportation system supply and its related data, typically including the structure and scale of traffic network conditions, capacity, delays etc..

· Data on travel demand and related data, typically including the population, the number of jobs, the number of labor force and the behavior characteristics of people based on the population data, such as family income, vehicle distribution, different purposes of travel, and temporal and spatial distribution.

· Traffic flow data this type of data mainly refers to the service traffic volume on the facilities, Peak Hour Factor(PHF). For the bus, the data includes network traffic volume of the largest cross sectional traffic flow.

· Data on transportation planning, construction of infrastructure, and environmental impact and resources, trip generation policies, including status of project that have been planned for construction, environmental constraints value of, charges, noise, emissions and energy consumption.

· Data on trends of land use, socio-economic and other related factors affecting the trip generation, including the changes in population and jobs, the land use type, adjustment of land use planning and economy and society development planning etc..

During the implementation of the plan, whether the above-mentioned types of data need to be acquired or not and their accuracy requirements are based on the following four aspects:

· Monitoring the performance of the transport system. In typical transportation networks and stations, the traffic data should be able to describe the time spatial distribution of the current traffic flow, and reveal the traffic volume of different modes of transportation. In road segment or nodes with poor transportation performance, it can quantitatively reveal the specific situation. The performance description based on data is an important basis for transportation planning to reveal traffic contradiction and analyze the traffic condition.

· Understanding and analyzing travel behavior. Traffic data should be able to reveal which factors affect whether people travel or not, which travel mode and travel time they decided to travel, and other behaviors. And it should be able to describe the travel behavior of space-time aggregation and related factors affecting the behaviors. The data reflecting these factors should be easily distinguishable and objective.

· Calibrating model and forecasting future travel demand. From the travel demand to the travel behavior and then to the different sections of the network, different ways and different periods of the actual traffic flow, it needs some observations to check the correct value of the model; traffic model is reasonable, need to calculate the calibration; model, but also through the introduction of the number of future years the number of travel characteristics of the relevant indicators in order to analyze the pros and cons of the next year's traffic service level. This will allow transportation planning data to serve the model checkups and will be easier to anticipate in the future.

· Evaluating the effectiveness of transportation planning programs or improvement measures. The traffic data should provide important parameters with clear concept and basis which can easy to distinguish the effect for scheme alternative, the performance of the transportation service and its impact assessment.

Traffic data occupies an important position in transportation planning. On stages of transportation planning, it needs to have the corresponding types of traffic data. And data accuracy to a large extent determines the quality of transportation planning, which requires, reasonably determine the data source, sample size and sampling methods based on the statistical analysis.

2.1.2 Data Sources

The data sources of transportation planning usually include two aspects:

(1) Existing resources

These data are usually collected by visiting relevant functional departments, such as government agencies of statistics, planning, transportation and land resources management and other government agencies, and some data can be collected directly from the relevant websites. It should be noted that the traffic data zoning system should be consistent with the administrative divisions in order to facilitate the collection of data, such as population, jobs, land function division, highway and urban road classification and mileage, traffic, cost information.

(2) Specific survey

It is usually a labor-intensive activity, which is the survey on transportation system and its related systems conducted in the selected time, region and location of the sections and intersections. In addition to trucks, taxis, buses, bicycles, hubs, tourist spots and the purpose is to understand the status of the transport system and the existing problems, to grasp characteristics and regulation of various transport problems. This part of the workload in the transportation planning research process occupies a considerable proportion, and the price is expensive, the typical representative is based on person trip survey (PT survey).

2.1.3 Requirements for Data

The formulation and implementation of traffic planning is directly affected by method of data collection, data structure and its envelope relationship and the coverage of data source, accuracy and completeness of data sources.

· Study area: In order to facilitate the determination of the scope of the survey, of the study area, land use, socioeconomic condition and other information will be divided into several traffic zones.

· Forecasted period: It is necessary to select the base year, usually the year before the planning special investigation, and identify study year with a variety of data to forecast economic development and travel demand of study and planning year.

· Typical survey time: generally, traffic volume of 24/16/12 hours, peak hour and weekend etc. usually are collected in normal days avoiding the days with special activities, abnormal climatic conditions, the situation of temporary closed roads, and absence of transport services unless the plan goal is to obtain abnormal traffic data.

· Policy background of data collection: data of transport planning projects policy supported will be collected more conveniently, fast and efficiently. Therefore, it is necessary to understand the policy background, so that the project in line with the policy context to carry out.

2.2 Data Types and Zone Division

2.2.1 Data Types

Data can be classified as qualitative and quantitative data.

Qualitative data refers to data describing the inherent characteristics of phenomenon or relative rank and order, that is, the qualitative characteristics of the phenomenon without quantitative features. Things can be sorted according level or order. Qualitative data contains the classification system, and the majority of classification systems have the same hierarchical structure, therefore, qualitative data can reveal not only the similarity and difference of things, but the relative position of things in the classification tree.

Quantitative data refers to a complete quantitative description of the object, as well as their level and order revealing the difference of things, which can describe absolute amount of objects due to its units of measurement and datum point.

Quantitative data could be further classified into:

· Nominal: classification (e. g. yes or no).

· Ordinal: rank, order (e. g. large or small).

· Interval: the degree of difference between items (e. g. temperature).

· Ratio: with meaningful zero volumes (e. g. height, weight).

2.2.2 Zone Divisions

A traffic zone is the geographical unit that combines transportation sources to avoid the complicated work of analysis on each traffic source. Sometimes given the convenience of analysis on trip distribution, the planning area is also divided into the middle-size zone, big-sized zone etc. Then, the trip can be divided into the internal trip and external trip. The trip with origin and destination in a same zone is defined as internal trip, and the trip with origin and destination in different zones is defined as external trip.

(1) Determine the number of zones

Transportation data are generally grouped by geographic location or type/function of transportation facility. Aggregating the data into geographic analysis units called "zones" is a typical method in transportation modeling. Land uses with those zones are assumed to be homogeneous.

There are many factors that need to be considered to determine the number of zones. On the one hand, maximizing the number of zones can achieve greater accuracy, minimize data loss in aggregation and the number of intrazonal trips; on the other hand, a small number of zones can minimize the workload, investigation costs and study time. The number of zones used in any study depends upon many factors, see Table 2-1.

Table 2-1 The comparison of deciding the number of zones

Number of zones	A large number of zones	A small number of zones
Advantage	Achieve higher precision	Minimize the workload
	Reduce data loss during aggregation	The level of detail needed for information from other sources
	Could be more flexible in analysis	Minimize study time
	Minimize the number of intrazonal trips	Minimize the sampling fluctuations in zones by obtaining reasonable number of observations per zone
	Be compatible with other survey data	

A compromise between all these needs must be sought. Some practical limitations should also be considered; e. g.

· study purpose, time and budget;

· required accuracy;

· homogeneity distribution of land use in the zone;

· socioeconomic data available;

· compatibility with assessment boundaries and existing planning zones;

· natural boundaries (e. g. freeways, railroad, rivers, administrative boundaries) are usually taken as zone boundaries.

(2) Purpose and principle of zones division

The purpose of dividing zones is to:

· Minimize costs enhance the practical operability to reduce the difficulty of analysis and forecasting under the condition that required precision is needed.

· The trip production and attraction are easy to be combined with regional economic indicators to facilitate the analysis of the relevant regulations.

· Using the trips between the zones to represent spatial distribution of travel demand.

· Provide data support for conveniently stimulating the traffic flow by applying the trip assignment.

Generally, the zones division should be correspond with the data classification systems, so land use within those zones is homogeneous. Usually, the main principles of zone division are:

· Homogeneity: homogeneity of important attributes, e. g. land use, demographic composition and income.

· Compatibility: compatibility with the administrative boundaries, old zones.

· Equitability: take the travel time as a measure, the traffic congestion is more detailed than that on the non-congested sections, and the land use intensity is higher than the low intensity region, and the direct impact area is more important than the indirect impact area.

· Boundaries: natural boundaries (e. g. freeways, railroad, rivers, and area municipality boundaries) and it should be avoided to take major arterials zone boundaries.

The survey data was collected by Chang'an University in 2003 *and* 2004, *separately.* 227 *zones are shown in the* Fig. 2-1.

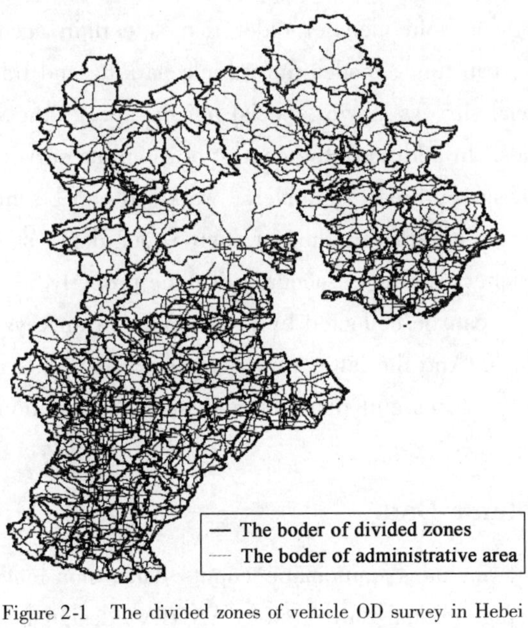

Figure 2-1 The divided zones of vehicle OD survey in Hebei

Source: *Chang'an University, Hebei Province Highway OD Survey Report.*

· *Homogeneity: large-type mineral areas are divided as a zone.*

· *Compatibility: the boundaries of counties were taken as zone boundaries.*

· *Equitability: the province was partitioned into zones carefully; considering the adjunct provinces, e. g. Henan, Shandong, as the areas indirectly affecting the dividing of zones; the boundaries of municipalities and counties as the zones boundaries.*

· *Boundaries: the five corridors were chosen to provide convenience for the test of trip assignment.*

2.3 Data in Transportation Planning

The smooth progress of transport planning requires a lot of basic data for support. The interaction among traffic, land use and socio-economic development generates a large amount of data and a variety of data types. This section discusses the data types and collection methods, which mainly introduces data of travel behavior, traffic, OD, road network and node, other traffic facilities, land use, socioeconomic and demographic data.

2.3.1 Travel Behavior Data

Travel behavior data refers to the travel of residents in the survey area (such as the OD of each trip, the travel mode, etc.).

· Household characteristics mainly include address, family size, vehicle ownership, car use, dwelling unit type and area.

· Demographics of household member older than a certain age (e. g. seven years) and include: gender, age, occupation, income, education, work address and work day or off.

· Trip data for each household member older than a certain age (e. g. seven years) and include: trip purpose, OD, trip time, modes the vehicle parking and transfer.

· Other data: additional surveys are for special objects, e. g. the willingness of owning cars, the trip data at the weekends. In addition, the contest of sampling survey is applied when there is a great amount of residents at survey area. Relatively, workload can be minimized by sampling, and quality control measures (e. g. eliminating the obviously wrong data) should be used efficiently, so this method is cheaper, quicker, and more accurate if done properly.

The travel behavior data can be collected by home-interview surveys, telephone surveys, mail-back surveys, on-line surveys. And the latter three surveys collect data of some groups, which are different from the first survey, so careful planning and impact evaluation should be taken to avoid some mistakes.

2.3.2 Travel Volume Data

The travel volume data includes: automatic counts data, non-motorize vehicle counts data, pedestrian counts data, average annual daily traffic (AADT), design hourly volume (DHV), peak hour volume (PHV) etc.. And it is needed to learn the time-spatial distribution of volume and traffic composition for determining the target. In addition, what data should be collected is determined by the planning goal.

(1) Traffic volume and classification

Traffic volume is the counts of transport cross the point, or a lane. Traffic volume can be classified as automatic counts data, non-motorize vehicle (mainly including bicycle) counts data, pedestrian counts data. It can also be classified as interzonal trip, boundaries trip, screen line trip and special survey trip.

· Interzonal trip: the volume is generated at the segments and intersections. Different land use results different volume of segments in same zones.

· Boundaries trip: the volume is generated at the intersection of zone boundaries and segments within the zone, which reflects the volume entering and exiting the zone.

· Screen line trip: the rivers, hills railway etc. or imaginary line are usually considered as screen line. And the screen line trip is the volume through the lines. The data can be collected by manual counting, automatic coil counting, geomagnetic counting and video counting etc., which is used to check the reliability of OD data.

· Special survey trip: the volume is generated at the special sites, which is used to satisfy the need of traffic management and signal control, e. g. the volume entering and exiting the city, public transit volume.

(2) Typical traffic volume data

In practical, different method of statistic or observation is used to describe the traffic, e. g. average traffic volume, peak hourly volume etc..

· Average Traffic: the average traffic in a period is used as the traffic in this period and be classified as Average Daily Traffic (ADT), Annual Average Daily Traffic (AADT), Monthly Average Daily Traffic (MADT), Week Average Daily Traffic (WADT) etc..

· Peak Hourly Volume: in city, the hour with highest volume is defined as the peak hour in the continuous hourly survey. The volume in peak hour is defined as peak hour volume. 4 fold of highest 15-minute volume is defined as peak hour flow rate, which is used to reflect the actual service traffic volume.

· Peak Ratio. The ratio of peak hourly volume to daily volume is the peak ratio(%). The ratio can reflect the concentration of PHV, and it can be used for the conversation between the PHV and daily volume. The data reflected peak ratio of highway is mostly 9%-10% (mean = 9.6%), and the peak ratio of arterial is lower than the highway in China.

· Peak hour factor (PHF). The ratio of the peak hour volume to the hourly traffic volume which is the traffic volume expanded from certain period of peak hour is defined as the peak hour factor. Generally, peak hour is divided into 5 min, 6 min, 10 min or 15 min as the certain period. The expression of the peak hour factor is:

$$PHF_t = \frac{\text{Peak hourly traffic volume}}{\text{Traffic volume of } t \text{ period in peak hour} \times \dfrac{60}{t}} \tag{2-1}$$

where, $PHF_t < 1$, reflecting the traffic distribution within the various periods of peak hour, and the closer the value is to 1 indicating the peak hourly traffic volume is more stable

· Designed hour vehicles (DHV). The hourly traffic is sorted in order of volume in a year, then the hourly traffic ranked 30th is defined as DHV, or 30th hourly traffic volume.

(3) The temporal and spatial characteristic

· Temporal characteristic

The traffic exists some rules in time though it changes with time, which can be showed by the annual variation, monthly variation, weekly variation, hourly variation etc..

· Spatial characteristic

a. Distribution of regional traffic volume

Unbalance of regional economy results in the difference of traffic in different regions, e. g. the obvious difference of traffic between developed and developing provinces.

b. Distribution of urban-rural traffic volume

Many aspects, e. g. economic development, industrial structure, transport infrastructures, population density, material standard of living, car ownership, exist difference in urban and rural regions, which leading to different traffic. Generally, there are some empirical findings that traffic volume in urban roads is largest, followed by the rural roads, suburbs roads, and the volume in country roads is smallest.

c. Direction distribution

In long period, the traffic may be in equilibrium in both directions. But some situations, e. g. tidal flow with large traffic difference on two-ways at rush hour, cause the difference of traffic in both directions, which can be described by the directional distribution factors:

$$K_{\mathrm{D}} = \frac{\text{Traffic volume of the driving direction}}{\text{Two-way traffic volume}} \tag{2-2}$$

where, $K_{\mathrm{D}} \geqslant 50\%$. Some foreign researchers found that the value of K_{D} was 70%, 60% and 50% in commuting routes, arterial roads and main street in downtown, respectively; and in China, the value of K_{D} was 60%-70% in commuting routes.

d. Lane distribution

The traffic volume on one-way with two or more lanes has difference in different lanes. Generally, the traffic volume is larger in the right lanes at the condition with less volume; the traffic is larger in the centre and left lanes when the road filled with large traffic volume.

(4) Traffic volumes composition features

The traffic composition features referred the ratio of transport modes in traffic, which is the basis of determining road function, path property and developing management measures. According to the attributes and location of the road, there are different descriptions for composing characteristics of traffic on the highway, urban road and gates of urban road. Various vehicles are converted into standard vehicle, and conversion factors are shown in Table 2-2.

Table 2-2 Vehicle conversion factor

Vehicle types	Car	Bus	Heavy truck	Articulator
Conversion factor	1.0	2.0	2.5	3.0

In the road traffic volume analysis and highway planning and design, the vehicle will be divided into cars, buses, articulator, light truck, medium truck, heavy trucks, trailers, and tractors etc..

The proportion of travel modes is related to the regional, road classification, regional economic development level and regional characteristics, for examples, cars, buses and trucks etc., except tractors, motorcycles and other low-performance transport vehicles, can be allowed to drive on the expressway; urban road traffic composition is relatively complex, usually including large, medium and small cars, trucks, motorcycles, electric vehicles, bicycles, tricycles, tractors etc.. In the city center where the traffic management is relatively strict, it is often limited to the modes to pass. The traffic composition is relatively simple. The urban entrances and exits are in the suburbs of the city. It is the transition between the highway and the urban road. Both the characteristics, but different, such as buses, minibuses, bike ratio is generally lower than the city road, higher than the road in city outer area.

Survey methods commonly used are manual counting method, floating car method, mechanical counting method and video method. The method used to carry out the investigation depends mainly on the equipment, funding and technical conditions available, the purpose of the investigation and the information requested.

2.3.3 Other Travel Data

(1) Commercial vehicle OD data

Drivers of commercial vehicle from different depots are sampled and interviewed. Data collection usually include the origin, destination, load, no-load and freight of commercial vehicle classified.

(2) Taxi data

These data can be collected by onboard equipment in taxi and interview of the taxi drivers to obtain the trip purpose, occupation and income etc., and mainly include the number of taxi, origin, destination, trip time, routes etc., which can provide valuable information for problems about taxi allocation in serve region and site selection etc..

(3) Transit OD data

Vehicle-following method, Stationed method, IC card data and Tickets method are the main survey methods for collecting data. And the comparison of these methods is shown in Table 2-3.

Table 2-3 The collected OD data of public transits can be used for the researches

Survey method	Advantages	Disadvantages
Vehicle-following method	Operational work and data processing are simple and clear. Easy access to uninterrupted passenger flow volume of route	The OD of transit passengers is collected by interviews, and usually the Oral address of passenger interviewed is not clear. Some passengers did not have the patience to finish, which resulting in the low return as a result of the non-multiple choice questionnaire
Stationed method	Operational tasks is simple and clear, and station investigation can be intuitive to understand the rationality of changes of cross-section traffic volume	The station is a benchmark for survey, It need to be careful to avoid data error when completing the line during data processing

continued

Survey method	Advantages	Disadvantages
IC card method	Part of passengers transfer information can be collected without investigators	Class Ⅰ IC card can only obtain data of passengers owning the IC card, and the OD data of passengers having two or more travel times can be inferred strictly
Tickets method	The relatively complete routes with OD of passengers can be collected	The preparation of the investigation is more complicated, which needs for public transit business support, and large work

Note: There are two types of IC cards: Ⅰ-the card recording information that is used only when get on the bus with; Ⅱ-the card recording information that is used when get on and off the bus.

2.3.4 Road Network and Node Data

(1) Highway and urban road classification

According to the location, the nature of traffic and its use characteristics, for vehicles and pedestrian walk facilities can be divided into road and urban roads (hereinafter referred to as the road network). The road refers to the road connecting the cities, villages, factories and mines and forest areas, mainly to provide car driving and have certain technical conditions of transport facilities, can be divided into freeway, one, two, three, four (total of five) technical level, including state, provincial, county, township, village five administrative levels and major arterial, minor arterial and collector of three types of functional classification. Urban road refers to the use of traffic within the city to provide traffic facilities, according to the road in the road network status, traffic function and the service along the building functions are divided into five categories including expressway, trunk, sub-dry, slip road and community road. Transport planning should not only be considered within the planning of the road network, but also abstract to the traffic network. Because of the different planning objectives, regional development, and characteristics of the different requirements of the network service performance is also high and low, network abstraction network processing methods will be different. As a transport planning for urban areas, the usual method of network processing in planning practice is described below. In order to ensure that the road network can meet the traffic demand in the vast majority of hours, and truly reflect the network access and service performance, the need of classifying the road network to adapt to the accuracy of traffic network supply analysis needs.

In the traffic model, the technical level of the road network can be divided into five categories according to the network traffic service function, the traffic volume and the driving speed characteristic:

· Freeway/Expressway road

Expressway provides the car for sub-direction and sub-lane driving. The annual average daily traffic volume of the expressway should be above 15000 minibuses. Expressway is in the city road network from the rapid role of traffic skeleton, contact the city's main area, connecting the main road, external traffic entrances and exits, to meet the rapid flow of traffic flow requirements.

· Arterial road

Connecting large and medium-sized cities, transport hubs, important external ports and military strategic locations, urban and regional economic centers; providing inter-provincial and large and medium-sized cities, planning long distance, large traffic and faster traffic; in the regional or urban traffic from the "pass" the role of traffic through the main function, service functions, supplemented by the requirements of the vehicle faster and more; usually one or two roads or 4 lanes above the city main road, in remote, less developed areas, some low-grade roads also have the function.

· Minor arterial

Reduce the circuitous, the main road between the road, similar as technical level and the main road.

· Collector

Complete the different communities, villages and towns travel traffic access to the primary and secondary roads of the transition, the collection of road network.

· Local road network

To communicate along the main function of the main traffic, traffic is relatively small, to achieve the ultimate goal of docking, directly with the user's source of the trip to the convergence of the convergence of scattered road for residents to provide access and access services.

According to the difference of travel purposes, in the regional planning, the city's traffic planning usually ignores the last level of road networks, and instead of the core link method, in the traffic impact assessment, but also need to expand the level of the network, the micro-level of the traffic distribution analysis.

(2) Road network and notes data (Mekky and Eng, 2001)

Road network and node data are the basis for traffic demand forecast. The network data refers to the data of each section of the road network, including traffic flow, speed, density, capacity, travel time, number etc.; the nodes data includes the location of the node and number etc..

· Network Data

In order to represent the connectivity of network in the transport planning, the road network is usually described as a network of connections between a series of nodes and nodes. Most of the lines in the transport network (except for the hypothetical lines) can be seen as representing "some delays" (such as travel time) or "costs" (such as crossing fees, fuel consumption, etc.) generated by the driver, delay "or" cost" is called traffic impedance (Fig. 2-2).

· Nodes

Nodes can be classified by 3 types:

a. Centroid, a dummy point, is assumed as the end and start of all trips (both auto & transit). It cannot be located on the arterial network and the transit routes, as trips between two centroids are not allowed to pass through a third one.

Figure 2-2 Xi'an road network

b. Gateways refer to the location of the external cordon(defining the study area) where the trips enter and leave the study area, which is connected to the study area by a dummy links.

c. Other nodes are the intersections among highway, urban roads and transit routes, bus stations and survey spots etc. Most nodes on the map are nodes mentioned.

Nodes data usually include coding (zone coding), locations (described by latitude and longitude), the index(marking the nodes selected); in the transit passenger forecast, the bus station data is needed to be added.

· Links

Links are directional(one-way or two-way), such as two-way road, pedestrian roads. There are usually three types of links:

a. Delay links represent that the arterial, roads and intersections parts of the network. Most of the sections in the transport network are delayed.

b. Dummy links have zero length or zero travel time. They are used to keep the network connectivity, and not the physical sections of network. For instance, they are used to connect gateways to the network.

c. Centroid connectors represent the local network, connect the centroids to the rest of the network. Typically, they are assigned so they are given a very large capacity(Fig. 2-3).

In transit networks, there are two additional types:

Walk links represent the walking between the zone centroids and the bus station(usually two-way).

Special transit links are created where transit services exist in locations where road network is not coded.

At the end of each vehicular trip, there are minutes need to be spent on arriving or leaving the vehicle (which is usually small, such as 2 minutes). And time may also be counted in the parking activity, resulting in a certain deviation. As mentioned above, the traffic volume(composition) of the important links are needed to validate the model to solve the traffic development control issues. In addition, it is necessary to measure the travel time to ensure that the traffic estimated by the model is reasonable. The links data includes:

a. Node from and note to.

b. Length.

c. Modes that use the link.

d. Link types, related with the functional classification the links(e. g. freeway /expressway, arterial), and digit identifies the link jurisdiction (e. g. regional municipality), location and technical level.

e. Number of lanes. Usually an integer or a fraction, for example, the operation of a tram reduces the effective number.

f. Volume delay function identifiers usually include two digits. The first digit refers to the capacity per lane per hour excluding trucks. The second digit represents the free flow speed on the link.

Figure 2-3 Centroid connectors in Xi'an

g. Volume delay function. This function associates the link travel time T to its volume capacity ratio(V/C), and free flow time T_0. One of the most commonly used formulas is the one described by US Highway Authority:

$$T = T_0\left[1 + 0.15\left(\frac{V}{C}\right)^4\right] \tag{2-3}$$

h. Observed link volume for base year(optional);

i. Turning penalties(optional).

For transit, other information on each link should be indicated e. g. :

Line name

Line description

Mode of line(transit)

Vehicle type

Line headway in min

Line default speed

Route record:

Line itinerary defined by the sequence of nodes

Dwell time(including acceleration/deceleration times)

Layover time

Transit time function

Boarding /alighting restrictions

Fare

Transfer

In the multimodal case, vehicle equivalency factor will be needed. Also the effect of reserved bus lanes on the capacity of the links must be considered.

Transfer links between transit lines represent transfer coat and walking distance from one line to another. As mentioned above, for the transit network, there are two types of centroid connections, namely, walk connectors and auto connectors to go to rail stations if there is no walk connector.

Travel modes:

a. Auto, including auto drivers and passengers;

b. Public transit, classified into bus, streetcar, subway, high-speed rail, train, urban railway, BRT;

c. Bicycle, motorcycle;

d. Walk;

e. Transfer can be considered as a mode.

2.3.5 Other Traffic Facilities Data

With the increase of social and economic levels and the vigorous development of transportation, travel demand has transformed from rapid growth period to stable growth period. The research focus of transport planning also transformed from road infrastructures, such as new or expanding roads, to traffic policies, regulations etc. , such as the effective of infrastructures. This is related to the need to effectively access the transport infrastructure data; at the same time, in order to clarify the supply conditions of current regional traffic system and the rationality of structures, the data about transport facilities and service capacity should be collected, including:

· The statistics of overall situation of the road network specifically include: the total length of the road network, the total area, density, area rate, the proportion of various types of roads etc. .

· The statistics of segments condition specifically include: the length of the road segments, area, line type, level, lane division, separation of facilities, road surface conditions, lateral clearance, vertical clearance etc. .

· The statistics of intersection facility specifically include: geometry of intersection, control methods, measures of separation and drainage.

· The statistics of transit network specifically include: the length of the transit network, the passed region, station situation, vehicle conditions, and service personnel.

· Traffic control facilities. Specific include: traffic signs, signals, performance, collation of traffic police etc. .

2.3.6 Land Use Data

Land use in traffic planning studies is often intended to include traffic activities on the land as well as demographic, social and economic factors. The form of land use will significantly affects the number of travel attraction. Therefore, the land use, usually collected by government agencies for purposes other than transportation (such as land use planning, economic and development research), is essential for understanding the current and future travel modes, zones division. Because land use involves travel forecasting, it usually includes type, intensity and location.

(1) Population

For the travel mode analysis and the travel forecasts, the population is one of the most important land use data. In the case of traffic demand forecasting, it is also necessary to collect information on the type of household dwelling and the area of the dwelling. Population-related data also includes age, birth rate, mortality, and migration data. Immigration is an important factor in population growth and makes difficult to forecast population.

(2) Employment

Employment is an important factor in determining the trip attraction. Generally, employment depends on economic factors, with the regional economic development and changes, the regional population grows more regularly which makes employment more difficult to estimate and forecast than the population.

In the country, the employment data is collected by the statistical report of the relevant institutions, which can collect the data used for urban traffic demand forecasting with less work.

The type of employment is classified in the foreign countries, such as Toronto. Two typical ways: the first one is based on industrial production and services to classify employment, namely coding as the standard industry classification (SIC); the other is based on the type of activity of staff. Sometimes the survey uses two encoding methods at the same time. It should be noted that part-time work (less than 20 hours per week) has a growing trend, which will have a certain impact on travel at the peak time, so it is necessary to identify and monitor its trend.

(3) Labor force

The labor force, especially the employed, is the main component of the peak traffic volume. Some models require labor information classified by occupation type; some cities use trip generation model that is based entirely on employment labor data.

With the development of economy and technology, the application of computer technology is becoming more and more mature and popular, and the number of people working at home has increased steadily. This is an important factor to be considered in demand modeling.

(4) Students

For the travel forecasting, the number of students is an important data and easy to be collected, and it directly determines the trip generation with the purpose of school.

(5) Floor space

Floor space is an important factor, usually collected in the employment survey. In urban areas of transport planning, planned land area and floor area ratio (the ceiling of building storey) are used to roughly calçulate the employment and population.

(6) Socio-economic and demographic data for the planning region

The socio-economic system is an important factor in the analysis of traffic systems. In socio-economic survey, it is the main context to collect the basic data of the socio-economic situation of the study area, of which the population is important. For instance, subway project feasibility analysis needs future year's traffic volume, which relates to the local economy (such as GDP) and population.

The data required for the socio-economic survey are as follow:

· Population.

· Total population, age structure, number of employee, occupation structure, social workers, average population growth rate, birth rate, mortality rate, etc..

· National economic indexes.

· Gross national product (GDP), per capita income, industrial structure, gross industrial and agricultural value of output, investment and distribution of capital construction.

· Passenger and freight volume.

· Transport volume, transportation turnover amount, the proportion of various modes.

· Travel modes.

· Number of transit vehicles, residential car ownership.

2.3.7 Data Summary analysis

It needs multiple types of data, collected by different study methods in transportation planning. The data types and collection methods are summarized in Table 2-4.

Table 2-4 Data types in transportation planning

Data types	Context	Application	Methods
Travel behavior data	Household characteristic, individual characteristics, once travel characteristics and other study data	Be used to analyze the travel characteristics in the study area. To provide the basic data for the traffic planning. Be the basis of the future forecasting of travel data	Home-interview, post-card and telephone survey
Traffic volume data	The traffic volume of segments, intersections and screen line	Analyze traffic volume, trends, and check accuracy of OD survey	Manual counting method, mechanical counting method, video method etc.
Other travel data	Commercial Vehicle OD Data, Taxi Data, Transit OD Data	Be used for transit network planning, optimization of existing routes, analysis of residents travel behavior, traffic demand	Roadside interview, vehicle-followed method
Network and nodes data	Road traffic capacity, length, travel time, the actual traffic volume, geographical location, etc.; nodes are divided into centroid, gateway, other nodes(such as the intersection)	Provide basic data for the road network planning and demand forecasting, be used to evaluate the level of services, road reconstruction and expansion etc.; the basic data traffic planning software needs for forecasting needed	Traffic survey on segments and nodes
Other traffic facilities data	The statistics of overall situation of the road network, the statistics of segments status, the statistics of intersection facility, the statistics of transit network, traffic control facilities	Clarify the current supply of the traffic system, promote the efficient use of transport facilities, and be used for the planning and construction of future transport facilities	Segments and notes survey on site, visits to relevant institutions
Land use data	Population, occupation, labor force, students and floor space	Used to analyze the current and future residents travel mode, divide zone	Visit related institutions, statistical yearbook or website etc.
Socio-economic and demographic data	Population, national economic indexes, passenger and freight volume, means of transport	Is the important components of implementation and support of project and engineering feasibility analysis	Visit related institutions, statistical yearbook or website etc.

2.4 Data Collection Methods

Data for transport planning can be collected from the relevant statistics and literature. The other part can be obtained through the investigation.

2.4.1 Origin and Destination Survey(OD Survey)

Origin and Destination survey(OD survey) is a survey of the starting point and the destination of the traveler in a given area, and obtains the traffic data between the starting points (usually between the traffic zones). Generally OD survey can be classified into: residents, vehicle and cargo travel OD survey.

(1) Study time

There are two aspects to determine the study time:

· Date of study. Tuesday, Wednesday and Thursday are usually approval, while the holiday is avoided. Besides, it is suggested to get in touch with Meteorological Service to ensure the survey date when there is no rain, snow and wind.

· Survey time. The survey time usually lasts for 12 hours or 24 hours, which has effects on the workload and quality of survey. 12-hour survey usually starts from 7:00 am to 19:00 pm while 24-hour survey starts from 7:00 am to 7:00 am on the next day. Person trip survey usually collects data from 3:00 pm to 3:00 am on the next day.

(2) Types and methods of survey

· Person trip survey

Person trip survey can be classified into the trips of urban residents and the floating population, and the survey mainly includes: origin and destination of trip, trip mode, travel time, distance and times etc. The survey method is as follows:

a. Home-interview survey: the residents of study area are sampled to obtain travel information of family members one day. This method is relatively reliable and comprehensive for its high quality and recovery rate. Before survey, it is necessary to motivate residents by getting the project well-known to make the survey smoothly go on. The method is used to forecast urban traffic demand.

b. Commuter survey: the data can be collected directly from the work place which requires small workload and collect OD data of commuters. This method is commonly used in surveys of transit planning and bicycle.

· Vehicle OD survey

The vehicle trip includes motor vehicle trip and non-motor vehicle travel. And the survey mainly includes: type of vehicle, origin and destination of trips, trip purpose, type of goods, the average tonnage or seats and the actual loading rate. The survey method is as follows:

a. Form survey: the form sent to the driver, the investigator to explain the contents of the form to be completed by the survey object after the recovery. This method has a higher valid response rate. Survey form is designed to ensure the preparation of a comprehensive, problem design science, to meet the needs of planning and analysis.

b. Roadside survey: in the main road and the city entrance to set up a survey station, through traffic control to stop the vehicle, the investigator asked the trip origin and other travel information. During the investigation, care should be taken not to cause traffic congestion or serious traffic delays. Therefore, traffic police or other personnel are required to help control the situation and maintain order.

c. Postcard survey: questionnaires are filled out by drivers and then mailed back; the survey spots set in positions where traffic calming zones exit, such as the toll station, stop signs. This method has low valid response rate, is less than the accuracy requirements, and used less in our country.

d. License plate method: normally, this method is used to investigate the flow distribution of hub areas. At the every survey station, the license plates of passing vehicles are recorded. The first survey station is the starting point, the last survey station is the ending point. The data collected by this method using large amount of labor is rough.

e. Screen line survey: at the survey station locating in the regional boundary or screen line, all through the route of the vehicle passengers or travelers for statistical counting, can be used for home inspection investigation. Such surveys can grasp the various characteristics related to the condition of the vehicle, investigate the traffic volume, speed, density and delay data, but also for the traffic control, road comprehensive management, road planning to provide the basis.

f. Bus station survey: the investigators in the car or on the station to inquire about the passengers to understand the starting point and transit situation. The main contents are: travel starting point, travel routes, on the train site, get off the station; get off after the transfer, transfer line information, the destination. This method has a high sampling rate, but requires a lot of manpower to be mobilized.

· Cargo flow OD survey

The focus of the survey data is to investigate the distribution of the supply point and the attraction point, the classification, quantity and proportion of the cargo flow, the route of the truck and the location of the station.

(3) Statistics results of OD survey data

OD survey data is the necessary data for mainstream traffic forecasting, which plays an important role in transportation planning. The performance type of OD data is as follows:

· OD survey data statistics output

Due to the large amount of OD survey data, the data processing is also complex. It usually need to use the computer for analysis. The main output of analysis is as follows:

a. OD distribution of various vehicles in different regions;

b. Summary OD distribution of vehicles in different regions;

c. Passenger and cargo OD distribution in planning region;

d. The proportion of various travel modes;

e. Average tonnage of truck;

f. Average seat of bus;

g. Actual loading rate of truck and bus;

h. The constitution of goods for truck;

i. Road traffic volume.

· OD table

OD table is the main form for summarizing the results of the investigation. It can be divided into rectangular table and triangular table. The former can reflect the direction and quantity of traffic flow between traffic zones, simple and intuitive, as shown in Table 2-5; the latter is the sum of the round-trip traffic in the rectangular table, forming a return form, as shown in Table 2-5. The element q12 in the table represents the number of trips from traffic zone 1 to traffic zone 2, O_1 represents the total travel volume of the traffic zone 1, and T represents the travel volume of the entire area.

Table 2-5 Triangle OD table

O	D					$O_i = \sum_{j=1}^{n} q_{ij}$
	1	2	3	…	n	
1	q_{11}	q_{12}	q_{13}	…	q_{1n}	O_1
2		q_{22}	q_{23}	…	q_{2n}	O_2
3			q_{33}	…	q_{3n}	O_3
…				…	…	…
n					q_{nn}	O_n
						$T = \sum_i O_i$

· Expected line graph and contour map

In order to reflect the traffic flow between the various traffic zones, the data provided by the OD table can be allocated to the map of the zones, and the traffic zones can be represented by the center of mass and the cells are connected to form a desired line graph, where the line thickness and traffic volume are in certain proportion. Drawing of such graphs can be done with planning softwares, such as TransCAD, Cube etc..

If the straight line connecting the centroid is transferred to the polyline with same directions and with a certain of thickness that is proportional to the traffic volume, that is, the contour map of traffic volume.

· Traffic generation statistics graph

Plotted the traffic generation and attraction into a statistical map (such as a histogram, a line chart or a pie chart) to form a traffic generation statistics graph. The figures can clearly express the difference of generation and attraction between zones.

OD vehicle survey on Highway in Hebei Province

a. The layout of OD survey points should be based on the basic principle that the traffic flow situation of main roads between affected areas directly and indirectly by project, or among the zones in the affected areas directly by project.

b. Include the parallel or competitive routes for the calculation of road traffic, which is the key to set the OD survey points.

c. A survey point should be set at a larger road junction.

d. Try to avoid the impact of urban traffic, so the survey points should be away from the town, generally at least 5 km away from the town entrance.

e. The survey station should be arranged at straight segments with broad subgrade (sight distance is more than 250 meters), at the same time, there are less than 150 meters between one survey station and next one.

f. OD survey points are also used as traffic observation points.

g. In order to verify the observations of daily traffic volume and master the ratio of daily traffic volume, 12 hours or 24 hours of traffic observation points should be set on typical road.

h. Set notification signal in the direction of vehicle passing at the 100 *to* 150 *meters away from the survey point to remind the driver to pay attention.*

i. The enough space should be left for the vehicles that are not interviewed pass when carrying out sampled survey.

Under the guidance of the above principles, there are generally two ways to set OD survey points: the zone boundary method and the surrounding node method. The former refers to setting observation sites at the intersections among the roads connecting the zones and the zone boundary (regional boundary or screen line), attempting to "encircle" the whole zone, and all of the intersections, as shown in Fig. 2-4; *the basic idea of the latter is to regard the central city (usually the location of the government, the development zone with high intensity urban land use, CBD etc.) as the traffic generation of the traffic zones and abstract it as a road network node. Then set survey stations on the higher-grade roads through the node to ensure that there are surveys points can be set on the arteries of doorway, as shown in* Fig. 2-5.

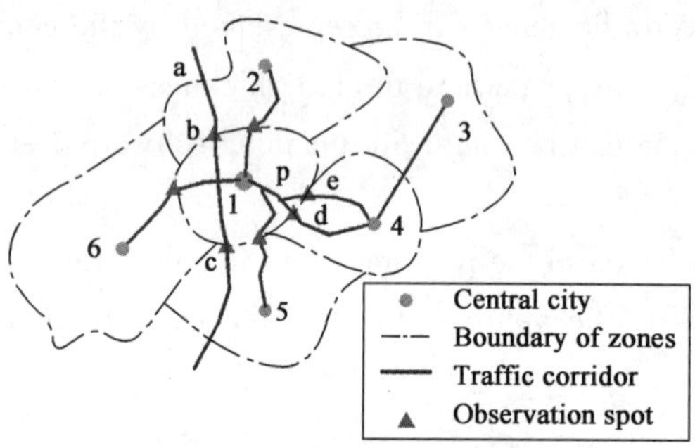

Figure 2-4 Zone boundary method

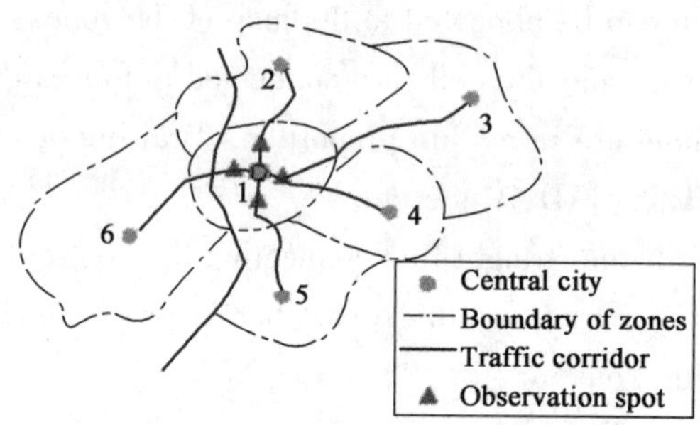

Figure 2-5 Bounding nodes method

Then integrate the data of each survey point into the OD table. In this process, the most important thing is to eliminate the repeated sample. The method of regional OD table synthesis is related to the OD survey method. There is still no accepted and mature synthetic method. In total, there are five regional OD synthesis methods:

a. Labeling method

Label each surveyed vehicle in front of the right front window glass, indicating the survey number and the direction of the vehicle. The labeled vehicle is no longer investigated, and the vehicle changing the direction is needed to be re-interviewed and changed labels.

This method is simple and quick, especially the data processing process is more convenient. However, this method is complicated to deal with repeated vehicles during the investigation, so that complete sample data cannot be collected. In addition, if the method adopts the sample survey, the logic of enlarges sample is not firm enough, resulting big error. If not sample survey, the workload of survey will be increased and the traffic will be affected.

b. License plate number method

Record the vehicle number, and consider the first record of the survey point position as the starting point, the last record of the survey location as the end of the trip.

The method is simple in recoding, has small impact on the traffic flow, and has been able to use advanced technology for non-stop investigation. However, the process of OD synthesis is a trouble work to track the travel trajectory of each vehicle to determine the O(origin) and D(destination) of trip. Moreover, because of layout of survey stations and the division of zones, even though the tracking route is correct, the OD is not necessary accurate on its location.

c. Series and parallel method

When the vehicle passes through an OD survey point, and whether or not it has been investigated, it is re-investigated as a sample survey, which makes it possible the vehicle is surveyed repeatedly by different OD survey sites or by the same OD survey site. The criteria for judging this method is: it is series connection for a number of OD survey sites on a route, and the average or maximum traffic volume of each survey site is the traffic volume of the survey site; and it is parallel connection for the same survey site corresponds to different routes, and the sum of traffic volume of the all routes is the traffic volume of survey site.

The method is the most rigorous OD survey method in theory, and is applied in engineering feasibility study, and performs well. However, this method usually requires manual judgment of the series or parallel connection of the routes, so it will cause a greater workload under the more complex road network conditions. Some scholars have responded with solution of a serial-parallel common formula, however, the solution does not consider the route without the OD survey sites.

d. Parallel method

As the serial and parallel method is difficult to achieve computer programming, the series and parallel method become parallel method using approximate disposal. The specific approach is: firstly, search for the shortest route corresponded to an OD survey site, then search for the second shortest route in parallel with the shortest route, and find out all such routes, finally, calculate the traffic volume using series and parallel connection.

This method makes up for the shortcomings of serial and parallel method, and can be achieved easily by using computer. But the search of the parallel route is an approximation algorithm, causing some errors are caused by some such routes missed; and for the operational vehicles, the route choice depends on the passenger flow rather than the shortest route, which is contrary to the algorithm, and errors are made.

e. Generation arrival method

As for generation arrival method, it is considered that for each traffic zone, both the generation and the arrival traffic volume are all achieved through the directly connected link, so the traffic volume in the zone is only related to the survey station, and have no direct relation with survey stations in other links. Since the relationship among survey stations on links directly connected to the zone are parallel, these relevant traffic flow can be used to calculate the traffic volume of the zone(row Ⅰ *and column* Ⅰ *in the zone Origin-Destination* Table 5-1, Chapt 5) *by using parallel algorithm, namely, summing them directly. In the process of building a traffic network, the specific way is structuring a basic network cut set consisting of the zone* Ⅰ, *the node area directly connected to it and the connected links, then aggregate the generation and arrival traffic volume by directly summing the traffic volume data collected in survey stations within the cut set. This method does not need to search the path, thus there is no need to give each road a resistance value which reduces the error caused by this process, and also easy to achieve by using program; When applying this method, all links connected with the traffic zone should be laid out for a survey station which may resulting in increased costs. In practical application, this method can be used only under the specific network structure.*

This OD survey was conducted by roadside survey, when conducting the field survey, the same survey was carried out repeatedly on all motor vehicles (or samples at a certain sampling rate) passing by every survey station, regardless of whether they had been investigated or not. Serial-parallel method and parallel-path method are determined to aggregate OD table.

Using the combined zone OD table to make detailed statistical analysis of the arrival traffic volume in survey area, we can get the histogram of the traffic volume (Fig. 2-6), *the expectation line in the survey area* (Fig. 2-7), *the expectation line* (Fig. 2-8) *and the traffic assign ment on highway* (Fig. 2-9) *in HeBei Province.*

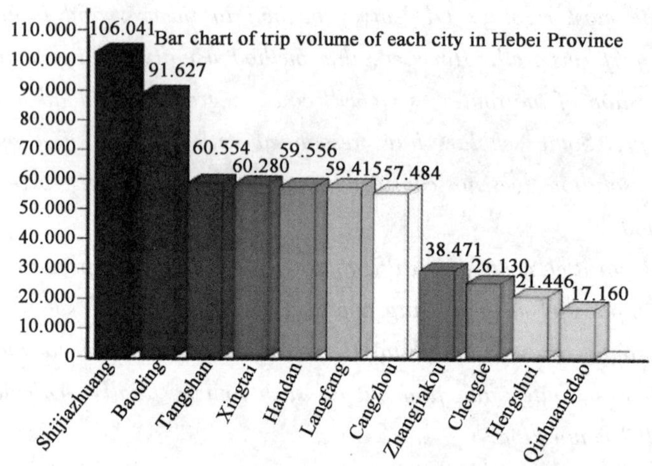

Figure 2-6 Bar chart of trip volumes of each city in HeBei Province

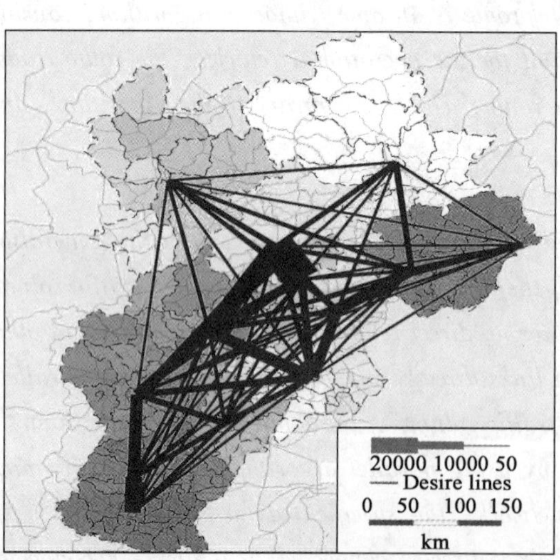

Figure 2-7 Trip desire line within survey zone

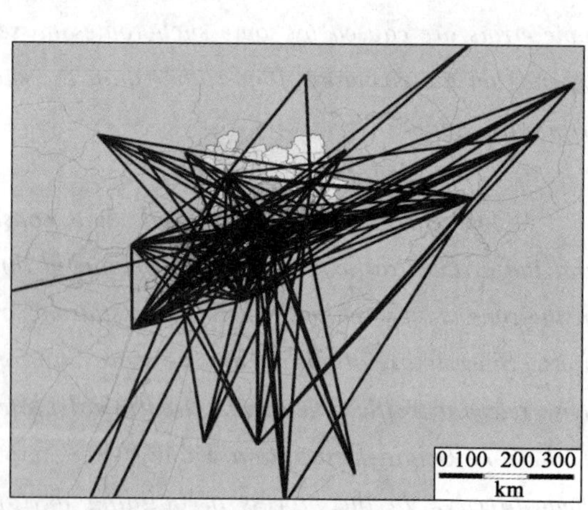

Figure 2-8 Trip desire line out of survey zone

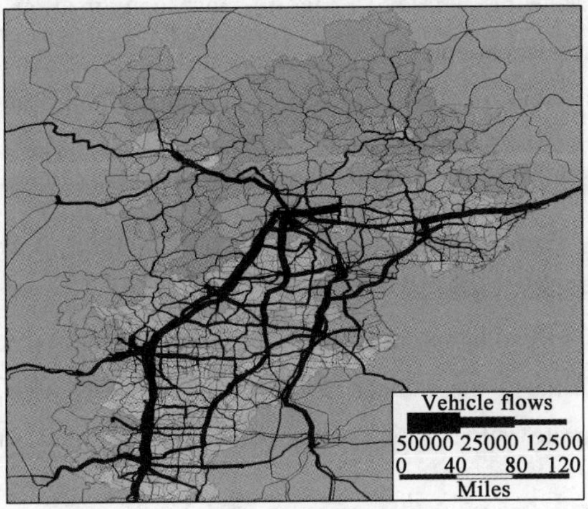

Figure 2-9 Traffic assignment on section

Source: *Chang'an University, Hichway OD Survey Report in HeBei Province.*

2.4.2 Survey Methods

(1) RP (Revealed Preference) survey

The RP survey, the behavioral investigation, is an observational or detective survey of what has happened, specifically referring to observations on the policies have already been implemented or facilities already exist. RP survey can collect the data about the respondents' actual action or travel behavior has been finished to get the probability of actual use or acceptance of a facility. Thus, the relevant probability model or other models can be established, which is the commonly used method.

At present, RP survey has been widely applied, and the main context of screen-line counts, roadside survey etc. is consisting with RP survey. However, due to the RP data reveals travel behavior occurred or can be observed, the data cannot reveal whether the trip is satisfied or not, what will change. So the Stated Preference (SP) survey is put forward to make up for the above shortcomings.

(2) SP (Stated Preference) survey

The SP survey, the preference survey, is a subjective preference for a number of alternatives under assumptions that did not actually happen. In the late 1970s, the United Kingdom applied SP survey to study traffic problems, and then the United States, Australia, also conducted related surveys. In the 1980s, the researchers deeply carried out studies of the SP survey from both theoretical and practical aspects. The "*SP Method Research in Transportation*" album was published on the *Journal of Transport Economics and Policy* in 1989, which enabled the SP survey to be further promoted in the transportation field. It was proved that SP surveys had increasingly become an important tool in the study of travel behavior and were used in travel choice, parking choice as well as route choice etc.. SP survey methods can be divided into the following seven types:

· House hold interviewing survey. Face-to-face conversation, investigators record the respondents' responses in the questionnaire.

· Visit and Indwelling Survey. Visit and place the questionnaire at the visited home, and visit the family again and recover it a few days later.

· Mail-out survey. Mail and collect questionnaires.

· Telephone survey. Currently the use rate of this method is less used as the results of considering effectiveness of survey results.

· Field survey. The investigators randomly choose respondents and record the respondents' responses in survey spot. Due to the refusal to cooperate in most cases, the investigators may ask those whom seem to cooperate with, which cause deviation between sample distribution and real travel group.

· Distributing questionnaires on the spot. Distribute questionnaires in waiting room and ticket gate etc. and collect questionnaires at the exit. Investigators can also get into the vehicle, ask participants and finished the questionnaires.

· Distributing questionnaire on the spot and collect questionnaires by mail. Choose respondents randomly, distribute questionnaires and ask respondents to send the questionnaires by mail in the survey spot.

(3) Comparison of the RP with the SP survey

RP and SP survey have their own advantages and disadvantages, e. g. RP survey is more reliable, and SP survey is more flexible. Table 2-6 is the comparison of the RP and SP survey characteristics.

Table 2-6 Comparison of the RP and SP survey characteristics

Context	RP survey	SP survey
Choice behavior	The actual result of the action is consistent with the actual action, and the information that can be obtained is only the result of the selection	The intentions are not necessarily consistent with the actual in the hypothetical state. There are four types of sorting, selection, scoring and matching data
Alternative	Feasible and realistic	Can be unrealistic
Alternative characteristics	Including non-quantifiable attributes such as reliability and comfort; the observation data with error usually is difficult to be collected. The range of attribute values is limited, and the correlation between attributes is large	Including non-quantifiable attributes such as reliability and comfort, the observation data is easy to obtain, there is no observation error, can expand the range of attribute value, can control the correlation between attributes
Alternative sets	Indefinite	Define
Personal observation data	Be restricted by the times of actual choice behavior	There can be multiple scenarios through imagery, resulting in multiple observations
Data reliability	The greater reliability	The larger data error

Thus, it can be seen that the RP survey does apply to the research traffic phenomena that have occurred. When the changes of traffic system, such as the implementation of new traffic measures or the introduction of new traffic modes, result in the change of traffic condition, the RP survey cannot meet realistic need. And SP survey of free attributes, the level of design, just make up for the RP investigation of the defects. So combing the RP and SP survey can better meet the actual needs, and it can be used widely. The disaggregate model generally based on the data of the RP survey is limited to the condition the future traffic mode unchanged. However, the service characteristics of new transport modes are different with the current transport modes, so the model cannot be able to meet the requirements. In this case, it is necessary to carry out the SP survey, obtain the residents' intention data for the future situation, combine the two data for the calibration of the disaggregated model parameters, and forecast the traffic sharing rate.

2.4.3 Land Use and Employment Data

(1) Land use

There is a complex relationship between urban-rural transport and land use, namely, in some degree urban-rural structure is the result of the interaction between transport and land use. On the one hand, land use form is the cause of urban and rural traffic and it determines the generation and modes of urban-rural traffic. On the other hand, the development of urban-rural traffic system has influence on urban and rural spatial structure, changing the accessibility, which is the key link between land use and transportation links and has the crucial effects on urban-rural land use size, intensity and spatial distribution. Therefore, it is necessary to know the land use condition of the survey area before traffic survey.

· The impact of land use on transport

Study shows that the residential density, development scale, architectural design, layout and other aspect have influence on composition of traffic demand, travel mode and travel distance. Higher residential density will facilitate the development of public transport due to decrease of travel demand and increase of level of traffic service. When the development scale and density up to a certain degree, the need of large-capacity public transport will appear, while the development of bicycle and pedestrian modes of transport will be encouraged in compact, small scale and mixed development land use model, reducing the use of private cars. Studies have shown that every 10% increase in density will decrease the private car trips by about 0.7%. Large-scale, decentralized, low-density land development method will significantly stimulate the development of cars: land development intensity also significantly affects the intensity of traffic flow: land use and pedestrian-oriented planning will reduce the travel rate and travel distance, significantly increasing the proportion of bus trips, average shopping distance, but there is no significant correlation with the travel mode of shopping trips. there is also no obvious relationship between land use and other non-work trips. On the contrary, single-function large-scale residential areas or employment centers will lead to an increase in average travel distance. In addition, land use characteristics will also change or contribute to the city's road network pattern.

· The impact of transport on land use

The impact of transport on land use mainly shows up in the location choice of family and enterprise, land use, intensity and price. Only taking traffic costs and land prices into consideration, various types of land users will choose different areas to develop, business generally select the downtown area. Agriculture is at the outermost area of the city. Industrial and residential areas are distributed in the area between urban centers and rural areas; the survey found that families also tend to choose traffic convenient location; rail transport or high-capacity road network has a strong spatial attraction and differentiation effect on the land use alongside, the attraction of residential land and public land meet the distance-decay law, while the industrial land are on the contrary; transport routes and accessibility also influence commercial, residential and industrial land prices in varying degrees. A study conducted in Shanghai shows that 72% changes of land price are caused by changes of traffic accessibility index, that is, the higher the index is, the higher the land prices will be. The improvement of accessibility has expanded the activity space of residents and enterprises, stimulated the development and redevelopment of land along the transportation lines, increased the total land use, promoted the migration of the old cities, accelerated the relocation of commercial centers, eventually leading to the city's outward expansion and multi-centered development.

(2) Employment data collection

In urban traffic travel, work travel also called commuting travel, occupying a large proportion, which is the main traffic source considered when planning road and public transport. Combined with the distribution of land use, generally, office area will be divided into the same traffic zone to make sure the investigation data is accurate and reliable. Employment information can be obtained through questionnaires distributed within the survey area or through files from companies. Such surveys are usually conducted at least once every two years.

2.4.4 New Transport Technologies

With computer information technology fully joining into the social life, the Internet (social contact, searching, E-commerce, Weibo), Internet of things (sensors, Smart Earth), Internet of Vehicles, GPS, telecommunications (phone calls, SMS, cell phone location) will all produce amount of data. Massive transactional data and interactive data make up big data. Big data has 4V features: Volume, Variety, Value and Velocity. It should be noted that big data is only data, when applying it to the actual transport field, what we need is big data extraction technology. Currently the the big data extraction technology used in transport field is shown in Fig. 2-10 (Wu Xiangguo, *Maintenance and Upgrading of Chongqing Comprehensive Transportation Models Under Big Data Era*, 2015).

Big data extraction techniques such as Loop Vehicle Detector, GPS Vehicle Location, video recognition and radar detection have some limitations in some degree, for example three typical problems in Loop Vehicle Detector technology:

· Traffic data collection is limited. Loop Vehicle Detector technology can only get the traffic volume, occupancy rate, radar speed measurement, but necessary travel planning data such as travel time, travel speed data cannot be obtained.

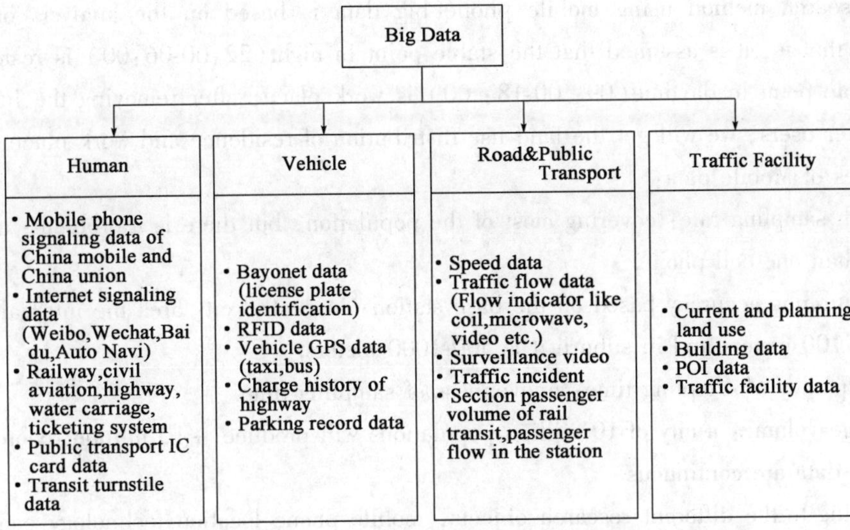

Figure 2-10 Big data extraction techniques commonly used in transportation

Source: *Wu Xiangguo*, *Maintenance and Upgrading of Chongqing Comprehensive Transportation Models Under Big Data Era*, 2015.

· Damage rate and maintenance costs of Loop Vehicle Detector are high. In the United States, for example, it is estimated that the Loop Vehicle Detector damage rate is about 30% per year and it needs to spend 2 billion to 3 billion US dollars to repair.

· The easy damaged feature of Loop Vehicle Detector affected the promotion. Limited by the funds, the improvement of Loop Vehicle Detector technology is slow, and the traffic monitoring area is limited. In United States, the static fixed-point Vehicle Detector traffic data acquisition mode covered 50% of the city expressway and less than 10% of the city main road in 15 years; Shanghai spent two years (from 2003 to 2005) costing nearly 200000000 yuan to cover an elevated expressway and 1/6 of the important intersection in city center and the detector damage rate is about 30%.

GPS Vehicle Location, although with high accuracy, better technical application reliability, it needs relative high initial investment and operating costs, not every city is willing to pay for this cost. At present, it has been installed in bus, taxi, high-capacity passenger cars in some well-developed cities.

Spot information acquisition technology such as, Microwave detection technology, video image recognition technology and other floating information acquisition technology, such as, GPS floating vehicles, RFID and other floating information acquisition technology both focus on operating vehicles and the output is vehicle operating information. According to the information of traffic flow, we can get citizens travel information by reverse deduction, but the algorithm is complicated, the accuracy is low and it is difficult to be used when the target area is large. Therefore, transportation researchers have been looking for a more economical, more efficient, more accurate travel information access technology. From data source like Mobile phone data, Internet signaling data, public transport IC card data, RFID data can be obtained in some aspects of valuable information, and researches can get some valuable information.

(1) Mobile phone data

The research method using mobile phone big data is based on the analysis of a behavior hypothesis, that is, it is assumed that the stable point in night(22:00-06:00) is residential place and the stable point in daytime(09: 00-18: 00) is work place, after removing the interference of non-commuter users, we will get the land use distribution of residence and work place.

Features of Mobile data:

a. High sampling rate: covering most of the population, but there is a problem: a person may have more than one cell phone.

b. Positioning accuracy based on the base station: in central city area the interval of base stat ion is about 100 meters and in suburb it is 500-1000 meters.

c. Frequency of sampling time: unevenness of sampling time.

d. Large volume: a city of 10 million populations will produce +10 million records a day.

e. The data are continuous.

According to the different research objects, mobile phone location technology can be used to extract individual travel parameters, which are divided into mobile phone signaling survey technology and mobile phone sensor(GPS, accelerometer, Wi-Fi) survey technology.

· Mobile phone signaling survey technology

The mobile phone signaling data refers to the signaling monitoring platform established by the operator, which collects the exchange of signaling data between the mobile phone and the base station. Through the background correlation, synthesis and analysis, we can get the anonymous cell phone ID, event category, time stamp, base station number, location area number and other information, including event data during calling time and non-conversation time.

At present, the technology has been able to capture the distribution of home-work location in urban area, commuting travel characteristics, people flow of hot spots, OD data in large zone.

The mobile signaling data are recorded by the mobile communication network after the following events occur in the mobile phone, as shown in Table 2-7.

Table 2-7 Data types of cell phone signaling data

Event type	Content
Location update event	Normal Location Update(occurrence of displacement in different area), Periodic Location Update (update cell phone's location data when no other event happen), Start Up events(Mobile phone communication network records the location of mobile phone after starting up the phone)
Switch events	The occurrence of location switch during calling
Call events	Occurrence of calling, called, hang up, send and receive text messages

Statistics show that the ratio of three signaling in all signaling is about 3:2:5.

In order to extract the traffic OD quantization index from the mobile signaling data, two steps of end-point identification and travel endpoint matching are required.

· Origin and destination identification

By setting the time threshold and space threshold combined with the time interval and spatial distance between several adjacent signaling records, we can filter out false moves, achieve the recognition of mobile point and stay point and determine the travel endpoint, the procedure is shown in Fig. 2-11.

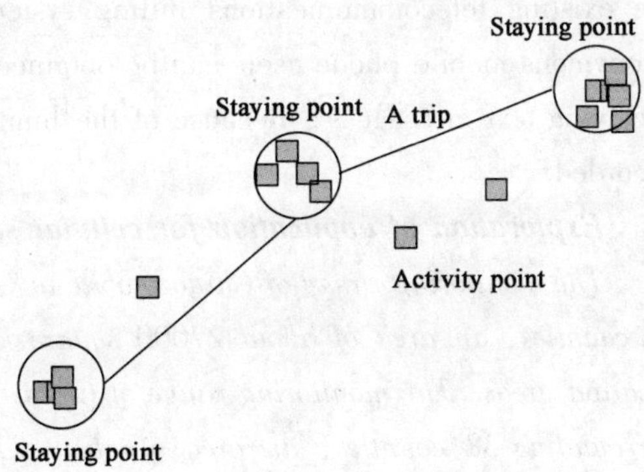

Figure 2-11 Schematic diagram of the travel endpoint identification

· Trip ends matching method

Mobile communication network signal coverage is logically designed by a number of regular hexagonal base station cell(the actual coverage is not regular hexagon) adjacent to each other to form a planar service area, also known as the cell, as shown in Fig. 2-12. A cell phone user always keeps in touch with one of the base station cells.

However, the relationship between the coverage of the cell and the coverage of the traffic analysis zone is not that of including or included, but intervened, see Fig. 2-13. Therefore, mapping the end-point of the cell location to the traffic zone becomes a complex task. According to the traffic zone division method, the end-point matching mode is divided into two types.

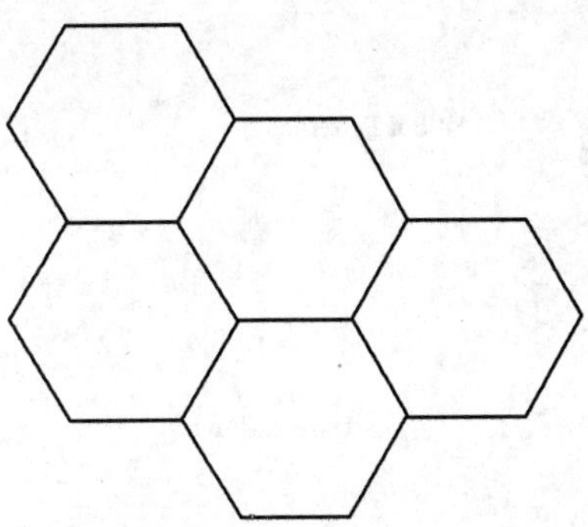

Figure 2-12 Mobile signal coverage form-regular hexagon

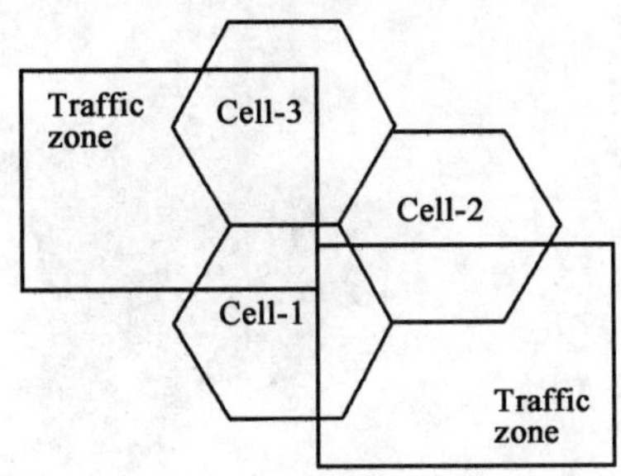

Figure 2-13 Cell and traffic zone layout

a. Trip ends matching to traffic zone divided by traditional method.

There are many ways to match the trip ends marked by base station code to the traditional traffic zone, such as face-to-face matching, point-to-face matching and point-to-point matching. Here we only introduce face to face matching method.

Face-to-face matching is based on the overlaying relationship between the coverage area of the cell and the traffic zone, such as all the trip ends marked by the base-station coded identifier are assigned to the traffic zone which has the largest coverage area, or the assignments of trip ends are according to possibility of the overlapping area size of the cell and traffic zone.

b. Trip ends matching to the traffic zone clustered by cells.

Using cell clustering to form a traffic cell avoids the problem of boundary inconsistent between cell and trip zone. Each cell can be uniquely assigned to a traffic zone, and the trip ends can also be matched by attribution.

Mobile phone bill location data is an important subset of mobile phone signaling data. Based on the existing telecommunications billing system of mobile operators, the location information of anonymous mobile phone users can be obtained when they generate billing data (such as sending and receiving text messages). Because of the limited data type, only partial fragments of the track are recorded.

Exploration of application for cellular signaling data in Chongqing

The monitoring range of China mobile in Chongqing consists of the main city and the surrounding 19 counties, an area of about 27000 square kilometers, including about 30000 base stations, 109 location areas. The monitoring range of China Unicom in Chongqing consists of the main city and the surrounding 38 counties, an area of about 82400 square kilometers, including about 25000 base stations, 94 location areas. Fig. 2-14 *and* Fig. 2-15 *show the monitoring range of China Mobile and China Unicom in Chongqing, respectively.*

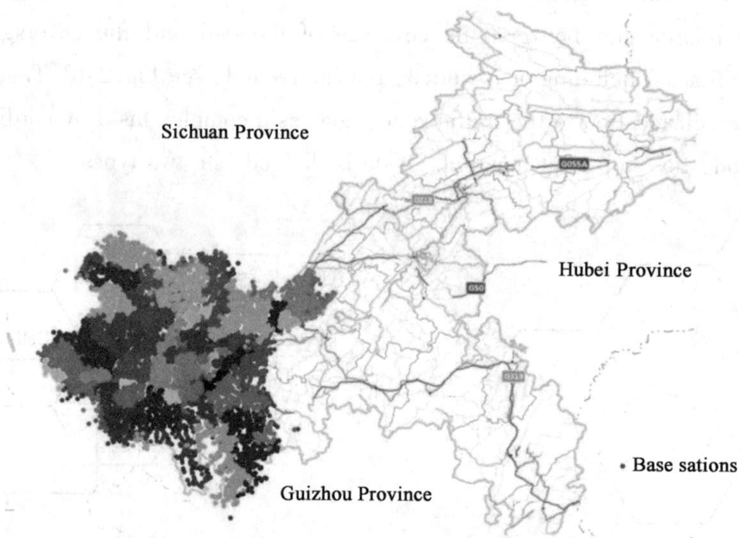

Figure 2-14 Monitoring range of China Mobile in Chongqing

Source: *Wu Xiangguo*, 2015.

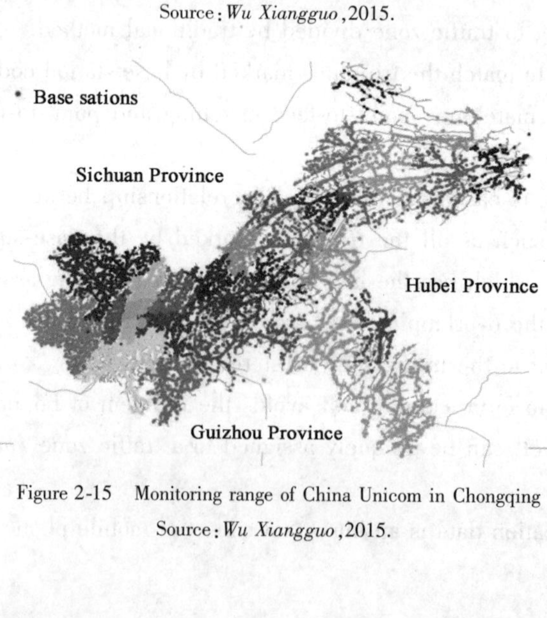

Figure 2-15 Monitoring range of China Unicom in Chongqing

Source: *Wu Xiangguo*, 2015.

Through the monthly cellular signaling data, researchers analyze the daily travel path of mobile phone users, summarize regularity to identify stable point as residential place at night, workplace during the daytime after removing the interference of non-commuters, acquire the distribution of the residential place and workplace in main city, as shown in Fig. 2-16, *these data can also be used for the analysis of Job-housing ratio, Job-housing mismatch, commuting travel.*

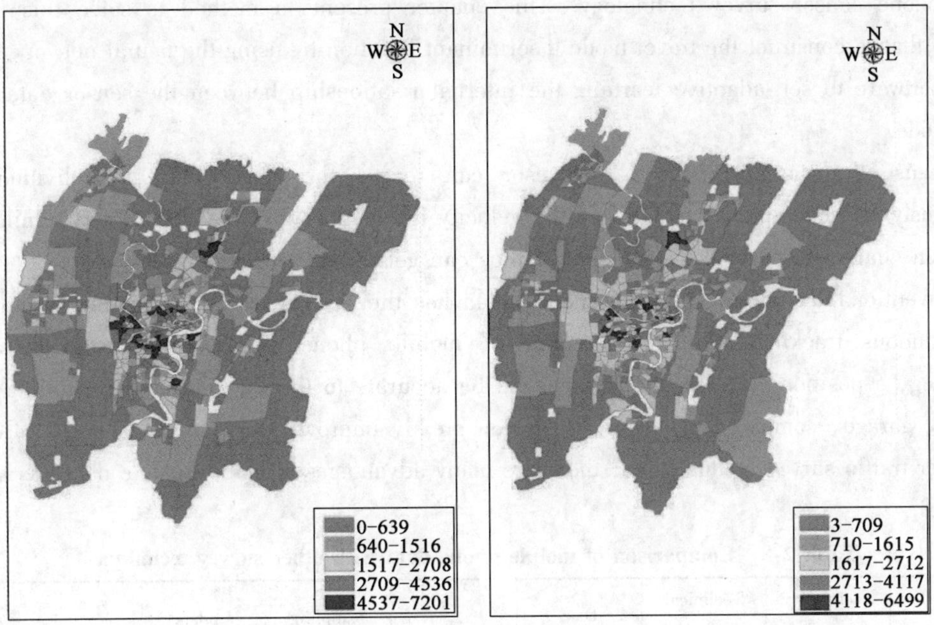

Figure 2-16 Distribution of nighttime residence and daytime work density in the main urban area

Source: *Wu Xiangguo*, 2015.

Tracking the origin and destination of passenger flower in important areas (out of the city entrances and exits, transport hubs, important public buildings, shopping district), can be distributed channel planning, in and out of traffic system organization, facilities provide the basis for evaluation.

· Cell phone sensor positioning technology

With the rapid development and popularization of smart phones, the accurate positioning ability of sensors such as mobile phone GPS, accelerometer, Wi-Fi, etc. has developed fast. Mobile phone sensor data can make up for the large-scale positioning problem of mobile phone base station positioning method and it will promote and support the accuracy extraction of traffic parameters.

The individual travel data extracted by cell phone sensor positioning technology can be used to construct activity-based traffic model, traditional four-stage model, public transportation network layout optimization, new district traffic planning, public security prewarning model and so on. Application of mobile sensor data for individual travel parameters extraction usually consists of the following two steps:

a. Trip stop spot identification

By setting the time and distance thresholds to determine the individual travel stop point, the individual is considered to reach the destination or transfer point when the time interval of two consecutive locating point interval longer than the time threshold, meanwhile the distance is less than the distance threshold.

b. Travel characteristic extraction

Travel time, travel distance and other traffic parameters can be obtained directly or after simple calculation from the mobile phone sensor data, while travel mode recognition is the main difficulty of mobile phone sensor survey technology. This chapter presents a method to solve this technical problem, that is construct the travel mode discriminant function by using the neural network model of Matlab software to self-adaptive learning the internal relationship between the sensor data and the traffic mode.

Because the mobile phone GPS sensor can record the speed data of individual travel continuously at the frequency of 1times, the velocity fluctuation characteristic is very similar to the fluctuation characteristic of the signal wave, thus can get the speed data.

Conventional 2G mobile phone signaling data has the defects of low positioning accuracy and non-continuous tracking. A large number of mobile phone 4G network uses micro-station positioning, a positioning technology which can be accurate to the location of the building or even the floor, garage, compared to macro site, which greatly improves positioning accuracy. Compared with other traffic survey technologies, there are many advantages of mobile phone data, as shown in Table 2-8.

Table 2-8 Comparison of mobile phone data with other survey techniques

Passenger flow information acquisition	Technology promotion scope	Technical maturity level	Data accuracy	Cost	Sampling rate	Update frequency	Respondent
Questionnaire	Large	High	Middle	High	Very low	Low	Mainly permanent residents
OD matrix estimation	Small	Low	Low	Low	High	Very high	Cannot distinguish
Volunteer GPS track	Small	Middle	Very high	Very high	Very low	Low	Depending on the volunteer population
IC card	Specific travel mode	High	High	High	High	Middle	Specific travel mode crowd
Video identification	Section	High	High	High	High	High	Cannot distinguish
Mobile phone acquisition technology	Large	Gradually mature	High	Very low	Very high	Very high	Can be divided into permanent residents or mobile workers

(2) Internet signaling data

Mobile Internet use frequency has been far higher than the traditional SMS, telephone and other traditional services. The single-day record can reach hundreds or even more than 1000 after including Internet signaling data, which is 10 to 20 times as much data size as the traditional 2G signaling data. The background operation of a large number of mobile APP will produce TCP /IP data packets which will produce signaling, such as Weibo, WeChat, Baidu map, AMAP.

Based on 4G Internet signaling, the user's detection rate has increased significantly. Therefore, the sample only need minor expansion or no expansion, reducing the error brought by sample expansion, meanwhile, more applications which cannot be applied before, such as trajectory tracking, travel time, travel frequency and travel mode identification(using mobile phone 4G data to obtain accurate arrival or departure time of the staying area, calculate the travel time between stops, compare it with the trip time gained from open-source data such as Baidu, Sogou et al. , thus can get the travel mode.), Channel flow, distribution of people flow in small-scale district.

An example of identifying the trip mode using the above method is shown in Fig. 2-17, Table 2-9.

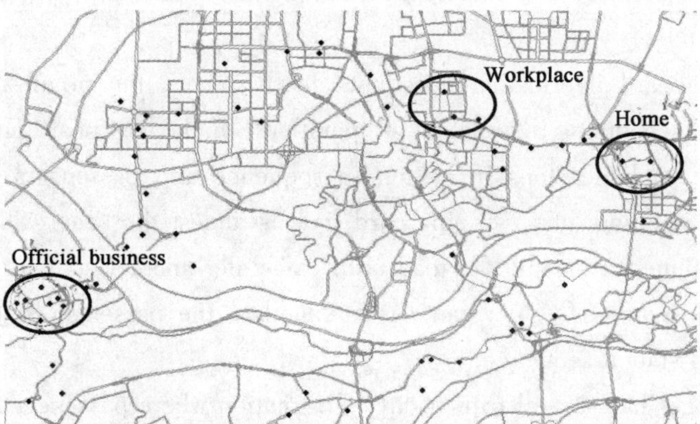

Figure 2-17 Schematic diagram of origin and destination of trip
Source: *Wu Xiangguo*, 2015.

Table 2-9 Identification of travel modes

Travel	Mobile phone travel time	Car travel time from open source data	Bus travel time from open source data	Travel mode identification
Home-Workplace	85	55	80	Transit

(3) Bus IC card data

The traditional method to obtain the spatial distribution OD matrix of the bus travel is to issue a survey form when the passengers get on the bus. Each person fills in the form according to his own trips, and then withdraws the form when he(she) gets off. This manual survey method costs more manpower, material and financial resources and lacks regularity. The common application of public transportation IC card technology provides a new method for public transit OD matrix survey.

At present, in china, people swipe IC card without identifying the station when getting on the bus, which can only obtains the limited information, including card number, swiping card time, line number and the vehicle number and so on, like Table 2-10 shows.

Table 2-10 Inquiry form of bus passenger record(partial)

Passenger card number	Driver card number	Line number	Balance	Line charge	Travel date	Processing date
C12345	Z04321	X12	41.23	0.8	2016/5/3	2016/5/4
C12345	Z02452	X06	39.63	0.96	2016/5/4	2016/5/5
…	…	…	…	…	…	…

Due to the reason passengers only need to swipe their ID card one time when they get on the bus in our country, it is easy to identify the station in which passengers get on the bus, however, if we want to record in which station passenger get off the bus, passengers need to swipe their card a second time when they get off, which will bring inconvenience to passengers and influence the efficiency of vehicle, therefore, it is impossible to implement secondary swiping card.

· Origin of bus travel

Although swiping card information does not clearly record the origin of trip, according to swiping card time and scheduling information of operation vehicle, the boarding station of passengers can be reckoned. The vehicle stops in station in sequence and passengers swipe, their card to getting on during the standing time, swiping card time is almost the same without the same station and then the bus continue to run into the road until encounter another station. Vehicles on the road continues to repeat this process, so it can easily calculate the passenger station from passenger's swiping card time and station sequence.

Each bus passenger has several trips a day. The station where passenger first swipes their card throughout the day must be the origin for the first trip of the passenger all day. After that, each time when they swipe their card in a station, it may be a transfer station or origin of the next trip.

· Destination of bus trips

First, we need to identify the times of swiping IC card within a day are needed to be identified firstly, specifically divided into: only one time card behavior, two and more time card behavior. For travels of passenger within one day, the calculation based on IC card statistics is mainly for passengers with two or more ID card information. For passengers with only one piece of IC card information, the station can only be estimated by a more coarse estimation method. For passenger with two or more IC card information, the estimation of the getting off station is based on the space location proximity between the first station and the second station, as shown in Fig. 2-18 (*Maintenance and Upgrading of Chongqing Comprehensive Transportation Models Under Big Data Era*, 2015). According to the spatial distance between the Route 2 IC card point and the Route1 station, if the spatial distance is short, the nearest station in Route 1 is get off station, as a1 point shown. Even so, the identification of the final end of the trip must use the estimated method, as shown in Fig. 2-18.

Note that residents generally have several trips within a day, so the getting-off passengers can be divided into two categories, one is the end of a trip; the other is the transfer. In order to determine the trip purpose is for transfer or for a new trip of passengers with second IC card information, according to the residents travel regulation. Analysis of the first and second time interval helps to determine what kind of travel it is. Here no longer explanation.

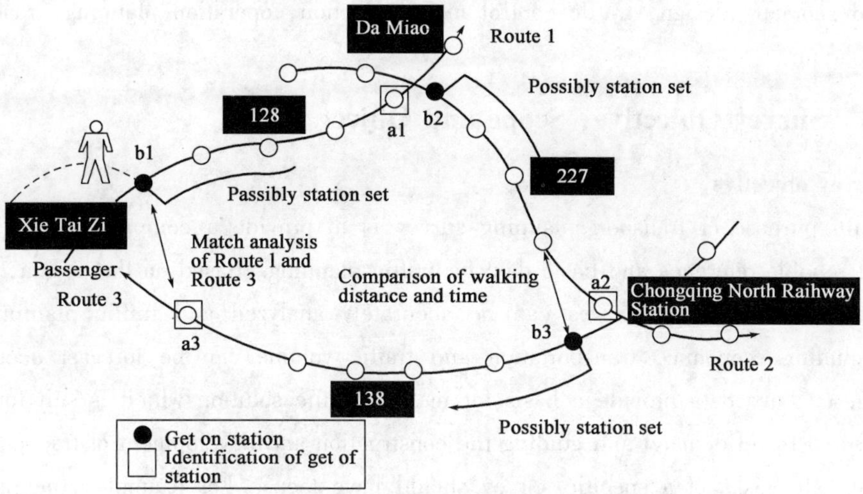

Figure 2-18　Illustration of getting-off station of passengers with two or more IC card behavior

Source: *Wu Xiaoguo*, 2015.

(4) RFID data

RFID refers to radio frequency identification, the principle is that the card management system pre-written the fundamental information, vehicle ID, vehicle type code, type of license plate, the nature of the license plate ownership and other basic information. Therefore, the proposed identification of vehicles has a unique identity card. Electronic tag adopts Ultra High Frequency (UHF) RFID tags, whose recognition rate is up to 99.95%. The maximum write speed is about 130 km/h, the maximum read speed is about 200 km/h, and the maximum communication distance is up to 20 meters at least.

The main components of RFID system are: passive electronic tags, antennas, readers, central data processing computer. Readers fixed to some location which can identify and record the passing time of the vehicle.

Using several continuous cross sections of lane equipped by RFID, we can track the vehicle trajectory, analyze the traffic flow of different direction of each section and based on these information different construction standards properly chosen to widen and reconstructed the different sections. This technology can also be applied to Area Access Control System and parking charge.

With the development of science and technology, traffic survey tends to be more rapid, better, and convenient, which may make up for the deficiency of traditional survey methods and provide new alternative methods, improve accuracy, reduce cost and workload in the future.

2.5　Design and Implementation of Person Trip Survey

Traffic survey means using the objective measure to calculate the road traffic flow and its associated phenomena, acquire and analyze the survey data, grasp characteristics, change regularity, existing problem of the traffic flow, then provide scientific basis for decision-making, such as road geometry design, traffic control mode selection, operation planning, road operation quality evaluation.

2.5.1 Survey Objective, Scope and Object

(1) Survey objective

The main purpose of transport planning survey is to provide a comprehensive, systematic, realistic and reliable reference and basic data for traffic planning. Based on these data, the current traffic situation in the planning area can be accurately analyzed and traffic planning involved indicator including economic, transportation and traffic volume can be forecast accurately and reliably. These above data provide a basis for making traffic solution which is suit for the social development and travel demand and guiding the construction and development of transport.

However, the tasks of a specific survey should have focus. For example, the purpose of a survey in Xi'an is to.

· Update personal travel behavior data during a typical working day.

· Provide a data base for the calibration of the traffic planning model parameters.

(2) Scope of survey

· Spatial scope of the survey

The spatial scope of the survey, usually, is the study area, to study the traffic conditions within the region to investigate. Determine the specific scope according to the survey purpose, survey object, land use attributes, road network distribution etc.. Generally with the traffic zone division, to investigate the traffic situation of each zone.

· Survey time range

The survey time range, that is, the investigation period, also needs to take the characteristics of survey purpose and survey objective into consideration. For example, the peak hour resident trip survey should be conducted in the peak hour during one day's travel. For example, 8:00-9:00 am, 5:00-6:00 pm on weekdays (Monday to Friday).

After the survey scope is determined, the sample of the survey should be selected. Often use the proxy list to select the sample. For example, the sample of the survey is taken from all households residing in the survey area, using household information from water list. Electricity list, the respondents are selected by random principle. Deviations in these lists will obviously result in deviations in the final sample. For example, it is not appropriate for the study area to using a telephone sample survey if most of these families do not have fixed telephones or unpublished telephone numbers.

(3) Respondent of survey

The object of the sample survey should be consistent with the planning needs of the crowd. For example, if we extract a sample from the phone book, the results of the sample survey are limited to those who own the phone. In general, the results do not apply to people who do not have a telephone or do not have a public survey number. For Home Interview Survey, usually, the survey is conducted for all households in the study area. Some studies may target individuals rather than families.

2.5.2 Overall Survey Design

Traffic survey is an ongoing process, which requires an overall design to improve the efficiency of the survey and ensure the accuracy of the survey results. Different resident travel survey has different survey design process, which needs to be based survey purpose, scope, object and make a special design.

(1) Organize the survey organization

As a result of extensive work and heavy workload, it requires a lot of units and departments to coordinate. Therefore, it is necessary to set up a special organization to coordinate and command.

(2) Data preparation

Before the survey, relevant information of the distribution of settlements, land use condition, station storage, terminals location, parking lots location need to be collected.

(3) Division of traffic zone

According to section 2.2.2 zoning system and the division principle, the study area should be divided into traffic zone rationally.

(4) Determine the sampling rate

We can choose whole sample survey in the case the population is not large, but in many cases, the survey need to be taken under some sampling rate, survey sampling method is shown in 2.5.5 sample design.

(5) Personnel training

The quality of the survey results depends largely on the investigators. The responsibility and attitude of the investigators directly affect the success or failure of the survey. Therefore, the investigator filtration should be acted in terms of responsibility and attitude. It is necessary to carry out indoor and on-site survey training.

(6) Develop plans

From a practical standpoint, arrangements should be both compact and leave room for dealing with emergencies.

(7) Pilot study

The purpose of the survey is to identify problems that may arise during a formal investigation, therefore, the content of the survey should be consistent with the formal investigation and address the problem of exposure in a timely manner.

(8) Field investigation

In the field survey process, it is necessary to control the survey quality, and supervision as well as inspection is also needed, in order to find the problems timely and ensure the quality of the investigation.

(9) Data Cleaning and Analysis

In order to minimize the computer memory occupied to facilitate data input and post-analysis, the text information in table should be changed into a number, that is, the corresponding data should be encoded. Usually, a unified spreadsheet template is created. The templates define the data format of the survey data and specify the range of valid values. Data entry personnel only need to open the template, input data according to the corresponding requirements. The template will automatically give a reminder when an error is entered.

(10) Data Analysis and Reporting

The preliminary statistical analysis of the survey data generally includes: effective data statistics, the actual sampling rate statistical analysis, statistical analysis of various indicators such as classification statistics; report preparation need to found the regularity and problem. The implementation process can be divided into four phases: pre-preparation phase, survey implementation phase, data processing stage and in-depth study phase, as shown in Fig. 2-19.

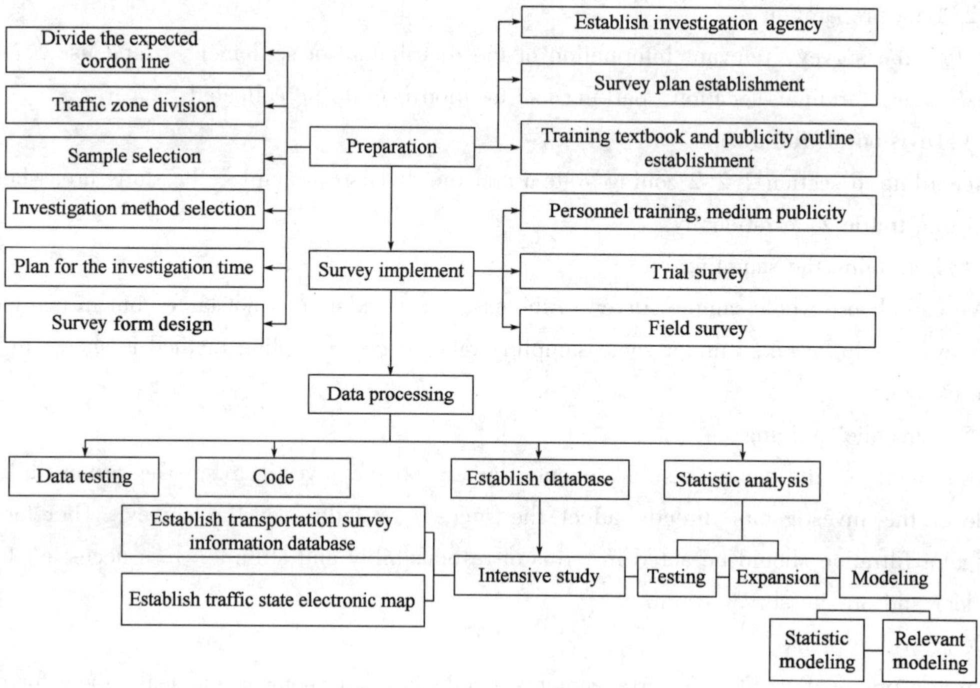

Figure 2-19 Flow chart of investigation process

2.5.3 Survey Method Selection

Person trip survey can conduct by mail, telephone or direct home interview survey. However, the program own characteristics should be considered, such as capital, time constraints, regional characteristics, etc. when select the most suitable survey method.

2.5.4 Survey Accurate Requirement

Due to sampling errors and other systematic errors, it is necessary to determine the accuracy of the survey before the survey is carried out, which is usually associated with the survey budget. Trip survey Accuracy requirements and test methods of trip survey for urban transportation planning are as follows.

(1) Precision requirements

· If the error is less than 5% , indicating that the OD survey is meeting the requirements.

· If the error is between 5% and 15% , indicating that the basic acceptable, but need to be adjusted.

· When the error is larger than 15% , then the OD investigation is wrong, or the work of the investigation and analysis of the work process is wrong, which should be checked the reworked.

(2) Precision test method

· Screen line method: there are only a few way (bridge, tunnel, etc.) connected to the different planning area in the screen line, which can be measured line traffic, compared these data with the trip assignment data of motor vehicles volume (residents travel volume) in the road section by the original OD survey.

· Sample check method: for some survey items in the individual partition, select another sample to conduct a survey again, this time the sample rate should be set higher, such as 25% , and then zoom to the population level, then make a comparison with the original survey data to check whether the error is tolerable.

· Mutual comparison method: if different survey items contain the same indicator, this indicator can be compared to determine the quality of the survey.

2.5.5 Sample Design

This is done before collecting various types of data to obtain a sample of a given population. In order to make the sample reflect the actual situation correctly, its representative (representing the overall characteristics) is very important, so the sample selection need to ensure unbiasedness. In order to ensure unbiasedness, the sample selection process needs to be random. For example, if n observations x_1, x_2, $\cdots$, x_n are selected from a finite population N to form a random sample with a sample size n, then the probability that each individual is selected in the population should be equal and independent.

(1) Sample sampling method

· Simple random sampling

The probability that each individual in n samples is chosen is equal, namely the extraction of the sample is determined randomly.

· Systematic sampling

We choose a starting point randomly in the whole population, then every k individual, choose the $k+1$ individual as the sample, that is, the sample is equally spaced or equidistantly, so it is also called equidistant sampling.

· Stratified sampling

The population is evenly divided into several levels, such as high-income families and low-income families. The best way to select a hierarchy is to find large differences between different hierarchy and small differences of individual within the same hierarchy, and then randomize the sampling at each level.

· Cluster sampling

The population is divided into several groups, each group having the same characteristics as the population, for example, selecting a city to represent the whole country. The criterion for selecting the optimal group is exactly the opposite of the hierarchical selection method: the difference between the groups is small, and the difference within each group is large. Random sampling is then used within the cluster.

The above sampling methods are called probability sampling, and non-probability sampling can also be applied in practice, especially when the input cost is low and the initial coverage rate is required. As in some pilot studies, the most commonly used sampling method is the "roadside survey". The main characteristic of non-probabilistic sampling is that the investigator does not know in advance the probability that each sampling unit will be selected. However, the survey should be as diversified as possible, and the sample size is proportional to the number of categories observed.

(2) Interval estimation and simple size

The determination of the sample size is based on the interval estimation in probability statistics.

Before discussing the formulas for sample size, a few clarifications about estimation must be made. Suppose we are interested in calculating the number of trips per household in a municipality where the size of the population considered (i. e. number of households) is N. A simple random sample of size n was drawn from that population. It is possible to show that the sample mean ($\overline{X}$) is an unbiased estimate of the population mean μ_x, i. e.

$$E(\overline{X}) = \mu_x \tag{2-4}$$

The variance of sample:

$$s^2 = \frac{\sum_{i=1}^{n} (x_i - \bar{x})^2}{n-1} \tag{2-5}$$

The variance of $\overline{X}$:

$$V(\overline{X}) = \frac{s^2}{n}\left(\frac{N-n}{N-1}\right) = \frac{s^2}{n}(1-f) \tag{2-6}$$

where, $f = n/N$ is called sampling fraction, note that some statisticians use N instead of $(N-1)$; $(1-f)$ is called "finite population correction factor"; s^2 is the sampling variance.

According to "central limit theorem", the distribution of the mean of random sample approaches to normal distribution as n goes to infinity irrespective to the distribution of parent population, then:

$$t_{n-1} = \frac{\bar{x} - \mu_x}{\sqrt{V}} \tag{2-7}$$

Above specification is called Student-t with $(n-1)$ degree of freedom.

Therefore, a $100(1-\alpha)\%$ confident interval for sample mean is:

$$\bar{x} - t_{n-1}\sqrt{v} \leqslant u_x \leqslant \bar{x} - t_{n-1}\sqrt{v} \tag{2-8}$$

where, t_{n-1} is the value of Student-t distribution with $(n-1)$ degree of freedom; α is the significant level, which means that only $\alpha \times 100\%$ of the sample range will not contain the true value of population mean. For a large sample size (larger than 50), the t value are 1, 1.96 and 2.58 for the significant level α 0.31(1/3), 0.05(1/20) and 0.01(1/100), respectively.

For a simple proportion p (i. e. the proportion of household with 2 or more cars), if $n \cdot p \cdot q > 3$ Binomial distribution could be approximated by normal distribution. In this case, it is possible to show that:

$$t_{\alpha/2} = \frac{\hat{p} - p}{\sqrt{v}} = \frac{\hat{p} - p}{\sqrt{p \cdot q/n}} \tag{2-9}$$

It's the t-distribution of $n-1$ freedom. Where, $v = p \cdot q/n$, $q = 1 - p$.

Therefore, a $100(1-\alpha)\%$ confident interval for p is:

$$\hat{p} - t_{\alpha/2}\sqrt{p \cdot q/n} \leqslant p \leqslant \hat{p} + t_{\alpha/2}\sqrt{p \cdot q/n} \tag{2-10}$$

In other words, the confident interval c can be expressed as follows:

$$c = \pm t_{\alpha/2}\sqrt{p \cdot q/n} = \pm \frac{t_{\alpha/2}}{2\sqrt{n}} \tag{2-11}$$

$$n = \pm \left(\frac{t_{\alpha/2}}{2c}\right)^2 \tag{2-12}$$

If a proportion of two random variables is the subject of investigation, for example, in clustering sample, then the average proportion is:

$$p_i = \frac{x_i}{n_i}$$

$$p = \frac{\sum_i x_i}{\sum_i n_i}$$

$$v = \frac{1}{m(m-1)}\sum_i \frac{n_i}{\bar{n}}(p_i - p)^2 \tag{2-13}$$

$$\bar{n} = \frac{\sum_i n_i}{m}$$

where, x_i is the number of trips in the i-th cluster; n_i is the number of elements in the i-th cluster; $\bar{n}$ is the average number of elements per cluster; m is the number of cluster.

The needed sample size depends on the investigation quantity (e. g. average, proportion or ratio), the level of significance α, the variability in the population (standard deviation σ) and the tolerance d (the difference between true value and the estimated parameter). The average and the population for large and the small population are discussed below.

Sample size for an average when the population is large. If an average value is the parameter under investigation, and the population is large (100000 or more), then the value of n which guarantees with confidence is $100(1-\alpha)\%$, that $\bar{x} - \mu$ will no larger than d, is:

$$n = \left(\frac{t \cdot s}{d}\right)^2 \tag{2-14}$$

Sample rate:
$$f=\frac{t^2 \cdot s^2}{d^2(N-1)} \tag{2-15}$$

Sample size for an average when the population is small. If the population is small, then the formula becomes:

$$n=(t \cdot s/d)^2(N-n)/(N-1) \tag{2-16}$$

When $n \approx N-1$, since n appears in both sides, then rearranging the formula adjusts as:

$$n=\frac{t^2 \cdot s^2}{d^2+t^2 \cdot s^2/(N-1)} \tag{2-17}$$

Sampling rate:
$$f=\frac{t^2 \cdot s^2}{d^2 \cdot N+t^2 \cdot s^2} \tag{2-18}$$

where, f is the sampling rate; t^2 is the standard Normal Distribution, the certain confidence interval corresponds with two side fractile.

When the significant level is 95%, $t_\alpha^2=1.96$.

where, s^2 is the population variance, sample variance can take place when the sample size is large; N is the population capacity; d^2 is the allowable absolute error controlled by error control indicator.

For example, let us assume that we need to get information about the average in s municipality with population 300000. Old data has shown that the average income is \$50000 and the standard deviation(s) was \$10000. What is the size of the sample needed to estimate the average income in that municipality with accuracy \$1000(d) with 95% confidence?

Since the sample size is large, so we select Eq. (2-14). When the significant level is 95%, $t=1.96$, $d=1000$, $s=10000$. The result is $n=384$ households. For 99% significance, $n=663$ household. If the population of the population was small, e. g. 8000 households, one would use Eq. (2-19), and $N=8000$. For 95% significance, $n=367$. For 99% significance, $n=612$.

Sample size for a proportion when the population is large. If a proportion(varies between zero and one) is the parameter under investigation, and the population is large(100000 or more), then:

$$t_{\alpha/2}=\frac{\hat{p}-p}{\sqrt{v}}=\frac{d}{\sqrt{p \cdot q/n}} \tag{2-19}$$

$$n=\frac{t^2 p \cdot q}{d^2} \tag{2-20}$$

In the absence of values for p(or q), one can use the fact that the maximum values of $p \cdot q$ is 0.25. For example larger than 50, one can use the following formulas:

$$n=1.96^2 \times 0.25/d^2=0.9604/d^2 \text{ for 95\% confidence}$$

$$n=2.58^2 \times 0.25/d^2=1.6577/d^2 \text{ for 99\% confidence}$$

As an example, suppose we are interested in estimating the proportion of families p with high income with 95% confidence, i. e. with $\alpha=0.05$ and within three percentage points. Therefore, $t_\alpha=1.96$, $d=0.03$. Since we have no idea of the magnitude of the proportion, we know that the maximum value of $p \cdot q$ is 0.25, therefore, using the equation above $n=1067$. Table 2-11 shows other examples.

Table 2-11 Minimum sample sizes for variables example as proportions(large population)

Error Tolerance	95% Confidence	99% Confidence
±1%	9604	16577
±2%	2401	4144
±4%	600	1036
±6%	267	460
±8%	150	259
±10%	96	166
±12%	67	115

Sample size for a proportion when population is small. If the population is not large(less than 100000), then adjusted formulas must be used.

$$n=\left(\frac{t^2p\cdot q}{d^2}\right)\frac{(N-n)}{(N-1)} \tag{2-21}$$

Note that "n" appears in both sides of the equation. Rearranging the population equation leads to the following formula:

$$n=\frac{t^2p\cdot q\cdot N}{t^2p\cdot q+(N-1)d^2} \tag{2-22}$$

When population is large enough, $N\approx N-1$, sample ratio can be calculated by the following formula:

$$f=\frac{n}{N}=\frac{t^2\cdot p\cdot q}{\frac{t^2p\cdot q}{N}+d^2} \tag{2-23}$$

Solving the same problem as above, with 95% confidence, except the sample come from a population of size 50000, gives $n=1045$. Note that the sample required from a small population is usually smaller than the sample required from a large population, ceteris paribus.

One of the problems in home interview survey is that it is a multipurpose tool. Experience in U. S. A. with home interview surveys has led the Bureau of Public Roads(BPR) to recommend the sample sizes shown in the Table 2-12.

Table 2-12 Home interview sample size recommended by B. P. R.

Population of area	Sample size
Under 50000	1 in 5 Households
50000-150000	1 in 8 Households
150000-300000	1 in 10 Households
300000-500000	1 in 15 Households
500000-100000	1 in 20 Households
Over 1000000	1 in 25 Households

The choices if sample sizes, method and the resulting cost should be carefully weighed against the accuracy needed. Note that the four formulas for sample sizes given above apply only to simple random sampling.

【**Example 2-1**】 Sampling survey is used to evaluate the level of vehicle spot speed of a section of a city where the error does not exceed 2 km/h. According to the relevant statistical report, the standard speed of the site speed of is about 12km/h. How many cars need to be surveyed? (Bilateral $\alpha = 0.05$, $t = 1.96$)

【**Sol.**】 Take $t = 1.96$, $\sigma = 12$, $\delta = 2$ into the formula, then get the sample size $n = 139$.

【**Example 2-2**】 The method of sampling survey is used to estimate the parking rate of an urban intersection. The required error is less than 0.06. How many cars do we need to investigate? (Bilateral $\alpha = 0.05$, $u = 1.96$)

【**Sol.**】 In the above case, we cannot determine the parking rate, but according to the characteristics of the quadratic function, when $p = 0.5$, the $p(1-p)$ gets the largest value, the calculated sample size is also the largest which is up to 267, so when we cannot determine the p value, often take $p = 0.5$ to get the most conservative sample size.

【**Example 2-3**】 In a person trip survey, the absolute error of the survey results is not allowed to more than 10 times in the confidence level of 95%, assuming that the estimation of population variance σ^2 is 80, the population size is 4330 people, what is the necessary sampling rate.

【**Sol.**】 according to the question, $t_\alpha^2 = 1.96$, $\sigma = s = 80$, $d = 0$, $N = 4330$.

$$f = \frac{t^2 s^2}{d^2 N + t^2 s^2} = \frac{1.96^2 \times 80^2}{10^2 \times 4330 + 1.96^2 \times 80^2} = 5.37\%$$

So when the necessary survey sampling rate is 5.37%, it meets the need.

From the practice, it is found that the uniform sampling rate is more conducive to data processing and the smooth progress of the investigation. Chang'an University was in charge of the motor vehicle OD survey in whole Hebei province. According to the different traffic volume, the sampling rate and sampling method were unified, which gained good effects. The selected sampling rates are shown in Table 2-13.

Table 2-13 Sampling rate of OD survey

Traffic volume Q	$Q < 2000$	$2000 < Q < 5000$	$5000 < Q < 8000$	$8000 < Q < 10000$	$10000 < Q < 15000$	$Q > 15000$
Type	Point type one	Point type two	Point type three	Point type four	Point type five	Point type six
Sampling rate	100%	100%	75%	60%	50%	50%

2.5.6 Survey Form Design

The content of the questionnaire should be as concise as possible while ensuring the coverage of key issues. This will not only distinguish the key issues and improve the survey accuracy, but also improve the efficiency while reducing working time.

Taking Chang'an University as an example. The investigation of the residents, temporary residents and floating population was conducted in Xi'an during weekdays from November to December of 2015. The first page is the cover, including the header (table name, household ID, investigators, auditors, etc.), the introduction of investigation contents, basic household information, instructions of filling out the form.

Family member's information table consists of family information column(member ID, gender, age, occupation, etc.) and personal travel characteristics(travel purpose, departure time, mode of transport, arrival time). Note that the travel purpose and travel mode in table should be filled in code, rather than specific contents, as shown in Schedule 2.

The population in the survey consists of the temporary resident population, the floating population. This two need to be investigated separately because the travel characteristics of the two are quite different. Schedule 3 shows the mobile population survey, which obtains travel information of floating population from lodging population(such as hotel). The first page includes the header, survey introduction, filling out instruction and the personal information column. The second page is the specific travel information form, the filling content of which is same as that of residents.

2.5.7 Survey Implementation

Extract samples and select survey locations. Generally, the questionnaire is sent to the survey address a few days prior to the visit, informing each family member of what is needed for the survey. Conducting a survey of family members on an appointed day, if fails, you need to try other methods. The collection of travel information is usually taken after the travel within 24 hours. It is often necessary to separate weekend travel from workday travel. It is also important to select, train and supervise the performance of investigators during the survey.

2.6 Data Analysis and Error Study

2.6.1 Sampling Error

Sampling error, also known as random error, is the error exists in any cases. Only a whole sample survey is made, this kind of error can be avoided. The above-mentioned sampling method can effectively reduce such errors, and at the same time, determine the sample size reasonably can reduce the sampling error. Factors affecting sampling errors in the transportation field include:

· The number of sampling units. Other conditions remain unchanged, the more the number of sampling units, the smaller the sampling error will be; whereas, the error will be big. This is because the sample structure becomes closer to the population as the number of sample increases. The sampling survey is more approximately to the complete survey. When the sample expanded to the population, it is a complete survey and there is no sampling error, but workload will increase significantly and generally due to funding, time constraints, it is impossible to conduct a comprehensive investigation.

· The degree of variation of the overall studied indicant. The indicant is divided into attributive indicant and numerical indicant. The difference is that the former is expressed in words, the latter is expressed in figures. For example, a respondents is male and the age is 23-year-old, where the sex is the attributive indicant, the age is the numerical indicant and 23 is the flag value. Obviously based on different indicants, the results of multiple samples of the synthesis characteristics will be different. Other conditions remain unchanged, the smaller the degree of variation of the indicants are, the smaller sampling error will be. On the contrary, the sampling error will be big. The sampling error is proportional to the variation of the total indicant. For example, the object of the person trip survey are the residents of the survey area. Due to the difference of the residents'attributes(gender, age, having driving license or not and so on), different person travels differently. If the classification is unreasonable, the sample deviation is large. And the greater the difference in resident attributes, the greater the sampling error will be.

· The choice of sampling method. The choice of sampling method should be based on the characteristics of the survey population. Area where residents of the same residential area have similarities and of different residential areas have differences are suitable for the cluster sampling method.

· Different sampling organization. There are different sampling errors in different sampling organizations. This is because the samples selected from different sampling organizations represents the population differently. For example, all selecting cluster method, home interview survey and roadside survey produce different sampling error.

2.6.2 Non-sampling Error

Non-sampling error, also known as systematic error, can be attributed to many reasons, most of the reasons are random errors, which are mainly subject to the subjective factors, specifically divided into human error and mechanical error. Three types of errors are as follows:

· Non-response error: for example, error caused by some measurement failure of the selected sample units, this kind of error includes:

a. Non-cover type(some typical units are not included in the sample);

b. The respondents are not at home;

c. Cannot reply(or do not want to reply, refuse to reply or be away for a long time during the investigation).

If there are differences between respondents and non-respondents, then the non-response error will be biased in the result.

· Survey error. For example, respondents may not have accurate information or not provide full information(such as respondents do not cover all family members of all trips). When this problem appears, the results of the survey will be biased.

· Editing, coding, programming errors. This kind of error refers to the error produced in the sample sorting, aggregation, classification, calculation and the error generated during the input process after acquisition of sample data. Cross-checking with other sources of information can resolve such error.

2.6.3 Correction and Expansion of Samples

Ideally, the size of the random sample extension is the reciprocal of the sampling size. For example, if you take 5% as the sample size, then the expansion coefficient is 20. However, before doing so, we need to test the samples, remove the invalid samples and the number of samples which are not received, calculated as follows:

$$F = \frac{Z}{S-d-n} \tag{2-24}$$

where, Z is the overall capacity within the partition; S is the sample size; d is the number of invalid samples in the response samples; n is the number of samples not received.

2.7 Summary of Data Usage in Traffic Planning

Table 2-14 shows the data usage of each phase of traffic planning.

Table 2-14 Application of traffic planning data

Step	Method and data type		Model exemplification
Trip generation	Generation rate method	The number of population per zone based on trip purpose, number of trip production and trip attraction per unit or total population of per zone, number of trip production and trip attraction per unit	$O_i = bx_i$ $D_j = cx_j$
	Elasticity-based model	Passenger capacity or cargo capacity growth rate, economic growth rate, which are defined with the GDP growth rate	$E = \frac{\Delta T/T}{\Delta Y/Y}$
	Function method	The average income, average car ownership rate, the number of households, population, employment, land use area and other independent variables in each traffic zone	$O_i^c = a_0^c + a_1^c \cdot x_{1i}^c + a_2^c \cdot x_{2i}^c + \cdots$ $D_i^c = b_0^c + b_1^c \cdot x_{1i}^c + b_2^c \cdot x_{2i}^c + \cdots$
Trip distribution	Growth factor modal	Complete base year OD table data is required	Fratar method: $f_F(F_{O_i}^m, F_{D_j}^m) = F_{O_i}^m \cdot F_{D_j}^m \cdot \frac{L_i + L_j}{2}$ $L_i = \frac{O_i^m}{\sum_j q_{ij}^m \cdot F_{D_j}^m}$ $L_j = \frac{D_i^m}{\sum_i q_{ij}^m \cdot F_{O_i}^m}$
	Gravity modal	Trip production and trip attraction for the target year of each traffic zone (the complete OD table data is not required), the traffic impedance function	$q_{ij} = a_i \cdot O_i \cdot b_j \cdot D_j \cdot f(c_{ij})$ $a_i = [\sum_j b_j \cdot D_j \cdot f(c_{ij})]^{-1}$ $b_i = [\sum_i a_i \cdot O_i \cdot f(c_{ij})]^{-1}$
	Intervening opportunities model	The number of arrival chances to pass from zone 1 is accumulated as S_j	$q_{ij} = \frac{O_i(e^{-\alpha \cdot S_j} - e^{-\alpha \cdot S_{j+1}})}{1 - e^{-\alpha \cdot S_{n+1}}}$

continued

Step	Method and data type		Model exemplification
Modal split	Logit model	For the MNL model, a fixed utility (available cost, impedance like travel time) of the alternatives is required	MNL model: $p(k)=\frac{e^{V(k)}}{\sum_j e^{V(j)}}$
	Probit model	The random utility function (including fixed benefit and random portion, road impedance expressed by negative value), variance, covariance	$p(k)=\varphi\left[\frac{V(k)-V(k+1)}{\sqrt{\sigma_k^2+\sigma_{k+1}^2-\sigma_{kk+1}}}\right]$
Trip assignment	Non-equilibrium assignment method	Route impedance (available time, cost, distance, etc.)	
	Equilibrium assignment method		
	Stochastic assignment method		

Four-step prediction is done using planning softwares, such as TransCad, Cube, EMME/2, VISSUM and so on. Before the analysis and calculation, the planning area should be divided into traffic zones and the following basic data need to be prepared: trip productions, trip attractions, travel impedance etc.. Then, transform the above basic data into OD matrix.

Exercises

1. What is the status of traffic data in the process of transportation planning?
2. What are the data types in transportation planning?
3. What access to traffic data?
4. What is the meaning for traffic survey? What are the methods for traffic survey? What are the important significances and effects of traffic surveys?
5. What are the sampling methods for traffic survey? What are the errors in the sample survey? How to improve the accuracy of sample survey? How to determine the sampling rate?
6. How to conduct OD survey, what is the basic process?
7. How to analyze OD data statistically? How to treat the accuracy of the OD survey data?
8. What is RP and SP survey? Explain the advantages and disadvantages of the two survey method.
9. How to conduct SP survey? What is the difference between SP survey and RP survey?
10. What are the applications of data in the field of transportation?

11. In order to obtain the origin and destination information data, usually, the roadside inquiry method is conducted, which may cause queuing problems. Assuming there is a survey point on a section of the road, the arrival of the vehicle is random and subject to Poisson distribution, the one-way traffic volume is 600 veh/h, the sampling rate is 50%. Selected vehicles need to stop for OD survey, assuming that a staff can finish a survey in 10 s averagely and the survey time per car is subject to negative exponential distribution. Please estimate the following indexes: average number of vehicles, the average queue length, the non-zero average queue length, the average time spent in the queuing system, and the average waiting time in the queuing system at the survey point.

12. A spot speed survey is conducted in a two-lane suburb road in length of 100 m, hoping to get the average speed (the allowable error is 2.1 km/h or less at a 95.5% confidence level), what is the minimum sample size? After the actual observation, the observed 60 original data are as shown in Table 2-15.

Table 2-15 Raw data of observed vehicle spot speed

2.73	3.03	2.71	2.68	2.71	3.02
2.88	2.73	2.70	2.62	2.67	2.77
2.46	2.68	2.81	3.43	2.84	3.19
2.87	3.57	2.81	2.32	2.57	2.93
2.98	2.32	2.72	2.28	3.30	3.04
2.60	2.37	2.40	2.57	2.66	2.88
2.78	2.59	2.70	2.71	2.51	2.54
3.15	2.41	2.49	2.23	2.90	2.45
2.77	2.47	2.51	2.80	2.53	2.56
2.66	2.59	2.73	2.70	2.92	2.90

The question is: whether the sample size meets the requirements or not? Give investigation and analysis for the speed data.

References

[1] Ali Mekky, P. Eng. Analytics Transportation Planning[M]. America, 2001.

[2] Wang Wei, GuoXiucheng. Traffic Engineering [M]. Nanjing: Southeast University Press, 2011:40-75.

[3] Zhang Yu. Traffic Planning Model-TransCAD Operation and Application[M]. Beijing: China Architecture & Building Press, 2011.

[4] Yang Fei, Yao Zhenxing. Travel-based feature extraction method based on mobile sensor data [J]. Urban Transport, 2016, 14(01).

[5] Zhang Tian, Yang Dongyuan, Zhao Yali, et al.. Comparison of Mixed Logit and Nested Logit Models for RP/SP fusion data[J]. Tongji University: Natural Science Edition, 2008, 36(08): 1073-1078.

[6] Hu Yongxuan, Song Yu, Zhang Jian, et al.. Improvement of traffic OD extraction method based on mobile signaling data[J]. Traffic Information and Security, 2015, 33(05):84-90.

[7] Ran Bin. Application of Mobile Data in Traffic Survey and Traffic Planning [J]. Urban Transport, 2013, 11(01):72-81.

[8] Ji Huihui. OD investigation methods and analysis of survey results[J]. Transportation World: Transportation Vehicles, 2010 (18):122-123.

[9] Tan Xianlin. Elimination of duplicate "series and parallel" method in the process of OD survey data processing[J]. Highway, 1997 (12):27-31.

[10] Gai Chunying, Yu Yulong. Traffic Forecasting Method in Feasibility Study of Highway Construction Project[J]. Journal of Traffic and Transportation Engineering, 2002, 2(01):51-54.

[11] Chen Chaogang, Ma Yun. Improvement and Treatment of Highway Vehicle OD Survey Methods[J]. East China Highway, 2003(1):69-73.

[12] Wei Junfeng, Wang Zhenmin. Discussion on Key Problems of Regional Highway OD Survey [J]. Communications Standardization, 2006(8):108-112.

[13] An Qilin. Synthesis of Regional Traffic Trip OD Table[J]. Highway, 1999 (3).

[14] Highway Bureau of the Ministry of Transport, Highway Engineering Technical Standard[M]. Beijing: China Communications Press, 2014.

[15] Lu Huapu. Transportation Planning Theory and Method [M]. Beijing: Tsinghua University Press, 2006.

[16] Shao Chunfu. Principles of traffic planning [M]. Beijing: China Railway Publishing House, 2014.

[17] Wang Rui. Research on several issues of urban residents' travel survey[D]. Xi'an: Chang'an University, 2006.

[18] Yang Xiaokuan, He Yulong. General Introduction to Traffic Engineering[M]. Beijing: China Communications Press, 2010.

[19] Zhou Tao, Geng Changxu, Gao Zhigang. Research on OD Projection Technology Based on Public Transport IC Card Data[J]. Urban Transport, 2007,5(03): 48-52.

[20] Chen Xuewu, Dai Wei, Chen Zhe. Information collection, analysis and application of IC card in public transport[J]. China Civil Engineering Journal,2004,37(02): 105-110.

[21] Chang'an University. Highway OD Investigation and Research Report of Hebei Province[R]. Xi'an Chang'an University, 2005.

[22] Ma Shuhong, Zhao Yifen. Xi'an residents travel survey[R]. Xi'an: Chang'an University, 2016.

[23] Wu Xiangguo. A New Exploration of the Maintenance and Upgrade of Chongqing Traffic Model under the Background of Big Data [R]. Chongqing: Chongqing Traffic Planning Research Institute, 2015.

Chapter 3

Transportation Model

3.1 Introduction

Models are widely used in our daily life. For instance, maps can be viewed as the first generation of transportation models for simulating geography and assisting navigation. A model can be thought of as a simple representation of the real life, and is the concrete of the problem and the point of view. In general, if the two systems S'and S have similar responses under similar stimuli, the system S' is the model of system S.

Models can be divided into the physical models and the abstract models.

Physical model: the instrument or infrastructure designed by using soil, wood, bones and wax.

Abstract model: It does not necessarily be represented as a specific entity, but it can exist theoretically. Is the theory or framework the objective of things? Abstract model includes mathematical model and analysis model. The mathematical model attempts to restore the system points and behavior by a mathematical equation based on a certain theory. An analytical model is a description of objective things or phenomena.

The transportation model belongs to the abstract model, which reflects the travel behavior of the traveler through a series of mathematical models or analytical models, which is a simulation of the travel behavior of the traveler in reality. According to Ali Mekky's summary of the transportation model, combined with the author's understanding, the role of the model is as follows:

· Explain certain transport phenomena. Based on the transportation model to explore the relationship between the parameters, the traffic phenomenon, and characteristics. A more in-depth explanation of the reasons of the traffic conditions could be made.

· Explore the evolution of traffic problems. The control variables can be controlled by controlling the range of some variables (influence factors) to reveal the difference of transportation operation results caused by different traffic flow or transportation facilities, and reveal the change of level of service.

· Select optimal scheme. Based on the transport model which can be used to represent the real traffic condition after calibration, it is possible to test and evaluate the different transportation planning options. It can quickly and economically test and evaluate various kinds of alternative solutions, and choose the transport planning scheme. Construction and management decisions cannot be analyzed in depth before they are put into operation, which cause a waste of transportation resources and even worse after the completion of transportation problems.

· Provide decision makers with comprehensive transport system and useful information. Based on the change of the parameters obtained by the model operation, it is possible to provide the decision maker with a variety of alternatives, to predict the information of the transportation planning alternatives more accurately and help decision-makers make scientific decisions.

It should be noted that the transportation model is not a transport plan, cannot replace the transportation planning, the transport model itself does not produce planning, but can be combined with the planning program to predict the development trend, to provide support for transportation planning which is an important part of transportation planning. It can be said that the role of transportation model is helping analyze the status quo and the future of the evolution of the mathematical law, then reach to a more accurate or quantitative understanding of the evolution of traffic.

3.2 Transportation Model

3.2.1 Development of Transportation Model

At the beginning of the 20th century, the United States began to use some simple traffic statistics model (transportation model) to carry out traffic estimation. In the middle of the 20th century, the emergence of computer makes the rapid motorization in Europe and the United States, the traffic demand model system began to develop, the initial stage of development involves the following aspects:

· Data Aggregation-make the data easy to manage and meet the requirements of the calculation;

· Simplified Model-the estimation of the parameters does not require lengthy calculations to forecast easily.

The model at the beginning contains only a few important variables. This simplified hypothesis has led to the emergence of a four-stage approach. Since the 1950s, transport pioneers started the study of transport in Detroit and Chicago, and the basic principles of the urban transport model have been developed. Transportation planning professionals have started using a four-stage Method of Transport Demand Analysis. In the 1950s and 1960s, the construction of transport infrastructure became the focus of social attention. Due to the need of such transportation planning, the four-stage model system developed rapidly. With its excellent practical simulation results, it became the most practical tool in the transportation planning in developed countries. After the 1970s, the focus of transportation planning moved from the infrastructure construction to the transport system management, the four-stage model system theory also began to expose the defects, the scholars began to focus on the individual level of travel behavior. The disaggregate choice models proposed by McFedden provide new ideas for the improvement of the transport model. The researchers began to think that the discrete choice model is the future direction of the transport model. And now the basic framework of the four-stage model has not changed, but began to seek a wide range of emerging transport forecast integration, innovation. The four-stage model is the mainstream model of transport planning and is widely recognized in the world. This chapter will focus on the theory and application of the four-stage model.

The focus of the transport model is constantly changing as people know the improvement and technological progress. The early transport modeling mainly considered how to meet the rapid growth demand of the motor vehicle in the supply balance. After 1980, the practice and theory of the transport adjustment and the dynamic adjustment of the transport supply have revealed that the urban area supply is difficult to follow the demand. No longer only the pursuit of transportation facilities to meet the transport needs, but from the environment, land, energy and other aspects to assess the appropriate, sustainable transport structure and demand management model. A new attempt to assess the transport planning program is being developed by integrating the carbon emission model with the transport demand model. In addition, how to increase the carbon footprint assessment of the transport plan is becoming more and more important because of its rapid growth and the global consensus on the development of low-carbon environmental protection. How to make full use of big data and Internet of Things, how to consider the development of transport planning risk, and how to do a better life cycle assessment on the program and construction timing selection are the developing trend of transport model.

3.2.2 Model Design

Ali Mekky(2001) suggested that the following elements should be considered when designing a transportation model:

(1) Objectives

When building a transportation model, it is necessary to consider the accuracy, and the difference of different transportation models. The accuracy depends on the goal, time and budget, and the availability of the data. Therefore, it is important to determine the goal of modeling at the beginning.

(2) Variables

Selecting variables which are incorporated into model.

(3) Simplifying assumptions

Travel patterns in cities and regions are very complex. Travel refers to a variety of people, a variety of travel purposes, different modes of transport, thousands of complex path composition. If we try to simulate the above complex model, it is necessary to simplify the assumption, the relevant assumptions of the transport model are as follows:

· Spatial aggregation: In order to understand how people move from one place to another in the city, the transportation model usually simplifies the problem by pooling geographically similar travelers in a single zone. It is called traffic zone. In the ideal traffic zone, each of traffic zone contains activities such as residential, industrial and so on, its internal should be homogeneous distribution(homogeneous activity) to ensure the uniformity of the characteristics of the activities.

· Sectoral aggregation: it is difficult to accurately simulate a system with thousands of unique elements. Therefore, the aggregation is necessary. Usually in accordance with the income, car ownership, family size and other similar attributes, assuming that the group of people's travel behavior has a certain common feature. In essence, the set is equivalent to grouping system elements, and in fact they are not the same, but they are treated as the same in transportation modeling.

· Decomposing the system into subsystems: The system usually refers to the combination of interrelated element, travel behavior simulation can be decomposed by the entire transport system into several sub-model system. In the mainstream transport planning process, the transport model is often divided into four subsystems, namely trip generation, trip distribution, mode split and transport trip assignment.

· Trip records linking: based on the travel mode change or passenger service, the relevant travel destination and travel path.

(4) Time treatment

Time can exist as an estimation term in the model or as a tool that makes the model dynamic. As a forecasting term, it is often referred as a planned specific year or target year, and is often used as a key variable for forecasting path and mode selection as a time concept spent in forecasting a trip.

(5) Theory

A model is a formal expression that allows planners to understand the systems they interested in. Therefore, it must make "understood" as accurate as possible, and supported by logical hypothesis. In the discussion of spatial distribution of travel activities, the gravity model is consistent with the entropy theory, and in the study of path and mode choice, the theory of utility and market can fit people's choice better.

(6) Technique

Once a theoretical hypothesis is given, it is necessary to use appropriate technical methods to express it in different ways; commonly used technical methods are:

· Mathematical equations: including linear/nonlinear equations, algebraic/differential equations, and mathematical equations;

· Simulation rules: such as the amount of travel per unit of land, the vehicle running on the road path selection rules.

3.2.3 Types of Models

Combined with the existing traffic model classification and traffic model development, the traffic model can be classified from the following three aspects:

(1) Classification according to the study area and coverage characteristics

· National/regional transportation model: This level is a strategic level of macro-transport model, covering a wide area, but only contains limited details. This strategic traffic model can test the impact of land use or significant changes on transport.

· Urban transport model: This model makes detailed traffic analysis based on the urban area.

· Project plan model: This model is based on traffic simulation in smaller areas of traffic state analysis, the degree of detail we want is generally determined according to the requirements of the project.

(2) Model algorithm principle classification

· Mathematical or Algorithmic:

Mathematical models could take the form of an equation or a system of equations. Algorithmic models might not contain any mathematical function, only just logical instructions, e. g. Monte Carlo models.

· Aggregate or disaggregate:

The disaggregate model is derived from the study of individual behavior theory and the individual behavior as the research object. Based on certain assumptions, the individual behavior level can be aggregated to the aggregate level; the aggregate model usually does not take individual behavior into account, and collects it together to study the total amount of traffic in the zone and the percentage of choice for the study. The aggregate model is usually used for macro-research (focusing on the strategic perspective of the planning scope) and the medium (which focuses on local traffic conditions). The micro-traffic research is usually based on the algorithm's disclosure of traffic conditions.

· Probabilistic or deterministic:

The deterministic model is used to answer how many people use a facility; the probability model is used to answer the probability of a person who want to use a facility.

· Discrete or continuous:

In the initial transportation planning model, the independent variables are usually continuous, slowly and gradually converted to discrete. The continuous model answers "how many" questions (e. g. how many trips are generated), while discrete (select) model answers "which one" problem

(e. g. choose which travel mode and which trip route). Lerman(1984) once states: "A lot of travel demand analysis questions, 'how many people are using public transport? ' Are the answer to the question in the aggregate model, but 'which one' in the disaggregate model is the answer to the question of travel demand analysis. "

· Static or dynamic:

The dynamic model handles "time" in a clear way, and is often simulated as a variable in the model at different times. The static model simulates the traffic state at a certain moment, and the time in the simulation can be used as a processing object to determine whether to choose, rather than deconstruct the variable in the model. One of the challenges to building dynamic models is the lack of data. Usually a recursive(every 5 years) static model is established as a quasi-dynamic model.

· Partial or comprehensive:

A partial model describes a phase or part of the whole process, and the comprehensive model includes all the processes in a model.

· Descriptive or normative:

Most of the models are used to describe a specific situation of correction formulas, such as regression models. The normative model is designed to optimize an objective function, such as a linear(and nonlinear) optimization model.

· Sequential or direct:

An important issue in transportation modeling is to decide whether the traveler's intention to travel is simultaneous or sequential. The traditional urban traffic pattern adopts the sequential method, and the intercity travel modeling will take some synchronization steps to simulate the trip.

(3) Classification based on model synthesis

· The trip based model: The model divides each traveler's trip as the basic unit of traffic demand forecasting, and divides the trip into home-based work trip, home-based other trip and non-home-based trip according to different trip purpose. This approach is a huge breakthrough for simplifying the model.

· The tour based model: With the development of transport planning, in the trip-based model, the non-home-based trip is forced to be more relevant to the family-related attributes. One change is to use the entire chain of individual levels as the basic unit of travel demand estimation.

· The activity based model: In order to compensate for the lack of performance in the response to personal travel, the activity-based model takes the individual activity as the basic unit of the travel demand forecasting, and considers that any travel behavior is second in relation to the activity.

This chapter will focus on the trip-based model, which is the foundation of transport research. For other theoretical models of development, the reader may be interested in referring to the relevant literature. e. g. WILEY(2011) *MODELING TRANSPORT*

3.2.4 The Mathematical Model

As mentioned above, the mathematical model can be a single-equation model or a system of equations model (Mekky and Eng, 2001). The former can be expressed as follows:

$$y = F\{x_1, x_2, \cdots, x_n\} \tag{3-1}$$

where, x_1, x_2, $\cdots$, x_n are the independent or explanatory variables and y is the dependent variables; F stands for function which shows the relationship between input and output quantities. Typical explanatory variables are population, employment, car-ownership travel time and fares. Output or dependent variables might be the modes, the number of trips, $\cdots$, etc..

3.2.5 Elements of the Transportation Model (Mekky and Eng, 2001)

One of the main objectives of the traffic model is to predict the traffic flow on various networks (roads) or the flow of passenger service facilities, and the level of service, speed, total network turnover and pollutant emissions, and the traffic environment quality. The demand for transport facilities stems from the spatial interaction between socioeconomic activities. The flow is the result of the balance of demand and supply (facilities, such as roads). Demand analysis is different from demand forecasting. The purpose of the former is to understand the factors that affect demand including the calibration coefficients of the demand model, which not only requires more than just the results of the analysis, but also can forecast exogenous variables.

(1) Definition

· Trips: A trip is movement made from an origin to a destination by some mode and route during certain time of the day and for a certain purpose (Fig. 3-1). Depending on the purpose of the trip, the trip can be divided into a home-based trip and a none home-based trip. Home-based travel owns at least one end of the home, while non-home based travel owns no end of home. Home-based trips can be further divided into home based work trip, home based school trip, and home based other trip, which includes shopping, visiting, recreation, medical treatment and others. For example, a person from home to work in the morning, from the company to the supermarket shopping, and then go home. This includes home-based work trips, non-home-based trips and other trips to home.

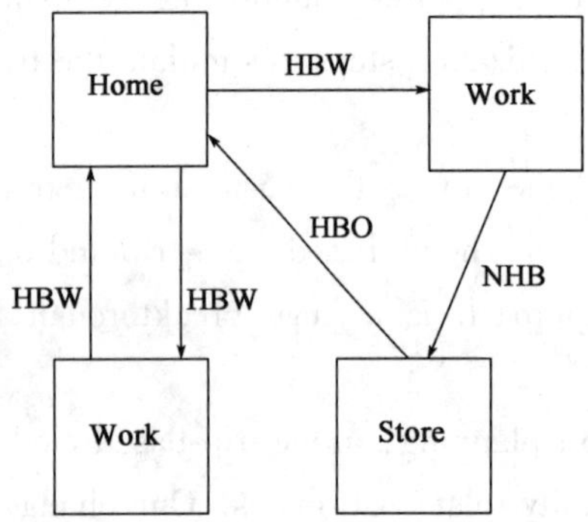

Figure 3-1 Example of trips

According to the end of the trip in the planning of the regional location of the study, the trips can be divided into the internal trips, external trips and the through trip.

a. Internal trips are the trips in the study area.

b. Internal-external trips or External-internal trips is a trip whose one end is outside the study area.

c. Through trips is the trip of which both ends are outside the study area.

Compared with the internal trips, the external trips and through trips are usually simplified by the transportation modeling. This chapter focuses on the relationship between the internal travel within the study area and planning research areas (Fig. 3-2).

· Production and attraction. The end of a travel trip is based on the end of a home travel home or the origin of a non-home based trip. One trip attraction is based on non-home end for home trip or the destinations of non-home based trip.

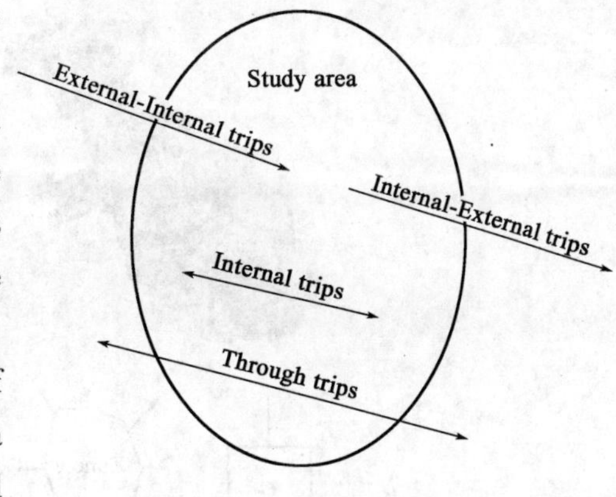

Figure 3-2 Trip types

Source: *Ali Mekky, P. Eng*, 2001.

Some traffic planners predict the number of travelers on the basis of generation-attraction. Such a classified trip can be regarded as home-based travel regardless whether it is from home to anywhere and return trip to home. This simplification is an accurate and simple way to deal with. But there is a weakness in this approach, that is, the direction of travel is estimated when modeling is needed in subsequent stages, and some similar theories are developed to deal with this problem. Other planners prefer to use the starting point, the idea of the destination to avoid this problem when modeling, which is particularly successful in modeling the early hours or hours.

From home to work place, school and home trip constitute two home based travel. Non-home-based travel is the work place to the shopping area or these places to the work place travel. In this case, the trip origin and the attraction end are the origin and destinations for the trip respectively.

(2) Transportation model

Four types of transportation models are described below including transportation model (four-stage model), regional transportation model, direct demand model and hybrid transportation model based on land use characteristics.

3.3 The Urban Transportation Model

The most widely used model for general transportation modeling is the traditional four-stage model. The model will produce different orders according to different situations. The most frequently used order of the four stages is G/D/MS/A.

G/D/MS/A means trip generation, trip distribution, modal split and trip assignment. In this order, it is assumed that the traveler first chooses the destination and then considers the travel mode, then chooses the travel mode after the destination determination, which will make the travel mode more sensitive to the network characteristics. Fig. 3-3 shows the principle and structure of the four-step model.

In fact, people may firstly decide to use which mode, and then choose the destination, and finally decide the route. Also, some steps may be decided at the same time, such as "take the

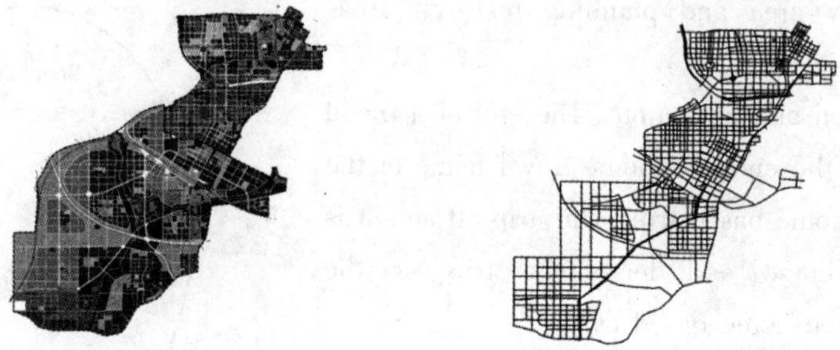

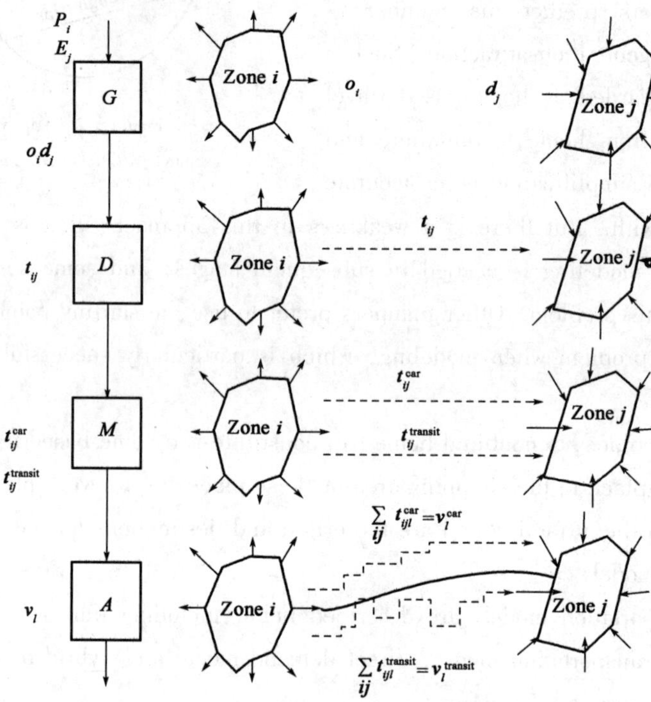

Figure 3-3 Model simplified diagram

subway to the train station" and so on. Senior and Williams (1977) study presented the other four-stage model structure as Fig. 3-4.

Figure 3-4 Other four-stage model sequence framework

3.3.1 Zone System

The first step in transportation modeling is to divide the study area into smaller areas, called "traffic zones", which are used to:

· Record the survey data on trip production and trip attraction.

· Record data on land use, population, employment and other socio-economic information.

· A part of the urban transportation planning model in the trip generation and trip distribution stage.

The number of traffic zones in a study area is a difficult question to answer, and it needs to consider all aspects of the study area. In general, defining more zones means better accuracy, while the data processing time is longer and the cost is higher. The following factors are usually considered when defining the number of traffic zones and their boundaries:

· The first factor to be considered for number of zones is the location of the outer boundary line of the entire study area. The boundary line is usually the boundary between the planning area and the adjacent area. If there is a strong economic link between the planning area and another area, such as where one region relies on employment and/or shopping in another area, it is usually necessary to expand the study area to areas outside the appropriate location and pay attention to the compatibility between the systems.

· The previous transportation planning model used to study the traffic system.

· The boundaries of existing administrative areas(i. e. cities, towns, townships and villages), census areas and planning blocks should be used to establish the boundaries of traffic zones, and the boundaries that have been used by urban planning or community planning should also be considered as a traffic zone. Each traffic district should be on the side of important natural barriers, administrative and historical boundaries, rather than on both sides.

· The location of any internal screen line should be matched with the boundary of the traffic zones, the screen line should not let any traffic zone be divided into two parts, but should be consistent with the traffic zone boundaries.

· To consider the transport network as well as existing and planning facilities, such as all highways, main roads, major secondary roads, bus routes and passenger rail lines. The initial traffic network for trip assignment should be identified first, and the traffic zone should be carried out by the main transportation facilities in the district. In most cases, the central line of the expressway, main road, passenger rail line and major natural barrier is to be used as the boundary of the traffic area.

· The shape of the traffic zone should be as consistent as possible in the geographical conditions, so that the zone's central line can truly represent the zone in the central area of the travel activities.

· Each traffic zone should have relatively homogeneous population, socio-economic, employment and land use characteristics, because the traffic characteristics of each traffic zone depend on the land use and socio-economic characteristics. If possible, large shopping centers should be separated from residents in a separate traffic zone. Other major trip production, such as factories, airports and parks, which have unique characteristics, should also establish separate traffic zones for them, and the intensive business district should also be in a separate traffic area.

· The number of households, population, land area, number of trips and the number of trips to each traffic area should be roughly equal.

· The size of the traffic zone should be associated with the number of traffic networks within the zone, the traffic zone should be small enough to avoid a large proportion of travel concentrated in the small traffic zone.

· In urban traffic planning model for passenger flow analysis and forecasting of urban passenger railway systems, each possible rail transit station should have a separate traffic zone. In this case, the output of the transportation planning model can be compared with specific rail transit station. For the convenience of the analysis and modeling of existing and proposed urban rail lines and BRT systems, the station site is set up as a single traffic zone, so that the output of the simulation process can be applied to specific the rail transit and bus station.

In the model analysis, in order to analyze conveniently, a point of a zone is represented as the centroid, so that is why the transport model focuses on the trip between the zones but ignores the intrazonal trips shown in Fig. 3-5. Therefore, in the micro-transport analysis, the traffic zone should be small enough to avoid trips which were aggregated into a intrazonal trips.

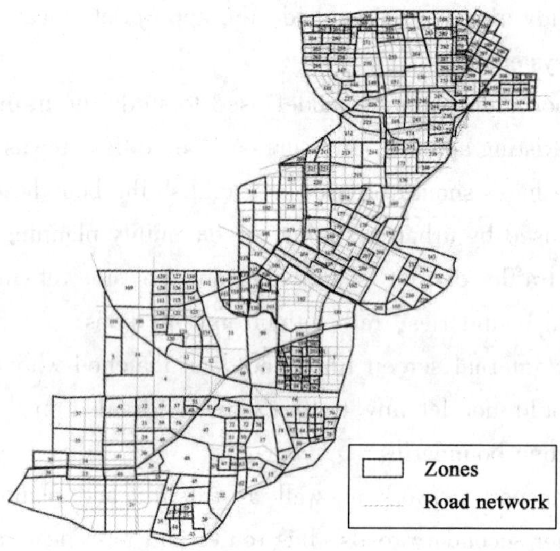

Figure 3-5 Traffic zones and zones'number at high-tech zone

Source: *Wang Yuanqing, Li Lei et al.*, 2010.

By using such a traffic zone system, the number of trip productions and attractions of the base year and the forecast year can be attributed to the traffic zone. For each traffic zone, its link line is designed to represent the travel demand that are generated and attracted by centroid. And a OD matrix is a table which contains the trips from the origin of trips to the destination. The number of zone trips placed in each cell in OD table.

3.3.2 Network Building

Network in the model is composed of usually two parts, one is the road network, and the other is the transit transport network. In general, the network building is to abstract the road and bus network into nodes (intersection or station), then link these segments together. And enter the attributes of the node and link. The road between the two nodes is mostly in real life between the two intersections of the road, but not all segments are the actual road and bus lines. A road segment may also represent delays in the network. For example, a turning movement experiences certain delay and this delay can be represented as a link in the network.

To meet the model accuracy requirements, detail description of the road needs to consume a lot of energy in the planning of network building, and abstracting each road workload requires heavy workload. If there is only an OD survey on the main trunk line, there is no need for internal road in zone to indicate that the too specific abstract of road network will result in greater error in model observations and estimation. Therefore, some of the path in the road network will be ignored in the abstract.

After the study area of the model being determined, the second step is to abstract the road network of the study area, usually based on GIS and other transport planning software to describe the road network, enter the relevant road network attributes, such as road network node attributes, link attributes. After the road network input being completed, the centroid of traffic zone and the road network is connected through the center of the link. Fig. 3-6 shows how the network is built in Xi'an.

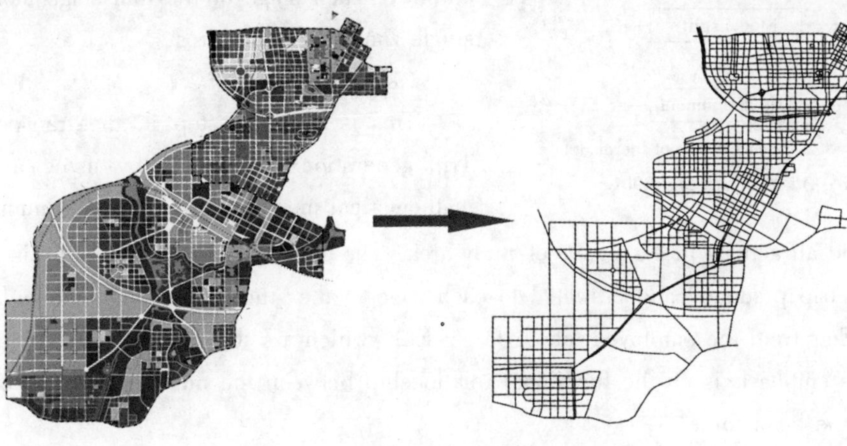

Figure 3-6 Network building of the model

Source: *Wang Yuanqing, Li Lei et al.*, 2010.

Fig. 3-7 shows the abstracted internal network of high-tech zones in Xi'an, including road network and bus lines. Each zone has been abstracted as centroid in the study area. Then links are used to connect each nodes. Line segments have their own interests.

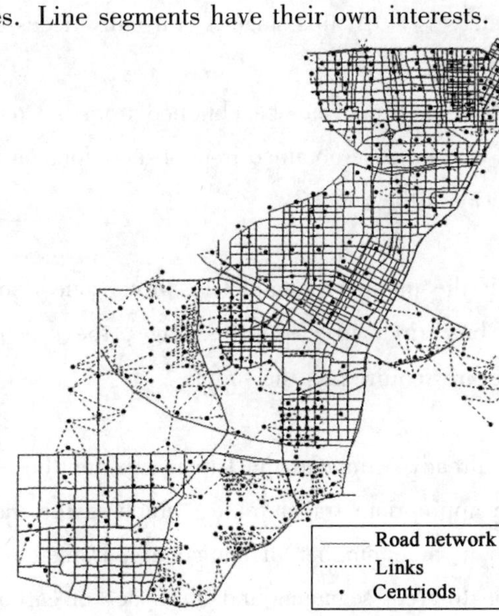

Figure 3-7 Model centroid connecting rods

Source: *Wang Yuanqing, Li Lei et al.*, 2010.

3.3.3 Four-stage Model Modeling and Data Flow

The division of the traffic zones, the data collection and the network buildings are the preparatory work of the transportation model. Then the four-stage model can be modeled. The output of each stage of the four-stage model can be used as the input of the next stage. Fig. 3-8 shows the input and output of each stage of the four-stage model from a single zone to a study area.

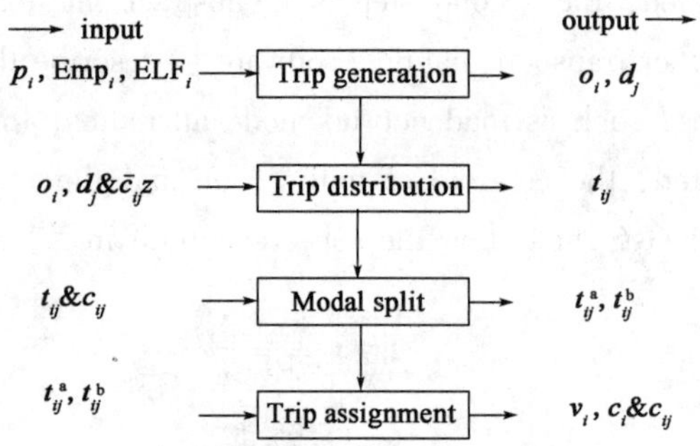

Figure 3-8 The four stages of the model

Source: *Ali Mekky*, *P. Eng*, 2001.

(1) Trip generation

This is the first step in the transport model. Trip generation is a stage by using a variety of mathematical methods to forecast the number of trip productions and attractions in each zone of study area. The objective of trip generation is to estimate the number of trip produced and attracted to each zone in the study area. Input: population (p), employment (Emp) and the employed labour force (ELF) which are the most important input of each zone "i". The emphasis is on the functional relationship between the number of trips, population, the work and the labor force.

Output: the total number of trip productions (o) and attractions (d) in each zone.

In theory, the travel volume of a study area is equal to the total amount of OD that travels.

(2) Trip distribution

The purpose of the trip distribution is to match the traffic volume from the zone "i" to the zone "j", and finally get the trip matrix (t_{ij}). At this stage it is usually necessary to know the travel time matrix from the zone "i" to the zone "j" (c_{ij}).

Input amount: a. trip generation which can be obtained from the output of the trip generation stage. b. the travel time matrix of each zone obtained from observations on the actual travel operation.

Output: the trip matrix between the zones.

(3) Modal split

This stage attempts to split the number of total trips from zone i to zone j into trips of each mode, egt. car trip matrix and bus trip matrix. At this stage, the travel time matrix (c_{ij}) and the traffic volume (t_{ij}) of each zone are required as the input.

(4) Trip assignment

The modal split stage has already estimated the trip matrix for the car and bus, and this step should allocate the trips to the appropriate travel route, which is the most important result of the transportation model, based on a large number of statistical parameters, such as the total traffic turnover, the level of service of different segments and the space of carbon emissions, etc.. At this stage we need to know the road resistance curve for each route. Usually, the car trip distribution and bus travel distribution should be separated to estimate. The main output of the car trip assignment is the travel volume(v_{ij}) on each route and travel time(c_{ij}).

The trip assignment stage also produces the travel time matrix of each zone, which is mainly used to be compared with the trip matrix in the trip distribution stage until it is equalized. As shown in Fig. 3-9.

Fig. 3-9 shows that the steps are not isolated, the travel time matrix, the travel space distance is associated with the actual traffic condition(level of service), and the time matrix should be iterated between the second and fourth stages until it fit the results of the accuracy requirements.

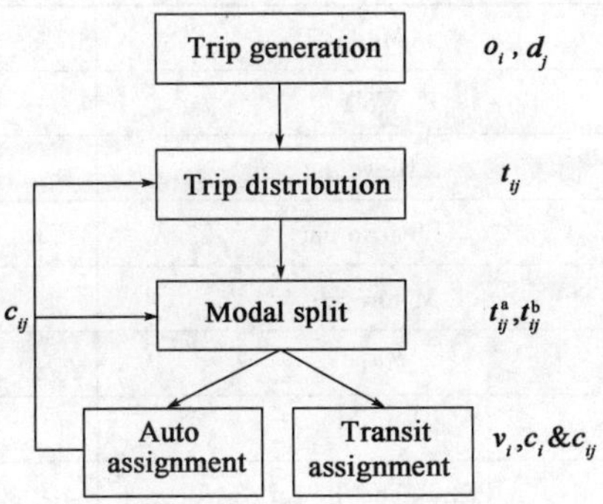

Figure 3-9 Iterative process of the four-stage model

Source: *Ali Mekky*, *P. Eng*, 2001.

The iteration does not affect the outcome of the trip generation step, which means that the model's trip generation is independent of the model network. This assumption is made in the compulsory trips(work and home), but this assumption may be biased in no-compulsory travel(tourism). Research shows that the purpose of the trip to a large extent affects the travel behavior, so in the model calibration of this link is usually in accordance with the purpose of different travel classification calibration. For example, the calibration model of Xi'an transportation model is divided into HBW(home based work trip), HBS(home based school travel), HBO(home based other travel), NHB(non-home based trip) and EB five categories.

Research has shown that travel behavior is related to the travel purpose. Focusing on the characteristics of the morning and evening peak period, the classification of trips by purpose is home to work, home to school and other. Table 3-1 and Table 3-2 show the distribution of the morning peak period based on home to work and home to school.

Table 3-1 Distribution of HBW&HBS trips by mode, within AM PK period in Xi'an

Mode	HBW	HBS	HBO	NHB	Sum
Walk	15.64%	4.50%	16.93%	2.13%	39.21%
Bicycle	7.40%	0.97%	2.73%	0.55%	11.64%
Electric car	7.89%	0.65%	2.68%	0.76%	11.97%
Motorcycle	1.09%	0.06%	0.31%	0.07%	1.53%
Bus	12.21%	1.00%	7.10%	1.06%	21.37%
Taxi	0.34%	0.04%	0.41%	0.08%	0.86%
Private car(by car)	5.26%	0.17%	2.11%	0.61%	8.15%
Private car(ride)	0.77%	0.23%	0.51%	0.07%	1.58%
Company commuter cars	1.16%	0.03%	0.30%	0.18%	1.68%
Company commuter bus	0.95%	0.06%	0.18%	0.08%	1.27%
Other	0.27%	0.14%	0.28%	0.04%	0.74%
Total	52.98%	7.86%	33.53%	5.64%	100.00%

Table 3-2 Distribution of AM PK period HBW&HBS trips by mode in Xi'an

Mode	HBW	HBS
Walk	29.53%	57.29%
Bicycle	13.97%	12.29%
Electric car	14.90%	8.23%
Motorcycle	2.05%	0.79%
Bus	23.04%	12.77%
Taxi	0.64%	0.48%
Private car(by car)	9.94%	2.14%
Private car(ride)	1.45%	2.95%
Company commuter cars	2.19%	0.44%
Company commuter bus	1.79%	0.79%
Other	0.51%	1.83%
Total	100.00%	100.00%
Total in peak period	52.98%	7.86%

Achieving internal consistency between models is a very important phase in the modeling process. As mentioned above, the use of iterative feedback is a general way to solve the problem. Some of the solutions to this problem have been mentioned in the literature, combined the use of several stages of the transport into a mathematical formula method, can effectively solve the problem of consistency. e. g.

- A combination of trip distribution and modes.
- A combination of trip distribution and trip assignment.
- A combination of modal split and trip assignment.
- Trip distribution, pattern division and trip distribution combination.
- And the combination of trip generation, trip distribution, and modal split and trip assignment.

3.3.4 Internal Trips

Internal travel refers that the trip origin and trip destination is in the same traffic zone. The type of trip in the transportation model is the reason for attention is due to the simulation of the actual situation requires a certain degree of simplification assumptions and set. In most transportation planning software, such travel is not allocated to the road network in the travel distribution because its starting and ending points are in the same centroid.

However, it is important to estimate them to separate them from the intrazonal trips. Trip generation and distribution estimates all trips including intrazonal. In the trip distribution stage, it is common to forecast the trips within the area, and the accuracy of the forecast depends on the method of estimating the number of trips in the zone.

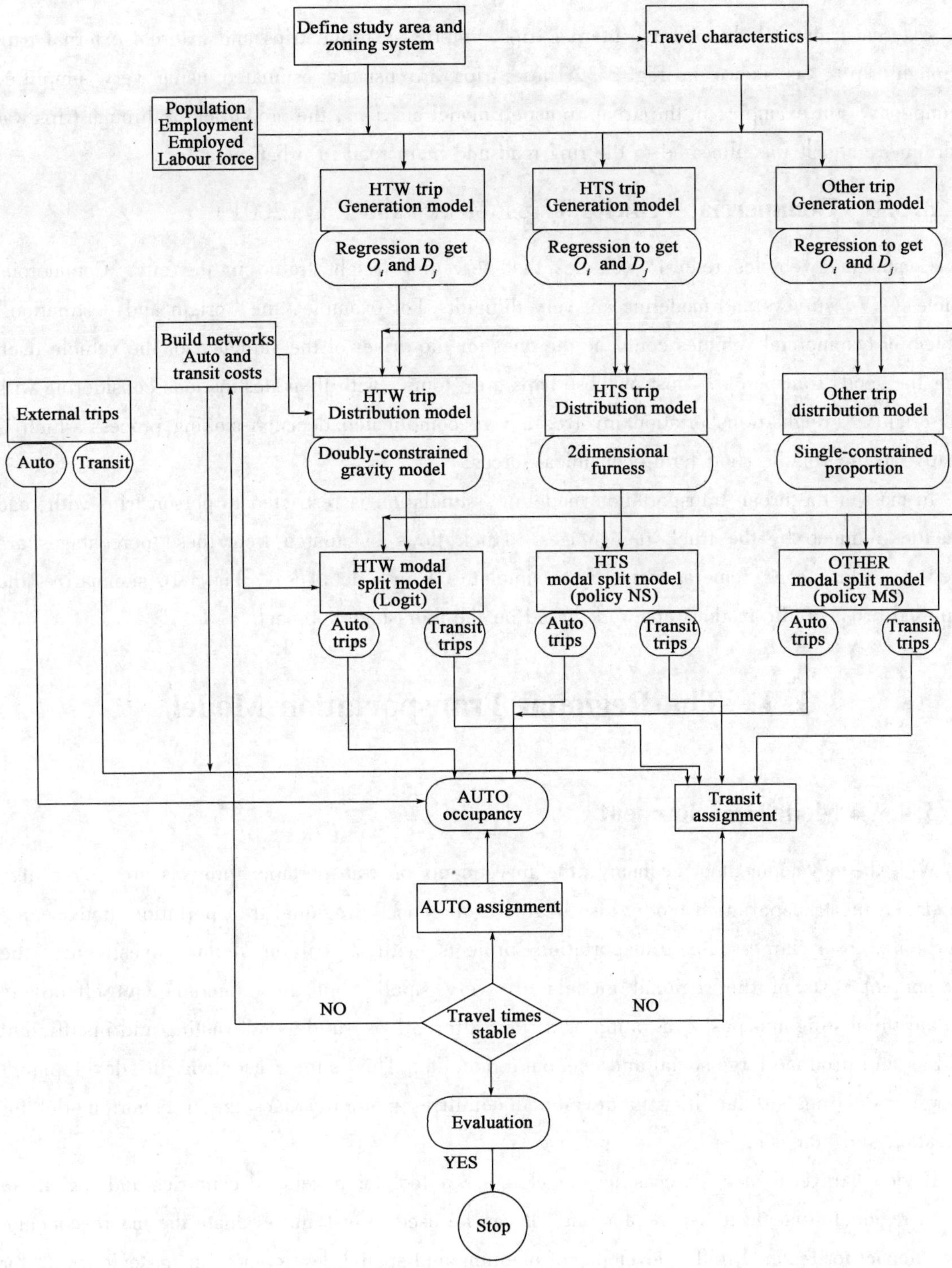

Figure 3-10 Urban traffic model framework

Source: *Ali Mekky and P. Eng*, 2001.

3.3.5 External Trips

External trips include external-internal trips, internal-external trips and external-external trips (through trip), as shown in Fig. 3-3. These trips are usually estimated using very simplified assumptions. For example, in the urban transport model of Xi'an, the proportion of through trips was determined, and it was allocated to the ring road and main road in urban area.

3.3.6 Commercial Vehicles Trips(Mekky and Eng, 2001)

Commercial vehicles refer to vehicles that serve for freight traffic in the city. Commercial vehicle's(CV) surveys and modeling are very difficult. For example, the "origin and destination" problem of commercial vehicles could be the ones for the driver of the vehicle, for the vehicle itself or for the goods transported. Most of those trips are "tours" with their destinations considering with their origins. Freight transportation involves a very complicated decision-making process which is sensitive to the volatile short term economical forces.

In most of the urban transportation modeling, simulation is restricted to person trips with road capacities reduced by the truck percentages. Truck flows calculated from these percentages are added at a later stage. Some agencies try to simulate CV in a detail way. Fig. 3-10 summarizes the simplified urban traffic model framework based on the four-stage approach.

3.4 The Regional Transportation Model

3.4.1 Model Development

With the development of economy, the investments on transportation projects are increasing. The size of the transportation model also begins to increase. Regional transportation model came into being. For large-scale transportation projects with a trillion dollar investment, the development costs of the regional models are very small, but these models can effectively regulate the testing and post-evaluation of various alternatives, and avoid wasting and insufficient building and produce large social and economic benefits. This is the reason why the development of large-scale transport facilities in developed countries generally uses the transport model for estimation and analysis.

Regional travel demand forecasting model is a key tool for developed countries and regions to support regional strategic transport planning. It can be used to test and evaluate the macroeconomic policy impact for regional traffic development planning and spatial development in strategic level, for the large-scale transport project evaluation and the traffic demand management, China is still in the initial stage, and it may usher in a new period of development with the integration of multi-model transport.

3.4.2 The Model Framework

The regional transport model should be built at different levels for demand forecasting. The highest level is the strategic level of the macro-traffic planning model, followed by the level of specific analysis based on a specific small area for more detailed analysis. So the regional traffic model is generally divided into three levels:

· Macro level: regional strategic traffic demand forecasting model;

· The meso level: traffic demand forecasting model of the central city, and the specific transport corridor forecasting model;

· Micro-level: the micro-simulation model of special point/study area.

Building principles of regional traffic demand forecasting model architecture can be on basis of our-stage model, also can be based on a direct demand model. Here focuses on the four-stage method rather than the city of the macro level of the regional strategic traffic forecast model. The model consists of five parts, namely:

(1) Initial cost

The initial cost usually refers to the travel time in the free flow of the road, as well as transport facilities charges, fuel consumption of different modes. The initial cost of regional transport model includes two parts:

· Highway network (car/bus/freight)

a. General trunk network.

b. Freeway network.

· Public transport network

a. Intercity bus and minibus service.

b. Railway network/multi-mode station/rail service.

c. Shipping.

d. Aviation.

(2) Passenger demand model

Passenger demand model is the four-stage model based on the regional population, economy, land use and other data. The output can be used as the input of next stage. As shown in Fig. 3-11.

The first step: determine the zone trip attractions and productions based on data of the GDP, population, cost, employment and other information.

The second step: obtain the trip distribution using the gravity model based on the comprehensive cost of road network.

The third step: conduct a modal split based on LOGIT travel choice utility model.

The fourth step: get the daily results of trip assignment and final comprehensive cost of road network using the traffic resistance function.

(3) Regional freight model

The regional freight model also uses the four-stage model to build the model, as shown in

Fig. 3-12. In the modeling process, following aspects should be considered.

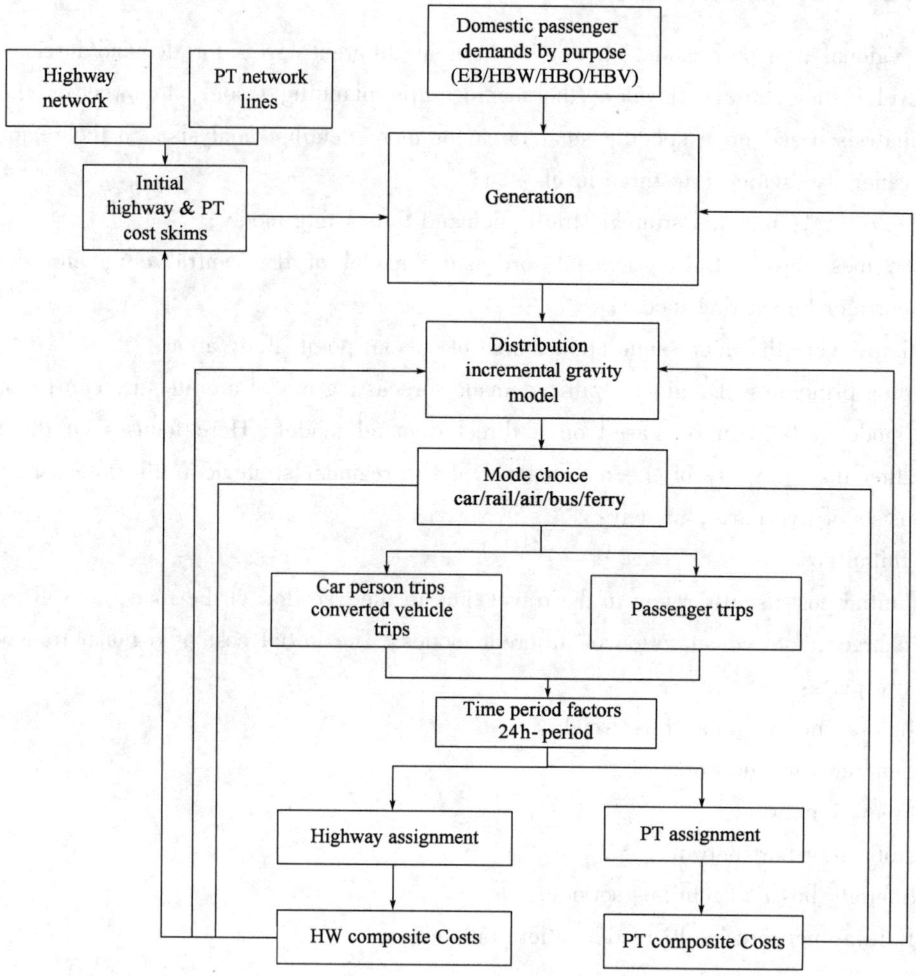

Figure 3-11　Passenger demand model framework

Source: *The book editorial board*, 2016.

· Growth rate of changes in domestic and international GDP and population changes;

· The spatial distribution of freight volume;

· Mode choice and external transport;

· Transfer the freight volume into the flow volume of light trucks, heavy goods vehicles for road network assignment.

(4) Road network assignment model and generalized comprehensive cost calculation

Road network assignment and generalized comprehensive cost calculation are prepared for the model iteration. The calculation results are also the important context to evaluate the necessity of project construction, and the following points need to be paid attention:

· Demand by time division (morning peak, off-peak, evening peak, night);

· The calculation of the relevant cost parameters with the combination of time, mode, demand model.

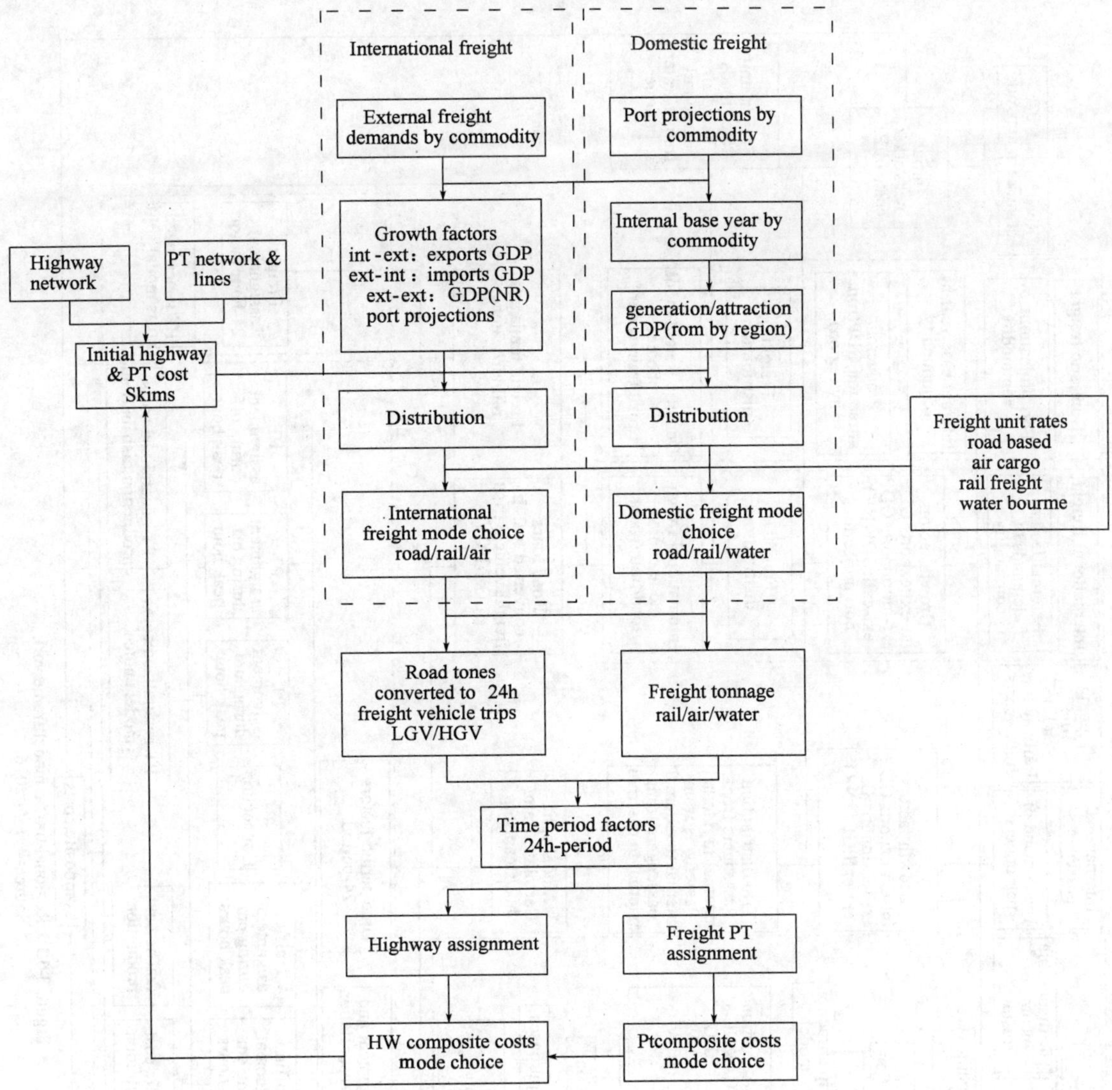

Figure 3-12 Freight demand model

Source: *Wright*, 2016.

(5) Evaluation module

Model is for all types of economic evaluation to provide the basis and data support, evaluation module need to consider the evaluation method has the following parameters:

· Economic and financial evaluation parameters.

· Safety (based on traffic volume, speed, traffic accident type changes), traffic emission parameters, traffic accessibility strategies of regional transport accessibility.

· The overall travel demand and overall characteristics of different years and the corresponding strategies.

The overall framework of the regional traffic model is shown in Fig. 3-13.

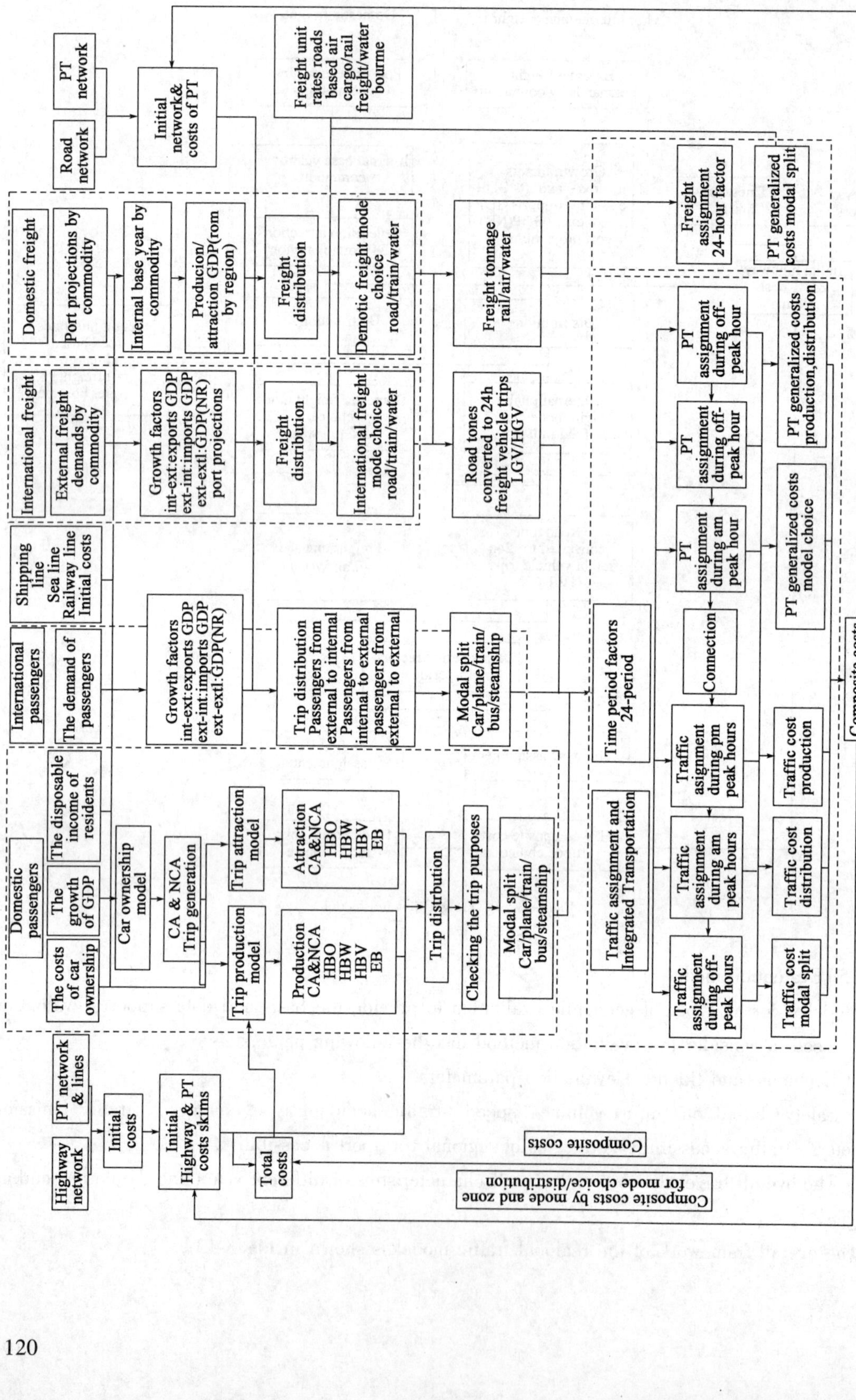

Figure 3-13 Regional traffic model framework
Source: *Wright*,2016.

3.5 The Direct Demand Model(Mekky and Eng, 2001)

The Direct Demand Model is a widely used model in economic to analyze the strategic travel behavior. Although the structure of the model is simple, it can have a strong ability of forecasting, especially on the travel demand between cities. This model can also distinguish main needs of traffic flow forecasts, freight and passenger volume; forecast the number of trips from one place to another. The estimation are on basis of regional characteristics including travel time, distance, cost, origin and destination population, employment, income, gross domestic product and other available socio-economic variables.

The direct demand model estimates the travel demand, following factors need to take into account:

· Travel time, travel distance, and costs.

· Socio-economic factors such as population, employment, income and GDP.

Here is an example of a direct demand model that incorporates the multiplicative structure of the first three stages. Using an estimated equation to forecast the number of trips, an example of this model is the one calibrated for Boston Metropolitan Region.

$$V_{ijt} = PE_j t_{ijt}^{-0.59} c_{ijt}^{-0.32} HS_i^{2.5} Y_i^{-0.04} ED_j^{0.03} PBE_j^{-0.79} \quad (3\text{-}2)$$

where, V_{ijt} is the daily number of shopping trips made by one household between zones i and j by the transit mode t; PE_j is the total retail employment in zone j; t_{ijt} is the total travel time between the zone i and the zone j by transit; c_{ijt} is the total cost of the trip between zone i and zone j by transit; HS_i is the average household size in zone i; Y_i is the average income of residents of zone i; ED_j is the rate of retail trade employment density in one j; PBE_j is the employment in personal business in zone j as a proportion of the total regional employment in personal business.

The direct demand model is a multiplicative formula that fuses the first three stages together to predict the number of trips from one place to another, and can generally be used to study the strategic aspects of traffic behavior. It can be applied to the strategic level of traffic model.

3.6 The Hybrid Model

Some scholars tried to combine two or more stages together, known as the hybrid transportation models. The difference between the hybrid model and the four-stage transportation model is that the former is based on the latter. The most popular one is to combine the trip distribution and the modal split together.

3.7 Model Calibration and Validation

The model calibration and validation is for the purpose of making the transportation model reflect the reality. In order to make the model reproduce the base year as accurately as possible, it is necessary to update the value of the parameter in the calibration process. Here is a brief introduction to some of these concepts.

(1) Model estimation

Using statistical analysis techniques and the observation data to determine the model parameters or regression coefficients. The model estimation is applicable to the case in which there are no existing data and research subjects. The model estimation uses the statistical analysis to aggregate data.

(2) Model assertion

Not based on statistical analysis of observed data, it can directly to choose the appropriate model and parameters. For example, applying a model of certain region to another region directly is the model assertion.

(3) Model calibration

It is the process to explore the model constants and other model parameters to produce more reasonable results. Due to the existence of the error, the model parameters can only be used to explain some of the observed phenomena, the validation through some adjustments makes the model fit the observation more consistent.

(4) Model validation

It is the application of calculating results of the calibration model on comparing with the observed data. Ideally, the observed data is not used for model estimation and validation, but this is sometimes not feasible. Verification data may use the data that includes the estimated and validate additional data for the same year model or the data for the alternative year to verify the correctness of the model.

(5) Sensitivity testing

It is a step using alternative data or assuming data analysis to test the results of applying model and model groups. The sensitivity test of the model includes the elasticity estimation and cross elasticity estimation of the model regression coefficients. It can also validate the demographic data, socioeconomic data and alternative assumptions on the transport system to assess whether the model results are credible and reasonable or not.

Fig. 3-14 shows the development, verification, and sensitivity testing of transportation models.

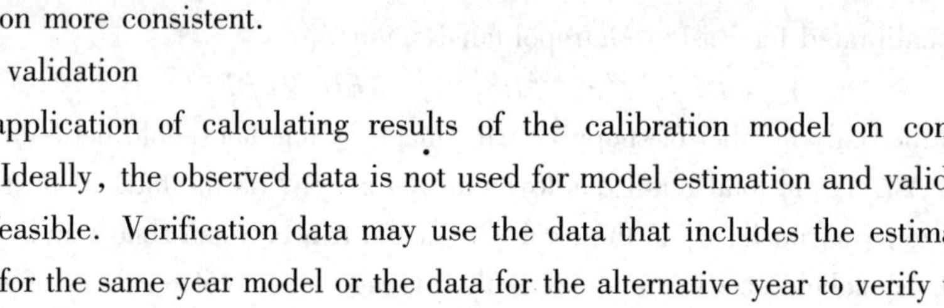

Figure 3-14 Overview of model development and application process

Model validation and sensitivity testing may develop a computational error, which requires a model to establish a return of model estimation and the calibration results. As for Application of Forecasting the Model for Future Years and Policy Choices, it is also possible to cause the model to return to the stage of model estimation and calibration when it comes to planning rationality. Problems that are not included in the application of the model generally do not lead to a direct cycle to the verification stage as such additional validation does not improve the forecasting of the model. Model validation is useful for confirming the accuracy of the estimation.

3.8 The Prospect

In 1970s, theory of travel demand and forecasting has developed quickly, in the following 20 years, the relevant theory has a breakthrough in the development and the application of mode. After the 21st century, some changes occurred in the transportation model, as some organizations began to explore new technologies in transportation forecasting. The advanced transportation model refers to those beyond the traditional four-stage demand forecasting model theory. In particular, there are five aspects of modeling:

- Tour and activity-based travel models.
- Land use models.
- Air quality models.
- Freight and commercial movement models.
- Dynamic network models.

The above types of models cannot meet the needs of academic research and turn to provide support services for transport policy making and transportation investment which is a useful complement to the four-stage model. For example, the activity-based models have been applied. The four-stage model also enhances innovation and seeks integration with the advanced transport models.

Despite these advanced models have their own advantages, it will be difficult to promote every step of development of these models. These models are still in the initial stages of development, and the hardware requirements are higher, as well as the higher funds, the lack of research talent and no support. There still is a long way to go.

References

[1] Ali Mekky, P. Eng. Analytics Transportation Planning[M]. America, 2001.

[2] David E. Boyce, H. C. W. L. Williams. Forecasting Urban Travel: Past, Present and Future [M]. UK : Edward Elgar Publishing Limited, 2016.

[3] The book editorial board. A study and practice on China city cluster integrated ecological transport planning guideline [M]. Beijing, China: China communications press. Co., Ltd, 2016.

[4] Juan de Dios Ortúzar, Luis G Willumsen. Modeling Transport [M]. Hoboken: WILEY, 2011.

[5] David A Hensher, Kenneth J Button. Handbook of Transport Modeling [M]. Amsterdam: Elsevier Science Ltd, 2007.

[6] R Donnelly, National Cooperative Highway Research Program. Advanced Practices in Travel Forecasting [M]. Washington, D. C. : Transportation Research Board, 2010.

[7] Senior M. L., Williams H. C. W. L.. Model-Based Transport Policy Assessment: The Use of Alternative Forecasting Models [J]. Traffic Engineering and Control, Vol 18(9), 402-406.

[8] Wang Yuanqing, Li Lei, et al.. Xi'an traffic model project. Xi'an: Chang'an University, 2010.

[9] Craig Wright. China city cluster integrated transport development strategy planning and policy training[R]. Xi'an: Shanghai WPS consulting Ltd.

[10] TMIP. Travel Model Validation and Reasonableness Checking Manual[M]. 2nd Edition. Federal Highway Administration. Washington DC, 2010.

Chapter 4

Trip Generation

4.1 Overview

After allocating and locating the future land use activities for the city by traffic zones, the first step of the Transportation Modeling Process is trip generation. This is the step that takes the socioeconomic and demographic characteristics of the inhabitants and land use characteristics of the zones to estimate the volume of trips produced or attracted by each of the traffic zones in the city.

Trip making involves a chain of decisions. It begins with a clear trip purpose, such as going to work, going shopping, or going to school. Knowing the trip purpose comes the decision on destination. Of course, for some trips, knowing the purpose, such as work trips and school trips, the destinations are automatically selected. But for certain shopping and other trips, choice of destinations may actually involve some deliberate consideration. Once the trip destination decision is made, the choice of travel mode and the trip route follows. To the trip makers, the choice of travel mode may come before the choice of trip route. To the other trip makers, the order of choice is just the reverse. It is important to point out that, for some trips the decision chain actually begins with, or ends at, whether or not the trip will be made.

In trip generation, the distinction of the two pairs of terms and the matrices that represent them: origin and destination versus production and attraction, requires some attention. Origin and destination refer to the direction of trips. Production and attraction refer to the volume of trips produced or attracted between two points which is to some extent different from Origin and Destination.

For home-based trips(HB), trip production point is defined as traveler's home. For non-home based trips, trip production point is the origin point. The trip attraction point for home-based trips is the other point, which is the workplace if it is a work trip. It is the destination point of non-home-based home trip.

Why is the person's home the producer of the home-based trip, both to and from home? The reason is simple, the person who goes to work and, therefore, the trip produced by home. And the same person has to go home after and, therefore, the return home trip is also produced by home. As for non-home based trip, the trip returning home is the attracted by home and the trip is produced by the other endpoint. Fig. 4-1 below shows the commonly used Production-Attraction and/Origin-Destination Matrix, and shows the relation of trip production volume, trip attraction volume and trip generation through the figure.

O	D						Total
	1	2	…	j	…	n	
1							O_1
2							O_2
⋮							⋮
i							O_i
⋮							⋮
m							O_m
Total	D_1	D_2	…	D_j	…	D_n	T

Productions

Attractions　　Number of trip generation

Figure 4-1　The relationship of production, attraction and trip generation

In PA Matrix, the element q_{ij} represents a trip distribution volume, that is the trip volume in average unit time between zone i and zone j, which can be for a day, a week, a month, or even for the peak hour. To two zones i and j, it is composed by two parts q_{ij} and q_{ji}.

q_{ij} is the number of trips that the production point is zone i (not necessarily the starting point of trip) and the attraction point is zone j (not necessarily is the endpoint of trip).

q_{ji} is the number of trips that the production point is zone j and the attraction point is zone i.

The structures of OD Matrix and PA Matrix are the same. Similar to PA Matrix, the element q_{ij} in OD Matrix represents that the trip volume that the trip starts from zone i and the trip ends in zone j.

Both in China and elsewhere, published reports indicate that the relevant factors for estimating trips produced by a traffic zone are those that describe the economic wellbeing of the household and household structure: household income, auto ownership, occupational structure, household size, value of land and residential unit type. These household characteristics and other similar measures of the land use characteristics are clear indicators of the trip making pattern of the zone.

The relevant factors for estimating trips attracted by a traffic zone are those that describe the land use type and level of intensity, total retail space and total office space, total retail sales, school enrollment, and total employees. These are clear indicators for the nature of trips attracted by a traffic zone.

For a city, it stands to reason that the total trips produced by various zones and the total trips attracted by the same various zones should be exactly the same. But since the estimation of these two quantities is carried out by using different factors, it also stands to reason that the two calculation results are to be different. In such event, it is advisable to use the trip production which is derived from the home trip, which it is more reliable and often used as the controlling gross of traffic zone. And this value can also be used to check production and attraction traffic volume in each traffic zone forecasted by different models. Fig. 4-2 shows the trip forecast volume from traffic zone a and the trip attraction volume by zone b. And, O_a represents the sum of trip volume from zone a, and D_b represents the trip volume sum of other zones to zone b.

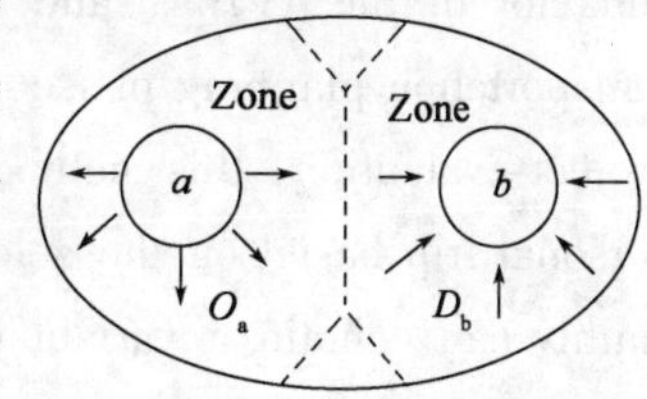

Figure 4-2 The diagram of traffic zone trip production and attraction

Source: *Shao Chunfu*, 2014.

4.2 A Historical Review of Trip Generation Research

In the early 1950s, an extrapolation of the OD expectation line was adopted. In the 1950s, an improved method for estimation travel demand by using land-use planning in the future was proposed, taking into account the effects of land use and economic factors in the present quantitative travel volume. Then, in the late 1950s and early 1960s, the regression analysis opened a door to the study of travel and travel factors and became a major method used commonly in transportation planning, such as KAWAKAMI Shogo(*Traffic Engineering*, 1987) proposed to use the building area as the index of regional characteristics, and the liner regression model of trip volume and concentration, trip concentration of shopping and concentration of entertainment trips are established. For the situation of liner regression, in 1964, Puget Sound put forward a trip generation model which can deal with the non-liner relationship between trip generation and land use variables, called "Category analysis". In 1967, there are two types of traffic generation models established in US: home-based travel and non-home based travel. And the home-based travel is subdivided into 5 types: home-based working, shopping, recreation, schooling, and other trips which are based on the construction area as a basis for forecasting travel volume. From 1966 to 1988, the United States Institute of Transportation Engineering(ITE) divided urban land into several types, and according to different types of land, size and location to study the number of trips and related laws. According to a large number of observations in the United States, the book "*Trip Generation*" was published. Through the continuous exploration of relevant researchers, a new disaggregate model, is produced in the field of travel generation model. In the 1960s, Japanese scholars first proposed the theory and algorithm of the disaggregate model by borrowing the theory of economic utility (the utility maximization). In 1959, Luce deduced the Logit model in the disaggregate theory and Marschsk and Suppes further improved the theoretical basis of the Logit model, until 1974, because of the complete discussion made by McFaddend and other scholars, the Logit disaggregate model theory system has taken shape. In the late 1970s, Manheim and Ben's team applied the disaggregate model to practical problems, and the disaggregate ideas and theories also began to apply to actual traffic forecasts. Researchers at the University of Oxford invented a disaggregate approach based on behavior in the 1970s, and then the disaggregate analysis received broad attention during the transportation planning phase, but because it was not suitable for large-scale intensive investment project evaluation, this method is still in the stage of continuous research and innovation. And the personal trip based on the selection model is an improvement to the home-based model because it mainly can contain a variant of variables and is compatible with the models established at other stages.

In the choice of variables, DeserPa(1971) and Bruzelius(1979) introduced the time factor in the study of trip generation. The main idea is to transform the travel generation into the utility maximization equation of time budget constraints and income constraints, taking into account the time problem in the model and strengthening the precision of the model. In the analysis of the city trip data, the sequential response model is used to forecast the possibility of various trips produced by household, and the travel cost, accessibility and location factors are also introduced to get a good forecasting effect. China's practice(Wang Yuanqing, Zhang Fuyong and Wang Yuanyuan, 2004) also proved that traffic location and number of trips is closely related. In this practice, it regarded the sectional factors influencing the trip generation as the multi-responses with the natural order, using the concept of local utility to this model, and it also proved that the travel behavior in metropolitan area is sensitive to the changes of geographic location. Among them, the response model with order is a very useful tool to the analysis of the traffic problems. In the article, Ferdous mentioned that researchers use the multivariate ordinal response framework to investigate the interaction between household and non-household members' non-work activities, indicating that the orderly response model has a strong flexibility.

In recent years, many scholars have focused on activities and the demand of traffic forecast related to the land use. In this process, the method that has been accepted in our country and abroad is the "four-stage method". However, with the continuous progress of society, it gradually becomes the focus about how to reflect the individual differences that the four-stage method neglected. Therefore, it is necessary to study the four-stage method. Many scholars put forward the establishment of a portfolio analysis model based on travel activities to study the relationship between the purpose of trip, travel distribution and way of division, so as to provide a new idea for traffic demand forecast. The study of Chapin (1971), Hagerstrand (1970), and Cullen and Godson (1975) laid the foundation to the activity theory. In 1979, Adler and Ben-Akiva of Massachusetts Institute of Technology put forward the forecasting method to classify the trip segments, mainly to determine the selectable set, and then calculate the household's branch of selection according to trip cost, activity utility, time benefit, and finally find the branch with maximum utility. Although at present, this model only focuses on the theoretical analysis, it shows that it is very meaningful to analyze the problem of traffic generation with utility theory. But this model fail to consider the travel order, the choice of ways of transport and other factors, and travel modeling is more complex, so it is generally used only for tourism or shopping traffic, such as the trip with relatively strong random. In the University of California of United States, Professor Beicun made the assumption that arbitrary travel is limited to the forced travel model, and the model selects the variables mainly from the household composition, household income and other aspects, and ultimately get the corresponding number of travel sections based on home trips and non-home-based trips. It can also reflect the hierarchical structure of each household's trip household's trip, but cannot be classified as home-based and non-home based trips. In the early 1990s, the two amendments in US, the Clean Air Act Amendments(CAAA) of 1990 and the ISTEA of 1991, led to the introduction of an improved project for the US Department of Transportation(DOT) model, and also to promote the development of activity-based model. Some scholars in our country put forward the model of trip generation based on the activity model(Yang, Chen et al., 2008). This model mainly uses the analysis of correlation and multinomial Logit method; at the same time establish the function of the activity model utility, through the method of the probability set with the average length of travel sections, to forecast the travel of the workers, so that the trip generation model and behavior model are effectively integrated together.

A major problem with the traditional method is lack of research on the correlation between land use(an important factor) and trip generation. In 1998, William A. Martinand, Nancy A. Mcguckin summed up four necessary aspects involving trip generation research: a. Socioeconomic type and land use of the zone; b. Transportation choice and development goals of transportation planning for the zone; c. Long-and short-term planning of traffic demand forecast for specially designated zones; d. The effects of newly developed zones (commercial center, park, etc.) on planning. These relevant aspects could also be studied in the process of traffic demand forecast so that it would be more precise and accurate. In recent years, scholars both at home and abroad have been paying increasing attention to land use. In 2000, Mitchell and Rapkin pointed out that urban traffic could serve as the function of land use and, rather than only focusing on the correlation between land use and traffic in a narrow sense, scholars began to explore the relationship between city pattern and trip generation behavior as well as the effects of different city patterns and structures on traffic demand, patterns and features. In the fifth EASTS, 2003, M Kawano, T Yoshitake and T Chishaki discussed relevant concepts resulting from trip generation, and analyzed trip generation through mathematical mode. They also discussed how to establish a mode between regional trip generation and total trip generation and introduced a generation form similar to OD. The form contributed to a clearer relationship between total and regional generation trip, thus enjoying higher level of practicality. In 2005, Chinese scholars Shi, Wang and Lu came up with the forecasting method based on land use pattern. This method, based on land use pattern and balance of total volume of resident trip generation, emphasized the effect of land use and thus enhanced forecasting accuracy. Besides these methods, some scholars established trip generation mode based on zone type. In this way, scholars first categorized zones in terms of land use intensity and then, according to zone types, established trip generation modes respectively. The above two methods combined trip generation with land use and could be applied to forecast in practice.

In 2003, Anderson and Malave put up the concept of dynamic model of trip generation. Aiming at medium-sized cities, they explored how to establish the mode and collect relevant data. They also tested the mode and provided some ideas on future research.

Recent developments on urban trip generation research by foreign scholars include the application of utility theory, frequency response curve and Entropy theory in trip generation. These new developments have, in a sense, enhanced the effectiveness of trip generation forecasting.

The method based on activities and land use can go together with four-stage method. Although disaggregate method has many advantages, it involves complex sub-methods and has wide margin of error when it comes to working out traffic volumes and this is why four-stage method is still prevalent in research on trip generation. This chapter will mainly deal with the contributing factors and common methods of trip generation. Also, it will analyze the merits and demerits of each method.

4.3 Analysis Unit

There are three main units for trip generation analysis: zone, household and individual.

4.3.1 Using Zone as Analysis Unit

When trip generation estimation uses zone as the analysis unit, it mainly uses two methods: the number of total trips of a zone and the average number of trips of a zone, such as trips/zone or trips/household/zone.

When regression analysis is used for trip generation estimation, the coefficients of regression equation from all the zones are more accurate. The regression coefficients can help to explain the variation of zone size, but cannot consider the variation of zone internally and, therefore, create bias to the trip generation estimation.

Other zone variables commonly used for the regression analysis include average household size, car ownership and number of drivers, the distance to the Central Business District (CBD).

There are problems when using average level of zone to explain trip generation summarized by Ali Mekky and P. Eng (2001). These include:

- The average data used for the analysis describe the situation of the center of the zone. But in actual trip generation, the rest of the zone may be quite different from the average due to other factors, such as traffic congestion.
- The prerequisite to using average data is the assumption that the households in the zone are of uniform economic characteristics. The assumption is problematic.
- In case of the existing groups to analyze individual behavior will produce ecological fallacy. The fallacy includes personal fallacy and ecological fallacy, and personal fallacy is opposed to

ecological fallacy, and ecological fallacy makes inferences only based on group's statistical data to its affiliated individual nature. Personal fallacy is biased, when derived same conclusion for group with individuals. This inference is clearly wrong. For example, we usually think that the families who own more cars have more trips, but it can't infer that the zone with most cars has the largest number of trips(Fig. 4-3). The inhomogeneity of observations from zones will make the changes within zones are different from the changes between zones. Therefore, using zone as analysis unit applies to short-term (5-10 years) forecastion of region where economic development is much more balanced. To avoid the shortcomings of using zone as unit of analysis, the trip generation estimation which using household or individual as unit has been developed. The mainstream urban transportation models use household classified by zones as the basic unit of travel behavior studies.

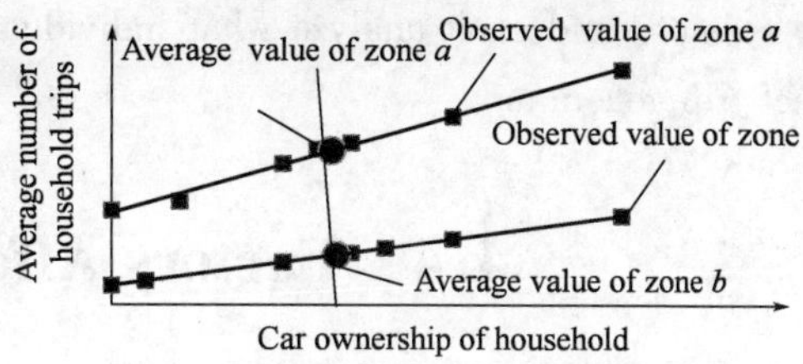

Figure 4-3 Average example

4.3.2 Using Household as Analysis Unit

Using household as analysis unit has been widely developed in trip generation and trip distribution. At least in the United States of America, census information is often collected with the household as the accounting unit and, therefore, analysis of many socioeconomic issues is facilitated by the existing census information. And, of course, collecting census information for the household is grounded on the recognition that, in many societies, many decisions are made by the household and for the household. Forecasting trip volume generated by the household appears to be the natural thing to do.

However, in advanced societies, the urbanization process has progressed to the point with the existence of high level of specialization of labor. Long disappeared was the household structure where everyone in the household engaged in the same profession, such as working on the household farm or working for the same factory. Now, it is common to find members of the same household work in different professions located in different parts of the city and with work schedules. Similar to using zone as the analysis, the use of the household as the analysis unit ignores the within household variation of trip making behavior and, therefore, faces similar criticism.

4.3.3 Using Individual as Analysis Unit

Trip generation estimation using zone and household as analysis unit is labelled as "aggregate" analysis, while estimation using individual as analysis unit is "disaggregate" analysis. According to Mekky(2001), the individual as unit of analysis has the following advantages:

- Compared to the method of home analysis unit, the analysis method based on individual is more compatible with other parts of the four stages.
- Fewer variables and categories can be used at this level of analysis.
- When calibrating, it needs fewer samples.

· At the individual level, certain important variables of population, such as age and gender, can be used.

· Considering the population change.

· Using the individual as unit of analysis is easier to forecast than using the household.

Household mandatory trips (go to school and work based on home) are very sensitive to household size and household workers, while don't affect other trip types(shopping, entertainment and so on), and can't analyze what individual property(age, professional and so on) change will affect trip generation.

4.4 Factors Affecting Trip Production

4.4.1 Zone Level

· Population;

· Household size;

· Employment;

· Car ownership;

· Residential density;

· Residential area;

· Accessibility.

4.4.2 Household Level

(1) Socioeconomic variables

The socioeconomic variables in trip generation play an important role. Typically, household socioeconomic variables are the foci of trip generation models, such as income. The common socioeconomic indicators are:

· Household size and household member composition. The household size is often defined as residential unit. With the increase in household size, per capita trip times reduced. For example, shopping can be replaced by one person. The composition of household members is different, which can produce different trip purposes, and influence household trip times. For example, if the young household members are in the majority, the trip of shopping and entertainment will correspondingly increase.

· The number of household members employed. There is a clear relationship between the trip rate of a household and the number of household members employed. For a household, when the number of household members with employment increases, the trip rate for journey-to-work as trip purpose also increases.

· Occupation. Different occupations produce different trip volumes. Some occupations, such as drivers, salesmen, purchasing staffs and salesmen, have higher trip rates, and some other occupations, such as teachers, students, and administrative staffs, have lower trip rates.

· Household car ownership and household members with driver's license. Families with high car ownership and families with large number of members with driver's license are expected to have higher trip times. Such expectation does not need further explanation.

· Household income. Household income affects the household mandatory and discretionary trip. Higher household income leads to more opportunities for trips and more modes for trip making, but the relationship is not entirely straight forward, and other household characteristics must be considered together.

(2) Network factor

Trip costs have not been widely used in trip generation analysis. The reason may be that trip cost (existing models developed land) in developed countries of personal income is relatively small.

The effect of network factor to trip mainly represents as the accessibility. The accessibility almost does not be a trip generation factor, but Leake and Huzayyin's research discovered certain relationship of the two things.

(3) Land use factors

Land use factors include land types and intensity. It stands to reason that different land use activities generate different volume of trips and at different times of the day or week which is one of factors that affect traffic trip generation. *National standards Urban Land Classification and Planning the Construction of Load Standard* (GB 50137—2011) divides urban constructive land into 8 types: residential land; public management and public service land; commercial service facilities land; industrial land; logistics land; road and transportation facilities land; utilities land; green and square land.

Among these, residential land is important traffic occurring source, and the household's home is the starting point and endpoint for most trips made. Trip related to residential area can be divided into the following types:

· Go to school and work from home;

· Go shopping from home;

· Social and recreational trips from home;

· Work or school to home;

· Shopping to home;

· From other places to home.

In China, urban land using appears several features as follows: first, the city scale expanses rapidly, economic developed zones and living zones continue to extent to suburb, and city population grows persistently; second, the internal city land structure changes dramatically; third, residents combination changes, these changes greatly affects the transportation state of city.

4.4.3 Individual Level

At the individual level, characteristics of the person having clear impact upon trip-making patterns include:

· Age. As a person goes through the various stages of life from birth to death, particularly from receiving education to finishing school, entering the work force and entering into retirement, the person goes through different trip-making patterns. Table 4-1 shows the percentage distribution of the contrast of trips in a certain zone in different ages from one survey.

Table 4-1 Contrast of trips in different ages

Age	6-18	>18-30	>30-40	>40-50	>50-60	>60-70	>70	Total
Average times	3.02	3.18	3.45	3.50	3.30	3.29	2.96	3.32
Proportion(%)	14.78	15.58	24.82	22.85	13.50	6.45	2.01	100

Source: *The Data Source of Weinan Resident Trip Survey in* 2011.

· Gender. Often individuals of different gender have different responsibility at home, or even in the choice of profession. Therefore, gender, in combination with marital status and occupation, is responsible for different trip-making patterns.

· Income. It can be divided into three types, high, medium and low or income between high and medium.

· Career. It can be divided into professional and executives; managers and technical persons.

· Employment types. You can use three categories: white-collar, blue and other.

· Employment status. It can be divided into two categories: work and unemployment, the former can be divided into a full-time and part-time.

· Car availability. Car availability is divided into these categories: no availability (that is families without cars or licenses); always available (the cars number that families have is equal to or more than the number of persons who have licenses; sometimes available the number of cars is less or persons who have licenses).

4.5 Factors that Affect Trip Attraction

Trip attraction is usually calculated at the zone level. Attraction of trips is related to land utilization (land use type, density, capacity of establishment, business sales, and location). For example, the number of employees of offices, employment density, zone area, the number of employees of government agencies, enrollment of educational institutions, sales force of commercial zones, sports stadium and convention center capacity.

4.6 Methods of Transportation Generation

4.6.1 Trip Generation Rate Method

(1) Overview

Trip generation rate method (also known as trip generation primary unit method) is using the ratio of trip generation volume and social indicators (population or land use) to forecast trip generation volume of forecast year. There are two main methods: a. use the ratio of individual's or household's average trip generation volume and based on the number of trips per capita for different trip purpose to estimate trip generation volume; b. use the ratio of trip volume that comes from different land use or the average trip volume per unit area and land utilization or economic indicators to forecast.

When forecasting residents' trip generation, it is based on the person trip survey data, and often uses average number of trips per day of individual or household. In United States and Japan, household is commonly used as unit since the individual trip is affected by household largely. In China, individual trip is commonly used as the primary unit. The specific way is: multiply the primary unit and total population of forecast year and get trip generation volume. Due to different trip purposes have different number of trips per unit, so when forecasting the population characteristics, it is usually based on different trip purpose(such as working, going to school, shopping, etc.). Fig. 4-4 shows the average number of trips of different trip purpose in 1986, Beijing.

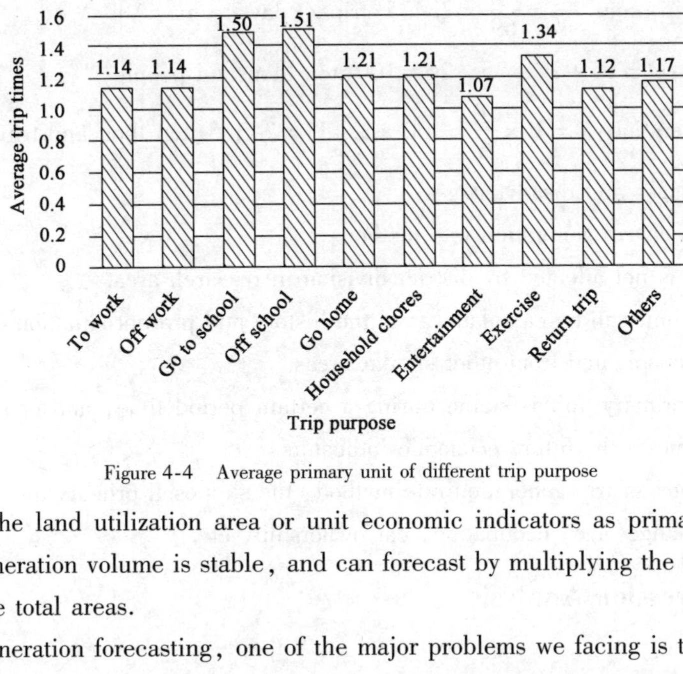

Figure 4-4 Average primary unit of different trip purpose

When using the land utilization area or unit economic indicators as primary unit, we usually assume that its generation volume is stable, and can forecast by multiplying the travel volume in unit area and the future total areas.

In the trip generation forecasting, one of the major problems we facing is the lack of data. For example, the person trip survey is conducted every five years in some big cities, data updates slowly. In the case of insufficient data, we can use the method of artificial counter to measure number of trips every day. When knowing number of households or land use types, we can multiply them and their corresponding primary unit and plus all terms in zone to get the trip generation volume.

To determine the value of the primary unit in the future, we usually adopt the following three methods: a. adopt the primary unit data; b. adopt the growth rate; c. function method, the main influencing factors in the function are age, gender, etc..

【**Example 4-1**】 As shown in Table 4-2, it is the present trip production and attraction of each traffic zone in a certain city. When the resident population average trip times are stable, use trip generation rate method to calculate trip production in the future.

Table 4-2 The present trip production, attraction and resident in each zone

Traffic zone	1	2	3	4
Present trip production volume/(ten thousand trip times/day)	32	40	51	45
Present trip attraction volume/(ten thousand trip times/day)	32	41	50	45
Present resident/ten thousand people	12	18	20	19
Future resident/ten thousand people	15	24	35	26

【**Sol.**】 According to the data in Table 4-2, we can get:

Present resident: $N = 12 + 18 + 20 + 19 = 69$ (ten thousand people)

Present trip generation volume: $T = 32 + 40 + 51 + 45 = 32 + 41 + 50 + 45 = 168$ (ten thousand trip times)

Average unit trip times: $\frac{T}{N} = \frac{168}{69} = 2.435$ [trips/(day · person)]

Future resident: $M = 15 + 24 + 35 + 26 = 100$ (ten thousand people)

Future trip generation: $X = M \times \frac{T}{N} = 100 \times 2.435 = 243.5$ (ten thousand trip times)

(2) The advantages and disadvantages

The advantages of trip generation rate method:

· Peoples' trip is not affected by district division in research area.

· The primary unit can be calculated from the history and present situation data in the research area, also can be transplanted from other similar areas.

· Assume the primary unit is stable during a certain period time, and can forecast the future trip production volume to the future economic indicators.

The disadvantages of trip generation rate method: the supposed primary unit can be changed by the traveler's own change (age, occupation, car ownership, etc.).

4.6.2 Regression Analysis

(1) Overview

Regression analysis is the most common method in trip generation. The calculation is relatively easy, and can be carried out using computer software, such as Excel or SPSS. Using regression analysis to forecast trip generation involves the use of linear and non-linear equations both.

The objective and the procedure for using regression model for trip generation begins with the articulation of a hypothesis (usually the hypothesis is the result of repeated observation of reality) that, say, the volume of supermarket shopping trips made in zones of a city is function of the number of households in the different zones, and that zones with more households tend to make more supermarket trips per week.

The next step is to select a sample(perhaps 30 zones) of zones from a given city and collect data on the number of households and the number of supermarket shopping trips made for a given period of time. The next step is to plot the data on a two-dimensional coordinate system, with the X-axis represent the household size and the Y-Axis representing the trip volume. The graph with plot of the 30 data point is called Scatter Plot. At this point, the analyst observes that the graph constructed shows a linear(or non-linear) relationship and then decides to use a liner equation with a dependent variable Y and one independent variable X.

The regression method commonly used for this simple "curve-fitting" exercise is called Least Square Regression. The objective is to use the collected data of trip volume and household size to "calibrate" the two parameters(the y-intercept and the gradient). Once these two parameters are calculated, the regression can be employed to calculate, or forecast, the supermarket shopping strip volume for zones from the same city that are not within the 30 zones used for the analysis, or for the same zones for a future point period, or for zones in other cities.

In the next section, the derivation of the regression begins with Eq. (4-1), the simple linear regression equation. Eq. (4-2) is the objection function. Q is the "sum of the squared deviations between the actual(observed) trip volume values and the corresponding forecasted values(forecasted by the regression line)", and the objective is to find such a line that would minimize Q. The pair of equations immediately below Eq. (4-2) are called Normal Equations, derived by differentiating Eq. (4-2) with respect to the y-intercept and the gradient, set the equations to 0, and solve for α and β. Eq. (4-3) and Eq. (4-4) give the statistical calculation.

[Example 4-2] A meta-linear regression is easy to analyze and calculate, it only has an independent variable x and a dependent variable y. The formula is:

$$y = \alpha + \beta x \tag{4-1}$$

where, y is dependent variable (trip production or attraction); x is independent variable (indicators such as population, car ownership volume); α is the y-intercept regression; β is regression coefficient, or the gradient.

As Fig. 4-5 shows, it is a line according to observation(point in the figure), this line objective function, that is linear regression model, α and β are unknown but fixed parameters, they can be obtained according to least squares. That is determining which one is the best regression line in the residuals square and minimum equation, the line should meet the objective function in Fig. 4-5.

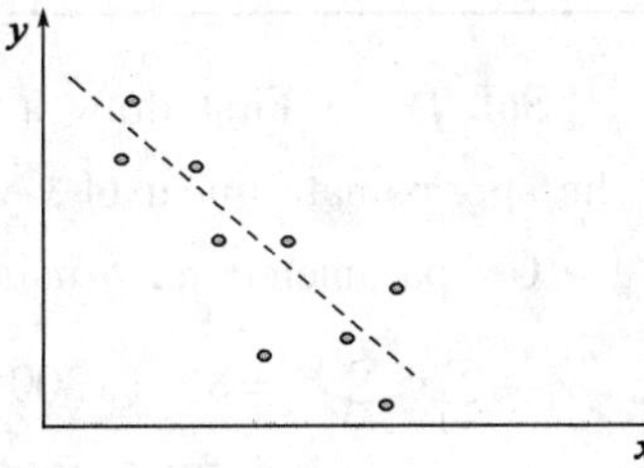

Figure 4-5 Linear fitting diagram

$$Q = \sum_{i=1}^{n}(\alpha + \beta x_i - y_i)^2 = \min \tag{4-2}$$

$$\begin{cases} \dfrac{\partial Q}{\partial a} = 2\sum_{i=1}^{n}(\alpha + \beta x_i - y_i) = 0 \\ \dfrac{\partial Q}{\partial b} = 2\sum_{i=1}^{n}(\alpha + \beta x_i - y_i) = 0 \end{cases}$$

The answer to the above linear programming is:

$$\begin{cases} \alpha = \frac{1}{n}\sum_{i=1}^{n} y_i - \frac{\beta}{n}\sum_{i=1}^{n} x_i & (4\text{-}3) \\ \beta = \frac{n\sum_{i=1}^{n} x_i y_i - \sum_{i=1}^{n} x_i \sum_{i=1}^{n} y_i}{n\sum_{i=1}^{n} x_i^2 - (\sum_{i=1}^{n} x_i)^2} & (4\text{-}4) \end{cases}$$

where, y_i is observation value.

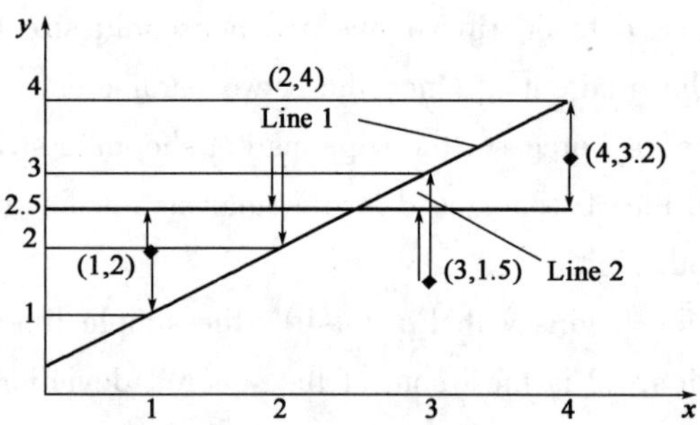

Figure 4-6 Optimal regression line diagram

The fitting relation between two linear and observations in the Fig. 4-6 can determine better line through calculating Q.

Line 1 $Q = (2-1)^2 + (4-2)^2 + (1.5-3)^2 + (3.2-4)^2 = 6.89$

Line 2 $Q = (2-2.5)^2 + (4-2.5)^2 + (1.5-2.5)^2 + (3.2-2.5)^2 = 3.99$

In comparison, line fitting residual of the smaller Q is small, and it is closer to the rule that the observed value reflects.

【Example 4-3】 In each zone of a certain residential land, number of trips of each day is the function of cars ownership volume. There are 8 research areas. The survey data is as Table 4-3 follows. Establish trip production model based on car ownership volume.

Table 4-3 Trip production and car ownership in each zone

	1	2	3	4	5	6	7	8
Car ownership	1200	2000	700	600	900	1000	1400	1600
Trip production/(trip times/day)	3100	4300	2200	2000	2500	2700	3300	3600

【Sol.】 · First draw a scatter plot, observe and get the approximate linear of x-y, as shown in Fig. 4-7.

· Get parameters a, b using least square method:

$$n\sum_{i=1}^{n} x_i y_i - \sum_{i=1}^{n} x_i \sum_{i=1}^{n} y_i = 8 \times (1200 \times 3100 + 2000 \times 4300 + 700 \times 2200 + 600 \times 2000 + 900 \times 2500 + 1000 \times 2700 + 1400 \times 3300 + 1600 \times 3600) - 23700 \times 9400 = 2034 \times 10^4$$

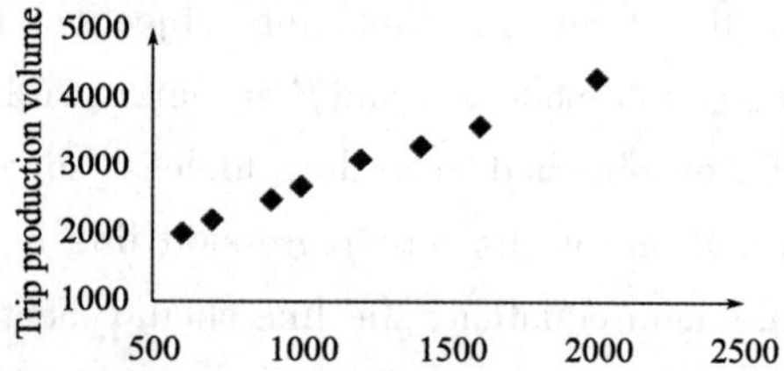

Figure 4-7 The relationship of car ownership and trip production

$$n\sum_{i=1}^{n} x_i^2 - (\sum_{i=1}^{n} x_i)^2 = 8 \times (1200^2 + 2000^2 + 700^2 + 600^2 + 900^2 + 1000^2 + 1400^2 + 1600^2) - 9400^2 = 1260 \times 10^4$$

$$\beta = \frac{n\sum_{i=1}^{n}x_iy_i - \sum_{i=1}^{n}x_i\sum_{i=1}^{n}y_i}{n\sum_{i=1}^{n}x_i^2 - (\sum_{i=1}^{n}x_i)^2} = \frac{2034\times10^4}{1260\times10^4} = 1.61$$

$$\alpha = \frac{1}{n}\sum_{i=1}^{n}y_i - \frac{\beta}{n}\sum_{i=1}^{n}x_i = \frac{1}{8}\times23700 - \frac{1.6}{8}\times9400 = 1082.5$$

· Get the regression equation:

$$y = 1082.5 + 1.61x$$

Multivariate(linear) regression analysis is one of the most commonly used forecastion methods, and it is the same to the reason of meta-linear regression. The most common form of building trip generation model with regression analysis is as follows:

$$T_i = a_0 + \sum_k a_k x_{ik} \tag{4-5}$$

where, T_i represents trip generation of traffic zone; x_1, x_2, $\cdots$, x_k represents the related variables that affect trip; a_0, a_1, $\cdots$, a_k represents regression parameters.

(2) Model test

Regression model(as well as any other model) shall be assessed from following aspects:

· Concision. The same forecastion should choose the model that the model structure is simpler and model parameters are less.

· Feasibility. The dependent variables contained by the model can forecast and be easy to forecast the future year's traffic generation.

· Reasonability. Model coefficients meet symbols and size of expectation, meet basic common sense and recognized theory. For example, population is proportional to trip volume.

· Forecastion effect. The forecastion efficacy of determined model can compare the dependent variable actual value in non-sample period and forecasted value in the same period. If the error is small, the forecastion efficacy of the model is good. On the contrary, you need to compute and select model again.

The statistical test of significance for correlated coefficients r, R^2, F test, t test are as follows:

· Correlated coefficient r.

Correlated coefficient r is a value that research linear relevance of variables. It is expressed as follows:

$$r = \frac{\sum_{i=1}^{n}(x_i-\bar{x})(y_i-\bar{y})}{\sqrt{\sum_{i=1}^{n}(x_i-\bar{x})^2\cdot\sum_{i=1}^{n}(y_i-\bar{y})^2}} = \frac{n\sum_{i=1}^{n}x_iy_i - \sum_{i=1}^{n}x_i\cdot\sum_{i=1}^{n}y_i}{\sqrt{n\sum_{i=1}^{n}x_i^2-(\sum_{i=1}^{n}x_i)^2}\cdot\sqrt{n\sum_{i=1}^{n}y_i^2-(\sum_{i=1}^{n}y_i)^2}} \tag{4-6}$$

The change range of r is $[-1, 1]$. When $r = -1$, x is negatively related to y, the value of $|r|$ is bigger. It reflects that the fitting extent of regression line and actual observation of variables is also higher.

· R^2

R^2 is coefficient of determination. It is the proportion (%) of the total variance in the dependent variables explained by the fitted equation. For example, when $R^2 = 0.81$, it shows that the fitting equation can explain 81% of the variance (Sum of Square, SS) in the dependent variables. In the case of the simple regression, the remaining 19% of the total variance is called "unexplained" variance.

The range of R^2 is (0, 1). Therefore, it measures the proportion of the total variance in Y "accounted for" by the X variable. It does not provide information on the direction of the relationship.

· D-W (Durbin-Watson) test

In the regression model test, it is very important to check the independence of the error term. If the error term is not independent, then any of the estimates and assumptions made by the regression model is unreliable. The test parameter is D_w or D, its value is $0 < D < 4$, its statistical significance is as follows:

When the residual and independent variables are independent of each other, $D \approx 2$;

When the residuals of two adjacent points are positive correlation, $D < 2$;

When the residuals of two adjacent points are negatively correlated, $D > 2$.

· F test and t test

If the regression parameters a_0, a_1, $\cdots$, a_k in Eq. 4-5 are all 0, then it can be considered that there is no significant linear relationship. The F test is using the method of hypothesis testing in the statistic to verify that the coefficient is all 0. Similarly, the process of verifying that whether each independent variable is zero is the t test. Related test methods can refer to the relevant statistical books, here we only briefly introduce the commonly used test indicators.

The statistics used to determine the results of the F test and the t test are mainly included F statistic, t statistic and sig(p value), the criteria for discrimination at the 95% confidence level are shown in Table 4-4 below.

Table 4-4 Test criteria

Statistic	Exist a significant linear relationship	Not exist a significant linear relationship
F	$F > F_{0.05}$	$F < F_{0.05}$
t	$t > t_{0.05}$	$t < t_{0.05}$
Sig(p value)	Sig(P) < 0.05 significant Sig(P) <0.01 very significant	Sig(p) >0.01

Note: the table values are related to confidence interval select, interested students can refer to related statistics books to know the meanings of various statistics.

(3) Regression and virtual variable

In regression analysis, the independent variable x is effected not only quantitative variable mentioned before, such as the income, population, but also qualitative variable, such as gender (man, woman), career (worker, teacher, farmer). Under the premise of keeping other factors invariant, the trip number of female workers maybe more than man workers, and such qualitative variable can affect the regression analysis result, and should be included in the regression analysis. When modeling, we need to convert the qualitative variables into virtual (dummy) variables. The introduction of virtual variable is to note the mutual independence among independent variables. The independent variable x can be divided into k mutual independent types, and it can use $k-1$ virtual variables to express, the value is 0 or 1.

【Example 4-4】 Assume the trip production rate is the function of career, and divide the career into 6 types: public officials, teachers, management personals, workers (including migrant workers), farmers and self-employed. Set the virtual variables and try to build up regression model, shown as Table 4-5.

$$y = a_0 + a_1x_1 + a_2x_2 + a_3x_3$$

Table 4-5 Virtual variables assignment

Career division	Virtual variables assignment
Public officials	All x are 0
Teachers	$x_1 = 1$, the rest are 0
Management personals	$x_2 = 1$, the rest are 0
Workers (including migrant workers)	$x_3 = 1$, the rest are 0
Farmers	$x_4 = 1$, the rest are 0
Self-employed	$x_5 = 1$, the rest are 0

(4) The advantages and disadvantages

The advantages of the regression model:

· The model is simple and spends less cost, and it is convenient for people to understand.

· The data is easy to get, can be taken from the city planning agencies.

· The parameters are relatively few in the regression analysis.

· The model can consider the complex relationship between traffic generation and main influence factors and the change of factors, but the considered factors are only continuous variables, and they are the quantitative indicators. The regression analysis is unable to consider the effect of non-quantitative indicators. It actually implies a basic assumption——assume the relationship of trip production and each factor (independent variable) in the future year is same to now and a basic condition——the planning year forecastion value of each independent variable is easy to get, and them should be determined by other model that reliability is higher.

The disadvantages of the regression model:

· It is unable to describe the using variables in regression analysis is effective or not.

· Regression analysis model considers the main factors that affect trip generation, and these factors must be continuous variables and quantitative indicators. Therefore it has a limitation that is unable to consider non-continuous variables or non-quantitative indicators.

In addition to the above drawbacks, the common drawback of regression analysis and category analysis is: does not consider that the level of traffic network service can affect the residents, trip generation. Residents' trip generation volume is effected by road traffic service level (trip convenience, comfort level). When the road network service level improves, trip is convenient, and persons are willing to travel; on the contrary, crowded blocked traffic must make persons cancel some trip such as entertainment trip.

4.6.3 Category Analysis

(1) Overview

Category analysis was introduced in the 1960s, can handle the non-linear relationship between traffic generation and land using variable. Due to individual's difference, its trip behavior is unique, so it needs to crowd people. That is category analysis. Therefore, this method shows that people have commonality or similar trip behavior.

Category analysis will general analyze in time, space, social economy and so on. Space category is that research area is divided into different zones, using zone as analysis unit, analyzing total number of zones, but it may not reflect the actual situation of transportation system. Time category is that time is divided. For example, time is divided into peak and non-peak, so it can reduce the complexity of analysis. Social economy category is that home is divided by income, car ownership number, including certain assumptions. In the actual situation, it determines category analysis' level according to how data detailed.

In trip generation forecastion, category analysis is mainly using household as analysis unit. It classifies household (usually use car ownership number, household size, household income as classified variable), collect the future household number and average trip rate of the same type household, and multiply the two things to get forecastable number. In the research process it must obey the following assumptions:

· The trip rate in a certain period is stable, that is considering in the same type household, average trip times in unit time named trip rate is constant and future household number is basic constant.

· Household size change a little.

· Income and car ownership number tend to increase.

· Household can use the method of hypothesis test to classify; every type of household number can use mathematical distribution to estimate according to corresponding household income and household structure.

The main modeling step of category analysis is: we must first classify related households laterally, then make the families of research area attribute to corresponding category, then every type household's average trip rate is divided by each investigated trip generation volume. Last, each type household multiplies corresponding trip generation rate, and get the sum of all types household in the research area and get trip total volume. Using the formula expressed as:

$$O_i = \sum_h r(h) n_i(h) \tag{4-7}$$

where, O_i represents calculated number of research area trip production number; $r(h)$ represents the average trip rate of h type household; $n_i(h)$ represents h type household number of zone i.

【Example 4-5】 According to household size, income and car ownership number of household, household of research object can be divided into different categories, as Table 4-6 shows. We know: low-income, no cars, three persons per household, this type household number is 100; low-income, no cars, four persons per household, this type household number is 200; medium-income, a car, four persons per household, this type household number is 300; high-income, 2 cars, 5 persons per household, this type household number is 50. Calculate trip generation total number in this zone according to investigated data.

Table 4-6 The average trip rate of different household type

Income	Low-income		Medium-income		High-income	
Household size car ownership rate	1-3persons	4 and over 4 persons	1-3persons	4 and over 4 persons	1-3 persons	4 and over 4 persons
No car	3.4	4.9	3.7	5.0	3.8	5.1
1 car	5.2	6.9	7.3	8.3	8.0	10.2
2 and more than 2 cars	5.8	7.2	8.1	11.8	10.0	12.9

【Sol.】 total trip volume:

$$100 \times 3.4 + 200 \times 4.9 + 300 \times 8.3 + 50 \times 12.9 = 4455 \text{ (person trips/day)}$$

(2) The application of category analysis

· Glamorgan Transportation Study. The study provides generation rate of 9 purposes in 1050 visits. Each trip rate of these 9 purposes is composed by 108 trip rate, one is for each household classification. It can be divided into 6 types according to income, 3 types according to car ownership number, 6 types according to household structure. The total types are 108 × 9 = 972. Samples are distributed in these types. This research represents if it is decimating samples, it need large samples. Table 4-7 shows trip rate of different trip ways and purposes.

Table 4-7 The generation rate of different modes and purposes

Trip mode	Trip purpose	Trip rate
Car	Working based on home	0.72
	Other based on home	0.68
	Non-based on home	0.27
Public transport	Working based on home	0.66
	Other based on home	0.83
	Non-based on home	0.06
Lift	Working based on home	0.49
	Other based on home	0.66
	Non-based on home	0.14

· In FHWA's trip forecastion model, it also uses category analysis to forecast residents' trip generation: the method and model that Portland research trip generation problem is shown as Table 4-8 follows.

Table 4-8 Portland METRO

Trip purpose	Way	Specific model
Working trip based on home(HBW)	Category analysis	Analyze trip rate according to household working number
Other trip based on home(HBO)	Category analysis	Category analyze trip rate according to household car ownership, household size
Shopping trip based on home(HBS)	Category analysis	Category count trip rate according to household size and household child number
Working trip non-based on home(NHBW)	Regression analysis	0.351106 × employment position number in zones
Non-working trip non-based on home(NHNW)	Regression analysis	2.381122 × retail position number + 0.239427 × household number

· In the survey of Australia west, the classification method is: household size is divided into 6 types. Car ownership number is divided into 3 types. The details are in Table 4-9. So household is divided into 3 × 6 × 6 = 108 (types).

Table 4-9 Australia's Midwest household horizontal classification diagram

Classification item	Category		
Household size	Residents of employment: 0 person; Unemployed adults: 1; Residents of employment: 1 person; Unemployed adults: ≥ 2 persons	Residents of employment: 0 person; Unemployed adults: ≥2; Residents of employment: 2 persons	Residents of employment: 1 person; Unemployed adults: ≤1; Residents of employment: 2 persons
Household income	Less than 500 pound	Unemployed adults: ≤1 person; 500-1000 pound	Unemployed adults: ≥2persons; 1000-1500 pound
Household car number	1500-2000 pound; no	2000-2500 pound; 1 car	More than 2500 pound; 2 and over 2 cars

· Xi'an transportation model. It can be divided into 7 types according to land using nature (core commercial zone, center living intensive area, secondary living intensive area, out skirts of economic development zone, remote rural economy, remote rural economy to be developed area), the household can be divided into 5 types (home based working trip, home based school trip, home based other trip, non-home based trip and official trip) to forecast trip generation.

(3) Distribution of family classification

The OD survey data are usually used for the family classification of the base year. However, in the prediction of family classification in one year, the average of each independent variable in the region is usually used. Thus, household income, car ownership and family structure require both personal and joint distribution.

· Income distribution. The Gamma formula shows the household income distribution as follows:

Let $f(x)$ be a family income for the probability of x and assume

$$f(x)=\frac{\alpha^{\mu+1}}{\Gamma(\mu+1)}x^{\mu}e^{(-\alpha,\ x)} \tag{4-8}$$

where, Γ is the gamma equation; α and μ are the parameters in the function type of the mean $\bar{x}$ and the variance σ^2 of the distribution.

$$\alpha=\frac{\bar{x}}{\sigma^2} \tag{4-9}$$

$$\mu=\alpha\bar{x}-1 \tag{4-10}$$

Therefore, the probability $p(x)$ of the income group x is as follows:

$$p(x)=\int_a^b \frac{\alpha^{\mu+1}}{\Gamma(\mu+1)}x^{\mu}e^{(-\alpha,\ x)}\mathrm{d}x \tag{4-11}$$

The average valuable and standard deviation of each zone's income needs to be known in defining the income distribution for a district, and the ratio of $\bar{x}/\sigma$ and x can also be used.

The ratios in the traffic studies in Douglas and Lewis (1971) and Wootton and Pick (1967) were 1.62 and 1.64, respectively. The value of μ used in the Monmouth shire traffic study is 1.636, while the value of μ used in the study in the northwestern part of the UK is 1.8.

· Home car ownership distribution. The amount of household car ownership is mainly related to household income x, so the probability of households that income is x with n cars is:

$$P\left(\frac{n}{x}\right)=\int_{x_1}^{x_2} a_n x^b \exp(-c_n x)\,\mathrm{d}x \tag{4-12}$$

where, a_n, b, c_n are constants; x_1 and x_2 are the upper and lower limits of income classification x.

The marginal probability of having n cars is as follows:

$$P(n)=\int_0^{\infty} P\left(\frac{n}{x}\right)P(x)\,\mathrm{d}x \tag{4-13}$$

In practice, there may be some factors that affect the impact of car ownership than the impact of income, for example, traffic accessibility. However, the data of these variables is not easy to get, so we need to use a proxy variable, generally we can use the population density as a proxy variable.

· Family structure distribution. Wootton, Pick (1967) and Pick and Gill (1970) suggested the use of the Poisson distribution for household size and the use of a binomial distribution for the employed population, with the following results:

Let α be the average family size minus 1, $\varphi(n)$ is the probability of the family size n, there are:

$$\varphi(n)=\frac{e^{-\alpha}\alpha^{n-1}}{(n-1)!} \quad (n=1,\ 2,\ 3,\cdots,N) \tag{4-14}$$

Let $P(n)$ be the employment probability of the family member that the family size is n, and then use the binomial distribution. The probability that there are r employees in the family with n

members is as follows:

$$P(r/n)=\frac{n!}{r!\ (n-r)!}P\ (n)^r[1-P(n)]^{n-r} \tag{4-15}$$

Thus, the probability $P(n,\ r)$ that the family size is n and there are r employment members, as follows:

$$P(n,\ r)=\varphi(n)P \tag{4-16}$$

$$P(n,\ r)=\frac{e^{-\alpha}\alpha^{n-1}n!}{(n-1)!\ r!\ (n-r)!}P\ (n)^r[1-P(n)]^{n-r} \tag{4-17}$$

where, $\alpha=$ Average household size $-1=$ population/number of households -1; $P(n)$ is the number of persons working in the family n/the population in the family n.

The average number of households and the average number of persons employed that inferred from the above formula are used to estimate the number of households in each family structure category in each region.

· Combined probability distribution. It is not enough to know the marginal probability $P(x)$ [Eq. (4-11)] that a family's income is x or the marginal probability $P(n)$ of the cars number owned by a family is n, or the marginal probability $P(n,\ r)$ [Eq. (4-17)] of the structure of the family $(n,\ r)$. We must combine with income/car ownership/family structure to consider. If the three distributions are independent, then the joint distribution is the result of the multiplication of the three. But the distribution of the three is not independent, so the iterative method can be used when make the three joint distributions.

(4) The advantages and disadvantages of category analysis

The main advantage of category analysis:

· The classification is clear and intuitive and easy to understand. This method uses the relation between trip production and household nature to describe to make people easier to accept.

· The required information is easy to get. We can directly collect data from existing OD survey or small scale survey.

· The requirement of variables is low. In modeling process, it doesn't need variables independent, even if the variables exist certain relation, it can also use.

· It is easy to test. Do samples research to part zone, and the test requirement of variables is low.

· The applicability is wide. The production and attraction of trip are respectively based on household nature and land using nature. Therefore, trip production and attraction can be used in a variety of range of research, such as the planning of new region and inter-regional planning.

The disadvantages of category analysis:

· When use household type to classify, we ignore the differences among families. For example, the household owing different number of cars that household scale is 1-4 persons will lead to different trip times. However, it tends to be ignored in this method.

· It is more difficult to assess. It needs to know the number of household types including forecastion of future household scale and data forecastion of planning years. These works are difficult to do.

· When determining variables level with personal subjectivity, it is loss of considerable.

· Due to difference of each sample number, when we use trip rate from sample to forecast trip volume, the accuracy is lower. The production parameters are too much.

· When we use category analysis, we need household information of planning years to forecast. It is a very tedious work.

4.6.4 Trip Rate Method

For a specific location, the trip volume of parameter x of the land using can be represented as trip rate. For example, to neighborhoods, trip rate can be expressed as the trip volume of every unit residential. The trip rate in general research reflects the relationship between city transportation and land using. The reference books that to provide trip generation rate recently commonly used is "Trip Generation" written by America. The American manual provides car trip generation rate from every type land using. And its content constantly updates to refer for transportation planning and related professionals.

It uses trip rate model to describe the relationship between the decided indicators of each land using trip generation volume. Different building nature(such as building area, parking area) affects trip generation volume. So it needs to investigate trip rate to determine trip rate model. The usual trip rate survey is shown in Table 4-10.

Compared to the traffic situation of the US, the transportation problem of country is more complex, it is difficult to learn from abroad. "Trip generation" published in 2009, it does survey and gets the high correlation trip rate indicators according to every type architectural features and traffic characteristics. The main content includes home, office, integrated business, shops, financial, hotels, culture and entertainments, hospitals, schools, books exhibition Hall, political authority, warehouse and comprehensive building and so on, the research result has a significant effect on city transportation quantitative analysis and evaluation. Trip generation uses the average number, diagram and formula to express trip production rate.

The average number method: average all production rate of all research building, then get average production rate of every type buildings based on every impact index factors.

Diagram method: make scatter plot with production rate data of each survey point. According to survey object's nature and characteristics, referring staffs do interpolation or plug and estimate and forecast trip volume supplemented engineering experience judgment. This method is intuitive and accurate, reflecting the related change trend between trip generation volume and effect index. Especially when determine trip rate to zones that are similar to existing sample, we can learn from existing sample point data. But the method needs high accuracy of samples. When the accumulative investigate sample is no sufficient, it is difficult to determine the variance.

Formula method: It is a mathematical model that future years, we can use regression model to show the relationship of trip generation volume and related indicators (such as the number of employees, total building area, etc.). Under normal circumstances, we can use software to so regression analysis, such as SPSS, EXCEL.

Table 4-10 Trip rate survey

Trip rate survey																
Date:					Location:				Week:				Direction:			
Time	Big truck				Small truck				Bus				Minibus			
	Number of cars		Number of passengers		Number of cars		Number of passengers		Number of cars		Number of passengers		Number of cars		Number of passengers	
	Arrive	Set off	Arrive	Set off	Arrive	Set off	Arrive	Set off	Arrive	Set off	Arrive	Set off	Arrive	Set off	Arrive	Set off
7:00-7:15																
7:15-7:30																

Time	Taxi				Motorcycle				Total				
	Number of cars		Number of passengers		Number of cars		Number of passengers		Number of cars		Number of passengers		
	Arrive	Set off	Arrive	Set off	Arrive	Set off	Arrive	Set off	Arrive	Set off	Arrive	Set off	
7:00-7:15													
7:15-7:30													

It can use the under formula to represent the interval estimation of production rate:

$$\bar{X} \pm (s/\sqrt{n})\, t_{\alpha/2,\, n-1} \tag{4-18}$$

where, $\bar{X}$ represents average trip rate of unit; s represents standard deviation of unit; n represents observed number of unit; $t_{\alpha/2,\, n-1}$ represents t statistics that significance level is α (t = 1.96, α = 0.05, range is n).

This formula shows that when the observed unit number increases, the trip rate estimation is more accurate. If two intervals overlap significantly, we can conclude that: the number difference between then is little. The 1 % difference between two ratios may be significant statistics of a large sample.

4.7 Other Models of Trip Generation(Mekky and Eng, 2001)

4.7.1 Non-based Home Trip

Non-based home trips are mainly related to the types of land use, but less related to other factors, and the volume of trip production and trip attraction by non-based home trips may be different although in the same condition.

4.7.2 Category Analysis of Personal Classification

Personal classification is a method included in the Category analysis described earlier, which treats individual behavior as units for classification, can be expressed as follows:

$$T_i = N_i \sum_j a_{ij} t_j \tag{4-19}$$

where, t_j represents the trip rate; T_i represents the total number of trips of zone i's residents; N_i represents the total number of residents in zone i; a_{ij} represents the percentage of j type residents in zone i.

The advantages of personal classification:

· The model used is based on the research of travelers, consistent with the rest of the classic traffic demand model;

· The number of the personal classification model is several times less than the number of samples required based on the household model;

· The characteristics of the travelers and changes in the population can be taken into account, but not in the household-based model;

· Personal classification is easier to forecast than household classification, and household classification needs to forecast household size. One drawback of the personal classification is that it cannot analyze the interactions among household members, such as income and spending.

4.7.3 Logit /Probit Method

Trip generation, in particular its production, can be viewed as discrete choices in which individuals(or households) choose not to travel, to travel once, and to travel twice. The Logit model and the Probit model are used to calculate the probability of occurrence of each trip, and the resulting probability is matched with each selected population P_i. $\sum_i \bar{P}_i \cdot i$(i is from 0 to ∞) is equal to the number of trips in the region.

What needs to be paid attention to is determining trip or not and how many trips. However, these choices or decisions are not independent. For example, the choice of three trips must undergo a second choice. The nested Logit model and Probit model are required. This is covered in detail in the IIA features of the Logit model in Chapter 6.

4.7.4 Peel Area Trip Generation Method

In the 1980's, the Pear Autonomous Region used a relatively simple form of trip generation based on census data. Trip generation in Peel is mainly estimated trip from home to work in 24 hours, including not only trip within the scope of the study, but also from the outside scope of the study trip.

The equation of 24-hour home-to-work trip generation is as follows:

Internal production: $WP = ELF \times (1 - PRWO - PRWH) \times 0.88$

Internal attraction: $WA = EMP \times (1 - PELO - PEWH) \times 0.88$

External production: $XWP = ELF \times PRWO \times 0.88$

External attraction: $XWA = EMP \times PELO \times 0.88$

where, ELF is (residents) employed labor in zone i; EMP is the employment rate in zone i; WP is the inside trip production from home to work in 24 hours; WA is the inside trip attraction from home to work in 24 hours; XWP is the outside trip production from home to work in 24 hours(work outside the research area); XWA is the outside trip attraction from home to work in 24 hours(live outside the research area); PRWO is the proportion of working outside the research area(in zone employed labor); PRWH is proportion of working outside the research area (in zone employed labor); PELO is the proportion of living outside the research area(in employee).

After calculating the volume of production and attraction, their total volume must be consistent. Typically, the population forecast is more accurate, the total volume of trip attraction equals to the total volume of trip generation. Individual district attraction can be adjusted using the unary proportion method. It is worth noting that if the calculation method is reasonable, the volume of generation will be equal to the attraction, or both will be equal to the average of the total generation and total attraction.

4.7.5 Site/Travel Method

Traditional trip generation methods consider only single destination trips. But sometimes travelers connect multiple destinations into a single trip. Some researchers(Hautzinger, 1981; Rose and Koppelman, 1984) presented the concepts of site and travel. A site is a place which is unrelated to home, travel refers to the moving process of starting at home and terminating at home and including at least one site. Therefore, the traditional trip is a moving process between two sites. It should be noted that the number of trips is equal to the number of trips plus the number of stations. You can use linear regression to estimate the number of trips and sites.

4.8 Production and Attraction Balance

In the trip generation forecast, it is required that the total trip generation volume is equal to the total travel attraction, and is equal to the trip generation volume. However, in the actual forecasting, error caused by the data or other factors is inevitable; any trip generation methods are unlikely to meet the above relationship. Usually we use the following methods to adjust:

· Adjust the volume of trips to make it balance with the volume of attractions:

$$O_i' = O_i \times \frac{\sum_{j=1}^{n} D_j}{\sum_{i=1}^{n} O_i} \tag{4-20}$$

where, i, j represent the traffic zones; O_i represents the trip production of traffic zone i; O_i' represents the trip production after adjustment.

· Adjust the volume of trip attraction to make it balance with the volume of production:

$$D_j' = D_j \times \frac{\sum_{i=1}^{n} O_i}{\sum_{j=1}^{n} D_j} \tag{4-21}$$

where, D_j represents the trip attraction from the traffic zone j; D_j' represents the adjusted volume of trip attraction.

In general, it is considered that the trip attraction volume is more reliable than the production volume, and therefore, the volume of production is generally balanced by the attraction volume.

· Adjust the volume of production and attraction to balance with the trip generation, also known as total control method, is the most commonly used method (where T represents the total volume of trip generation):

$$O_i' = O_i \times \frac{T}{\sum_{i=1}^{n} O_i} \tag{4-22}$$

$$D_j' = D_j \times \frac{T}{\sum_{j=1}^{n} D_j} \tag{4-23}$$

It is worth noting that, regardless of the method used to adjust, unit of the analysis method used must be consistent.

【Example 4-6】 Use the data in Eg. 4-1 to calculate the volume of trip production and trip attraction for each zone in the future, and adjust it using the total control method (assuming that the primary unit does not change).

【Sol.】 · Find out the per capita number of production and attraction in each zone

Zone 1: Production volume 32 ÷ 12 = 2.667[times/(day person)]

Attraction: 32 ÷ 12 = 2.667[times/(day person)]

Zone 2: Generation volume 32 ÷ 12 = 2.667[times/(day person)]

Attraction: 41 ÷ 18 = 2.278[times/(day person)]

Zone 3: Generation volume 51 ÷ 20 = 2.55[times/(day person)]

Attraction: 50 ÷ 20 = 2.5[times/(day person)]

Zone 4: Generation volume 45 ÷ 19 = 2.368[times/(day person)]

Attraction: 45 ÷ 19 = 2.368[times/(day person)]

· Find out the future trip production and attraction volume of each zone:

Zone 1: The volume of trip production 2.667 × 15 = 40.005(10000 times/day)

The volume of trip attraction 2.667 × 15 = 40.005(10000 times/day)

Similarly, we can calculate the future trip production and attraction volume of other zones, as shown in Table 4-11.

Table 4-11 The future trip production and attraction in each zone (10000 times/day)

O	D				Total
	1	2	3	4	
1					40.005
2					53.328
3					89.25
4					61.568
Total	40.005	54.672	87.5	61.568	

· Adjustment calculation:

As can be seen from the table, the volume of trip production is not equal to the volume of attraction, so adjust it with the total control method:

$$O_i' = 40.005 \times \frac{243.5}{244.151} = 39.897$$

$$D_j' = 40.005 \times \frac{243.5}{243.745} = 39.965$$

$$O_i' = 53.328 \times \frac{243.5}{244.151} = 53.184$$

$$D_j' = 54.672 \times \frac{243.5}{243.745} = 54.617$$

$$O_i' = 89.25 \times \frac{243.5}{244.151} = 89$$

$$D_j' = 87.5 \times \frac{243.5}{243.745} = 87.413$$

$$O_i' = 61.568 \times \frac{243.5}{244.151} = 61.4$$

$$D_j' = 61.568 \times \frac{243.5}{243.745} = 61.506$$

The final adjustment results are shown in Table 4-12.

Table 4-12 The volume of future trip productions and the volume of attractions in each zone (10000 times/day)

O	D				Total
	1	2	3	4	
1					39.965
2					54.617
3					87.413
4					61.506
Total	39.897	53.184	89	61.4	243.5

4.9 Evaluation of Disaggregate Model and Aggregate Model

According to the type of data, the travel demand forecasting models can be divided into aggregate and disaggregate models. Aggregate model is the model that handles and analyzes each person's traffic activity according to the traffic zone, in order to get model using traffic zone as the unit of analysis. The model system first calculates the average value using zone as unit, then uses average value to calibrate the model parameters. The application of aggregate model is simple, but there are many shortcomings. For example, the real relationship and causal relationship between independent variables may not be reflected; in the analysis, the model parameters depend on the size of the analysis unit, ignoring other factors.

The basic theory of the disaggregate model is that the consumers choose the maximized utility. The model is built up directly based on the survey data using traveler(individual) as the unit without statistic processing. The disaggregate model estimates the trip possibilities of any household or individual with discrete household or personal data. The output can then be aggregated to forecast the trip generation. The differences are shown in Table 4-13.

Table 4-13 Differences between disaggregate and aggregate models

	Aggregate analysis	Disaggregate analysis
Survey unit	Single travel	Single travel
Analysis unit	Zone	Individual(household)
Dependent variable	Neighborhood statistics value(continuous)	Personal choice(discrete)
Independent variable	Different zone data	Different individual data
Deductive method	Regression analysis and so on	Maximum likelihood estimation method, etc.
Suitable level	Presumption of community	Arbitrarily
Policy performance	Changes in the village representative value	The change of the individual independent variables

continued

	Aggregate analysis	Disaggregate analysis
Capture traffic phenomenon method	Production, attraction	Travel frequency
	Distribution	Purpose selection
	Transportation method division	Transportation way selection
	Path allocation	path selection

Logit model and Probit model are the most commonly used models in the disaggregate model, depending on whether individuals decide to travel. The probability of individuals choosing to travel in the binary Logit model can be expressed as:

$$P_n(1) = \frac{1}{1 + e^{\beta(x_{0n} - x_{1n})}} \tag{4-24}$$

where, $P_n(1)$ represents the probability that the n_{th} person decides to travel; β represents the coefficient vector of model parameter estimation; x_{1n} represents traveler's explanatory variables in personal utility; x_{0n} represents the traveler's explanatory variables in personal utility that does not determine.

Compared with the aggregate model, disaggregate model has these characteristics: a. high efficiency, low cost; b. modeling conveniently, simple operation; c. contain a variety of variables; d. high portability. The disaggregate model requires less survey data than the aggregate model, but requires more detail data than the aggregate model.

4.10 Problems of the Trip Generation Model

Most trip generation techniques assume that the trip rate is insensitive to changes in the network, which is clearly inconsistent with the actual situation. For example, the introduction of a toll-free bus on a route is likely to increase trip production and even change trip assignments, but these affected trips are difficult to be interpreted by the methods which are currently being used. In addition, the degree of road congestion will also affect the volume of trip production. Therefore, the trip production model maybe needs to include feasibility and cost indicators, but few researchers try to do so (Leake & Huzayyin, 1979 & 1980). In addition, trip generation model must take land use and economic variables and other factors into consideration. For currently, the existing models are not closely linked to them, so the development and use of the model need continuous innovation and improvement.

Practice see the relevant section of Appendix 2.

References

[1] Ali Mekky, P. Eng. Analytics Transportation Planning[M]. America,2001.

[2] Shao Chunfu. Principles of Traffic Planning[M]. China Railway Publishing House, 2014.

[3] Wang Yuanyuan. Research on travel generation in Xi'an[D]. Xi'an: Chang'an University, 2004.

[4] Lu Huapu. Transportation Planning Theory and Method[M]. Beijing: Tsinghua University Press, 2006.

[5] Meyer. Urban Transport Planning [M]. Beijing: China Architecture & Building Press, 1990.

[6] Anderson M D, Malave D N, Malave D N. Dynamic Trip Generation for a Medium-Sized Urban Community[J]. Transportation Research Record Journal of the Transportation Research Board,2003,1858(1):118-123.

[7] Editorial Department of China Journal of Highways. A review of China's highway traffic academic research. 2012[J]. China Journal of Highway and Transport,2012,25(03):2-50.

[8] Chen H C, Wellander S. King County Travel Demand Model Update: Trip Generation[C]// Proceedings of the Conference on Transportation, Land Use, and Air Quality, 2011.

[9] (Austria) John Brak, Translated by Jiang Su, Urban Transport Planning Theory and Practice [M]. Beijing: China Communications Press, 1987.

[10] Guan Hongzhi. Disaggregate Model: A Tool for Traffic Behavior Analysis[M]. China Communications Press, 2004.

[11] Li Xia. Research on Forecasting Methods of Urban Residents' Travel Generation[D]. Changchun: Jilin University, 2004.

[12] Lu Huapu, Yin Yafeng. The Disaggregate Analysis Method of Planning Theory and Its Application[J]. Journal of Highway and Transportation Research and Development,1996,13(1):22-28.

[13] Zhang Xiaoming. Study on the Model of Urban Transportation Trip Generation[D]. Beijing: Beijing University of Technology, 2000.

[14] Shi Fei, Wang Wei, Lu Jian. Induction and Innovation of Residents' Travel Generation Forecasting Methods[J]. Urban Transport, 2005, 3(1):43-46.

[15] Traffic Trip Index Research Group. Traffic Handbook[M]. Beijing: China Building Industry Press, 2009.

[16] GB 50137—2011 Urban land classification and planning construction land standards. Beijing: China Architecture & Building Press, 2012.

[17] Wang Yuanqing, Zhang Fuyong, Wang Yuanyuan. Study on correction method of location effect of generation rate method[J]. China Journal of Highway and Transport, 2004,(03): 90-94.

[18] Huntsinger L F, Rouphail N M, Bloomfield P. Trip Generation Models Using Cumulative Logistic Regression[J]. Journal of Urban Planning & Development,2013,139(3):176-184.

Chapter 5

Trip Distribution Models

5.1 Definitions

After trip generation is conducted, the productions and attractions of traffic zones can be obtained. For transportation planners, the next stage is to decide which zone the trips produced choose to go and where the attractions come from. In other words, the task of predicting future exchanges of each zone need to be done. We call this exchange between different zones as "trip distribution". This chapter mainly introduces the prediction of trip distribution.

The task of the trip distribution is to convert the trips between traffic zones from trip generation step to Origin-Destination (O-D) matrices, mainly trip purpose based O-D matrices. If the exchanges are classified by travelers' type, for example, trip distribution can be divided into two categories: car owners and non-car owners. Trip distribution modeling is not only one of the four steps of transport modeling, it can also be used in other fields, for example, in describing social phenomena of spatial-temporal interactions, such as population migration, the movement of goods, currency and information and so on.

The most practical model of trip distribution is the static fitting model. The dependent variable of trip distribution "q_{ij}" is the number of trips from zone i to zone j per unit time. The trip distribution conceptual model can be expressed as follows:

$$q_{ij} = F(x_1, x_2, \cdots, x_n) \tag{5-1}$$

where, $x_1, x_2, \cdots, x_n$ are the influence factors of trip distribution.

5.1.1 Origin-Destination (O-D) Matrix

O-D matrices is one of the most fundamental concepts in traffic distribution, where O represent trip origin, D represent trip destination. O-D matrices are commonly represented by an n-order matrix, which n represent the number of traffic zones, as shown in Table 5-1. From a strict theoretical perspective, the number of production zones and the number of attraction zones are not necessarily same, because some traffic zones only generate trips but never attract any trip, such as pure residential area. Some traffic zones are just attraction zones in peak hours, but not the production zones. In fact, most of traffic zones are both production and attraction zones. For simplicity, we assume the number of production zones is the same as the number of attraction zones, denoted by n.

Table 5-1 Trip distribution matrix

O	D				Total
	1	2	…	n	
1	q_{12}	q_{12}	…	q_{1n}	O_1
2	q_{21}	q_{22}	…	q_{2n}	O_2
⋮	…	…	…	…	⋮
n	q_{n1}	q_{n2}	…	q_{nn}	O_n
Total	D_1	D_2	…	D_n	T

Compared with the production and attraction in Chapter 4, that O_i、D_j are two non-directional quantities (scalar), the q_{ij} in this section is a quantity with directionality (vector) which has two subscripts. In general, i means zone that produced trips, j means zone that attract trips. The function which represents their relationships is:

$$O_i = \sum_j q_{ij}, D_j = \sum_i q_{ij} \qquad (i, j = 1, \cdots, n) \tag{5-2}$$

Total travel amount:

$$T = \sum_j O_i = \sum_i D_j = \sum_i \sum_j q_{ij} = \sum_j \sum_i q_{ij} \tag{5-3}$$

5.1.2 The Factors Affecting Trip Distribution

· Factors related to the demand side:

a. Activities which produce and attract trips in the traffic zones.

b. Car ownership rate. With the car ownership rate increased, the population will increase, which sequentially influence the trip distribution between the traffic zones.

c. Household income. It is one of the main factors affecting travel, especially the free travel. High-income families have high purchase rates of cars and high demand for shopping and entertainment.

d. Socio-demographic factors, such as age, gender, occupation and so on.

· Factors related to the supply side: e. g.

a. The spatial distance between traffic zones, directly affects the traveler's travel choice.

b. Land use. Transportation and land use have an inseparable relationship and land use development and utilization guide the choices of residential location, shopping place and working place, which influence travel distribution.

c. Travel costs. For example, travel time or travel expenditure can influence the choice of trip destination.

· Factors related to travel behavior:

Travelers tend to choose the shortest path. Under normal circumstances, travelers always choose travel routes with the shortest time and the lowest cost. When the two conditions are inconsistent, different people will prefer different condition based on their demands.

40 years ago, it was found that the number of trips between two zones was proportional to their activities, inversely proportional to the distance of spatial distribution.

5.1.3 Forecast of Trip Distribution

As we get the estimated values of trip productions and trip attractions in the previous chapter, we will obtain the element $q_{ij}$of O-D matrix, that is, from our knowledge the value of subtotal in each column and row of O-D matrix to find other value of each element. Mathematically, this is the problem of finding $n \times n$ unknowns by using $2n$ Eq. (5-2), there is no unique solution when $n > 2$. So we must borrow some other conditions to solve this problem. But further studies show that it is still hard to find an accurate solution。 However, it is easy to find an approximate solution.

Through the analysis and prediction of the survey data, the data that can be found and utilized are OD table at present $[q_{ij}^{0}]$ ($1 \leqslant i, j \leqslant n$, which 0 means the distribution in the base year), impedance matrix$[R_{ij}]$ between two zones. Many types of trip distribution models exist, it includes growth factor methods, gravity model, maximum entropy model, opportunity model and so on. This book only introduces the first two kinds of forecasting method in detail and briefly introduces the latter several methods.

5.2 Growth Factor Methods

The growth factor methods only consider trip ends and forecast trip distribution by simple extrapolation. Before using the methods, we need to assume that the current travel structure can be applied to future years. Growth factor methods are simple forecasting methods, which consist of two main points: the growth function method and the Furness method.

5.2.1 Basic Ideas of Growth Factor Methods

The specific growth factor methods include uniform factor method, average growth factor method, Detroit method and Fratar method. Their basic ideas are the same, while the differences between them are the definitions and iterative methods of growth function. We first describe the common ideas, and then discuss the different growth function methods. The basic ideas of growth methods can be described by the following algorithmic process(Fig. 5-1).

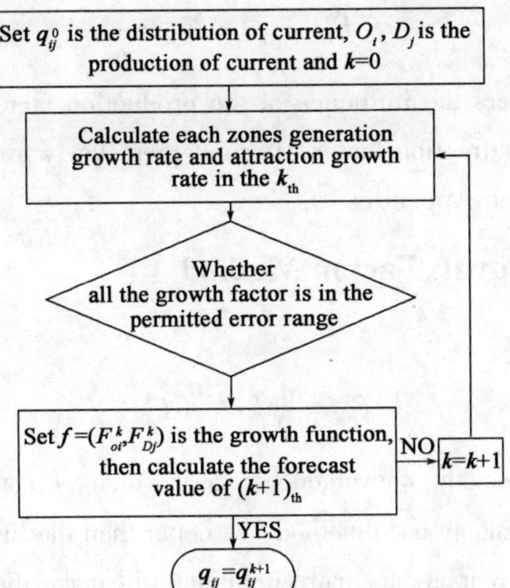

Figure 5-1 Calculation step of growth factor

As Fig. 5-1 shows, if we know the sum of productions(O_i^0 , O_i^f) and attractions(D_j^0 , D_j^f) during the current and future situation of zone i and zone j, we can define each zone generation growth rate and attraction growth rate in the 0th iteration.

$$F_{Oi}^k = \frac{O_i^f}{O_i^0}, F_{Dj}^k = \frac{D_j^f}{D_j^0} \tag{5-4}$$

In Fig. 5-1, after k^{th} iterations, if $f^k = (F_{oi}^k, F_{Dj}^k)$ is the adjustment value, then the $(k+1)^{th}$ estimated value is:

$$q_{ij}^{k+1} = q_{ij}^k \cdot f^k(F_{Oi}^k, F_{Dj}^k) \tag{5-5}$$

In Fig. 5-1, the new generation and attraction equation is:

$$O_i^{k+1} = \sum_j q_{ij}^{k+1}, D_j^{k+1} = \sum_i q_{ij}^{k+1} \tag{5-6}$$

Given that:

$$f_{Oi}^{k+1} = \frac{O_i}{O_i^{k+1}}, f_{Dj}^{k+1} = \frac{D_j}{D_j^{k+1}} \tag{5-7}$$

In Fig. 5-1, the results of the test are used to estimate whether the forecast is accurate. It is usually preferable to take 5%, 3% or other given threshold of iterations. As spatial distribution has a close relationship with factors related to productions, the accuracy in this step should not be too high and with less number of iterations to avoid excessive distortion. If the results meet the requirement, the results will be output, if not, we can return to the second step to readjust the growth factor and output the results. Next, we discuss several specific growth factor methods.

5.2.2 Unique Growth Factor Method

This method assumes that the growth of q_{ij} is only related to the production growth factor. The growth factor is given by:

$$f(F_{Oi}, F_{Dj}) = F_{Oi} = \frac{o_i}{o_i^0} \tag{5-8}$$

This method only considers the influence of the production factor to the growth function factor, ignoring the influence of the attraction factor. It converges slowly for the attractions not the same as the productions. (Example see Appendix 1)

5.2.3 Average Growth Factor Method

The growth factor is:

$$F_{Oi}^k = \frac{1}{2}(F_{Oi}^k + F_{Dj}^k) \tag{5-9}$$

If 1st iteration does not meet the convergence criteria, then we continue iterative until it meets the convergence criteria. This commonly used method was better than the first method. In the practical use it can completed by the help of computer for more iterations will make the calculation slower.

This method is significantly more reasonable than the first method, which is a more common method. In practice, we can finish it by means of a computer for its numerous iterative steps which will slow the calculation speed. (Example see Appendix 1)

5.2.4 Detroit Method

The Detroit method was proposed by J. D. Carol in 1956, which considers that the traffic volume from zone i to zone j am proportional to the growth rate of traffic generated in zone i and the growth rate of traffic attracted in zone j and inverse proportional to the growth of generation factor. This experience-based approach was later proved to be equivalent to the results obtained by the simultaneous probability-maximization method with the current OD table.

In this method, the growth factor was given by:

$$f_D^{k+1}(F_{Oi}^k, F_{Dj}^k) = F_{Oi}^k \cdot F_{Dj}^k \cdot \frac{T^k}{T^f} \tag{5-10}$$

where, T represent the amount of attraction; T^f represent predicted value; k means number of iterations; T^k/T^f means the growth of generation factor. (Example see Appendix 1)

5.2.5 Fratar Method

The Fratar method was proposed by T. J. Fratar(1954), which assumed that the traffic volume q_{ij} from zone i to zone j is not only proportional to the growth rate of productions of zone i and the growth rate of attractions of zone j, but also related with the growth factor of other traffic zones in the planning area.

Fratar method model was given by:

$$f_{\mathrm{F}}^{k+1}(F_{\mathrm{O}i}^k,\ F_{\mathrm{D}j}^k) = F_{\mathrm{O}_i}^k \cdot F_{\mathrm{D}j}^k \cdot \left(\frac{L_i + L_j}{2}\right) \tag{5-11}$$

$$L_i = \frac{O_i^k}{\sum_j q_{ij}^k \cdot F_{\mathrm{D}j}^k}, L_j = \frac{D_j^k}{\sum_i q_{ij}^k \cdot F_{\mathrm{O}i}^k}$$

where, L_i and L_j respectively represent the location faction of zone i and j. (Example see Appendix 1)

5.2.6 Furness Method

The Furness method assumed that the traffic volume q_{ij} from zone i to zone j is proportional to the growth rate of productions of zone i and the growth rate of attractions of zone j.

Furness method model was given by:

$$f_{\mathrm{FN}}^1(F_{\mathrm{O}i}^k,\ F_{\mathrm{D}j}^k) = F_{\mathrm{O}i}^k$$

$$f_{\mathrm{FN}}^2(F_{\mathrm{O}i}^k,\ F_{\mathrm{D}j}^k) = F_{\mathrm{D}j}^k \tag{5-12}$$

In this model, we first set the attraction growth factor as 1, and then we obtain the production growth factor that meets the conditions. Next we obtain the attraction growth factor again with updated matrix to finish a cycle iteration process. And then we repeat this process again until the growth of attraction and production meets the condition we settled. (Example see Appendix 1)

5.3 The Gravity Models

One of the disadvantages of the growth factor methods is that it doesn't consider the traffic impedance between traffic zones. It is useful for forecasting recent or entire year distribution in the entire network with little traffic impedances. In general, the traffic impedance will change with the traffic facilities improved or traffic volume increased. Thus, we must consider the influence of traffic impedances. This shortcoming can be partially remedied by gravity model.

Gravity model is proposed by Casey in 1955, which aroused form Newton's law of gravitation.

5.3.1 Generalized Gravity Model

The earliest model was given by:

$$q_{ij} = K \cdot \frac{O_i^\alpha D_j}{R_{ij}^2} \tag{5-13}$$

This model is obviously too rigid in the form of the law of universal gravitation and have a great error in practice. Thus, it is improved to:

$$q_{ij} = K \cdot \frac{O_i^\alpha \cdot D_j^\beta}{R_{ij}^\gamma} \tag{5-14}$$

where, α, β, γ, K are indefinite coefficients. Assume that they do not change with the time and places. According to the experience, the value range is from 0.5 to 1.0 and equals to 1 in most cases.

Traffic impedance R_{ij} is related to many factors, including travel time, distance and fuel consumption. For simplicity, we only take one of the main indicators as traffic impedance in most cases. We often choose time indicator in passenger traffic and choose distance indicator in freight transportation planning.

5.3.2 Impedance Function

The gravity model is simply, clearly and universal good, but there is something to be improved.

· Distributed impedance is more than R_{ij}. We can consider more complex and general functional relationship $f(R_{ij})$.

· If we only make use of the production, attraction and distributed impedance, we cannot describe distribution character very well. We cannot ignore inherent influence between the specific zones with such social or historical factors.

· We cannot ensure that the values q_{ij} forecasted by gravity model are same with the productions and attractions.

Thus, A. M. Voorhees updated the gravity model to amend the first and the third problem.

$$q_{ij} = O_i \frac{D_j f(R_{ij})}{\sum_{j=1}^{n} D_j f(R_{ij})} \tag{5-15}$$

where, $f(R_{ij})$ is distributed impedance function and can be represented by the following functions:

$$f(R_{ij}) = R_{ij}^{-\gamma}$$
$$f(R_{ij}) = \exp(-bR_{ij})$$
$$f(R_{ij}) = a\exp(-bR_{ij})R_{ij}^{-\gamma}$$

The impedance curve for each function is shown in Fig. 5-2.

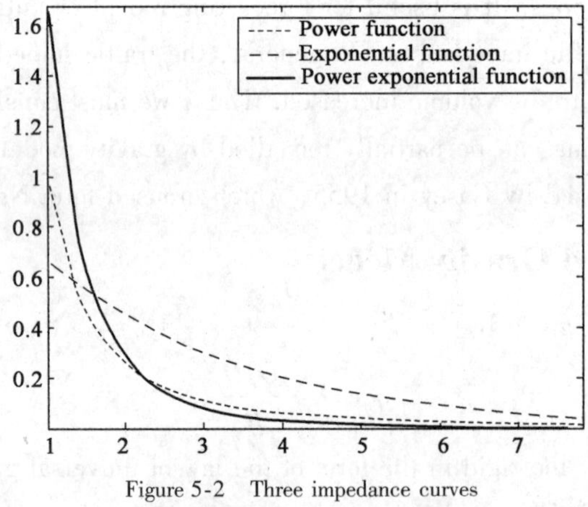

Figure 5-2 Three impedance curves

5.3.3 Model Parameters Calibration

Eq. (5-13) is the basic form of gravity model, where $f(R_{ij})$ is a function of travel distance, travel time and other indicators, can change with the number of trips. Given that $\alpha = \beta = 1.0$ and use above impedance function replace the impedance item in Eq. (5-14) to get the Eq. (5-16):

$$q_{ij} = KO_i D_j f(R_{ij}) \tag{5-16}$$

Considering the third disadvantage of gravity model, add the constraint conditions to the production to get the general coefficient k to amend this disadvantage. The function needs to meet the condition $\sum_{j=1}^{n} q_{ij} = O_i, K = 1/\sum_{j=1}^{n} D_j f(R_{ij})$ and use $1/\sum_{j=1}^{n} D_j f(R_{ij})$ to replace k in Eq. (5-16) in order to obtain the Eq. (5-17).

$$q_{ij} = O_i \frac{D_j f(R_{ij}) K_{ij}}{\sum_{j=1}^{n} D_j f(R_{ij}) K_{ij}} \tag{5-17}$$

The U. S. Bureau of Public Roads, BPR is obtained by introducing an adjustment coefficient that reflect the inherent relationship between the zone i and zone j on the basis of the modified gravity model described above.

The K_{ij} is given by:

· First set $K_{ij} = 1$ and obtained the factor $f(R_{ij})$ according the calibration model of O-D matrix at present.

· We get the O_i, D_j, R_{ij} of O-D matrix at present and then use it in the model to get the O-D volume T.

· By dividing q_{ij} in O-D matrix at present by O-D volume T, we obtain K_{ij}.

· Assume that the value of K_{ij} in the future is unchanged, we can directly use it without any modifying when we forecast.

Although this modified gravity model adds the condition of $\sum_{j=1}^{n} q_{ij} = O_i$, it cannot guarantee the sum of i in q_{ij} is same with the attraction D_j for they do not add the condition of $\sum_{i=1}^{n} q_{ij} = D_j$. Therefore, it is necessary for q_{ij} to do iteration according to the attraction and correct results.

5.3.4 Single Constrained Gravity Model

As simple gravity model cannot meet the following conditions:

$$\sum_j q_{ij} = O_i, \sum_j q_{ij} = D_j \tag{5-18}$$

Using the first Eq. (5-15) improve the gravity model to meet the condition in Eq. (5-18).

$$\sum_j q_{ij} = \sum_j K \frac{O_i \cdot D_j}{R_{ij}^{\gamma}} = KO_i \sum_j \frac{D_j}{R_{ij}^{\gamma}} = O_i \tag{5-19}$$

Thus, we obtain the coefficient K.

$$K = \frac{1}{\sum_j D_j / R_{ij}^{\gamma}} \tag{5-20}$$

In general, the impedance function $f(R_{ij})$ is given by:

$$K = \frac{1}{\sum_j D_j f(R_{ij})} \tag{5-21}$$

Using Eq. (5-16), we obtain q_{ij}, see Eq. (5-22).

$$q_{ij} = K \cdot O_i \cdot D_j \cdot f(R_{ij}) = \frac{O_i \cdot D_j \cdot f(R_{ij})}{\sum_j D_j f(R_{ij})} \tag{5-22}$$

Thus, the sum of i row in O-D matrix is given by:

$$\sum_j q_{ij} = O_i \cdot \sum_j \frac{D_j \cdot f(R_{ij})}{\sum_j D_j f(R_{ij})} = O_i \tag{5-23}$$

After using the Eq. (5-21), the result exactly meets the condition $\sum_j q_{ij} = O_i$, that is, the coefficient K in Eq. (5-21) constraint the q_{ij} in row, which named "row constraint factor". But it still cannot meet the condition of $\sum_j q_{ij} = D_j$. Similarly, we can define a "column constraint factor" to constraint q_{ij} in column.

$$K' = \frac{1}{\sum_j O_i f(R_{ij})} \tag{5-24}$$

This gravity model that introduces "row constraint factor" or "column constraint factor" is named single constrained gravity model.

$$q_{ij} = \frac{O_i \cdot D_j \cdot f(R_{ij})}{\sum_j \cdot O_i \cdot f(R_{ij})} \tag{5-25}$$

The parameter calibration problem of this model (Fig. 5-3) is one less than the previous, only calibrate the parameter in $f(R_{ij})$ without calibrating K alone for they can obtain K by using Eq. (5-21).

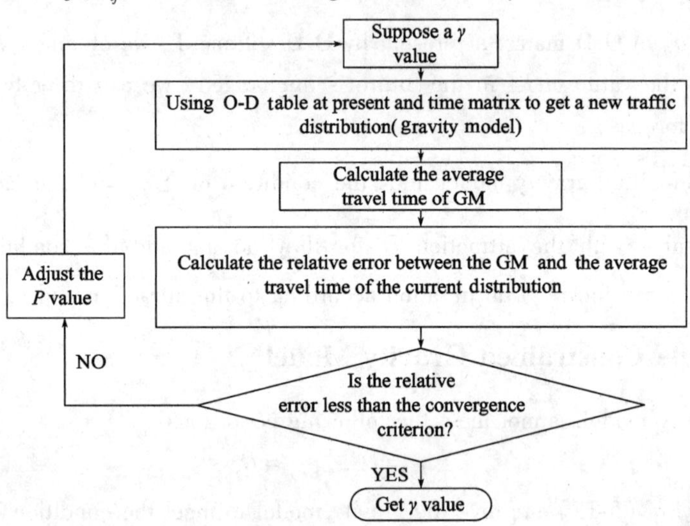

Figure 5-3 Parameter calibration of single constrained gravity model

Take $f_{R_{ij}} = R_{ij}^{-\gamma}$ as example, using trail method to illustrate the steps of calibrate parameter in single constrained gravity model.

We make the following additional explanation to the single constrained gravity model and its parameter calibration method.

· The calibration of γ when $f_{R_{ij}} = R_{ij}^{-\gamma}$.

· From Eq. (5-21) and Eq. (5-22), we can find that the parameter K is not a constant and greater than 0 and generally becomes smaller with time. This is contrary to people's expectations.

Take Eq. (5-20) as example, large amounts of data indicate that γ in Eq. (5-20) is not a constant and related to the travel purpose. For all-purpose model, $\gamma \approx 0.5$. In general, when the number of non-residential buildings increases, D_j becomes larger with time and R_{ij}. becomes smaller with time when traffic facilities improve in the traffic zones.

· Because single-constraint gravity model cannot meet the condition of $\sum_j q_{ij} = Q_i$, $\sum_i q_{ij} = D_j$ at the same time and not commonly used in practice. The double constrained gravity model can remedy this disadvantage.

5.3.5 Double Constrained Gravity Model

The gravity model that introducing row and column constraint factor at same time is double constrained gravity model. The double constrained gravity model was given by:

$$q_{ij} = K_i \cdot K'_j \cdot O_i \cdot D_j \cdot f(R_{ij}) \tag{5-26a}$$

$$K_i = [\sum_j K'_j \cdot D_j \cdot f(R_{ij})]^{-1} \quad (i=1, \cdots, n) \tag{5-26b}$$

$$K'_i = [\sum_i K_i \cdot D_i \cdot f(R_{ij})]^{-1} \quad (j=1, \cdots, n) \tag{5-26c}$$

where, K_i, K'_j is respectively row constraint factor and column constraint factor.

Take $f_{R_{ij}} = R_{ij}^{-\gamma}$ as example, using trail method to illustrate the steps of calibrate parameter in double constrained gravity model whose parameter calibration is shown in Fig. 5-4. (Example see Appendix 1)

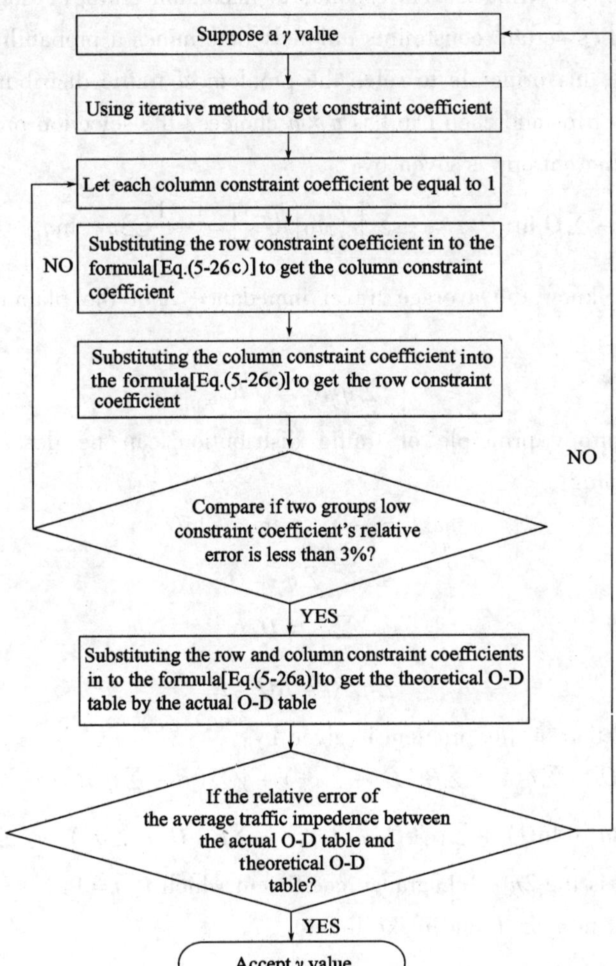

Figure 5-4 Parameter calibration of double constrained gravity model

5.4 Other Trip Distribution Models

5.4.1 Maximum Entropy Model

Shannon, the founder of information theory, presented the concept of "information entropy" according to the concept of entropy in the thermodynamics: set $A = \{a_1, a_2, \cdots, a_n\}$ is a symbol table of some information system X, the probability distribution of each symbol in A is $\{O_1, O_2, \cdots, O_n\}$ and the entropy of information system X is:

$$H(X) = -\sum_{i=1}^{n} O_i \ln(O_i) \tag{5-27}$$

In 1957, Jaynes proposed the principle of maximum information entropy theory that in all candidate probability distributions choose the distribution that the value is the maximum in the certain constraints as a distribution system X.

A certain probability distribution corresponds to maximum entropy; conversely, the maximum entropy state that satisfies certain constraints uniquely determines a probability distribution.

Thus, we can use this principle to solve the problem of traffic distribution. During the traffic distribution, there is Q trips and each trip has $n \times n$ choices, the selection probability is $\{p_{ij} = q_{ij}/Q: i, j = 1, 2, \cdots, n\}$, the entropy is given by:

$$H = -\sum_{i,j} O_i \ln(O_i) = -\sum \left[\frac{q_{ij}}{Q}\ln\left(\frac{q_{ij}}{Q}\right)\right] = -\frac{1}{Q}\sum_{i,j} q_{ij}(\ln q_{ij} - \ln Q) \tag{5-28}$$

Assuming that we know the average travel impedance $\bar{R}$ of the planning year, then we can obtain a new constraint:

$$\sum_{i,j} q_{ij} R_{ij} = Q\bar{R} \tag{5-29}$$

The maximum entropy principle of traffic distribution can be described by the following mathematical programming:

$$\max_{q_{ij}} h = -\sum_{i,j}(q_{ij}\ln q_{ij} - \ln Q) \tag{5-30a}$$

$$\text{s. t. } \sum_j q_{ij} = O_i \tag{5-30b}$$

$$\sum_i q_{ij} = D_j \tag{5-30c}$$

$$\sum_{i,j} q_{ij} R_{ij} = \bar{R}Q = R \tag{5-30d}$$

The Lagrange function of this problem is given by:

$$\begin{aligned} L &= h + \sum_i \alpha_i (O_i - \sum_j q_{ij}) + \sum_j \beta_j (D_j - \sum_i q_{ij}) + \gamma \sum_{i,j}(R - \sum_{i,j} q_{ij} R_{ij}) \\ &= -\sum_{i,j} q_{ij}(\ln q_{ij} - \ln Q) + \sum_i \alpha_i (O_i - \sum_j q_{ij}) + \sum_j \beta_j (D_j - \sum_i q_{ij}) + \gamma \sum_i (R - \sum_j q_{ij} R_{ij}) \end{aligned} \tag{5-31}$$

where, α_i, β_j, γ is the $2n+1$ Lagrange coefficient which $i, j = 1, 2, \cdots, n$. Calculating partial derivatives with respect to q_{ij} in L and make it zero.

$$\frac{\partial L}{\partial Q_{ij}} = -1 - \ln(q_{ij}) + \ln Q - \alpha_i - \beta_j - \gamma R_{ij} = 0 \quad (i, j = 1, 2, \cdots, n) \tag{5-32}$$

$$q_{ij} = \frac{Q}{e}\mathrm{e}^{-\alpha_i} \cdot \mathrm{e}^{-\beta_j} \cdot \mathrm{e}^{-\gamma R_{ij}} \tag{5-33}$$

if

$$u_i = \frac{Q}{O_i}\mathrm{e}^{-\alpha_i}, v_j = \frac{\mathrm{e}^{-\beta_j}}{D_j} \tag{5-34}$$

then

$$q_{ij} = u_i v_j \cdot O_i D_j \mathrm{e}^{-\gamma R_{ij}} \tag{5-35}$$

This is the double constrained gravity model in section 5.3.2 where the impedance function is exponential. If Eq. (5-30d) is replaced by Eq. (5-36):

$$\sum_{i,j} q_{ij}\ln(R_{ij}) = R' \tag{5-36}$$

then we can get the answer by the mathematical programming problem.

$$q_{ij} = u_i v_j \cdot O_i D_j R_{ij}^{-\gamma} \tag{5-37}$$

This is the gravity model in section 5.3.2 where the impedance function is a power model.

If we add Eq. (5-30d) and Eq. (5-36) to the Eq. (5-35) at the same time, then we can get the answer by the mathematical programming problem.

$$q_{ij} = u_i v_j \cdot O_i D_j R_{ij}^{-\gamma} \cdot \mathrm{e}^{-bR} \tag{5-38}$$

This is exactly the composite gravity model in section 5.3.2, in which impedance function is power and index. The maximum Entropy model is also one of the stochastic probability models. The typical maximum entropy models are the Wilson model and the Sasaki model.

5.4.2 Opportunity Model

Opportunity Model is proposed by Schneider(1959) which introduces a spatial separation of a new measure. The number of intervening opportunities D_{ij} between the zone i and zone j is same as the number of opportunities at the destination that a center of the particle is 1 with a circle of radius 1. The number of competition opportunities O_{ij} between the zone i and zone j is the number of trip origins, which has better or at least equal accessibility than the travel from zone i to zone j. We can measure the travel starting point by the center that the particle is 1 with a circle of radius 1.

(1) Stouffer opportunity model

At first Stouffer opportunity model was used to simulate migration movement which indicates the number of people D_j arriving at a given distance is proportional to the number of opportunities to reach this distance and inverse proportional to the intervening opportunities D_{ij}.

$$q_{ij} = K\frac{D_j}{D_{ij}} \tag{5-39}$$

It should be noted that the model does not need calibration and can guarantee $\sum_i q_{ij} = D_j$ but cannot guarantee $\sum_j q_{ij} = O_i$ at the same time.

(2) Schneider opportunity model

Schneider opportunity model extended Stouffer's theory and introduced a new theory. Although the shorter time the better it is, but not every time to get the shortest time. This theory not only considers the shortest time, but also considers the next shortest time. The law takes into account the following equation developed by Schneider with each potential destination has the probability L of being received.

$$q_{ij} = O_i \{ \exp(-L \cdot D_{i,j-1}) - \exp[-L(D_{i,j-1} + D_j)] \} \tag{5-40}$$

The nature of this model is the ratio q_{ij} of traveler leave from zone j convert to the aggregate quantities of intervening opportunities D_{ij}.

$$q_{ij} = k\exp(-LD_{i,j-1}) = \frac{O_1 - \sum_{k=1}^{k=j} q_{ik}}{O_i} \tag{5-41}$$

5.4.3 Radiation Model

Simini proposed a radiation model for forecasting traffic distribution in 2012 according to the related data from Alabama and Utah. This model think that the travel distribution between the zone i and zone j is related to their populations P_i and P_j, and distance L_{ij}. However, this model does not use distance as the impedance function of the model. Construct trip distribution model by radiation mode in physics.

$$T_{ij} = T_i \frac{P_i P_j}{(P_i + s_{ij})(P_i + P_j + s_{ij})} \tag{5-42}$$

where, s_{ij} is the total number of people within the range of circle with center at i and radius equal to L_{ij}.

Unlike the gravity model, R_{ij} is replaced by variable s_{ij}. The radiation model is more convenient and concise than the gravity model as they do not need to calibrate the parameters and avoid the problem that traffic distribution mutual symmetry between zones in the gravity model.

5.5 Comparative Analysis of Different Models

The calculation method of q_{ij} mentioned above has their own pros and cons, as shown in Table 5-2.

Table 5-2 Analysis of pros and cons in different model

Prediction method	Pros	Cons
Growth factor method	· The structure is simple and easy to understand · Does not need travel time between the zones · Can predict hourly traffic volumes and daily traffic volume · Can predict O-D matrix for all traffic purposes · Particularly effective when the peripheral distribution of the O-D matrix change a little · Particularly effective to calculate the O-D distribution among railway stations	· Need a complete O-D matrix of the base year · Cannot be used when there is a large change as follows in the planning area a. The future division of the district changes b. The travel time or the tightness between the zones changes. Such as improve or increase the transport facilities c. When the land use pattern greatly changes, such as large-scale residential construction · If the traffic volume in O-D matrix at current is 0, then it will be 0 too in future traffic volume · If traffic volume in O-D matrix at present is very small, then the credibility will decrease

continued

Prediction method	Pros	Cons
Gravity model	· The impact of land use on the production and attraction can be taken into account · It is sensitive to the change in travel time between the zones for the construct of traffic facilities · Model construction is simple and can be applicable to any region · It can predict future O-D traffic volume even if there is no completed O-D table	· This is the application of the physics laws to social phenomena, which has some similarities but not entirely based on human actions · Use the single average traffic distribution for the study area has some problem · Travel distance distribution in the study area is not a fixed value and the travel distance coefficient is not necessarily constant, but the gravity model think it is constant · The travel time varies with travel model and time, while gravity model only considers one condition · As the distance between the zones tends to 0, the traffic volume tends to infinity, which not fit the fact. When distance is too short, the predict value could be high · It's difficult to have the travel time when we solve the traffic within the community · In order to make the forecast results coincide with the generation and attraction of future, we need to use the growth factor method for iterative calculation
Opportunity model	· The use of model is independent of the boundaries of the zones and the area · The calculation is relatively simple · As it uses distance to determine the priority order, so the accuracy of the distance is not greatly influence the travel as gravity model as · As the definition of the opportunity and the order of the zones are decided by the user, the use of model has great elasticity	· It is difficult to use it for unused people · It is hard to decide the L value · It is subjective arbitrary to decide L value as a constant value. Otherwise it did not consider the characteristics of the various parts of the region · It is hard to coincide the predicted attraction · It is difficult to obtain a reasonable standard of opportunity
Radiation model	· Can take into account the impact of population on traffic occurrence and attraction · No parameter calibration is required during the calculation · Considering the influence of distance on travel distribution to avoid the error of distributed decrease with the increase of distance · Avoiding the distance between the two points is always symmetrical distribution	· It is the application of the physics laws to social phenomena, which has some similarity, but not entirely necessarily based on human action · Need a lot of data to prove the consistency of the model in any region · Ignore the impact of travel time on travel distribution

5.6 Other Problems Need to Be Considered

5.6.1 Spare Matrix

In general, the trip matrix is almost a sparse matrix, that is, has a lot of 0 elements. For example, a survey region composed by 500 zones, about 250000 elements will have about 2.5 million expected trips during peak hours, about an average of 10 trips per district. Some O-D pairs especially originated from residential to work have higher trips while the other district has fewer trips. The method used to study the travel matrix may be roadside survey method. If the sampling rate is 20%, then the probability that an O-D is not observed is very high. At each survey point, when using the accurate sampling rate, the sampling trip matrix will be expanded with some corresponding error.

It is possible to fill in a blank matrix by using a sub-matrix method. In addition, it is also possible to fill in a blank matrix with a low value or another expanding matrix. However, the trip matrix generally has a certain error, which will enlarge during the process of expanding matrix.

5.6.2 Travel Outside the District

In the study area, especially in the planning area, it is reasonable to assume conditions of the comprehensive trip distribution model. However, many trips may have at least one end outside the planning area. The application of distribution model depends on travel distance or travel cost, but it isn't defined in the condition of outside trip. In this case, it is common to consider the outside trip and add them to the modeling process. Using roadside survey method (studying the entrance of study area boundary line) to determine the number of trips and distribution matrix on of inside and outside trips. Then using the growth factor method, such as Furness method to predict and update future year O-D matrix. The results of travel can be obtained by the model of production and attraction from the inside and outside. The data of the integrated constraint model in the area must be subtracted from the total trip and the trips in area.

5.6.3 Inner Trip

Considering the limitations of the zone system, the travel cost value of the mass connector can only be a rough value and an approximation of the true number. The concept of travel cost value within zones was roughly represented by the mass connector. Some commercial software allows the user to simulate travel model by adding or subtracting terminal costs. More precise control inner trip cost can make the gravity model fit better. It is common to assume that the inner trip is calculated at a fixed rate in trip generation model and when the traveler moves from the community center to the interior of the community, the inner trip are typically not loaded onto the network, causing not need detailed model. In practice, some inner trip use analogue network, which make sense to rough partitioning systems.

5.6.4 Production and Attraction; Start Point and End Point

Trip distribution model can be developed on the premise that each trip has travel a start point and end point. The nature of the model is to connect the start point to the end point, such as the start point of home based travel is home and the end point is work place(schools, shops etc.). It must be transformed into a generation-attraction matrix before assigning the trips to the road network. In general, the matrix is almost the same as we assuming each generation and attraction has same direction in one day.

However, when a short-term O-D matrix is needed, some trips are considered to be direction of production-attraction, others are the opposite direction. This problem can be solved in two different ways: one for single trip purpose to construct a matrix, such as set the working place was an only destination in all trips.

The other is to use the survey date directly to determine the proportion that most closely matches the trip destination matrix in different time of one day. Such as an early peak matrix may include 70% trips that from start point to end point and 15% trips that from end point to start point.

5.6.5 Modeling Error

Obviously, many practical problems reduce the accuracy of the modeling process, which reflect the imperfection of traffic model. This problem not only reflects in the distribution model, but also reflects in the other modeling.

Many small values in the travel matrix will enlarge the corresponding error after the matrix expansion or synthesis, such as the value between the 0-5 will enlarge to 20-30. Fortunately, some study has solved the question of how to calibrate the model and compare the calibrated result matrix to the original matrix. Sikdar and Hutchinson (1981) used data from 28 research communities in Canada to check and test the double-constrained gravity model and found that these models were poorly fitted with the random error in 75%-100%, which strongly suggests that such models should be cautiously used.

Using several parameters to simulate the travel matrix is a difficult task, so now we usually use gravity models. However, many people consider the influence of travel purpose on travel mode. Especially for shopping, entertainment and having more choices at the same time, application of comparison and selection for impedance function choices must need. In the mid-1980s, more people pay attention to the statistical methods and simulations method on their calculation in travel model errors. Statistical method is very powerful except for the error of data causing the output error. British transport assessment handbook (1985) analyzes the sensitivity of input data errors for distribution models. To some extent, the data error in the construction matrix is mostly based on the error data. Approximate analysis technique for estimating the output error due to sampling rate changes would be a major advance in the early 80s of 20th century. For example, Gunn established an approximate expression for estimating confidence interval of element in the gravity model. The 95% confidence interval elements(i, j) of travel times range from c_{ij}/q_{ij} to $q_{ij}c_{ij}$, whose confidence factor C_{ij} is given by:

$$C_{ij} = \exp[2(1/\sum_{ij} n_{ijk} + 1/\sum_{ij} n_{ijk} + 1/\sum_{ki} n_{ijk})^{0.5}] \quad (5\text{-}43)$$

where, n_{ijk} is the travel time of investigation area in sampling, only applicable to the survey plot evaluation error that generated by the sampling. Data acquisition and processing may also expand the error range. In addition, other sources of errors from model estimation are more difficult to quantify, such as the error generated by model simplifies the actual problem without completely representing the actual system, causing the confidence interval expand again.

Simulation technology is very important when the confidence interval of the model output results does not exist or difficult to develop. If the date required by the model does not have error, we can modify the types and errors of data to close the actual. This process, of course, need a lot of time and computer resources, and will repeat a lot to get a series of parameters and the data model we checked each time could be slightly different. This process also can analyzes the data error stability in model parameters.

In this case, the application needs some reasonable data to adjust and then use this predictive data to run the model. This result provides a method for the sensitivity of the variable for the model output.

5.6.6 Stability of Trip Matrix

Travel demand model rarely considers the problem that the stability of the travel matrix will change with the time. Based on past experience, the actual situation is not always unaltered. It is observed that the road network in any section of the daily traffic flow all have significant changes, which can predict the changes of traffic flow level for days or weeks (excluding seasonal variations).

Permanent and semi-permanent automatic flow counters can easily observe these changes for they are reliable and can easily install and maintain. Traffic flow changes are caused by at least two reasons: changes in the travel matrix and changes in the travel route, which causes the great daily changing range of trip matrix element value level. If rarely collect trip matrix data of different date in same place, we will get this information difficultly.

The traffic count can help modeler aggregate the travel behavior into the travel matrix, which can reduce the degree of random change of trip matrix. Leonard and Tough develop the complex simulation models based on O-D sets data (including itinerary and traffic counts) collected from the UK Reading Center for four consecutive days. Investigators record the number plate of the car to track their entrance into the reading center, route, export and parking point through the reading center. Thus, the error in the investigation and study did not exist. Only 10% of the 40 zones, 80 lines were collected from Monday to Thursday. The data are independently analyzed by Willumsen (1982) to observe the daily variation of the traffic flow and the O-D matrix level. And Willumsen also use percentage to represent the absolute error appeared in the traffic flow level and the travel matrix.

$$\%\text{MAE} = 100\% \times (\sum_a |V^a - V^b| / \sum_a V^a) \quad (5\text{-}44)$$

$$\% \mathrm{MAE} = 100\% \times \left(\frac{\sum_{ij} | t_{ij}^a - t_{ij}^b |}{\sum_{aij} t_{ij}^a} \right) \tag{5-45}$$

where a and b separately represent the traffic flow V and the O-D pair T_{ij} in different date. The findings of typical changes are shown in Table 5-3.

Table 5-3 Model validation error(%)

% MAE	Tuesday		Wednesday		Thursday	
	section	matrix	section	matrix	section	matrix
Monday	11	76	11	72	12	75
Tuesday			13	68	14	85
Wednesday					12	70

It can be seen that the daily changes in traffic levels are consistent with the forecast while the travel matrix level is very high for our dealing with smaller element values and sparse matrix, which have studied that the change in this level will be quite large.

These results show that it is not possible to obtain a very accurate trip matrix for the reasons that it is only a sample and the purpose of the model is not to copy the survey results or to obtain the basic travel matrix, but to estimate the character of basic travel matrix. When the traffic flow is distributed to the road network, the traffic flow rate is consistent with the survey results.

This result also suggests that we must be careful when assessing the planning values of trip matrix or testing the changing planning. And sensitivity analysis is well suited for studying the impact of various travel matrixes.

Practice see the relevant section of Appendix 2.

Exercises

1. What is the status and role of traffic distribution forecast in transportation planning?

2. Try to describe the idea of growth function method.

3. Table 5-4 shows the current distribution , the production and attraction of future (unit: million times). Try to use this information to get distribution of future by Fratar method. Set the convergence criterion was $\varepsilon = 3\%$. Judging whether the results of iterative three times is convergence (intermediate results after the decimal point to retain three significant figures).

Table 5-4 the current distribution, the production and attraction of future

O	*D*			Current	Future
	1	2	3		
1	4	4	2	10	20
2	3	4	5	12	20

continued

O	D			Current	Future
	1	2	3		
3	4	3	3	10	25
Current	11	11	10	32	
Future	25	28	22		65

4. What kind of travel distribution prediction methods should be adopted in the traffic distribution forecast of the new urban area and the old city and tell the reasons.

5. What are the commonly used impedance functions in the gravity model?

6. What are the calibration methods for the gravity model?

7. Try to describe the applicability, advantages and disadvantages of the gravity model.

References

[1] Shao Chunfu. Principles of Transportation Planning[M]. Beijing: China Railway Publishing House, 2004.

[2] Lu Huapu. Transportation Planning Theory and Method[M]. Beijing: Tsinghua University Press, 2006.

[3] Michael D. Meyer, Erik J. Miller, Urban Transport Planning[M]. Yang Xiaokuan, Trans. Beijing: China Architecture & Building Press, 1990.

[4] Wang Wei, Xu Jiqian. Urban Transport Planning Theory and Method[M]. Beijing: China Communications Press, 1992.

[5] Xiao Qiusheng, Xu Weici. Urban Transport Planning[M]. Beijing: China Communications Press, 1998.

[6] Ali Mekky, P. Eng. Analytical transportation planning[M]. America, 2001.

[7] Michael D Meyer, Eric J Miller. Urban Transportation Planning: A Decision-oriented Approach[M]. USA, 2008.

[8] Wang Wei. Intersection flow direction prediction model and its accuracy test. Academic Committee of Urban Roads and Traffic Engineering of the Society of Civil Engineering of China Civil Engineering Society. Proceedings of the National Conference on Urban Road and Traffic Engineering[C]. China Civil Engineering Institute of Urban Engineering, Academy of Engineering, Urban Road and Traffic Engineering Academic Committee, 1991.

Chapter 6

Modal Split Models

6.1 Overview

6.1.1 Introduction

Modal split is the third step of four-stage method for traffic demand forecasting, which mainly study the relationship between different modes and corresponding to the traffic volume between the zones, that is, the proportion of travelers using different modes. The process of modal split studies travelers' mode choice behavior usually basing on person trip survey data, then establish appropriate modal split model to forecast the changes in the demand for trips of different modes with the change of infrastructure and level of service conditions. The output is modal shares (percentages) or the total number of trips by mode.

Modal split step attempt to split the number of total trips of each zone into the shares of each mode. Fig. 6-1 reflects modal spit diagrammatic sketch when there are two modes (car and rail) between zone i and j. During the process, the characteristics of the modes and the characteristics of the travelers using those modes are the main factors affecting modal split (section 6.2).

Establishing the modal split model combining with the survey data and choosing the reasonable model is the most critical link of modal split stage.

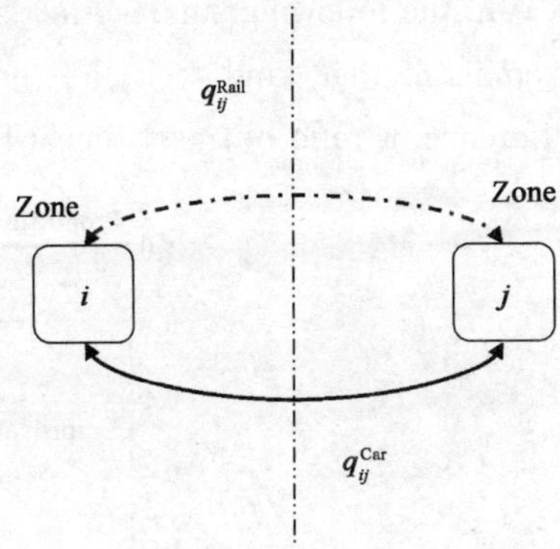

Figure 6-1 Modal split diagrammatic sketch

6.1.2 Development Process

The earliest model of modal split models is diversion curves model, originated in 1860s. Modal split models have conformed utility models, random utility models, direct demand models, discriminant models, aggregate models, disaggregate models and so on. The above models are widely used in the forecast of modal split shares, the analysis of traffic policy benefits and the impact analysis of traffic engineering projects. The development of modal split models is shown in Fig. 6-2.

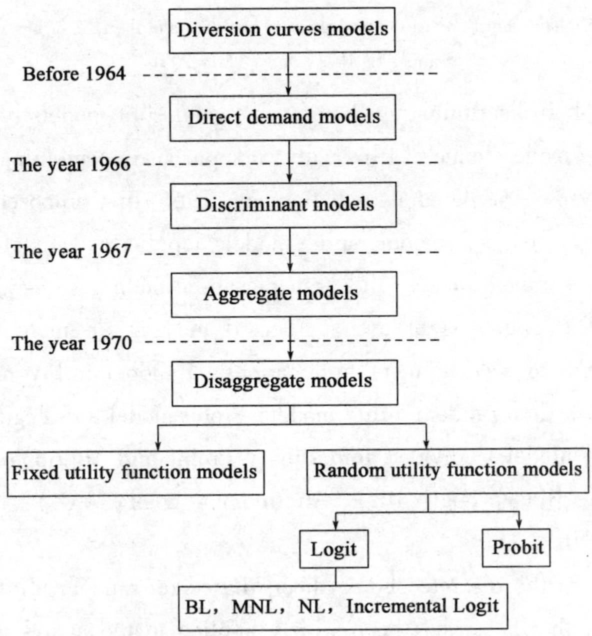

Figure 6-2 Development of modal split models

Early research mainly focused on the study of car travel. Because the competition between the auto and the transit was not fully understood, modal split model was not taken seriously. Later studies tried to calibration and use modal split model in the form of "diversion curves".

In addition, in the early research, there was no consensus on the role of modal split in the four-step model, and some scholars combined this step with the trip generation (trips are generated according to each mode separately).

Some researchers applied modal split after trip generation (considering that most of the objects of the model are work trips, so do not applied modal split after other two steps). A variety of socio-economic variables (e. g. household car ownership, population density) and factor of road network were used to describe and interpret modal split.

In the following studies, modal split is usually carried out after the trip distribution. The early attempts of that kind took the form of diversion curves where the explanatory variable was the difference or ratio of travel times(Fig. 6-3).

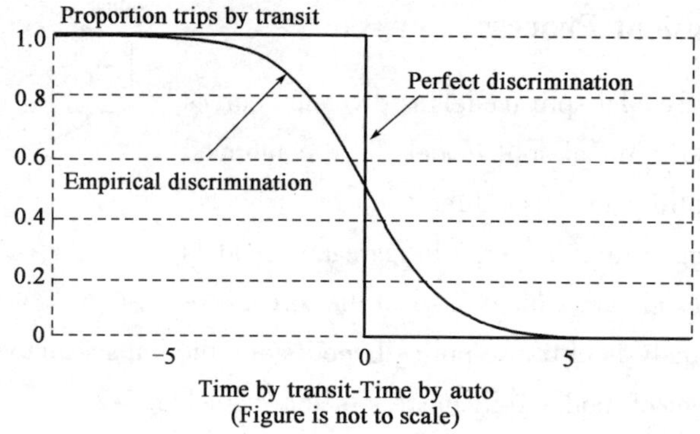

Figure 6-3 The relationship between the proportion of bus trips and the ratio of bus to car travel time

Source: *Ali Mekky and P. Eng*, 2001.

Warner(1962) applied discriminating thought in modal split models. Subsequently, Quarmby (1967) applied it in the mode choice of trips with work purpose, combining disaggregated data and binary mode in the analysis. And, Quandts and Baumol (1966) first proposed direct demand model. Before the late 1970s, most of modal split models applied aggregated models. With the diversification of regional travel modes and transportation planning, new transport policies are constantly published. Disadvantages of the aggregated models are more and more obvious and disaggregate models began to receive more applications. Random utility model is one method of disaggregate analysis. Based on random utility model, Probit model and Logit model can be derived. Among them, the Probit Model is divided into Binary Probit and Multinomial Probit model; Logit model is divided into the Binary Logit(BL), Multinomial Logit(MNL), Nested Logit(NL) and Mixed Logit model(MMNL), etc..

McFadden put forword the discrete choice theory based on random utility theory in1974. In the subsequent development, the theory has been widely applied to the analysis of individual or family behavior. Probit and Logit model are both discrete choice models, all kinds of discrete choice model can be derived from the random utility model. McFadden(1974) assumed that the random error term in the random utility model is independent and identically distributed in the Gumbel distribution, thus the MNL model is derived, and the BL model is a special case of the MNL model. Since the MNL model assumed that the schemes are independent from Irrelevant Alternatives(IIA), this assumption is clearly inconsistent with the actual situation. Based on MNL model, Williams(1997) assumed that there is some correlation between some programs; the programs which have obvious relevance are classified into the same group, thus derived NL model. Daganzo(1979) assumed that the random error term of the random utility model obeys a multinomial normal distribution, and then derived the Probit model. Because individual behavior choice is influenced by observable and unobserved factors at the same time and MNL, NL, Probit model can't consider individual choice preferences and other unobservable factors. Ben Akiva and Bolduc (1996) put forward Mixed Logit Model, which is also called MMNL model, on the basis of the existing Logit and Probit Model, considering the choice of factors can't be observed, such as the choice preferences of individual programs.

In view of the fact that the Logit Model is simpler and more convenient than the Probit Model in the model building and model calibration, it has been widely used in the field of traffic engineering, such as the road toll policy, in the prediction of modal split shares and so on.

6.2 The Main Factors Affecting Modal Split

Typically, there are many modes you can choose, for example, residents can choose many modes, such as private cars, commuter buses, public buses, taxis, and urban rail transit, cycling and walking in urban transport. The main factors that influence the choice of the traveler's mode can be divided into the characteristics of the traveler, the characteristics of the mode, the characteristics of location and the characteristics of trip.

6.2.1 The Characteristics of Traveler

(1) Household car ownership or availability

Availability of cars is an important factor influencing mode choice, and many residents are more likely to drive private cars as the car is convenient, comfortable, fast and so on. People use cars as their main travel mode in Japan, the United States, Germany and other developed countries. With China's rapid economic development, a growing number of urban and rural residents can also choose a car.

(2) Motor vehicle driving license

Whether residents have motor vehicle driving license, to a large extent, affects the mode choice of residents. To obtain automobile driving license is easy in the United States, Japan and other developed countries. Car driving license ownership is more than 90% of the population with proper age, so as to make it possible to have more car trips.

(3) Age, gender, income

People fewer than 18 years old and cannot drive cars usually choose the public transit trips. Due to the inconvenience of physical activity and abundant time after retired for the elderly, they generally choice to use public transit. People between 20 to 50 years old apply more auto trip than other modes as the needs of work. In general, the car utilization rate of males is higher than that of females. Residents who apply auto trip need to pay car purchase cost, fuel cost, maintenance fee, taxes, insurance and other expenses, so that income is one of the important factors which restricts car travel.

(4) Family structure

Members of the family, generally including retired elderly, young couples, children, etc.

Elder people are more inclined to take public transit, while young couples prefer to use car in the case of fulfilling all the conditions. At the same time, as the bicycle can't carry people and other regulations in some areas, some young couples who send their children to school or go shopping can only apply public transit or car travel.

6.2.2 The Characteristics of the Mode

(1) Travel distance and time

Travel time is one of the important factors affecting the mode choice. That is to say, when there are several available modes between origin and destination, the travel time of each mode has great influence on the mode choice of the travelers. According to the research results of Illinois Industrial University Research Institute, respectively 20% and 25% of the travelers applying private car and subway travel regard time as a major factor. Considering the choice between private car and bus, bus-selection of time as only 2%, and the family car was 44%. When people consider the choice between family cars and buses, the proportion that residents view the time as factor apply the bus is 2%, yet family car is 44%. In addition, the proportion of men (36%) view the time as choice factor were more than that women (25%) view. Consequently, planning urban transportation system, the running time of coordination between modes and transfer efficiency is one of the important factors.

As the distance increases, people's travel distance by walking, bicycles, motorcycles, buses, cars, rail, aircraft orders increase. Fig. 6-4 shows a reasonable travel distance for various modes.

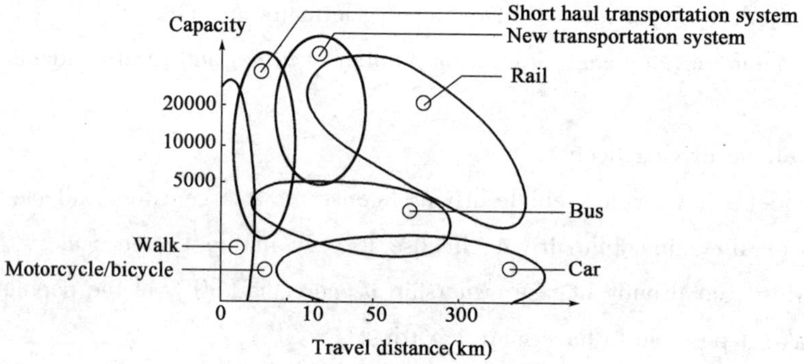

Figure 6-4 Reasonable travel distance for various modes

Source: *Shao Chunfu*, 2014.

(2) Cost, comfort

The cost of transportation modes is directly related to the comfort and travel time. In general, taxi or private car is faster, more comfortable and the travel time is relatively short, while the travel cost is relatively high. In many cases, travelers tend to select the best way of comprehensive benefits combined with the actual situation (economic condition, if in a hurry, state of health, etc.). For example, the cost of the taxi is relatively high for low-income people in a trip, but if consider the travel time, comfort and other indirect value on the purpose of the trip, people maybe choose to travel by taxi.

(3) Parking facilities and parking fees

One of the prerequisites for travelers to apply private car is parking space, if travelers don't have enough parking space or parking facilities in the destination (work places, major shopping malls, tourist attractions and other places of curbside) and nearby area, it will be hard to apply private car for travel, so the utilization rate of public transport is relatively high. At the same time, if the parking fee is too high, travelers will reduce the use of cars.

(4) Safety

People are very concerned about the safety of the trip process. If a certain mode is convenient, fast, and fulfills other characteristics, but the security is very poor, the passenger's personal safety can't be guaranteed, the traveler will not consider the mode. In fact, due to the sudden nature of the traffic accident, when people choose private cars to travel, considering the security of the mode is relatively small.

(5) Punctuality

In the urban traffic system, most people travel because of work, and the demand for punctuality is high. Subway, light rail transit and other mode avert traffic jams and departure interval is fixed, so it has good timeliness and reliability. The bus is easily affected by the traffic jam, punctuality is worse during the rush hour. In Japan, one of the main reasons why people choose to live near the subway or urban railway is the timing.

6.2.3 The Characteristics of Location

The characteristics of location include population density, population size, traffic facilities level, climate, parking space and parking fees. If population density is large, social facilities (schools, hospitals, supermarkets, gymnasium, tourism etc.) relatively complete and the flow of people is crowded in the area, the utilization rate of public traffic is relatively high. However, most of the travelers choose a bike or motorcycle, private car travel where geographical location is relatively remote and frequent bus departure is less. For where is always rainy and snowy, in poor weather, the utilization rate of public transportation is high. For some special geographical locations such as mountains, rivers, the utilization rate of car and bus is high.

6.2.4 The Characteristics of Trip

(1) Trip purpose

Trip purpose is divided into two types: rigid and elastic. For shopping, leisure and other elastic travel, people don't have high sensitivity of the travel time, and the buses, bicycles and other modes are convenient, economic, so people travel by public cars, bicycles, walking and etc. Otherwise, people have high sensitivity of the travel time for work and school, they usually choose cars, subway and light rail transit as subway and light rail transit delays less and car is flexible, comfortable and fast. For the long distance trip, people usually travel by trains, long-distance buses and private cars.

(2) Travel period

In different period of a day, the road traffic characteristics such as traffic structures, traffic jams are different. The priority of urban public transport during the peak hours of traffic congestion is obvious. People usually take the bus or subway to get off work. In holidays, the number of external traffic increased, at this time road traffic jam is heavy than usual, people usually travel by public transport. In the late night, bus or subway is out of service, people often use taxi or private car to travel.

6.3 Commonly Used Methods

For traffic models of modal split, there are different dimensions to classify the models. Fig. 6-5 shows that the modal split models could be classified along three dimensions: role within the other stages of the transport model, mathematical form and analysis unit. The aggregate and disaggregate approach use the zones and individuals as analysis units respectively. From mathematical form, modal split models can be classified by discriminative model or probabilistic model. The modal split models are classified by trip end models and trip interchange models form "the location within the other three stages of the model" point of view.

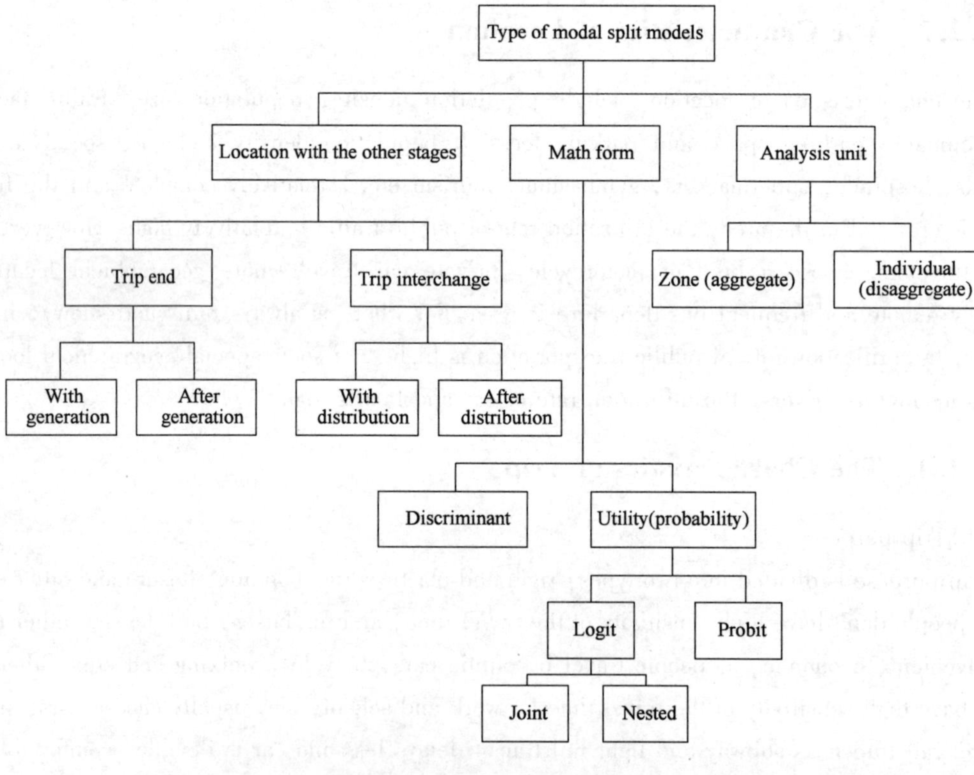

Figure 6-5 The type of modal split models

Source: *Ali Mekky, P. Eng*, 2001.

Just as the classification mentioned above, a discussion of each typical model is given below.

6.3.1 Diversion Curves Model

In the early studies, researchers used the method of diversion curves to describe modal split, and the main idea is to describe the function curve between modal split rae as and some explanatory variables(e. g. the difference of travel time or travel time ratio by two modes, the distance for each zone, the land use for each zone etc.) based on the individual trip survey(see Fig. 6-3 to Fig. 6-6 in section 6.1.2). There are some applications of diversion curves in China, examples are shown below.

Chang'an University and Zhejiang highway and water transportation engineering consulting corporation(2010) used the difference of general travel time for high speed rail(HSR) and high speed bus(HSB) as the abscissa, and calibrated the diversion curves of HSR and HSB based on survey. The effect of curve fitting as shown in Fig. 6-6.

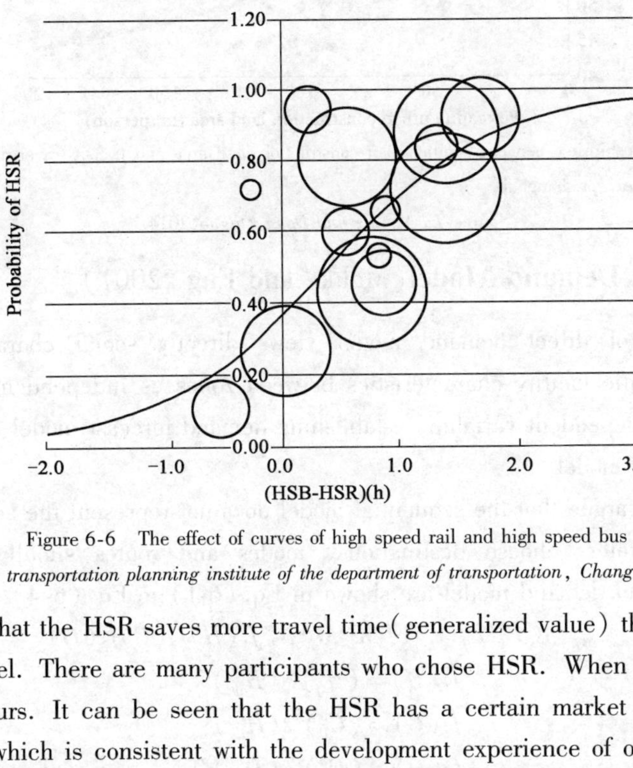

Figure 6-6 The effect of curves of high speed rail and high speed bus

Source: *The transportation planning institute of the department of transportation, Chang'an University.*

It can be seen that the HSR saves more travel time(generalized value) than the HSB especially in long distance travel. There are many participants who chose HSR. When HSR saves travel time between 0.7-1.0 hours. It can be seen that the HSR has a certain market share in the inter-city passenger transport which is consistent with the development experience of other countries for high speed railway. When HSR saves time between 0-0.4 hours, there are more than 0.5 probability of choosing HSR, which stating although high-speed rail can save travel time, but the HSB is still part of the passenger market.

Lu Ximing(2014) established the curve between construction land area per capita and the share rate of public transport about the main city of Shanghai, studying the relativity between the public transport share and land use in the main city of Shanghai. As shown in Fig. 6-7. The use rate of public transport is calculated as follows:

$$\text{Public transport share} = \frac{\text{Public transport trips}}{\text{Public transport trips} + \text{Car transport trips}} \times 100\%$$

From the above chart shows, the less per capita city construction land area, the higher public transport share. This shows that for the main urban areas, the greater population density of the area, the higher public transport share. Because the center of travel gathering, traffic congestion is serious, car travel convenience degree is low, so the travelers are willing to use public transportation.

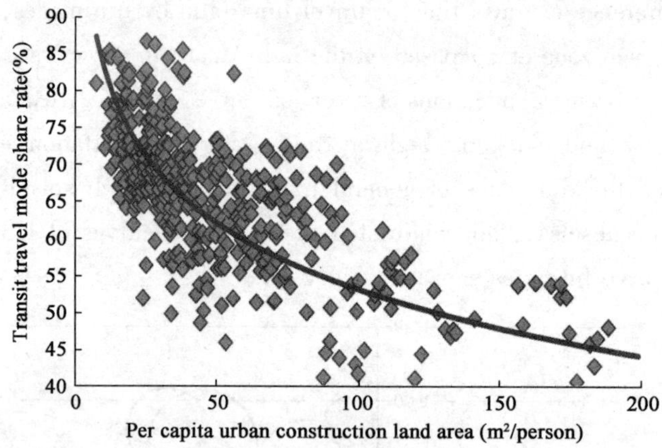

Figure 6-7 Relationship between per capita urban construction land area and transit travel mode share in main urban area of shanghai

Source: *Lu Ximing and Dong Zhiguo*, 2014.

6.3.2 Direct Demand Model (Mekky and Eng, 2001)

The basic idea of direct demand model views directly social characteristics, economic characteristics and traffic facility characteristics between zones as independent variables and some travel demand as the dependent variable, establishing demand forecast model, using survey data to solve and verifying the model.

Some researchers argue that the sequential model does not represent the actual decision making process and that travelers choose destinations, modes and routes simultaneously. The basic expressions of the direct demand model are shown in Eq. (6-1) to Eq. (6-4).

$$t_{ijk} = \alpha_0 P_i^{\alpha_1} P_j^{\alpha_2} Y_i^{\alpha_3} Y_j^{\alpha_4} M_i^{\alpha_5} M_i^{\alpha_6} N_{ij}^{\alpha_7} f_1(H) f_2(C) f_3(D) \tag{6-1}$$

$$f_1(H) = (H_{ij}^{\mathrm{b}})^{\beta_0} (H_{ijk}^{\mathrm{r}})^{\beta_1} \tag{6-2}$$

$$f_2(C) = (C_{ij}^{\mathrm{b}})^{\Gamma_0} (H_{ijk}^{\mathrm{r}})^{\Gamma_1} \tag{6-3}$$

$$f_3(D) = (D_{ij}^{\mathrm{b}})^{\sigma_0} (D_{ijk}^{\mathrm{r}})^{\sigma_1} \tag{6-4}$$

where, t_{ijk} is trips from zone i to zone j by mode k; P_i is population of zone i; Y_i is mean income at zone i; M_i is industrial character index for zone i; N_{ij} is number of modes serving zones i and j; H_{ij}^{b} is minimum travel time from i to j; H_{ijk}^{r} is relative travel time for mode k; C_{ij}^{b} is least travel cost from i to j; D_{ij}^{b} is optimum travel frequency from i to j; D_{ijk}^{r} is relative travel frequency for mode k.

6.3.3 Discriminant Model (Mekky and Eng, 2001)

(1) Fundamental model

The discriminant model is the earliest behavioral model used for the pattern division. It assumes that the traveler decides in a certain way, and then builds a model under this assumption to predict the choice of the traveler under the influence of relevant factors.

The method starts by defining a disutility function D_{kn}, expressions are as follows

$$D_{kn} = \alpha_{n1}x_{kn1} + \alpha_{n2}x_{kn2} + \cdots + \alpha_{nm}x_{knm} = \sum_{m} \alpha_{nm}x_{knm} \tag{6-5}$$

where, D_{kn} express as a travel benefit function of traveler n by mode k; α_{nm} are weight coefficients of independent variables; x_{knm} are independent variables (time, cost, distance, degree of comfort, etc.).

Assuming there are two modes 1 and 2, the traveler choose mode 1 instead of selecting mode 2, R_n less than zero, that is $R_n = D_{1n} - D_{2n} < 0$.

Define the following functions:

$$\text{sgn}_{ijn} = \begin{cases} 1, & R_n < 0 \\ 0, & R_n > 0 \end{cases} \quad (i < j) \tag{6-6}$$

Analysis of the data of N disaggregated samples can obtain N 0-1 triangular matrixes, Table 6-1 is the triangular matrix of the mode choices of n travelers.

Table 6-1 The 0-1 symmetric of matrix traveler n

	1	2	3	4	5	…	s
1	1	sgn_{12n}	sgn_{13n}	sgn_{14n}	sgn_{15n}	…	sgn_{1sn}
2	0	1	sgn_{23n}	sgn_{24n}	sgn_{25n}	…	sgn_{2sn}
3	0	0	1	sgn_{34n}	sgn_{35n}	…	sgn_{3sn}
4	0	0	0	1	sgn_{45n}	…	sgn_{4sn}
5	0	0	0	0	1	…	sgn_{5sn}
⋮	⋮	⋮	⋮	⋮	⋮		⋮
s	0	0	0	0	0	…	1

Notes: s represents travel n optional mode number.

Through the statistics the n upper triangular matrix, calculate the sharing rate of each mode of transportation.

Theoretically, the traveler choice mode 1 instead of mode 2, it will get a negative "R_n", vice versa. In practice, however, the perfect discriminant does not exist for the following reasons:

· The behavior of the traveler is sometimes not reasonable.

· The properties of the independent variable contained in the model are not very comprehensive.

· Measurement error, system error has been existed.

In this case, in order to reduce the error as much as possible and better applied the theory to practice, it need to minimize the error of α_{nm} and increase the accuracy of x_{knm}.

(2) Other models

In the study of the travel mode for the purpose of work, using the cost ratio or the exponential of cost ratio to define R_n as follows:

$$R_n = \frac{D_{1n}}{D_{2n}} \tag{6-7}$$

$$R_n = \ln \frac{D_{1n}}{D_{2n}} \tag{6-8}$$

Eq. (6-7) and Eq. (6-8) distinguish criterion is the ratio of the two travel modes, but not the difference between the positive and negative points.

In the UK, the generalized cost function is usually used to define the negative utility function as follows:

$$c_{kn} = \Theta_{k1} \mathrm{ta}_k + \Theta_{k2} \mathrm{tw}_k + \mathrm{tr}_k + \Theta_{n4} M_k \tag{6-9}$$

where, c_{kn} is the generalized cost function of traveler n by mode k; ta_k is the access time by mode k(e. g. walking to and from stations); tw_k is the waiting time by mode k; tr_k is the on-mode ride time; M_k is the money cost of travel by mode k; the count backwards of Θ_{n4} (also expressed as VOT or VOTT) is the time value of traveler n.

The disutility functions and the generalized cost function c_{ki} usually contain two types of variables: generic and mode specific variables. Note that socio-economic variables (person-specific) cannot be introduced in a difference function in a direct way as they would have no effect on it. To cope with that, Quarmby used two methods; namely:

· Combine them with generic variables to form new generic variables. For instance, travel cost M_k for a particular mode k can be divided by the person's income S_n to produce a new variable:

$$x_{kn} = \frac{M_k}{S_n} \tag{6-10}$$

· Use them as a set of alternative specific variables with one mode and zero with the other.

6.3.4 Utility Model

(1) Introduction

Travelers choose to travel with which mode is based on the comparison of comprehensive value of the trips between different modes. The comprehensive value is the utility of one trip; it is the measurement of attraction of travel mode. Typically, based on the consideration of their own factors and characteristics of alternative modes, the travelers will choose the travel mode with maximum utility according to the principles and interests of their own.

Before traveling, according to the characteristics of the travel (travel time flexibility, travel purpose, travel time, travel path characteristics, the time value of cost etc.) combined with the characteristics of different traffic modes (economic, safe, comfortable, fast, reliability, etc.) and their own conditions (income, health status, gender, age), travelers choose the comprehensive value of the best or better mode to travel. When we analyze travel mode choice, how to compare the comprehensive value of different modes for individual travel? We can use the utility function model to quantify comprehensive value of the corresponding travel mode, and then choosing the optimal travel mode. The utility of the traveler's trip mode is usually expressed as a function of the relevant attributes (trip characteristics, mode characteristics, traveler's characteristics).

Utility is one of the common concepts in Economics; it is usually the measurement of satisfaction of consumers' needs and desires. The utility of the travel mode is usually expressed as the comprehensive value of the attributes. In order to facilitate the mathematical treatment, the utility model is usually represented by a linear function, general expressions are as follows:

$$U_{kn} = \alpha_1 x_{kn1} + \alpha_2 x_{kn2} + \alpha_3 x_{kn3} + \cdots + \alpha_m x_{knm} \tag{6-11}$$

where, U_{kn} is the utility of traveler n travel by mode k; α is coefficient of each attribute.

(2) Constant utility theory

Based on the constant utility theory, when mode k brings the greatest utility for traveler n in a particular trip, then the traveler n will choice the mode k, the utility value of mode n meet the equation as follows:

$$\text{When } U_{kn} > U_{jn},\ \forall j \neq k \in J_n \tag{6-12}$$

$$p_n(k) = 1 \tag{6-13}$$

$$p_n(j) = 0 \tag{6-14}$$

where, J_n is the selective mode of traveler n.

We call this deterministic choice, and the probability of choosing the mode k is shown in Fig. 6-8.

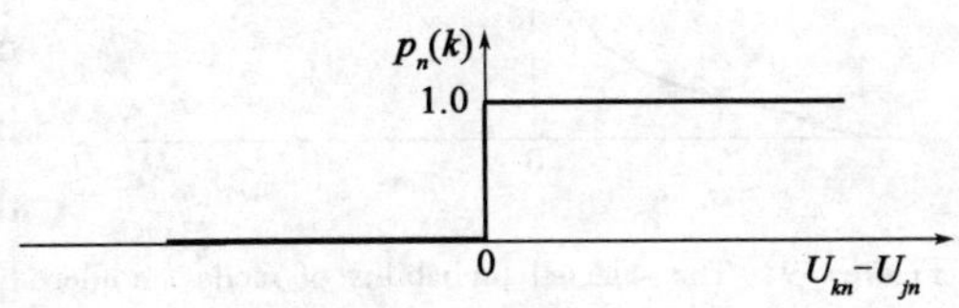

Figure 6-8 The selective probability of mode k in a deterministic choice condition

Eq. (6-9) assumes that the utility of alternative mode is fixed, the expression does not contain some unpredictable factors or a hidden attribute. The two probabilistic methods are distinguished by expression from the utility, the method called fixed utility approach, another is called random utility approach (described below).

(3) Random utility theory

The utility model can be divided into fixed utility model and random utility model. The utility of alternative travel modes is fixed in the utility model, and the utility model has no random error. Travelers will choose the most efficient mode to travel, and assume that the traveler will travel in accordance with the choice of probability formula, obviously the utility is a parameter in the formula. The random utility model takes into account the different individual traveler cognition on the same traffic in different ways, the same cognitive differences between individuals of different travel modes of transportation are different, the model error caused by traveler's specific environment, and the error is random. It is assumed that the random error term ε_{kn} obeys a certain probability distribution, and the total benefit is divided into a fixed benefit part and a random benefit part, obtained the following expression:

$$U_{kn} = V_{kn} + \varepsilon_{kn} \tag{6-15}$$

where, V_{kn} is the fixed utility of the traveler n by mode k, common expressions is:

$$V_{kn} = \beta_1 x_{kn1} + \beta_2 x_{kn2} + \cdots + \beta_m x_{knm} \tag{6-16}$$

Using this model to do the following analysis: for traveler n, when the random utility by mode k is maximum, the mode k is selected. The selected probability $p_n(k)$ of mode k represented as follows:

$$p_n(k) = [U_{kn} > U_{jn}, \ \forall j(\neq k) \in J_n] \tag{6-17}$$

Then obtain the Eq. (6-19):

$$\begin{aligned} p_n(k) &= p[\varepsilon_{jn} < V_{kn} - V_{jn} + \varepsilon_{kn}, \ \forall j(\neq k) \in J_n] \\ &= \int_{\varepsilon_{kn}} F[V_{kn} - V_{jn} + \varepsilon_{kn}, \ \forall j(\neq k) \in J_n] f_{kn}(x)\,\mathrm{d}x \end{aligned} \tag{6-18}$$

where, $F(-)$ is probability distribution function; $f_{kn}(x)$ is probability density function of probability variable $x = \varepsilon_{kn}$.

The meaning of Eq. (6-15): first assuming ε_{kn} is fixed, solving the probability distribution function corresponding to the mode j; secondly, when the probability of ε_{kn} change, and its probability density multiplied after integration.

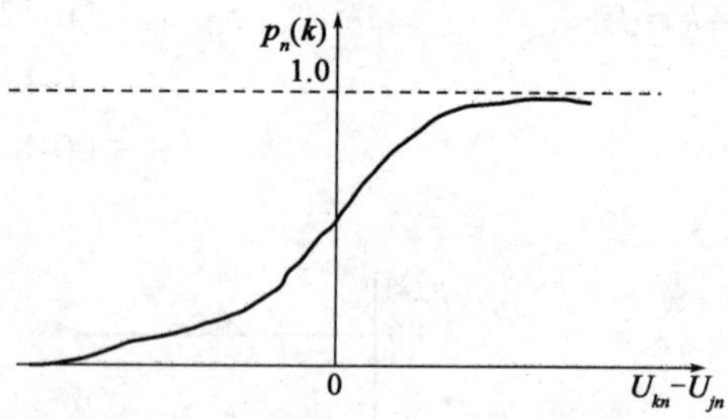

Figure 6-9 The selected probability of mode k under the condition of random error term

When the random error term is introduced: although the fixed benefit of mode k is smaller than the mode j, the traveler n has chosen the mode k to complete a trip. The reason is that it is difficult to measure the random error term when lack of information. After introducing the random error term, the probability selection curve of the mode k, j is shown in Fig. 6-9 as below:

The utility model is divided into Probit model and Logit model according to the function distribution type of random error term ε_{kn}. Among them, which ε_{kn} obey the normal distribution corresponds to the Probit model, and the Gumbel distribution corresponds to the Logit model.

(4) Probit model

For Eq. (6-15), with the assumption that the random error term obey the standard normal distribution, whose mean is 0, with finite variance covariance matrix (multivariance normal distribution), when $\varepsilon_{kn} \sim N(0, \Sigma)$, the expression of multivariate normal distribution with finite variance covariance matrix:

$$\begin{bmatrix} \varepsilon_{1n} \\ \varepsilon_{2n} \\ \vdots \\ \varepsilon_{kn} \end{bmatrix} = \begin{bmatrix} U_{1n} - V_{1n} \\ U_{2n} - V_{2n} \\ \vdots \\ U_{kn} - V_{kn} \end{bmatrix} \sim \mathrm{MVN}\left[\begin{bmatrix} 0 \\ 0 \\ \vdots \\ 0 \end{bmatrix}, \begin{bmatrix} \sigma_{11}^2 & \sigma_{12} & \cdots & \sigma_{1k} \\ \sigma_{21} & \sigma_{22}^2 & \cdots & \sigma_{2k} \\ \vdots & \vdots & \ddots & \vdots \\ \sigma_{k1} & \sigma_{k2} & \cdots & \sigma_{kk}^2 \end{bmatrix}\right] \tag{6-19}$$

where, σ_k^2 is the variance of random error term ε_{kn}; σ_{1k}, σ_{2k} is the covariance of random error term ε_{kn} and ε_{1n}, ε_{2n}.

From Eq. (6-15), we can get the Probit model as follows:

$$\begin{bmatrix} U_{1n} \\ U_{2n} \\ \vdots \\ U_{kn} \end{bmatrix} \sim \mathrm{MVN}\left[\begin{bmatrix} V_{1n} \\ V_{2n} \\ \vdots \\ V_{kn} \end{bmatrix}, \begin{bmatrix} \sigma_1^2 & \sigma_{12} & \cdots & \sigma_{1k} \\ \sigma_{21} & \sigma_{22}^2 & \cdots & \sigma_{2k} \\ \vdots & \vdots & \ddots & \vdots \\ \sigma_{k1} & \sigma_{k2} & \cdots & \sigma_k^2 \end{bmatrix}\right] \tag{6-20}$$

Using the above model, when given a fixed benefit V_{kn} and the variance and covariance of random error term, we can calculate the selection probability. In only two schemes, assuming utility of mode 1 is larger than mode 2, namely mode 1 is selected, we can get following equations:

$$p_{1n} = p(U_{1n} > U_{2n}) \tag{6-21}$$

$$p_{1n} = \Phi\left[\frac{V(1) - V(2)}{\sqrt{\sigma_1^2 + \sigma_2^2 - 2\sigma_{12}}}\right] \tag{6-22}$$

where, Φ is distribution probability of standard normal distribution function.

If there is mode 1, mode 2, mode 3 can be selected, and the utility of mode 1 is the maximum, the probability of mode 1 being selected meet the following probability equation:

$$p_{1n} = p[U_{1n} > \max(U_{2n}, U_{3n})] \tag{6-23}$$

Obviously, when there are 3 selected modes, calculating the largest utility of choice probability distribution function is complicated. When more than 3 kinds of modes are used to calculate the probability of the maximum utility, the Eq. (6-21) can be used as the basic idea, and then the maximum benefit can be solved successive iteratively, general form is as follows:

$$\max[U_{1n}, U_{2n}, \cdots, U_{kn}] = \max\{\max\cdots\max[\max(U_{1n}, U_{2n}, U_{3n})]\cdots, U_{kn}\} \tag{6-24}$$

When more than 3 modes can be chosen, the calculation of the Probit model is very complex, so this method is rarely used. In solving practical problems, the model with many variables is more complex. In order to make the model better fit the actual situation, not only establish the correct model, but also establish a more accurate solution to the general model is necessary. Therefore, we usually using Logit model to calculate the utility model of traffic mode choice.

(5) Logit model

For the Eq. (6-14), assuming that random error term ε_{kn} is independent, which obeys the Gumbel distribution $\varepsilon_{kn} \sim \mathrm{EV}(0,1)$. Define $x = \varepsilon_{kn}$, the distribution function of ε_{kn} is as follows:

$$F_e(x) = \exp[-\exp(-x)], \ (-\infty < x < \infty) \tag{6-25}$$

According to the theory of probability and statistics, the Eq. (6-26) can be as follows:

$$\begin{aligned} p_n(k) &= \int_{-\infty}^{\infty} \prod_{j \neq k} \exp[-\exp(-V_{kn} - V_{jn} + x)] \times e^{-x} \exp(-e^{-x}) \mathrm{d}x \\ &= \int_{-\infty}^{\infty} \prod_{j} \exp[-\exp(-V_{kn} - V_{jn} + x)] \times e^{-x} \mathrm{d}x \\ &= \int_{-\infty}^{\infty} \exp[-e^{-x} \sum_{j} \exp(V_{jn} - V_{kn})] e^{-x} \mathrm{d}x \\ &= \frac{e^{v_{kn}}}{\sum_{j} e^{v_{jn}}} \end{aligned} \tag{6-26}$$

Eq. (6-22) is the foundation of Logit model calculation, calculation and parameter of the probability of reckoning is simpler than the Probit model, and widely used. Only need to know each kind of optional transportation utility value, then the probability can be calculated. The logit model is specific described in section 6.4.

(6) The selection of model

The Probit model of random error obeys normal distribution, there is a relationship between the random error of different traffic modes, and for more than three of the traffic mode choice calculation is very complicated. Therefore, this model is more suitable for two modes to have interaction relationship between choices.

Logit model of random error term is Independent and Identically Distributed (IID), the transportation of random error has no correlation, and the model is relatively easy calibration, can easily handle a variety of traffic mode choice, and has been widely used in practice.

The tails of the Probit are relatively "thin". This makes the model relatively more sensitive to large values of the difference in the utility functions of the alternatives. If any such values occur due to data errors rather than actual effects, then the subsequent error calibration would be greater for a Probit model than for a Logit Model.

6.4 Classification and Characteristics of Logit Model

After 1970s, the urban transportation mode's development tends to be diversified, and the behavior of people's choice of travel mode is becoming more and more complex, traditional aggregate analysis has been unable to adapt to the changes. Disaggregate analysis model can contain that aggregated model cannot contain the individual factors, which can consider many of the traveler's own characteristics and social characteristics, so it began to be widely used.

The Logit model is characterized by its simplicity of calculation, relatively easy parameter calibration, and wide applicability, so the model is usually used to operate in the process of traffic planning. University of California Professor Daniel L Mcfadden is the inventor of the Logit model, who promoted the development of discrete choice analysis and applied to the field of transportation planning through the Binary Logit Model analysis of discrete probability selection problems. Logit model that have developed so far can be divided into Binary logit, Multinomial Logit, Nested Logit, Incremental Logit and other models

6.4.1 BL Model (Binary Logit Model)

BL model research on the modal split that only contain two transportation modes, which is a special form of MNL model (multinomial Logit model). With the diversification of urban travel mode, the urban traffic is becoming more and more complex, comprehensive, the continuous improvement and development of transportation system, the BL model is not suitable for the research of transportation system analysis.

The utility model is assumed to be a linear function, and the probability of mode 1 and mode 2 are calculated as follows:

$$P_n(1) = \frac{\exp(V_{1n})}{\exp(V_{1n}) + \exp(V_{2n})} \tag{6-27}$$

$$P_n(2) = \frac{\exp(V_{2n})}{\exp(V_{1n}) + \exp(V_{2n})} = 1 - P_n(1) \tag{6-28}$$

$$V_{in} = \alpha_1 x_{in1} + \alpha_2 x_{in2} + \cdots + \alpha_m x_{inm}, i = 1, 2 \tag{6-29}$$

BL model can be regarded as a special form of MNL model, so the modeling idea is similar to MNL model, the solution refers to the Fig. 6-15.

【Example 6-1】 *When traveler A, B go to work, they can choose from two modes that are respectively auto and transit, the effectiveness of the two modes to travel the function expression as follows:*

$$V_{Auto} = 2.0 - 0.8TT_{Auto} + 0.05Age + 0.1Income$$

$$V_{Transit} = -0.5TT_{Transit}$$

The attributes of traveler and mode see Table 6-2, *the probability of mode* 1 *and mode* 2 *by BL model calculation.*

Table 6-2 Traveler, travel mode attributes

Index	TT_{Auto} (min)	$TT_{Transit}$ (min)	Age (year)	Income (yuan)
A	15.4	30.2	25	20k
B	25.6	55.0	45	10k

【Sol.】 · *Taking the attribute values into utility function, calculated separately the travel utility value of A, B on the two modes, the results are shown in* Table 6-3.

Table 6-3 Travel effectiveness of each mode

Index	*A*	*B*
V_{Auto}	-7.07	-15.23
$V_{Transit}$	-15.10	-27.50

· *Taking the utility value into calculation formula of probability BL model, the probability of selection is shown in* Table 6-4.

Table 6-4 Travel choice probability

Index	*A*	*B*
P_{Auto}	1.000	1.0
$P_{Transit}$	0.000	0.0

【Example 6-2】 *Residents from i to j to have a car (auto) and bus (transit) two modes to choose. Among them, the car travel time is* 10 min, *bus travel time is* 15 min, *assuming that the Logit model is applicable, try to calculate the probability of choosing two modes (assuming* VOTT = 20 cents/min).

$$P_{ij}^{Auto} = \frac{\exp(V_{ij}^{Auto})}{\exp(V_{ij}^{Auto}) + \exp(V_{ij}^{Transit})}, P_{ij}^{Transit} = 1 - P_{ij}^{Auto}$$

$$V_{ij} = -0.03C_{ij}, C_{ij} = t_{ij} \cdot VOTT$$

【Sol.】 *There:*

$$C_{ij}^{Auto} = t_{ij}^{Auto} \cdot VOTT = 10 \times 20 = 200 \text{ cents}$$

$$C_{ij}^{Transit} = t_{ij}^{Transit} \cdot VOTT = 15 \times 20 = 300 \text{ cents}$$

$$V_{ij}^{Auto} = -0.03 \times 200 = -6, V_{ij}^{Auto} = -0.03 \times 300 = -9$$

Take the calculated into probability calculation formula:

$$P_{ij}^{Auto} = 0.951, P_{ij}^{Transit} = 0.049$$

6.4.2 MNL Model(Multinomial Logit Model)

The MNL model is suitable for the case of multiple choice branches, Fig. 6-10 shows the probability distribution of the available travel mode in a trip. Mode choice set J_n contains n alternative travel models.

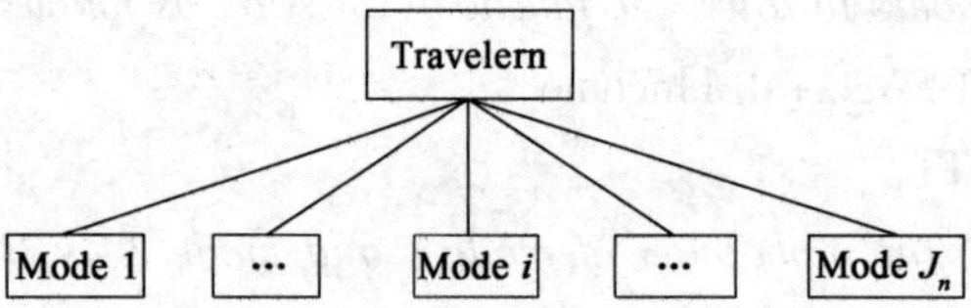

Figure 6-10 Available mode choices for traveler m

The derivation of the model can be introduced from two aspects. First, the use of Luce on the choice of probability theorem, that is, independence of irrelevant selection and also called IIA (Independence from irrelevant alternatives). Secondly, use the principle of utility maximization to make some distributional assumptions on the random error term of the utility function.

(1) Model origin

Luce theorem: If there are a number of options obey IIA, removing or introducing any other option will not affect the relative probability of choice between two choices.

Using this theorem, we can get the probability that the traveler n can choose three kinds of travel modes i, j, k; the mathematical expressions are as follows:

$$\frac{P_n(i)}{P_n(j)}=\frac{\exp(V_{in})}{\exp(V_{jn})} \tag{6-30}$$

$$\frac{P_n(k)}{P_n(j)}=\frac{\exp(V_{kn})}{\exp(V_{jn})} \tag{6-31}$$

Therefore,

$$\frac{P_n(i)}{P_n(k)}=\frac{\exp(V_{in})}{\exp(V_{kn})} \tag{6-32}$$

Comprehensive above three equations, then get:

$$\frac{P_n(i)+P_n(j)+P_n(k)}{P_n(j)}=\frac{\exp(V_{in})+\exp(V_{jn})+\exp(V_{kn})}{\exp(V_{jn})} \tag{6-33}$$

Due to $p_n(i)+p_n(j)+p_n(k)=1$, so there is the following equation:

$$P_n(j)=\frac{\exp(V_{jn})}{\exp(V_{in})+\exp(V_{jn})+\exp(V_{kn})} \tag{6-34}$$

The probability that the traveler n choose the mode k is expressed in the form of the MNL model as follows:

$$P_n(k)=\frac{\exp(V_{kn})}{\sum_{j\in C_n}\exp(V_{jn})} \tag{6-35}$$

Making the assumption that the random error term ε_{kn} in the utility can also get MNL, Hypothetical ε_{kn} obeys:

- Independent distribution;
- Same distribution;
- The gumbel distribution of position parameter Ω and scale parameter $\mu>0$.

Note that the Gumbel distribution can be expressed as follows:

$$F(\varepsilon) = \exp[-e^{-\mu(\varepsilon-\Omega)}], \mu > 0 \tag{6-36}$$

$$f(\varepsilon) = \mu\{\exp[-\mu(\varepsilon-\Omega)]\}\exp[-e^{-\mu(\varepsilon-\Omega)}] \tag{6-37}$$

In the formula, Ω is location parameter; μ is a positive scaling parameter.

The distribution characteristics of random error term ε are as follows:

· The mode is Ω;

· Mean value is $\Omega + \Gamma/\mu$, the Γ is Euler constant (usually 0.577);

· Variance is $\pi^2/6\mu^2$;

· If ε_{in} and ε_{kn} are independent identically distributed in the Gumbel distribution, corresponding parameters is (Ω_{in}, μ) *and* (Ω_{kn}, μ), then, $\varepsilon^* = \varepsilon_{in} - \varepsilon_{kn}$ is subject to the logic (logistic) distribution:

$$F(\varepsilon^*) = \frac{1}{1 + \exp[\mu(\Omega_{kn} - \Omega_{in} - \varepsilon^*)]} \tag{6-38}$$

Scale parameter μ is not fixed, usually set to 1.

In the above discussion, the form of V_{kn} is unrestricted. In practice, however, it is usually a form of linear combinations of parameters $\beta' x_{kn}$. Therefore, the model is:

$$P_n(k) = \frac{\exp(\alpha' x_{kn})}{\sum_{j \in J_n} \exp(\alpha' x_{jn})} \tag{6-39}$$

In the formula,

$$\alpha' x_{in} = V_{kn} = \alpha_1 x_{kn1} + \alpha_2 x_{kn2} + \alpha_3 x_{kn3} + \cdots + \alpha_m x_{knm} \tag{6-40}$$

(2) MNL properties

· There are two limiting cases:

When $\mu \to 0$, the variance of the perturbation term $\pi^2/6\mu^2$ is approximated to infinity. Therefore, the choice model can't provide useful information, so the choice probability of each travel mode is roughly equal.

$$\lim_{\mu \to 0} P_n(k) = \frac{1}{J_n} \qquad k \in C \tag{6-41}$$

where, J_n is the alternatives of scheme set C.

When $\mu \to \infty$, the variance of the utility disturbance is close to 0 and becomes a deterministic value.

$$\lim_{\mu \to \infty} P_n(k) = 0 \qquad V_{kn} < \max V_{jn} \tag{6-42}$$

$$\lim_{\mu \to \infty} P_n(k) = 1 \qquad V_{kn} > \max V_{jn} \tag{6-43}$$

If the effectiveness of certain travel modes meets the following conditions:

$$V_{kn} = \max(V_{jn}) \quad, j \in C_n, j \neq k \tag{6-44}$$

$$V_{kn} = \max(V_{jn}), j \in C_n, k = 1, 2, 3 \cdots, J_n^* \tag{6-45}$$

Then, the limit probability for selected scheme in scheme set C_n which have n^* schemes is $1/n^*$. If in scheme set $C_n - C_{n^*}$ which haves $n - n^*$ schemes, the corresponding limit probability is 0.

· Independent from irrelevant alternatives——IIA

The IIA property indicates that the ratio of the selection probability of any two travel modes is unrelated to the utility of others, that is to say:

$$\frac{P_n(i)}{P_n(1)}=\frac{\exp(V_{in})/\sum_j\exp(V_{jn})}{\exp(V_{1n})/\sum_j\exp(V_{jn})}=\frac{\exp(V_{jn})}{\exp(V_{in})}=\exp(V_{in}-V_{1n}) \tag{6-46}$$

In the formula, all of $\sum$ this is accepted $j\in C_n$.

In other words, IIA indicates that if the travelers n increase(or decrease) some travel modes on the basis of travel mode choice set and get a new set J'_n, the ratio of selection probability of two travel modes does not change. In other word,

$$\frac{P_n(i/J'_n)}{P_n(j/J'_n)}=\frac{P_n(i/J_n)}{P_n(j/J_n)} \tag{6-47}$$

However, the IIA property can lead to some deviations or errors in prediction, and the classic red and blue bus paradox explains its defects.

(3) Red and blue bus paradox based on IIA

There are two possible travel modes that can be chosen by the traveler n, respectively the car and the bus(assuming that all are red), which means that $V_{\text{car}/n}$ and $V_{\text{bus}/n}$ are equal, probabilities are as follows:

$$p_n(\text{car})=\frac{1}{2} \tag{6-48}$$

$$p_n(\text{bus})=\frac{1}{2} \tag{6-49}$$

Now adding a kind of blue bus, the other properties of the bus is the same as the red bus in addition to the color. In the IIA principle, the ratio of the choice probability is a fixed constant, so that the probability of the three travel modes is as follows:

$$p_n(\text{car})=p_n(\text{blue bus})=p_n(\text{red bus})=\frac{1}{3} \tag{6-50}$$

Obviously this is not realistic, because the traveler will view a bus trip as a travel mode according to the following probability to choose.

$$p_n(\text{car})=1/2 \tag{6-51}$$

$$p_n(\text{red bus})=1/4 \tag{6-52}$$

$$p_n(\text{blue bus})=1/4 \tag{6-53}$$

When resident travel, the actual choice probability results for the red and blue buses are inconsistent with the characteristics of IIA, and the MNL model is not suitable for random error correlation between some schemes.

It is worth noting that the nature of the IIA can only be applied to the same kind of traveler rather than to the whole. This can be explained by many examples. Imagine that a city's population is made up of two parts, and that the number of people in each part is of little difference. The city's two shopping centers are the main destinations for urban residents shopping trip, as shown in Table 6-5. Now a new shopping center is set up next to it, which has similar attributes to the existing shopping center. The computing results of the new choice ratio of urban residents shopping are shown in Table 6-5. Note that the nature of IIA applies to each group, but not to the entire population.

Table 6-5 Changes of urban population trip distribution ratio

Before new centre	CBD	Suburb 1	Suburb 2
Group 1	0.95	0.05	—
Group 2	0.05	0.95	—
Population share	0.5	0.5	—
After new centre	CBD	Suburb 1	Suburb 2
Group 1	0.9048	0.0476	0.0476
Group 2	0.0256	0.4872	0.4872
Population share	0.4652	0.2674	0.2674

Note: *data sources* (*Ben-Akiva and Lermen*, 1985).

(4) MNL modeling procedure

First, by analyzing the collected disaggregate data, the attribute vector B and utility function are determined. Secondly, the likelihood function L is constructed and the maximum likelihood estimation method is used to solve the optimal estimation $\hat{\theta}$ of the parameter vector θ. Finally, according to the covariance matrix of the vector θ, carries on the statistical test to each element. The specific steps are shown in Fig. 6-11.

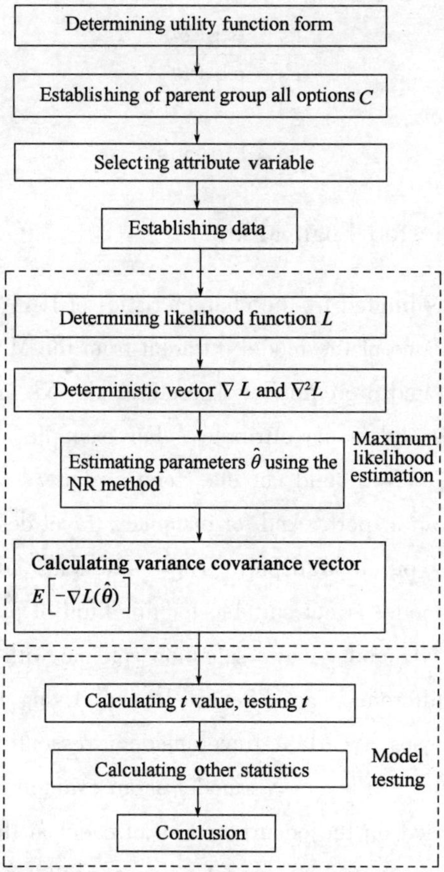

Figure 6-11 MNL modeling steps

Soruce: *Guan Zhihong*, 2004.

【**Example 6-3**】 *There are three travel modes connecting zone A and B, the travel time of three connecting modes respectively are* : 10, 9, 8 min. *The corresponding traffic volume of each connected mode respectively are* : 250330420 pcu/h, *try to establish multi-path probability assignment model, solving the distribution of parameter values* θ.

【**Sol.**】 · *Assuming* $t_1 = 10, t_2 = 9, t_3 = 8$, *solving the traffic volume sharing rate for each mode*:

$$p_1 = \frac{250}{250 + 330 + 420} = 0.25$$

$$p_2 = \frac{330}{250 + 330 + 420} = 0.33$$

$$p_3 = \frac{420}{250 + 330 + 420} = 0.42$$

· *Establishing mode utility function and taking it into probability calculation formula of MNL model, solving a parameter* θ.

$$V_1 = \theta t_1 \qquad V_2 = \theta t_2 \qquad V_3 = \theta t_3$$

Take mode 1, 2 *for example*:

$$\frac{P_1}{P_2} = \frac{\exp(\theta t_1)}{\exp(\theta t_2)}$$

Taking into the data obtains:

$$\theta = -0.278$$

6.4.3 NL Model (Nested Logit Model)

Because the MNL model is limited by the characteristics of IIA, researchers proposed the MNL model. Stratification is the essence of the model different from the MNL model, and precondition of IIA property is MNL model applied prerequisite. Therefore, the NL model focuses on the analysis of the probability of travel modes with same attributes. For example, the choice of a certain travel mode include the general bus, subway and car etc. for traveler n, while the conventional bus and subway are the nature of public transport. And for instance, travel destination, departure time, path analysis of traveler n travel by public transport. These problems are on the premise of choosing public transport modes, MNL model is not suitable for this kind of problem and so on.

The layering principle of NL model views selection scheme with large similarity as same level and takes schemes of large differences as different levels. Using the NL model to analyze the probability that a traveler chooses a certain travel mode is essentially the calculating process of conditional probability. Take the two layers NL model as an example (Fig. 6-12), the occurrence of an event at the first level is based on the occurrence of an event at the second level.

Take the two layers structure of the NL model as an example to study its modeling ideas, the basic steps are shown in Fig. 6-13.

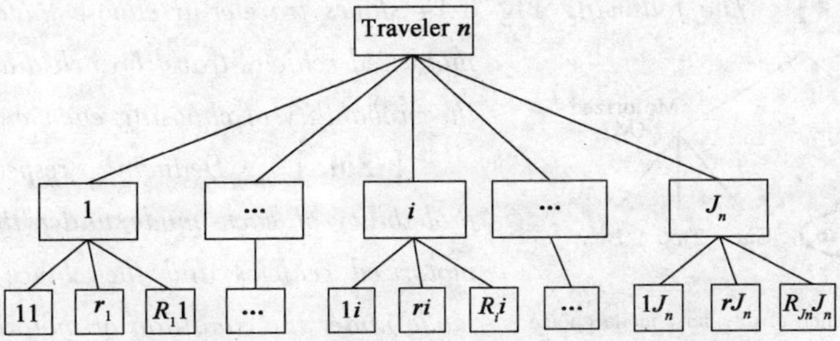

Figure 6-12 Trip optional mode structure of traveler n

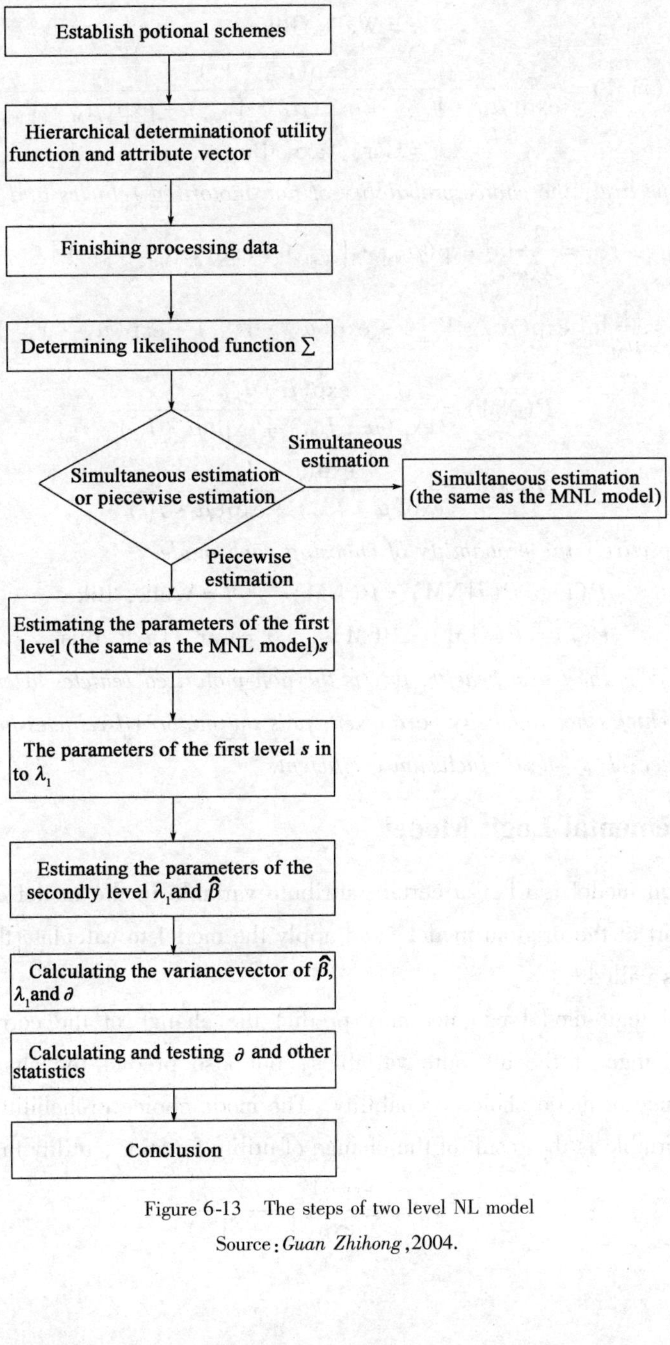

Figure 6-13 The steps of two level NL model

Source: *Guan Zhihong*, 2004.

【Example 6-4】 *The following* Fig. 6-14 *shows traveler* n *choose motorized vehicles, non-motorized vehicles travel branch diagram. Try to deduce the probability of choosing each mode.*

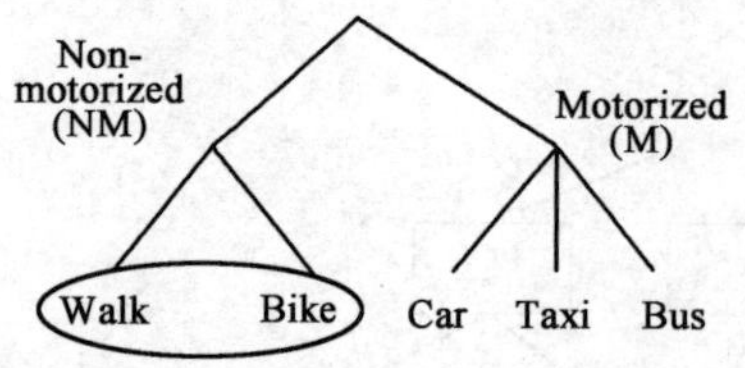

Figure 6-14 The branch of traveler i mode choice

【Sol.】 · *Deducing respectively the choice probability of each mode under the condition of non-motorized vehicles and the choice probability of each mode under the condition of motorized vehicles.*

$$P(i|\text{NM})=\frac{\exp(\mu_{\text{NM}}\cdot V_i)}{\exp(\mu_{\text{NM}}\cdot V_{\text{Walk}})+\exp(\mu_{\text{NM}}\cdot V_{\text{Bike}})}$$

$$i=\text{Walk, Bike}$$

$$P(i|\text{M})=\frac{\exp(\mu_{\text{M}}\cdot V_i)}{\exp(\mu_{\text{M}}\cdot V_{\text{Car}})+\exp(\mu_{\text{M}}\cdot V_{\text{Taxi}})+\exp(\mu_{\text{M}}\cdot V_{\text{Bus}})}$$

$$i=\text{Car, Taxi, Bus}$$

· *Deducing respectively the choice probability of non-motorized vehicles and motorized vehicles.*

$$I_{\text{NM}}=\frac{1}{\mu_{\text{NM}}}\ln[\exp(\mu_{\text{NM}}\cdot V_{\text{Walk}})+\exp(\mu_{\text{NM}}\cdot V_{\text{Bike}})]$$

$$I_{\text{M}}=\frac{1}{\mu_{\text{M}}}\ln[\exp(\mu_{\text{M}}\cdot V_{\text{Car}})+\exp(\mu_{\text{M}}\cdot V_{\text{Taxi}})+\exp(\mu_{\text{M}}\cdot V_{\text{Bus}})]$$

$$P(\text{NM})=\frac{\exp(\mu\cdot I_{\text{NM}})}{\exp(\mu\cdot I_{\text{NM}})+\exp(\mu\cdot I_{\text{M}})}$$

$$P(\text{M})=\frac{\exp(\mu\cdot I_{\text{M}})}{\exp(\mu\cdot I_{\text{NM}})+\exp(\mu\cdot I_{\text{M}})}$$

· *Deducing respectively the probability of choosing each mode.*

$$P(i)=P(i|\text{NM})\cdot P(\text{NM})\qquad i=\text{Walk, Bike}$$

$$P(i)=P(i|\text{M})\cdot P(\text{M})\qquad i=\text{Car, Taxi, Bus}$$

In the formula, V is the travel benefit; μ_{NM} is the non-motorized vehicles heterogeneity parameter; μ_M is the motorized vehicles heterogeneity parameter; μ is the motorized vehicles-non-motorized vehicles heterogeneity parameter; I is "nest" inclusion coefficient.

6.4.4 Incremental Logit Model

Incremental Logit model is when a certain attribute variable in the model change, just change the corresponding part of the original model, and apply the model to calculate the new mode choice probability, which is called.

The incremental logit model can not only predict the change of the correlated mode choice probability by the change of the attribute variables, but also predict the change of the attribute variables by the change of mode choice probability. The mode choice probability after the change of a certain attribute variable is the result of the change of utility function, utility function is as follows:

$$P_n'(k)=\frac{\exp(V_{kn}+\delta V_{kn})}{\sum_{j\in J_n}\exp(V_{jn}+\delta V_{jn})}\tag{6-54}$$

$$\delta V_{kn} = \sum_m \alpha_m \delta x_{knm} \tag{6-55}$$

where, δV_{kn} is utility change for travel n use mode i; δx_{knm} is the change of the property variable under the condition of the travel n use mode i.

At the same time the numerator and denominator are divided by $\sum_{j \in J_n} \exp(V_{jn})$, obtaining the deformation of the incremental logit model as follows:

$$P_n'(k) = \frac{P_n(k)\exp(\delta V_{kn})}{\sum_{j \in J_n} P_n(j)\exp(\delta V_{jn})} \tag{6-56}$$

Therefore, in order to predict the outcome of the change, it is necessary to know the choice probability of each mode and change in utility due to variation of variables in the base year. Therefore, there is:

$$\delta P_n(k) = P_n'(k) - P_n(k) = P_n(k)\left[\frac{\exp(\delta V_{kn})}{\sum_{j \in J_n} P_n(j)\exp(\delta V_{jn})} - 1\right] \tag{6-57}$$

6.5 Calibration and Solution of Logit Model

In theory, the maximum likelihood method or least square method is used to calibrate the parameters of Logit Model. In fact, in order to improve the work efficiency, applying some analytical software to complete the model parameters calibration such as SPSS, STATA, BIOGEME, NLogit, ALogit and so on. The following examples will better understand the application of each method.

6.5.1 Maximum Likelihood Method

The goal of the model calibration is to get the parameters of the model, and the calibration method of any model is based on the information provided by the sample. Taking the MNL model as an example, the maximum likelihood method is used to calibrate the model parameters, steps are as follows:

(1) Get the basic data

Obtain the mode choice and property of each travel mode from 20 travelers by surveying, as shown in Table 6-6.

Table 6-6 The data of personal travel survey

Id	Choice	Purpose	TC_{Car}	TC_{Rail}	TC_{Bus}	TT_{Car}	TT_{Rail}	TT_{Bus}
1	0	2	1500	4000	4500	60	120	150
2	0	2	1500	2800	3500	75	100	130
3	1	1	9000	3120	5600	90	105	95
4	0	2	1600	4000	3800	150	120	120
5	1	1	4500	4200	5000	120	150	115
6	2	2	5000	5200	3000	95	75	55

continued

Id	Choice	Purpose	TC_{Car}	TC_{Rail}	TC_{Bus}	TT_{Car}	TT_{Rail}	TT_{Bus}
7	1	1	3500	2700	3600	90	110	105
8	2	2	3000	3000	2000	120	120	125
9	0	2	3400	4000	3600	90	120	110
10	2	1	4000	5250	2500	120	110	125
11	0	1	1000	2500	1500	85	90	90
12	1	2	3000	3500	3500	105	90	100
13	2	2	3500	3500	3000	80	70	65
14	0	2	4000	4000	4000	80	90	95
15	2	1	3500	3500	3500	90	120	80
16	0	2	1500	3500	3600	150	75	70
17	1	3	1000	2800	1600	105	90	100
18	1	3	2000	2450	2300	135	90	110
19	0	2	1000	3500	2000	120	120	105
20	2	2	5000	3500	1000	90	90	55

Note: *Id is the number of traveler*; *PURPOSE is trip purpose*(*1-commuting*, *2-shopping*, *3-others*).

Choice is travel mode(0 is Car, 1 is Rail, 2 is Bus).

TC_{Car} is car travel cost, TC_{Rail} is rail travel cost, TCB_{us} is bus travel cost.

TT_{Car} is car travel time, TT_{Rail} is rail travel time, TC_{Bus} is bus travel time.

(2) Determine the characteristic parameter and utility function

This example only use the characteristic parameter TC (travel cost) and TT (travel time) as the independent variables. The utility functions for each travel mode are as follows:

$$V_0 = \theta_3 \cdot TC_{Car} + \theta_4 TT_{Car} \tag{6-58}$$

$$V_1 = \theta_1 + \theta_3 \cdot TC_{Rail} + \theta_4 TT_{Rail} \tag{6-59}$$

$$V_2 = \theta_2 + \theta_3 \cdot TC_{Bus} + \theta_4 TT_{Bus} \tag{6-60}$$

Using the basic formula of MNL model as results:

$$P_{0n} = e^{V_{0n}} / \sum_{i \in J_n} e^{V_{in}} \tag{6-61}$$

$$P_{1n} = e^{V_{1n}} / \sum_{i \in J_n} e^{V_{in}} \tag{6-62}$$

$$P_{2n} = e^{V_{2n}} / \sum_{i \in J_n} e^{V_{in}} \tag{6-63}$$

The property variable of utility function for each travel model as follows:

$$X_0 = (x_{01}, x_{02}, x_{03}, x_{04}) = (0, 0, TC_{Car}, TT_{Car}) \tag{6-64}$$

$$X_1 = (x_{11}, x_{12}, x_{13}, x_{14}) = (1, 0, TC_{Rail}, TT_{Rail}) \tag{6-65}$$

$$X_2 = (x_{21}, x_{22}, x_{23}, x_{24}) = (0, 1, TC_{Bus}, TT_{Bus}) \tag{6-66}$$

The uncalibrated parameters as follows:

$$\theta = (\theta_1, \theta_2, \theta_3, \theta_4) \tag{6-67}$$

(3) Data collation

The raw data cannot be used in model, usually processing raw data based on the model, then used in calibrating the parameter, the result of processing survey data from personal travel as shown in Table 6-7.

Table 6-7 The structure of model calibrate date

n	i	Selection δ_{in}	The inherent dummy		x_{in3}	x_{in4}	n	i	Selection δ_{in}	The inherent dummy		x_{in3}	x_{in4}
			x_{in1}	x_{in2}						x_{in1}	x_{in2}		
	0	1	0	0	1500	60		0	1	0	0	1000	85
1	1	0	1	0	4000	120	11	1	0	1	0	2500	90
	2	0	0	1	4500	150		2	0	0	1	1500	90
	0	1	0	0	1500	75		0	0	0	0	3000	105
2	1	0	1	0	2800	100	12	1	1	1	0	3500	90
	2	0	0	1	3500	130		2	0	0	1	3500	100
	0	0	0	0	9000	90		0	0	0	0	3500	80
3	1	1	1	0	3120	105	13	1	0	1	0	3500	70
	2	0	0	1	5600	95		2	1	0	1	3000	65
	0	1	0	0	1600	150		0	1	0	0	4000	80
4	1	0	1	0	4000	120	14	1	0	1	0	4000	90
	2	0	0	1	3800	120		2	0	0	1	4000	95
	0	0	0	0	4500	120		0	0	0	0	3500	90
5	1	1	1	0	4200	150	15	1	0	1	0	3500	120
	2	0	0	1	5000	115		2	1	0	1	3500	80
	0	0	0	0	5000	95		0	1	0	0	1500	150
6	1	0	1	0	5200	75	16	1	0	1	0	3500	75
	2	1	0	1	3000	55		2	0	0	1	3600	70
	0	0	0	0	3500	90		0	0	0	0	1000	105
7	1	1	1	0	2700	110	17	1	1	1	0	2800	90
	2	0	0	1	3600	105		2	0	0	1	1600	100
	0	0	0	0	3000	120		0	0	0	0	2000	135
8	1	0	1	0	3000	120	18	1	1	1	0	2450	90
	2	1	0	1	2000	125		2	0	0	1	2300	110
	0	1	0	0	3400	90		0	1	0	0	1000	120
9	1	0	1	0	4000	120	19	1	0	1	0	3500	120
	2	0	0	1	3600	110		2	0	0	1	2000	105
	0	0	0	0	4000	120		0	0	0	0	5000	90
10	1	0	1	0	5250	110	20	1	0	1	0	3500	90
	2	1	0	1	2500	125		2	1	0	1	1000	55

Note: $\delta_{in}=1$ is chosen; $\delta_{in}=0$ is not chosen.

(4) Determine the likelihood function

The maximum-likelihood estimator is the most likely parameter value of model for the observed sample. The probability of any sample being chosen need to be considered in the set of observations N (where $N=20$). Since the set of observations is chosen randomly from the whole populations, the probability of whole sample "L" is the result of multiplying the probability of each observed samples. It is defined as follows:

$$L^* = \prod_{n=1}^{20} \prod_{i \in J_n} P_{in}^{\delta_{in}} \tag{6-68}$$

$$P_{0n}^{\delta_{0n}} \cdot P_{1n}^{\delta_{1n}} \cdot P_{2n}^{\delta_{2n}} = \prod_{i \in J_n} P_{in}^{\delta_{in}} \tag{6-69}$$

Since it is more convenient to calculate Log $L^* = L$ than L^*, generally use L to express the maximum likelihood function.

$$L = \ln L^* = \sum_{n=1}^{20} \sum_{i \in J_n} \delta_{in} \ln P_{in} = \sum_{n=1}^{20} \sum_{i \in J_n} \delta_{in} (\theta \cdot X_{in} - \ln \sum_{j \in J_n} e^{\theta \cdot X_{jn}}) \tag{6-70}$$

(5) Calculate gradient vector ∇L and Jose matrix $\nabla^2 L$

$$\nabla L[\theta^{(0)}] = \begin{pmatrix} \sum_{n=1}^{20} \sum_{i=0}^{2} (\delta_{in} - P_{in}) x_{in1} \\ \sum_{n=1}^{20} \sum_{i=0}^{2} (\delta_{in} - P_{in}) x_{in2} \\ \sum_{n=1}^{20} \sum_{i=0}^{2} (\delta_{in} - P_{in}) x_{in3} \\ \sum_{n=1}^{20} \sum_{i=0}^{2} (\delta_{in} - P_{in}) x_{in4} \end{pmatrix} \tag{6-71}$$

$$\nabla^2 L = \begin{pmatrix} \partial^2 L/\partial\theta_1^2 & \cdots & \partial^2 L/\partial\theta_1 \partial\theta_m \\ \vdots & \partial^2 L/\partial\theta_k \partial\theta_l & \vdots \\ \partial^2 L/\partial\theta_1 \partial\theta_m & \cdots & \partial^2 L/\partial\theta_m^2 \end{pmatrix} = \begin{pmatrix} \Lambda_{11} & \Lambda_{12} & \Lambda_{13} & \Lambda_{14} \\ \Lambda_{21} & \Lambda_{22} & \Lambda_{23} & \Lambda_{24} \\ \Lambda_{31} & \Lambda_{32} & \Lambda_{33} & \Lambda_{34} \\ \Lambda_{41} & \Lambda_{42} & \Lambda_{43} & \Lambda_{44} \end{pmatrix} \tag{6-72}$$

where,

$$\Lambda_{11} = -\sum_{n=1}^{20} \sum_{i=0}^{2} P_{in} (x_{in1} - \sum_{j=0}^{2} P_{jn} x_{jn1})^2 \tag{6-73}$$

$$\Lambda_{14} = -\sum_{n=1}^{20} \sum_{i=0}^{2} P_{in} (x_{in1} - \sum_{j=0}^{2} P_{jn} x_{jn1})(x_{in4} - \sum_{j=0}^{2} P_{jn} x_{jn4}) \tag{6-74}$$

$$\Lambda_{kl} = -\sum_{n=1}^{20} \sum_{i=0}^{2} P_{in} (x_{ink} - \sum_{j=0}^{2} P_{jn} x_{jnk})(x_{inl} - \sum_{j=0}^{2} P_{jn} x_{jnl}) \tag{6-75}$$

$$\Lambda_{41} = -\sum_{n=1}^{20} \sum_{i=0}^{2} P_{in} (x_{in1} - \sum_{j=0}^{2} P_{jn} x_{jn1})(x_{in4} - \sum_{j=0}^{2} P_{jn} x_{jn4}) \tag{6-76}$$

$$\Lambda_{44} = -\sum_{n=1}^{20} \sum_{i=0}^{2} P_{in} (x_{in4} - \sum_{j=0}^{2} P_{jn} x_{jn4})^2 \tag{6-77}$$

(6) Use the NR (Newton-Raphson method) to estimate the value of $\hat{\theta}$

When $\nabla L = 0$ estimate the value of θ_1, θ_2, θ_3 and θ_4 by NR method.

Step 1: For $\theta = (\theta_1, \theta_2, \theta_3, \theta_4) = 0$, $m = 0$, due to the manual calculation, reducing the requested calculate precision from $\mu_1 = 10^{-4}$ to $\mu_1 = 10^{-3}$, $\mu_2 = 10^{-2}$.

Step 2: For $m = 0, \theta = (\theta_1, \theta_2, \theta_3, \theta_4) = 0$, then $P_{0n} = P_{1n} = P_{2n} = 1/3$. Use this condition to calculate the gradient vector and Jose matrix, with the following formula:

$$\nabla L[\theta^{(0)}] = \begin{pmatrix} \sum_{n=1}^{20}\sum_{i=0}^{2}(\delta_{in} - P_{in})x_{in1} \\ \sum_{n=1}^{20}\sum_{i=0}^{2}(\delta_{in} - P_{in})x_{in2} \\ \sum_{n=1}^{20}\sum_{i=0}^{2}(\delta_{in} - P_{in})x_{in3} \\ \sum_{n=1}^{20}\sum_{i=0}^{2}(\delta_{in} - P_{in})x_{in4} \end{pmatrix} = \begin{pmatrix} -0.667 \\ -0.667 \\ -16270 \\ -85 \end{pmatrix} \tag{6-78}$$

$$\nabla^2 L[\theta^{(0)}] = \begin{pmatrix} \Lambda_{11} & \Lambda_{12} & \Lambda_{13} & \Lambda_{14} \\ \Lambda_{21} & \Lambda_{22} & \Lambda_{23} & \Lambda_{24} \\ \Lambda_{31} & \Lambda_{32} & \Lambda_{33} & \Lambda_{34} \\ \Lambda_{41} & \Lambda_{42} & \Lambda_{43} & \Lambda_{44} \end{pmatrix} = \begin{pmatrix} -4.44 & 2.22 & -1826.67 & 69.25 \\ 2.22 & -4.44 & 813.33 & 11.67 \\ -1826.67 & 813.33 & -18014978 & 76414.8 \\ 69.25 & 11.67 & 76414.8 & -5372.22 \end{pmatrix} \tag{6-79}$$

Step 3: Calculate the $\theta^{(m+1)}$ with the following formula:

$$\theta^{(m+1)} = \theta^{(m)} - [\nabla^2 L(\theta^{(m)})]^{-1}\nabla L[\theta^{(m)}] \tag{6-80}$$

$$\{\nabla^2 L[\theta^{(m)}]\}^{-1} = \frac{\nabla^2 L[\theta^{(m)}]}{|\nabla^2 L[\theta^{(m)}]|} \tag{6-81}$$

For $m = 0$, the process for calculating the $\theta^{(1)}$ as the follows:

$$\theta^{(1)} = \theta^{(0)} - \{\nabla^2 L[\theta^{(0)}]\}^{-1}\nabla L[\theta^{(0)}] = \begin{pmatrix} -0.831 \\ -0.87 \\ -0.001 \\ -0.043 \end{pmatrix} \tag{6-82}$$

Step 4: To test accuracy as the follows:

$$\frac{1}{4}\{\sum_{k=1}^{4}[\theta_k^{(m+1)} - \theta_k^{(m)}]^2\}^{1/2} < 10^{-3} \tag{6-83}$$

$$\frac{\theta_k^{(m+1)} - \theta_k^{(m)}}{\theta_k^{(m)}} < 10^{-2} \tag{6-84}$$

The iterative process need to be continued until the formulas meet the condition by using the $\theta^{(1)}, \theta^{(0)}$ to test accuracy.

Then $m = 1$, return to **Step 2.**

For $\theta^{(1)} = (-0.831, -0.87, -0.001 -0.043)$, Table 6-8 shows the probability of choosing trip modes from twenty travelers.

Table 6-8 The probability of choosing trip modes ($m=1$)

No.	P_{0n}	P_{1n}	P_{2n}	No.	P_{0n}	P_{1n}	P_{2n}
1	0.997	0.003	0.000	11	0.779	0.061	0.160
2	0.956	0.039	0.005	12	0.550	0.277	0.173
3	0.011	0.880	0.109	13	0.335	0.224	0.441
4	0.762	0.110	0.129	14	0.666	0.188	0.146
5	0.677	0.109	0.213	15	0.567	0.068	0.365
6	0.052	0.044	0.904	16	0.243	0.364	0.393
7	0.622	0.255	0.124	17	0.703	0.097	0.200
8	0.425	0.185	0.390	18	0.260	0.503	0.237
9	0.826	0.054	0.120	19	0.752	0.027	0.221
10	0.370	0.071	0.559	20	0.009	0.018	0.972

Calculate the new Gradient vector and Jose matrix as follows:

$$\nabla L[\theta^{(1)}] = \begin{pmatrix} 2.424 \\ 0.137 \\ -3990.15 \\ 49.16 \end{pmatrix} \tag{6-85}$$

$$\nabla^2 L[\theta^{(1)}] = \begin{pmatrix} -2.100 & 0.837 & -795.306 & 7.245 \\ 0.837 & -2.827 & -93.476 & 17.188 \\ -795.306 & -93.476 & -5569114 & 49940.2 \\ 7.245 & 17.188 & 49940.2 & -2378.175 \end{pmatrix} \tag{6-86}$$

Proceed to **Step 3**: calculate the $\theta^{(2)}$ by iterative calculation:

$$\theta^{(2)} = \theta^{(1)} - \{\nabla^2 L[\theta^{(1)}]\}^{-1} \nabla L[\theta^{(1)}] = \begin{pmatrix} 0.972 \\ -0.181 \\ -0.0001 \\ -0.03 \end{pmatrix} \tag{6-87}$$

Since the $\theta^{(2)}$ is not up to requested by testing accuracy, the process needs to be repeated, Table 6-9 shows the result from **Step 2.**

Table 6-9 Calculate the parameter using the maximum likelihood by iterative calculation($m=3$)

m	θ^m				m	θ^m			
	θ_1^m	θ_2^m	θ_3^m	θ_4^m		θ_1^m	θ_2^m	θ_3^m	θ_4^m
3	0.256	-0.261	-0.0011	-0.0296	8	1.447	0.095	-0.003	-0.054
4	0.985	-0.108	-0.002	-0.037	9	1.678	0.210	-0.003	-0.062
5	0.684	-0.360	-0.002	-0.043	10	1.714	0.231	-0.003	-0.064
6	0.531	-0.204	-0.001	-0.023	11	1.715	0.231	-0.003	-0.064
7	1.084	-0.090	-0.002	-0.037					

For $m = 10$, the result of accuracy testing as follows:

$$\frac{1}{4}\left\{\sum_{k=1}^{4}[\theta_k^{(11)} - \theta_k^{(10)}]^2\right\}^{1/2} = \frac{1}{4}\times 10^{-3} < 10^{-3} \quad (6\text{-}88)$$

$$\max\left|\frac{\theta_k^{(11)} - \theta_k^{(10)}}{\theta_k^{(4)}}\right| = \left|\frac{1.715 - 1.714}{1.714}\right| = \frac{10^{-3}}{1.714} < 10^{-2} \quad (6\text{-}89)$$

From the formula above, the result meets the precision accuracy by accuracy testing, then loop stops running, the value of estimating parameter as result:

$$\theta = (1.714,\ 0.231,\ -0.003\ -0.064) \quad (6\text{-}90)$$

(7) Calculate the covariance

For $m = 10$, calculate the covariance of $\{-\nabla^2 L[\theta^{(10)}]\}^{-1}$ as result:

$$\nabla^2 L[\theta^{(10)}] = \begin{pmatrix} -1.733 & 0.777 & -767.548 & 4.283 \\ 0.777 & -1.534 & -127.296 & 8.987 \\ -767.548 & -127.296 & -1792129.944 & 44983.172 \\ 4.283 & 8.987 & 44983.172 & -2243.424 \end{pmatrix} \quad (6\text{-}91)$$

Then,

$$\{-\nabla^2 L[\theta^{(10)}]\}^{-1} = \begin{pmatrix} 1.2153 & 0.6127 & -8.94\times 10^{-4} & -1.32\times 10^{-2} \\ 0.6127 & 0.9779 & -4.11\times 10^{-4} & -3.16\times 10^{-3} \\ -8.94\times 10^{-4} & -4.11\times 10^{-4} & 1.78\times 10^{-6} & 3.24\times 10^{-5} \\ -1.32\times 10^{-2} & -3.16\times 10^{-3} & 3.24\times 10^{-5} & 0.0011 \end{pmatrix} \quad (6\text{-}92)$$

(8) Calculate the t-value

Calculate the t-value of estimated parameter from each variable by the following formula.

$$t_k = \frac{\hat{\theta}_k}{\sqrt{v_k}} \quad (6\text{-}93)$$

where, v_k is the k-th diagonal elements of covariance matrix.

Calculate each t-value as result:

$$t_1 = \frac{1.714}{\sqrt{1.2153}} = 1.55 \quad (6\text{-}94)$$

$$t_2 = \frac{0.231}{\sqrt{0.9779}} = 0.23 \quad (6\text{-}95)$$

$$t_3 = \frac{-0.003}{\sqrt{1.78\times 10^{-6}}} = -1.69 \quad (6\text{-}96)$$

$$t_4 = \frac{-0.064}{\sqrt{0.0011}} = 1.93 \quad (6\text{-}97)$$

Using the value of t-value to judge a variable had the influence on the probability selection or not. Take the 10% significance level as an example, from quantile values for the t distribution we can see that for freedom is 20, the $t_{0.9}(20) = 1.325$, in addition to the value of t_2, the t_1, t_3, t_4 is greater than 1.325, then draw a conclusion: with 90% confidence the value of variable x_{in1}、x_{in3}、x_{in4} have the influence on probability selection but x_{in2} has not the influence on probability selection.

(9) Calculate and test the other statistics.

N: Sample size.

$L(0)$: The value of likelihood for $\theta = (0, 0, 0, 0)$.

Estimated value of parameter corresponding the inherent dummy is optimal and for corresponding the not inherent dummy is zero.

$L(\hat{\theta})$: the value of maximum likelihood.

$\chi_0 = -2[L(0) - L(\hat{\theta})]$: Calculate χ^2 - test for $\hat{\theta} = (0, 0, 0, 0)$. On the condition that the freedom is 20, if the $\chi_0^2 > \chi_\alpha^2$, the $\hat{\theta}$ is not always zero vector, vice versa.

$\chi_c = -2[L(c) - L(\hat{\theta})]$: The inherent dummy.

$\chi_c = -2[L(c) - L(\hat{\theta})]$: For $\hat{\theta} = c$, calculate the χ^2 - test when the estimated value for other parameters expect for inherent dummy is zero (the freedom is 19). The test principle as above.

The calculation steps of hit ratio as follows:

Step 1: Calculating the likelihood function by using the estimated value $\hat{\theta}$, and calculate the selection probability P_{in} for each mode from arbitrarily traveler n.

Step 2: For arbitrarily traveler n, there are more than 50% selection probability of the selected mode, and the estimated selection mode as results:

$$\hat{\delta}_{in} = \begin{cases} 1; & P_{in} > 50\% \\ 0; & P_{in} < 50\% \end{cases} \quad (i = 0, 1, 2) \tag{6-98}$$

Step 3: Compare the practical and estimated results, the S_{in} as defined:

$$S_{in} = \begin{cases} 1; & \delta_{in} = \hat{\delta}_{in} \\ 0; & \delta_{in} \neq \hat{\delta}_{in} \end{cases} \quad (i = 0, 1, 2) \tag{6-99}$$

Overall hit ratio
$$\text{HitR} = \frac{1}{3N}\sum_{n=1}^{N}(S_{0n} + S_{1n} + S_{2n}) \tag{6-100}$$

Mode 0 hit ratio
$$\text{HitR}_0 = \frac{1}{N}\sum_{n=1}^{N} S_{0n} \tag{6-101}$$

Mode 1 hit ratio
$$\text{HitR}_1 = \frac{1}{N}\sum_{n=1}^{N} S_{1n} \tag{6-102}$$

Mode 2 hit ratio
$$\text{HitR}_2 = \frac{1}{N}\sum_{n=1}^{N} S_{2n} \tag{6-103}$$

Superiority ratio ρ^2: Also called coefficient of determination, the computation expression is $\rho^2 = 1 - L(\hat{\theta})/L(0)$. The value of it is between zero and one, the model accuracy is increasing with the value, since the endogeneity obeys the 0-1 function, generally believing the model is well when the value ρ^2 of is between 0.2-0.4.

$\rho^{-2} = \left(\frac{N-K}{N}\right)\rho^2$: It is index to measure fitness for the model, the value closer to one, the better it is.

(10) Results summary (Table 6-10)

Table 6-10 Results summary

Distinction	$\theta=(\theta_1, \theta_2, \theta_3, \theta_4)$	Remarks
Estimated value	$\hat{\theta}=(1.714, 0.231, -0.003, -0.064)$	Optimal estimation of parameter values
t-value	$t=(1.55, 0.23, -1.69, 1.93)$	$t_k=\hat{\theta}_k/\sqrt{v_k}$
$N=20$ $L(0)=-21.97$ $L(c)=-29.44$ $L(\hat{\theta})=-8.71$		$\chi_0=26.52$ $\chi_c=41.46$ HitR = 95% $\rho^2=0.604$ $\rho^{-2}=0.483$

From the results, the model accuracy is high.

6.5.2 Least Square Method

When calculating mode choice probability, the utility value of different mode is calculated, then used in Logit model. For BL model, Eg. 6-5 is an example to introduce how to calibrate the model parameter using the least square method.

[Example 6-5] *Between two zones where only bus and car travel, we assume the Logit model is suitable for mode choice between two zones. Try to estimate parameters and estimate the utility value for bus and car travel using the data from* Table 6-11 *to* Table 6-16.

Table 6-11 Bus travel time (min)

t_{ij}^{Bus}	1	2	3
1	5.0	11.0	13.0
2	10.0	12.0	12.0
3	14.0	16.0	7.0

Table 6-12 Car travel time (min)

t_{ij}^{Car}	1	2	3
1	3.0	8.0	10.0
2	8.0	7.0	11.0
3	10.0	11.0	3.0

Table 6-13 Bus cost (yuan)

c_{ij}^{Bus}	1	2	3
1	1.0	1.5	2.0
2	1.5	1.5	3.0
3	2.0	3.0	1.5

Table 6-14 Car cost (yuan)

c_{ij}^{Car}	1	2	3
1	11	15	23
2	15	12	25
3	23	25	19

Table 6-15 Bus division ratio

p_{ij}^{Bus}	1	2	3
1	0.273	0.265	0.253
2	0.282	0.248	0.255
3	0.239	0.192	0.244

Table 6-16 Car division ratio

p_{ij}^{Car}	1	2	3
1	0.727	0.735	0.747
2	0.718	0.752	0.745
3	0.761	0.808	0.756

Solution: Based on the known conditions, the utility function expression S for bus and car are as follows:

$$V_{ij}^{Bus} = \alpha_1 t_{ij}^{Bus} + \alpha_2 c_{ij}^{Bus} \tag{1}$$

$$V_{ij}^{Car} = \alpha_1 t_{ij}^{Car} + \alpha_2 c_{ij}^{Car} + \alpha_3 \tag{2}$$

Since,

$$p_{ij}^{Bus} = \frac{\exp(V_{ij}^{Bus})}{\exp(V_{ij}^{Bus}) + \exp(V_{ij}^{Car})} \tag{3}$$

$$p_{ij}^{Car} = 1 - p_{ij}^{Bus} \tag{4}$$

Then,

$$\ln\left(\frac{p_{ij}^{Car}}{p_{ij}^{Bus}}\right) = \alpha_1 (t_{ij}^{Car} - t_{ij}^{Bus}) + \alpha_2 (c_{ij}^{Car} - c_{ij}^{Bus}) + \alpha_3 \tag{5}$$

Take the data form Table 6-17 *into* Eq. (5), *and make:*

$$y = \ln\left(\frac{p_{ij}^{Car}}{p_{ij}^{Bus}}\right),\ x_1 = t_{ij}^{Car} - t_{ij}^{Bus},\ x_2 = c_{ij}^{Car} - c_{ij}^{Bus}$$

The Table 6-17 *shows the results for nine sample points* (x_1, x_2, y), *and* Table 6-18 *shows the test value of parameters* α_1, α_2, α_3 *using least square method.*

Table 6-17 Sample data

No.	x_1	x_2	y	No.	x_1	x_2	y
1	-2	10.0	0.979	6	-1	22.0	1.072
2	-3	13.5	1.020	7	-4	21.0	1.158
3	-3	21.0	1.083	8	-5	22.0	1.437
4	-2	13.5	0.935	9	-4	17.5	1.131
5	-5	10.5	1.109				

Table 6-18 The estimated value of parameter

Parameters	α_1	α_2	α_3
Estimated value	-0.069	0.0162	0.607
t-test value	-3.570	2.974	5.448
Sample		9	
Correlation coefficient		0.89	

Therefore, we can get the utility function expression of two modes, and calculate the utility value for each mode combining the value of property.

6.5.3 Statistic Analysis Software

It is difficult to calibrate the model parameter in a convenient, fast and correct way when number of samples and parameters are big, we can use the software to solve this problem. Calibrating the data using Biogeme as follows:

(1) Analyzing data and modeling the utility model

Trip purpose is key factor for mode choice. Generally, it needed to be considered as a characteristic variation for utility function. Defining the dummy is an independent variable for utility function from car travelling:

Dummy: dummy = 1 if Purpose = 2 otherwise dummy = 0.

The utility functions for each mode are as follows:

$$V_{\text{CAR}} = \theta_1 + \theta_2 \text{TC}_{\text{Car}} + \theta_3 \text{TT}_{\text{Car}} + \theta_4 \text{dummy} \tag{6-104}$$

$$V_{\text{RAIL}} = \theta_5 + \theta_2 \text{TC}_{\text{Rail}} + \theta_3 \text{TT}_{\text{Rail}} \tag{6-105}$$

$$V_{\text{BUS}} = \theta_6 + \theta_2 \text{TC}_{\text{Bus}} + \theta_3 \text{TT}_{\text{Bus}} \tag{6-106}$$

(2) Calibrating the parameters using Biogeme, results are shown in Table 6-19

Table 6-19 The results of calibrated parameter using Biogeme

Parameter	θ_1	θ_2	θ_3	θ_4	θ_5	θ_6
Calibration value	0	-0.0504	-0.125	6.62	6.74	3.54
t value	2.67	-1.59	-1.51	1.58	1.51	1.58
Sample N	20					
Adjusted goodness of fit	47.7%					

The absolute value of t-test for calibrated parameters are all greater than 1.51, it shows that the accuracy of model is greater than 90%. And the adjusted goodness of fit index is 47.7%, is shows that the model fits data well.

6.6 Probit Model

From the previous learning, we know that the Probit model is good at analyzing the mode choice from two travel modes. For some travel modes having strong correlations, Probit model is better than Logit model in model accuracy. Therefore, it is important to learn the Probit model and corresponding application. The Probit models have binary and multinomial models, the binary model is more convenient and simpler than multinomial model in calculating. And there are two ways to calculate the choice probability of each travel mode using the multinomial model, the one is Monte Carlo method, and the other is an approximation method that calculate probability with the multi-dimensional normal distribution.

6.6.1 Binary Probit Model

Assuming two travel modes 1and 2 for traveler n in binary Probit model. The random utility theory for two travel modes obeys the two-dimensional normal distribution as follows:

$$\begin{pmatrix} U_{1n} \\ U_{2n} \end{pmatrix} \sim \left[\begin{pmatrix} V_{1n} \\ V_{2n} \end{pmatrix} \begin{pmatrix} \sigma_1^2 & \sigma_{12} \\ \sigma_{21} & \sigma_2^2 \end{pmatrix} \right] \tag{6-107}$$

Then,

$$p_{1n} = \text{prob}(U_{1n} > U_{2n}) = \text{prob}(U_{2n} - U_{1n} \leqslant 0) \tag{6-108}$$

$$p_{1n} = \Phi\left(\frac{V_{2n} - V_{1n}}{\sqrt{\sigma_1^2 + \sigma_2^2 - 2\rho_{12}\sigma_1\sigma_2}} \right), p_{2n} = 1 - p_{1n} \tag{6-109}$$

where, Φ is standard normal distribution function; σ_1^2 is covariance var(U_{1n}); ρ_{12} is the correlation coefficient for 1 and 2.

Since $V_{1n} = \alpha_1 x_{1n1} + \cdots + \alpha_m x_{1nm}$, $V_{2n} = \alpha_1 x_{2n1} + \cdots + \alpha_m x_{2nm}$, the definition is as follows:

$$V_{2n} - V_{1n} = AX'_n \tag{6-110}$$

$$A = (\alpha_1,\ \alpha_2,\ \cdots, \alpha_m) \tag{6-111}$$

$$X'_n = \begin{pmatrix} x_{2n1} - x_{1n1} \\ x_{2n2} - x_{1n2} \\ \vdots \\ x_{2nm} - x_{1nm} \end{pmatrix} = \begin{pmatrix} x_1 \\ x_2 \\ \vdots \\ x_m \end{pmatrix} \tag{6-112}$$

Use this formula to calculate the parameter vector A. Then get the likelihood function L having binary variables as follows:

$$L^* = \prod_{n=1}^{N} p_{1n}^{\delta_{1n}} \cdot p_{2n}^{\delta_{2n}} \tag{6-113}$$

$$L = \ln L^* = \sum_{n=1}^{N} (\delta_{1n}\ln p_{1n} + \delta_{2n}\ln p_{2n}) \tag{6-114}$$

Finally, calibrate the parameter using appropriate method.

6.6.2 Multinomial Probit Model

In the Probit model, assuming the amount of alternatives n, and random utility of each travel mode obeys multi-dimensional normal distribution as follows:

$$\begin{pmatrix} U_{1n} \\ U_{2n} \\ \vdots \\ U_{J_n n} \end{pmatrix} \sim \left[\begin{pmatrix} V_{1n} \\ V_{2n} \\ \vdots \\ V_{J_n n} \end{pmatrix} \begin{pmatrix} \sigma_1^2 & \sigma_{12} & \cdots & \sigma_{1J_n} \\ \sigma_{21} & \sigma_2^2 & \cdots & \sigma_{2J_n} \\ \vdots & \vdots & \vdots & \vdots \\ \sigma_{J_n 1} & \sigma_{J_n 2} & \cdots & \sigma_{J_n}^2 \end{pmatrix} \right] \tag{6-115}$$

For $n > 3$ or even more, using the Monte Carlo Simulation or STATA to estimate the choice probability of each travel mode. In this section, just knowing the derivation process for $n = 3$.

Giving the definitions as follows:

$$\mu_{12} = E[\max(U_{1n}, U_{2n})] = V_{1n}\Phi(\alpha_{12}) + V_{2n}\Phi(-\alpha_{12}) + \sqrt{\text{var}(U_{1n}+U_{2n})}\phi(\alpha_{12}) \tag{6-116}$$

$$\alpha_{12} = (V_{1n} - V_{2n})\sqrt{\text{var}(U_{1n}+U_{2n})} \tag{6-117}$$

$$\begin{aligned}\omega_{12} = E[\max(U_{1n}, U_{2n})]^2 = (V_{1n}^2 + \sigma_1^2)\Phi(\alpha_{12}) + \\ (V_{2n}^2 + \sigma_2^2)\Phi(-\alpha_{12}) + (V_{1n}^2 + V_{2n}^2)\sqrt{\text{var}(U_{1n}+U_{2n})}\phi(\alpha_{12})\end{aligned} \tag{6-118}$$

where, ϕ is distribution density function.

The relationship between the third normal distribution parameter U_{3n} and the maximum in U_{1n} and U_{2n} is as follows:

$$\rho'_{3n} = \rho[U_{3n}, \max(U_{1n}, U_{2n})] = \frac{\sigma_1\rho_{13}\Phi(\alpha_{12}) + \sigma_2\rho_{23}\Phi(-\alpha_{12})}{\sqrt{\omega_{12} - \mu_{12}^2}} \tag{6-119}$$

Therefore, derive the choice probability of mode 3:

$$p_{3n} = \text{prob}[U_{3n} > \max(U_{1n}, U_{2n})] = \Phi\left(\frac{V_{3n} - \mu_{12}}{\sqrt{\sigma_3^2 + \sigma_m^2 - 2\rho'_3\sigma_3\sigma_m}}\right) \tag{6-120}$$

where, $\sigma_m^2 = \omega_{12} - \mu_{12}^2$.

6.6.3 Model Solution

Binary Probit model uses the mathematical method of maximum likelihood function to calculate estimated value of parameter. For multinomial Probit model, generally use the relative software such as STATA and Biogeme etc. Following are the solution methods for binary or multinomial Probit model.

(1) Binary Probit model solution

The likelihood function of binary Probit model is as follows:

$$L = \ln L^* = \sum_{n=1}^{N}(\delta_{in}\ln p_{in} + \delta_{jn}\ln p_{jn}) \tag{6-121}$$

Calculating the first-order partial derivative for attribute A, and take it to zero as follows:

$$\frac{\partial L}{\partial A} = \sum_{n=1}^{N}\left(\delta_{in}\frac{\partial p_{in}/\partial A}{p_{in}} + \delta_{jn}\frac{\partial p_{jn}/\partial A}{p_{jn}}\right) = 0 \tag{6-122}$$

Then, insert the equation in the function of p_{in} and p_{jn}. Do the following definition:

$$\nabla L = \begin{pmatrix} \dfrac{\partial L}{\partial \alpha_1} \\ \dfrac{\partial L}{\partial \alpha_2} \\ \vdots \\ \dfrac{\partial L}{\partial \alpha_m} \\ \dfrac{\partial L}{\partial \alpha_{m+1}} \end{pmatrix} \tag{6-123}$$

Define $\nabla L = 0$, solve the equation. Using the Newton-Raphson method to calibrate the parameters.

(2) Multinomial Probit model solution

Get the estimated value of parameters by using the Biogeme to write Probit modeling coding and input relative disaggregate survey data, it will not be discussed here.

6.7 Application of Logit Model in Traffic System Analysis

6.7.1 BL Model Application——Calculate the Effectiveness of Transit Improvement

[Example 6-6] Basing on the Eg. 6-2 above, assume that applying some measurements for transit operation improvement, the travel time decreases from 15 min to 12 min. Use 100 travelers as unit, try to calculate the travel effectiveness after the transit operation improvement (Assuming VOTT = 20 cents/min).

· Calculate the travel cost of the car and bus after implementation of improvements respectively.

If: VOTT = 20 cents/min

Then, $C_{ij,\ \text{before}}^{\text{Auto}} = C_{ij,\ \text{after}}^{\text{Auto}} = 10 \times 20 = 200$ cents, $C_{ij,\ \text{before}}^{\text{Transit}} = 15 \times 20 = 300$ cents, $C_{ij,\ \text{after}}^{\text{Transit}} = 12 \times 20 = 240$ cents

· Calculate the proportion of transit trip before or after the implementation using the Eq. (6-24), then get:

$$P_{\text{before}}(\text{Bus}) = \frac{\exp(-0.03 \times 300)}{\exp(-0.03 \times 300) + \exp(-0.03 \times 200)} = 4.74\%$$

$$P_{\text{after}}(\text{Bus}) = \frac{\exp(-0.03 \times 240)}{\exp(-0.03 \times 240) + \exp(-0.03 \times 200)} = 23.14\%$$

· Calculating the traveler cost saving.

Transit traveler cost saving is unit traveler cost saving. Where, the transit traveler is divided into inherent and new traveler, the cost saving is calculated as follows:

$$\text{TCS}_{\text{existing}}(\text{Bus}) = 100 \times 4.74\% \times 3 \times 20 = 285 \text{ cents}$$

$$\text{TCS}_{\text{new}}(\text{Bus}) = 100 \times (23.14\% - 4.74\%) \times (3 \times 20/2) = 552 \text{ cents}$$

$$\text{TCS}_{\text{total}} = 285 + 552 = 837 \text{ cents}$$

Note: the cost saving for new transit traveler is calculated obeying ROH theory.

6.7.2 MNL Model Application——Comparing the Effectiveness of Different Strategies

[Example 6-7] There are three travel modes provided for traveler n from O to D, respectively, the car, bus and metro. Table 6-20 shows the attributes for each mode:

Table 6-20 The attribute for each mode from O to D(basic plan)

Mode	Travel time(min)		Travel cost(cost)
	IVTT(In vehicle travel time)	OVTT(Off vehicle travel time)	
Car	18	0	4
Bus	18	20	0.5
Metro	18	15	2

The utility functions for each travel mode are as follows:

$$V_{car} = -0.025IVTT - 0.05OVTT - 0.004COST$$

$$V_{bus} = -1.8 - 0.025IVTT - 0.05OVTT - 0.004COST$$

$$V_{metro} = -2 - 0.025IVTT - 0.05OVTT - 0.004COST$$

Combine Table 6-20 and Table 6-21, then use the ROH or Logsum method to calculate the travel utility value for traveler n in each scenario. (value of travel time VOTT = $16.80/h)

Table 6-21 Travel attribute for each scenario

Plan 1	Decrease OVTT for bus								
OVTT(bus)	18	16	14	12	10	8	6	4	2
Plan 2	Decrease OVTT for bus and subway								
OVTT(bus)	18	16	14	12	10	8	6		
OVTT(metro)	13	11	9	7	5	3	1		
Plan 3	Increase cost for car								
Dollar increase	+$1	+$2	+$3	+$4	+$5	+$6	+$7	+$8	

· Calculate the choice probability of each mode.

From Table 6-20, substitute each value of attribute into formula below:

$$P_i = \frac{\exp(V_i)}{\sum_{j \in J_n} \exp(V_j)}$$

The results of choice probability of each mode are shown in Table 6-22.

Table 6-22 Choice probability of each mode in basic plan

Mode	Travel time (min)		Travel cost(cost)	V_i	P_i
	IVTT	OVTT			
Car	18	0	4	-2.05	0.7200
Bus	18	20	0.5	-3.45	0.1776
Metro	18	15	2	-4	0.1024

· Using Logsum method to calculate utility value of travelling in different scenarios, which is shown in Table 6-23.

Table 6-23　The result of travelling utility value in different scenarios based on ROH and Logsum method

Plan 1	Decrease OVTT for bus								
OVTT(bus)	18	16	14	12	10	8	6	4	2
Car	0.707	0.693	0.678	0.662	0.646	0.628	0.61	0.591	0.572
Bus	0.193	0.209	0.226	0.244	0.263	0.282	0.303	0.325	0.347
Metro	0.101	0.099	0.096	0.094	0.092	0.089	0.087	0.084	0.081
Logsum($)	46.3	96.4	150.7	209.3	272.5	340.6	413.8	492.2	576.1
Plan 2	Decrease OVTT for bus and subway								
SOVTT	18	16	14	12	10	8	6		
Metro OVTT	13	11	9	7	5	3	1		
Car	0.699	0.678	0.656	0.633	0.609	0.585	0.561		
Bus	0.191	0.204	0.218	0.233	0.248	0.263	0.279		
Metro	0.11	0.118	0.126	0.134	0.143	0.152	0.161		
Logsum($)	72.6	150.4	233.6	322.5	417.3	517.9	624.6		
Plan 3	Increase cost for car								
Dollar increase	+$1	+$2	+$3	+$4	+$5	+$6	+$7	+$8	
Car	0.633	0.536	0.437	0.342	0.258	0.189	0.135	0.095	
Bus	0.233	0.294	0.357	0.417	0.47	0.514	0.548	0.574	
Metro	0.134	0.17	0.206	0.241	0.271	0.297	0.316	0.331	
Logsum($)	-677.5	-1262.5	-1748.7	-2137.1	-2435.9	-2658.3	-2819.3	-2933.3	

6.7.3　NL Model Application——Road Congestion Pricing Effects Analysis

【Example 6-8】　Shopping mall A and B are the destinations for shopping trips, the total attraction for resident trips is 125000 trips/d. Total volume is divided averagely into two groups based on VOTT: VOTT = $6/h and VOTT = $12/h. There are only one route and three modes (Auto, Bus and Walk) for residents to the shopping mall A, the distance is 1 mile and the free flow speed is 10mile/h; For store B, there are two routes (which are Route 1 and Route 2) and two modes (Auto and Bus) for the residents, the distance is 8 miles and the free flow speed is 60 mile/h, but the bus do not go along with the Route 1. The index of trip attraction for shopping mall A is 10 and for shopping mall B is 200. The branch diagram for alternatives of travel modes is shown in Fig. 6-15, the travel time is calculated by the road impendence function from Federal Highway Administration which is as follows:

$$t_l = t_{\text{free},\,l}\left[1 + 0.85\left(\frac{v_l}{c_l}\right)^{5.5}\right]$$

where, t_l is the travel time for route l; $t_{\text{free},\,l}$ is the free flow time for route l; v_l is the flow route l; c_l is the capacity route l.

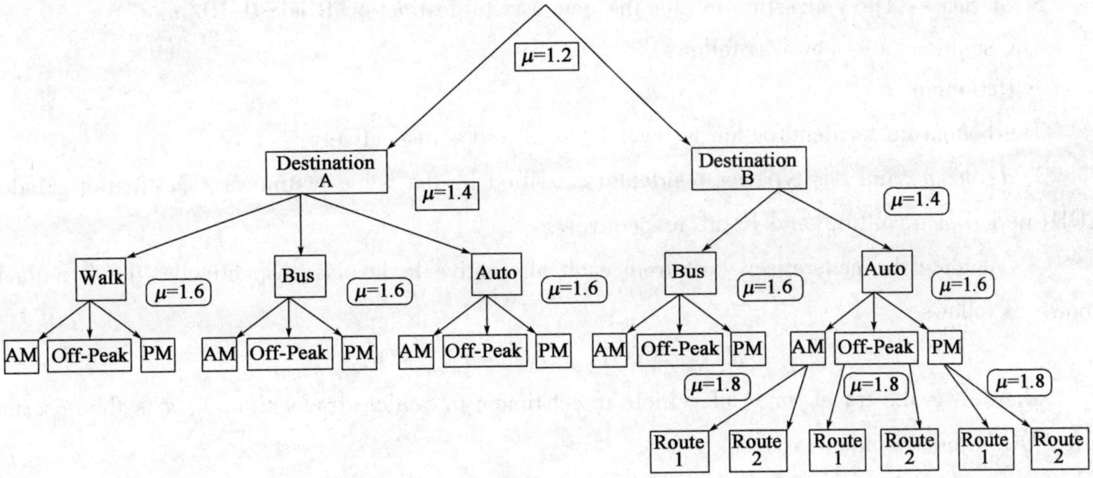

Figure 6-15 The branch diagram for alternatives of travel modes

Source: *Kockelman*, 2011.

Use the data to analyze the traffic conditions for Route 1 and Route 2 in different fare policy (Table 6-24).

Table 6-24 The shopping route and attribute of mode

		Destination		
		A	B	
			Route 1	Route 2
Capacity (pcu/TOD)	AM peak	12000	12000	12000
	Off peak	24000	24000	24000
	PM peak	16000	16000	16000
Speed (mile/h)	Walk	4.47	—	—
	Auto	10	60	60
	Bus	—	60	60
OVTT (min)	Walk	13.4	—	—
	Auto	0	—	0
	Bus	15	—	15
Fare ($/per)	Walk	0	—	—
	Auto	0	0	0
	Bus	0.5	—	0.5
Opera. cost ($/per)	Walk	0	—	—
	Auto	0.2	1.6	1.6
	Bus	0	—	0
Length (mile)		1	8	8

Foundation: There is only one route and do not collect the congestion fee to destination B.

Scenarios 1: There are two routes that do not collect the congestion fee to destination B.

Scenarios 2: The congestion fee for the new way to destination B is $0.05/mile.

Scenarios 3: The congestion fee for the new way to destination B is \$0.10/mile.

The solutions are shown as follows:

· Definition.

The bottom-up for dendrogram is level 1, 2, 3 and 4 respectively;

i, d, m, p, and r is type for residents (classified by the value of time), Destination、Mode、TOD (period of travelling) and Route respectively.

· Calculate the generalized cost from each alternative in level 1 respectively, the formula is shown as follows:

$$GC_{i,\ dmpr} = VOTT_i \cdot t_{dmpr} + \tau_{dmpr} + OC_{dmpr}$$

where, t is the travel time (off vehicle travel time + in vehicle travel time); τ is the cost and fare; OC is the operation expense.

· Calculate the utility constant from each alternative in level 1 respectively, the formula is shown as follows:

$$V_{i,\ dmpr} = (\ln attr_d - \ln attr_B) + ASC_m + ASC_p - GC_{i,\ dmpr}$$

where, ASC_m is the constants for each mode as $ASC_{Auto} = 0$, $ASC_{Bus} = -1.1$, $ASC_{Walk} = -1.3$; ASC_p is the constants for travel time as $ASC_{Auto} = 0$, $ASC_{O,P} = -0.3$, $ASC_{PM,P} = 0.2$; attr is the attraction.

· Calculate the inclusive coefficient from each alternative in level 2, 3, and 4 respectively, the formula is shown as follows:

$$\Gamma_{i,\ dmp} = \frac{1}{1.8}\ln[\exp(1.8 \times V_{i,\ dmp,\ route1}) + \exp(1.8 \times V_{i,\ dmp,\ route2})]$$

$$\Gamma_{i,\ dm} = \frac{1}{1.6}\ln[\exp(1.6 \times \Gamma_{i,\ dm,AMP}) + \exp(1.6 \times \Gamma_{i,\ dm,\ OP}) + \exp(1.6 \times \Gamma_{i,\ dm,\ PMP})]$$

$$\Gamma_{i,\ d} = \frac{1}{1.4}\ln[\exp(1.4 \times \Gamma_{i,\ d,\ Walk}) + \exp(1.4 \times \Gamma_{i,\ d,\ Bus}) + \exp(1.2 \times \Gamma_{i,\ d,Auto})]$$

· Calculate the probability of occurrence for each alternative as follows:

$$Pr_{i,\ d} = \frac{\exp(\mu_4 \cdot \Gamma_{i,\ d})}{\sum_{j \in D}\exp(\mu_4 \cdot \Gamma_{i,\ j})}$$

$$Pr_{dm} = Pr_{i,\ d} \cdot \frac{\exp(\mu_3 \cdot \Gamma_{i,\ dm})}{\sum_{j \in M}\exp(\mu_3 \cdot \Gamma_{i,\ dj})}$$

$$Pr_{i,\ dmp} = Pr_{i,\ dm} \cdot \frac{\exp(\mu_2 \cdot \Gamma_{i,\ dmp})}{\sum_{j \in TOD}\exp(\mu_2 \cdot \Gamma_{i,\ dmj})}$$

$$Pr_{i,\ dmpr} = Pr_{i,\ dmp} \cdot \frac{\exp(\mu_1 \cdot \Gamma_{i,\ dmpr})}{\sum_{j \in R}\exp(\mu_1 \cdot \Gamma_{i,\ dmpj})}$$

· Results summary (Table 6-25).

Table 6-25 The state for Route1 and Route 2 in different plans

	Route	TOD	Foundation	Scenario 1	Scenario 2	Scenario 3
Travel time (min)	1	AM. P	19.12	13.69	14.26	14.94
		O. P	14.2	9.69	10.11	10.67
		PM. P	19.26	13.81	14.39	15.07
	2	AM. P	—	13.72	11.85	10.28
		O. P	—	9.71	8.51	8.06
		PM. P	—	13.84	11.97	10.38
Toll ($)	1	AM. P	$0.00	$0.00	$0.00	$0.00
		O. P	$0.00	$0.00	$0.00	$0.00
		PM. P	$0.00	$0.00	$0.00	$0.00
	2	AM. P	—	$0.00	$0.40	$0.80
		O. P	—	$0.00	$0.40	$0.80
		PM. P	—	$0.00	$0.40	$0.80
V/C	1	AM. P	—	0.97	$0.99	1.00
	2	O. P	—	0.78	$0.81	0.84
		PM. P	—	0.97	0.99	1.01
		AM. P	1.08	0.96	0.89	0.80
		O. P	0.98	0.77	0.62	0.42
		PM. P	1.09	0.96	0.89	0.81

From the example above: use the BL, MNL and NL model to analyze the mode choice for travelers, and quantify the variation of travel efficiency in each scenario by setting some scenarios, provide science basic for establishing and implementing the relative transportation policy.

6.8 Problems and Summary

In this chapter, the main content is application model for model split in four-step method. The basic theory for this model is utility maximization theory. Disaggregate approach is the effective tool to solve the mode choice problem about residential travel behavior, summary is as follows:

6.8.1 Maximum Utility Theory for Traveler

Urban traffic phenomena is a comprehensive result of an amount of personal travel behaviors, in other words, the set of disaggregated data deduce the characterized data which is aggregated. The disaggregated approach is used to forecast or analyze traffic features in survey region by researching the mode choice behavior, and provide foundation theory for solving traffic problem.

The traveler takes a series of decision factors as the premise, then choose when to travel, use which mode, which travel route, etc., and the standard of traveler's decision is to maximize the travel utility.

Now, most researchers approve the random utility theory which is first raised by Manski in 1997. The traveler will select the trip mode that has the maximum utility, and the expression of choice probability of mode i is as follows:

$$p(k|J_n)=p(U_{kn}\geqslant U_{jn},\ \forall j\in J_n) \tag{6-124}$$

6.8.2 The Basic Expression for Utility Function

The utility function consists of deterministic and random error component is as follows:

$$U_{kn}=V_{kn}+\varepsilon_{kn} \tag{6-125}$$

where, V_{kn} is the deterministic component that can be determined accurately, and it is made up of some characteristic indies in function form which are direct or indirect quantified such as time, cost, congestion cost and comfort etc. when we solve the model, generally transforming the V_{kn} to linear expression; ε_{kn} is the component that cannot be forecasted, which is used to improve the model accuracy.

6.8.3 Logit and Probit Model

(1) MNL model

If the random error component ε_{in} is independent and obeys the Gumbel distribution, that is IID (Independent Identical Distribution), the probability of traveler n to select the mode i is as follows:

$$p_{kn}=\frac{e^{V_{kn}}}{\sum_{j=1}^{J_n}e^{V_{jn}}} \tag{6-126}$$

where, J_n is the set of alternatives for traveler$n$.

(2) NL model

The random error component in the utility function of each travel mode is independent and obeys IIA property, that is the precondition for using the MNL model, this model is clearly not applicable to the condition that there is the correlation among the travel modes in the set of alternatives, this is the limitations of MNL model, the famous red bus/blue bus paradox is the best example for this problem. The NL model solves the weakness from MNL model by layering the data.

During modeling, classify each alternative according to relevance at first. For example, the bus and subway belong to public transport in the car, bus and subway, which can be classify into a same category. After classifying the alternative, analyzing the application from each level using MNL model, the selection probability of each travel mode can be calculated.

(3) Probit model

If the random utility $(U_{1n},\ U_{2n},\ \cdots,\ U_{J_n})$ obey the multi-dimensional normal distribution, in other words, the random error component ε_{in} obeys multi-dimensional normal distribution as follows:

$$\varepsilon_{in}\sim \mathrm{MVN}(0,\ \Sigma) \tag{6-127}$$

where, Σ is covariance matrix.

Then, for binary Probit model, the choice probability of mode i and $j$are as follows:

$$p_{1n} = \Phi\left(\frac{V_{2n} - V_{1n}}{\sqrt{\sigma_1^2 + \sigma_2^2 - 2\rho_{12}\sigma_1\sigma_2}}\right) \tag{6-128}$$

$$p_{2n} = 1 - p_{1n} \tag{6-129}$$

For Multinomial Probit model, generally calculate the model using the relative softwares.

Besides the summary below, we also need to pay attention to the problems as follows:

· The Multinomial Logit model obeys the Luce theory, but the multinomial Probit model disobeys this theory as it can overcome the defects of correlation for random error component.

· The tail of graph for Probit model (Both ends are same) is tinier than Logit model. The Probit model is more sensitive about difference among the value of utility function from the different modes (the bigger that difference value of fixed utility function for mode k and n is, the worse that stability of this model is, the worse that reliability is).

· The modal split model is established for each market segment, that is, the model is established for the family own/no car.

· The property variables should stay independent.

· The system error for a property will influence the parameters; meanwhile it will influence other parameters.

· After calibrating the parameters, must test the rationality of the parameters. For example, the rational symbol, the rational value and the rational standard deviation.

Practice see the relevant section of Appendix 2.

Exercises

1. Describe the difference between aggregate and disaggregate analysis.
2. Describe the influence factors of travel mode choices.
3. Analyze the difference between Logit and Probit model.
4. Describe the development history of the Logit and Probit model.
5. What is the different between trip end model and trip interchange model?
6. What is the application condition for MNL model?
7. What is the IIA property?
8. How to layer the NL model?
9. What are the useful Logit model?
10. Describe and compare the characteristics of Logit and Probit model?
11. There are two modes from A to B, the transport volume is one thousand people, and fixed utility function are shown respectively as follows: $V(\text{bus}) = -0.08t - 0.04c$, $V(\text{subway}) = -0.08t - 0.04c + 0.40$, where t is travel time (minute), c is ticket price (yuan), if the travel time

of subway is 10 min, the ticket price is 5 yuan, the travel time of bus is 30 min, the ticket price is 1 yuan, what are the passenger traffic sharing for bus and subway? If the share ratio is 87.70%, and other things being equal, how to adjust the ticket price?

12. There are three modes for traveler n from A to B, respectively, for the Auto, Bus and Metro. The fixed utility function of each travel mode as(1), (2) and(3), Table 6-26 and Table 6-27 show the attribute of each travel mode before or after implementing measures, try to calculate the share ratio of each mode.

$$V_{car} = -0.025IVTT - 0.05OVTT - 0.004COST$$

$$V_{bus} = -1.8 - 0.025IVTT - 0.05OVTT - 0.004COST$$

$$V_{metro} = -2 - 0.025IVTT - 0.05OVTT - 0.004COST$$

Table 6-26 The attribute of each mode from A to B(present situation)

Mode	Travel time(min)		Travel cost(cost)
	IVTT(In vehicle travel time)	OVTT(Off vehicle travel time)	
Car	18	0	4.0
Bus	18	20	0.5
Metro	18	15	2.0

Table 6-27 The attribute of each mode from A to B(after implementing measures)

Mode	Travel time (min)		Travel cost(cost)
	IVTT(In vehicle travel time)	OVTT(Off vehicle travel time)	
Car	25	0	6.0
Bus	15	16	0.5
Metro	18	15	1.5

13. The book introduces using maximum likelihood method to calibrate the parameter of MNL mode, try to use the least square method to calibrate the parameter, and compare the *D*-value between result of these two methods, analyze the reasons.

14. The Eg. 6-7 use least square to calibrate the model parameter, try to analyze that which data need to be collected for forecasting the share ratio of travel mode in the future?

References

[1] Guan Hongzhi. Disaggregate model, a tool of traffic behavior analysis [M]. Beijing: China Communications Press, 2004.

[2] Shao Chunfu. Principles of Transportation Planning[M]. Beijing: China Railway Publishing House, 2004.

[3] Lu Huapu. Transportation Planning Theory and Method [M]. Beijing: Tsinghua University Press, 2006.

[4] Wang Wei. Traffic Planning[M]. Beijing: China Communications Press, 2007.

[5] Liu Canqi. Modern Transportation Planning [M]. Beijing People's Communications Press, 2001.

[6] Lu Ximing, Dong Zhiguo. Relationship between Transit Travel Mode Share and Land Use in Main Urban Area of Shanghai[J]. Urban Transport of China, 2014(4):1-2.

[7] FS Koppelman. A conceptual and methdological framework for the generation of activity-travel patterns[J]. Transportation, 2000, 27(1):5-23.

[8] Stephane, Hess. Estimation of value of travel-time savings using mixed logit models [J]. Transportation Research Part A Policy & Practice, 2005, 39(2):221-236.

[9] K. M. Kockelman. Anticipating new-highway impacts: opportunities for welfare analysis and credit-based congestion pricing [J]. Transportation Research Part A: Policy and Practice, 2011, 45(8):825-838.

[10] KM Kockelman. NCHRP Report 365[R]. Washington D. C.: NATIONAL ACDEMY PRESS, 1998:62-73.

[11] Ma Shuhong, K M Kockelman, DJ Fagnant. Welfare Analysis Using Logsum Differences VS. Rule of Half: A Series of Case Studies [J]. Transportation Research Record Journal of the Transportation Research Board, 2015, 2530:73-83.

[12] M A Munizaga, R Alvarez-Daziano. Mixed Logit vs. nested Logit and Probit Models[J]. Daziano, 2008.

[13] Washington, Simon P, Karlaftis, et al.. Statistical and Econometric Methods for Transportation Data Analysis, 2nd edition[M]. CRC Press / Routledge, United States of America, 2010.

[14] Ali Mekky, P. Eng. Analytics Transportation Planning[M]. America, 2001.

[15] McFadden D. Conditional logit analysis of qualitative choice behavior, on Frontiers in Econometrics, Zarenbka, Ed., Academic Press, N. Y., 1974, 105-142.

[16] Daganzo, C. Multinomial Probit, Academic Press, New York. 1979.

Chapter 7

Trip Assignment

7.1 Literature Review

In the 1950s, the United States carried out traffic investigation and planning studies on the Detroit metropolitan area and the Chicago metropolitan area, and created a transportation planning method based on the quantitative analysis of the behavior of travelers. Many theoretical researchers and transportation engineers have put a lot of efforts into the study and developed a four stages of network traffic flow calculation method based on the trip generation, trip distribution, trip patterns, traffic allocation. Traffic allocation as the final stage of the four-stage forecasting method is an important link in the traffic flow analysis. The trip distribution is the act of assigning the travel space PA/OD to a specific traffic network according to the known road network description in order to obtain the traffic volume. If the flow direction is further needed, it requires the directional conversion of PA to OD according to the amount of travel destination or time characteristics. If one needs to calculate the number of vehicles on a road, the trip distribution should be implemented after obtaining the OD traffic volume (number of vehicles) according to vehicle load factor. OD traffic volume is the amount of traffic from the origin to the destination. In general, there are many roads available between an OD pair. Trip distribution aims to distribute the OD traffic volume as close as possible to the actual traffic distribution of the road network.

Trip assignment was originally used on cobweb-like air routes, and it was assumed that travelers tend to choose the shortest route from the origin the destination, which is the OD-based route assignment. Early trip assignment was chosen on the basis of experience: a person familiar with the trip assignment area could draw one or two routes connecting a pair of traffic plots presuming a "route splits" ratio and assigning traffic according to this value. This ratio is a variance function of the distance, time, and cost between different routes. As the size of the analog traffic network becomes larger and larger, more and more complicated, the manual distribution is time-consuming and inconsistent with the practice resulting the manual distribution being difficult to meet the needs. There is a breakthrough of the trip assignment method symbolized by the publication on the shortest path through a maze by Moore(1959). The computer program was introduced to OD table assigned to the OD point on the most "short" route. This method was named All-or-Nothing method which is also known as the shortest path allocation method. This method does not take into account the congestion of the road network and takes the path resistance as a constant. The OD of each OD pair is all assigned on the shortest path connecting OD pairs. The advantage of this method is that the calculation is quite simple and the assignment is completed in one time. The disadvantage is that when the traffic network is congested, the distribution result does not accord with the actual traffic condition. This is because it's the road resistance (time consumption, fuel consumption, etc.) which will increase as the gradual increment of traffic volume on the shortest path, which means this road may no longer be the shortest path. Thus, traffic could accordingly be transferred to other feasible paths. Two methods have been developed to tackle this weakness. The first one is known as the "capacity limit" method based on the heuristic method, which adjusts the distribution of road network traffic through changing the road impedance in order to maintain the distributed traffic within the capacity of the corresponding sections. The other method is based on the mathematical optimization method. The famous traffic experts Wardrop came up the first and second theorem of network balance distribution in 1952. Wardrop's first principle established a model minimizing transformational cost for the sake of travelers. Wardrop's second principle developed an optimized model that minimized the overall cost of the total trip from the road planner's point of view. Wardrop principles played a very important role in the development of traffic flow assignment theory. In 1956, Beckmann proposed a mathematical programming model to describe the Wardrop principle, and proved the equivalence, existence and uniqueness of the solution, but it was difficult to solve it due to a lack of theoretical and computational methods. Leblanc and other scholars resolved the solution of Beckmann model using the F-W(Frank-Wolfe) algorithm in the nonlinear programming in 1975, which enabled meeting the needs of modern traffic distribution with complex mega-networks. The transportation planning technology has developed rapidly since then. It costs 23 years since the come up of Wardrop principle tile being resolved by Beckmann model, symbolizing a leap from theory to practice of modern trip distribution. This method takes the congestion characteristics of the network, which is variation of traffic impedance against the traffic flow, into consideration. During the study of the actual travel behavior of the network travel process, it was found that it was a difficulty for travelers accurately calculating the impedance of each path so as to make to make the right choice. In addition, different travelers could estimate totally different values regarding the same path due to the difference of individually computational capacity and personalized perception. Therefore, Professor Daganzo and Professor Sheffi in 1977 proposed the theory of random distribution. This method stated that road users' perception for road impedance was only an estimation of the actual impedance. The difference between the estimated value and the actual value is a random variable. The stochastic distribution can well reflect the randomness of the row selection behavior, which is a big step in the process of fitting and reflecting the real traffic network. With the development of computer technology, some traffic flow assignment theories have been realized in traffic planning software, such as TransCAD, TRIPS, EMME, CUBE etc., which enables more and more application of the traffic distribution in practical planning projects.

In the 1980s, as the methods of transportation planning were relatively mature, the field of transportation research gradually shifted attention to traffic control and guidance, for example, the field of Intelligent Transportation Systems (ITS). The time concept of transportation planning is usually in the form of year. The OD matrix at a given time of year can be regarded as invariant, and the time concept of traffic control and induction can be divided into minutes or even seconds. It is necessary to extend the trip distribution to the travel process of the traffic, so the "dynamic trip assignment" which introduces the travel time is necessary to make the traffic flow truly in accordance with the actual situation of the road network and reflect the time variation of the travel demand. Made an urgent request. Dynamic Trip Assignment, is to reduce personal travel costs or the total cost of the system as the goal, considering the changing supply situation at any time. The traffic needs to be rationally assigned to different paths on the simulation method. It is an optimal model to analyze the trip distribution under the conditions of traffic supply and traffic demand conditions. It is an important basis for traffic flow control and management, dynamic path guidance and so on. At present, although the dynamic trip assignment has not yet matured in algorithm and practical application, it is still one of the development directions of trip assignment.

7.2 Basic Assignment

Trip assignment generally has four scenarios:

- OD traffic volume will be assigned to existing traffic network. Compare estimations of the link traffic volume and the corresponding assigned traffic volume. Test model accuracy and calibrate model parameters.
- The planning annual OD traffic volume is assigned to the current traffic network, and the shortcomings of the existing road network to meet the traffic demand of the planning year are analyzed, which provides the basis for the planning and design of the traffic network.

· The planning annual traffic volume is assigned to the planning network, and the rationality of the traffic network planning is evaluated. The parameters such as traffic volume, running time and congestion status are provided for the performance and influence calculation of the planning scheme.

· The planning year OD traffic volume is assigned to the traffic network of different action plans and different years, so as to provide the basis for rationally determining the transportation management plan of the construction sequence and construction period.

Trip assignment technology also has important value and applicability in the following problems:

· Evaluation of options available;

· To establish priorities for the construction of transport projects;

· To study the main influencing factors of traffic;

· To study the main influencing factors of traffic migration;

· To determine the best location of service centers or public facilities (such as fire stations, bus hub station);

· To determine the optimal layout of regional traffic observation station program.

7.3 Computer Representation of Traffic Network

7.3.1 Adjacency Matrix Method

The most common way to enter a traffic network into computer is the Adjacency Matrix method. The adjacency matrix of a traffic network is a n-th square matrix l (n is the number of nodes in the network), which represents the general adjacency of the nodes in the network. Its elements l_{ij} are determined according to the following rules:

$$l_{ij}=\begin{cases}1,\text{node } i \text{ and node } j \text{ are connected with each other}\\0,\text{node } i \text{ and node } j \text{ are connected without edge or } i=j\end{cases} \tag{7-1}$$

Suppose there is a traffic network, the connection relationships of each node are shown in Fig. 7-1, and its corresponding adjacency matrix is shown in Table 7-1.

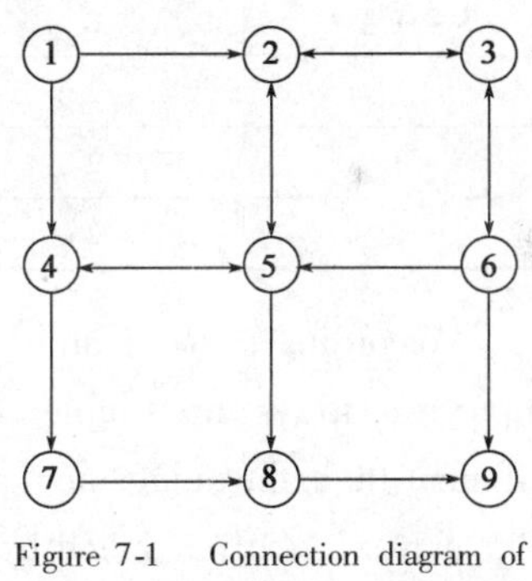

Figure 7-1 Connection diagram of each node in the traffic network

Table 7-1 Adjacency matrix table corresponding to Fig. 7-1

i	j								
	1	2	3	4	5	6	7	8	9
1	0	1	0	1	0	0	0	0	0
2	0	0	1	0	1	0	0	0	0
3	0	1	0	0	0	1	0	0	0
4	0	0	0	0	1	0	1	0	0

continued

i	j								
	1	2	3	4	5	6	7	8	9
5	0	1	0	1	0	0	0	1	0
6	0	0	1	0	1	0	0	0	1
7	0	0	0	0	0	0	0	1	0
8	0	0	0	0	0	0	0	0	1
9	0	0	0	0	0	0	0	0	0

For unidirectional edges(i, j), the connection value in one direction of the line is $1(l_{ij} = 1)$ and the other direction is $0(l_{ij} = 1)$. If line$(1, 4)$ has direction, it means that it is a one-way line, so in the adjacency matrix $l_{14} = 1$, and $l_{41} = 0$. If each side of the traffic network is bi – directional, then its adjacent matrix is a symmetric matrix.

7.3.2 Adjacency List Method

Adjacency list method is similar to adjacency matrix method. Adjacency list method uses two sets of numbers to represent the adjacencies of the network. Dimensional array $R(i)$ represents the number of edges connected to the node i; the other group is a two-dimensional array $V(i, j)$ containing $R(i)$ elements. The node number of the connected node j. Table 7-2 shows the adjacencies of the traffic network in Fig. 7-1 using the adjacency list method.

Table 7-2 the adjacent table of contents corresponding to Fig. 7-1

Node i	$R(i)$	$V(i, j)$	Node i	$R(i)$	$V(i, j)$
1	2	2,4	5	3	2,4,8
2	2	3,5	6	3	3,5,9
3	2	2,6	7	1	8
4	2	5,7	8	1	9

According to $R(i)$ and $V(i, j)$, the computer can judge the adjacency between nodes, and the input two arrays are simpler than the input adjacency matrix. The adjacency list method is more efficient than the adjacency matrix. As can be seen from Table 7-2, the amount of information elements is greatly reduced by removing the non-connected relationships. Usually, the more complex the network is, the better this method is. For example, in the planning of transportation network in Xi'an, elements of L matrix are 45396, adjacent list method only input 1498 valid data(3.3% of the total data), the efficiency of about 30 times better. Therefore, the adjacency list method is more efficient than the adjacency matrix to represent the transport network. Adjacency list method is adapted to input, call and search network structure adjacency, which not only can reduce the computer input and calculation workload, but also can greatly reduce the memory unit required by software in the traffic planning process and improve the calculation speed.

7.3.3 Edge Cataloging Table

Another computer simulation method for representing the network structure is edge cataloging method which arranges the edges in the network arbitrarily. Each edge corresponds to a sequence number. The computer stores the sequence number and the starting and ending node number of each edge. Table 7-3 is the edge cataloging table corresponding to the network in Fig. 7-1.

Table 7-3 The edge cataloging table corresponding to Fig. 7-1

Sequence number	Starting point	Sequence number	Starting point
1	(1, 2)	9	(1, 4)
2	(2, 3)	10	(4, 7)
3	(3, 2)	11	(2, 5)
4	(4, 5)	12	(5, 2)
5	(5, 4)	13	(5, 8)
6	(6, 5)	14	(3, 6)
7	(7, 8)	15	(6, 3)
8	(8, 9)	16	(6, 9)

Storage edge cataloging table needs less memory space than storage adjacency matrix, but according to the edge cataloging table to search the network is not very convenient, therefore it is not often used in transportation planning.

7.3.4 Weight Matrix

According to the adjacency matrix (or adjacent list table or edge cataloging table), the computer can determine the adjacency between nodes, that is, to determine the connection mode of the network. But the adjacency matrix only gives the general connection between nodes. There is no quantitative information of relationships between nodes such as the length between two nodes, travel time or travel cost etc.. The quantitative information of relationships between nodes is reflected by the weight matrix (D), and the element d_{ij} of the weight matrix is determined by the following equation:

$$d_{ij}=\begin{cases}0 & i=j\\ \infty & \text{There is no edge connection between two nodes}\\ \omega_{ij} & \text{There is an edge connection between two nodes}\end{cases} \tag{7-2}$$

The "weight" in the weight matrix can be the connection length between two nodes, the driving time, the travel cost, the traffic flow and so on according to the actual needs. As shown in Fig. 7-2, the distance (km) between the nodes is represented by the number beside the edge. The distance weight matrix of the network is shown in Table 7-4.

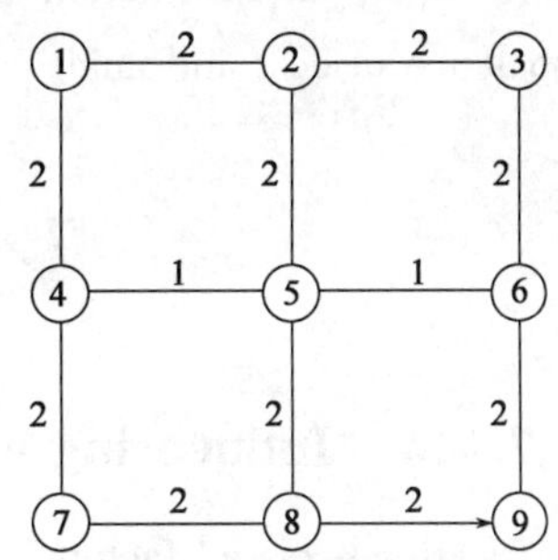

Figure 7-2 Network diagram with weights

Table 7-4 Distance weight matrix table

i	j								
	1	2	3	4	5	6	7	8	9
1	0	2	∞	2	∞	∞	∞	∞	∞
2	2	0	2	∞	2	∞	∞	∞	∞
3	∞	2	0	∞	∞	2	∞	∞	∞
4	2	∞	∞	0	1	∞	2	∞	∞
5	∞	2	∞	1	0	1	∞	2	∞
6	∞	∞	2	∞	1	0	∞	∞	2
7	∞	∞	∞	2	∞	∞	0	2	∞
8	∞	∞	∞	∞	2	∞	2	0	2
9	∞	∞	∞	∞	∞	2	∞	2	0

In the process of abstraction of the actual road network, whether the number of cross-sections or the number of cross-points are thousands, if the actual road is transformed into corresponding computing network, on the one hand, to collect and collate the corresponding data is very difficult; on the other hand, the processing cost will increase exponentially. Therefore, in the actual analysis, according to the different required accuracy, it is needed to simplify the actual road. Simplification should mainly consider the following points:

· The road which is not the only connection between two nodes, is narrow and has small capacity may not be considered;

· Small road intersection is not considered as a node, in the road impedance function it can be taken into account with the appropriate impact;

· According to the needs, several parallel roads can be combined into a road, and modify the capacity of this road;

· Hierarchical structure of the network, for example, in the distribution process, do traffic assignment for the main trunk roads in the city which constitute the city's transportation network, and then for local sub-network which are constituted by roads from a district or a few districts.

In short, the abstraction and simplification of the transport network is decided after considering the balance of cost and analysis of the accuracy.

7.4 Shortest Path Selection

7.4.1 Influencing Factors of Path Selection

(1) Road-related factors

The trip "impedance" of each route has the following aspects:

· Travel time;

· Travel distance;

· Travel expenses;

· Travel safety;

· Road conditions, such as road alignment, sidewalks, intersections, signal levels, greening, etc..

The trip impedance is generally considered to be a weighting function for all of the above factors. However, in practical applications, safety, road conditions are difficult to quantify, the future situation is more difficult to assess, therefore, in the traffic assignment process, the direct consideration of factors are travel time, travel distance and travel cost, the rest of the factors are indirect considered in road capacity estimation and the road impedance function.

(2) Driver-related factors

Drivers' perceptions of road conditions vary with their socio-economic characteristics and physiological characteristics. For example, high-income drivers may pay more attention to travel time, rather than the level of travel cost. Overgaard (1966) found that the choice of route may also depend on the purpose of travel.

(3) Vehicle-related factors

Trucks and cars from the same starting point to the same destination may choose a different route. This is partly because local laws prohibit the use of certain roads for trucks. In Denmark and China, the main consideration for car driver routing is time, while truck drivers are primarily concerned with distance. For China, the toll of expressways and the cost of expressways also affect the movement of trucks.

7.4.2 Shortest Path Calculation

The shortest path computation is the most basic algorithm in trip assignment. On one hand, currently all the common used methods for traffic assignment are based on the shortest path; on the other hand, at least 90% of the computation time in any assignment method, including the balanced assignment method, is spent on the shortest path. Therefore, a good trip assignment method must be based on a good shortest path calculation method. The shortest path algorithm problem consists of two sub-problems: the calculation of the minimum path impedance between two nodes and the identification of the shortest path between two nodes. The former is the premise to solve the latter. Many algorithms consider these two sub-problems separately. The algorithm is designed to calculate the minimum impedance and the shortest path separately.

In all kinds of literature, there are many algorithms about the shortest path of traffic assignment, such as Dijkstra method, matrix iteration method, and Floyd-Warshall method. In this section, Dijkstra algorithm is used as an example.

7.4.2.1 Dijkstra method

This method was first proposed by Dijkstra in 1959, also known as Label-correcting Method. It is often used to calculate the minimum impedance from the start point to the end point. By Dijkstra method, all the minimum impedance between nodes can be obtained simultaneously in the network.

(1) Basic idea

· First, starting from the starting point O, give each node a label, there are two categories of labels (T and P).

The label T is a temporary label indicating the upper limit of the shortest path weight from the start point O to this point. The label P is a fixed label indicating the shortest path weight from the starting point O to this point.

· In the labeling process, T label is changing, while P label does no longer change. Give label T for those points without P labels.

· Each step of the algorithm changes the label T of a point to the label P until all the label T are changed to the P label. That is, the process will end until all the shortest path weights from the starting point O to the other points are obtained.

(2) Process

· The first step: Initialization.

The starting point (point 1) is marked with the label P, $P(1)=0$, and the remaining points are marked with the label T, $T_1(j)=\infty$, $j=2, 3, \cdots, n$. That is, the shortest path weight from the starting point 1 to 1 is 0, and the upper limit of the shortest path weight to the other points is temporarily set to ∞. Numbers in bracket denote node number, and subscripts indicate the number of steps. After the first step, get a label P, $P(1)=0$.

· The second step:

Pass the $(K-1)$ steps, the node i is just the point where the P label is obtained, and then all the points that do not get the label P need to process in next step (step K); for all nodes adjacent to node i and not marked with the P label:

$$T_k(j)=\min[T_{k-1}(j), P(i)+d(i, j)]$$

where, $d(i, j)$ is the distance from i to j (path weight); $T_{k-1}(j)$ is the label T of node j in step $(K-1)$.

Consider the remaining points not marked with the P label, and modify their T labels:

$$T_k(j)=T_{k-1}(j)$$

In all T labels, the smallest T label is selected $T_k(j_0)$:

$$T_k(j_0)=\min T_k(j)$$

where, j_0 is the minimum T label corresponding to the node number.

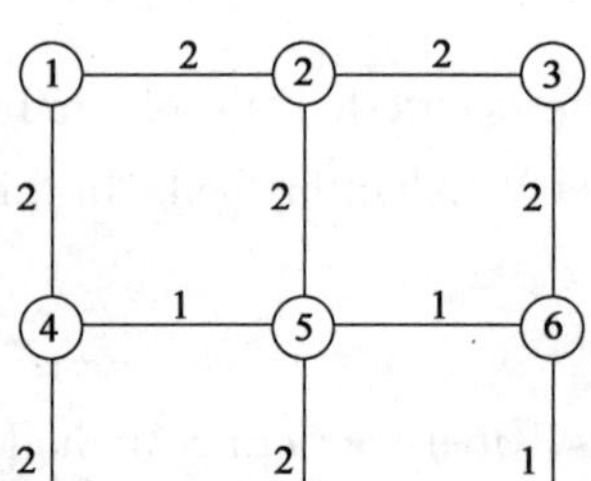

Figure 7-3 Traffic network diagram

Mark the point with the label P: $P(j_0)=T_k(j_0)$, End of step k label.

· The third step: When all the nodes have no label T, the algorithm ends. Get the shortest paths from the starting point 1 to all the other points; otherwise return to the second step.

[Example 7-1] The Dijkstra method is used to calculate the shortest paths from node 1 to node 9 of the road network shown in Fig. 7-3.

Step 1: Mark the starting point 1 with label P: $P(1)=0$, and the other nodes are marked with label T: $T_1(2)=\cdots=T_1(9)=\infty$.

Step 2: Node 1 is the point which get the label P, node 2 and 4 are adjacent with node 1 and are marked with label T, modify these two labels:

$$T_2(2) = \min[T_1(2), P(1) + d(1, 2)] = \min[\infty, 0 + 2] = 2$$

$$T_2(4) = \min[T_1(4), P(1) + d(1, 4)] = \min[\infty, 0 + 2] = 2$$

Modify the rest of the nodes without P labels:

$$T_2(3) = T_2(5) = T_2(6) = T_2(7) = T_2(8) = T_2(9) = \infty$$

In all T labels, find the smallest label. Node 2, 4 is the minimum; optionally choose one (for example: node 2), given the P label,

$$P(2) = T_2(2) = 2$$

Step 3: Node 2 just got the P label. Node 3 and 5 are adjacent with node 2, and they are marked with label T, modify the two nodes of the label T:

$$T_3(3) = \min[T_2(3), P(2) + d(2, 3)] = \min[\infty, 2 + 2] = 4$$

$$T_3(5) = \min[T_2(5), P(2) + d(2, 5)] = \min[\infty, 2 + 2] = 4$$

Modify the rest of the nodes without P labels:

$$T_3(4) = 2$$

$$T_3(6) = T_3(7) = T_3(8) = T_3(9) = \infty$$

In all T labels, node 4 is the smallest:

$$P(4) = T_3(4) = 2$$

Step 4: Node 8 just got P label. The nodes 9 and 8 are adjacent to each other, and the T label is modified to modify the T label of the point:

$$T_9(9) = \min[T_8(9), P(8) + d(8, 9)] = \min[6, 5 + 2] = 6$$

In all label T, node 9 is the smallest, and node 9 is marked with the label P:

$$P[9] = T_9(9) = 6$$

All nodes are marked with the label P, the calculation is over. The shortest paths from node 1 to the other nodes are obtained, as shown in Table 7-5.

Table 7-5 Results

Node	1	2	3	4	5	6	7	8	9
1	0	2	4	2	3	4	4	5	6
Label P	$P(1)$	$P(2)$	$P(3)$	$P(4)$	$P(5)$	$P(6)$	$P(7)$	$P(8)$	$P(9)$

7.4.2.2 Other methods

Traffic planning often needs to find the shortest path weights matrix between any two nodes in the road network ($n \times n$ order), n is sometimes large. Dijkstra algorithm needs to be repeated n times, the calculation efficiency is not the highest. Methods prior to this method and with less number of iterations can be found in a large number of literatures (e. g. Martin, 1961, etc.), such as Shimbel algorithm, also known as matrix iterative method, which uses the matrix to represent the network, through the matrix operation to determine the shortest path. The main drawback of the algorithm is that it requires a larger storage space (about 10-20 times of Dijkstra algorithm).

7.4.2.3 Shortest path identification

After obtaining the shortest path weights matrix, it is necessary to find out the shortest path between each node pair, allocate the traffic flow, and then plan the network.

The shortest path is usually identified by tracing: starting from the starting point of each shortest path, searching for each traffic node in the shortest path until the end of the path.

Algorithm ideas:

· Starting from the starting point r, looking for node i adjacent to r, if satisfied: $d_{ri} + L_{\min}(i, s) = L_{\min}(r, s)$.

Then the road segment is from r to s on the shortest path on the composition of the shortest path.

where, d_{ri} is the distance from r to i; $L_{\min}(i, s)$ is the shortest path of node I to S; $L_{\min}(r, s)$ is the shortest path of node r to s.

· To find node j adjacent to node i to meet:

$$d_{ij} + L_{\min}(j, s) = L_{\min}(i, s)$$

Then the link $[i, j]$ is a segment of shortest path from r to s.

· Repeate, until the end of node s. Connect the nodes r, i, j, $\cdots$, s to get the shortest path from r to s.

If there are different paths that satisfy the above algorithm between r and s, these paths can be the shortest path from r to s.

【Example 7-2】 Identify the shortest path from node 1 to node 9 in Eg. 7-1.

【Sol.】 From the starting point 1, due to:

$$d_{14} + L_{\min}(4, 9) = 2 + 4 = 6 = L_{\min}(1, 9)$$

So link [1, 4] is on the shortest path.

Due to:

$$d_{45} + L_{\min}(5, 9) = 1 + 3 = 4 = L_{\min}(4, 9)$$

So link [4, 5] is on the shortest path.

Due to:

$$d_{56} + L_{\min}(6,9) = 1 + 2 = 3 = L_{\min}(5, 9)$$

So link [5, 6] is on the shortest path.

Due to:

$$d_{69} + L_{\min}(9, 9) = 2 + 0 = 2 = L_{\min}(6, 9)$$

So link [6, 9] is on the shortest path.

The shortest path from node 1 to node 9 is 1-4-5-6-9.

7.5 Trip Assignment Method

7.5.1 Road Resistance Function

In general, the road resistance function through a path, which is not a constant should include the impact of many factors like reflect traffic time, traffic safety, transportation costs, comfort, convenience and punctuality, etc.. However, it is very difficult to establish a scientific rigor and explanatory function model based on these factors. Through a large number of theoretical analysis and engineering practice, it has been found that, for passenger transport, the main factors affecting the road resistance is time. So travel time is often used as the main basis for metering road resistance, which is based on the following three reasons:

· Theoretical research and practical observation show that the driving time is the primary factor considered by the traveler, especially in the path and mode choice of urban traffic.

· Almost all of the other factors affecting the road resistance are closely related to the driving time, and showing the same trend with the driving time.

· Travel time is easier to measure than other factors, and even if it is necessary to take the impact of other factors into consideration, those factors are often being converted to time for measurement.

Therefore, the road travel time-traffic flow function can be expressed as:

$$t_a = f(q_a)$$

where, t_a is the travel time required for section a; q_a is the traffic flow through road segment a. The most widely used road travel time function is the BPR function developed by the Bureau of Publ ic Road(BPR) in the form of:

$$t_a = t_0\left[1 + \alpha\left(\frac{q_a}{c_a}\right)^{\beta}\right]$$

where, t_a is the impedance of section a; t_0 is free flow impedance, that is, the vehicle free travel time when the flow on the road is zero, which mainly depends on the technical level of road sections, traffic control and other conditions; q_a is the traffic volume of section a; c_a is the actual capacity of road section a, that is, the maximum number of vehicles that can be passed by the road section per unit time; α, β are block coefficients obtained from the actual data regression analysis, which can be also taken from the value used in the US Highway Bureau traffic allocation procedures: $\alpha = 0.15$, $\beta = 4$.

7.5.2 Wardrop Equilibrium Principle

In 1924, Knight in an economic paper first discussed the idea of user balance, but in the field of traffic research this idea was officially came up until 1952 by Wardrop. Wardrop First Principle: The network will be in a state of balance when the user of the road knows exactly the traffic status of the road network and attempts to select the shortest path. In the network considering the impact of congestion on the travel time, each OD pair has an equal and shortest travel time when the network reaches the equilibrium state; the unused path has equal or longer travel time. The Wardrop second principle: the crowded road network traffic should be based on the average or the total cost of travel based on the minimum distribution.

If the traffic assignment model satisfies the Wardrop first or second principle, the model is a balanced model. Models meet the Wardrop first principle are user equilibrium(UE) or user optimal allocation models while System optimization (SO) allocation models are those meet the Wardrop second principle.

(1) User equilibrium assignment model

In 1952, after Wardrop proposed the principle of user equilibrium distribution, there was no strict model for a long period to find a traffic allocation method that met this balance criterion. In 1956, Beckmann et al. proposed a mathematical programming model to meet the Wardrop criterion, which functioned as the theoretical foundation for the problem of traffic distribution. Later distribution models, such as elastic demand allocation model and distribution-distribution model, are all different extended variations based on the Beckmann model.

· Parameters used in the user equilibrium allocation model

x_a——traffic on section a;

t_a——traffic impedance on section a, also known as travel time;

$t_a(x_a)$——section a with the flow as an independent variable impedance function, also known as the travel time function;

f_k^{rs}——departure from the r, the destination for the OD between the k on the path of traffic;

c_k^{rs}——the total travel time on the path of the k th of the OD between the destination and the destination;

u_{rs}——the travel time for the shortest path between the departure point of the destination and the destination for the r;

$\delta_{a,k}^{rs}$——link-path-dependent variable, 0-1 variable, If the link a is on the k th path between the departure point r and the destination s, then$\delta_{a,k}^{rs}=1$, otherwise $\delta_{a,k}^{rs}=0$。

· Basic constraints of the model

First, the flow conservation equation should be satisfied, that is, the sum of the distribution traffic of each path should equal to the total amount of OD traffic. The formula can be expressed as:

$$\sum_{k\in W_{rs}} f_k^{rs} = q_{rs}\ \forall r\in R,\ \forall s\in S \tag{7-3}$$

Second, the traffic on the section should be from each (r, s) point on the road through the flow of accumulated, which meets the following conditions:

$$x_a = \sum_r \sum_s \sum_k f_k^{rs}\delta_{a,k}^{rs}\ \forall a\in L, \forall r\in R, \forall s\in S, \forall k\in W_{rs} \tag{7-4}$$

At the same time, the impedance of the path should be the accumulation of the impedance of each path passing through the path. Therefore, the total impedance of the path and the impedance of the link should meet the following conditions:

$$c_k^{rs} = \sum_a t_a(x_a)\delta_{a,k}^{rs}\ \forall a\in L, \forall r\in R, \forall s\in S, \forall k\in W_{rs} \tag{7-5}$$

Finally, the path traffic should meet the nonnegative constraint, $f_k^{rs}\geqslant 0\ \forall k, r, s$

· Beckmann traffic balance distribution model

It is found that in the equilibrium distribution the total area of the region under the travel time function curve was the smallest (Sheffi, 1985). Therefore, the objective function can take the sum of the integral of the travel time function of each section and use the method of minimizing the objective function Distribution problem. The traffic balance distribution model is as follows:

$$\min: Z(X) = \sum_a \int_0^{x_a} t_a(x)\,dx$$

$$\text{s. t.} \begin{cases} \sum_k f_k^{rs} = q_{rs} \\ f_k^{rs} \geqslant 0 \end{cases}$$

$$x_a = \sum_r \sum_s \sum_k f_k^{rs} \delta_{a,k}^{rs} \tag{7-6}$$

【Example 7-3】 As shown in Fig. 7-4, there are two paths (and also sections) connecting a departure point and a simple destination network. The impedance of the two sections is assumed as the function of the traffic volume x_1 and x_2:

$$t_1 = 2 + x_1,\ t_2 = 1 + 2x_2$$

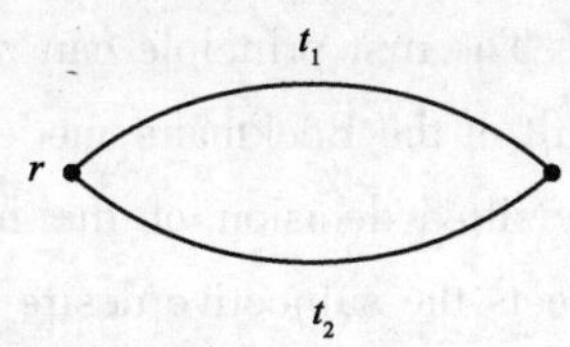

Figure 7-4 Traffic network diagram

Knowing that $q = 5$ between r, s, please find the network to achieve the equilibrium state of the solution.

【Sol.】 **Method 1**: Using the Beckmann model to solve this problem. Substituting the impedance function into the model:

$$\min: Z(X) = \int_0^{x_1} (2 + x)\,dx + \int_0^{x_2} (1 + 2x)\,dx$$

$$\text{s. t.} \begin{cases} x_1 + x_2 = 5 \\ x_1,\ x_2 \geqslant 0 \end{cases}$$

Combine "$x_1 = 5 - x_2$" into the objective function and integrate it into an unconstrained minimum problem:

$$\min: Z(X) = 1.5x_1^2 - 9x_1 + 30$$

Let $dZ/dx_1 = 0$, get $x_1 = 3$, $x_2 = 2$.

Method 2: This problem can also be based on Wardrop user balance principle by resolving the equilibrium state of the solution. When the network reaches equilibrium, it should meet:

a. Conservative conditions: $x_1 + x_2 = 5$;

b. The balance condition: $t_1 = t_2$, that is $2 + x_1 = 1 + 2x_2$.

Solve this equation group, get $x_1 = 3$, $x_2 = 2$, $t_1 = t_2 = 5$.

Method 3: The problem can also be found by graphic method of balanced distribution solution, as shown in Fig. 7-5.

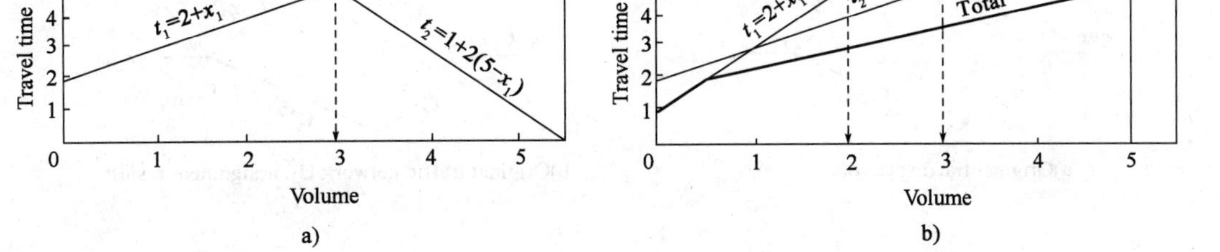

Figure 7-5 Graphic method

(2) Optimal allocation model of system

The Beckmann model is based on the Wardrop first principle based on the user equilibrium principle, which is therefore called user optimal (UE). Wardrop also proposed a second principle that is the system optimal allocation problem. System Optimum Assignment is defined as: In a congested network, the traffic should be allocated according to the principle that the total travel time in the road network is minimized.

The first principle can reflect the actual travel behavior of the user in the traffic network. The result of the Beckmann model based on the first principle is more in line with the situation of the diversified decision of the multiple traveler in the actual traffic network. The second principle reflects the subjective desire of the traffic system manager. The obtained results are in the same for some circumstances, while there is a difference compared to the actual distribution of the traffic network. However, it can be used as the index of the system evaluation to provide the management decision-making basis for the manager. In this sense, the second principle is the distribution principle desired by the road system manager.

The optimal principle of the system is easier to describe by mathematical models. The objective function is the minimum impedance of all users in the network, and the constraint is the same as the user equilibrium distribution model. Therefore, the optimal allocation model is:

$$\min: \tilde{Z}(X) = \sum_a x_a t_a(x_a) \tag{7-7}$$

$$\text{s. t.} \begin{cases} \sum_k f_k^{rs} = q_{rs} \\ f_k^{rs} \geqslant 0 \end{cases}$$

$$x_a = \sum_r \sum_s \sum_k f_k^{rs} \delta_{a,k}^{rs}$$

(3) BRAESS paradox

The paradox shows that building a new road in a region does not necessarily mean that the total travel time in the area or the travel time of each road user will be reduced. The reason is that road users choosing the personal travel path is based on the principle of user balance distribution. This allocation method does not reduce the total travel time of the system. So adding a new path will not essentially reduce the total travel time of the system. When the traveler based on the principle of optimal allocation of travel behavior selection, the new section is bound to enhance the overall system travel situation. Sheffi (1985) gives numerical examples of paradoxical problems, as shown in Fig. 7-6 and Fig. 7-7.

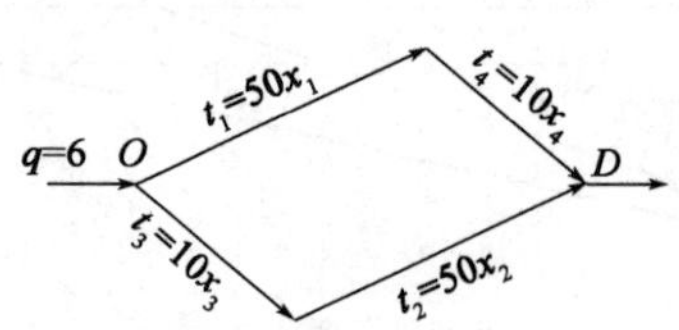

a)Original traffic network

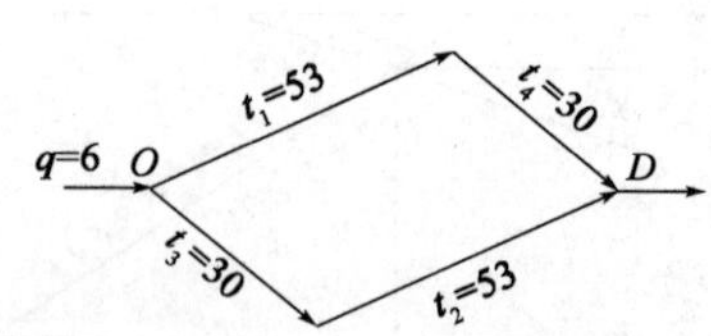

b)Original traffic network UE assignment results

Figure 7-6

It can be seen from Fig. 7-6b) that the travel time of each driver in the original traffic network is 83 min, and the total travel time of the system is 83 × 6 = 498 min. As can be seen from Fig. 7-7b) that after the increment of the road, the travel time of each driver in the transportation network is 92 min, and the total travel time of the system is 92 × 6 = 552 min. Validated the scientific nature of the BRAESS paradox.

a)After the new section of the traffic network

b)After the new section of the traffic network UE aliocation results

Figure 7-7

7.5.3 Random UE Model

The Wardrop equilibrium principle advances in that it reflects the crowding characteristics of the network and the fact that the traffic impedance varies with the flow, but it is difficult for the traveler to accurately calculate the impedance of each path to make the correct path selection, and because each traveler has different calculations and levels, and the estimates for different travelers will not be the same for the same section.

The impedance of the road section changes with the amount of traffic. Assuming that the expected value of the impedance of the road segment is a function of the traffic volume of the road segment, the path selection behavior of the road user in the random user balance assignment still follows the Wardrop first principle, but the user selects the path with minimum impedance. The probability that the user chooses a path between the ODs is equal to the probability that it senses the path impedance to be the smallest in the perceptual impedance of all possible paths between the OD pairs. This probability of selection is a conditional probability. The perceived impedance of the k-th path is chosen as follows:

$$P_k^{rs} = P(C_k^{rs} \leqslant C_l^{rs}),\ \forall l \neq k; \forall k, r, s \tag{7-8}$$

In a random user equilibrium state, an OD pair between all selected paths does not necessarily have the same actual impedance. The amount of traffic allocated to a selected route is equal to the product of the OD pair's communication probability versus the selection probability of the path, i. e. :

$$f_k^{rs} = q_{rs} \cdot p_k^{rs},\ \forall k, r, s \tag{7-9}$$

In this relation, the path traffic f_k^{rs} is related to the selection probability which is related to the size of the perceived path impedance. The size of the perceived path impedance, as a random variable, is a function of the actual road impedance. The actual road impedance is a function of traffic. So a random user balance of the state can be achieved by processing this procedure cycle by cycle. The relationship shown in Eq. (7-9) is called SUE condition.

7.5.4 The Relationship Between the Traffic Distribution Models

(1) The relationship between optimal allocation of system and optimal assignment of users

The impedance function is transformed, therefore, the user optimal assignment model can be transformed into the system optimal allocation model if $\tilde{t}_a(x_a)$ is used as the impedance function. So the user optimal allocation under the impedance function is obtained. The solution is the optimal solution of the system. In other words, after the impedance function is transformed, the optimal model of the system can be solved according to the algorithm of user optimal model.

Let:

$$\tilde{t}_a(x_a) = t_a(x_a) + x_a \frac{dt_a(x_a)}{dx_a}$$

Get:

$$\begin{aligned}\int_0^{x_a} \tilde{t}_a(x)dx &= \int_0^{x_a} [t_a(x) + x\frac{dt_a(x)}{dx}]dx \\ &= \int_0^{x_a} [t_a(x)dx + xdt_a(x)] \\ &= \int_0^{x_a} d[t_a(x)x] = x_a t_a(x_a)\end{aligned}$$

(2) Relationship between UE and SUE

SUE is more universal, and UE is only a special case of SUE, when the perceived impedance variance is 0, that is, road users on the road impedance estimates are exactly the same, SUE becomes UE.

7.6 Trip Assignment Preparation

7.6.1 Initial Inspection

In the road network coding and zones division, to maintain zones and road network balance is very important. This means that the accuracy of road network coding must match the zone system. Excessive road network (relative to the number of zones) will result in a low traffic volume on the road segment. Small number of zones will result in a low traffic volume because in this case a lot of trips are "inter-zones" and will not be assigned to the road network.

7.6.2 Pre-run Inspection

(1) Edit the travel data, check the following factors are correct

- Data types (numbers, characters, data, etc.);
- The data ranges;
- The user's missing data;
- The system's missing data;
- Response frequency distribution.

Ensure that external trips are represented in the requirements matrix. Check its validity.

(2) Edit the road network

· Mapping and analysis of road networks covering most of the study area. Find missing links, skip links, directed coding errors, and fatal terminal errors to find illogical routes and speed.

· Check the location of the zone center and the appropriateness of connecting to the road network.

· Check steering penalties and prohibitions.

· Check the road network connectivity.

(3) Check the rationality of combination of demand and supply

It is reasonable to plot the frequency distribution of the trip length and determine the following statistics:

· Total number of trips;

· The maximum, minimum and average travel length.

7.6.3 Program

Prepare a number of test scenarios. Choose a clear standard for evaluation. These standards are usually derived from goals and objectives.

7.7 Trip Assignment Frequently Asked Questions

7.7.1 Error Sources in Traffic Assignment

(1) Error in assignment method

· System errors between assignment principle and realistic behavior;

· Errors form simulating dynamic traffic flow with static model;

· Errors form simplifying the assumptions, for example, "the travel time on the road segment depends only on the flow of the road", which may be a suspicion that, in congested road network, intersection traffic flow and segment flow will be the important reasons for delay.

(2) Errors in demand estimation

· Errors due to aggregation of the zone travel;

· Errors due to exclusion of "inter-zone trips";

· The estimation error of exogenous variables;

· The remaining errors from traffic distribution and modal split.

(3) Supply estimation errors

· Road network abstraction errors (e. g. too many or too few road sections);

· Road network connections (e. g. high-load sections, missing links, and virtual sections connected to the centroid);

· Road network parameters(e. g. lack of steering penalties or prohibitions, wrong direction of traffic, inaccurate lane numbers);

· Errors in defining generalized cost function, only using the most common time parameters;

· Errors in cost estimation;

· Errors in forecasting cost components;

· Imperfect road network information.

(4) Errors in traffic statistics

· Seasonal changes in traffic flow;

· The difference between the counting time and the evaluation time.

7.7.2 Results of Trip Assignment

The results of trip assignment should be carefully checked before approval, which is particularly important in case of congested road networks. Some of the possible problems are:

· Unreasonable traffic flow on some sections;

· A large number of sections $V/C>1$;

· Not all matrices have been allocated;

· The results of traffic assignment have not achieved convergence;

· The traffic flow of section varies drastically between iterations;

· Unreasonable low speed on some sections.

The last question is the most common, and the following remedies can be taken:

· Check the road network coding problem;

· Recalculate and adjust the demand matrix that begins at the traffic generation stage and for subsequent stages;

· Recalculate the demand distribution matrix by adjusting the initial assumptions of the travel costs to match the allocation results;

· Constrain the demand matrix in such a way that $V/C>1.1$ is not allowed for any link.

7.8 Results of Trip Assignment and Evaluation

7.8.1 Validation of Assignment Results for Base Year

The first assignment results are usually that the base year OD table is assigned to the base year road network. This assignment is usually to "validate" the model and detect its "accuracy". The results of this assignment can help to understand a number of potential problems, such as some road network coding/partitioning problems, or methodological problems. Assignment errors are discussed in section 7.6. The accuracy of the traffic assignment can be verified as follows:

· Study the reasonableness of travel tree.

· Draw the travel length frequency diagram. If the maximum travel length is unreasonable, it may be beneficial to re-examine the feasibility of long-distance travel.

· Comparing the simulation flow and the section traffic volume.

· Comparing the simulated flow/volume ratio with the actual situation of the section.

· Plotting the difference between the observed flow rate and the simulated flow rate (percentage).

· Plot the difference between the base year and the forecast year's flow and speed (in percent).

You can also do the following analysis:

· Draw road section proportion diagram of the target year and the base year at different levels of service.

· Analyze and verify the starting and ending points of the road users of selected sections.

· Analysis of verification spider road network expectations line.

· Investigations turned to traffic. The main nodes are listed first, followed by a set of nodes behind and before those roads, as compared to the survey traffic flow.

At the same time, the following adjustments may be necessary to resolve the problem:

· The number of zones;

· The detailed level of the road network;

· The number of centroid connection;

· Part of the centroid to the road network connection;

· Intraoral time (car/bus);

· Access (terminal) time;

· Section parameters.

7.8.2 Systematic Reviews

The transportation system can be evaluated after the trip assignment, and the overall system condition can be assessed for one or more of the following objectives: a. economic rationality and feasibility; b. effective use of planned land to a reasonable level of service; c. effective combination of modes of transport.

(1) System cost

Total travel costs include operating costs, incident costs, and travel time costs. The transportation construction and maintenance costs can also be assessed as needed.

(2) System performance

· Total travel of the road network;

· Average travel length;

· Average speed;

· Frequency (or cumulative) distribution of travel length;

· Frequency distribution (or accumulation) of road sections flow;

· Distribution of traffic frequency (or accumulation) in car kilometers;

· Cumulative frequency distribution of lane service level of expressway (or main road);

· Statistics of urban center area multiple travel indicators.

Then, based on the above indicators to compare difference between the base year and future year, determine the merits of the planning program.

(3) Economic evaluation

· Cost/benefit;

· Present value;

· Annual cost;

· Internal rate of return.

Practice see the relevant section of Appendix 2.

Exercises

1. What is the meaning and function of trip assignment?

2. What are the basic data required for trip assignment?

3. Explain the meaning of Wardrop's first and second principles and their differences and connections.

4. Fig. 7-8 is the network diagram, where ①, ④, ⑤, ⑦ are the OD action points, the figure in the line value for travel time, some fixed value, some with traffic, Q for traffic flow, OD distribution The flow matrix is shown in Table 7-6.

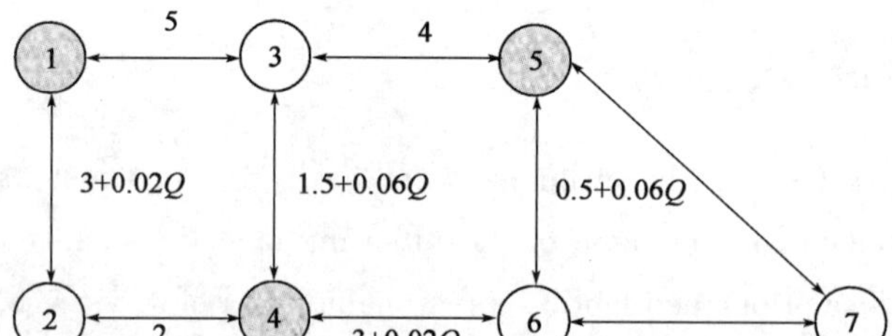

Figure 7-8 Diagram of the OD traffic network

Table 7-6 OD traffic matrix

O	D			
	①	④	⑤	⑦
①	0	300	400	500
④	300	0	100	250
⑤	400	100	0	600
⑦	500	250	600	0

· Let $Q=0$, allocate the OD matrix by the shortest path method;

· The OD matrix is allocated by the capacity limiting-incremental loading method, with the secondary distribution being 50% for the first time and 50% for the second time.

References

[1] Huang Haijun. Theory and Practice of Balanced Distribution of Urban Traffic Network[M]. Beijing: China Communications Press, 1994.

[2] Wang Wei, Xu Jiqian. Urban transport planning theory and methods[M]. Beijing: China Communications Press, 1992.

[3] Wang Wei, Guo Xiucheng. Traffic Engineering[M]. Nanjing: Southeast University Press, 2000.

[4] Xu Jiqian. General Introduction to Traffic Engineering[M]. Beijing: China Communications Press, 1991.

[5] Shao Chunfu. Principles of traffic planning [M]. Beijing: China Railway Publishing House, 2004.

[6] Lu Huapu, Huang Haijun. The Frontier of Transportation Planning Theory[M]. Beijing: Tsinghua University Press, 2007.

[7] Yosef Sheffi. Urban Transportation Network Analysis: Equilibrium Analysis Mathematical Programming Methods[M]. New Jersey:Prentice Hall,1985.

[8] David Foot. Operational Urban Models: An Application [M]. London : Methuen & Co. Ltd. ,1981.

[9] Beckmann MJ , Mcguire CB. Studies in the Economics of Transportation[J]. Economic Journal, 1956 , 26 (1) :820-821.

[10] Michael GHBell, Yasunori Lida. Transportation Network Analysis[M]. London : WILEY, 1997.

[11] Michael DMeyer, Eric JMiller. Urban Transportation Planning: A Decision-oriented Approach [M]. USA, 2008.

[12] Ali Mekky,P Eng. Analytics Transportation Planning[M]. America,2001.

[13] David EBoyce,Huw CWL Williams. Forecasting Urban Travel:Past,Present and Future[M]. UK:Edward Elgar Publishing Limited,2016.

[14] SHIMBEL A. Structure in communication nets [C]// Proceedings of the Symposium on Information Networks. New York: Polytechnic Press of the Polytechnic Institute of Brooklyn, 1955:199-203.

Chapter 8

Model Calibration and Validation

8.1 Concept[1]

It is the core work of transportation planning to make the right decisions to guide the urban traffic construction. There are some expressions in English to explain the related work. It was known as VVA (Verification/Calibration, Validation, Accreditation). Verification means to collect real world data then to seek the appropriate theoretical expression. Calibration, means to obtain the specific output data to adjust the process of parameter simulation(From Verification's assumptions), it was often based on common sense and statistical test to explore the most suitable equation repeatedly. Validation is a method to evaluate the difference between a model estimation and a real data from an application perspective. It is usually done from the output results before the formal forecast. Model accreditation is to recognize the method, parameters and results of the model based on a certain standard or a certain process. Only when the model meet the requirements of the first two "V" can we decide whether it meet the standard of "A" and whether it can be applied to solve

[1] The content of this chapter mainly refers to Xi'an Urban Traffic Model Project and other three references, FDOTSPO (2008), FHWA (2010) and Ismart (1990).

practical problems. The travel model development, validation, and application processes can be viewed as shown in Fig. 8-1. Model validation and sensitivity testing may reveal the need to return to the model estimation or model calibration process. Using a future year situation and policy to apply a transportation model requires checking the reasonableness of the forecast, or it may show that you need to return to the model estimate or calibration process. There is no need to return to the model validation process during the application of the model because the additional validation process cannot improve the accuracy of the model or model estimation, but in some cases, additional model validation can help confirm the authenticity of the forecast.

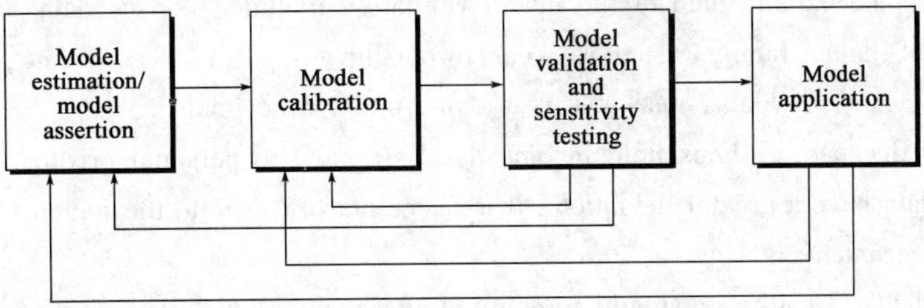

Figure 8-1 Model development and application process

Source: FHWA, 2010.

8.2 The Importance of Calibration and Accreditation of Transportation Model

The transport model is a closed system that contains a series of mathematical formulas and complex relationships in addition to specific input parameters, which are used to reflect an open real world, where the main activists does not always make a rational decision, the response to the change can be made and the response to travel is not consistent. Only to find the law that can explain the characteristics of the design of the equation then model can be used to explain the equation corresponding to the simulation. The transport model (Model worker) is not omnipotent, the lack of information and false assumptions can lead to imprecise models, leading to erroneous decisions, So models that have not been calibrated and validated cannot be used in transportation planning practices. Therefore, the model calibration and accreditation is particularly important, only after this step can we find a suitable explanatory model for traffic phenomena, seek more accurate fitting and interpretation of phenomena, so that it is in line with the actual characteristics of the simulation, and then apply it to reality.

8.3 Data Validity Check

Data checking is a critical step before model validation begins, and it is important to check the input data continuously throughout the model validation process. The data includes not only the input data but also travel survey data, special traffic flow data and velocity data. The input data should be compared with other similar data, inspection and validation should include a reasonable test data, analysis test, a map and visual inspection, and a field test. Transportation model data validation requires verification of two types of data: socioeconomic data and traffic network data. The quality of the road network and socio-economic data affect model assessment, verification and verification. Reasonable traffic forecast requires a reasonable future socioeconomic and road network data, thus, the accuracy of the model depends on the accuracy of the input data.

8.3.1 Socioeconomic Data Test

The main socioeconomic data of the model validation include: census data (income, gender, age, employment data, family structure, car ownership), public sector data, school student registration data, land use data, market survey data, and spatial photos.

· Income. Because the household income data is related to personal privacy, the survey data and the actual data have a greater deviation. It is necessary to calibrate the region's income statistics based on the government.

· Census data. Census data should compare official population statistics with community or unit actual employment, and actual living statistics.

· Family demographic verification. Indicators needed to be verified are: the number of households per capita, the number of vehicles per household, the number of vehicles per household, the number of vehicles per vehicle. It is necessary to compare the above-mentioned indicators calculated from the survey data with historical data, other caliber or survey sampling data to judge whether the indicators are reasonable.

· Car-owned ratio of family. According to the survey data, the ratio of family that own no car, one car, two cars, three cars and above three cars is separately calculated. Compare the ratio with the historical data to determine whether the indicators are reasonable.

· Frequently asked questions and solutions. There may be a lot of problems related to economic data inspection during the traffic model establishment process, and common problems and solutions are shown in Table 8-1.

Table 8-1 Troubleshooting strategies for issues with input socioeconomic data

Issue	Potential solving strategies
1. Aggregated socioeconomic data are significantly different from independent data sources	· Check data aggregation procedures to ensure that TAZs were not skipped or double counted · Check for differences between coverage areas for socioeconomic data and independent data · Determine which data set is likely to be more accurate
2. Overall aggregate rates (e. g., average household size) are different from observed data or trends	· Recheck observed data for processing errors · Perform checks for smaller geographic areas to isolate · problems or determine if the difference is general in nature
3. Inconsistency (not necessarily inequality) between number of workers and number of jobs at the regional level	· For base year, determine which data source is more reliable and adjust data from the less reliable source to be consistent with it · For forecast year, determine which variable has more reasonable growth rate and adjust growth rate for the variable with the less reasonable rate

Source: *FHWA*, 2010.

8.3.2 Basic Road Network Inspection

Compared with the difficulty to master the accurate data of the socio-economy, the input of the road network is easy to obtain and more accurate. For most of the models, the survey period traffic should be consistent with the road conditions. If the analysis is carried out in the previously surveyed road network, it is necessary to check whether there is any change of traffic condition between data surveyed time and model calibration time, and the latest road conditions should be reflected through the simple update of the model, including increasing road traffic capacity (by increasing the lane), or adding new bus routes.

In order to avoid the wrong coding or connection error of the abstract network, the common test method is to carry out the overall inspection of the road network and classification inspection for different grades of the road, and compare the attributes of the similar sections in Geographic Information System (GIS) platform. For the public transport network, the edited bus section can be compared with the actual operating data. Road sections can be randomly selected for the property inspection, while one-way section should be checked one by one for the region with much more one-way road sections. GIS can also be used to check the connection of road network, link attributes and so on.

(1) Centroid link inspection

The position and number of center-of-mass links have a very important effect on trip assignment, and different link matching can affect the assignment results. The location and number of the main road entrance and the bus station of different districts and roads should be reasonably matched, to reflect the reality as far as possible.

(2) Turn penalty

Not only the speed of road but also the intersection of the turn penalty time should be considered in the calculation of travel time. In fact, traveling on the congested main roads, most of the delay time are accumulated to the intersection. In the mesoscopic and microscopic model analysis, the correct and reasonable setting of the turn penalty is very important to get the simulation effect closer to the observed flow. A common method of coding the turn penalty is to use the default penalty time for all turns, and then to adjust the turn penalties for large or small intersections separately.

(3) Coding error

The path tree (Fig. 8-2) is useful for finding coding errors. The path tree is the shortest path found from one cell to other cells. The number of centroid is the same with path tree. The check of path trees can find most of the errors associated with the network geometry. Some traffic software can easily generate path trees, and with

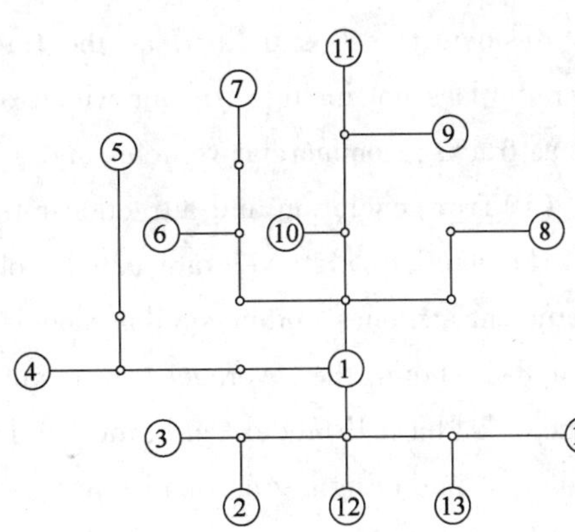

Figure 8-2 Example of a path tree

common sense, planners can find some strange connection path. Some fatal coding error can often be quickly eliminated through the inspection for the attributes of these strange roads. Professional planners need to have a primary orientation point through surveys and exchanges for the planning area, the most convenient path for their links, the location of large flows and crowded sections and their potential causes, and then check the path tree created by the software. Thus, it is easy to find the wrong coding nodes, thus rapidly complete road network revision.

(4) Public transport network inspection

Bus network can conveniently check the bus interval, bus and pedestrian connection rationality, the type of bus(such as subway, light rail, BRT, bus, micro-bus) and car connection rationality through GIS assistance. For inappropriate situation, the connection situation of centroid links and PT or walking links should be adjusted by increasing or decreasing the walking links so that the network connectivity is consistent with the real situation. Different modes of travel route should be checked separately or successively.

In addition to the above items, the direction error of one-way road, the socio-economic data input error, speed, traffic capacity, road free passage time input error, repeated connection error of inter-node links, link connection node error, node or road missing error, traffic flow error in network centroids(travel cannot pass through centroids), road distance error, the inconsistence between the geometric size of the intersection and turn penalty should also be checked.

8.4 Trip Generation Validation

Trip generation forecasting includes travel generation and travel attraction, and the method of predicting trip generation and attraction includes the category generation method and the linear regression method. The category generation method is often applied to travel generation prediction, and linear regression method is applied to travel attracting forecasting.

8.4.1 Residents Travel

Resident travel is defined as the travel of residents within the model planning area, which generally does not include trip for which one or two travel endpoints is outside the model area, as well as trucks, commercial vehicles and special trip destination.

(1) Trip generation and attraction rate

The standard of travel rate can be obtained from national censuses, resident travel surveys, government agencies, other similar models, and national normative documents on model practice. Table 8-2 shows the average travel rate reference obtained from the report "FSUTMS-Cube Framework Phase II Model Calibration and Validation Standards", while the situation in our country is different including big or small cities.

China's situation is not exactly the same, and it has been found that cities differ greatly in size. Foreign experience and domestic compatibility has yet to be accumulated, and the following will list other US indicators and reference values for reference. The average generation rate calculated by the Xi'an Urban Traffic Model Database is shown in Table 8-3.

Table 8-2 Aggregate trip rate benchmarks

Statistic	Benchmarks[a]	
	Low	High
Person Trips/TAZ	—	15000
Person Trips/Person	3.3	4.0
Person Trips/DU(or HH)	8.0	10.0
HBW Person Trips/Employee	1.20	1.55

Note: a. Generally excludes nonmotorized trips; including motorized trips could increase person trips per dwelling unit up to 11.5.
Source: *FDOTSPO*, 2008.

Table 8-3 Aggregate Trip Rate of Xi'an

Statistic	Value
Person Trips/TAZ	14207
Person Trips/Person	1.25
HBW Person Trips/Employee	1.76

Source: *Chang'an University, Xi'an Planning Bureau.*

Ideally, most of the model parameters should be within this range, and if the data reported by the model is beyond this range, it is necessary to check the socioeconomic data, travel productivity, travel attraction rate, residence unit weight and special generation point.

As shown in the table above, if generation of a zone is more than 15000 people, then the zone is considered to be divided into multiple zones. The minimum number of trips of traffic zone does have a recommended value because the zone should be as small as possible. The number of per capita travel (or unit houses or jobs) can be calculated by the model and compared with the recommended values in the table above.

Adjusting the generation rate is an important means of adjusting the model. Typically, the travel rate is either based on the previous data, either by borrowing data from other areas, or by data based on recent small sample surveys. Therefore, it is often not possible to accurately represent the travel of a particular area of the base year. In most cases, these data may represent the total area rate, but not the travel rate of the different sub-regions. The entire planning area can be divided into several areas for separate check, and for the abnormal parameters, additional investigation should be carried out. Some anomalies are often associated with special socio-economic characteristics, and the discovery of these cases is critical to the formation of effective planning programs.

The travel characteristics that affect the trip include the sharing rate of different travel modes and the travel rate of different travel modes. The average travel rate per household and capita travel rate generated by the model area should be compared with the data of other regions to determine the rationality.

(2) Percent trips by purpose

Compared with other similar models, the proportion of different trip purposes can be a good measure for trip generation or attraction. Table 8-4 provides a reasonable range of the proportion of each trip purpose.

Table 8-4 Percent trips by purpose

Statistic	Benchmarks	
	Low	High
Percent Trips by Purpose-HBW	12%	14%
Percent Trips by Purpose-HBSH	10%	20%
Percent Trips by Purpose-HBSR	9%	12%
Percent Trips by Purpose-HBSC	5%	8%
Percent Trips by Purpose-HBO[a]	14%	28%
Percent Trips by Purpose-HBNW[b]	45%	60%
Percent Trips by Purpose-NHB[c]	20%	33%

Note: a. HBO includes a variety of special trip purposes depending on the model leg, airport, colleage and shop.

b. HBNW accounts for all home-based trip purposes expect HBW.

c. NHB includes combined purposes for NHB work and NHB nonwork, where appropriate.

Source: *FDOTSPO*, 2008.

(3) The balance between production and attraction

Most of the trip generation models will balance the total amount of home-based attraction with the total amount of home-based production. Before the balance, for most of the trip-generating models, the total amount of home-based attraction will be greater than the total amount of home-based production. While the balance may address regional differences, it is still necessary to check the ratio between the total amount of production and that of attraction, and large differences often indicate the existed problems with job estimate, travel rate, and so on.

For each trip purpose, the predicted total amount of travel production must be equal to the total amount of travel attraction, but the total amount of travel production and the amount of travel attraction in the model application phase are not exactly the same, which causes the subsequent travel distribution to be problematic, because the most commonly used double constraint model will try to satisfy both travel production and attraction.

Before examining the production and attraction balance, the impact of pedestrians in non-residential areas needs to be considered. One of the reasons is that if the activity times of working, shopping and other activities in the model area of people from the outside of the planned model study area is greater than that of people from the planned area carrying out activities outside of the planned area, the amount of internal production will be more than the amount of generation, while such imbalances can be calculated. Because many models regard cars' passing through the screen lines as external trips, and the residents' trips as internal trips. The second reason is that special generating point (such as the airport) as a unique travel attraction point will produce many non-home based trips.

Once these factors are taken into account, the balance between the trip generation and production of each travel destination can be checked. For the base year, the balance between the trip generation and attraction is actually an effective means of verification, and if the two cannot be well balanced, the reasons should be carefully checked.

8.4.2 External Travel Ratio

The number of external trips can be checked according to the size of the area, the close proximity of the area to the neighboring cities and the road grade and factor analysis of the external boundaries reaching the area. External travels included:

· I-X(Resident internal-external) ;

· X-I(Nonresident external-internal) ;

· I-I(Nonresident internal-internal) ;

· X-X(External-external).

The statistical examination for external travels includes:

· Compare the car trips of the base year with the observation traffic of each external trip generation point of the base year. It should be noted that the observed traffic may contain truck, which needs to be excluded because the truck needs to be modeled separately.

· Compare the total employment travel rate passing through the traffic zones, including all internal and external trips. The employment travel rate is the total production of each family(internal and external) and the total attraction of each employment. In particular, it is necessary to compare the employment travel rates in the vicinity of the model area with the model's internal zones, since the model will produce many external trips to many remote zones. It needs to be guaranteed that these additional external trips do not duplicate the trips of the residents within the model area.

The external trip generation point is used to represent the trip reaching or leaving the study area. External trip generation point is similar to the centroid of the road network, that is, trips based on the end of this node is the origin point or destination point. But in fact, the external trip generation points represent the points of the road and are without socioeconomic characteristics. Outer traffic generator aims at production and attraction of different purposes which can be obtained through the observed road flow. E-I and I-E travel may take a similar approach as I-I travel within the planning area, while E-E travel requires special treatment.

If the E-E travel is less, it can be added to E-I and I-E travel for assignment. If E-E trips accounts for too much, the following steps are required:

· If E-E trips often go through a specific path, the E-E trips can be manually assigned to the road network. For example, the cross-boundary roads of national or provincial grade can take this way when passing through small cities.

· Establish an E-E trip table and assign it to the road network along with other travel destination. Gravity models do not apply to such trips.

E-E travel proportion of external travel is recommended in Table 8-5.

Table 8-5 Proportion of E-E travel in different cities

Population size	E-E travel ratio(%)
50000-100000	21
100000-250000	15
250000-750000	10
750000-2000000	4

Source: *FDOTSPO*, 2008.

The modeling phase needs to collect travel data of external sites. The cost of investigating the driver at an external site is relatively low and is of greater help in increasing the accuracy of the forecast.

In addition to E-E travel, school trip and truck travel trip do not apply to gravity model. Few people travel to school using a car abroad, but it's normal in china. If this does not cause too much impact on the road traffic prediction, we can regard such cases as home-based work trips; if the school is very large and there are a lot of shuttle parents' vehicles, such cases can be addressed individually by taking a similar method like external travel processing. To some extent, the truck trip likes an external trip, which can be calibrated during the check for an external site. If the truck trip is a strict internal travel, it should be classified as other internal trips which should be predicted and assigned by specialized module and reasonably combined with passenger forecasting module for the total traffic flow.

School trips and truck trips are similar to out-zone trips and can easily lead to model's misappropriation in some respects. A separate trip table can be provided for each trip purpose separately. Often, such error account for little proportion and does not matter for the overall forecast, and these two types of trips can be categorized for other purposes.

8.4.3 Business and Cargo Travel

Model predicted truck trips can be compared with the expanded truck survey data. If the data of the local trucks and goods OD and the optional road network are missing and the inspection of the truck/cargo model can be started until the road network distribution stage, the truck volume can be compared with the traffic volume of the passenger vehicle. If the model's truck traffic is too high (or too low) compared to the observed data, this may indicate that the trip generation rate/tonnage is too high (or too low) or the truck travel distance is too long (or too short), the relevant parameters of which should be analyzed and revised.

After the trip assignment, the regional truck mileage (VMT) survey data and the car mileage data of the total area got from the model should be compared to check the rationality of the simulation situation.

8.4.4 Special Generator

Special generation points are places where traffic demand is high. Typical special generating points include airports, universities, entertainment venues, military bases, hospitals and shopping centers. If the planning model area is small, these points will be less.

The test data of the special generating points mainly include the traffic flow and flow survey data in the vicinity of the trip-generation area. It can be verified by comparing the traffic flow leading to the generating point or the adjacent generating point with the model assigning result. If the model result is obviously different from the observation result, it is necessary to specify the specific generation point and adjust the corresponding travel generation rate. Trips of the generating area of the target year can be compared with the base year for rationality check. Trips of a special point can be divided into two parts to check the rationality of the predicted results: travel expectations increase over time and travel expectations remain relatively static. For example, travel expectations of universities, military bases, hospitals remain relatively static, unless the employment, military grade, the number of beds change in accordance with the forecasting. On the contrary, the attraction of a special generation point to entertainment place, such as a park or a shopping center, will increase as the population increases, even if the special generation point does not change in the forecast year.

8.5 Trip Distribution Validation

8.5.1 Aggregate Check

Verification of the results of the trip distribution model refers to the verification of the "trip table". Two aggregate travel distribution models (trip length check and OD trip mode check) can be used to check model fitting results of the base year.

8.5.2 Average Travel Length

The average travel length for different purposes is the most common test indicator for all the model validations. The average travel length can be obtained from a variety of sources, such as resident survey data, model fitting statistical documentation, model validation studies, and so on. The unit of travel length can be time/distance. The travel length check for the base year includes comparing the average travel length of the model results and the probability distribution of the travel length with the observed data of the residents' travel survey. Each trip travel length can be individually checked, including travel distance and time inspection. The probability of the travel distribution and the model fitting can be plotted in the same table for the matching degree comparison. The "FSUTMS-Cube Framework Phase II Model Calibration and Validation Standards" provides a reference range for average travel length shown in Table 8-6.

Table 8-6 Average trip length and frequencies by purpose

Statistic	Benchmarks	
	Low	High
Average Trip Length-HBW(min)	12	35
Average Trip Length-HBSH(min)	9	19
Average Trip Length-HBSR(min)	11	19
Average Trip Length-HBSC(min)	7	16
Average Trip Length-HBO(min)	8	20
Average Trip Length-NHB(min)	6	19

continued

Statistic	Benchmarks	
	Low	High
Average Trip Length-IE(min)	26	58
Statistic	Standards	
Mean Trip Length, Observed Total Trip	±3%	
Trip Length Frequency Distribution versus observed	±5%	
Coincidence Ratios by Purpose[a]	70%	

Note: a Some lower coincidence ratios have been deemed acception for trip purposes that had relatively few trips and therefore higher error rates.

Source: *FDOTSPO*, 2008.

The geometric distribution, the distribution of activities and the distribution of trip production are different according to the size of the model area. Therefore, the average travel length varies from region to region, and the average travel length of the simulation can be compared with the residents' travel investigation. The "coincidence rate" provides a good way to compare the two different distributions (model distribution and survey distribution), and the "coincidence rate" for each trip destination should be at least 70%. The "coincidence ratio" is calculated as follows:

$$CR = \frac{\sum_{T}[\min(PM_T, PO_T)]}{\sum_{T}[\max(PM_T, PO_T)]} \tag{8-1}$$

where, CR is coincidence ratio; PM_T is proportion of modeled distribution in interval T; PO_T is proportion of observed distribution in interval T; T is histogram interval for time, distance, or other impedance measure.

Fig. 8-3 shows the fitting chart of the model distribution and the survey distribution.

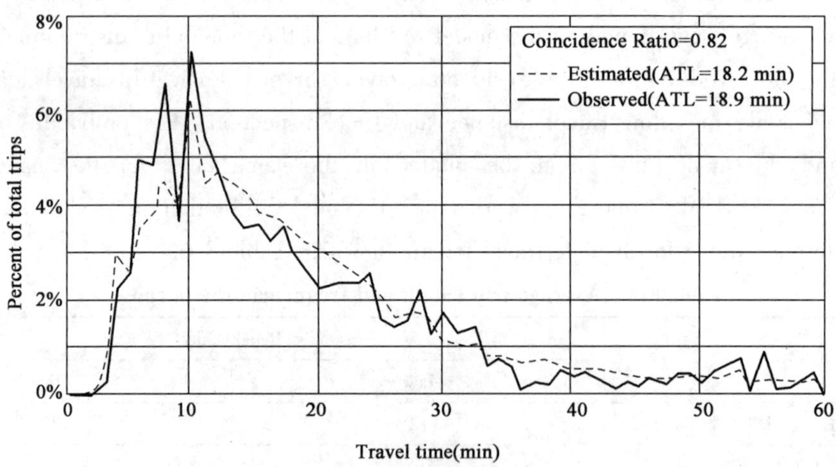

Figure 8-3 Coincidence ratio

Note: ATL = Average Trip Length.

Source: *FDOTSPO*, 2008.

Adjustment method:

The traffic volume can be adjusted by adjusting the trip distribution module. Shortening or increasing the average trip length during the trip distribution phase can increase or decrease the traffic volume of the road section. The length of the trip from the gravity model distribution can be controlled by changing the gravity model input parameters. As shown in the following travel example (Fig. 8-4), the travel time of the zone 1 to other zones (Table 8-7) and the total trip production and attraction (Table 8-8) are listed.

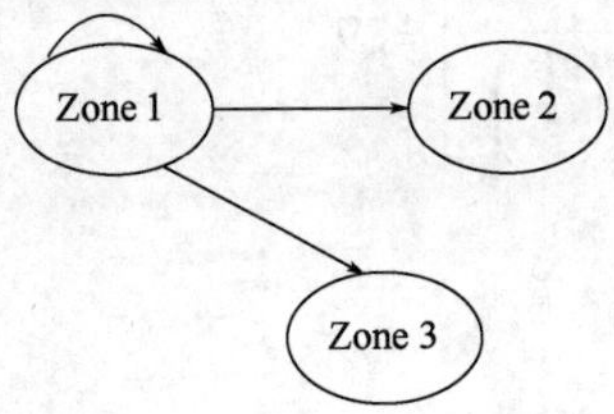

Figure 8-4 The trips from zone 1 to others

The basic formula for the gravity model is as follows:

$$T_{ij} = P_i \cdot \frac{A_j \cdot FF_{ij}}{\sum_{1}^{n} (A_j \cdot FF_{ij})} \tag{8-2}$$

where, T_{ij} is trips from zone i to zone j; P_i is trips produced at zone i; A_j is attractions in zone j; FF_{ij} is friction factor for trips going from zone i to zone j; n is number of zones.

Power function:

$$FF = \frac{1}{t^x}$$

Exponential function:

$$FF = \frac{1}{e^{tx}}$$

Table 8-7 Travel time

Zone to zone	Time (min)
1-1	3
1-2	5
1-3	10

Table 8-8 Trip production and attraction

Zone number	P (production)	A (attraction)
1	100	100
2	300	200
3	200	300

where, t is travel time between zone i and j; x is distribution parameter.

Using the data in the example, the impedance factor uses a power function, assuming that the distribution parameter used for the impedance factor is 2, and the gravity model will distribute the 100 trips of zone1 as follows:

$$T_{1\text{-}2} = 100 \times \left[\frac{200 \cdot \left(\frac{1}{5}\right)^2}{200 \cdot \left(\frac{1}{5}\right)^2 + 300 \cdot \left(\frac{1}{10}\right)^2 + 100 \cdot \left(\frac{1}{3}\right)^2} \right] = 36$$

$$T_{1\text{-}3} = 100 \times \left[\frac{3}{22}\right] = 14$$

$$T_{1\text{-}1}=100\times\left[\frac{11}{22}\right]=50$$

If the distribution parameter changes from 2 to 3, the impedance factor changes so that the gravity model changes the travel distribution as follows:

$$T_{1\text{-}2}=100\times\left[\frac{200\cdot\left(\frac{1}{5}\right)^3}{200\cdot\left(\frac{1}{5}\right)^3+300\cdot\left(\frac{1}{10}\right)^3+100\cdot\left(\frac{1}{3}\right)^3}\right]=29$$

$$T_{1\text{-}3}=100\times\frac{0.3}{5.6}=5$$

$$T_{1\text{-}1}=100\times\frac{3.7}{5.6}=66$$

As increasing the distribution parameters, shorter trips will be more attractive. When the distribution parameter is 2, the gravity model generates 50 trips within the zone 1 and the trip time is the shortest 3 minutes. When the parameter is 3, the number of trips in these zones is increased to 66, and the other longer trips (1-2 and 1-3) are reduced by 7 and 9 times respectively. The longest trip (1-3) maximally reduced the proportion of trips.

In practice, the friction factor table is more commonly used than an equation (e. g., conducting an OD survey). The use of the friction factor table is more flexible than the power and exponential functions because it is easier to adjust to obtain the desired trip impedance value. An example friction factor table is shown in Table 8-9.

Table 8-9 Friction factor table

Trip length(min)	Home based work(HBW)	Friction factor home based nonwork(HBW)	Nonhome based(NHB)
1	275	335	390
2	255	325	380
3	240	305	350
4	220	280	310
5	205	245	250
6	180	205	205
7	160	170	165
8	138	140	130
9	120	115	105
10	102	94	84
11	88	76	69
12	75	62	57

continued

Trip length(min)	Home based work(HBW)	Friction factor home based nonwork(HBW)	Nonhome based(NHB)
13	64	50	47
14	55	40	38
15	45	32	31
16	36	26	25
17	28	22	20
18	18	18	13
19	9	15	8
20	2	13	3

Source: *Ismart*, 1990.

The average travel length of the travel distribution can be shortened or increased by changing the distribution parameter (friction factor). If the length of the trip changes, the traffic volume of the road section will increase or decrease.

Working trips have a longer average travel time than shopping trips, and different distribution parameters can be used to achieve this scenario in the model for different travel purposes. The "Calibrating and Adjustment of System Planning Models" gives the default values of the distribution parameters for different purposes shown in Table 8-10.

Table 8-10 Gravity model adjustments

Different travel purposes	Parameter		Trip length(min)	
	Power	Exponential	Large Pop.	Small Pop.
Home-based work	2.0-2.2	0.1	15-20	7-10
Home-based non work	1.9-2.0	0.1	13-17	6-9
Non home-based	1.8-2.0	0.1	13-17	6-8

Source: *Ismart*, 1990.

8.5.3 Percent Intrazonal Trips

Measuring the percentage of intrazonal trips by purpose can be a means to identifying issues with friction factors, intrazonal time calculations, and even zone size. The percent of intrazonal trips is very dependent on zone size and composition. It is typical that HBW trips would have the smallest percentage of intrazonal trips while home-based nonwork (HBNW) trips, including shop, social recreational, and school, generally have the highest intrazonal activity. The best comparisons of the size and range of traffic zone are against observed geocoded survey data. Since intrazonal percentages vary considerably, it is recommended that comparisons be made against percentages from other similar models where household surveys have not recently been completed. Table 8-11 depicts a benchmark range of percent intrazonal trips by purpose and standards for comparing observed and estimated intrazonal activity.

Table 8-11　Percent intrazonal trips

Statistic	Benchmarks	
	Low	High
Percent intrazonal-HBW	1%	4%
Percent intrazonal-HBSH	3%	9%
Percent intrazonal-HBSR	4%	10%
Percent intrazonal-HBSC	10%	12%
Percent intrazonal-HBO	3%	7%
Percent intrazonal-NHB	5%	9%
Percent intrazonal-Total Trip	3%	5%
Statistic	Standards	
	Acceptable	Preferable
Percent intrazonal, observed total trip	±5%	±3%

Source: *FDOTSPO*, 2008.

There are two types of four-stage models for internal travel as shown in Fig. 8-4: interzonal trips and intrazonal trips. An interzonal trip between centroids 9 and 10 uses path 9-7-6-5-10. For an intrazonal trip, the road network is not used, and trips are not assigned. Therefore, the higher the proportion of intrazonal trips, the smaller the traffic on the road network.

For example, there are 4 possible trips for the two zones shown in the Fig. 8-5: interzonal trips: 9-9 and 10-10; intrazonal trips: 9-10 and 10-9. Table 8-12 shows the hypothetical interzonal trips distribution. One-third of the trips from zone 9 are intrazonal trips. Thus, the number of trips through route 9-7-6-5-10 is 200. If the number of intrazonal trips increases, the trips assigned to the road network will be reduced.

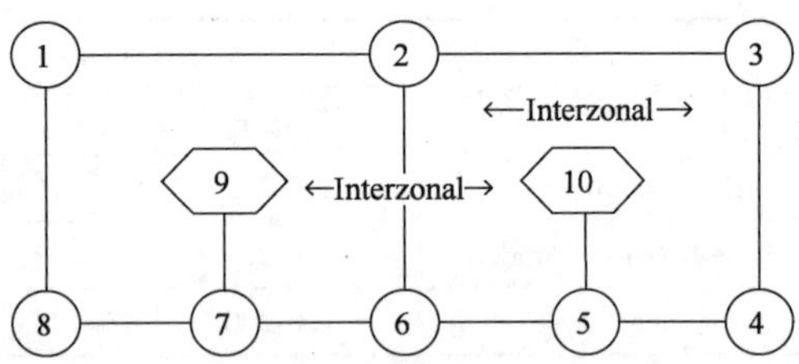

Figure 8-5　Internal trip types

Source: *Ismart*, 1990.

For example, if the trip table is converted shown in Table 8-13, the intrazonal trips will account for 1/2, so that the number of trips for the route 9-7-6-5-10 reaches 150. Increase the proportion of intrazonal trips, road network traffic will be reduced, on the contrary, road network traffic will increase. Therefore, the flow of the road section can be changed by changing the proportion of intrazonal trips.

Table 8-12　Trip table for two zone area

Zone area	9	10
9	100	200
10	200	100

Source: *Ismart*, 1990.

Table 8-13 Modified trip table

zone area	9	10
9	150	150
10	150	150

Source: *Ismart*, 1990.

The best way to control the intrazonal trips is to adjust the intrazonal times in the gravity model traffic distribution process. The smaller the intrazonal travel time, the more intrazonal trips. Another way to control intrazonal trips is to change the average travel length in the gravity model. Shortening the length of the trip will increase the number of intrazonal trips because intrazonal trips are usually shorter in travel time than interzonal trips.

The third influencing on the intrazonal trips is the definition of zone. If there is iintrazonal trips, this zone must have both trip production and attraction (dwelling unit and employment unit). A zone that only contains dwelling units or units of employment only has intrazonal trips for non-home based trip purpose.

If the zone is large, there will be many intrazonal trips. If the zone is too large, any traffic distribution will produce more centroid links. These trips need to be supported by 2 to 4 or 4 to 6 lanes of facilities. If these trips are ignored, the traffic planning scheme will often fail. In a model system that is well-designed in both a residential area and a road network, the mass-centered link load flow is generally lower than 10000 or 15000 car trips/day.

8.5.4 K-Factors

The K factor can be used to correct the difference in trip exchanges at the regional level. They represent socio-economic or other characteristics that influence trip decisions but are not expressed in the model. A cross-river bridge may cause discrepancies between the observed and modeled traffic model. For example, if only quantitative measures are used then the number of intrazonal trips between zones separated by bridges may be unimaginable. At this time, planners can use K-factor or manually adjust the flow of the bridge section to match the actual traffic volume.

The K-factor is similar to the mode-specific constant in the logit model to measure the factors that are unable to be included in the models. Because the input variables of the travel distribution model are relatively few, it is reasonable to believe that there are other factors that have not been considered by the model to influence the destination selection. In most cases, these factors cannot be measured, quantified, or predicted. The K-factor provides a way to consider these factors, although they are assumed to be constant at different times and in different situations.

The use of K-factors must be done with great care as they can perfectly match the traffic travel observed between the models and model simulations. Before it is determined that the K factor is the best way to solve O-D traffic matching, it should not be considered to use K-factors as much as possible. The K factor should be considered as the last resort after considering all other possible verification methods. Even if the K factor is used, its amplitude should be small, and the closer to

1, the better.

It may be necessary to use the K-factor when it is necessary to correct trips between different zones, for example taking into account the distribution of external – internaltrips of the area shown in Fig. 8-6. Due to geographic boundaries, external trips generated between External Station 2 and the zones in District *A* are unlikely, but trips generated from outside the model area may enter the model area through External Station 1 and then reach the zones in District *A*. The internal-external trip volume from the External Station 2 will not be excluded from the trip from traveling to zones in District *A* during the typical trip distribution process. Therefore, the use of the K-factor can ensure these impossible trips generated between External Station 2 and the zones in District *A* disappear in the model.

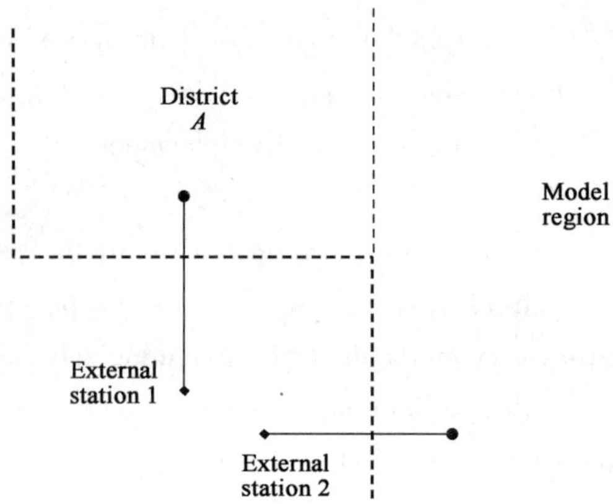

Figure 8-6 Example of K-Factor Use with External Stations

Source: *FHWA*,2008 .

8.5.5 Origin-Destination Pattern Checks

Household surveys that can be expanded through typical sample supplemental surveys are unlikely to estimate the effective OD trip tables between zones. In order to check the OD mode from a more aggregate level, "regional level" verification can generally be performed. The ideal area size depends on many elements, including the size of the model area, the number of zones, the number of trips, administrative boundaries, traffic barriers (such as rivers), and the size of the market segments.

Similar to the trip length check, the OD trip mode can be checked by orientation rate, which is defined the directivity of the trips from the production area to the attraction area divided by the total trips to attraction area.

For example, there are a total of 100 trips from Zones *A* to *B*, a total of 600 trips in Zone *A*, a total of 3000 attracted to Zone *B*, and a total of 10000 regional trips. The orientation rate from Zone *A* to Zone *B* are calculated as follows:

$$(100/3000)/(600/10000) = 0.56$$

If the orientation rate is less than one, it means that the production zone produces a fewer trips to the attraction zone than the entire zone, whereas the production zone produces more trips to the attraction zone than the entire zone. Orientation rate can verify the rationality of the model distribution. As a verification test at the zone level, the closer the ratio of the observed orientation rate to the model trip rate, the better the model fits the observed value, indicating that the model distribution and the survey distribution have a good match. Differences can be checked out to facilitate identification of problems in model building. Orientation rate is a relatively new method. If the calculated value is close to 1, it means that the model distribution has a good match with the survey distribution.

8.5.6 Summary

Frequently asked questions and solutions for traffic distribution verification are shown in Table 8-14.

Table 8-14 Troubleshooting strategies for issues with trip distribution model results

Issue	Potential troubleshooting strategies
1. Average trip lengths too long or short	· Recalibrate friction factors or adjust parameters of friction factor formula or logit utility equations · Recheck skim data and trip end inputs · Check distribution patterns
2. Coincidence ratio too low	· Recalibrate friction factors or adjust parameters of friction factor formula or logit utility equations
3. District-level origin-destination patterns inaccurate for some interchanges	· Check trip lengths · Check travel impedances between affected districts · Introduce or adjust K-factors · Introduce impedance penalties on network · Links(e. g., bridge crossings)
4. Too may or few intrazonal trips	· Adjust intrazonal travel times for types of zones with this issue
5. Model too sensitive or insensitive to changes in level of service	· Adjust parameters for appropriate level of service variables in impedance/utility functions or friction factors

Source: FHWA, 2010.

8.6 The Verification of Modal Split

8.6.1 Vehicle Loading Rate

Vehicle loading rate can be used to convert person-trip to vehicle-trip, which can lead to huge changes, examples are as follows. The total home-based trip on the study area is 138000 person-trips. If vehicle loading rate is 1.38, the trips will be 100000 vehicle-trips. However, if loading rate is 1.15, the trip will be 120000 vehicle-trips. As a result, the trip directly increases by 20%.

Loading rate can be adjusted to make the vehicle-trips decrease or increase. The variation range of loading rate with different trip purpose is shown in Table 8-15.

Table 8-15 the range of loading rate of the small passenger car with different travel purpose

Home based work trip	1.07-1.20
Home-based non-work trip	1.40-1.71
Nonhome-based trip	1.24-1.65
The total	1.31-1.54

Source: *Sosslan*, 1978.

8.6.2 Target Proportion Matrix of Modal Split

The method can be used to realize the calibration of the modal split model by establishing a check matrix. The matrix should include estimates representing the estimated demand by mode and trip purpose. The target matrix needs to consider all trip purposes, mode (highway, transit, and nonmotorized modes that exist in the base year model), auto ownership (0, 1, 2, 3 +), geographical subarea and so on.

Table 8-16 showed the target matrix based on Home base work trip that the FSUTMS - Cube Framework Phase II Model Calibration and Validation Standards recommended. Additional geographic market segmentation may be considered if sufficient data to estimate observed demand exists. When used in the future year, it should be based on the rational change concept. For example, when the proportion of cars is too high, the road network tends to be fully saturated. In this case, people's travel behavior and the improvement of public transport priority facilities should be integrated when considering the implementation of bus priority.

Table 8-16 The target matrix of home-based work trip

Trip mode	Car-free family	One car family	Two car family	Three car family
Walk	5000	6000	4000	3000
Bike	2000	1000	500	200
Drive alone		130000	350000	200000
Two people share	6000	15000	20000	10000
Three people share	1000	2000	4000	2000
Bus + walk	6000	7000	4000	1000
Local bus, passenger booking record		500		
BRT + walk	1000	1000	1000	500
Fast bus, passenger booking record		2000	4000	2000
Light rail + walk	500	1000		400
Light rail, passenger booking record		300		500

Source: *FDOTSPO*, 2008.

According to different trip purposes, the time period and the income category should be classified; the final model has four modes: car, transit-walking access, transit-auto access, and nonmotorized. Fig. 8-7 shows the survey and analysis of the trip generation and trip distribution.

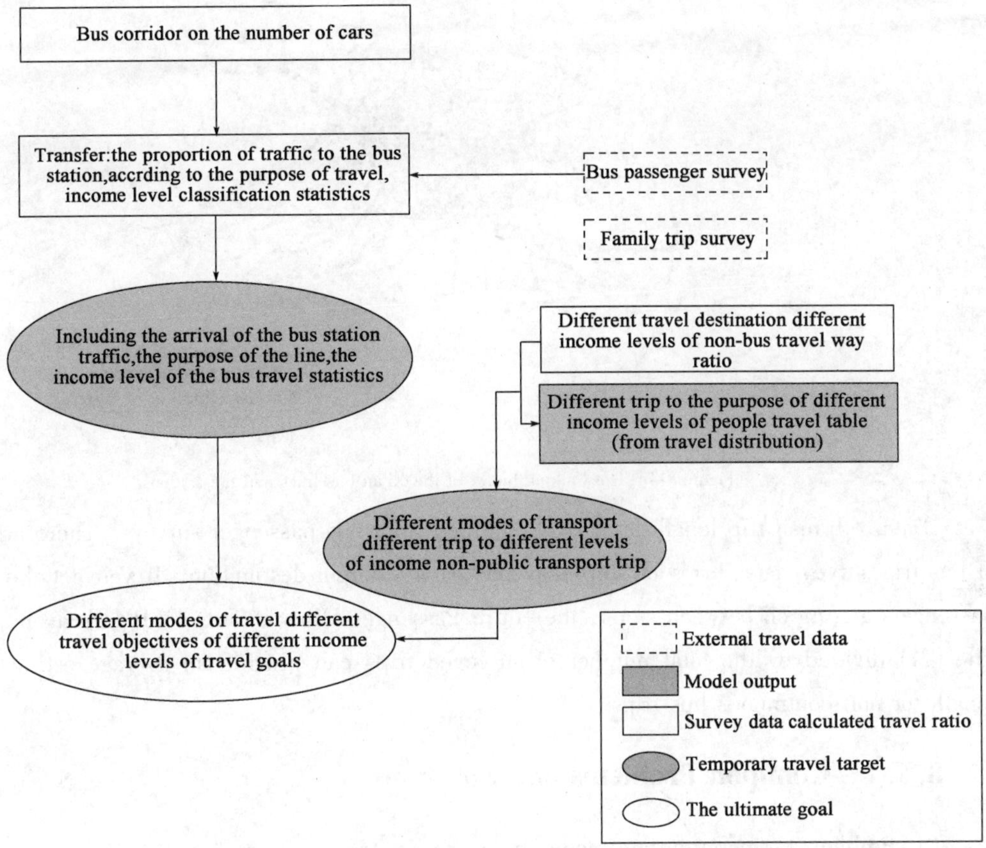

Figure 8-7 The survey and analysis of trip generation and trip distribution

Source: *Travel Model Validation and Reasonableness Checking Manual* (Second Edition).

The verification of modal split is greatly influenced by the logit coefficient and the related factors, such as the road and bus network, the cost matrix, the public transport cost matrix and the parking fees and so on. The main work of checking the bus network and cost matrix mainly includes: network connectivity and the shortest path, non-transit section(NTL, None Transit Legs) time, departure interval of the sorting bus, walking proportion, walking buffer of the transit paths, velocity difference between bus and car and so on.

Fig. 8-8 is the walking buffer of the Xi'an bus lines and the stations. The gray area represents the area that people can walk to the bus lines from the districts.

8.6.3 Transit Trip Length

If the data of transit trip length survey is available, the transit trip length of the model should be compared with the data. The trip distribution and the modal split are checked at the same time in this process. Before the check, modal split must be operated firstly.

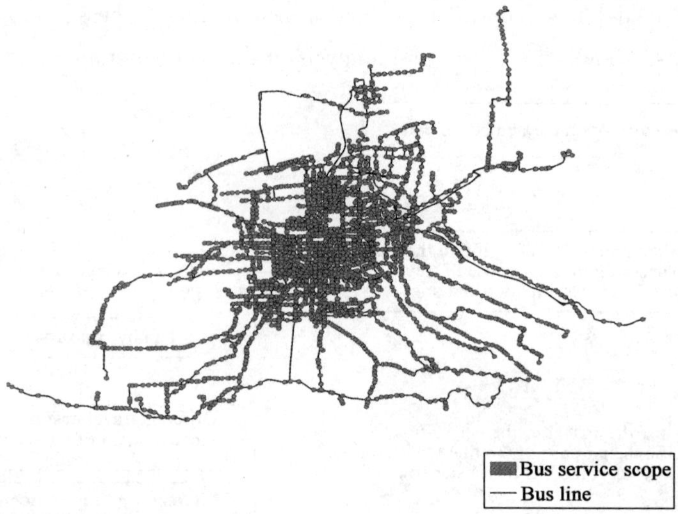

Figure 8-8 The walking buffer of the Xi'an bus lines and the stations

Data of transit trip length is usually obtained from bus passenger surveys. There are two types of bus trip survey data, trips of stop-stop and trips of orgin-destination. If you get the number of passengers getting on between stops, the entire Passenger-Miles of Travel (PMT) can be estimated. The PMT divided by the total number of surveyed trips can provide an average estimate of travel length for non-continuous bus trips.

8.6.4 Common Problems and Solutions

(1) Problem 1: inappropriate mode choice parameters

All parameters should be checked for reasonableness in sign and magnitude, and relationships among parameters should be checked as well. All coefficients in a mode's utility function related to level of service (time, cost, number of transfers) for that mode should be negative. Out of vehicle travel is generally considered to be more onerous than in-vehicle travel, and so out-of-vehicle time coefficients should be greater in absolute value than in-vehicle time coefficients. The ratio of the in-vehicle time to cost coefficient for each mode represents the value of (in-vehicle) time and can be converted to familiar units (e. g., yuan/hour) for reasonableness checking. From the FSUTMS-Cube Framework Phase II Model Calibration and Validation Standards, the time values of different cities in the United States are shown in Table 8-17.

The reason for the inaccuracy of the coefficients is that if coefficients were estimated from survey data, data insufficiency or errors might be preventing estimation of valid coefficients. If coefficients were transferred from another context or model, the model transferability might not be completely appropriate, or the original model from which the coefficients were transferred might have had errors.

Table 8-17 The time value of different cities in America

			Baltimore	Dallas	Denver	Michigan	Houston	Los Angeles	Milwaukee	Philadelphia	Pittsburgh	Portland	Sacramento	St. Louis	Tucson
Based home work	Average	Range	1993	1996	1985	1996	1985	1991	1991	1986	1978	1985	1991	1965	1965
The car in vehicle time	-0.032	-0.01--0.05	-0.034	-0.055	-0.018	-0.052	-0.022	-0.021	-0.016	-0.042	-0.047	-0.039	-0.025	-0.023	-0.018
Car outside the time	-0.058	-0.04--0.09	-0.044		-0.093				-0.041		-0.069	-0.065	-0.038	-0.057	
Car running costs	-0.513	-0.3--1.3	-0.143	-0.558	-0.350	-0.410	-0.614	-0.2%	-0.450	-0.260	-2.100	-1.353	-0.279	-1.170	-0.184
Car parking costs	-0.627	-0.3--1.3	-0.143	-0.588	-0.950	-0.410	-1.540	-0.2%	-0.450	-0.260	-2.100	-1.353	-0.279	-1.170	-0.184
Bus time	-0.024	-0.01--0.05	-0.012	-0.025	-0.018	-0.009	-0.022	-0.021	-0.016	-0.011	-0.047	-0.039	-0.025	-0.023	-0.018
Bus walking time	-0.050	-0.04--0.07	-0.044	-0.064	-0.054	-0.019	-0.057	-0.053	-0.041	-0.032	-0.069	-0.065	-0.038	-0.057	-0.040
Bus waiting time	-0.050	-0.04--0.07	-0.029	-0.064	-0.028	-0.019	-0.057	-0.053	-0.041	-0.051	-0.069	-0.040	-0.038	-0.057	-0.040
Bus transfer time	-0.050	-0.04--0.07	-0.016	-0.064	-0.059	-0.019	-0.057	-0.053	-0.041	-0.051	-0.069	-0.090	-0.038	-0.057	-0.040
Bus cost	-0.531	-0.3--1.3	-0.053	-0.550	-0.044	-0.410	-0.614	-0.2%	-0.450	-0.115	-2.100	-1.353	0.279	-1.170	-0.184
Transfer times			-0.268				-0.088								
Walking time/in vehicle time	2.08	1.5-3	3.55	2.56	3.00	2.00	2.58	2.50	2.62	2.97	1.47	1.64	1.52	2.50	2.25
Waiting time/in vehicle time	2.10	1.5-3	2.33	2.56	1.57	2.00	2.58	2.50	2.62	4.80	1.47	1.01	1.52	2.50	2.25
Time value(car)	$3.79	$2-$5	$14.16	$5.91	$3.09	$7.61	$2.15	$4.25	$2.09	$9.66	$1.33	$1.75	$5.39	$1.17	$5.78
Time value(bus)	$2.72	$2-$5	$14.16	$2.73	$2.45	$1.36	$2.15	$4.25	$2.09	$5.53	$1.33	$1.75	$5.39	$1.17	$5.78

The solution is that coefficients or relationships between them might have to be constrained to a reasonable value. For a model being estimated from survey data, the model should be re-estimated with the constraint imposed.

(2) Problem 2: over-estimate or under-estimate transit trips

The reason may be:

· It is likely that, if modeled and observed shares match poorly, there are errors in transit or highway networks, path building and skim settings, transit accessibility, socioeconomic data, or other inputs such as parking costs. Some settings (e. g., maximum walk and auto access times) should also be checked for consistency with the results of on-board surveys.

· Transit markets might not be represented properly in the model. One of the best ways to check this is by assigning the trip table obtained by expanding the transit on-board survey to the transit network and comparing the results to observed ridership.

· After all other areas are checked, it is still common that modeled mode shares and/or transit ridership from an uncalibrated model do not match the observed data. This may be due to errors in the survey data such as undetectable or uncorrectable biases, sampling error, response errors, recording errors, or missing responses.

There are solutions:

· All network data, including transit route fares, headways, and stops, and transit access should be rechecked for completeness and consistency. Other data, including socioeconomic data and parking costs, should also be checked. Path building settings, such as weights for walk and wait time and values of time, should be made consistent with the mode choice model parameters as well as the results of on-board surveys.

· The results of the assignment of the on-board survey trip table should be examined by any market segmentation that is available. This includes trip purpose, geographic, corridor, and demographic (e. g., income level). Route-level differences from the observed ridership should result in checks of the coding of the transit route and its stops and accessibility. It is possible that the comparison will show errors in the trip distribution, which should be corrected before mode choice is rerun.

· The most common method for achieving reasonable mode shares is to adjust the mode choice constants to achieve better replication of observed mode shares and/or transit ridership. However, it is critical not to use the calibration of mode choice constants as corrections for other unrelated model problems such as those described above. Therefore, extreme care should be taken to ensure that all other causes have been ruled out before constants are adjusted. The adjustment of constants is usually done in an iterative manner, where the mode choice model is run, the results are compared to observed data, and constants are re-estimated to provide a better match between modeled and observed data.

(3) Problem 3: Auto occupancies not matching observed data

While logit mode choice models generate auto occupancy rates as an output, highway only mode choice models use auto occupancy rates as an input to convert person trips to auto trips. The possible reason is the inaccurate assumed auto occupancy rates. If coefficients were estimated from survey data, data insufficiency or errors might result in errors in occupancy rates. If coefficients were transferred from another context or model, the model transferability might not be completely appropriate, or the original model from which the coefficients were transferred might have had errors.

The solution is that the output and structure of the modal split should be checked and adjusted based on the typical auto occupancy rates by purpose from travel surveys.

8.7 Verification of Trip Assignment

Most of the time and efforts will be spent on trip assignment in the model validation process. Because trip assignment is the most important stage in the modeling process. In addition, this stage has more evaluated methods than other stages.

The trip assignment model is regarded as a vertex process of any model. Many models use a feedback loop to balance the traffic speeds in the stage of trip distribution with traffic speeds used in previous phases, such as trip distribution, destination selection, and speed in the stage of model split. It is advisable to use an overall post-local verification method before trip assignment verification.

The verification of trip assignment is generally inseparable from other model phases. The verification of trip assignment is an important step for the four-stage model. Assignment verification is generally applied independently from resident surveys or other verification data that can be used for model verification, such as independent traffic speeds and travel times.

Trip assignment is usually the concentration for most of the model validation checks, and representative inspections include screen-line checks, the mean error of regional fitting flow (RMSE), and vehicle miles of travel(VMT). Trip assignment checks are usually performed only at the regional level or sub-link or sub-area of the model. Many verification techniques are based on the traffic volume and trip time.

8.7.1 Passenger Car Distribution Inspection

The three commonly used traffic allocation steps include: All-or-Nothing assignment, capacity restraint, and equilibrium assignment. capacity restraint and equilibrium assignment are verifications of the distribution results.

In the method of All-or-Nothing assignment, the initial speed of the road segment should correspond to the Class C service level of the road facility, which is approximately equal to 87% of the free-flow speed show in Fig. 8-9. The Capacity-Restraints allocation aims to balance the traffic distribution with the road capacity and speed. This process is an iterative process. According to the BPR function, the capacity of the road section calibration will influence the road speed during the subsequent iteration.

Figure 8-9 Capacity relationship

For example, according to the BPR function, $s = \frac{60}{1 + 0.15 \times (3000/3000)^4}$, if the length of the road section is 1 km, the free flow speed is 60 km/h, the capacity is 3000 vph, the assigned flow is 3000 vph, and by calculating, the actual speed of the link is 52 km/h, and the trip time is 1.15 min(60/52). If the capacity decreases to 1500 vph, the speed will decrease to 18 km/h, and the time will increase to 3.3 min.

In the stage of trip distribution, we have analyzed that the increase in the travel time of the road may reduce the trips of distribution. Thus, reducing the speed of the capacity-Restraints distribution process, or the actual speed of the road section or adjusting the traffic capacity, will increase the travel time and reduce the distribution traffic of congested road sections.

If assigned volumes for entire classifications of facilities are high or low, speeds or capacities can be used to correct the inconsistencies.

If the trips of assignment on the highway are too low and the assigned traffic on the arterial is too high, one of the solutions is to increase the speed or capacity of the highway or reduce the speed or capacity of the arterial. It should be noted that traffic capacity only affects assignment results during the process of capacity restraint assignment, and speed will have an impact on the assignment results regardless of different assignment methods.

Some planners prefer to use differently defined capacities in the speed-flow function. The designed capacity (*C*-level service flow) is replaced by the final capacity (Class *E* service level traffic). This requires changing the parameters of the speed-flow function. In particular when using final capacity, the parameters for the ratio of flow and capacity to be multiplied need to be larger. For most road network settings, taking α from the BPR function to 0.8 instead of 0.15 is an optional strategy. You can get better prediction speed by changing this value.

It is difficult to obtain good forecasts in congested road networks using method of All-or-Nothing assignment. The capacity-restraints approach can balance iteration results through an iterative process. However, with the above two methods, the traffic of a single road section is sensitive to minor changes in the road travel time or turn penalty, which makes it difficult to obtain a comprehensive result of different road speeds. In the equilibrium assignment process, there are usually several suitable paths between each OD pair of the road network. These parallel paths can help produce more accurate aggignment results, and they are also of greater use in the verification process. These parallel paths can buffer the impact of road speed on the road section flow, and small changes in speed can produce very small flow changes.

Equilibrium assignment requires many iterations until convergence. At the time of initial verification, it needs at least 3 to 4 iterations, and at the final verification, it needs at least 10 to 11 iterations. If there are fewer than 200 zones at the road network, it is recommended that more iterations necessarily. It should be noted that equilibrium assignment and capacity restraint are more effective on the congestion road. For less congested metropolitan areas, it is easier to give accurate results using method of All or None.

8.7.2 The Property Comparison Based on Traffic Turnover

Independent traffic data based on road grades and regional characteristics can be created to check whether the assigned traffic turnover and the observed traffic turnover are in compliance. The greatest possible non-conformance is the error in the distribution of trip length and frequency.

Comparing the model's assigned traffic turnover data with the annual traffic turnover estimate (if any), the difference between the two should be between 5%. It should be noted that the premise of the comparison should be the same. Usually, the estimated value of traffic turnover is for the entire region, and the assignment result does not cover all the roads. Therefore, appropriate adjustments need to be made before comparison.

Assigned VMT by functional classification provides an excellent check of the reasonableness of an assignment. The FSUTMS-Cube Framework Phase Ⅱ Model Calibration and Validation Standards recommended the range of urban traffic turnover, which can refer to Table 8-18.

Table 8-18 The distribution of traffic turnover

Classification	Model value/Observed values				
	Ohio	Florida		Michigan	FHWA
Functional classification		Acceptable range	Ideal range		
Express way	±7%	±7%	±6%	±6%	±7%
Main road	±10%	±15%	±10%	±7%	±10%
Secondary road	±10%	±15%	±10%	±10%	±15%
Feeder road	±15%	±25%	±20%	±20%	±20%
All the way		±5%	±2%		
Regional classification					
Central business district	±10%	±25%	±15%		
Urban border area	±10%	±25%	±15%		
Urban	±10%	±25%	±15%		
Suburb	±10%	±25%	±15%		
Countryside	±10%	±25%	±15%		

VMT per person needs to be within reasonable ranges, the US metropolitan area is usually 17-27 miles; the small city area is 10-16 miles. Similarly, the amount of VMT per household needs to be within reasonable ranges, the US metropolitan area is 40-60 miles, the small areas ranging is 30-40 miles.

8.7.3 Traffic Volume-related Checks

The traffic volume-related checks compare modeled traffic volume to observed traffic volume on a link-by-link basis. There are several common methods.

$$(1)\ \mathrm{RMSE}=\sqrt{\frac{\sum_{i=1}^{N}[(\mathrm{Count}_i-\mathrm{Model}_i)^2]}{N}}$$

Among them, Count_i is the observed traffic count for link i; Model_i is the modeled traffic volume for link i; N is the number of links in the group of links including link i.

$$(2)\ R=\frac{N\times[\sum_{i=1}^{N}(\mathrm{Count}_i\times \mathrm{Model}_i)]-(\sum_{i=1}^{N}\mathrm{Count}_i)\times(\sum_{i=1}^{N}\mathrm{Model}_i)}{\sqrt{[(N\times\sum_{i=1}^{N}\mathrm{Count}_i^2)-(\sum_{i=1}^{N}\mathrm{Count}_i)^2]\times[(N\times\sum_{i=1}^{N}\mathrm{Model}_i^2)-(\sum_{i=1}^{N}\mathrm{Model}_i)^2]}}$$

Among them, R represents the correlation coefficient, and the other parameters are the same as the previous one.

The above two methods are often used in model validation, and they measure the linear fitting relationship between the assigned and the observed traffic.

(3) Scatter diagram (Fig. 8-10)

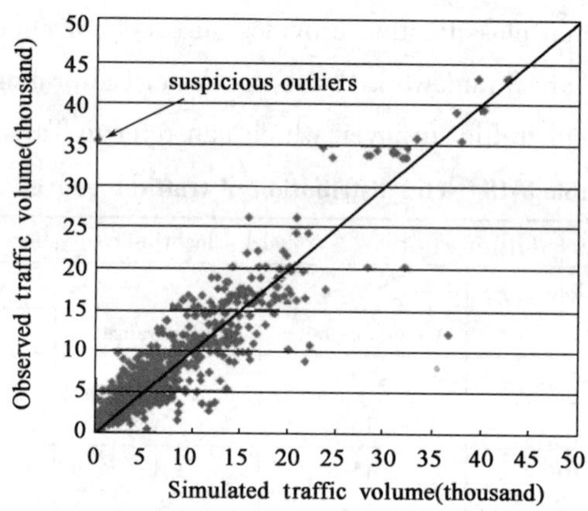

Figure 8-10 Observation-fitting flow diagram

Source: *FSUTMS-Cube Framework Phase II Model Calibration and Validation Standards.*

8.7.4 Typical Problems and Countermeasures

(1) Problem one: the high assignment of road trip at the regional level

Possible reasons include the calculation error of trip production and attraction rates, and mode splits may be a problem. For highway only models, auto occupancy factors might be the problem.

The solution is to re-check or use the lower trip production and attraction rates, and check the reasonableness of mode splits and adjust mode choice constants, particularly to the drive alone mode. For highway only models, testing of other relevant auto occupancy factors can have a dramatic impact.

(2) Problem two: the low assignment of road travel at regional level

The possible reason may include insufficient nonhome-based trips, trip production and attraction rates, mode splits, and auto occupancy rates.

The solution is to re-check or use the appropriate trip production and attraction rates and a reasonable trip proportion, for which, nonhome-based trips typically represent about 25-33 percent of daily travel and increasing nonhome-based trips at special generators should also be considered.

(3) Problem three: the high or low assignment for different facilities/areas/the number of lanes

The reason may be that the area type, facility type and the number of lanes are incorrectly edited, and the variable factors are not indicative of regional travel. Free flow and/or congested speeds look suspect.

If the highway assignment model is loading too many or too few trips in certain categories of facility type, area type, or number of lanes, we should recheck network coding of the traffic corridors and adjust the speeds and capacities for select combinations of area type, facility type, and number of lanes.

(4) Problem four: too high or too low assignment in special links and traffic corridors

The reason may be that the centroid connection is not properly connected to the road section, and coding errors might be present for area types, facility types, and/or lanes.

If the highway assignment model is loading too few or too many trips on specific links and corridors in the network, adjustment of centroid locations and centroid connectors

Can be considered. Centroid locations generally reflect the geographic center of trip making activity within a traffic analysis zone and thus are relatively subjective. Likewise, centroid connectors also are subjective. Centroids and connectors can be reviewed and adjusted with caution not to skew these locations too far from logic and to ensure that there is no negative impact on the calculation of transit access and egress links. Area types, facility types, and lane ages should also be reviewed for reasonability. Other network checks could include reviewing links without assignment volumes or those with very high volume/capacity ratios.

(5) Problem five: the high or low assignment in traffic corridors and cordon lines

Fig. 8-11 shows the distribution of traffic corridors and cordon lines on a planned area.

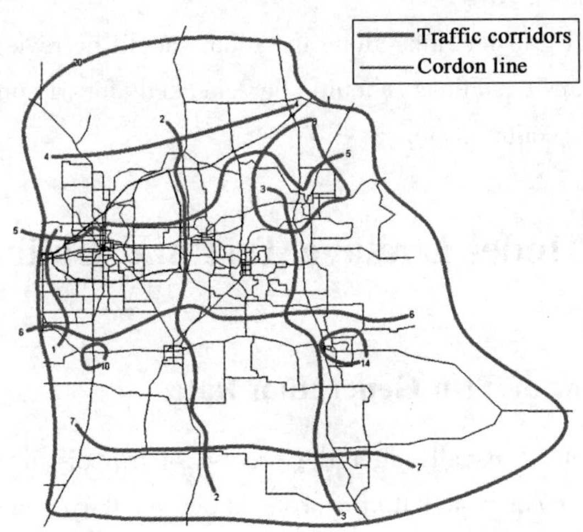

Figure 8-11 The distribution of traffic corridors and cordon line

Source: *FSUTMS-Cube Framework Phase II Model Calibration and Validation Standards.*

The possible reason for the deviation between the observed value and the fitting value is that trip distribution between the regions is suspicious, traffic volume on the traffic corridors and the cordon lines is wrong, or gaps in continuity of the screenline, cutline, or cordon line exist. The solution includes:

· Screenline validation problems could be indicative of errors in the distribution of trips. Therefore, some of the adjustments and checks recommended for trip distribution should be considered to correct screenline validation, in addition to network-and path-related adjustments such as network corrections, and the addition of bridge penalties and prohibitory. Since cordon lines and cutlines sometimes represent specific area types such as central business districts(CBD) and beach areas, adjustments to terminal times and centroid connector speeds can be quite helpful.

· Because it is easy to make editorial errors, continuous review and confirming the traffic statistics should be done for the whole verification process.

· Screenlines, cutlines, and cordon lines should be designed to maximize continuity. For example, if a screenline crosses a northbound one-way street, that the same screenline should cross the complimentary southbound one-way street. This requires that a screenline number and traffic count be coded on each link. If a count is not coded, summed assignment results will be incomplete. Likewise, if the screenline number is not coded on a specific link, it will not be summed as part of the screenline volume.

(6) Problem six: the problems of transit assignment

The reasons may be caused by the estimation error of linked trips, transit network coding error, and access coding errors. The solution is:

· If the model is replicating mode shares properly yet individual routes are generally under-or over-assigning, assumptions used to convert unlinked trips to linked trips should be rechecked.

· If transit assignment error is limited to specific bus lines, the user should recheck the coding of mode, headways, and fares.

· Access, egress, and transfer links along the route should be reviewed for correctness. Park-and-ride facilities and transit stations should be checked for assumptions such as parking availability, feeder bus connections, etc.

8.8 Model Linkage Test and Calibration

8.8.1 Adjustment of Trip Generation Rate

Adjusting the travel rate is usually after the process of trip distribution and trip assignment. Contrasting traffic assigned volume and traffic observations on the cordon lines can be concluded whether to improve or reduce travel rates. The comparison of the cutting lines reveals that trips starting from or arriving at this particular region from another region is too high or too low. One explanation is that there is a difference in travel generation rates between these regions, which suggests that it is necessary to adjust the production and attraction of trip generation. This adjustment will also cause other problems, so any adjustments should be made in coordination with other possible adjustments.

8.8.2 Travel Cost Cycle Iteration Calculation

In the four-stage model, the travel cost is loaded into the model as the input file in the trip distribution and mode split stage. The initial travel cost is obtained from the zero flow road network or the transit network. In the assignment process, the network trip costs can be generated after assigning the trips to the network, which will be loaded into the trip distribution and mode split stage as traffic cost, and the final stable assignment result can be obtained after repeated iterations. The process is shown in Fig. 8-12, the trip time matrix results can be repeated iteratively in the traffic distribution and the modal split stage.

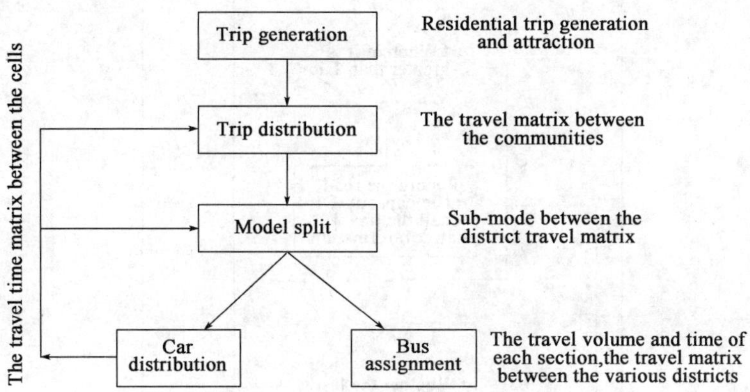

Figure 8-12 Trip time iteration process

8.9 Over-assignment

Over-assignment problem is the link flow exceeding link capacity after trip assignment process. Over-assignment problem often occurs in congested areas with high-growth rate. Most of the trip assignment methods will produce over-assignment problem. If the number of iterations of trip assignments is increased in order to prevent over-assignment, it can lead to unreasonable low speed and path detour.

There are two main causes of over-assignment problem, the first one is the error related to the supply, such as road network editing errors and road delay function error. The second one is the demand-related error, including overestimation of trip generation, predicted error of trip distribution and mode split and without consideration of peak distribution. These errors can cause the traffic on the road network to be overestimated or the supplied capacity to be underestimated, resulting in excessive assignment. The general way to solve the problem of over-assignment is to manually adjust the over-assigned links, which can lead to discontinuous assignment and the impact of the adjusted link speed unable to be evaluated. Better solution for the over-assignment problem includes: establish a sub-model for trip generation, reflect the change of network like link speed to the trip generation stage; adjust the travel demand matrix and then carry out repeated iterations until the desired matching is obtained. As is shown in Fig. 8-13.

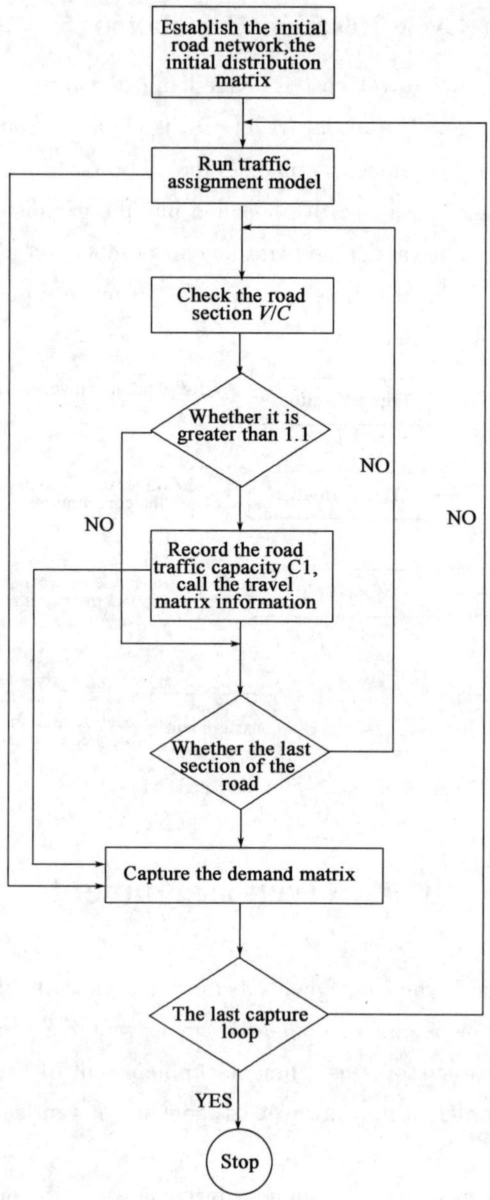

Figure 8-13 The iterative process of over-assignment

Source: *Ali Mekky*, *P. Eng*, 2001.

References

[1] Florida Department of Transportation Systems Planning Office (FDOTSPO). FSUTMS-Cube Framework Phase II Model Calibration and Validation Standards [M]. America: Cambridge Systematics Inc,2008.

[2] Federal Highway Administration (FHWA). Travel Model Validation and Reasonableness Checking Manual Second Edition [M]. Washington D. C., US: Cambridge Systematics Inc, 2008.

[3] Ismart, D. Calibrating and Adjustment of System Planning Models [J]. Federal Highway Administration ,Washington D. C. ,1990:20-40.

[4] Ali Mekky,P. Eng. Analytics Transportation Planning[M]. America, 2001.

[5] Chang'an University, Xi'an Planning Bureau. Xi'an Urban Traffic Model Project [R]. Xi'an, 2010.

[6] Art Sosslau. Quick-Response Urban Travel Estimation Techniques and Transferable Parameters (QRUTETTP), Comsis Corporation,National Cooperative Highway Research Program, Report 187,Washington, D. C., 1978.

Chapter 9

Public Transport Planning Technology

9.1 Role of Public Transport in Urban Transport System

An important task of transport is to solve problems of human mobility, and the way to achieve this movement includes modes of cars, public transit, bicycles and walking. The studies on travel behavior show that people firstly consider the travel time, fee, when they choose the travel mode. These factors are often referred as "travel costs" in transport. In the balance of many travel modes, travelers prefer to the mode with less cost. Among these modes, car travel can achieve a rapid "door to door" travel, and is widely favored by people as a result of its high accessibility and lower cost.

Increasing usage of cars has had a tremendous impact on urban land use, transportation and the environment. From the 1950s a vicious circle of traffic happened in developed countries such as the UK. With the increase of car ownership, traffic jams occur frequently, which increases road construction. At the same time, the city continues to expand, and average travel distance increases. The attraction of slow traffic and public transportation decline, and more and more people choose car travel. These trends are difficult to rely on spontaneous reason to ease, and bring about more problem associated with congestion and environmental.

At present, the transportation of large and medium-sized cities in our country is very similar to that of the developed countries such as Britain about forty or fifty years ago. With the acceleration of the urbanization process, the traffic demand and the automobile ownership are rising. Constantly repeated the vicious circle of "the increase in the volume of cars-congestion-more road construction-the increasing car ownership-the greater degree of congestion".

Experience at home and abroad shows that the city continuing to improve the convenience of car travel is not sustainable (will induce more car travel), facilitating the car travel. Compressing transport space for other modes could be against travel rights of other road users. To meet the same traffic needs, the car occupies a larger road space, but intensive public transport can effectively use the road space (Fig. 9-1). Thus improving the convenience of public transport will guide people to choose more bus trips and reduce car travel, which will fundamentally improve the efficiency of urban transport, speed up the development pace of urban economy, and reduce the cost of urban life.

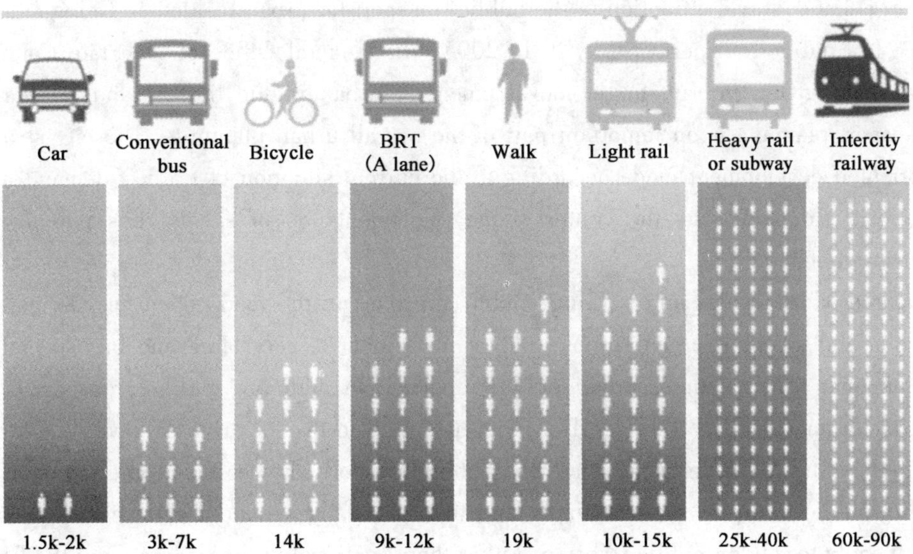

Figure 9-1 Occupied road space for different vehicles

Note: The number of persons per hour on the road marked 3.5m in units of thousands of people/h

Source: *Adjusted results according to Botma & Papendrecht, and Chinese studies.*

In the premise of guaranteeing to the supply of operation space and environment of the pedestrian and bicycle transportation and public transport, combined with guiding the orderly development and the rational use of cars and other private travel modes, urban transport could be more green and sustainable. It is fortunate that more and more people are aware of the importance of public transport priority. More and more bus priority policies, rail transit network, bus lines become the most important focus of urban transport planning. This chapter will introduce the strategy, public transportation network, public transportation model and public transportation assessment, including the aspects of concept, method of facility planning and transportation analysis.

9.2 Urban Public Transit Priority Strategies

With the continuous rise of the economy and the ever-changing modes of transportation, rapid urbanization and motorization have brought great pressure to the urban traffic. As the characteristics of large volume and high efficiency of urban public transport, the total amount of resources available for urban use is constrained, which make it difficult to give priority to the development of public transport for domestic and foreign cities.

From the beginning of the early 1970s, France began to implement the "bus priority" policy to vigorously develop public transport, increase public transport subsidies, restrict the development of car development, open bus lanes in the city center and protect the bus priority. Since then, the world generally began to support the bus from the land use, tax, financial subsidies and other aspects, but also to delineate the bus lane, the intersection of bus priority passage and other measures to enhance travel attraction of the public transport for urban residents. China attaches great importance to "public transport priority". In 2005, the General Office of the State Council issued the notice about giving priority to the development of urban public traffic, and put forward that public transport planning is an important part of the overall urban planning. The city should set up the bus-oriented development mode according to the current situation of traffic, demand and public transportation, and guided by the center of the implementation of special bus planning and rail transit construction.

Compared with bicycles and walking, public transport in the road outside needs more complex line planning and transport organizations, public investment is very large and bus special planning must be the main component of urban public services. In addition, public transport is the most important mode for those like the elderly, young people who do not drive or have no car. Both the city and the countryside have to provide basic public transport services for people to travel. Opening high-quality public transport services firstly and then gradually expand the development of strength will guide people to rely on public transport rather than car travel at the beginning of the formation of TOD(Transit Oriented Development) cities will be more livable. But the early development of cities often needs large amount of investment.

The high level of public transport development will bring "public brand" to transport for a city. Such as BRT system of Guangzhou, Changzhou, Yichang, developed rail transit network of Shanghai and monorail system of Chongqing(Fig. 9-2). These excellent public transport systems are not only an important part of urban congestion release, but also an important part of that urban life and an impression of city. The development of public transport is good or bad, which is related to life happiness of the people, is the pen of the traffic congestion change, is typical benchmark of the city government concept and management level and is the most important measure of indicators whether the city is attractive or not. All these need measures from the land, finance, road rights, management, timing and other aspects.

a) monorau　　b) BRT

Figure 9-2　Excellent example of the bus system

Source: *Karl Fjelistrom, itdp-china. org.*

Guangzhou Bus Rapid Transit

Guangzhou BRT system is west of Tianhe Sports Center, east of Huangpu Xia Park, the total length of 22.9 km, began operation since February 2010, the system daily passenger travel volume of 850000 people (May 2014 workday average, does not contain the station Transfer), the peak passenger capacity (passenger number/h/one-way) of 274000 person-time, the system coverage of 273 km, covering 1/3 of Guangzhou City.

Guangzhou BRT became the world's second, the largest capacity of BRT in Asia, the project has gained the United Nations "World Sustainable Transportation Award 2011" and BRT "Gold Standard", similar to the subway-like bus station and ride mode, increased on and off and Road construction and construction, bringing convenient traffic, has also become a sign of the Guangzhou bus service. The system has 31 routes into the BRT channel.

Compared with ordinary bus services, the main features are:

Isolated bus lanes	√
Bus lines and corridors of the integrated network	√
More than 75% of the stations have bus lanes	√
Public bike near BRT station	√
The station is far from the intersection	√
The intersection of three-dimensional cross or signal priority	√
Improvement of public space around the station	√

9.3　The Process for Bus Hub and Network Planning

Public transport planning needs to collect a large number of data including the size of the population, car ownership, bus utilization and other historical trends to diagnose the status quo, forecast future characteristics of the bus demand, analyze the use of public transport planning, and test the implementation effect of different bus supply program, and make preferred choice. The workflow is as follows:

Step 1: Determine the objectives and strategies of public transport planning

Public transport planning for different purposes corresponds to different planning strategies and methods. Urban public transport special planning need to predict the city's bus travel demands, and hierarchical network planning; large international conferences, sports events, public transport solutions focus on the rapid flow of passenger, and need to facilitate the transport hub, good direct access to lines, the program needs to be easy to implement and dismantle at the same time; inter-city bus program adjustment, custom bus program need to accurately estimate the size of the demand, intercity bus needs to be demonstrated in terms of vehicle selection and road conditions. Therefore, before the implementation of public transport planning work, the first thing is, according to the actual situation, to make a clear target and the strategy.

Step 2: Investigation and analysis on the present situation of bus service

Planning goal is the general guidelines for public transport planning research, needing to collect a large number information of bus travel information, including bus passenger(OD, sectional traffic volume), bus facilities(station construction, site layout situation,, bus lanes); and opinions and suggestions on the bus. These data are used to analyze the status quo, related operational indicators, sand seek the difference between the status quo and people's reasonable expectations and optimization measures. First consideration is the bus hub, and thinking points and order for the hub is the convergence point in a variety of modes of transport, between multi-level bus, between different bus lines, to facilitate people to reach, transfer, which should be based on the characteristics of demand stratification (1 Level, district level, city level, national level, international level), and classification(aviation, track, external long distance line, city bus, P & R, comprehensive). Then considering the city population, jobs, industry distribution, and the implementation of urban planning years, the bus network layout could be planned, and then a system planning is conducted for bus service needs of the parking, maintenance, connection, information services, management, ticket prices, financial investment, etc.

Step 3: Bus network layout with demand priority

The bus line should serve regional with large travel demand. Bus travel demand is concentrated in large residential areas, commercial areas, etc. The type and scale of urban land use in essence determines the reasonable direction of the bus line. Based on the current passenger traffic survey, the bus passenger flow map in Fig. 9-3 is obtained through the planning software. Traffic volume is used to determine the layout of framework and non-framework of bus network layer by layer. The layers of bus lines in accordance with the "one by one wiring, optimize the network" approach are used to form a planning area of the bus network options. Different ideas choose the line series could be used as bus alternatives are often not unique.

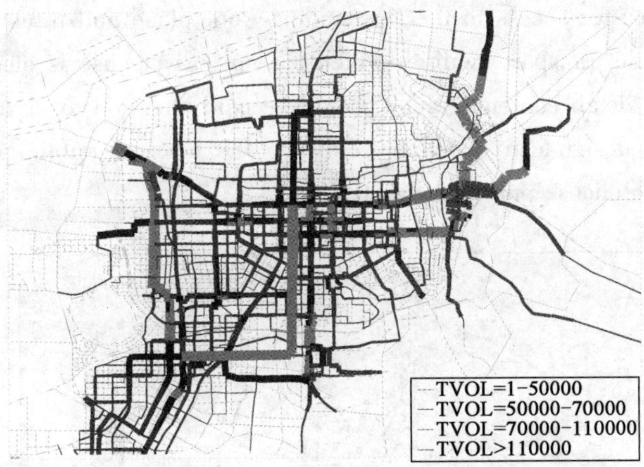

Figure 9-3 Bus passenger flow

Source: *Xi'an* 12th *Five-Year Bus Special Planning*.

Step 4: Establishment of transit model to forecast passenger flow

After the completion of the bus network layout, we need to verify whether the line will attract enough passengers. This work can be used to simulate the process of bus passenger travel, and to calculate the relevant parameters to evaluate the level of bus operation. The mathematical model used to deal with these problems can be referred to as the bus assignment model. The bus model includes four parts: the bus network, the traffic impedance, the path search and the bus assignment. The bus model needs to calibrate the relevant parameters according to the actual situation, which is the key to ensure the accuracy of the forecast. Based on the current situation of passenger demand, the model can be used as the basis of the passenger flow forecast.

Step 5: Planning program

After completing the establishment of the bus model and the passenger forecast, the new problem faced by the planner is how to judge the merits of the planning network or how to choose the best in many alternatives. Passenger flow indicators include passenger volume, turnover, and cross-section passenger flow and so on; network evaluation indicators commonly used network density, site density, etc. to evaluate. The bus service and the city match, usually referred to as the bus market, is an important factor in bus planning to consider. The existing behavior studies show that the range of attraction of rail transit can reach the surrounding 1000 m, and the conventional bus is 500 m. The track attraction is higher in the range of 700 m and the conventional bus is 300 m. Taking the existing bus station as the center, attracting the radius of the site coverage effect map, is an important factor in public transport planning analysis, see Fig. 9-4. Other bus metrics can also be calculated and visualized by some tooling software.

Step 6: Bus platform and station planning

The complete bus planning also includes planning for public transport facilities. It is particularly important to plan the traffic arrangements for the tunnels and sites in these facilities. To clarify the hub, car park, maintenance site, laned, stop, the location of the harbor, land use scale and recommended program. These could provide accurate preconditions for the land pre-approval, municipal design and easier access to the surrounding work place and transportation organizations. Those some urban public transport facilities which are not easy to use is closely related to the bus planning lag and a not detail content, which should be paid attention to. Excellent public transport facilities planning and design can effectively enhance the level of public transport services, and attract more travelers to choose public transport.

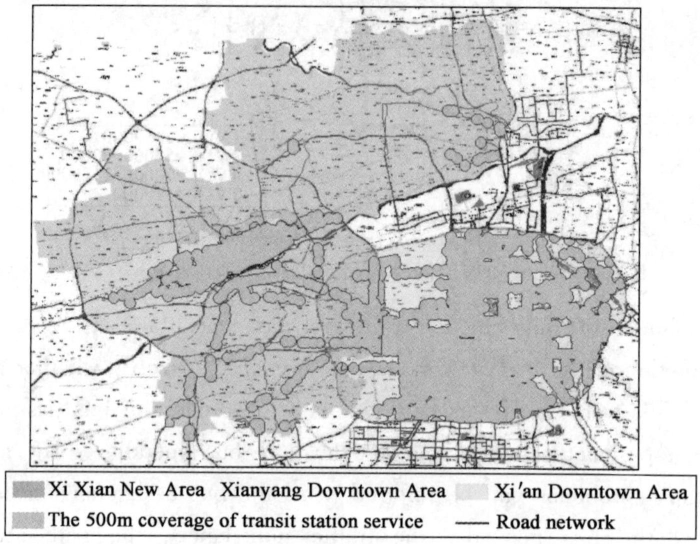

Figure 9-4 Schematic diagram of station coverage

Source: *Challenges and Strategies "city traffic integration" -West Ham Integrated Study Figure.*

Step 7: The implementation of the action plan

The next work is how to plan the implementation of public transport planning, and make the development of schedule, including public transport infrastructure planning and timing, public transport management system construction plan, public transport information construction plan, public transport emergency security system plan and so on.

9.4 Public Transport Network Layout Method

9.4.1 The Influence of Land Use Type on the Bus Connection

The bus network is designed to conform to the upper planning of the city or region and be coordinated with urban land use type to serve the city's main residential areas, industrial areas and commercial activities. From the macro view, urban land use planning decides the direction and distribution of public transport lines. Line layout requires the connection of population, job-intensive areas, the city's important functional areas and major transport hub. Fig. 9-5 represents the Xi'an high tech Zone land use map, population distribution and industrial distribution map.

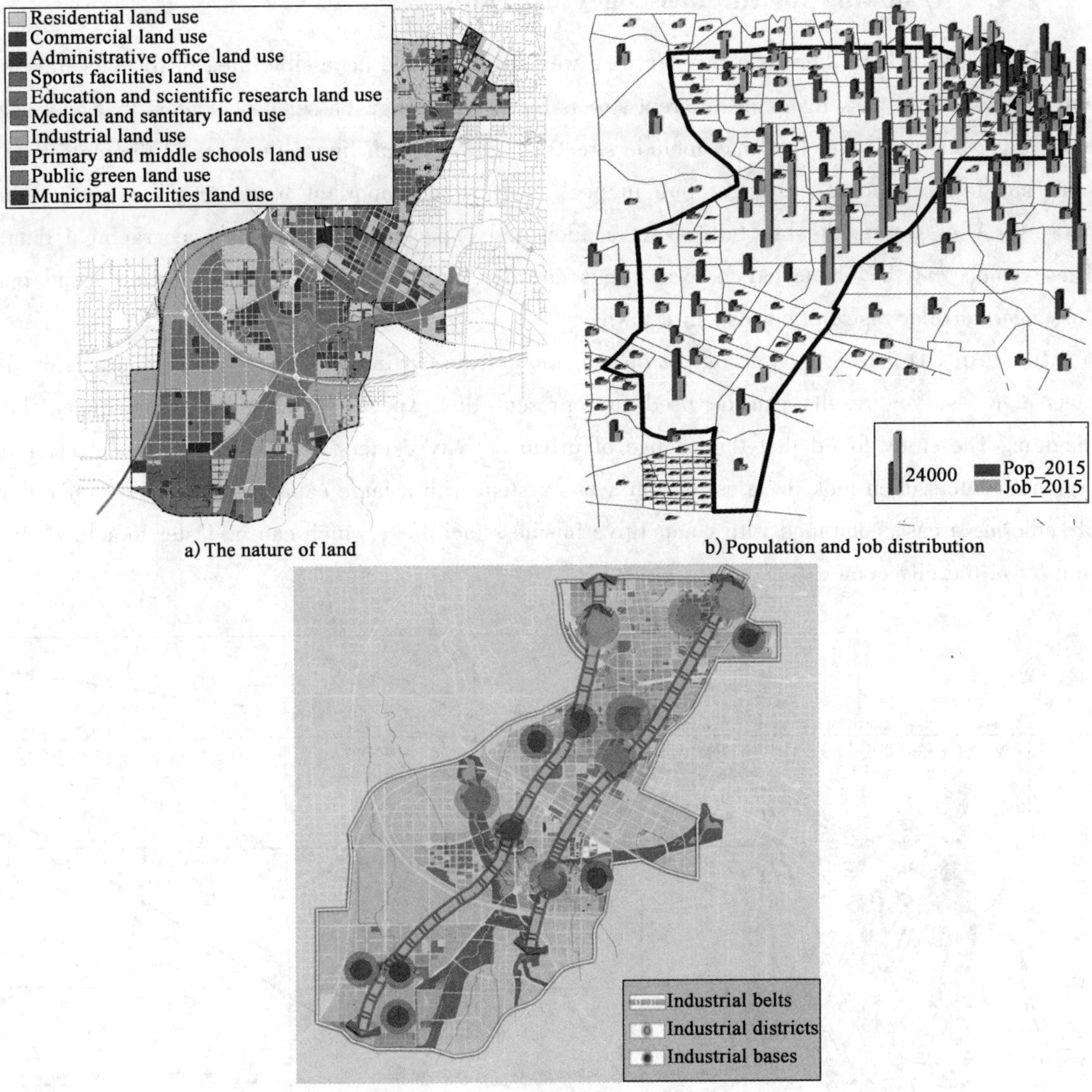

a) The nature of land

b) Population and job distribution

c) Industrial park distribution

Figure 9-5 Land use characteristics of Xi'an high-tech zones

Source: *MVA*, *Chang'an University*, *Xi'an High-tech Zone Integrated Transportation Planning*.

From the figure, it can be seen that the area of residential land and commercial office has a clear assembly area, and these areas will have a lot of bus travel demand; from the population and job distribution map, we can find that the number of jobs and population is often unbalanced in a traffic area, indicating that there will be a lot of commute traffic between the district; In the city, highly intensive industrial park planning often have the growth of traffic demand. Even though the city has a high degree of external automation, less jobs in the industrial park, as an important growth point of the city economy, there are bus travel demand, thus there is a need to support the bus station and line planning.

9.4.2 Looking for the Passenger Corridor

In the area where there is a bus service, we can obtain the accessible area of the bus traveler and the passage of passengers on different streets by investigating. Passenger corridors that channels have larger bus passenger flow may include streets, highways, rail lines, the peak of the main flow, scale and intersection of passenger hub in peak hour is an important basis for the layout of the network. After getting the bus hub size, location and expected associated the geographical data. These points can be connected to form a bus corridor. Fig. 9-6 is bus layout planning and bus passenger corridor distribution map in a town.

Bus trip OD matrix is based on the investigation of the car in the city. The current status of the bus service survey results can be used to represent the expected line and bus passenger flow diagram. The study found that the change of urban activity centers was slow, and the transfer of regional centers often took decades to form a bus system with a large capacity in the new generation of gathering areas, combined with competitive business facilities, which can be faster to achieve the transfer of the city center.

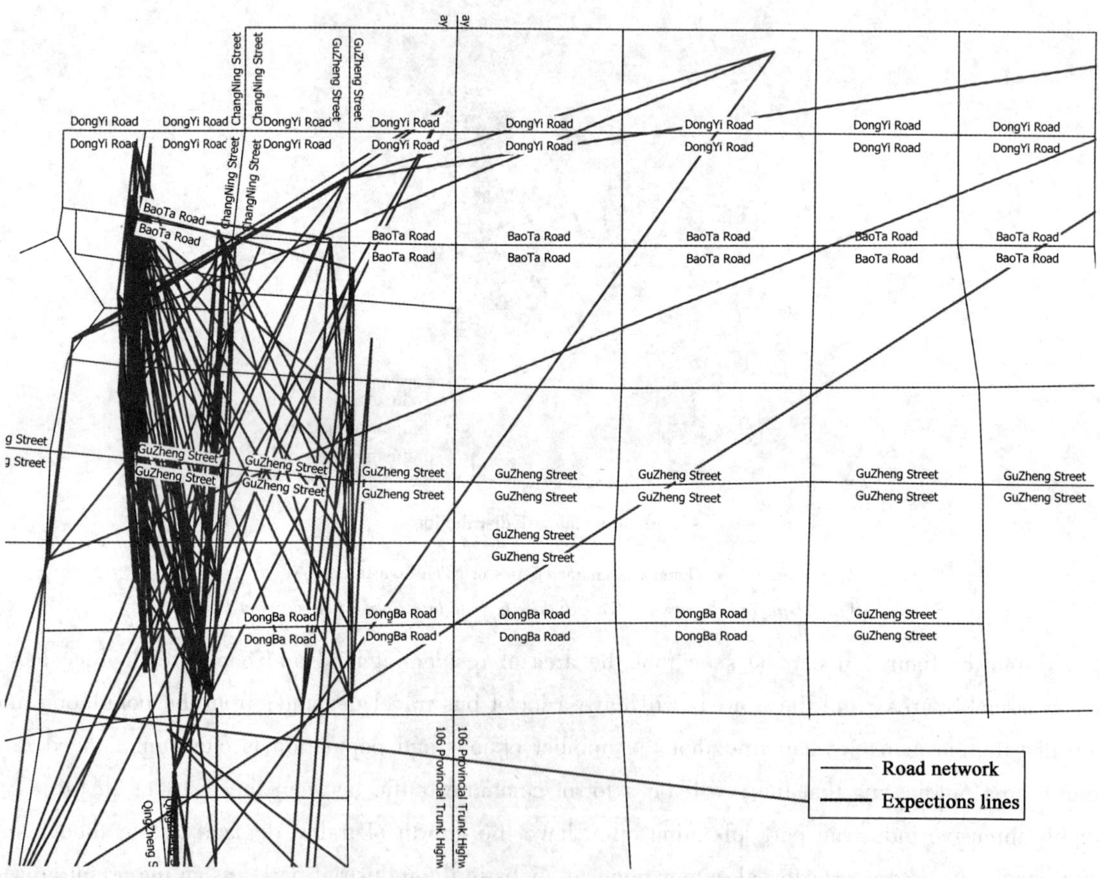

a) Transit passenger flow expectations map

Figure 9-6

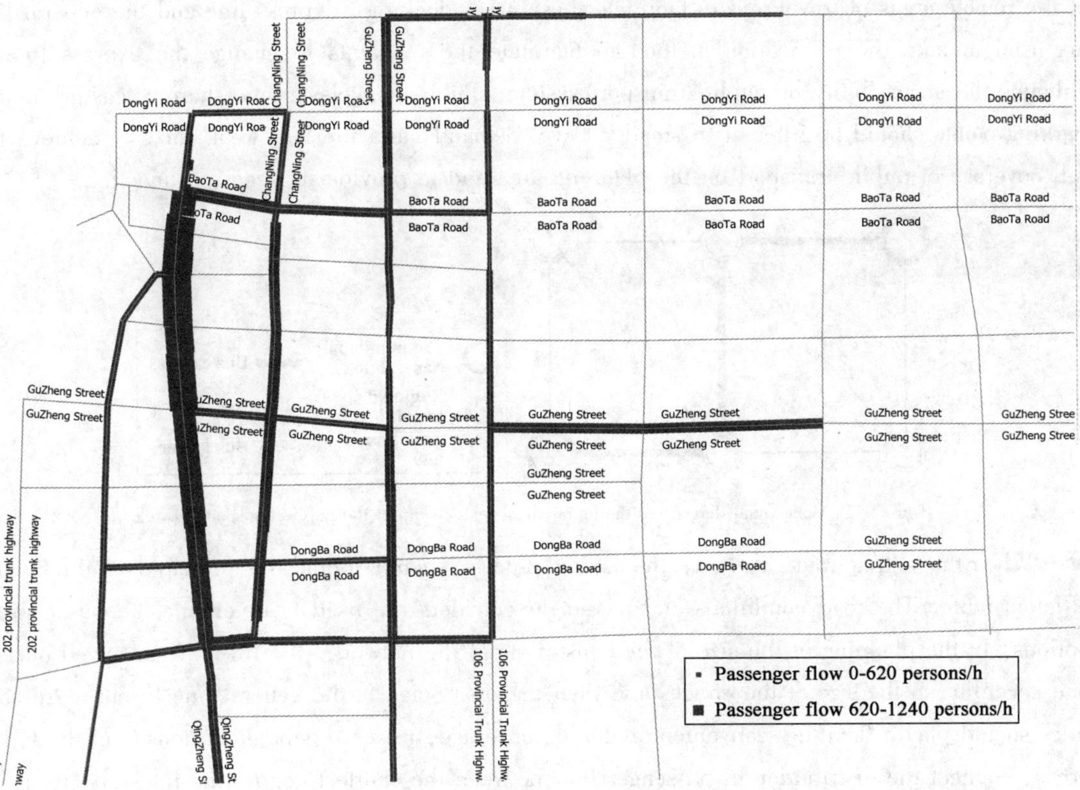

b) Transit passenger corridor bandwidth

Figure 9-6 Expectation line forecasts passenger corridor

Source: *Chang'an University BRT Research Center, Chengcheng County Bus Planning.*

9.4.3 Hierarchical Routing

Public transport system is responsible for conveying passenger from one place to another in the city. The passenger's travel distance is different as well as their trip purpose, their speed, stop and reachability. For example, some travelers want to get to the airport from the train station quickly. For some which need to reach the commercial center from the residential area, the ordinary bus lines are relatively convenient, but in the traffic congestion, they hope there are bus lanes service; for some travelers whose travel distance is short, or their office and living environment is good. They care more about the comfortable and convenient travel environment. In order to meet the needs of different passengers, the planning system needs to be divided into three levels of express line, plain line, branch line; the hierarchical planning of skeleton line, main line and micro loop is also carried out, which is shown in Fig. 9-7.

The bus express line should be used in the form of rail lines or BRT lanes to provide line services for long-distance rapid transport of large-scale transportation hubs and large passenger flow collectors. Ordinary lines often provide convenient services for urban area passenger flow by using of medium distance station, connecting the transport hub and passenger concentration areas, and using ordinary public car models. The feeder line is used to meet the traffic within the area or the outskirts of the remote areas of travel and to facilitate these areas docking. Express line and the general line are used to take the connection method to facilitate the residents to change the express line to enhance the accessibility of public transport system. Public bicycles, time-sharing leasing or taxi parking points should be filled with smaller travel demand, and the less weak links to achieve the full coverage of public transport on the planning area and to provide its access connection.

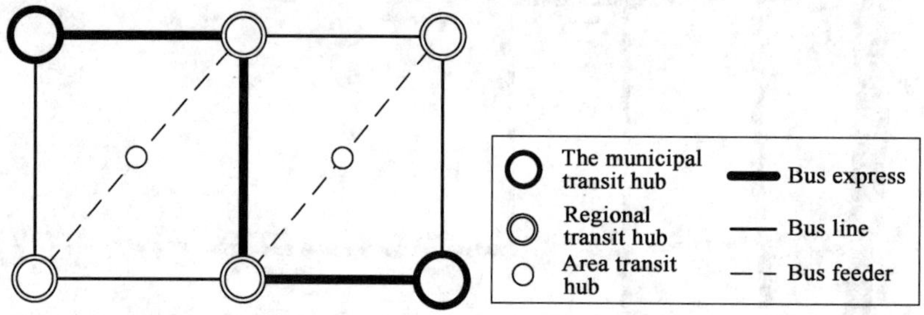

Figure 9-7 Conceptual diagram of the hierarchical relationship of the public transport network

When the actual route is laid, the laying process should follow the principle of direct and efficient route. The road conditions and passenger corridors are used to determine the bus express options. In the planning of the size of the constraints of the network, the lines are arranged one by one according to the size of the effect, and then the next stage is the general line layout. Ordinary lines should play a flexible, convenient and wide coverage, to serve population density of the larger areas, connect the distribution of passenger flow between the shortest connecting lines and focus on higher-level activities center, the hub of the docking. The layout of the feeder line is more flexible, and the main role is to enhance the coverage rate, accessibility of the bus system.

Xi'an High-tech Zone Transit Planning

In the comprehensive transportation planning of Xi'an Hi-tech Zone, the conventional transit system is divided into two systems: rapid transit systems and transit bus systems, which is shown in Fig. 9-8. *The rapid transit systems include two levels: urban rail transit and passenger transport. The*

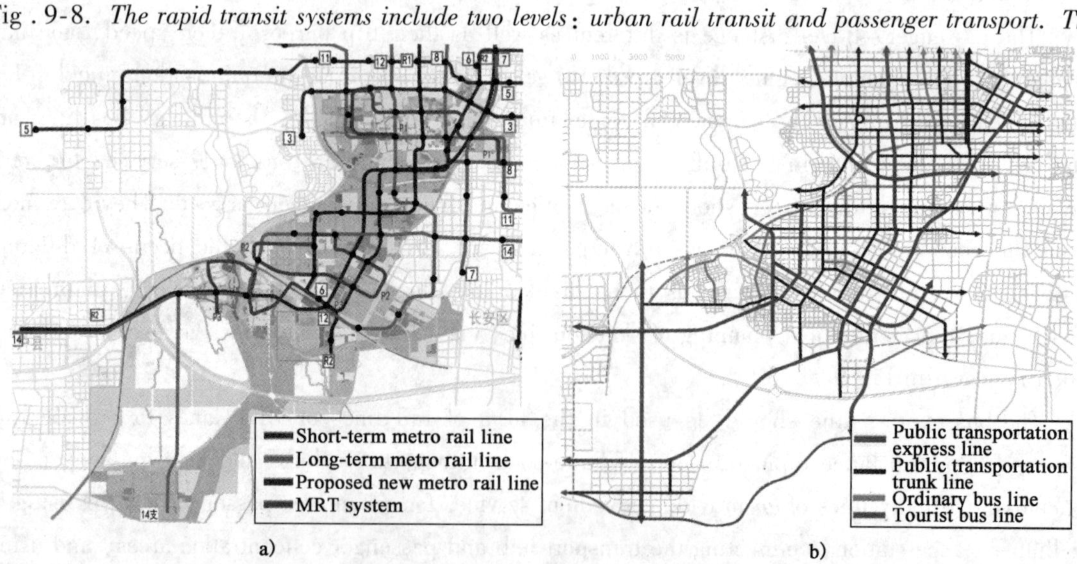

Figure 9-8 Conventional Public Transport Planning of Xi'an High-tech Zone

transit bus include public transportation express line, public transportation trunk line, ordinary bus line and tourist bus line. Transit line planning in accordance with the rail transit -MRT system -bus system in the order of hierarchical wiring, formed integrated transit network.

9.5 Transit Model

9.5.1 The Development History of Transit Model

In the 1960s, the transportation planning forecast of large cities promoted the birth and development of traffic model, and the bus model came into being. In the United States, the Detroit regional traffic forecast did not take into account the bus system. The subsequent Chicago regional traffic research, the planners began to think about how to use mathematical models to describe the bus travel. Richard Bunyan and Robert Dial are responsible for the study of the bus system in the Chicago traffic study. Dial and Bunyan imitate the road assignment model of BPR to develop a set of procedures to predict bus travel, which consists of seven parts: road network abstraction, bus line abstraction, travel OD, pattern division, and traffic assignment and generation report. The bus line abstraction and the pattern of the model proposed at the time seems very new. Dial found that waiting time is an important factor affecting line chooses of the passengers, so he used the queuing theory to push out the waiting time, and assigned the bus travel with all and no assignment method. In the same period of the United Kingdom, Wootton(1967) explored how the bus and orbit services were truly reflected in the equation of the model in the London traffic study. He established a complete public transit model in TRANSITNET software, showing the relationship and the transfer behavior in the structure of different bus services, bus service, departure interval and the average waiting time, finally proposed that the travel time between OD points can be expressed by the sum of walking time, waiting time, in vehicle time. Transfer time, and the transfer time penalty can be added to express the response of different people to transfer.

Dial and Wootton established the initial structure of the bus model, although there are some ideal treatments in the road network abstraction and assignment methods, but the abstract thinking and cost structure of the model has been used so far.

In the Dial bus model, the assignment of public transport to the combination of the line through the same site on the bus line combined into a line. In reality, the differences in the traffic flow of each line are simplified in the Dial model. In order to solve the problem of public transportation line, Robillard(1975) in the assignment stage, the bus trip in each bus line in accordance with the frequency of the line of departure line size.

Spiess(1989) proposed the classical OP(Optimal Strategy) assignment model. Spiess thinks that a bus trip includes walking, travel, transfer and other links, and take this thought as a basis in the bus network to add a walk, transfer sections to represent the travel path of passengers. The bus travel impedance should take into account the waiting time at the same time, walking time and travel time and other factors. Spiess's bus assignment theory has been widely used in bus assignment software.

From 1980s, the theory of public transport model has been developed in many aspects, including the following two aspects:

· Assignment model based on the timetable. Tong and Richardson (1984) divide the bus assignment model into frequency-based and timetable-based model. The former will be the assignment based on the target line; the latter take the bus vehicle as an assignment object. In Tong's public transport model, each vehicle's arrival time, departure time and passenger arrival time are accurately displayed on the timetable to accurately reflect the passenger's waiting and travelling process. The timetable model can better simulate the operation of bus vehicles, thus more and more scholars have started to study the model.

· Congestion problem. Congestion is an important factor affecting the level of public transport services, and it also has a huge impact on the choice of passengers. De Cea (1993) used the BPR function to deal with bus congestion problems and proposed the concept of effective frequencies in congested situations. Kurauchi proposed the concept of failing riding, which is used to simulate the situation in which the passengers cannot get on board because of the crowded congestion.

Avishai Ceder (2007) summarizes the research process of the bus assignment model (Table 9-1). It can be found that the public transport model theory, it is continued to develop and improve in the network topology, travel costs, congestion adjustment and assignment methods in the last 50 years of research.

Table 9-1 The main development of public transit assignment model

Reference	Frequency-based	Timetable-based model	Boarding choice
Dial (1967)	Combined with shortest path assignment method, the queuing theory is used to determine the waiting time		Take the bus firstly arrived
Cbriqui & Robillard (1975)	Abstract the behavior that passengers make multiple lines of choice, and regard the corrected waiting time as travel impedance		Take the first bus arrived in the bus set
Nguyen & Pallotino (1988)	Introduce a path that connect directly to the OD points to indicate a transit route, called a hyper path		Take the first bus arrived in the bus set
Spiess & Florian (1989)	Passengers use the balanced assignment method to select the travel line to reduce the total travel time (walking time + walking time + in-vehicle travel time)		Take the first bus arrived in attractive routes
De Cea & Fernadez (1993)	Consider a congestion influence, and waiting time is affected by passenger volume		Take the first bus in the bus set that is not overloaded
Wu, et al. (1994)	Apply the hyper path to the process including walking, waiting, get on, car, transfer and get off. Waiting time varies with passengers flow		Take the first bus arrived in attractive routes

continued

Reference	Frequency-based	Timetable-based model	Boarding choice
Hickman & Bernstein (1997)		Passengers understand the size of each path impedance, using the selection model for assignment in the various travel stages	
Tong & Wong(1999)		The departure time is determined in virtual bus network, passengers concerned about walking, waiting, in-vehicle travel time when traveling, and use the shortest path assignment method	Random utility path choice
Lam, et al. (1999)	Stochastic User Equilibrium under the limit of routes capacity		Take the first arrival of the bus If the first bus is overloaded, the passenger will choose another
Cominetti & Correa (2001), Bouzaiene-Ayari, et al. (2001)	The congestion formula derived from the queuing theory		Take the first bus arrived in the bus set under the capacity limit
Nuzzolo, et al. (2001)		Choose the departure time and departure station according to the length of travel distance	Random utility choice model
Kurauchi, et al. (2003)	The concept of the probability of failure in the case of congestion is put forward		Take the first arrival of the bus, and consider the risk of failure
Cepeda, et al. (2006)	The crowded formula of the large transit network station		In the case of spare capacity, take the first bus in the bus set

Source: *Public Transit Planning and Operation*, p360-361.

9.5.2 The Structure of Transit Assignment Model

The development of the bus model has formed a complete and unified model structure. From the beginning of the birth, the transit assignment model is accompanied by software applications; the structure of the bus assignment model in mainstream transport planning software (such as CUBE, Trans CAD) is shown in Fig. 9-9.

Transit model is divided into network construction, impedance calculation, route search and selection, transit assignment of four stages. The transit network is established based on the road network, containing elements such as lines, nodes and line information. It is the basis of the transit assignment model. Transit impedance is the basis for path search, selection and assignment in the model. The size of the transit impedance is not only related to waiting time, fare and other transit system factors, but also related to the impact of congestion level. The model searches for a reasonable travel path according to the set impedance threshold (such as travel time, transfer time) and forecast the choice of travel path. The transit trip OD matrix is loaded into the forecasted travel path to complete the transit assignment.

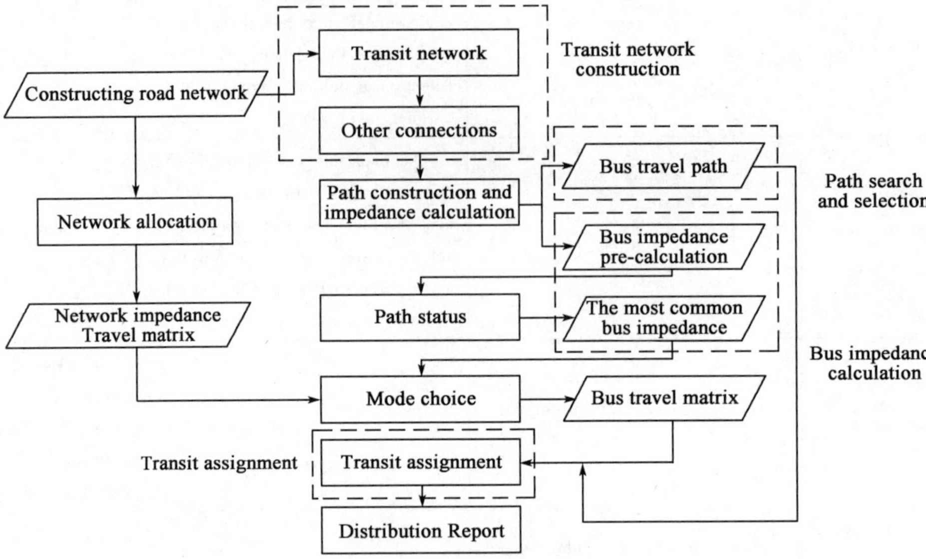

Figure 9-9 Transit assignment model

9.5.3 Data Input and Output

9.5.3.1 Data Input

The data required for the transit assignment model is more and more complex than the highway transportation model. Fig. 9-10 shows the input data and output data for the Cube public transport module. In the software side, the basic data of the public transport model include: script file, road network, bus line, non-transit trip segment, transit system data, transit operation data, OD matrix and so on. The meaning of each data is shown in Table 9-2.

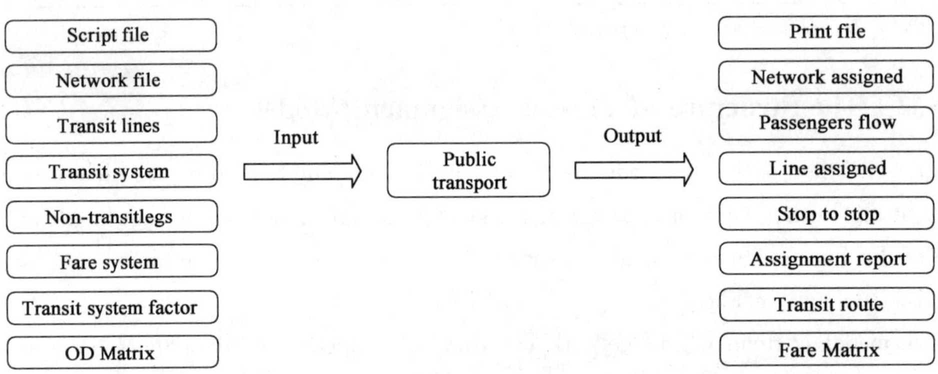

Figure 9-10 The data input and output of public transport model

Table 9-2 The input data module of public transport and its meaning

Data module	Function
Script file	Define the methods used in all aspects of the model, including impedance calculation methods, path search methods, assignment methods, etc.
Network file	Define the road network that relies on transit assignment

continued

Data module	Function
Transit network	Define transit network that relies on transit assignment
Transit system	Define the classification of the bus system, the line company, the waiting time curve, and the waiting curve
Walking	Define centroid link in the transit network and transfer segments
Fare system	Define the fare system used by every system
System parameter	Define in boarding penalty, transfer penalty in transit network nodes
OD matrix	The OD matrix for transit trip

9.5.3.2 Abstract Transit Network

(1) The development of network abstraction

Transit network abstraction as a tool for transit assignment, continues to improve with the travel and the assignment method. The earliest transit model network is obtained analogously from the road network, and there are only points and lines in the transit model network to indicate the station and bus lines (such as Dial, Robillard, see Fig. 9-11). Transit trip costs only consider the waiting time and in-vehicle time, and only describe the bus station and the line, do not express the transfer in the road network.

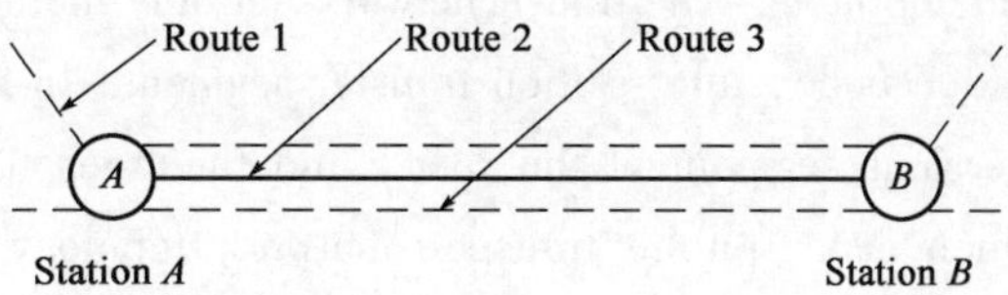

Figure 9-11 Robillard construction of public transport network

Spiess (1989) proposed a complete transit travel behavior theory of previous studies, and firstly proposed a pedestrian segment. Spiess believes that travel time is composed of walking time, waiting time and in-vehicle trip time, and the purpose of the passenger is to reduce the total travel time. Spiess believes that a public transit trip includes some or all of the following links:

- From trip origin to the bus station;
- Waiting process;
- In-vehicle travel process;
- Get off;
- Walking between bus stations;
- Leave the bus station to the destination.

Based on the above assumptions, Spiess proposed a more complete abstracted bus network, as is shown in Fig. 9-12.

The picture above shows the bus network abstracted by Spiess. The network structure is divided into points and lines; the point includes the OD point, the station and the virtual station that represent the ride and the transfer. The line includes the walking segment, the bus segment and on or off section. The transit network topology that Spiess proposed completely expressed a bus trip including walk, ride, and transfer process. The process of walking, riding and transferring for passengers provide a basis for the realization for the future network topology and software.

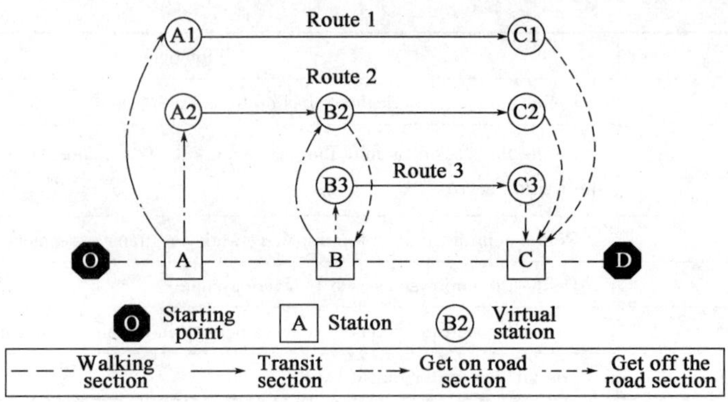

Figure 9-12 Transit network topology

(2) The representation of transit network topology

The road network consists of three elements: traffic zone centroids, the common node and the road link. Traffic zone centroids represent production and attraction. The common point represents the intersection. The link represents the relationship and the impedance between the common node and the node. The transit network not only includes the above nodes and links, but also includes the station node, inter-station transfer segment. In addition, there are a number of bus lines running in the same segment of the road, and the lines have their own frequency, fares and service levels, which make public transport network topology more complex. According to Spiess's abstraction method, the extended public transport network is shown in Fig. 9-13.

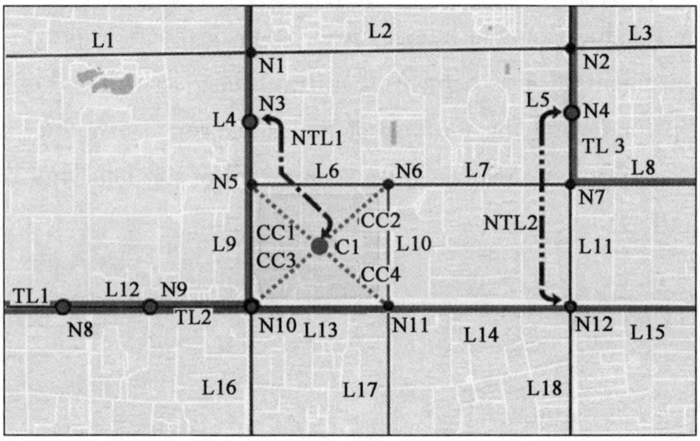

Figure 9-13 The structure of basic network topology

· The node

N: the road node, as is shown as N1, N2, N3 and other points in Fig. 9-12. Road nodes in accordance with the function can be divided into two types: the intersection and the bus station. Intersection is the nodes that multiple segments intersect, such as N1, N2, N10 and so on. Bus station is the connection point between the bus system and road system, so some of the road nodes play the role of the bus station, as is shown in the figure N8, N9 and so on. If the bus station is set at the intersection, the intersection node can also be used as a bus station, as is shown in the figure N10.

C: the traffic zone centroid, as is shown in the figure C1. Traffic zone centroid represents production and attraction.

· Segment

L: road segment, as is shown in the figure L1, L2 and other segment. Road segment is the basis for the establishment of bus lines; in addition, the process that the passenger walks from the station to the center of the zone is also based on road segments to complete in the bus travel.

TL: the bus lines, as is shown in the figure TL1, TL2, TL3. The bus lines are based on road network to be established and are an abstract representation of the bus lines. CC: Centroid link, as is shown in the figure CC1, CC2. Centroid link is the route from the zone to the road network. The centroid linkage generally represents the pedestrian segment in the ordinary bus trip. The length of the segment affects the traveler's choice of the station. In the P & R travel mode, the centroid link indicates the distance that traveler arrives at the bus station.

NTL: Non-bus travel segments, including walking sections and transfer segments. Walking segment is the segment that the traveler departs from the zone to the station and consists of centroid link and road segment, as is shown in the figure NTL2.

· The property of bus line

Transit property cannot be represented by graphics, and it is stored in the various sections of the line in the form of data, to accurately simulate the characteristics of public transport. In the software, a variety of bus types, ticket system and operating companies are defined in the property, which is directly called in the property setting of every line. In the transit network abstraction, one bus line will store one or more of the following property:

a. The types of public transit: Urban public transport, including railway transit, conventional public transit, bus rapid transit, ferry and so on. There are the larger differences among different transit systems in line form and operation.

b. Fare system: The fare system is used in bus lines, such as a vote system, mileage vote system and so on.

c. The departure time interval: The departure time interval of the bus line is an important factor for passengers to choose a line.

d. Capacity: The size of the vehicle affects the transportation capacity of the line, which is the basis of congestion analysis.

9.5.3.3 The Output Result

There are many ways to express the results of transit assignments:

· The report of transit passenger flow. Output the passenger flow report of each line (Fig. 9-14). The report includes: basic line information (such as system type, affiliated company, line length), running time, traffic volume, turnover, etc. These indicators can be used to calculate the accuracy of the model and forecast the size of the transit passenger flow in the future, and estimate the benefits.

· The graph of transit flow assignment. The transit passenger flow is assigned to transport network to get the graph of passenger flow assignment (Fig. 9-15). We can intuitively find the distribution of transit passenger flow to determine the main areas for the passenger mustering to provide the basis for adjustment and planning of the bus line.

```
REPORT LINES   UserClass=1
Name            Mode  Op Stp Cr Distance    Time         Pass      PassDist        PassHr
Sort=MODE
------------------------------------------------------------------------------------------
RailNo4            1   1  25  -    41.08   82.17   214,095.59  1,367,385.47    45,581.65 RailNo4
RailNo4-           1   1  25  -    41.08   82.17   211,122.75  1,393,603.75    46,455.95 RailNo4
RailNo2            1   1  22  -    27.53   55.05   356,082.34  2,329,980.32    77,642.60 RailNo2
RailNo2-           1   1  22  -    27.53   55.05   348,704.24  2,295,573.66    76,498.71 RailNo2
RailNo3            1   1  27  -    43.19   86.35   349,724.22  2,848,434.25    94,940.37 RailNo3
RailNo3-           1   1  27  -    43.19   86.35   341,008.99  2,683,252.36    89,431.90 RailNo3
RailNo5            1   1  25  -    46.08   92.15   152,607.41    995,344.45    33,177.15 RailNo5
RailNo5-           1   1  25  -    46.08   92.15   142,437.47    925,408.27    30,844.55 RailNo5
RailNo1            1   1  23  -    31.31   62.60   567,221.85  5,515,629.72   183,804.70 RailNo1
RailNo1-           1   1  23  -    31.31   62.60   586,506.16  5,508,071.59   183,552.09 RailNo1
RailNo6            1   1  30  -    39.69   79.39   392,933.69  3,213,628.57   107,152.44 RailNo6
RailNo6-           1   1  30  -    39.69   79.39   387,495.53  3,160,392.25   105,378.76 RailNo6
Regional Rail1     1   1  11  -    44.29   53.14   218,933.72  2,911,447.68    58,230.64 Reginal Rail1
Regional Rail1     1   1  11  -    44.29   53.14   223,850.46  2,974,133.92    59,484.17 Reginal Rail1
30-                3   2  27  -    15.24   77.63     5,158.09     13,186.36     1,074.69 30
315                3   2  15  -    19.04  180.53    33,363.08    127,796.08    17,677.79 315
315-               3   2  15  -    19.04  178.03    33,845.16    129,251.63    18,361.96 315
610                3   2  33  -    20.67  138.09    13,270.72     23,198.32     2,504.49  610
610          -     3   2  33  -    20.67  141.03    11,960.14     18,133.23     1,957.24  610
713                3   2  44  -    26.08  138.81    33,628.44    101,586.32     8,049.06 713
713-               3   2  44  -    26.08  137.87    38,783.63    109,952.72     8,671.98 713
715                3   2  42  -    28.36  174.77    10,382.20     19,794.05     1,937.14 715
```

Figure 9-14 The report of transit passenger flow

Source: *BRT Research Center, Chang'an University.*

Figure 9-15 The bandwidth graph of transit passenger flow assignment

Source: *BRT Research Center, Chang'an University.*

· The passenger flow on and off the bus and cross section. Output the number of passengers on and off at each station of a bus line and cross section, which can be used to analyze the spatial assignment characteristics of bus passenger flow. The report in Fig. 9-16 can determine the size of the cross-sectional passenger flow between the stations of every bus line. We can calculate the number of vehicle in the line according to the capacity and the frequency of vehicle after the determination of maximum cross section flow. The number of passengers on and off the station is assigned to the road-the public transport network, then check the relationship between the amount of passengers and the land use type, finally verify the reasonability of the assignment of the results.

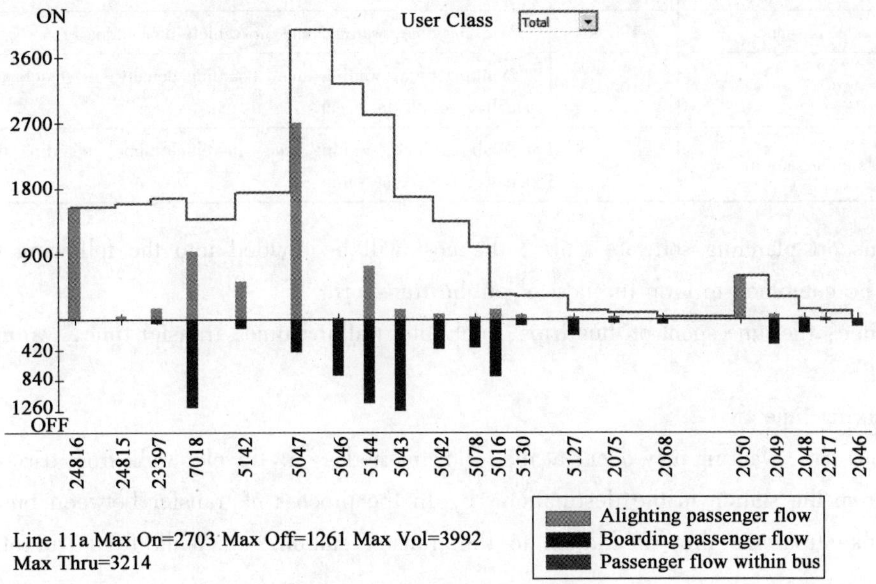

a) Section passenger flow

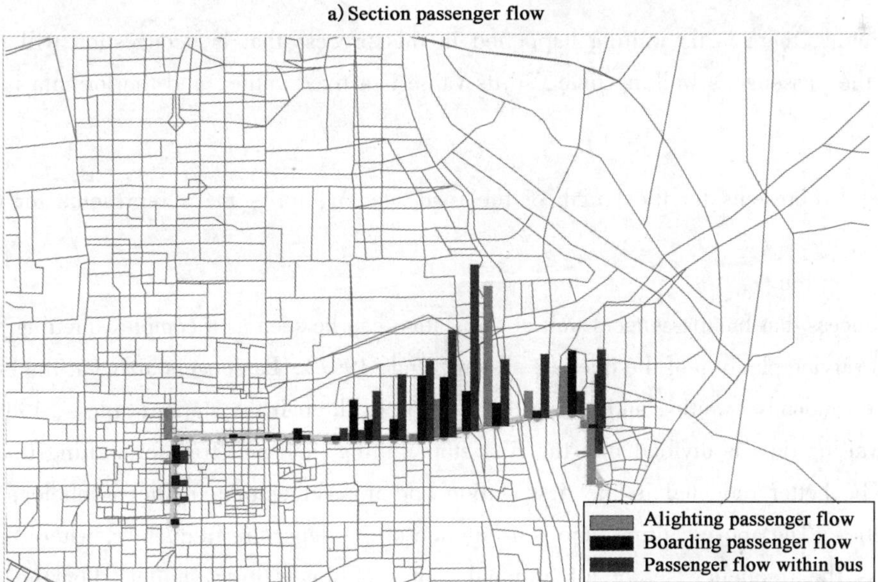

b) Transit on/off bars

Figure 9-16 The number of passenger on and off the bus at bus station

9.5.4 Trip Costs

The trips will produce impedance in each stage of their trip. The generalized bus trip cost is an important parameter in the problem of public transport assignment. How to complete and accurately express the composition of bus trip cost is an important part of the development of transit model. Table 9-3 shows the scholar's consideration of the bus cost in the different periods.

Table 9-3 The study on the bus cost

Scholar	Time	Cost composition
Dial & Le Clercq	1970s	Waiting time, in-vehicle travel time
Spiess & Florian	1980s	Walking time, waiting time, in-vehicle time, transfer
Wu	1990s	Walking time, waiting time, boarding penalty, in-vehicle time, transfer penalty, get off the penalty
Cube planning software	Now	Walking time, waiting time, in-vehicle time, boarding time, transfer penalty, fare, time value

In transport planning software Cube, the cost will be divided into the following four types, which can be combined to form the cost of public transport.

(1) Time: the time spent on bus trips, including walking time, transfer time, waiting time and in-vehicle time

· Walking time

In a bus trip, walking may occur at the following nodes: a. traveler walk from trip origin to the station or from the station to the destination. b. In the process of transfer between bus lines, the traveler walks from the drop-off station to the transfer station. c. Walk from trip origin to the destination.

In general, there is no waiting happened in this process that is, congestion will not have an impact on the passenger's walking time, so its value is a fixed value, and the formula is as follows:

$$t_{\text{walk}} = \frac{l}{s} \tag{9-1}$$

where: l represents for the length of the road section, unit: m; s represents for the walking speed, unit: m/s.

· Waiting time

The process that bus passengers wait at the station can be seen as a complex queuing process, the station is a service platform of the queuing system (Dial, 1967). Passengers arrive at the bus station at a given rate randomly, waiting and taking the other lines through the station (Spiess, 1989).

The waiting time is divided into the first stop waiting time and transfer waiting time in Cube, which can be better reflected in the first station and transfer station in the psychological behavior characteristics. The above waiting time is a function of the departure frequency, where the departure frequency is the frequency set of all optional routes of the waiting station. For the relationship between them, domestic and foreign scholars have related research (such as "effective frequency"); here introduce the default function in the Cube software.

The Cube default setting uses the waiting time deduced by Dial(1967) to calculate. Assuming that the bus distance is distributed in a way of exponential function. The arrival time of the passengers is random, so the waiting time is a half of time headway. The relationship between the waiting time and the time headway is shown in Fig. 9-17. There are a minimum waiting time and maximum tolerance time for every transit traveler. In the minimum tolerant headway time, waiting time t_{wait} meet:

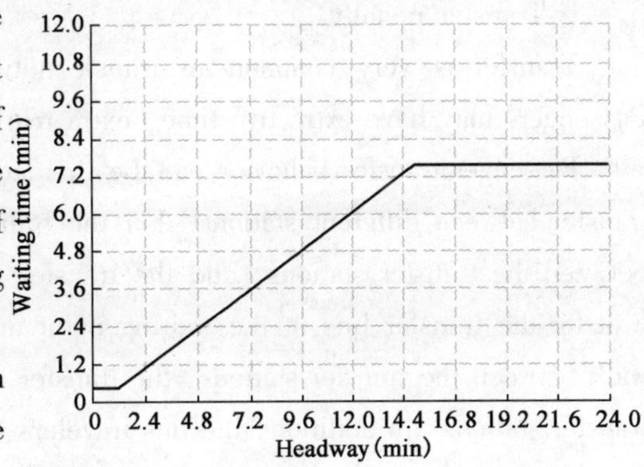

Figure 9-17 The function of waiting time

$$t_w = \frac{1}{2} t_h \tag{9-2}$$

where, t_w is the waiting time, unit: s; t_h is the bus head time, unit: s.

Cube software can be used to draw the waiting time curve to change the time function, to establish a waiting time model for improving the accuracy of the model.

· In-vehicle time

In-vehicle time of passenger refers to the running time of the bus on the bus line after the passenger boarding on the bus. Under the condition of non-congested road network, its value depends on the length of the bus section and the running speed of the bus. The formula is as follows:

$$t_s = \frac{l_b}{s_b} \tag{9-3}$$

where, l_b is the length of the bus trip line, unit: m; s_b is the bus speed, unit: m/s.

Bus congestion will affect the level of transit services, so that passengers feel discomfort. The performance is "time is very slow". Therefore, in the case of congestion in the vehicle, the vehicle is an increasing function of passenger traffic volume, that is, the generalized trip time increases. In the crowded transit network conditions, the in-vehicle time will be affected by road traffic at the same time.

(2) Penalty: transfer, boarding and alighting make it inconvenient for the traveler, which is often non-temporal impact, including boarding penalty and transfer penalty

· Boarding penalty

Boarding penalty is a comprehensive concept. In the part of the model, it is the station of the up and down time for the passengers. Part of the model will be the impact of the frequency of the trip on the impedance of the vehicle in the penalty. If only refers to the time on the bus, it is the boarding time for the bus line, and it is the walking and boarding time in a channel or platform for the subway lines.

According to the site-related statistical information, the penalty time of different transit modes is calibrated.

· Transfer penalty

Transfer is very common in transit network, so it is necessary to consider transit cost. Passengers may have extra trip time, extra trip expenses and multiple transfers.

Passenger transfer behavior can be divided into the transfer between the same station and the transfer between different stations. For the transfer between the same stations, there is no distance between the transfer stations, and the transfer impedance includes the waiting time that passengers wait for the transfer line at the waiting point and transfer costs. Assuming that the passengers only walk between the transfer stations, the transfer impedance also includes the walking time between the transfer stations. In addition, the bus travelers will try to avoid transfer. Transfer times as an integer variable is often used as a component of the transfer amount penalty. The calculation of each element in the transfer penalty is related to the calculation method of the walking time and the ticket price.

(3) Fare: the economic cost of a bus trip can often use "time value" to achieve the cost of mutual transformation in the economy and the time

There are many ways to pay the bus; the most common is a ticket system, in addition to distance charges, sub-charges, district charges, monthly fees, combined charges and other means. Different charging methods have different impact on different bus trips, such as that the Shanghai subway and the original Beijing subway ticket system is different, which will affect attraction of the scope of rail services.

· One-ticket system

The fee will be charged when the passengers get on the bus. The boarding penalty can be used to describe the inconvenience caused by the transfer. As people are charged when boarding bus in a ticket system, and do not change with the travel distance. This can also be seen as an additional punishment on the bus. Distance charge

Distance charge: That is charges according to the trip distance of passengers. In this case, passengers will prefer to choose a direct line. You can set the starting point of the fare and the unit distance fares, or fare charts to indicate the distance charges. Fig. 9-18 shows the linear and non-linear distance charges.

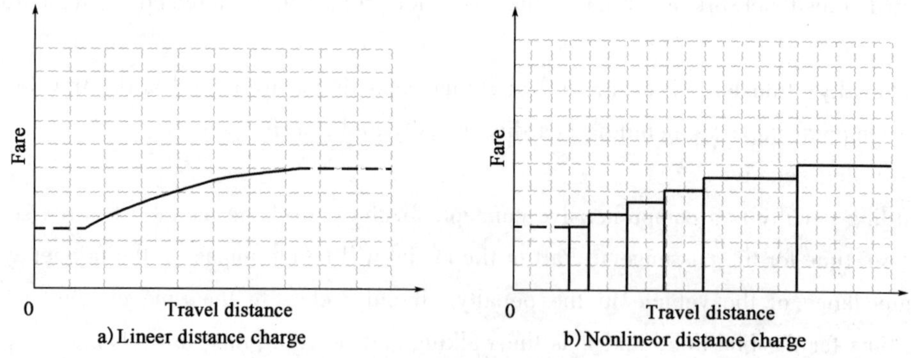

Figure 9-18 Distance charges

· Zonal charges

The fare depends on the origin and destination rather than the path, so this way of charging does not have an impact on the passenger's route or route choice, and the passenger will always choose the shortest path between the two points. This method of charging is often accompanied by the division of the toll area[Fig. 9-19a)]. One of methods dividing zones is that considering the city center as the center of circles to divie zones [Fig. 9-19b)] This charging model can be drawn in the GIS bus parking area, and in the form of a matrix to store the bus costs.

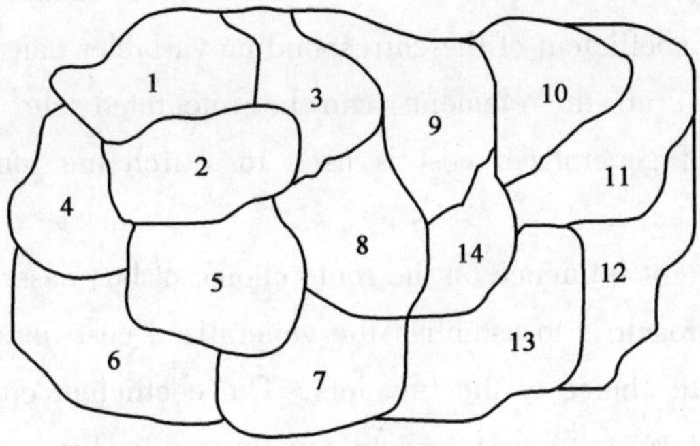

a) Cherge zones

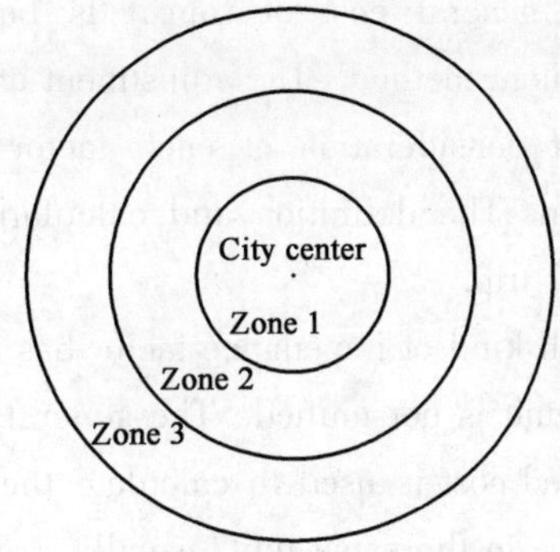

b) An annular zone system

Figure 9-19 Partition charge

· Fare table charges

Transit charges are expressed in the form of fare tables, which is common for long-distance buses or suburban buses. This kind of ticket system is also the zonal charge.

· Interval charges

The cost is related to the range through which the passenger passes. In this way, although the cost is related to the number of stations passing, it is slightly different from the distance charge. The cost of an interval-based fee is non-linear and often divides multiple sites into the same charge zone. This kind of charging method mainly restricts the transfer behavior. The interval charge is shown in Fig. 9-20.

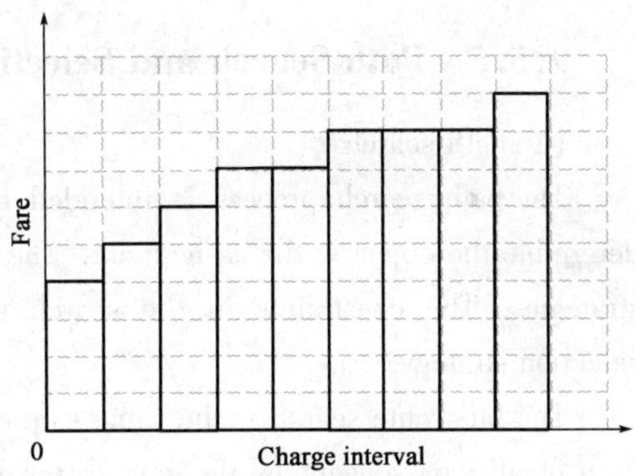

Figure 9-20 Interval charge

· The accumulated charges

The accumulated charge is a kind of ticket system based on the interval charge, and the fare is the sum of all the zonal costs of all the trip lines.

· Monthly charges

That is the ticket system, which is valid in a certain period; passengers can freely ride any of the provisions of the lines without having to pay in the effective period. In the choice of the path, the passengers is not affected by the price factor, passengers do not need to pay for the transfer. Therefore, he will generally choose the line with the shortest trip time.

(4) Weight: the weight is different in the cost, which can reflect the sensitivity of passengers on different types of costs

(5) Time value: it is used for conversion between time and cost dimensions

The time value parameter is a user-defined attribute that is used to convert travel time and waiting time into a monetary unit and then combined it with the application of the ticket. The generalized cost of travel is achieved by using the calculation of the time value.

(6) Generalized cost

The general cost of transit is based on the linear model of the above elements as the measurement method. The adjustment of the coefficient of the corresponding variables can reflect the degree of consideration of each factor, and all the elements can be integrated into the same dimension. The definition and calculation of generalized cost is used to search the route of bus passenger trip.

Each kind of impedance factor has different influence on the route choice of bus passenger trip, and the unit is not unified. The general approach is to establish the generalized cost function. The generalized cost is used to calculate the route choice of the travelers. The coefficient converts the impedance to the same unit (usually a monetary unit). At present, in the public trip assignment, the generalized cost between the origin and destination point definition ij for travel is as follows:

$$C_{ij} = \alpha_1 t_{aij} + \alpha_2 t_{wij} + \alpha_3 t_{bij} + \alpha_4 t_{tij} + \alpha_5 t_{bij} + \varphi F_{ij} \tag{9-4}$$

where, t_{aij} is the waiting time between i and j, unit: s; t_{wij} is the waiting time between i and j; t_{tij} is the transfer penalty between i and j; t_{bij} is boarding penalty between i and j, unit: s; F_{ij} is the fare between i and j, unit: yuan; $\alpha_1 \sim \alpha_5$ is the weight factor of the cost factor; φ is the time value parameter, unit: yuan/s.

9.5.5 Path Search and Selection

(1) Path search

The path search process is intended to retrieve a valid travel route in the road network to determine the object of the assignment. The process is a combination of physical networks and travel strategies. The constraints in the search are also affected by choice strategy of the passenger selection strategy.

The bus route search is the same as the network, but it is more complicated in the constraints. First of all, passengers in the bus trip will be able to avoid transfer, so a variety of transport planning software in the search bus path will set a threshold. When the number of transfer exceeds the threshold, it is no longer used; In addition, all passengers will not be concentrated on the optimal route, but will be distributed in the optimal, sub-optimal route (not necessarily two). Therefore, in search for the path between a pair of transit OD, the model often will set a threshold that passenger accepted then search all possible paths below the threshold.

(2) Path selection

There are a number of feasible bus lines on a road (the collinear problem), that is, there are a variety of line options between bus origin and destination. So passengers face a choice at the station: whether to take the earliest arrival of the line, or wait for other lines. The problem faced by passengers is one research context of the strategy choice.

Chrique & Robillard first proposed a probabilistic framework of collinear problem, assuming that the passengers at the station do not select a bus line, but a bus lines set formed by the few bus lines, a line of passengers will eventually take this line in the set to reach the final point. The model proposed by Chrique essentially takes a number of alternative lines as a line; the departure frequency of this line is the sum of the frequency of all lines in the collection. The probability of selecting a line in a collection is calculated as follows.

$$P = \frac{f_{\text{line}l}}{\sum_i f_{\text{line}i}} \tag{9-5}$$

where, P is the probability of selecting line l; $f_{\text{line}l}$ is the departure frequency of line l; $f_{\text{line}i}$ is the departure frequency of line i.

Chronique only considers the impact of the departure frequency on the passenger selection in the model, ignoring the in-vehicle time in the line. Therefore, Spiess proposed the optimal strategy (Optimal Strategies) after the Chrique, to make up for this shortcoming; the improved model is still in use, which is the main method to solve the selection problem.

9.5.6 The Method of Transit Assignment

(1) All-or-nothing assignment

The early bus assignments are the shortest path (all-or-nothing) assignment. However, due to the existence of bus collinear question, transit assignment and road assignment are the same. Dial, Le Clercq assigned using the proportion of the departure frequency between a pair of OD. Chriqui assigned the whole trip to the shortest bus line or bus line set.

(2) Optimal strategy

Spiss and Florian (1989) proposed the concept of optimal strategy, which was a generalization of a single path. It is assumed that passengers often choose first bus line which could be able to bring them to the destination with roughly reasonable time. Then for different service time and use frequency, passengers can use different paths. The line set with the least cost of trip is called the best strategy. The bus trip is assigned to each path according to the relative departure of each path service in the best strategy.

(3) Pathfinder method

This approach is an improvement to the best strategy. The path search method uses the generalized cost of travel instead of the travel time as the basis for the selection of the best path. The generalized travel cost is calculated by applying a user-specified time value (VOT) that converts the trip and the waiting time into monetary units and then combines with the associated travel expenses. This method can adjust the parameters to change the size of the path set of the optimal policy. As the parameter values increase, some lines with higher travel costs are also added to the assignment path set.

(4) Stochastic user equilibrium method

Since the UE model has a hypothesis, that is to say, it is unrealistic for travelers to know the trip cost of each line. Therefore, from the behavior characteristics of the traveler, the stochastic user equilibrium model is more reasonable than the UE model. Based on this consideration, Lam(1999) and Nielsen(2000) established a Logic model and Probity model to achieve SUE transit assignment. Nielsen also used the SUE model in Copenhagen for the practice of bus network assignment.

(5) Assignment method based on the schedule

The assignment method based on the timetable is generally used in the case that the frequency of the bus supply is low, and the information of the timetable is very important for the passengers. This approach is precisely considered for timetable information. Therefore, it is particularly suited to the modeling and assignment of public transport systems or rail networks in suburban areas.

9.6 Transit Service Evaluation

Whether the bus planning is reasonable needs to be evaluated. As an important part of transit planning, transit service evaluation is mainly carried out in two stages of planning: before the planning we need to evaluate the current transit system to analyze the existing problems of current services; and after the completion of the transit network planning and model assignment, we need to evaluate the transit system to evaluate the effect of the planning program, and to provide the basis for further adjustment.

The evaluation of transit service is based on two aspects of passenger flow index and network index.

9.6.1 The Evaluation Index of Passenger Flow

In terms of bus planning, passenger flow affects the financial evaluation of the planning project, the assessment of the national economy. And the assessment of the economic benefits is mainly dependent on the number of passengers. So post project evaluation about the passenger flow is essential.

(1) Daily passenger volume in single line

The daily passenger volume of a line is equal to the total passenger flow of all stations in the line, and all the adjacent lines are transferred to the total passenger flow. It is the result of the assignment of urban travel on the line, reflecting its passenger attraction. This indicator is also the main parameter to calculate the line operating ticket revenue and carry out economic evaluation.

(2) Total passenger volume in network

The sum of all the lines of passenger volume under the jurisdiction of the network is calculated from the sum of all the volume in station and the transfer volume.

(3) Passenger turnover

Passenger turnover is multiplied by the number and distance of passengers in the process of flow. It is the output of public transport direct transportation and it is the passenger index which reflects the transportation efficiency.

(4) Peak hour passenger volume & maximum cross section passenger flow during peak hour

Peak hour passenger volume refers to the largest hourly passenger volume in one-way during the day. The peak hour section volume is the largest, which is called the peak largest hour section traffic (Fig. 9-21).

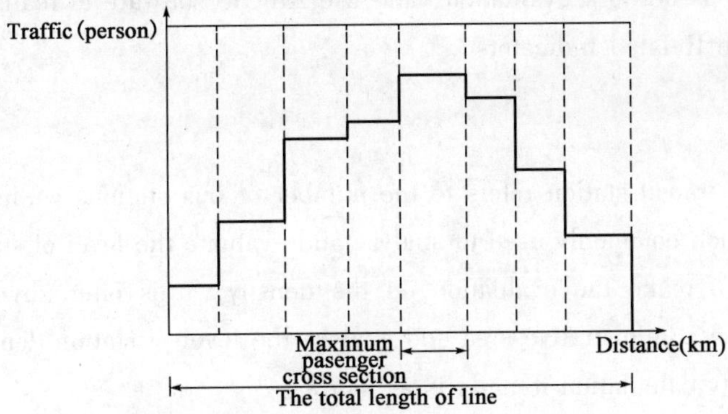

Figure 9-21 Maximum passenger flow diagrams

For the subway, the peak hour traffic of the station is mainly used to calculate the station ticket sales system, entry and exit channel, platform scale. Peak hour passenger volume & maximum cross section passenger flow during peak hour are mainly used to calculate subway train logarithm during peak hours and train program, as well as the number of the conventional bus.

(5) Station entry/exit volume

For the rail transit system, the number of passengers entering and leaving the rail transit system in the unit time is the number of passengers entering the rail transit system. The number of passengers leaving the rail transit system refers to the number of passengers who get off the rail transit system per unit time. Which can be understood as the number of stations on and off in the conventional bus system.

(6) Passenger transfer volume

The number of passengers on the bus station changed from one bus line to another per unit time. In the rail transit, passenger flow is considered including statistics of transfer, and accessibility transfer. The transfer barrier out of the station is not included in the passenger flow.

(7) Transfer coefficient

The average coefficient for passengers is the sum of the number of passengers traveling and the number of passengers divided by the number of passengers traveling, which is the measure of the degree of direct travel and the convenience.

$$\text{Average passenger transfer coefficient} = \frac{\text{Station entrance amount} + \text{The station transfer amount}}{\text{Station entrance amount}} \tag{9-6}$$

9.6.2 Transit Network Evaluation Indicator

The convenience of public transport generally refers to the convenience of residents traveling by public transport, and it could be measured specifically by the through the degree the residents are close to public transport, the range bus can be reached, the optional route to reach the different destination. Using various indicators and charts to intuitively express the convenience of the public transit system is the problem dealt in this section. This section summarizes the station and the network index in the bus network evaluation, and use ArcGIS software to realize visualization.

9.6.2.1 Station Related Indicators

(1) Station density

· Definition

Density of public transit station refers to the number of bus stations within the scope of urban land use per unit, which commonly used to analyze and evaluate the level of station facilities supply in urban land use. To make the evaluation on the density, it is often divide the scope of the evaluation based on the administrative area and analyze the level of station density.

The station density calculation formula is as follows:

$$\text{Station density} = \frac{\text{Number of bus stops}}{\text{Urban land area with bus service}} \tag{9-7}$$

· Approach

The use of GIS tools can be more intuitive to show the station density combined with geographic maps. Fig. 9-22 is the density analysis of the bus station in Xianyang. According to the administrative, land use and etc. , the Xianyang city is divided into multiple analysis area, then the station density of each district could be calculated. The planners use this representation to visually present differences in the density of different communities, and provide a basis for decision makers.

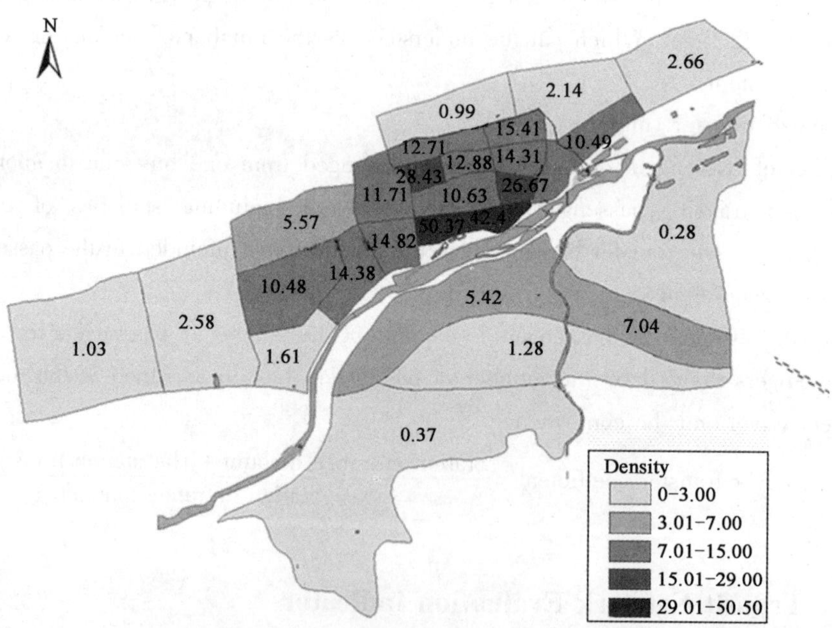

Figure 9-22 Village station density assignment

(2) Coverage rate of station

· Definition

Coverage rate of station is an important indicator that reflects the distance of the city residents from the bus station, and it measures the rationality of station setting in bus line planning. Coverage rate of transit station is usually calculated by using the center of the bus station. A reasonable walking distance for the radius of the circle take a radius of 300 m or 500 m for conventional bus, and 800 m for rail traffic.

Calculation formula of coverage rate of station is as follows:

$$\text{Transit station coverage} = \frac{\text{Bus stops coverage area}}{\text{Urban land use area with the bus service}} \tag{9-8}$$

According to *Road Traffic Urban Planning and Design Standards*, rate of bus station within 300 m is not less than 50%, according to the 500 m radius calculation, not less than 90%. The range of service coverage for different population scales is provided in the Urban Integrated Transport System Planning Specification (draft), as is shown in Table 9-4.

Table 9-4 Station coverage specified size

Planning the size of the city population (million people)	Rail	Service range	Coverage
≥100	Yes	The 800 m radius range of urban rail transit station and the 500 m radius range of bus station	≥95%
	No	500 m radius of urban transit (electric) station	≥90%
50 ~ 100	—	500 m radius of urban transit (electric) station	70%-80%
≤50	—	500 m radius of urban transit (electric) station	60%-80%

Source: *Urban Integrated Transport System Planning Norms (draft)*.

· Processing method

GIS software often provides a "buffer" tool to facilitate coverage of the area. Fig. 9-23 displays service scope of the Xi'an bus station and GIS tools are used to generate a range of services, then to calculate coverage rate. The scope of analysis should be divided according to the urban characteristics and needs.

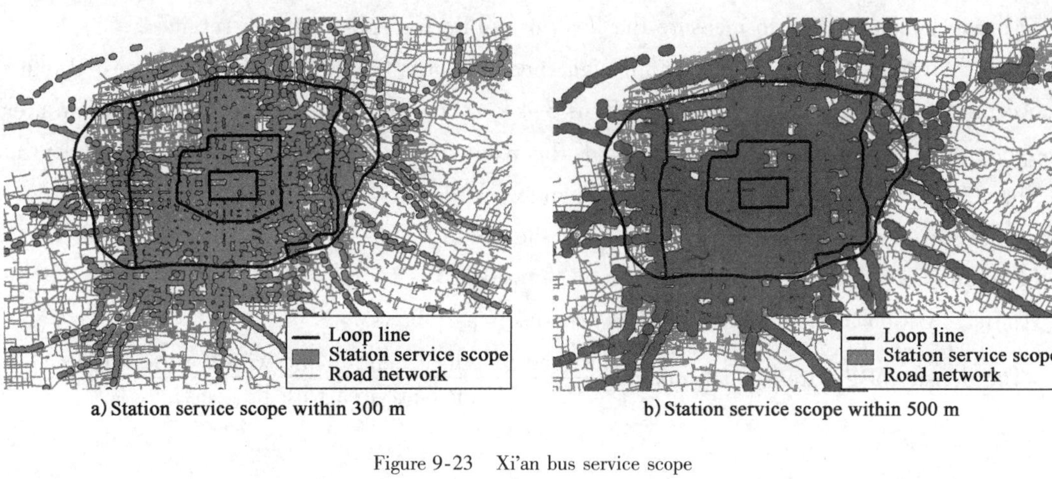

a) Station service scope within 300 m   b) Station service scope within 500 m

Figure 9-23 Xi'an bus service scope

(3) Average distance between stations

· Definition

Average distance between stations of bus station refers to the average length of the bus lines within the urban land area, which is an important index reflecting the level of the transit network.

Under the condition of the same length of the line, the long distance between stations can get a higher delivery speed and save trip time of passengers traveled for long distance. But the longer distance between station increases walking time for long distance traveler. The average distance of the general public transit is planned and designed according to the following values: transit(trolley) bus line 500-800 m; suburban line 800-1000 m; bus station express line; urban line 1500-2000 m; suburban line 1500-2500 m.

Average distance of station calculation formula is calculated as follows:

$$\text{Average distance between stations} = \frac{\text{Line length}}{\text{Number of sites} - 1} \tag{9-9}$$

In the actual analysis, the bus station distance in the downtown area is small, and the distance from the suburb is larger. In order to reflect the characteristics of the average distance between different regions, an algorithm for the average bus stop distance is introduced.

$$\text{The bus average station spacing in a region} = \frac{\text{Total line length in the region}}{\text{Number of segment separated by station}} \tag{9-10}$$

· Processing method

With the statistical functions in ArcMap, we can get the length of the bus lines and the number of segments in each zone. The histograms can be intuitive to show the difference between the average distances of different regions. Fig. 9-24 is the average bus station in Xianyang City from the map.

9.6.2.2 Transit Network Related Indicators

(1) The line density

· Definition

Bus network density refers to the length of the road center line which commonly be passed bus line in urban land use used to measure the level of public transport network services.

The urban road traffic planning and design specifications (GB 50220—1995) suggested that the urban central area of the bus network density is 3-4 km/km^2 and 2-2.5 km/km^2 in the urban areas. In big city or city center area, the density of the residents is high, the passenger is concentrated assignment. The lines are repeated, and the network density are used with high value; on the contrary in the small city or urban fringe area the value is lower. The density of transit network should be adapted to the density of urban road network.

The calculation formula of bus network density is as follows:

$$\text{The density of the transit network} = \frac{\text{The road length of central line with the the bus line}}{\text{Urban land area with bus service}} \tag{9-11}$$

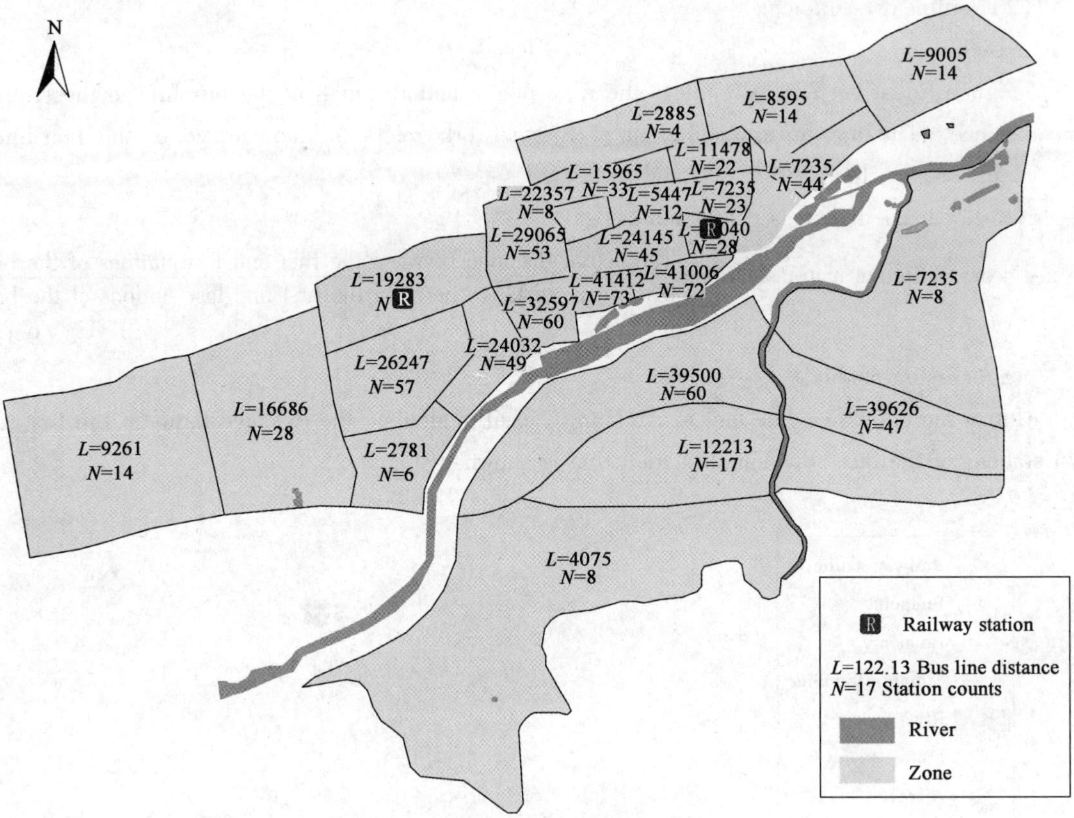

a) Bus line distance and station counts

Table

zone	Average Stop Spacing
A	567.29
B	569.53
C	501.42
D	536.56
E	548.39
F	543.29
G	450.04
H	453.88
I	588.34
J	521.71
K	483.79
L	490.46
M	463.58
N	460.48
O	567.16
P	721.15
Q	613.89
R	594.14
S	643.18
T	595.94
U	661.48
V	658.33
W	843.1
X	718.41
Y	509.39
Z	904.4

(0 out of 26 Selected)

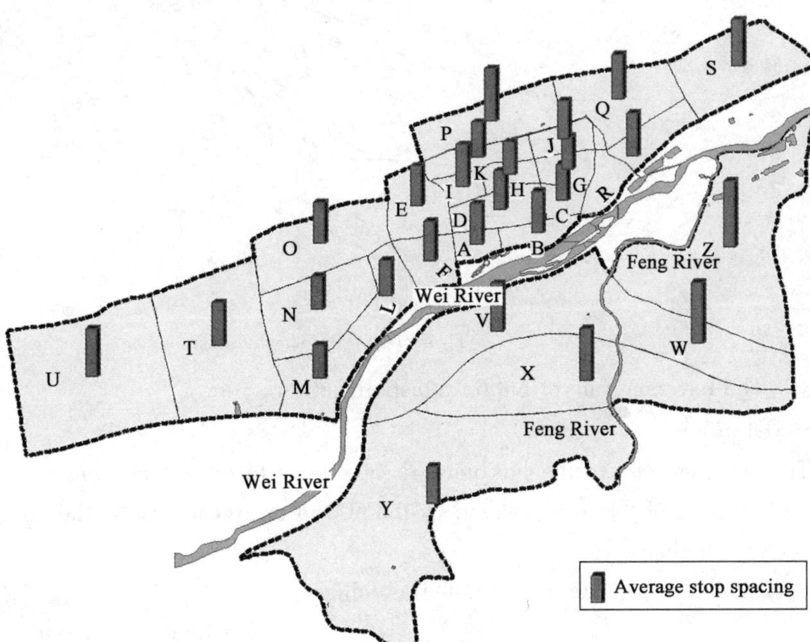

b) Average stop spacing

Figure 9-24 Regional average bus station distance map

(2) Nonlinear coefficient

· Definition

The non-linear coefficient refers to the ratio of the actual length of the bus line to the straight line distance. The non-linear coefficient of the network refers to the average of the non-linear coefficients of each line.

Non-linear coefficient is calculated as:

$$\text{Non-linear coefficient of transit line} = \frac{\text{The actual distance between the first and last stations of the bus}}{\text{The linear distance between the first and last stations of the bus}} \tag{9-12}$$

· Processing method

Utilize the simplified line tool in ArcMap to easily calculate the distance between the first and last stations of the bus. Bus simplification line is shown in Fig. 9-25.

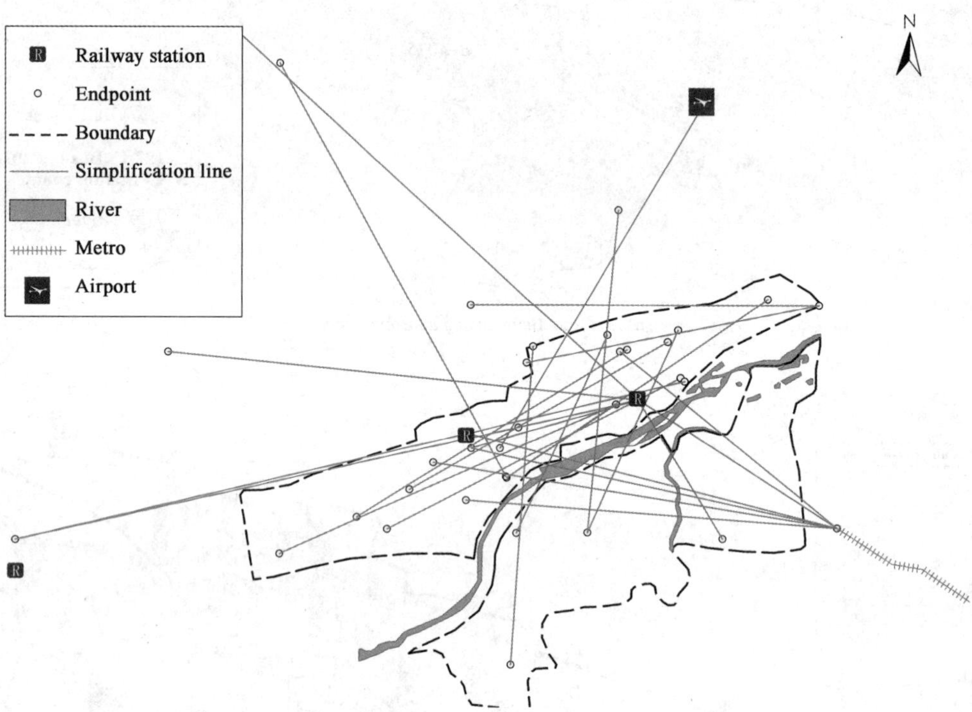

Figure 9-25 Bus simplification line

(3) The coverage rate of public transport network

· Definition

The coverage rate of the bus network is similar to that of coverage rate of the bus station. It refers to the ratio of the area covered by the 500 m or 300 m area of the public transport line in the built area in the central city.

The bus coverage rate is calculated as follows:

$$\text{The coverage rate of the bus network} = \frac{\text{Bus line coverage area}}{\text{Area of urban land use with transit service}} \times 100\% \tag{9-13}$$

· Processing method

The geographical map expression can be used to major public facilities(such as transport hub, government hospitals) to facilitate the rational assignment of bus lines planning. Fig. 9-26 is Xianyang City bus line coverage map.

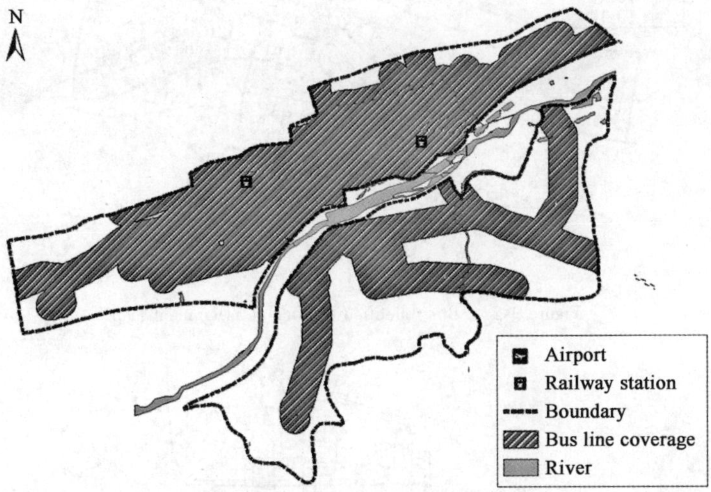

Figure 9-26 The coverage rate of the bus line

(4) Repeated coefficient of transit network

· Definition

It refers to the ratio of the total length of the bus line and central line length of the road with bus line, reflecting the balance of the bus line in the city on the road assignment. Usually, in the crowded, traffic flow area, there are the bus lines, thus repeated coefficient is larger. Too much, lines in a segment is easy to cause the peak bus lines and interference with other motor vehicles in peak hours and easily lead to waste of resources.

The repeated coefficient of the bus line is calculated as follows:

$$\text{Repeated coefficient of bus lines} = \frac{\text{The total length of the bus lines}}{\text{The length of the road center line with bus lines}} \tag{9-14}$$

· Processing method

The processing method of the bus repeated coefficient can refer to the traffic flow band in the trip assignment. The number of bus lines on the road segment is expressed by a different line width in a geographic map. Fig. 9-27 displays Xianyang bus repeated coefficient.

Before the commencement of the "five" transit planning(Fig. 9-28), the various evaluation on the status of the bus network were carried out in Xi'an. The report proposed that the layout of Xi'an public transport network is unreasonable, leading to the overall lower efficiency of the bus system is difficult to play. Xi'an bus network density of 2.67 km/km^2, and is less than the 3 km/km^2 in "urban road transportation planning and design specifications"; line coefficient of 3.9 is greater than the standard value 2.5.

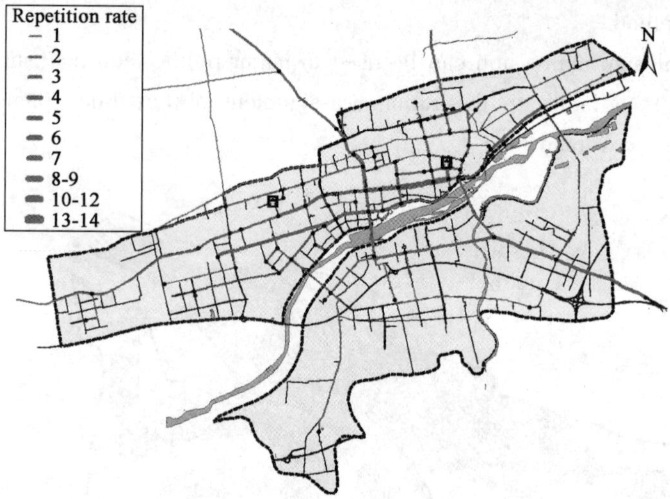

Figure 9-27 Bus repetition coefficient assignment map

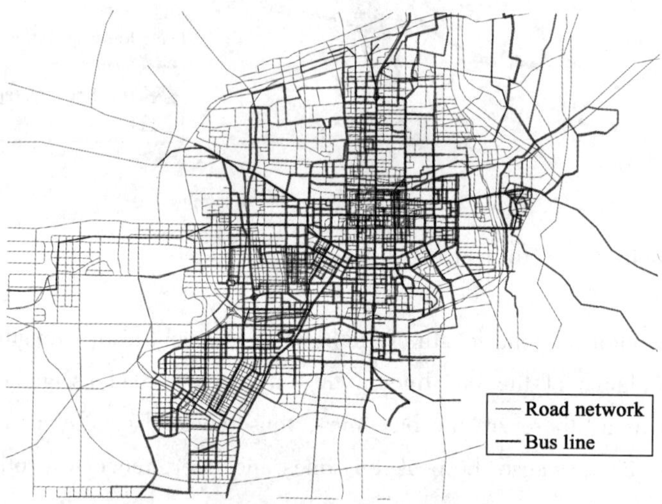

Figure 9-28 The transit planning

9.7 Public Transport Facility Design

9.7.1 Bus Lane

(1) The setting conditions

"Bus lane setting" (GA/T 507—2004) claims that: the city main road which meet all the following conditions should be set up bus lanes:

· The one-way motor vehicle lanes is above 3 lanes (including 3 lanes), or the total width of one-way motor vehicle road width is not less than 11m.

· The one-way bus passenger trip is greater than 6000 passengers in peak hours, or bus traffic volume is greater than 150 vehicles in peak hours.

· The average volume per section is greater than 500 vehicles/peak hours.

The city main road which meets one of the following conditions should be set up bus lanes:

· The one-way motor vehicle lanes is above 4 lanes (including 4 lanes), section of one-way traffic volume is greater than 90 vehicles/peak hour.

· The one-way motor vehicle lanes is above 3 lanes, one-way bus traffic volume is greater than 4000 vehicles in peak hours, and bus traffic volume is greater than 100 vehicles in peak hours.

· 2 lanes for one-way road, one-way bus passenger volume is more than 6000 passengers/peak hours, and bus traffic volume is greater than 150 vehicles/peak hours.

Each lane of traffic volume is greater than 500 pcu/h and the public transport vehicles is more than 90 cars /h in the main and secondary roads, should set up regular bus lanes.

(2) The layout for bus lane

At present, bus lanes are reconstruction from the original urban all the city. According to the special position, the bus road can be divided into three types: bus line in the middle of the street, roadside bus lanes and bus lanes with two-way in same road side. How to choose the form of in engineering practice, is based on the characteristics of urban road traffic.

Fig. 9-29 displays the bus line in the middle of the street, for which the stations are set in the two sides of the central line.

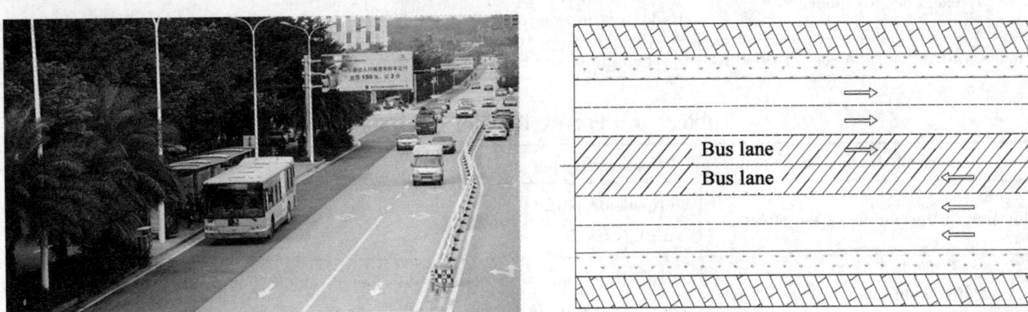

a) b)

Figure 9-29 The bus road lane

Fig. 9-30 displays the roadside bus lanes, the most out of the city road lane into a bus lane. It is reconstructed in the outside lane of the road.

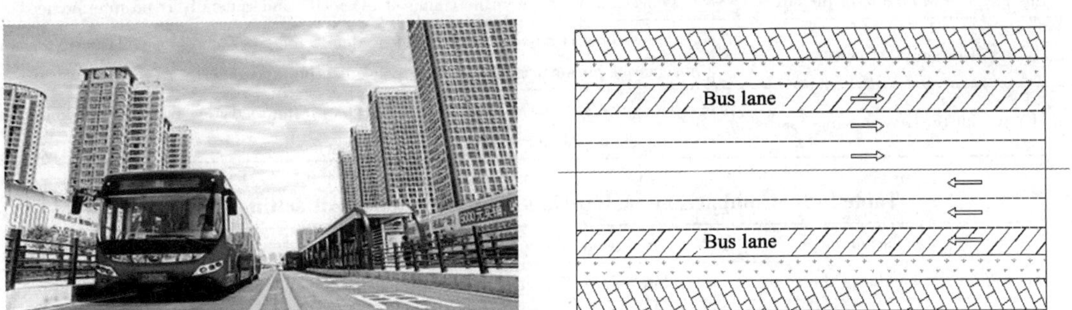

a) b)

Figure 9-30 Roadside bus lanes

Fig. 9-31 displays bus lanes with two-way in same road side, the upper and lower bus lanes on the same side of the road.

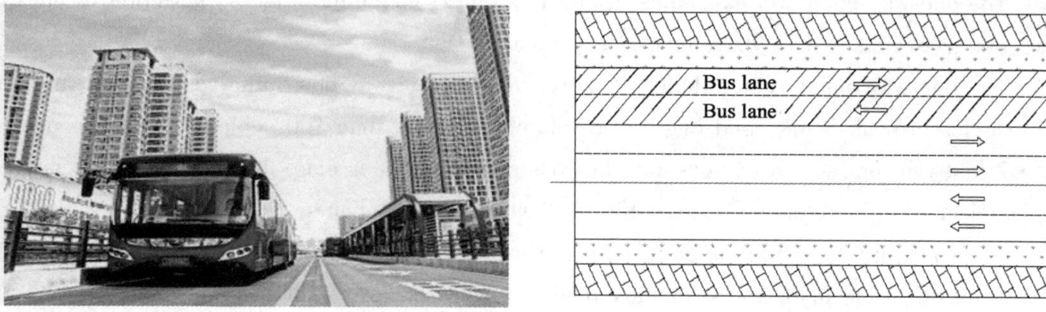

a)　　　　　　　　　　b)

Figure 9-31　Bus lanes with two-way side

(3) Comprehensive analysis of lane layout (Table 9-5-Table 9-8)

Table 9-5　Effects of different settings form of bus lane on road

The form of the bus lane	On the entry and exit
Bus line in the middle of the street	Right-turn vehicles have no effect on the lane
Roadside bus lanes	The vehicle come from roadside entrances has a greater impact on road bus lanes. Reducing the interference of the bus need to be shut down some of the entry and exit
Bus lanes with two-way in same road side	The side of the entrance have a greater impact on the two directions of the bus

Table 9-6　Traffic flow on road segment

The form of the bus lane	Road traffic impact
Bus line in the middle of the street	Roadside parking has no effect on the lane, but the turn of vehicle could conflict with bus traffic
Roadside bus lanes	Roadside lane is affected by non-motor vehicles, and roadside parking, easily to conflict with the bus
Bus lanes with two-way in same road side	Basically not affected by road vehicles

Table 9-7　Impact of different settings on pedestrian traffic

The form of the bus lane	Impact of different settings on pedestrian traffic
Bus line in the middle of the street	Pedestrian is far from the center of the road, and generally is no interference
Roadside bus lanes	Pedestrians is adjacent to bus lanes, due to the randomness of pedestrians, in the absence of physical isolation, may cause conflict and security risks
Bus lanes with two-way in same road side	The same side interference is consistent with the roadside, bus lane needing to set the physical isolation

Table 9-8　Comparison engineering quantity of different setting forms

The form of the bus lane	Comparison of engineering quantity
Bus line in the middle of the street	More use in the sub-band or the inside lane, a small amount of renovation project
Roadside bus lanes	More use in the sub-band or the outside lane, a small amount of renovation project
Bus lanes with two-way in same road side	Arranged on the same side of the road, a large amount of land to expand, heavy workload on pipeline demolition, housing demolition

(4) Lane width

The provisions of the width of the bus lane are different in different specifications. "Bus lane setting" (GA/T 507—2004) stipulates that the section of the bus lane width should not be greater than 3.75 m, not less than 3.25 m. At the intersection of the lane width should not be less than 3.0 m. "Urban road design code" (CJJ 37—2012) provides that conventional bus lane width should not be less than 3.5 m. Combined with design specifications, road conditions and design experience, recommended bus lane width settings is shown in Table 9-9.

Table 9-9 Bus lane width suggested

Index	Lane design speed (km/h)			Parking lane, harbor docking
	80	60-80	40	
Exclusive transit lane	3.75	Recommend 3.75 Limited 3.5	Recommend 3.5 Limited 3.25	3.0 m + the width of isolation facilities

(5) Isolation facilities

In order to avoid the illegal by use of the vehicle, it is necessary to set up separate facilities between its adjacent lanes. The specific forms include marking, physical separation and colored pavement.

· Marking

Separated by single yellow solid line and dotted line, double yellow or white solid line, or anti-reflective road signs [Fig. 9-32a)]. The advantages of marking are easy to setting, small impact on the landscape, and easy to change the lane when the road encounters barrier. Its shortcomings are weak isolation function, and not conspicuous exclusive lane.

· Physical separation

Setting side rail, median separation and lane separator to prevent interference and lane use of other vehicle, side rail and median separation performed well, but need a certain road width [meet the safety requirements of edge and width on both sides of the road, shown in Fig. 9-32b)]; median separation can be directly placed in the marking, do not occupy the road width, but it is easy to cause traffic accidents. For example, in BRT lane in Hangzhou, lane BRT, it causes of some traffic accidents at the beginning.

a) Marking　　b) Physical separation　　c) Colored pavement

Figure 9-32 Bus lane isolation facilities

Source: *Karl Fjellstrom, itdp-china. org.*

· Color pavement

The laying of red asphalt pavement in the bus lane, increases the identification of dedicated road, but it is not easy to ensure the specificity of dedicated road, the general use of illegal vehicles [Fig. 9-32c)].

9.7.2 Stop Station and Harbor Design

The bus station can be divided into the following categories according to the function: the station, the terminal station and the central station. The intermediate station bears function of the majority of passengers up and down the guest function, which is the largest number of stations, bus planning. This section will provide a brief introduction to the design form and guidelines of intermediate stations.

(1) Bus stop spacing

Stations should be set combined with conventional bus planning, traffic demand and urban rail transport. The distance between the buses in urban area should be 400-800 m, and the distance between bus stops in area should be determined according to the specific situation.

(2) The platform form

The basic forms of the platform include in-line platform, bay platform, zigzag platform and platform, which is summarised in Table 9-10.

Table 9-10 Basic forms of the bus station

Basic forms	Legend
Platform	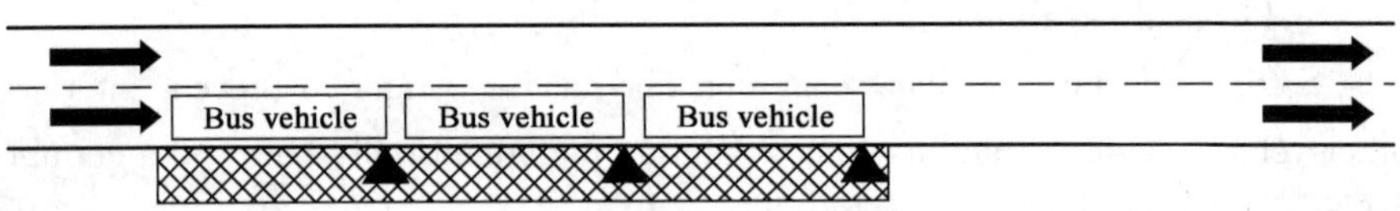
Bay platform	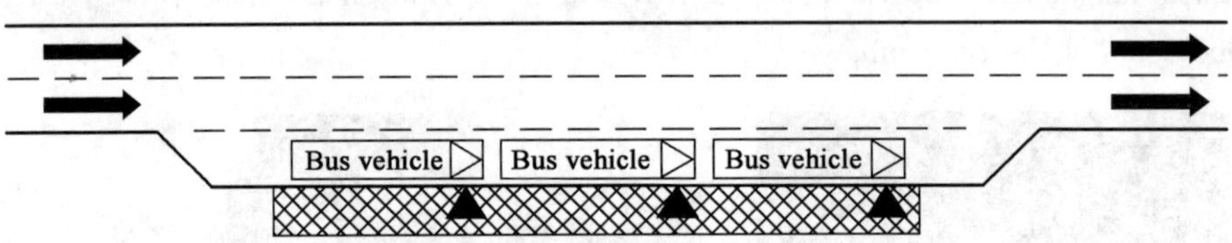
Zigzag platform	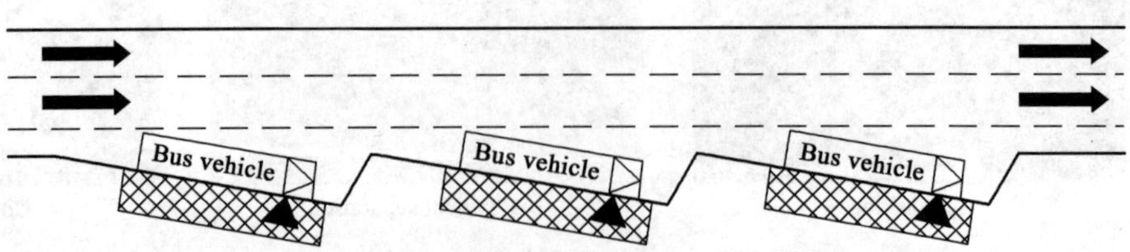

continued

Basic forms	Legend
Channel platform	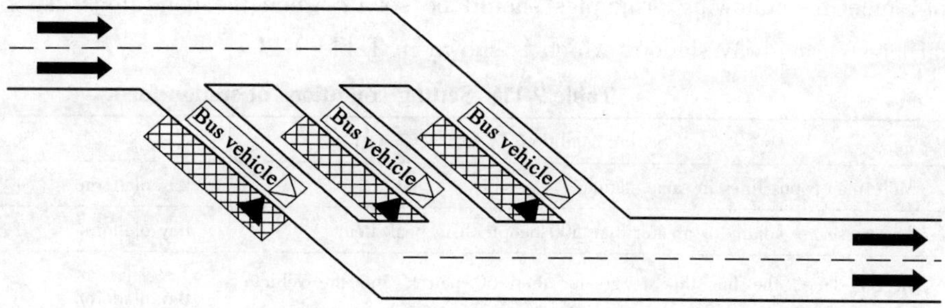

Source: DB11/T 715—2010, *Design code of bus stops and stations.*

Most of the station forms are inline and bay platform.

· Inline platform (Fig. 9-33)

Inline platform has the advantages of simple setting and small cost. But the bus stop occupies the roadway space, the rear of the vehicles need to pass through changing lane, which are likely to cause congestion. In addition, if arrival of some buses at the station at the same time should queue up in front of the station, thus affecting passengers boarding and alighting.

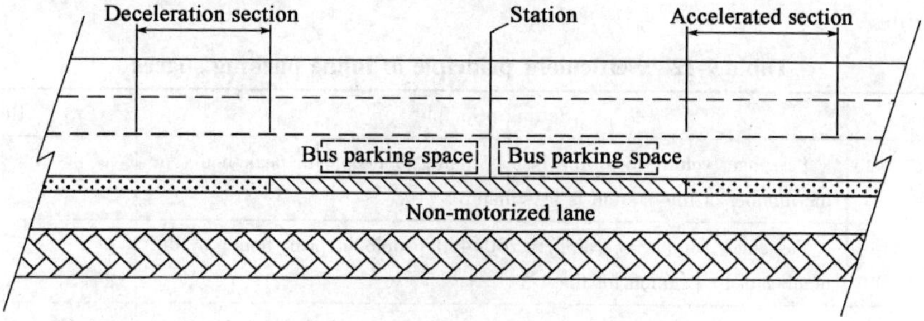

Figure 9-33 Inline platform

Source: DB11/T 715—2010, *Design code of bus stops and stations.*

· Bay platform (Fig. 9-34)

Bay platform perfectly solves the problems of overtaking and non-motor vehicle interference. In the case of road conditions allowed, the bay platform should be set as far as possible. "Shenzhen bus stop station setting standard" (SZDBZ12—2008) provides a comprehensive design basis for the principle of harbor bus station, which can be used as a reference in practical planning.

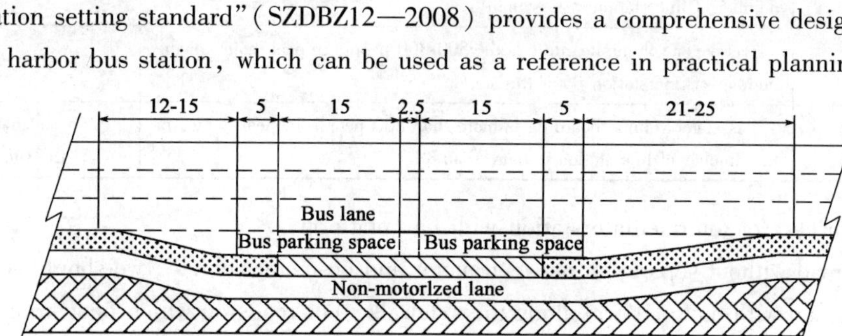

Figure 9-34 Bus bay platform (unit: m)

Source: SZDBZ 12—2008.

Bay platform of inter mediate station should be set in the level of main road and above. Secondary the level of trunk below roads or high-grade roads, intermediate station of bay platform if they meet the following principles should be set up when the conditions can be arranged for non-harbor-style midway station, which is shown in Table 9-11.

Table 9-11 Setting conditions of station form

Setting condition	Set form
More than 5 bus lines in same stations	Bay platform
The passenger volume is greater than 500 people/h in peak hour	Bay platform
In bus lane, the bus flow is greater than 60 pcu/h and the vehicle saturation of the non-bus lane is greater than 0.6	Bay platform
The number of bus boarding is line in a station is more than 10, or peak hours passengers on the train more than 1000 in peak hour	Deep bay(double bay), or add a station with the same name
The number of bus boarding is line in a station is more than 16 lines, or peak hours passengers on the train more than 1600 in peak hour	Deep bay(three bay), or add two station with the same name

(3) Parking setting principle

"Shenzhen City Bus Intermediate Station Code" (SZDBZ 12—2008) suggested that parking spaces in bay platform shall not exceed three (Table 9-12), and should follow the following principles(Table 9-13).

Table 9-12 Settlement principle of inline parking spaces

Parking space	Setting principle	Remarks
One	Passenger volume boarding is less than 250 people in peak hour, or the number of line station is less than 3	
Two	Passenger volume boarding is 250-450 people in peak hour, or the number of line station for the 4-5	
Three	Passenger volume boarding is more than 450 people in peak hour, or the number of line station is more than 5	Or transformed into a harbor style

Table 9-13 Principles for setting parking spaces on bay platform

Parking space	Setting principle	Remarks
Two	Passenger volume boarding is than 500 people in peak hour, or the number of line station is less than 5	
Three	Passenger volume boarding is the 500-800 people in peak hour, or the number of line station is for the station 5-8	
Four	Passenger volume boarding is more than 800 people in peak hour, or the number of line station is more than 8	Or set the station of the same name

(4) Design case of intermediate station with bay platform

· In the road without separation between motor and no-motor vehicle, we should set up shallow intermediate station with bay platform along the sidewalk. For roads on which pedestrian and vehicle or roads of which non-motor vehicle flow peak hour is less than 1000 vehicle/h, if sidewalk width (including green band) is greater than or equal to 7 m, can be set shallow intermediate station with bay platform in the sidewalk, as shown in Fig. 9-35.

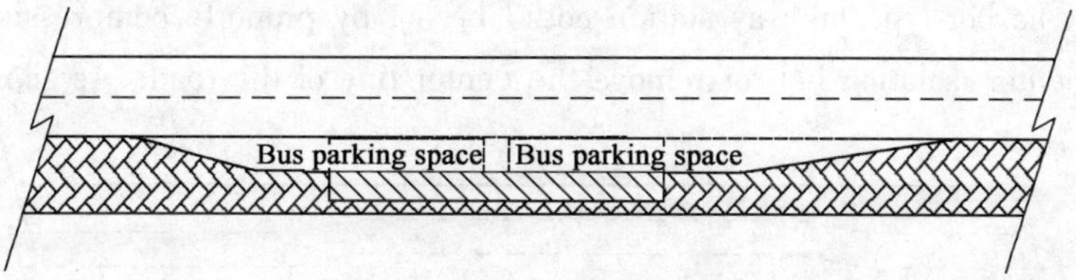

Figure 9-35 Setup schematic

· For road mixed with motor vehicle and non-motor vehicle, if the width of the sidewalk (including green belt) is greater than or equal to 7 m, and non-motor in peak hour vehicle flow is greater than 1000 vehicle/h, it should not run on the sidewalk, but should use excess width of the sidewalk between in motorway and non-motor way to set up a shallow bay platform, as shown in Fig. 9-36.

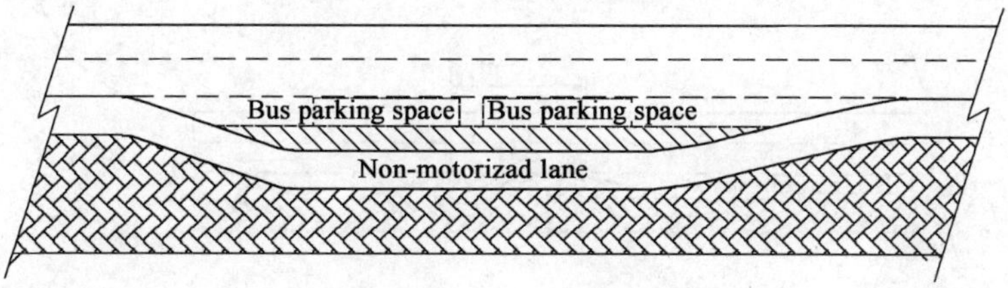

Figure 9-36 Setup schematic

· For the road with separation between motor vehicle and non-motor vehicle, the shallow harbor midway station are set up when the separation width is greater than or equal to 4 m, see Fig. 9-37a). When the width of the separation is less than 4 m and the sidewalk have excess width, the method of setting the shallow harbor station is shown in Fig. 9-37b).

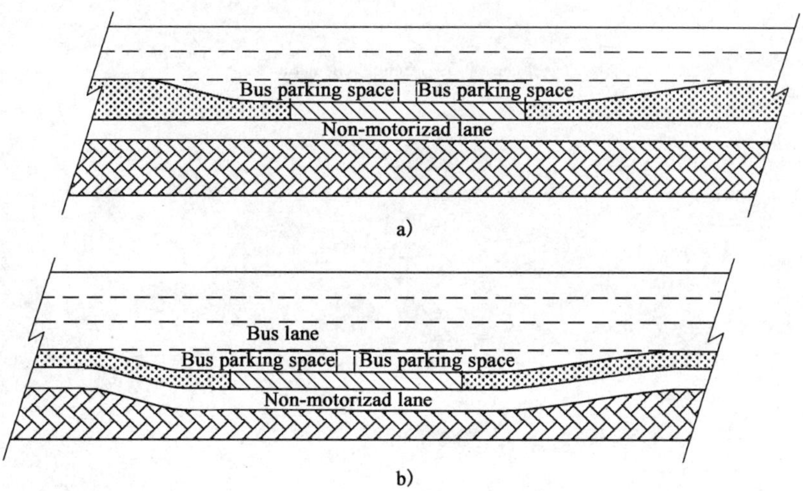

Figure 9-37 Setup schematic

· For the road without separation between motor vehicle and non-motor vehicle, if the width of the sidewalk (including the green belt) is less than 7 m and greater than or equal to 5.25 m; or width of separation is less than 4 m and greater than or equal to 2. 25 m If the width of the motor vehicle is large, the shallow harbor-type midway station could be set by properly compressing the motorway, compressing the center isolation belt or remove the center line of the road. As shown in Fig. 9-38.

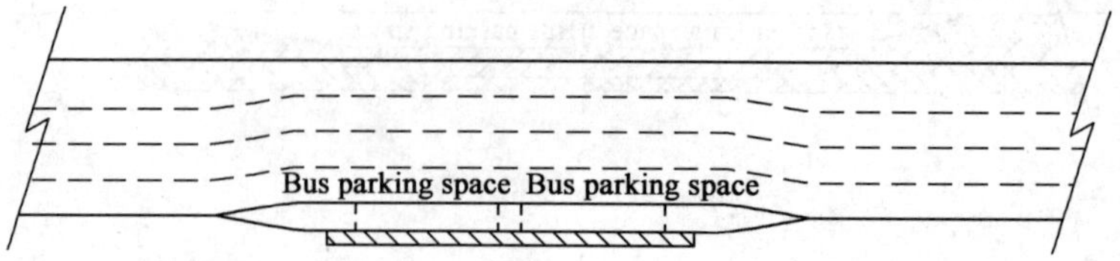

Figure 9-38 Setup schematic

· When the right side of the entrance channel widens the lane, the intermediate station should be located at least 15 m far from upstream of the lane bifurcation point and will expand the lane with the length of the bus station for the integrated design(Fig. 9-39).

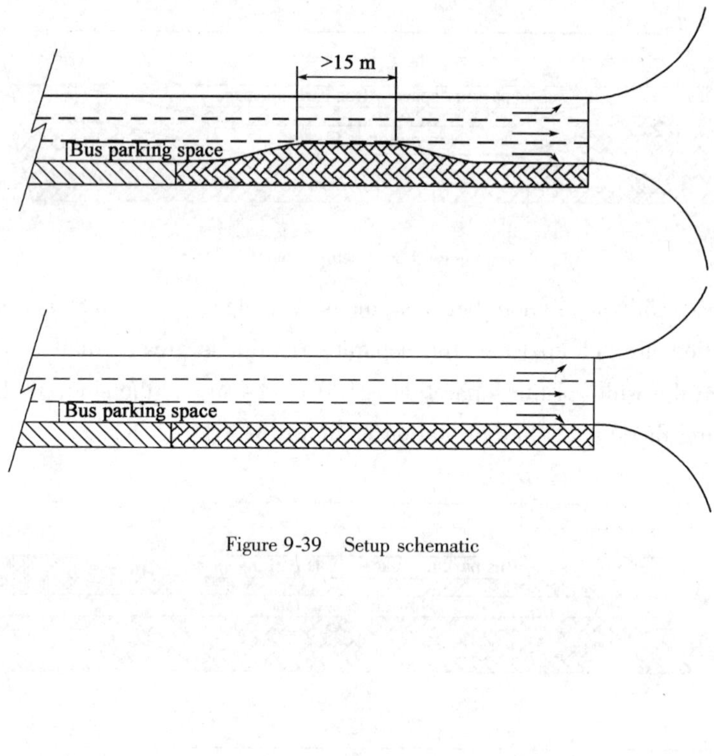

Figure 9-39 Setup schematic

References

[1] Yulin Liu, Jonathan Bunker, Luis Ferreira. T Transit Users' Route-Choice Modeling in Transit Assignment: A Review [J]. Transport Reviews, 2010, 30(6):753-769.

[2] Roberto Cominetti, Jose Correa. Common-Lines and Passenger Assignment in Congested Transit Networks[J]. Transportation Science, 2001, 35(3).

[3] Carlos F. Daganzo, Yosef Sheffi, On Stochastic Models of Traffic Assignment [J]. Transportation Science, 1977, 11(3):253-274.

[4] Joaquín de Cea, Enrique Fernάndez. Transit Assignment for Congested Public Transport Systems: An Equilibrium Model[J]. Transportation Science,1993,27(2):133-147.

[5] Heinz Spiess, Michael Florian. Optimal Strategies: A New Assignment Model for Transit Networks[J]. Transportation Research PART B Methodoogical,1989,23(2):83-102.

[6] Claude Chriqui,Pierre Robillard. Common Bus Lines[J]. Transportation Science, 1975, 9(2):115-121.

[7] Wu Jiahao,Michael Florian,Patrice Marcotte. Transit Equilibrium Assignment: A Model and Solution Algorithms[J]. Transportation Science, 1994, 28(3):193-203.

[8] T. M. Ridley, JOTresidder. The London Transportation Study and beyond [J]. Regional Studies, 1970, 4(1):63-71.

[9] Avishai Ceder. Public Transit Planning and Operation[M]. Dutch: Elsevier, 2007: 343-363.

[10] Vukan R. Vuchic. Urban Transit: Operations, Planning, and Economics [M]. US: Wiley, 2005.

[11] Chen Xuewu, Ge Hongwei, Wang Wei. Research on the Priority of Urban Public Transport Development[J]. Modern Urban Research, 2004(01): 34-36.

[12] Zuo Zhongyi, Shao Chunfu. Research on the Development Policy of Urban Public Transport Priority[J]. Comprehensive Transportation, 2012(04):30-33.

[13] Qi Shiying. London's Public Transport Priority Policy and Its Enlightenment[J]. Urban Transport, 2007(04):66-69, 26.

[14] Zhou Wei. China's Sustainable Transport Development Strategy and Policy Choice in the New Era[J]. Journal of Chang'an University(Social Science Edition), 2007(02):1-7.

[15] Feng Shumin, Chen Hongren. Research on Calculation Method of Bus Configuration Quantity [J]. Journal of Transportation Systems Engineering and Information, 2006(03):79-81.

Chapter 10

Method of Initial Transportation Programming

10.1 Summary of Transportation Programming Process

The preceding chapters of this book are mainly about how to analyze the traffic volume and V/C on the traffic network based on the values of PA between the traffic sub-areas corresponding to the socio-economic development. But they do not involve how to do a transportation programming which is the most important part of transportation planning. In fact, according to the traffic flow on the road network and nodes, we can find the weaknesses or conflict point in traffic system, which is the key to solving the urban traffic problem. Then a preliminary plan is simulated so it can be selected or continue to be improved. Based on the assumption of the future transportation development, the planning was conducted with the method of the previous chapters. Recommendation can be proposed from multiple perspectives. Solving the traffic congestion in a specific location could be achieved through traditional methods, such as, increasing the capacity of traffic facilities, changing facilities' using rules to change traffic flow composition, adopting intelligent transportation facilities to increase the urban traffic efficiency and reduce demand (demand management). And it could also be achieved by adjusting the traffic system management to change the traffic demand's intensity, time and spatial distribution, land use and demand spatial distribution which is caused by travel characteristics. These methods can make the balance of traffic supply and demand with the expected LOS of existing transport infrastructure. Table 10-1 lists the various possible solutions to alleviate traffic congestion.

Table 10-1 Examples of commonly used strategies and ITS solutions for traffic problems

<table>
<tr><th>Problems</th><th>Solution</th><th>Common solution</th><th>ITS solution</th></tr>
<tr><td rowspan="3">Traffic congestion</td><td>Increasing the number of lanes</td><td>· New road
· New lane</td><td>· Advanced traffic control, enhanced traffic signal solutions
· Accident management, rapid response of accidents
· Traffic corridor management
· Advanced vehicle systems</td></tr>
<tr><td>Increasing efficiency</td><td>· HOV lane
· Car-sharing
· Fixed route bus
· Setting turning lane, one-way street, two-way single lane, parking prohibition
· New or enhanced public transport services
· Providing passengers with one or more optional modes of transport and services</td><td>· Real time transit service information
· Integration of transit and transfer service
· Flexible bus line
· New bus service</td></tr>
<tr><td>Reducing demand</td><td>· Advise on non-driving trips or car trips on non-congested hours</td><td>· Telecommuting
· Congestion charging
· Improvement of parking management</td></tr>
</table>

Table 10-1 provides a logical tree for the problem of traffic congestion. In the actual planning, the time-varying features of specific problems should be refined and deepened to seek an optional planning scheme. In addition to establishing a logical game tree for the problem, and choosing an optimal scheme, the regional traffic network can be designed based on the comprehensive node importance layer by layer(developed area) and the method of area line location or external traffic layout, on the development area urban road network can be established with the land economic development. Regional rail network layout can be designed based on TOD theory to achieve optimal development pattern of passenger flow and land use. Based on the OD passenger flow analysis, the appropriate service was selected. This chapter will explain these methods to facilitate the selection in the planning process.

Based on the existing regulations, practical practices and reference, it can be found that the planning scheme should be proposed by the rational selection method. It is produced by eight different stages:

· Identify goals, objectives and standards.

· Collect and analyze data.

· Identify the problem. Including the part about status quo/planning year service level or environmental requirements where is fail to meet the standard or still need to improve.

· Propose various alternative solutions for the problems.

· Evaluate alternatives. It was based on the traffic model that includes simulation and assessment of the influence of each alternative on users and non-users.

· Select the best one or more alternatives based on whether achieve the standard and the merits of the parameters.

· To recommend the planning and related parameters(service level, performance, impact) to the decision-makers, and then select the primary planning program.

· Public participation. According to the relevant laws, consult the relevant departments and the public views, if necessary, continue to adjust and improve in order to form an implementable planning program.

10.2 Regional Road Network Programming Schemes

10.2.1 Importance Degree Traffic Location Distribution Method

Traffic location is a high-risk area(or place) in geography with regard to a kind of economic and geographical phenomenon(such as industry, agriculture, urban and transport network). More precisely, traffic location is an area(or place) in geography which has a good chance to produce phenomenon of economic geography. In order to achieve specific economic objectives, the economic geography project should be set in a certain range within the reach of the target location. This kind of geographical area within a certain range can be called traffic location.

Traffic location refers to the place where traffic-phenomenon in the geography turns out with a high incidence(or probability). Traffic location line presents a high incidence area in the geography (Guan Chudu, 2000). It represents a geographical phenomenon where a geographical factor plays a dominant role inevitability. According to the characteristics, the traffic location line can be divided into traffic location routes, traffic location rays, traffic location vertical line, horizontal line, loop and so on. The center line, the bisector, the edge line, the shortest path, the valley line and the ridge line indicate the traffic location which have economical advantages.

Traffic location distribution method is developed on the basis of traffic location theory. It originates from the source of the transport and the high incidence zone can be found out(e. g. the traffic location line). It is, specifically, achieved through the analysis of planning area's geographical characteristics, economic development model and distribution of resources. And then, it is combined with the status of the planning area to find out the most likely areas of traffic. Finally, it is used as the basis for the layout of the road. The route determined by this layout method is not only necessary for transportation, but also spending less.

The node importance distribution method is to analyze the transport hubs in the planning area and to select the road network node. On the basis of simplifying the virtual road network into the abstract road network, we can select the indexes that can reflect the importance of nodes. Principal component analysis is to correct the correlation between sub-indicators and draw the weight and calculate the importance of each node. Then, based on the above, the nodes are classified through the hierarchical cluster analysis and the node importance maximum tree is solved by graph theory. Based on the node importance maximum tree, the method of optimizing the road network layout is formed by drill-down layout of the road network.

The important degree-traffic location distribution method is to combine the important distribution method with the traffic location distribution method. Traffic location line is a potential advantage of transportation instead of a planning line. It is given by geographical factors. Thus, combined with the calculation results of route importance by node important degree theory, it can further clarify the relative importance of the location line, and the specific process is shown in Fig. 10-1. The location line is obtained by stratifying the location characteristics of the export corridors in different areas. The design of export corridors is obtained by qualitative comparison and result analysis of important degree-traffic location distribution method. The important degree-traffic location distribution method includes:

· The node importance distribution method includes node selection, the method of determining the importance index system and the method of calculating the importance;

· Location analysis of export corridors is mainly based on different ranges of traffic location line distribution.

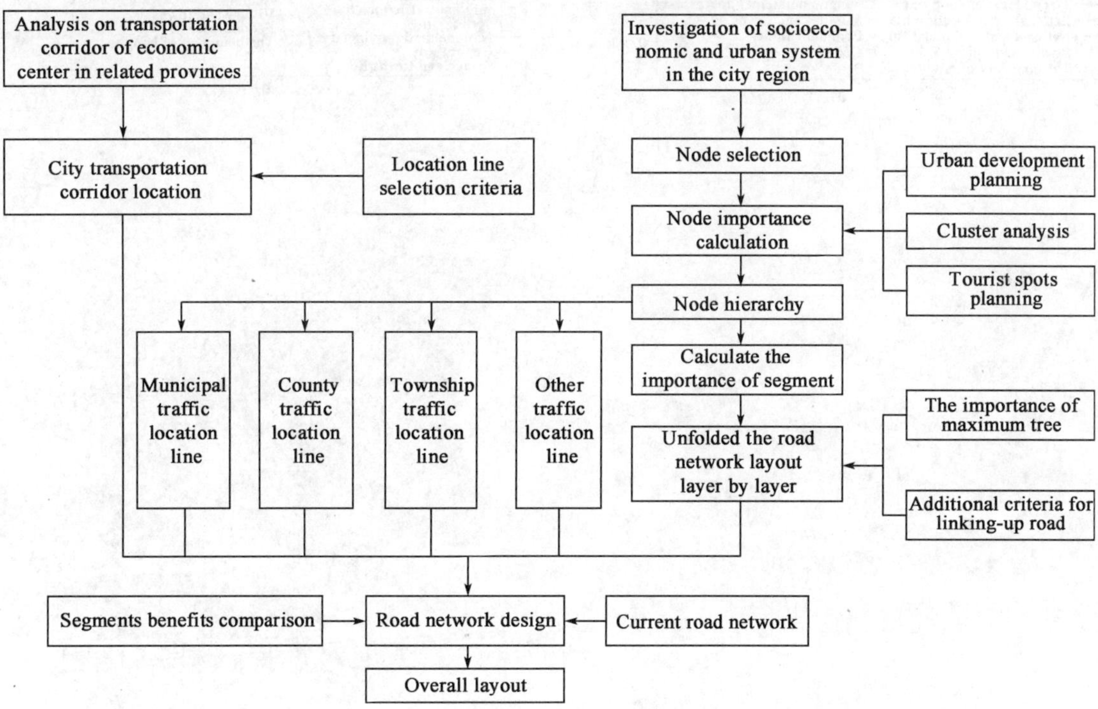

Figure 10-1 Flow chart of the layout method combining node important degree with area location

Source: *Wang Yuanqing*, 2002.

10.2.2 Application Cases

By analyzing the geographical location, natural conditions, social and economic development characteristics and future planning of Ningbo City, it is found there are 3070 nodes(including 2980 actual nodes and 90 virtual nodes) in Ningbo. Connecting these traffic sources gets traffic location line of Ningbo City shown in Fig. 10-2a).

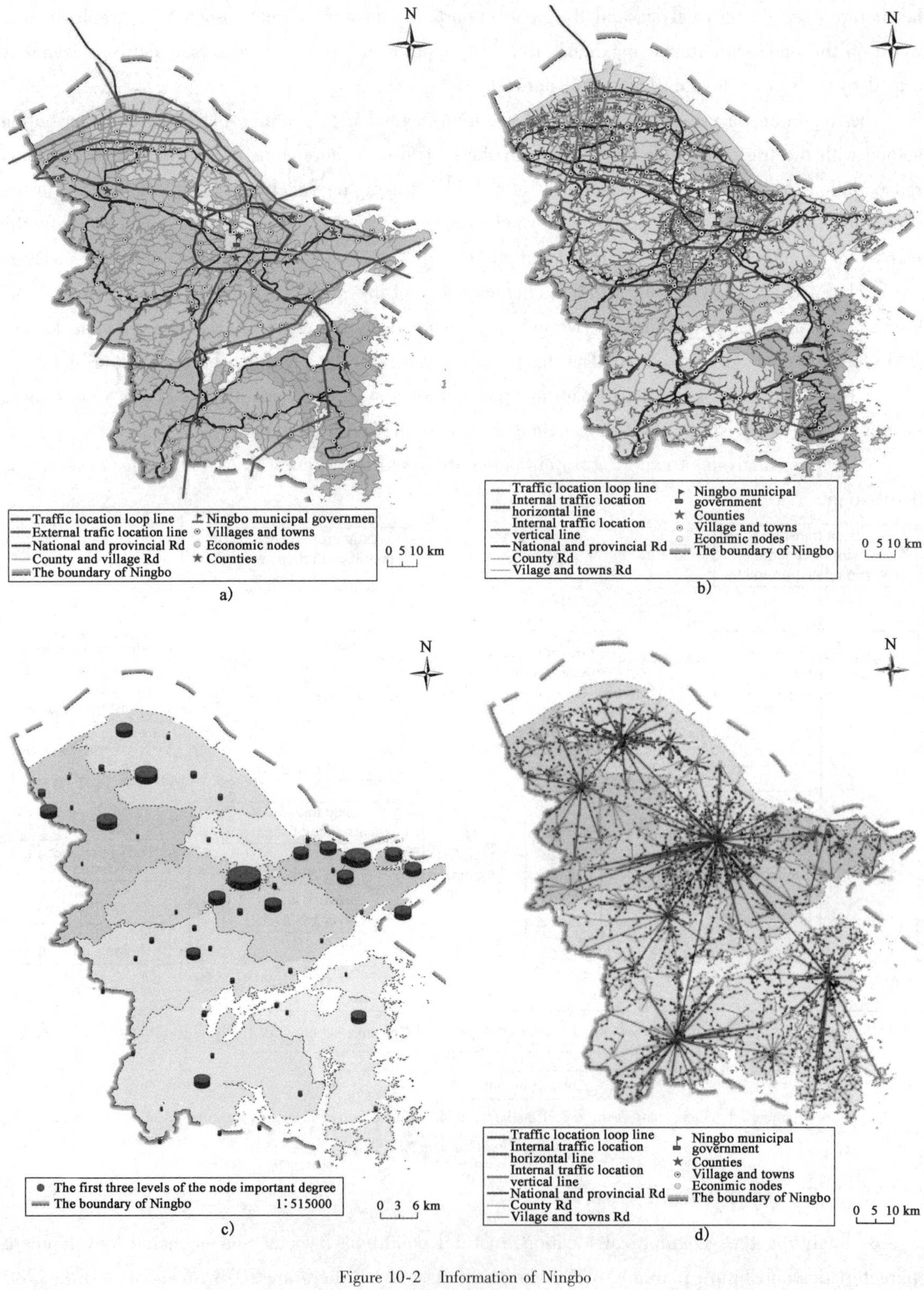

Figure 10-2 Information of Ningbo

These lines include 11 external traffic location lines (7 horizontal and 4 vertical, shown in Fig. 10-2b) and 11 internal traffic location lines(6 horizontal, 4 vertical and 1 ring). Among them, the external traffic location lines connect Ningbo and other provinces, counties and cities, and correspond to the function of the provincial highway. It is the basis for the county and township roads in Ningbo, adjusted for the provincial highway. The internal traffic location lines contain:

(1) Node selection

For highway network planning, based on the consideration of nodes balanced distribution, scale and proper quantity, nodes which have a certain characterization for distribution planning are selected. According to the cluster analysis of the townships, administrative village, resources industry park, external main entrance and main passenger transport/freight station' s geographical location and social status are obtained in Ningbo. Finally, we get 3070 nodes. Among them, there are 2980 actual nodes, including 10 counties, 136 township nodes and 2834 administrative villages in Ningbo City; 90 virtual nodes include the main transport nodes and economic nodes which will have a significant development.

(2) Node importance calculation and analytical hierarchy process

The node importance is the comprehensive measure of the strength of various functions of nodes. According to the social and economic, population distribution and other actual situation quantitative analysis of the importance of each node indicators, the formula is:

$$I_i = \alpha_1 \frac{p_i}{\bar{p}} + \alpha_2 \frac{G_i}{\bar{G}} \qquad (10\text{-}1)$$

where, I_i is importance of node i; p_i is population of node $i(p)$; $\bar{p}$ is average population of node i; G_i is budgetary income of node i (ten thousand RMB); $\bar{G}$ is average budgetary income of all node (ten thousand RMB); α_1, α_2 are the weights of each indicator.

Using Eq. (10-1) is to calculate the importance of 3070 nodes in Ningbo. Nodes are sorted according to the importance and function position of different nodes in Ningbo is ensured. And these nodes can be divided into six levels by dynamic clustering analysis.

(3) Maximum node importance tree

According to the division of the node level and different levels for route layout of the main control points, we can calculate segment importance, the formula is:

$$\mathrm{In}_{ij} = \frac{I_i \cdot I_j}{L_k} \cdot \alpha \qquad (10\text{-}2)$$

where, In_{ij} is Corridor strength between node i and node; I_i, J_i represents importance of node i, j; L_k is spatial distance between node i and j; α is route administrative level and function correction factor.

According to the method of calculating the importance of the route and optimize selection, the node in next level can also be connected with the node in upper level. In order to get a tree, it cannot form the circle when it is connected. Through the above method, we can get the maximum node importance tree of Ningbo, which is shown in Fig. 10-2c) and Fig. 10-2d).

(4) Theoretical road network distribution

Traffic location line and maximum node importance tree in Ningbo is the skeleton distribution of Ningbo highway network. According to the skeleton distribution and node hierarchy, broken circle method is used for optimization layer by layer. The finally formation of Ningbo theoretical highway network distribution is shown in Fig. 10-3.

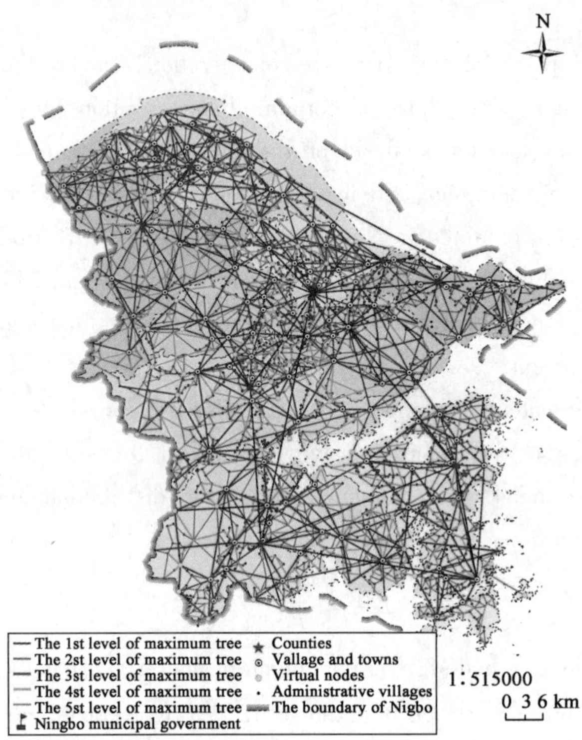

Figure 10-3 Ningbo theoretical highway network distribution

In theoretical distribution:

The first layer of highway network will connect with downtown, city center, external entrance and main traffic economic nodes. It corresponds to the function of national road of Ningbo City.

With the second layer of highway network, all cities and counties in Ningbo City can be accessed efficiently, and the highway even can connect the central town to the central area where the town is located or stands nearby. It corresponds to the function of provincial road of Ningbo City.

The third layer of highway network is a supplement for the first and the second layer of highway network so that all towns are smooth connectivity. It corresponds to the function of county road of Ningbo City.

The fourth layer of highway network connects the relatively important socio-economic and central village with larger population and nearby towns. It plays a role of distribution passenger and freight traffic, and corresponds to the function of township road of Ningbo City.

The fifth layer of highway network connects the administrative village to other administrative village or upper network. It is the entrance of each administrative village and corresponding village road.

10.3 Urban Central Area Traffic Network Distribution

10.3.1 Urban Transport Network Distribution and Land Use

The relationship between road traffic and land use is the same as that between "bone" and "meat". Road traffic is the skeleton of the city while urban land is attached and restricts the development of road traffic network. Once the skeleton of the city has been identified, the layout of the city and the scope of the land have been identified. In general, land use is a major determinant of travel activity and transport system supports which affects urban land use and related activities. The relationship between the distribution of the transport network and land use is shown in Fig. 10-4.

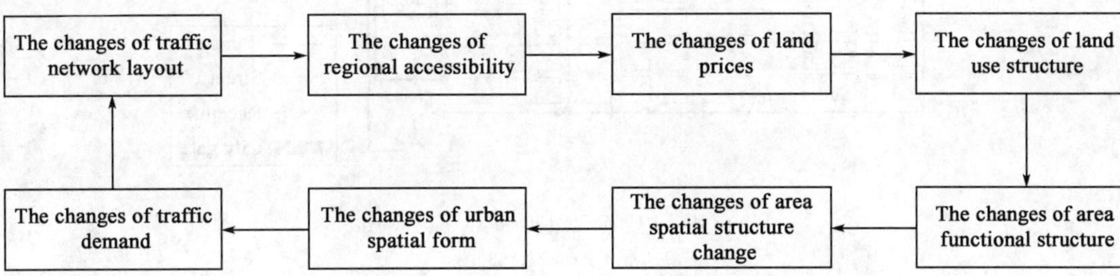

Figure 10-4 The associated effect of traffic patterns

10.3.2 Xi'an Urban Road Network Distribution

Xi'an is a famous ancient capital of world and one of China's historical and cultural cities. Xi'an has 41 national key cultural relics protection units, 65 provincial key cultural relics protection units and 176 civic and country key cultural relics protection units including many famous great ruins such as Chang'an City of Han Dynasty and Chang'an City of Tang Dynasty. Xi'an's urban network distribution has been gradually evolving for Zhou Dynasty.

(1) Chang'an City in Tang Dynasty

Chang'an City in Tang Dynasty is 972 m long from east to west and 8651 m long from north to south. With the circumference of 36 km, its occupied area is 83 km^2. The schematic diagram is shown in Fig. 10-5. Chang'an City in Tang Dynasty is a typical representative of the board-type city, and it is formed in order to adapt to the political, economic, military and other requirements in Tang Dynasty. This form is conducive to rapid construction and development in the traditional town.

(2) Chang'an City in Ming Dynasty

In the early years of the Ming Dynasty, Chang'an City is 13912 m in circumference with 2886 m east wall, 2708 m west wall, 4256 m south wall and 4262 m north wall, and the occupied area is 115 km^2 which is including the thickness of the wall. The plan is shown in Fig. 10-6.

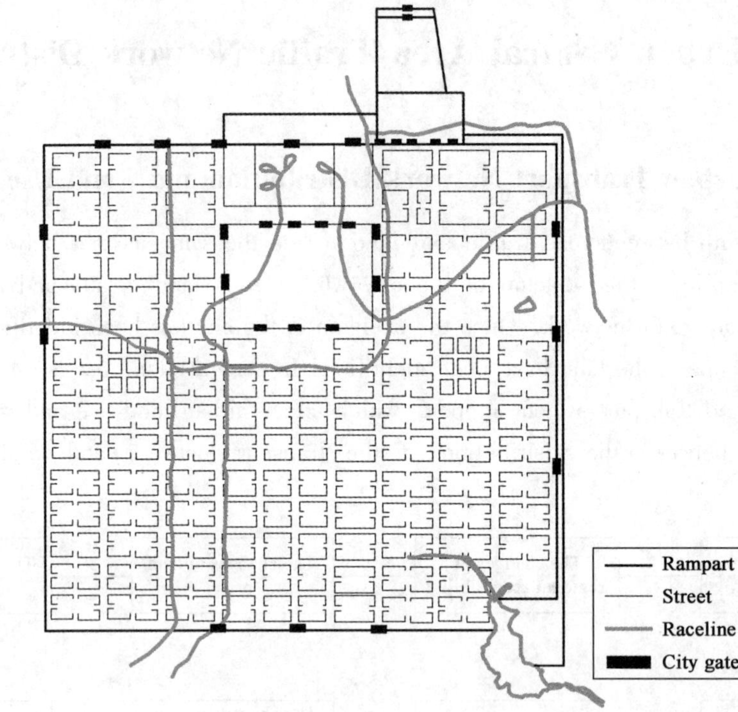

Figure 10-5 Chang'an City in Tang Dynasty

Source: *http://news.163.com.*

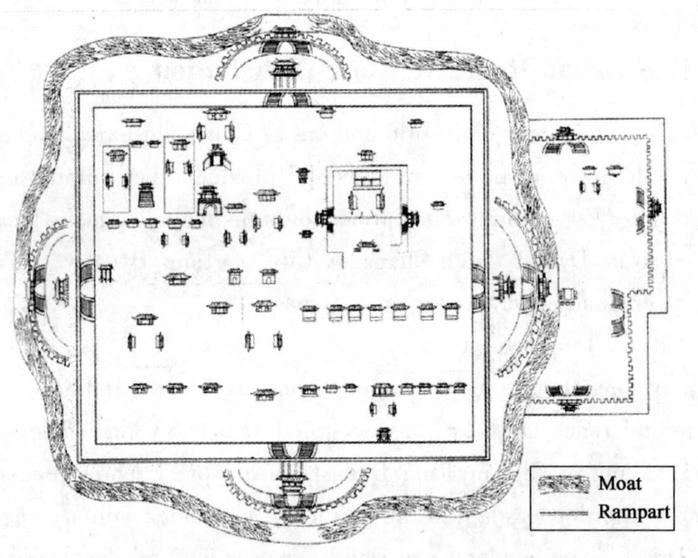

Figure 10-6 Chang'an City in Ming Dynasty

(3) Urban transport planning for Xi'an

Xi'an first to fourth round of the overall planning is shown in Fig. 10-7. The first overall planning of Xi'an is Xi'an urban overall planning in the 1950 s. This planning which acknowledges the wall of Ming Dynasty for the city center has formed the basic network skeleton of the core area and the embryonic form of urban development. The second overall planning of Xi'an is a new planning in order to accommodate the development of Xi'an Urban Construction. The construction land has a tendency to expand northward and southward on this planning. The third overall planning is in 1990. At that time, urban construction land increased significantly and the external groups emerged. It has formed a pattern that main urban area and groups develop together. The fourth overall planning was formed, examined and approved in 2008. In this planning urban construction land expanded to north and south and incorporated some external groups into main urban area.

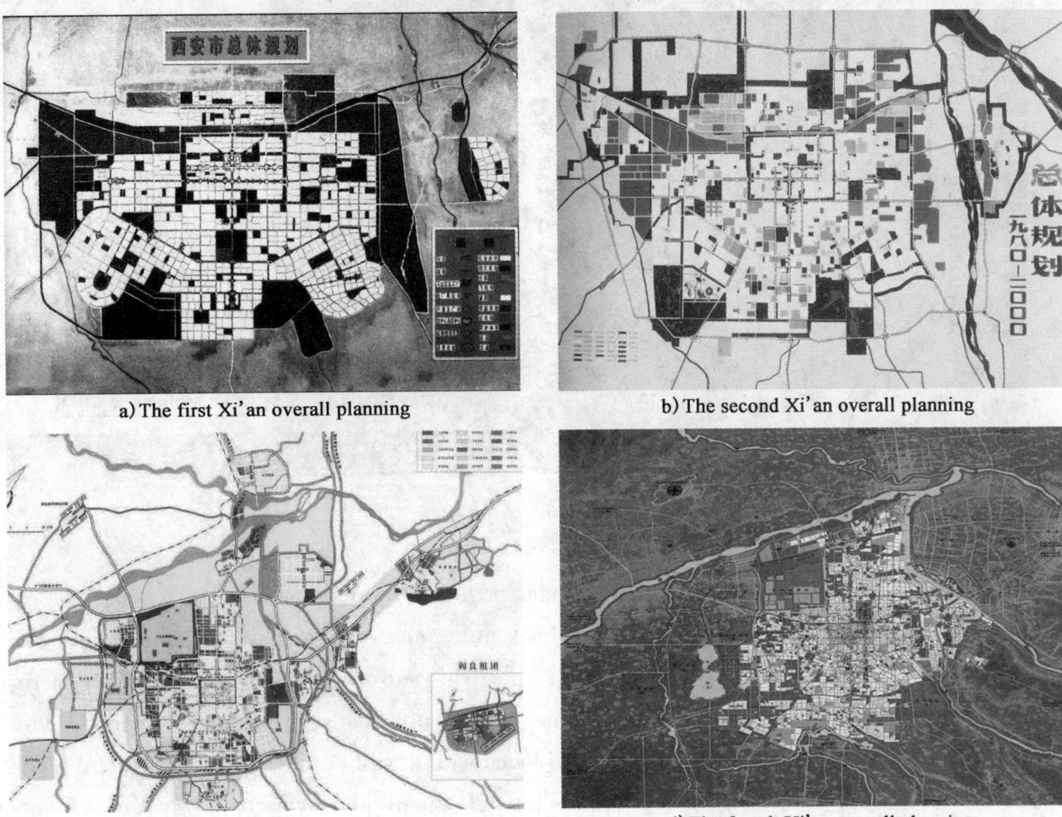

a) The first Xi' an overall planning

b) The second Xi' an overall planning

c) The third Xi' an overall planning

d) The fourth Xi' an overall planning

Figure 10-7 Xi'an four overall planning

10.3.3 Melbourne Urban Road Network

Melbourne is Australia's second largest city. As one of the most livable cities in the world, Melbourne is not only the center of the economy and business of Australia and the Asia-Pacific region, but also a historical and cultural sign which is famous for strong cultural atmosphere and high Green rate, fashion, food, entertainment and colorful sports activities. Narrowly speaking, the city of Melbourne refers to the central urban areas of Melbourne, including the CBD of Melbourne (Fig. 10-8), East Melbourne, West Melbourne, North Melbourne, Parkville, Carlton and other ten administrative regions with more than 60000 people. Melbourne central urban area is a highly concentrated area of economy, business, entertainment, shopping, food, education and so on. In

Melbourne, economic and cultural prosperity is inseparable from scientific and rational urban planning, convenient transit, pleasant and comfortable neighborhoods. All of these are worth China urban traffic to learn and refer to.

Figure 10-8 Location of Melbourne CBD
Source: *Google earth.*

(1) Hoddle road network: lay the development pattern of the century

Melbourne city's development pattern dates back to the city road grid system, the Hoddle Grid, planned by the surveyor Robert Hoddle in 1837. The road network consists of five east-west roads and nine north-south roads, which are divided into 32 square blocks with a width of 201 m. Each square block is divided into 20 small plots which covers an area about 1920 m^2. Among these area, the street blocks were square and the other plots were long rectangle. Hodder Road, the main road with a width of 30 m, is two-way traffic. There are four one-way traffic east-west road interspersed which has a distance about 10 m between five main roads. These roads form a miniature cycle in each block, as shown in Fig. 10-9.

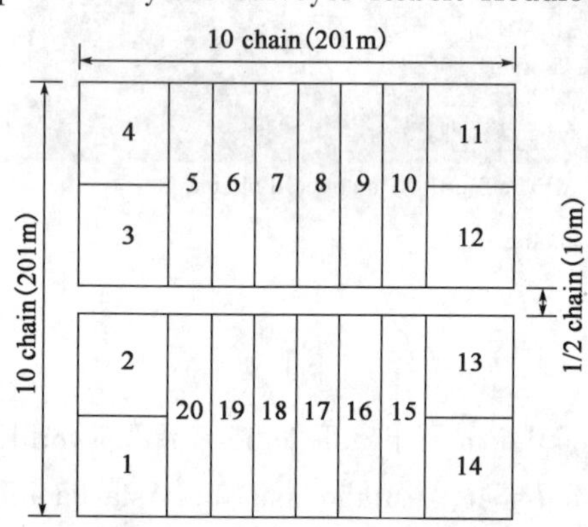

Figure 10-9 Hoddle road network
Source: *Wikipedia, authors hand painted.*

At the beginning of Hoddle's planning, it was suggested that all road networks should be of 30 m in width and that sufficient space should be reserved for the future expansion of the city. The width of way to Melbourne at that time is really too wide. So the final use of the compromise is the current Hoddle road network width program. Melbourne's development proves that it is Hoddle's sense of advance which laid the foundation for the development of Melbourne's city center and urban area since 180 years ago.

Indeed, the narrow 10 m roadway in the subsequent urban development has caused the traffic bottleneck, but in fact, these human scale streets and buildings along the street have constituted a unique urban space. Now, it gradually evolved to Melbourne's most unique Laneway, and gave birth to a unique Laneway culture. The streets of the CBD gather diverse restaurant, coffee shop and bar. It not only creates a large number of employment opportunities and provides weekday's lunch and a perfect place for party after work but also becomes a famous tourist attraction in Melbourne to draw tourists from all over the world. For those who first arrived in Melbourne, if they have no idea about eating, nevertheless, want to experience the most authentic Melbourne food culture, then they should get into these streets. Because usually there will be an unexpected harvest.

(2) Escape from Melbourne

In the 1960s, the period of industrialization, because the central area was the city's industrial production and market transactions center, leading to serious environmental pollution and poor public security in central area, people began to move to suburb which had a better environment continuously, and the city center became an empty city after work. In the 1980s, the federal government adopted radical financial reform policies for an oversupply market and the serious economic recession. Business failures and office rents continued to spread, so people began to flee the central area quickly.

(3) The revival of Melbourne CBD

In order to reverse the economic crisis, Melbourne began to implement a series of market intervention and stimulus measures.

The first strategy "zip code 3000" came out which was to strengthen the urban center of the dynamic. Then, transforming vacant office buildings into apartments were to attract people to live in city center. Meanwhile, the optimization of Swanston Street (Fig. 10-10) pedestrian environment and a series of transformation projects were used to revitalize the CBD area of commercial retail. The strategy has promoted the rapid growth of CBD population, and the integration of business, shopping and living in urban areas has ensured the areas' prosperity. Until the mid-1990s, the city center of Melbourne added more than 3000 apartments, the original commercial office of a single city function switched to the multi-functional one.

The implementation of the Walking Environmental Renovation Project in Swanston Street, which began in 1992, and included the prohibition of cross-boundary motor vehicle traffic, allowed only tramcar, non-motor vehicles and local residents to enter and strictly controlled the height of the building. After the completion of the transformation of Swanston Street to enhance the CBD area of walking comfort and non-motor vehicle traffic safety, the CBD pedestrian traffic has been greatly enhanced. The latest research data show that from 1993 to 2013, the average pedestrian flow of Melbourne CBD per working day was from 240000 to 360000 and when it came to Saturday, it was increased from 0.28 to 44 million. It can be seen that it is an effective measure to promote the prosperity of urban CBD by ensuring the street space of human nature and creating a suitable environment for walking. These measures can effectively gather the flow of people and promote the development of commercial retail.

Figure 10-10 The Swanston Street

Source: *Google earth.*

The second point was to adjust the city center land use and urban functions widely which refers to gradually relocating the industrial plants and port facilities that gathered around the CBD, guiding developers to develop high-rise residential in the city center, bringing residential development in the South Bank and the port(Fig. 10-11) which are two key areas city renewal area, etc. The decline trend of the Melbourne CBD has been reversed and has become the most attractive and important feature of Melbourne's urban core area.

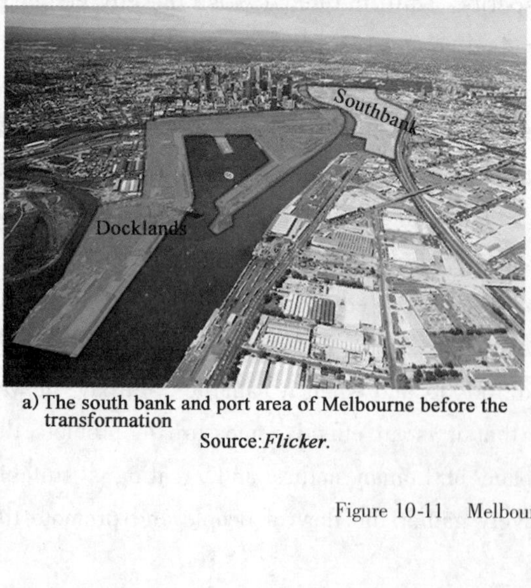

a) The south bank and port area of Melbourne before the transformation

Source:*Flicker*.

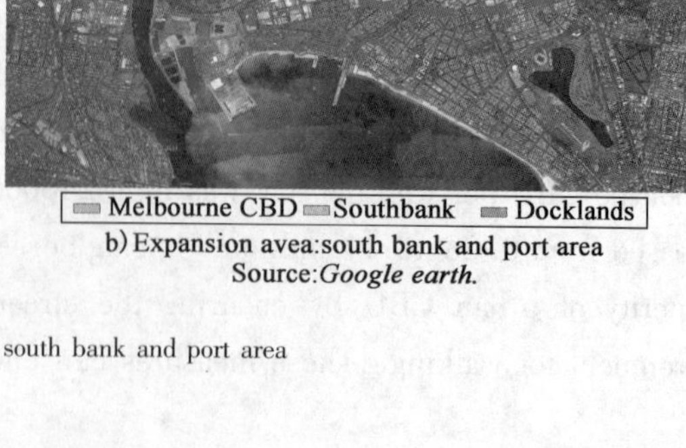

b) Expansion avea:south bank and port area

Source:*Google earth.*

Figure 10-11 Melbourne south bank and port area

(4) Melbourne recentralization

Melbourne encourages people to give birth and attract immigrants as a sustainable population strategy. A large number of immigrants constantly pouring into the city brings the sustainable economic growth, but also carries many challenges. In response to the rapid population growth, in addition to the traditional urban expansion and the new residential areas of the strategy, Melbourne focuses on the redevelopment of the region which has been developed already, such as the development of residential buildings around the CBD and the central area of Melbourne, to increase the development intensity to maximize the use of existing facilities and save substantial investment in infrastructure. At the same time, by strengthening the first degree of Melbourne CBD, the central area of the core functions is strengthened.

(5) Livable transit system

Currently, Melbourne has the world's largest tram network which is serving the urban (Fig. 10-12). Tramway mileage is up to 250 km, with a total of 25 lines and 1763 stations, which are more than Berlin, Vienna, St. Petersburg and other European cities. Melbourne trams deliver more than 180 million passengers every year. It effectively connects the CBD and suburban areas, and forms an effective complement with metropolitan railways.

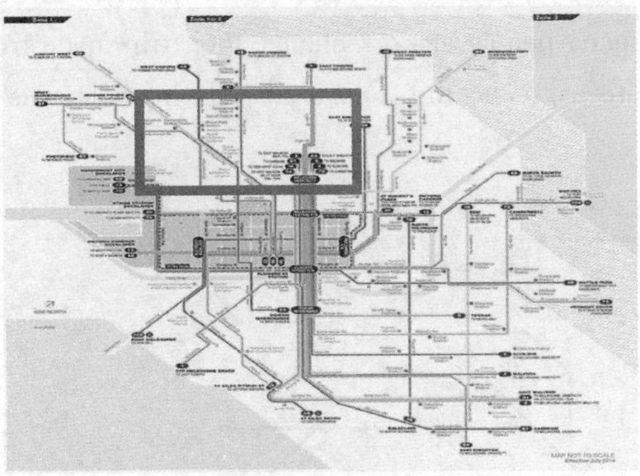

a) Melbourne tramway network
Source: *Public Transport Vicloria, PTV.*

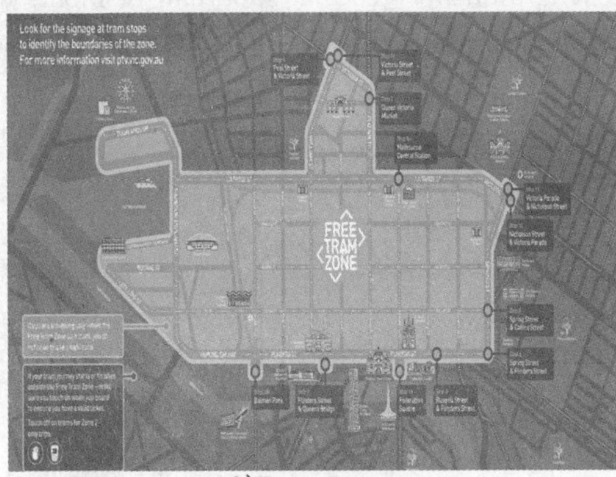

b) Free tram zone
Source: *Public Transport Vicloria, PTV.*

c) Melbourne CBD loop tram
Source: *www.blogigo.com.*

d) Melbourne city tram
Source: *ZOL.com.cn.*

Figure 10-12 Melbourne tram

Melbourne CBD is only 2.4 km^2 big and there are underground city loop and five railway stations for service. The city loop is the core node of the Melbourne metropolitan area and the Victoria regional railway network. It further strengthens the original Flinders Street Railway Station (Melbourne Metropolitan Railway Station) and the Southern Cross Railway Station (Victoria District Railway hub) between the links. Moreover, it provides more convenient travel options to residents and visitors. The city loop is spread around the CBD, and the evenly distributed five stations cover the majority of the CBD area.

The concept of TOD (Transit Oriented Development) is strictly practiced. In addition to Swanston Street for bus and pedestrian oriented commercial district to implement strict measures of control building height, CBD within the high-strength office, apartments and other commercial development is basically located in the railway site 400 m radius of service.

Melbourne's urban train began to run in 1855, and now has 20 train lines, with the total length of 372 km line and a total of 200 stations. Its passenger traffic reached 214 million people in 2009. It is one of the world's largest urban rail transit systems. Melbourne's urban train network (Fig. 10-13) is mainly located in the Greater Melbourne area which is showing as a circular radial and runs through the city's main external channel and population living area. Its settlements are laid along the train lines so that suburban residents can arrive in the urban areas more quickly. As the city center of Melbourne is a busy business center, many people at work change their trip mode from private car to train because they cannot park a private car, and the train is also the main means of transporting students to school.

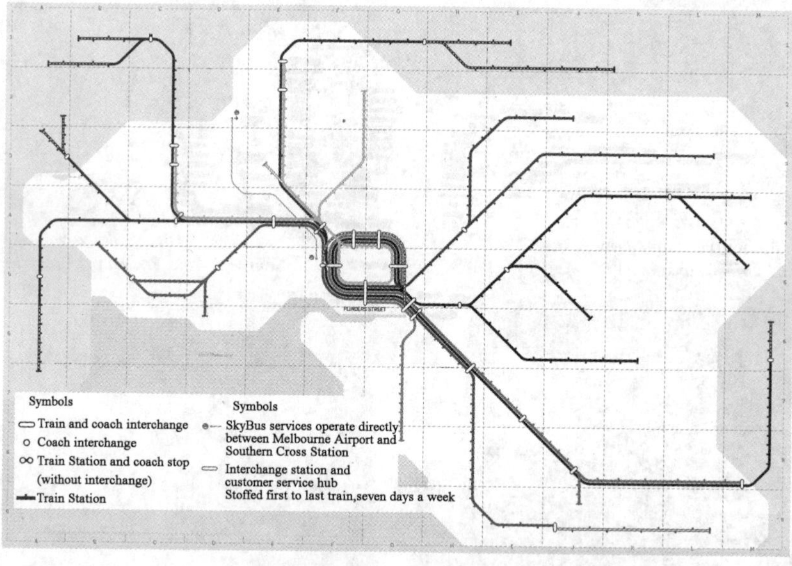

Figure 10-13 Melbourne railway network

Source: *Public Transport Vicloria, PTV.*

Melbourne's V/Line train (Fig. 10-14) is the gateway to the outskirts of Melbourne, Victoria and other places, and some urban train sites. V/Line tickets for the day can be used as a general all-day ticket in Melbourne. And many of China's urban railways mostly laid in the ground is not the same as Melbourne's. Most of Melbourne's train is located above the ground and it is only driving in the underground in a small area of the city center.

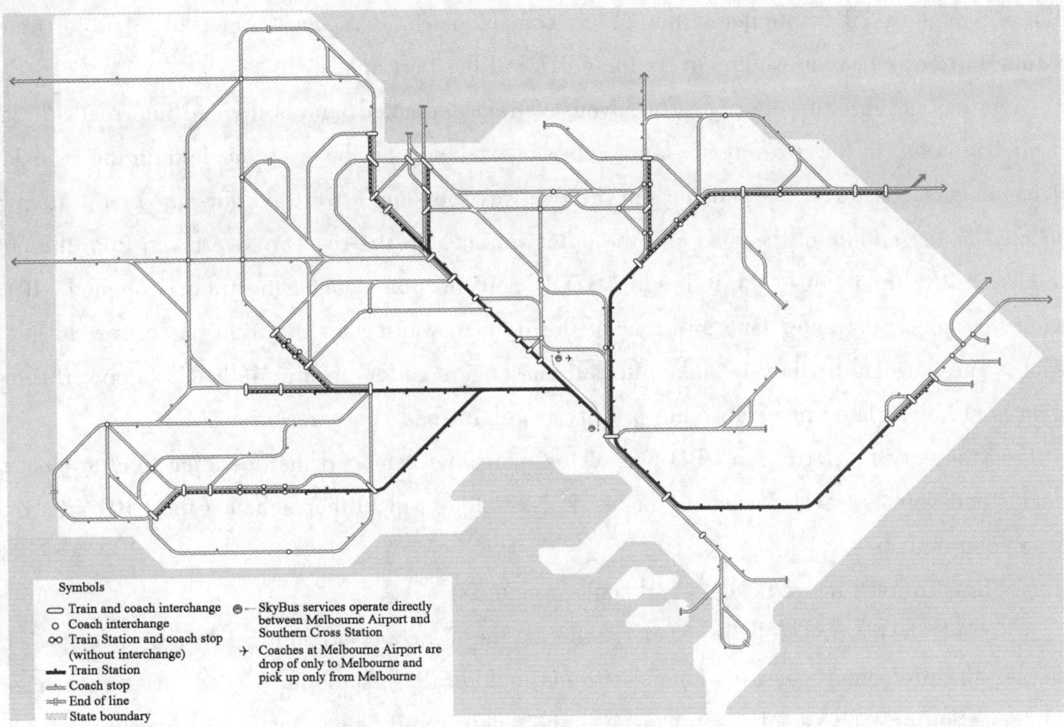

Figure 10-14 Melbourne V/Line train network

Source: *Public Transport Vicloria, PTV.*

(6) Strictly implement the bus priority policy

Melbourne has a convenient and personalized ticketing system. Its three major public transport networks work together to implement integrated ticketing and seamless transfer services. Passengers can transfer among tram, train, V/Line train, bus, and even ferry only while holding valid ticket or myki. The validity of the ticket is determined by region and time. By region, there are zone 1 (suburb) ticket, zone 2 (outskirt) ticket and zone 1 & zone 2 ticket (Ticketing system divides city into two areas. The fare rate, the first and last time varies). By time, there are usually two hours (people can take any public transport, such as train, tram and bus, within two hours), daily, weekly, monthly and yearly ticket. In the limited time and area, the ticket can be arbitrarily transferred to all directions of various means of transport. In case of cross regional, the fare will be relatively increased. In order to solve the increasingly urban transport congestion, Melbourne has introduced a variety of initiatives to encourage people to use transit. From March 2008, it is free of charge for the citizens of Melbourne to take the train before 7:00. It is a latest and bold attempt to improve urban traffic. In 2010, Melbourne implemented a new public transport pricing method and myki's new IC card can be used for city trains, buses, trams and V/Line. Passengers swing card in the bus can save the cost of the station and the placement of multiple credit card machines in the car can effectively save passengers boarding time. Myki can be purchased at convenience stores, major tram stations and train stations expediently.

To tie in with the Melbourne city center's strategy of enhancing the proportion of transit travel, Victoria in January 2015 introduced the "Free Tram Zone". Passengers can take trams for free at any time in free tram zone which covers the CBD and the port area.

Tram has an absolute priority. The layout of tram dedicated lane is divided into roadside lane and median lane. In the two-way six-lane(two-way six-lane) or above, trams laid on the roadside, and passengers can travel by roadside; in the two-way four-lane(two-way four-lane), the tramway is located in the middle of the road and the other vehicles on the road are overtaken from the outer lane. When the tram stops, the red sign "STOP" on the rear door of the tram is opened. It can prompt the car on the outer lane and rear of the tram in waiting for the tram passengers to get on and off. The car can drive or overtake after all passengers get on or off. Melbourne's powerful tram system is closely related to its absolute priority in urban road space resources.

From January 1, 2016, the CBD part of the main line extended the operating time to meet the residents and visitors travel demand at night. This strategy will further enhance the CBD area night consumption activities.

(7) Road infrastructure design of "People oriented"

All road design of Melbourne city reflects the "people-oriented" design concept. For example, the protection measures for pedestrians include the installation of pedestrian crossings at the intersection of each signal system to meet the safety requirements of pedestrian crossing, and the zebra crossing is the absolute priority of pedestrians crossing the street so that any motor vehicle must stop to wait the pedestrian. And on the busy junctions, the overpass is used to separate pedestrian and traffic. The overpass is closed with escalators for pedestrians going up and down. Pedestrians who shuttle among the city roads can always feel the security and have a feeling of being taken care.

The user-friendly design of the inconvenient traveler includes the differentiated accessibility services which are according to the specific situation provided by the operators of the vehicles, such as disabled persons' special compartments, the retractable pedals for disabled on and off, special seats and special channels for disabled persons, and place clear signs to indicate that other passengers pay attention to comity. The train operator also allows passengers to carry bicycles, children's carts and baby carriages for free to meet the travel demand of various groups.

In order to alleviate traffic pressure, the government has set up a number of public bicycle facilities in the city (Fig. 10-15). In 2010, Melbourne was equipped with 5.45 million public bicycles with a turnover rate of 0.8 times/(d · b) and travel time is between 16-22 min. At the same time, in order to protect the safety of cycling users, Melbourne built a Veloway of about 1.7 km long between the Southern Cross train station and the Flinders street train station at the southern end of CBD.

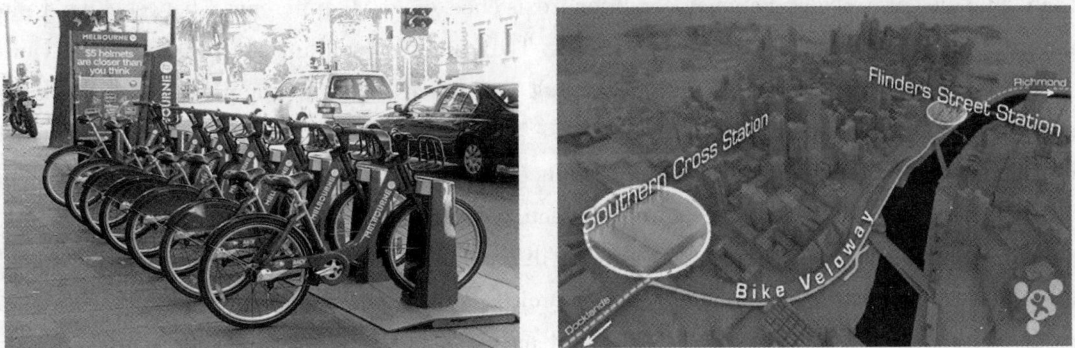

a) Public bicycle rental point
Source: *Yangcheng Evening News*.

b) Veloway
Source: *FENG.com*.

Figure 10-15　Melbourne public bicycle

10.3.4　Summary and Mirror

A city is a single center or multi-center and the number of core area depends entirely on the size of the city. To develop a multi-center development pattern, strengthen the existing CBD area and enhance its primacy as the primary condition, the most efficient time to develop the multi-center city is when the marginal effect begins to decline and the negative externalities are completely greater than the positive externalities.

Relying solely on new office to provide employment space is not enough to enhance the employment intensity and primacy of core area. In addition to many high-income white-collar workers in office buildings, a large number of medium-skilled jobs are distributed in clothing store, restaurants, bars, cafes, community services and other units. The survival and development of these supporting services departments are dependent on the environment suitable for walking and human scale of the street space.

We should avoid the idea of urban CBD to extend the large road network, large plots, instead super large volume of building scale of block scale. Because if above formation of the urban space has shaped, the loose space layout will intensify traffic demand and congestion of the existing regional; at the same time, eliminating a large number of commercial and employment opportunities along the street directly will cut off the market self-improvement mechanism of the foundation.

The above points are the key problems that the development process of China's urban livable city should focus on.

10.4　Urban New Development Area Rail Transit Planning in Hong Kong

10.4.1　The Development Model of TOD

TOD is an important part of the "smart growth" model of American cities. This model is in line with China's sustainable urban development. The research theories include diversity, density and design. But because of our national conditions existence essential differences between the United States and China, it cannot simply be borrowed. TOD suitable for China's cities should be viewed from the integration perspective of urban planning and urban transport planning to achieve a high degree of integration between traffic and land use. Specifically, TOD is a moderate high-intensity land development within the easy walking distance along the backbone bus lines and bus stops, which emphasizes the mixed use-design of residential, commercial, public space, etc., so that the land development and public transport facilities will form an effective community integration, so as to guide the orderly growth of urban space and control the city disorderly spread.

In many cities, 80% of the trips are based on home-based trip, residential location plays an important role for urban travel activities. Reducing travel needs through the use of mixed land should focus on the residential land. The first type of mixed land use is characterized by a reduction in the travel distance of non-commuter traffic, that is, the mix of commercial, residential, office and other service sites. This kind of mixture can reduce home-based trip such as shopping, schooling, part of the employment and entertainment. Another mixed land use is characterized by reducing the commuter travel distance, that is, land mixed of residential land and employment. This type of mixture can significantly reduce commuter travel distance, which is actually very common in urban cities of China.

10.4.2 Background of Hong Kong Rail Mode

Hong Kong's rail transit construction has achieved worldwide success, and its formation has a very complex background (limited land use, land development being strictly controlled, high land prices) and its own particularity. But the fast, efficient and environmentally friendly development of city and track achieved through the construction, layout and development of Hong Kong track traffic can be referenced by construction of new city.

(1) Urban background

Geographically, the geographical area of Hong Kong is 1103 km^2, of which the altitude below 50 m accounts for only 17.8%. Most of the rest are steep hills, and grass and forest land area accounts for 79%, with 21% built area. In terms of population conditions, till 2015, the total population of Hong Kong is about 7.3 million. The unique landforms and demographic characteristics determine the highly intensive land use structure in Hong Kong, guide the urban transportation development with efficient rail transit system, and realize the organic combination of urban spatial pattern and transportation system.

(2) Political background

After the British occupation of Hong Kong, the communication between Hong Kong and China's mainland including Shenzhen was cut off taking the new territories as a quarantine belt. At the end of the reform and opening up, the political future of Hong Kong was not clear. The government had mainly focused on internal traffic and land use issues. After the reunification of Hong Kong, Hong Kong strengthened ties with the mainland of China and the Pearl River Delta. Its traffic construction also shifted from internal construction to external traffic. The construction of rail transit also closely focused on the selection of its line location.

(3) Economic background

Hong Kong's economy has been maintaining rapid growth, but its industries are constantly moving to the Mainland because of the policy of the reform and opening up, and eventually it has been transformed into a financial service center. The transformation of the economic structure led to a large number of unemployed population and labor surplus and signs of declining in inner city. Therefore, it is very important to transform the old city and maintain the center attraction and high intensity of land use by using rail transit construction rationally and effectively.

(4) Planning policy background

The key factor which affects the development of rail transit and land use in Hong Kong is the relevant planning policy. Hong Kong's overall transport study emphasizes that land development and transport planning should be closely integrated, both of which must be considered at the beginning of the planning. The territory-wide development strategy study should take into account the need for collaboration between urban development and transport supply, especially in new towns. Transportation policy should comprehensively consider economic development, population growth and land transport needs. Policy development should be a priority model to coordinate the development of land use and transport, play the first role in transport, and guide the development of land use and transport facilities, to make the two closely combined.

10.4.3 Hong Kong Rail Pattern Characteristics

Considering the current situation of rail transit construction in Hong Kong, the integration of land and traffic is actually the application and implementation of TOD development concept. From the macro point of view, the development of rail traffic promotes the development of new city. From the micro point of view, the development of rail traffic promotes land development within walking distance of sites.

(1) Location choice

· "Bead-chain" development model of land. This model is based on the balance of urban development, to achieve comprehensive high-intensity and high-density development of the core area and maintain the low-density ecological environment of the external core area.

To protect its strong attraction, the Hong Kong government built the old center area by using the opportunity of rail transit. Land use along the track site is planned by mixed high-density development model. This model facilitates the development of subway integration along the area. At the same time, the Hong Kong government has used rail transport to guide the development of the new district. It has built a large number of new towns including Tsuen Wan, Sha Tin, Tuen Mun, Yuen Long, Fanling, Sheung Shui, Tai Po, Tseung Kwan O, Tin Shui Wai and Tung Chung. The new town group has almost digested Hong Kong's new population for nearly 30 years.

Rail transit builts a new urban pattern by exchanging time for space and creates a large-scale network-node urban structure. This has formed an urban morphology and lifestyle of residents who rely on rail transit and provided a strong passenger support for the development of rail transit.

· Integrated transport mode which regards rail transit as the backbone implements a variety of transportation modes at the same time. The following two points are the key to the formation of urban traffic mode with conventional bus being the main body and rail transit being the backbone. First, priority to the development of rail transit should be given. Second, coordination of various modes of transport should be achieved for common development, especially the integration of public transport system. The rail transit connects with conventional public transport and other modes of transport reasonably to form an integrated public transport system.

(2) Station planning

· "3D " model of land use. This model mainly promotes the development and utilization of land within the walking distance of the site. In the close area of the site (walking), the design range is a circle whose radius is about 400-800 m that usually needs to walk 5-15 min. This model takes the station as the core to organize living, retail, office and public space in this circle. The central area of the community is equipped with bus stations and commercial facilities, and residents can reach other centers or urban centers via bus. The "3D" model of land use around the station is a high density, diversity and rational design. Its significance lies in the mixing use of land, high facilities, shortened travel distance and reduced energy consumption.

· The seamless connection model of transport facilities. This mode should be beneficial to integration of rail transit stations, bus stations, taxis, car parking and other connected transport facilities and form convergence and conversion center in different functions and scale in urban transport system. The core of model is the use of rail transit to achieve zero transfer between rail transit lines and the use of rail transit stations to achieve zero transfer with other modes. In order to ensure that airport line is more competitive than car, Hong Kong Airport Express (Fig. 10-16) increases their attractiveness by setting little stations where passengers can check their luggage before arriving at the airport if they take rail. Typical examples of the convenience of transfer is Kowloon Tong Station and Nanchang Station. Kowloon Tong Station is one of the largest railway interchanges in Hong Kong which meets the subway and Kowloon-Canton Railway. Nanchang Station is the first subway which shares the station with the KCRC. Nanchang Station is the first station shared between railway and Kowloon-Canton Railway, the outside of which sets taxi stations and public bus stations connected with public buses, public green minibuses taxies, etc..

10.4.4 Thinking and Revelation

· The enlightenment of the Development Direction of big cities in China. For a large city with a population over 5 million-100 million, the single-center model cannot meet the needs of urban development. When considering the implement of the sub-center city model, we can consider drawing lessons from the development experience of Hong Kong and using the opportunity of rail transit to develop new city pattern about networks and nodes. Thereby, it can enhance the city cohesion and get rid of the single-center development model of city.

· The enlightenment of the choice of traffic mode in big cities in China. In view of the high concentration of land use in China's large-scale land use model, we can learn from Hong Kong's experience in solving traffic problems by building a comprehensive transportation system with rail transit being the backbone, the priority development of public transport, the moderate development of cars and bicycles and improving the connection LOS of the site around the connections.

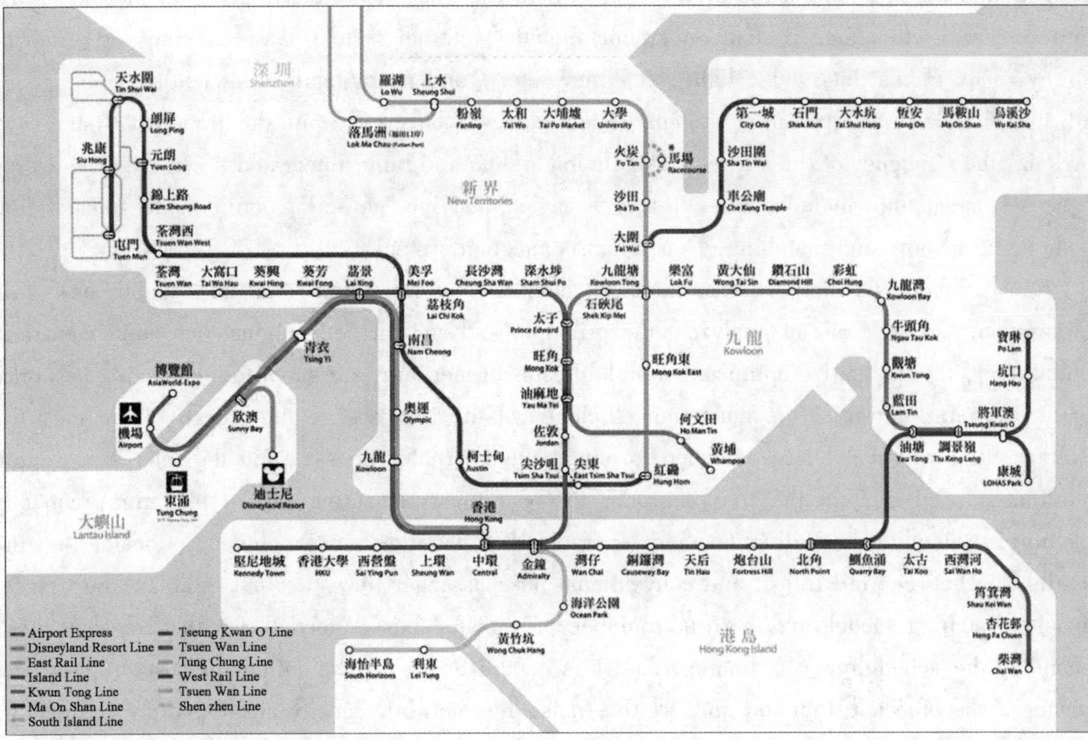

Figure 10-16　Hong Kong subway map

Source: *MTR Corporate.*

· The enlightenment of the old city reconstruction and the new city construction mode. Rail transit construction opportunities should be taken advantages to learn Hong Kong's urban construction experience, complete the transformation of old city and the construction of new urban tasks and control the land use of urban built-up areas and urban development areas eventually.

· The enlightenment of "Zero Transfer" of Traffic Hub. The construction of the transportation hub should be people-oriented, to achieve "zero transfer" among a variety of modes and improve transport facilities and network design of different modes.

10.5　Multi-dimensional Alternatives

10.5.1　Planning Programs to Increase the Supply of Transport Facilities

(1) Transportation hub and system convergence planning

Integrated passenger transportation hub refers to a specific node on an integrated transport network. It is a passenger terminal which integrates layout for two or more passenger stations of foreign transport means (or a foreign transport mode and urban rail transit station) and connects with urban transport integration. The basic function of the urban traffic hub is the "portal" of people's transportation which is one of the urban's infrastructures. The system convergence of the hub is the key to realize its function. System integration includes internal system of public transport (such as subway, conventional bus, bus, light rail, tram, etc.) and its rational and scientific convergence with non-motorized transportation system. The seamless convergence of the transport system can maximize the efficiency of the entire transportation system and build integrated transport. The design of the scheme mainly includes three issues: conventional bus network coordination, transfer hub location and layout, and matching of operation connection system.

Conventional bus network coordination includes existing line adjustment and new line optimization. On the basis of analyzing the principle and goal of conventional bus adjustment and optimization, the qualitative optimization and adjustment measures are given to the existing network; For the new line network, the maximum efficiency of the unit cost is the objective function, the coverage efficiency model is established to obtain the alternate site set, and the intelligent search algorithm is used to form the line network; for operation connecting system matching, capacity matching, scheduling coordination and operational integration are included. Considering the coordination between rail transit and conventional bus passenger flow, we first establish the transfer capacity matching model and get the number of transfer buses needed for the transfer sites. Secondly, the scheduling coordination model is established with the minimum cost of passenger transfer as the objective function and get the transit bus network density and departure frequency, thereby rail transit and conventional bus operation integration's advantages are analyzed. The result recommends to implement integrated operation and management of rail transit and conventional bus.

For transfer hub layout and location, the infrastructure layout at the hub is proposed by analyzing the factors and principles of transfer hub layout. And then, the location model of rail transit and conventional bus transfer hub is established to provide reference for the transfer hub site selection.

(2) Urban road system planning

To strengthen the capacity of transport carriers, the adoption of urban road planning, construction, rectification and other measures should be considered. In new development areas where the road network has not yet been formed, the alternatives should be considered from the perspective of building roads and improving the road network.

Structure of road network refers to different functions and different levels of road coordination and organic layout in urban space. It ensures that road system and internal interrelated elements form reasonable and stable combination configuration (such as overall configuration, grade configuration, arrangement, transfer mode, etc.), thus road system can effectively make the greatest overall benefit. The usual way is to change the line direction on the original road network, break the road and upgrade/degrade road to make the road network have structure.

From view of road, planning of urban road system should ensure "hardware", that is, road system construction and renovation can achieve a certain capacity, as well as pay attention to the road network structure. Especially, in the case of urban road network having been formed through adjusting the road function and level and matching with the land, better results can often be achieved.

In urban cities, when some interchange was built, there will be congestion. This phenomenon shows that road planning did not carry out scientific traffic analysis and people ignored the traffic development concept of bus priority when the overall network capacity was difficult to increase. It is not feasible to continue to maintain the mode of driving through road construction in areas where urban traffic supply and demand contradiction are relatively great.

(3) Intersection planning

Through the design of lane width and lane function, pedestrians and bicycles crossing street and intersecting internal traffic flow guide lines, space resources at the intersection can be reasonably allocated, to increase the transit efficiency of the intersection and protect pedestrians crossing the streets in a safety and ordered manner.

Through the optimization and redesign of intersection signal control scheme, the time vehicles and pedestrians used to pass through the intersection can be reasonably allocated to reduce delays and ease congestion.

There are two different modes of transport for intersection planning. One is the kind of intersection represented by Xi'an through the widening of the design, to increase traffic flow through the intersection of the traffic section, so that the intersection capacity and road capacity can match well. However, after the widening of the lane and increase of the intersection area, it will increase the number of vehicles which enter into the intersection. The increasing confusion with more conflict points and larger conflict area will raise the difficulty of management. The add to the distance from the center line of the stop line enabled vehicles to pass the intersection for a long time, reduce the capacity of the intersection, and even cause clearance that affects vehicle traffic in next phase. At the same time, it is easy to be limited by road red line. Another is achieved through narrowing the intersection area and controlling the number of vehicles entering the intersection at a given time, represented by San Francisco, to reduce conflict points and areas and standardize the intersection order. This reduction in the intersection area of the planning approach has reduced pedestrian crossing distance, so it is convenient for pedestrians to quickly pass through the intersection. It has also shortened the distance between the parking lines, reduced the time through the intersection of vehicles and increased the capacity of the intersection.

10.5.2 Reducing Traffic Demand

Broadly speaking, traffic demand refers to the change of traffic choice behavior through the guidance of traffic policy and so on, aiming to reduce the amount of motor vehicle trips and reduce or eliminate traffic congestion. In narrow sense, it means a comprehensive traffic policy adopted to cut down the number of commuters with the mode of "one person in one car" during the peak period. It can reduce too much concentration of traffic travel in both time and space. Measures to disperse traffic needed in time include the staggered rush hour plan, congestion pricing, flexible work time, work at home, etc.. Measures to disperse traffic needed in space include providing road traffic information and congestion, the accident situation to driver, promoting the decentralization of traffic demand, limiting the land use intensity where far from bus station, balancing job-housing land use, and reducing long-distance commute travel, et.

10.5.3 Transformation of Travel Mode

Transformation of travel mode is mainly used to promote transit and improve the proportion of environmentally friendly travel. "The task that traffic aims to complete is space displacement of people and objects. If there is a better way, we will have another option besides vehicle." Traffic is not only a simple engineering and technical problem resolved by building a few roads or bridges, but also systemic social engineering, and we should understand what it firstly serves for. A city should provide space for vehicle travel, but the vehicle is not equal to the basic travel needs of the public. Under the same road resources, the conventional transit transport capacity per hour is 10 times as big as vehicle capacity, while rail transit capacity per hour is 30 times as big as vehicle. When transporting the same number of passengers, compared to vehicle, public transport can save more than 80% of energy as well as 90% of road resources, and reduce pollutant emissions by 80%. Therefore, the development of public transport and the transformation of travel mode, especially the transformation of the travel of vehicle users is internationally recognized as a good method to alleviate congestion and improve the environment. There are many problems needed to be solved in the implementation process of public transport priority development strategy. These problems include the choice of urban public transport development mode and the layout of public transportation network.

10.5.4 Intelligent Transportation Mode

The application of advanced technology greatly facilitates people's travel. It improves the quality of travel from the safety, comfort, efficiency, etc.. Intelligent transportation system integrated advanced computer processing technology, information technology, data communication and transmission technology, automatic control technology, artificial intelligence, and electronic technology, etc. These are effectively used in the transport management system. It establishes a wide range and all-round transport management system which is timely, accurate and efficient. The application of intelligent transportation system is mainly embodied in advanced navigational system, electronic toll collection system, safety driving system, transportation management optimization system and public transportation information system. The use of ITS technology can establish a fast, punctual, safe and convenient transportation system, and thereby provide new ideas for transportation system optimization.

References

[1] Wang Yuanqing, Cui Shihua, Hao Subin. Methodology of Regional Integration of Rural Road Network with Important Degree Location[J]. China Journal of Highway and Transport, 2002, 15(4):86-89.

[2] Liang Jiang, Sun Hui. Tang Chang'an's new layout of urban layout and shape in the square [J]. Urban Planning, 2003, 27(1): 77-82.

[3] Wu Hongxuan, Shi Hongshuai. The Yuan Dynasty to the end of the Qing Dynasty. The Evolution of Urban Form and Structure in Xi'an[C]. Taiyuan: 2003 Annual Meeting of the Chinese Ancient Society, 2003.

[4] Li Chen. Study on the evolution and development of Xi'an urban center axis spatial sequence [D]. Xi'an: Xi'an University of Architecture and Technology, 2014.

[5] Xie Yu. Research on the integration of bicycle elevated highway construction and rail transit transfer[D]. Beijing: Beijing Jiaotong University, 2016.

[6] Elliot Fishman. A review of recent literature on public bikes[J]. Urban Transport, 2015, 13(6):80-94.

[7] Wang Jingyuan, Zhuang Yan. Discussion on the measures to narrow the intersection area and narrow the lanes[J]. Traffic Science and Technology, 2007, 22(3): 89-91.

[8] Han Shengfeng, Chen Xiaohong. Study on the Red Line Width of Roads in China's Big Cities [J]. Journal of Tongji University, 2006, 4(7):909-912.

[9] Yang Xiaoguang, Bai Yu, Xue Kun. Study on the planning and design method of traffic and landscape coordination for urban trunk roads[J]. Urban Transport, 2003, 27(10):34-38.

[10] Chen X. Research on the layout and optimization strategy of urban transportation network [D]. Wuhan: Huazhong University of Science and Technology, 2005.

Chapter 11

Technique for Transportation Planning Decision-making Life Cycle Cost and Impact Analysis

With the rapid development of information and computing technology, transportation planning is entering a critical historical period ages from concept guidance to win by data. Determine whether the program is superior to the process. For example, as the development of Alpha Go, a better idea is found developed through based on a comprehensive data instead of concept guidance. The life cycle assessment method is just a highly generalization of the data of traffic development of transport, which is a new trend in the development of traffic planning and evaluation. In this chapter, we will reveal the progress of these above aspects in recent years will be described comprehensively.

Life cycle concept has been taken into account in the decision-making process of referring to construction project from "cradle to grave", the whole process, in order to achieve the goal of sustainable development(Campbell 1996). Usually the context of sustainable development including three aspects: environment, society and economy, as shown in Fig. 11-1 below. Methods of evaluating these three angles aspects are environmental life cycle assessment, social cycle assessment economic life cycle costing to economy and social cycle assessment economic life cycle costing respectively.

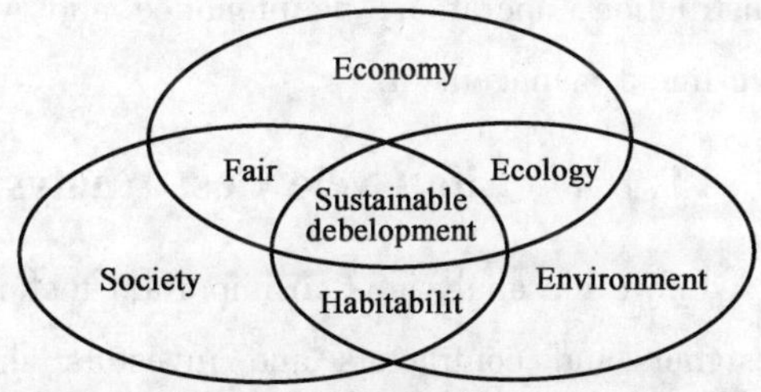

Figure 11-1 The three aspects of sustainable development

Source: *Shen Hongyan*, 2007.

· Environmental life cycle assessment (ELCA): evaluate the environmental impact of construction projects or products in processes of the production, use, and disposal processes, such as CO_2 emissions or energy use.

· Social life cycle assessment (SLCA): evaluate the social impact of construction projects or products, such as the impact on the residents' health. At present, this method is in the initial stage and there has been no uniform standard for quantitative calculation. But it can be qualitative analyzed.

· Environmental life cycle costing (ELCC): evaluate the economic cost of construction projects or products.

· Social life cycle assessment (SLCA): evaluate the social impact of construction projects or products, such as the impact on the residents' health. At present, this method is in the initial stage and there has been no uniform standard for quantitative calculation. But it can be qualitative analyzed.

It should be considered in those three aspects in the process of planning a project. Try to make the project coordinated in environment economy, society and economy environment. In order to select the optimal solution scheme, it is essential to improve economic efficiency, pay attention to environmental protection and social harmony, and improve economic efficiency. The first two sections of this chapter will elaborate on LCC and LCA.

11.1 Life Cycle Costing (LCC)

Life Cycle Costing Analysis (LCCA): LCC is to consider the total cost of the infrastructure, including the whole process of building, operation, maintenance and waste disposal. Due to that most transportation infrastructure projects usually need long-term planning and have great effects to the society, environment and political environment, their constructions not only need a huge one-time investment but also require to cost a lot during their phase of operation and maintenance cost. In this way, the life cycle cost means the whole life cycle cost comprehensive analysis of a construction project. The pros and cons of the infrastructure project planning and design will affect the cost of the operation and maintenance work when the project is completed. Thus, for a higher one-time investment in higher projects, the cost of maintenance is usually lower. In addition, with the increase in the use of infrastructure, equipment aging, budget constraints and other issues becoming increasingly prominent, it is necessary to consider the relationship between investment in the construction phase and management of the latter maintenance phase. LCCA takes into account the total cost of the whole life cycle of the infrastructure, including the whole process of investment, construction, operation, maintenance and waste disposal. It is a kind of tool for optimizing the investment management.

11.1.1 Life Cycle Cost Analysis History

Life cycle analysis is an important technique for investment assessment and economic analysis. Designers and contractors and investors should take " life cycle " as the starting point, take reasonable technology, economic and strategic measures to minimize the total cost of the project within its service life.

Some euramerican developed countries such as the United States take the lead in putting forward to the idea of life cycle design based on the optimization of the whole life cycle. In 1960s, the concept of life cycle costing was first used in the U. S. Defense Agency United States Department of Defense(DOD) to calculate the life cycle cost of defensive weapons purchase. On account of it has achieved good effect, it developed rapidly from military equipment procurement to all walks of life fields at present. In 1970s, the United States government and military departments issued a series of standards, rules, guidelines, circulars and manuals and other documents, such as "*Life Cycle Cost Evaluation of Procurement Guidelines*", it applied described LCC method for optimization method in the cost of the decomposition, estimation, modeling, verification and evaluation.

The United Kingdom in 1970s created the discipline of equipment integrated engineering developed terotechnology based on the idea concept of life cycle. The subject mainly research focused on the economic problem issue of life cycle cost of equipment. In 1980s, LCCA has been applied in the fields of aviation, spaceflight, vehicle, building and so on. At this point, the focus of the study leans to optimizing the life cycle cost of infrastructure projects, to considering the construction cost, and to selecting the best optimal scheme of life cycle cost.

In 1980s, this analysis method was gradually applied to the road transportation sector industry. The study was mainly concentrated in the performance and economy of the road infrastructure associated with. That is the durability problems of highway and bridge, and the optimization problem of short-term investment and long-term investment. The earliest application of LCCA in the field of transportation is to determine the best solution for the pavement material. In 1990s, there were a series of representative of achievements, "*Life Cycle Cost Analysis in Pavement Design*" promulgated by the FHWA in 1998 was the representative one, it expounded the design theory and principle of the life cycle method.

Major transportation policies of the United States on the implementation of LCCA:

· In 1991, "*The Intermodal Surface Transportation Equity Act*" proposed that the LCCA should be considered in the design of bridges, tunnels and pavements.

· In 1995, "*The National Highway System Directive Action*" required all projects with higher cost items(over $25 million) to make use LCC analysis A.

· In 1996, according to the Federal Highway Administration (FHWA) introduced a demonstration project 115 "*Life Cycle Cost Analysis In Pavement Design*". By the end of 2002, these techniques have been used for transportation agencies pavement design departments of in more than 40 states.

· In 1998, FHWA published provisional technical bulletin of LCCA of the pavement "*The Life Cycle Cost Analysis of Pavement Design*".

In Japan, Asko Sarja, the representative of the practitioners on the life cycle design of engineering project, published many articles and research works about the life cycle design of engineering project in 1990s. Those documents were mainly related to the environment, ecology, concrete materials and, structural durability design etc and others.

One of the most representative one is a book of "*The Project Life Cycle Design of the Project*". From the technical point of view, this book comprehensively introduces the framework, the design process, the design method, the design of the repeated use of concrete, recycled materials and the development direction of further development of the life cycle design.

At present, the life cycle is the most widely used in the evaluation of buildings assessment in China in our country. Zhang Zhihui applied the idea method of life cycle on the building in the environmental impact assessment of buildings, including the process of acquisition of raw materials, the manufacture and processing of raw materials, the production of building materials, the construction, and operation use of buildings, and the process of demolition.

Life cycle analysis is an important technique for investment evaluation assessment and economic analysis. Designers and engineering contractors and investors should be based on taking "cycle life cycle" as the starting point, to ensure that taking reasonable technology, economic and strategic measures to minimize the total cost of the project within the its service life.

11.1.2 Introduction of Life Cycle Costing Analysis

The main goal of LCCA is to seek the most cost-effective solution, through balancing the relationship between the trade-off of the costs and benefits among of investment costs, operation and, maintenance and the benefits, to achieve the purpose of minimizing the life cycle cost.

The basic concept of decision making is that if the investment at this stage can be of greater value in the future, then the investment is reasonable(Luenberger 2009). Decision making not only need to consider the life cycle investment costing in investment, operation and other stages of a project, but also need to consider the impact of other factors, such as the environment and risk. In the transport sector, LCCA has been applied in the specific project preliminary development, construction costs, operation and maintenance's costs and scrap costs. The analysis begins with the project planning stage. By calculating the cost of each phase, it can better allocate the funds for the operation, maintenance and other costs. As the project develops, life cycle will become increasingly small influential. The famous Pareto curve indicates that in the life cycle of a project, about 70% of the life cycle cost have been identified at the end of the project planning stage; 85% of the life cycle cost has been determined at the end of scheme selection. Therefore, the early stage of the life cycle has a great influence on the later stage, the design phase of the project plan is the best time to determine the costs and benefits of the life cycle analysis.

(1) Application areas and restriction factors constraints of LCCA

The application of LCCA in transportation is mainly focusing on analyzing the cost of construction projects in associated with the phase of the planning, design, construction, operation and maintenance, there are four main types of application:

· Choose the best solution optimal scheme which to meet the requirements: To through compare comparing the costs and benefits of different alternatives, and selecting the best cost-effective solutions;

· Factors contributing to the of increasing in costs and the risk analysis: Analyzing analyze the risk factors in the life cycle of the project, which may lead to costs increasing, in order to find the possibility of reducing the total costs;

· Design optimization: Evaluate the design of the project, compare and improve the product design to minimize the life cycle cost;

· Sub project construction order sorting: Under the condition of limited funds, comparing sub project costs and arranging the sub project priority according to the capital requirements.

The applications of LCCA in the above four types should be located used in the different stages of the life cycle: In in the early stage, it emphasizes on the cost analysis of the whole system while the latter stage is focusing on analyzing the cost of a particular part of the system.

LCCA has made remarkable achievements in many fields, but there are still many problems which hinder the application and development of this method. The main factors that limit the use of LCCA are embodied in the following five aspects:

· The existence of risk and uncertainty, and the difficulty of accurately predicting forecast on the future data are the key factors that lead to the low utilization rate of LCCA;

· The data of the existing database is unreliable, incompatible and incomplete, and the management cost of the database is too large. The input data is not accurate, the cost information is expired. It is difficult to use the model directly because the historical data come from different models, manufacturers and technologies which make the database incompatible;

· The lack of transparency between the various departments of the construction project, increasing the difficulty of LCCA;

· The investment and maintenance work of construction projects is usually controlled by different departments, which hinders the application of LCCA;

· The practitioners lack of limited professional training for relevant software and analysis methods of LCCA and complete understanding of LCC that also limits the use of LCCA.

Although LCCA has some limitation, it can provide relatively comprehensive information for decision makers by analyzing the benefits and costs of the life cycle of the construction project. Therefore, the decision maker can use the limited funds to achieve the highest cost efficiency, increase the persistence of the benefits, and improve the management level of the major infrastructure.

(2) LCCA and related economic evaluation methods

· Cost Effectiveness Analysis: Cost effectiveness can be used to measure the cost-benefit relationship for achieving a specific goal (such as: pay off the loan, etc.), and to find the lowest-cost scheme to achieve the objectives of the program through the analysis of cost effectiveness.

· Benefit-Cost and Net Benefit Analysis: The different point between benefit-cost and net benefit analysis is that net benefit analysis mainly analyzes a specific target cost and chooses the scheme of with minimum cost while the benefit-cost compares the total costs and benefits and is then finally presented in the form of ratio of benefit/cost form. If the ratio is bigger than 1, the project is feasible. Net benefit is the difference between total revenue and total cost, which is the absolute comparison of the difference between the income and the cost of different schemes, while the benefit/cost is relative comparison.

· Life Cycle Costing Analysis: LCCA includes the net benefit analysis of the time value of money, which contains the discounted value of the cost and benefit (the next section covers). LCCA can be used to compare the total cost of different projects in different time periods.

(3) The discount rate of the life cycle

The currency has time value, thus the value of the currency of the same denomination is different at different times. In the calculation of the LCC of a construction project, the cost of the future year should be converted to the base year and multiplied by the corresponding discount rate. The factors determining the discount rate are as follows:

· Inflation. Although the general economic analysis does not consider the impact of inflation, its impact is an objective existence. In the case of inflation, the currency of the same denomination is now worth more than the future.

· Account interest. Regardless of the size of the interest rate, the currency of the same denomination is now worth more than the future.

· The risk. Due to the existence of investment risk, it may increase its future costs and reduce future profits. For example, the evaluation of the future value of highway reconstruction should take into account the possibility of road damage caused by the disaster, technological progresses, and changes in people's preferences. The bigger the risk, the greater the discount rate of future income is.

For whole life analysis, firstly, calculate and analyze the benefits and costs of each period (usually in years). Then convert the income and cost of each planning year to the base year by multiplying the discount rate. Finally, add all the income and cost respectively to get the present value of total income and the present value of total cost. And the net present value Net Present Value is the difference between the two. Fig. 11-2 is the life cycle analysis that is not multiplied by the discount rate. Fig. 11-3 is the life cycle analysis with a discount rate of 7%. It should be noted that the income and cost are both multiplied by the discount rate. In this case, the cost is valid when the discount rate is not used(i. e., the total cost is less than the total income), but it is invalid when the discount rate is used.

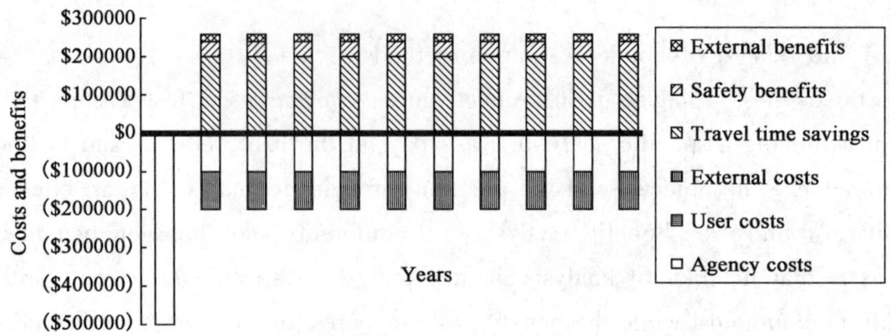

Figure 11-2 Road life cycle analysis(no discount rate)

Source: *Todd Litman*, 2006.

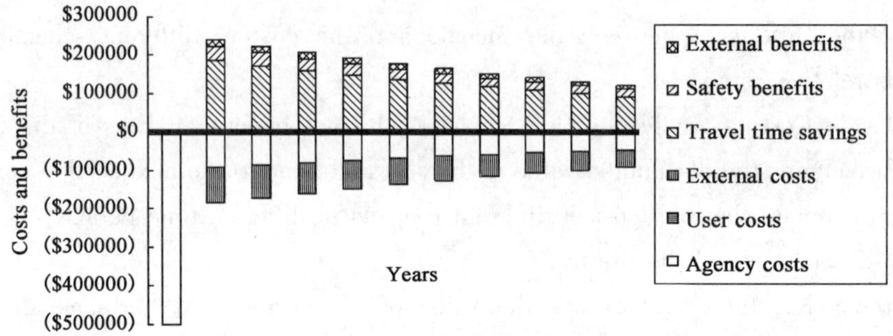

Figure 11-3 Road life cycle analysis(including discount rate)

Source: *Todd Litman*, 2006.

11.1.3 Life Cycle Costing Analysis Method

(1) Economic evaluation framework

Evaluation framework is the basic structure of evaluation and comparative analysis. The framework needs to define the following parts:

· Evaluation methods: such as cost-effectiveness, benefit-cost, life cycle analysis, etc..

· Evaluation criteria: influence factors in analysis and evaluation methods could be specified targets and the problems(such as congestion reduction is the goal and congestion is a problem) for qualitative analysis or costs and benefits(such as incomes from congestion reduction or costs caused by congestion) for quantitative analysis.

· Modeling techniques: analyzing the impact of policies or projects on traffic travel behaviors and the nature of land use, calculating the costs or benefits.

· Infrastructure scheme: the scenario without the implement of a project or policy.

· Functional units: the per lane kilometers, vehicle kilometers, person kilometers, costs increased in peak hour traffic volume.

· Base year and discount rate: base year is a basis for comparison, discount rate as a ratio of future value convert into present value reflects the cost changing change with the change in the time value of money.

· Scope: to define the geographical and temporal scope of the evaluation.

· Uncertainty: the uncertainty that whether there is any sensitivity analysis or statistical testing.

· The presentation of the results: in order to compare the different evaluation schemes.

(2) The analysis method of life cycle costing

The life cycle analysis method can be summarized as:

· Defining the scope of analysis, such as the time boundaries of analysis, the analysis phases, etc.;

· Determining alternative design schemes;

· Analyzing the cost of inventory and collecting the necessary data for analysis;

· Calculating the net present value Net Present Value and performance indicators;

· Analyzing the results and risks to select the optimal scheme.

The life cycle analysis process presented in the paper "*Integrated Life Cycle Design of Structures*" by Asko Sarja is shown as Fig. 11-4.

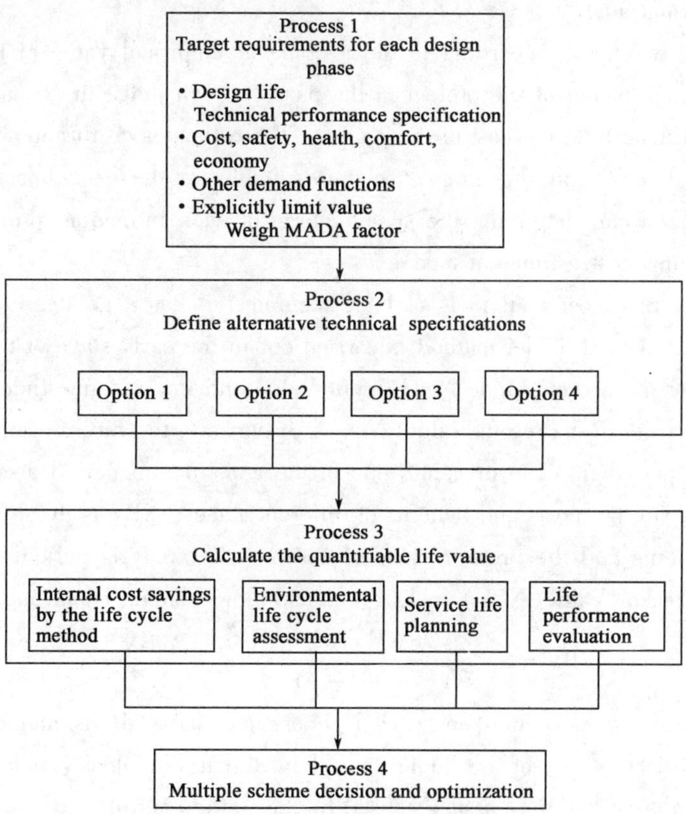

Figure 11-4 Life cycle analysis process

· Defining the scope of the analysis. The scope of the analysis largely determines the limiting factors and methods of the project. Therefore, the objectives of the project and the subsystem or part of the system whether included in the system or not should be clearly defined.

· Identifying alternative design schemes' phase and costs inventory analysis phase. According to the whole life cycle of the project, the whole process includes investment, operation, maintenance and waste disposal. In order to carry out inventory analysis, it can be divided into the following stages: Project evaluation and early design stage, project evaluation and selection stage, detailed design stage, project implementation and production stage, use and maintenance stage, scrap stage. Use the history data to determine the average cost of each process unit or establish statistical models. Based on those two methods to establish a cost estimation model.

a. Statistical model method. According to the historical data of the past works, the paper finds out the relationship between the number or the cost of the projects and a single factor or other relevant factors. In the early stages, because of the imperfection of the system design, the input of available data is limited. Thus, it needs to use similar built system, similar built cost estimation model and compare the characteristics of new and old system to establish the new system cost estimation model. This method is called "top-down" cost estimation model (Asiedu and Gu 1998). The accuracy of this method depends on the number of historical samples and the processing techniques of regression analysis.

b. Average cost method. According to the average or empirical value of the unit cost of the labor, material and equipment of the project in the past, we can judge the consumption quantity of each project and estimate the total cost of the project. The estimates on the number, the unit cost of the project will affect the results' accuracy, so it is suitable for the design phase which has been completed. The method can determine the specific form of each individual project, this method is called the "bottom-up" cost estimation model.

Although the average cost method is of high accuracy, it has a greater impact on the system design because the statistical model method is carried out in the early stage of the project.

· Calculation of net present value Net Present Value and Performance Index

a. Net present value Net Present Value (NPV). It converts the future cost and benefit of each year in the analysis period into the present value of the construction period according to the social discount rate to compare the costs and benefits of different stages. NPV is the difference between the present value of benefits and the present value of costs in the analysis period. The formula of net present value Net Present Value (NPV) in LCCA is as follows (Sheng Hongyan, 2007):

$$\mathrm{NPV} = C + \sum_{t=1}^{N} \frac{O_t + \mathrm{M}_t + R_t + \mathrm{RUC}_t}{(1+r)^t} + \frac{\mathrm{RV}}{(1+r)^N} \tag{11-1}$$

where, C is initial construction cost; O_t is operating costs; M_t is maintenance cost; R_t is renovate cost; RUC_t is the cost of a vehicle caused by the traffic block (such as when a road or bridge is modified, the cost of the passage caused by the traffic control); RV is residual value; r is discount rate; N is economic period; NPV = 0, which means that the costs and benefits of the program are equal, just to achieve the expected revenue; NPV < 0, indicates that it is not up to the expected rate of return, the economic benefits are not good; NPV > 0, indicates that the economic benefits get excess returns.

b. Equivalent uniform annual costs (EUACs). It is used to calculate the economical indicators and its formula is as follows:

$$\mathrm{EUAC} = \mathrm{NPV} \cdot \left[\frac{r(1+r)^N}{(1+r)^N - 1}\right] \tag{11-2}$$

c. Reliability, availability, maintainability and safety (RAMS) are used to evaluate the functionality and reliability of the products. For construction projects, it needs to take into account the impact of the four indicators and balance the relationship among the indicators to keep the system optimal.

d. Analyze the results, the risks and then select the optimal scheme. The uncertainties, risks and other factors of the project reduce the accuracy of the LCCA. Therefore, the factors which affect the accuracy of calculation should be analyzed. Risk can be described by probability distribution function, and the probability distribution of uncertainties is not clear. Thus, the methods of risk analysis and Monte Carlo simulation are usually used to analyze the influencing factors and probability distribution of project risks. If the investment is of high risks in the construction project, we need a more detailed assessment of the risk model to select a more appropriate scheme. However, if the construction project has a high degree of uncertainty, it would be better to choose a more simple method, because the uncertainty will invalidate the complicated analysis.

(3) Composition and model of life cycle costing

Firstly, establish the cost analysis model of construction period, maintenance period, operation period and travel time delay in road construction. At the same time, establish the cost-effective model. Then based on the design alternatives, inputs the parameters into the system, the parameters include the discount rate, the design speed, the material consumption of project construction, the time occupied by the construction of road, maintenance frequency, annual traffic volume after the completion of road and the age limit of analysis, etc. so as to get the whole life cycle costs and benefits of the scheme to select the optimal scheme.

The followings are some of the major models to calculate the life cycle cost. From the point of view of highway managers and users, the cost model can be divided into owner cost model and road user cost model.

· Owner cost model

The owner's cost is the cost of the highway manager and the owner, including the construction cost, maintenance cost and management cost, etc. According to similar projects' empirical unit costs and the size of the projects, the costs of the road side safety facilities optimization, the improvement of intersection safety and the improvement of road cross section could be estimated. The daily maintenance costs can be calculated on a base year basis using a constant annual growth rate.

a. Costs of construction period costs and operation maintenance

The costs of the construction project within the life cycle analysis period are estimated based on the average cost per unit of historical equipment or material, combined with the number of equipment or materials used in the project proposals. The maintenance costs of the operation period are similar to that of the construction period, and will not be repeated here.

b. Maintenance costs during operation

Road operation stage each year need some funds for highway maintenance, mainly including cleaning the road, digging ditch, plant pruning, dredging culvert, remediation shoulder, and daily work of maintenance warning pile, 100 meters pile, repair pits, irrigation joints and other daily maintenance works. The costs mainly include staff salaries, machines and materials, and they are related to conservation mileage and price changes. The annual growth rate of the costs is relatively stable. In accordance with the price index method which is internationally accepted and maturely used in the road industry to calculate the part of the annual cost, based on the present relevant statistical data, the number and cost of various types of conservation works has been organized based on the present relevant statistical data and the relevant coefficients has been calibrated (Wang Landao, 2016):

$$\begin{cases} \mathrm{ADJ} = \mathrm{LCP} \times K \\ K = \alpha + \beta \dfrac{\mathrm{LL}_1}{\mathrm{LL}_0} + \gamma \dfrac{\mathrm{PL}_1}{\mathrm{PL}_0} + m \dfrac{\mathrm{CE}_1}{\mathrm{CE}_0} + n \dfrac{\mathrm{TI}_1}{\mathrm{TI}_0} + a \dfrac{\mathrm{ST}_1}{\mathrm{ST}_0} + b \dfrac{\mathrm{BI}_1}{\mathrm{BI}_0} + c \dfrac{\mathrm{LT}_1}{\mathrm{LT}_0} + d \dfrac{\mathrm{LM}_1}{\mathrm{LM}_0} - 1 \end{cases} \tag{11-3}$$

where, ADJ is annual adjustment amount of maintenance cost adjustment amount; K is adjustment coefficient of maintenance cost adjustment coefficient; LCP is the baseline maintenance cost of the same type of conservation work last year; LL_1, LL_0 is the index of this year and last year's maintenance cost. In essence, the changes in the cost of living expenses. It should be calculated based on the price index of daily necessities and the average wage index of the community; PL_1, PL_0 is the cost index of daily maintenance equipment for this year and the previous year which shall be calculated on the basis of the mechanical depreciation and the change of repair costs; CE_1, CE_0 is the costs index of cement for this year and the previous year which is derived from the combination of unit price and consumption; TI_1, TI_0 is the costs index of timber for this year and the previous year which is derived from the combination of unit price and consumption; ST_1, ST_0 is the costs index of steel for this year and the previous year which is derived from the combination of unit price and consumption; LT_1, LT_0 is the costs index of transportation for this year and the previous year. Based on the consideration of the fluctuations in oil prices, it is consisted of the combination of unit price and consumption of the number of trips, fuel consumption per trip; LM_1, LM_0 is the costs index of flooring materials for this year and the previous year which is consisted of the combination of unit price and consumption of the stone, lime, loess and other materials; α, β, γ, m, n, a, b, c, d are the coefficients that different item costs take up in the total maintenance costs. It is calculated based on the each every cost amount of the composition of the maintenance costs in the base year. α is a constant coefficient, including profits, taxes, etc., usually 0.1-0.25.

· Road user cost model

The cost of road users includes vehicle operating costs, travel time costs, traffic accident costs and environmental costs caused by vehicle emissions. Road user costs include these two cases: the costs of road users under normal operating conditions and the additional costs of road users caused by the road construction. The cost of road users in the life cycle is similar to the cost of maintenance and management, and the cost of the future year is estimated based on the base year cost and the annual average growth rate.

a. Vehicle operating cost

The operating cost of the vehicle is the expenditure of the resource consumption of the vehicle on the road, including fuel consumption, wheel consumption, maintenance labor and material costs, vehicle depreciation, management fees, etc.. The costs of fuel used by each vehicle, tire consumption and maintenance materials should be calculated according to the following formulas respectively (Wang Landao, 2016):

$$\text{fuel consumption}: F_L = a_1 + b_1 \times \text{IRI} \tag{11-4}$$

$$\text{wheel consumption}: T_C = a_2 + b_2 \times \text{IRI} \tag{11-5}$$

$$\text{material consumption}: P_C = C_0 \times \exp(C_q \times \text{IRI})\,\text{CKM}^{\text{KP}}\ (\text{passenger car})$$

$$P_C = C_0(1 + C_q \times \text{IRI})\,\text{CKM}^{\text{KP}}\ (\text{freight car}) \tag{11-6}$$

where, F_L is fuel consumption, L/100 km; T_C is wheel consumption, article/1000 km; P_C is material consumption, the proportion of new car prices/1000 km; IRI is international roughness index, m/km; CKM is accumulated vehicle accumulated mileage, km; KP is vehicle age index (vehicle depreciation coefficient); $a_1, a_2, b_1, b_2, C_0, C_q$ are the regression coefficients.

The parameters' values are shown in Table 11-1.

Table 11-1 Parameters' values of the consumption if fuel, wheel and material

Vehicle type	a_1	b_1	a_2	b_2	$C_0(10^{-6})$	$C_q(10^{-3})$	KP	CKM(10^4)
Passenger car	9.78	0.182	0.0466	0.0071	12.95	17.81	0.308	15
Bus	23.80	0.294	0.0739	0.0016	1.87	4.63	0.483	50
Small truck	17.42	0.568	0.0669	0.0107	1.87	327.33	0.371	30
Medium truck	23.00	0.434	0.0653	0.0012	1.87	327.33	0.371	30
Heavy truck	19.00	0.298	0.1556	0.0034	5.52	45.90	0.371	30
Container car	35.39	0.893	0.2155	0.0053	5.52	20.35	0.371	30

b. Travel time cost

Travel time cost is the cost of travel time delay mainly caused by the decline in travel speed. Considering the time value of different types of people, the formula for calculating the travel time cost of vehicles on the road is as follows:

$$\text{TTC} = \sum_j \text{UTTC}(j) \times \left[\frac{L}{\text{sp}'(j)} - \frac{L}{\text{sp}(j)}\right] \times N(j) \tag{11-7}$$

where, TTC is travel time cost, yuan; UTTC(j) is the unit travel time cost of class j people, yuan/(person hour); sp(j) is the average travel speed of class j people under normal conditions, km/h; sp′(j) is the average speed of class j people when the speed drops, km/h; $N(j)$ is the number of people of category j, person; L is road section length, km;

c. Traffic accident cost

In order to analyze the accident cost in the life cycle of the highway, the prediction estimation model of safety index SI is established to calculate the cost of three kinds of serious accidents which are death, injury and financial loss respectively; Then, by using the historical data to analyze the number of those three kinds of serious accidents occurred on the similar roads every year and calculate the accident cost. The AASHTO Highway Safety Manual (2010) of the United States, in which the cost of each accident is determined to be \$4008900, \$82588, \$7400, respectively.

d. Environmental costs

The environmental costs of this section will only take into account the environmental impact of automobile exhaust emissions, and the specific life-cycle carbon emissions will be explained in the next section. In foreign countries, there is a lot of research on the quantitative evaluation of environmental benefits, and the amount of pollutant emissions per unit mileage is affected by the average travel speed, the number of trips, traffic volume and other factors. Such as the TRANSYT-7F emissions model of the United States, the calculation of vehicle exhaust emissions is the following:

$$\mathrm{ROP} = \frac{Ae^{Bv}}{Cv} \tag{11-8}$$

where, ROP is the pollutant emission rate(g/per vehicle · km); v is the average travel speed for road vehicles(km/h) ; A, B, C are constants. Therefore, the total amount of emissions on the road as the following:

$$P_a = \mathrm{ROP} \cdot x_a \cdot l_a \tag{11-9}$$

where, x_a is the total number of vehicles on the road a; l_a is the length of road a.

The United States Environmental Protection Agency(EPA) in the Clean Air Act(CAA) defines the "standard pollutants" in the air and also raised the environmental costs of various air pollutants, as shown in Table 11-2.

Table 11-2 Motor vehicle exhaust emissions and the reference value of the cost of loss

Exhaust emissions	CO_2	CO	Pb	CH_4	NO_x	N_2O	PM10	SO_x
Losing cost per tonne($)	6.22	0.99	1719	129	54	1075.14	2297	73.5

Therefore, the total environmental cost $w = P_{ai} \times C_i$, Where, P_{ai} is the total emissions of the class i emissions on the road a; C_i is the losing costs of the class i emissions.

11.1.4 Project Case

In Sweden, about 100 fatal traffic accidents in average occur on each two-way single lane every year. Therefore, it has aroused the concern of many scholars about how to improve the safety of these roads. As a result, anti-collision road grew up in the 90s of 21st century. It is a kind of road type with low initial construction cost, small footprint, and the same or even higher safety of the traditional road. Compared with the traditional road, the anti-collision road can reduce the fatality rate by 76%, which can effectively improve the safety of the two-way lane road, and the construction investment is less, and it has better social and economic benefits.

Anti-collision road has 3 lanes, compared to the middle of the traditional road to add a passing lane. It serves as a common lane for both traffic directions, alternating between two directions with overtaking requirements, similar to reversible lane. However, this passing lane is alternately provided by the overtaking service on the space, rather than the reversible lane provides alternate service in time. The most significant feature of the anti-collision road is that the two directions are separated by the cable guardrail.

However, with the use of this type of road, the high cost of its operation and maintenance is gradually exposed. For example, due to the width of single lane is smaller than that of traditional road, the probability of rutting is 3 times higher. These costs can offset road maintenance costs by increasing the possibility of overtaking, road width, etc. to reduce road wear. Therefore, in order to analyze the feasibility of converting the road to the anti-collision road program in Sweden, they use the life cycle method to find the smallest total cost program of anti-collision road. Fig. 11-5 is the type of cost included in the life cycle analysis of such roads.

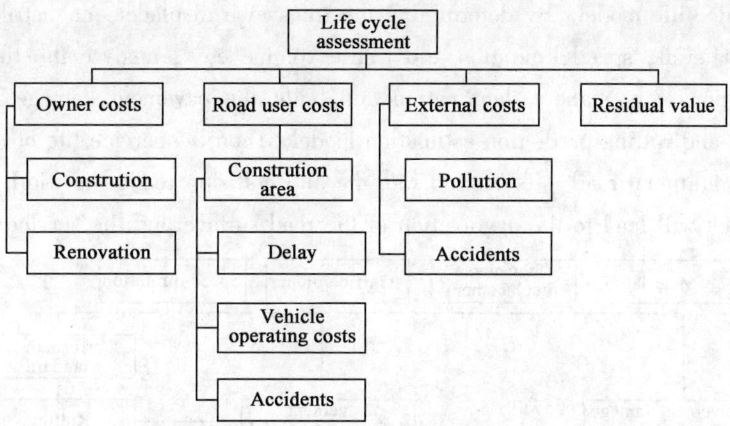

Figure 11-5 Cost components of life-cycle analysis for Swedish anti-collision roads

Source: *Jonas Wennström*, 2014.

(1) Analysis steps

The difference between the options is mainly reflected in the differences between the width of the road, the quality of the aggregate and the thickness of the adhesive layer. The net present value ValueNet Present Value of each alternative is calculated by the method of life cycle analysis. Firstly, the cost of road construction is calculated using Table 11-3 based on the consideration of the different surface layer, adhesive layer standard and road width in the scheme. According to the service life of different schemes, the relationship between the construction cost and the maintenance cost of each scheme is estimated, and the operation, maintenance and renovation costs in recent 40 years of the roads under different schemes are calculated. And the costs are converted to the present value by a discount rate of 4%. The road user costs (RUC) and external costs are calculated based on the cost unit prices shown in Table 11-3; finally, the residual value of each alternative is calculated according to the relevant regulations.

Table 11-3 Unit cost of road users' detour during road maintenance

Cost structure	Unit price (krone/m)
Delays	730
Volatile organic compounds (VOC)	179
Number of accidents	70
External costs	17

Source: *Wennström*, 2014.

The service life of road is the key parameter in the life cycle analysis.

The larger the investment in the construction period, the longer the service life of the road, and the smaller the cost of operation, maintenance and renovation; while the smaller the investment in construction period, the shorter the service life. Therefore, a reasonable determination of the service life is the key link in LCCA.

Because the service life is limited by the road performance standards, it is necessary to carry out the renovation when the road performance index exceeds the threshold value. Fig. 11-6 shows the build process of the service life model. By determining the transverse displacement distribution, properties of the pavement material, speed limitation and traffic volume etc., analyze the rut caused by road wear and the location of permanent deformation and build the pavement damage model, pavement deformation model and rutting prediction estimation model. Then the service life of each alternative is estimated. If the traditional road is converted into the anti-collision road, the width of each lane will be shortened, which will lead to the aggravation of the road surface and the service life of the road.

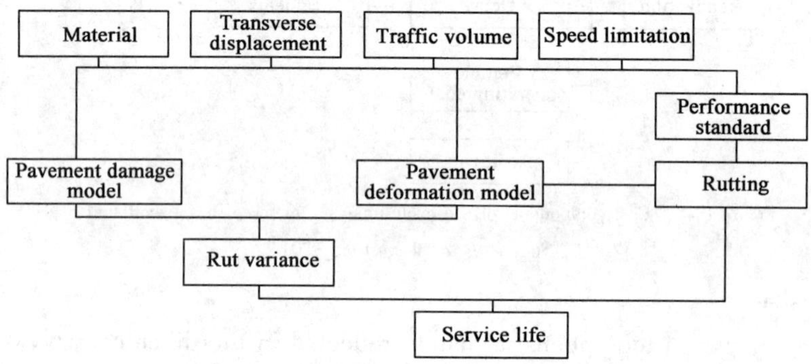

Figure 11-6 Modeling structure of the service life

Source: *Jonas Wennström*, 2014.

Through multiple regression analysis, it is found that there is a linear relationship among service life, lane width and aggregate quality. The service life of road can be calculated by formula 11-10.

$$\text{Service life} = -1.27 + 3.00 l_w - 0.43 A_n + 0.03\text{th} \tag{11-10}$$

where, l_w is the length of lane (m); A_n is the weight of aggregate (km); th is the thickness of adhesive layer (mm).

(2) Owner cost analysis

Total cost of owner is calculated by putting the unit price and quantity of each construction work during the construction and renovation of the project into owner cost model. Table 11-4 is the owner cost unit price (2010 unit price standard).

Table 11-4 Owner cost unit price in life-cycle analysis

Construction type	Construction	Nordic ball-milling parameters	Thickness (m)	Unit price (krone/m^2)
Layer construction	ABS16 70/100	5	40	106
	ABS16 70/100	7	40	98
	ABS16 70/100	9	40	94
	ABS16 70/100	12	40	92

continued

Construction type	Construction	Nordic ball-milling parameters	Thickness(m)	Unit price (krone/m^2)
Bonding layer	ABb16 50/70		45	102
	ABb16 50/70		60	129
	ABb22 50/70		80	165
Pavement widening	Including excavation, fill and so on	—	—	800
Reinforcement	ABS16 70/100		40	85
	ABS16 70/100		40	79
	ABS16 70/100		40	75
	ABS16 70/100		40	74
	Milling		40	20
	TM device		—	26

Source: *Wennström*, 2014.

Wherein, ABb means AsfaltBetong, Bindlager(bonding layer); ABS means AsfaltBetong; T means stone matrix asphalt(SMA).

(3) Road user cost and external cost model

In order to ensure the safety of construction workers during road maintenance and prevent the occurrence of traffic accidents, the anti-collision road is closed during the pavement maintenance work. But this also contributes to the increase in the cost of road users' bypass delays such as fuel consumption and time costs which caused by detouring. The cost of delay in construction area depends on the relationship between the parallel road and the construction road. By analyzing the characteristics of the monthly, weekly and daily distribution of the annual average daily traffic(AADT) of the parallel road and the construction road, the hourly traffic volume of the road during the construction period is forecast and the delay caused by the detour is calculated.

External costs include the cost of environmental pollution and traffic accidents. Road user cost and external cost unit price are shown in Table 11-3.

(4) Life cycle analysis results

There are total 64 alternative schemes of lane width, aggregate quality and bonding layer thickness. There are three main criteria for the scheme selection. Standard 1: during the life of the project, select the minimum owner cost of the program with the discount rate of 4%. Standard 2: during the life of the project, select the minimum owner and user cost of the program with the discount rate of 4%. Standard 3: during the life of the project, select the minimum sum of owner cost and road user cost with the discount rate of less than 4%. In these three criteria, the analysis and comparison of the minimum net present ValueNet Present Value of the program as shown in Table 11-5.

Table 11-5 Optimal solutions for anti-collision roads in Sweden under three criteria

Optimal solution	Standard 1	Standard 2	Standard 3
Lane width	3.25 m	3.25 m	3.5 m
Bonding layer thickness	—	80 mm	80 mm
Aggregate quality	$5A_n$	$5A_n$	$5A_n$
Expected service life	6 years	9 years	—
The analysis and comparison of cost during construction and operation period	Operation, maintenance, renovation (OM&R) cost is relatively high, the cost of road users as well	The cost of the construction period is 2 times that of standard 1, but the cost of OM&R is low	Owner costs increased, but the OM&R and road user costs reduced

Source: *Wennström*, 2014.

It can be obtained from the analysis of different alternatives: the better the quality of the aggregate, the wider the road, the thicker the bonding layer, the smaller the net present ValueNet Present Value of the life cycle cost. If the road service life is 5-7 years, the owner cost will become the lowest; if the service life of the road is 8-11 years, the sum of owner cost and the road user cost will be the lowest.

11.2 Life Cycle Assessment of Energy and Emissions

Life Cycle Assessment (LCA) can assess the volume that products produce environmental and energy emissions in production and activity process during life cycle, including production, making, transportation, distribution, using, maintenance, reusing of materials and scrapping and destroying at last. It calculates energy, resource and pollution emissions by qualitative and quantitative methods which make it easier to calculate environmental impact of various subsystems. LCA developed rapidly in 1980s and the complete LCA consists of four steps as follows:

· Definition and scope of object: description what LCA contains or does not contain, such as purification, production, consuming and scrapping of raw material; description what the importance hypotheses and space-time restriction are.

· Inventory analysis: describing the inflow and outflow of matter and energy in the system. For example, purification of raw material flows into system and outflows system finally by pollutant emissions and energy consumes.

· Impact evaluation:

a. Classification: classification of inflows and outflows in the list according to their impact on environment.

b. Characterization: describing and integrating the characteristics of the elements in each category.

c. Assessment: qualitative or quantitative analysis and comparison for each category.

· Improvement and evaluation: evaluate the possibility of improving.

11.2.1 Review of Life Cycle Assessment of Energy and Emissions

To solve the increasingly serious environmental pollution problems, reduce greenhouse gas emissions and reduce dependence on imported oil, many countries are committed to the development of alternative transportation fuels and advanced vehicle technologies. In 1980s, LCA is gradually applied to the field of road traffic, and obtained a series of achievements in 1990s. To evaluate the energy and emissions effects of alternative fuels and vehicle technologies more accurately and completely, researchers who work for Argonne National Laboratory established the GREET model to calculates energy use and emissions from vehicle operations, fuel production processes and vehicle production processes.

(1) The history of fuel cycle assessment

In 1991, Delucchi established a model for calculating greenhouse gas emissions and the calculation method of greenhouse gas emissions from fuel cycle of a variety of transportation fuels and electricity is studied. The greenhouse gases include CO_2, CH_4, CO, N_2O, NO_x and non methane organic gas (NMOGs). Delucchi also studied the changes in the nature of the land used because of automotive manufacturing, transportation systems maintenance, emissions and energy use and the biofuels. In order to calculate greenhouse gas emissions of fuel cycle in a certain stage, Delucchi computed the total energy of combustion in the stage, and obtained the total energy of each fuel. Finally Delucchi got the greenhouse gas emissions except CO_2 (calculating CO_2 emissions by burning carbon conservation). And Delucchi also considered greenhouse gas emissions due to fuel leakage and evaporation in burning process. Finally, the greenhouse gas emissions of each phase are converted to CO_2 equivalent emissions per mile and the total emissions of the fuel cycle process are obtained. This method which was used by Delucchi is mostly used and widely cited in the calculation of greenhouse gas emissions.

Besides, Bentley et al studied the calculation method of CO_2 for electrical vehicles, fuel cell hybrids and internal combustion engines. In 1992, researchers in Sweden Ecotraffic studied the calculation methods for the emission and energy consumption of different transportation fuels. However, the results of this study only use the Swedish data, so the results can only be applied to Sweden. In 1996, Acurex studied the fuel cycle emissions of new formulations of gasoline, diesel and alternative transportation fuels, including three standard pollutants (NO_x, NMOG, CO) and two kinds of greenhouse gases (CO_2, CH_4). And the calculation framework of fuel cycle emissions is established, which provides a comprehensive calculation method for different vehicle fuels and technologies, but the PM10 and SO_x emissions are ignored in this study. Argonne National Laboratory, in 1998, assessed differences in energy use and emissions of the four major US cities of electric vehicles and gasoline vehicles. For a kind of fuel which was given, this research provided a detailed report for electric vehicle fuel emissions and energy use.

Fuel life analysis began at the Argonne National Laboratory Transportation Research Center. It has 20-year history of life cycle analysis for different fuels and vehicles. The United States Department of Energy (DOE's) funded Argonne to establish a fuel life-cycle model based on spreadsheets——the GREET 1.0 model. And the purpose of the model is to provide researchers with a simple tool to evaluate the impact of fuel life cycle and various transportation technologies emission.

GREET model——Greenhouse Gases, Regulated Emissions, and Energy Use in Transportation——is the most extensive and authoritative model that calculating fuel life cycle emission model. The model calculates quantitatively the five pollutants emitted during the whole life cycle of a given fuel and vehicle technology——VOCs, CO, NO_x, SO_x, PM10. And it also calculates greenhouse gas emissions from fuel life cycle, mainly CO_2, CH_4 and N_2O. GREET model consists of three parts: calculating energy use and emissions in the fuel cycle of light vehicles (passenger cars, small and medium goods vehicles) and heavy vehicles, and calculating them in the vehicle cycle of light vehicles.

A large amount of input data of the GREET 1.0 model was derived from Delucchi's research in 1991. Then the GREET model is updated and improved with the parameter assumptions of fuel production, and new fuels and vehicle technologies are used. Although hydroelectric, solar and wind power generation do not emit contaminants, these processes are also included in the GREET model. So, this book takes GREET 1.5 model as an example to analyze emission of greenhouse gases and pollutants in fuel life cycle analysis.

(2) The life cycle of the vehicle

Advanced vehicle technologies, hybrid electric vehicle (HEV) and fuel cell vehicle (FCV), have high efficiency of power system and have better fuel economy and lower emissions than conventional vehicles. Meanwhile, the development of lightweight body materials in the United States makes it possible to reduce the weight of the body material while it does not affect the safety and performance of the vehicle. The development of new vehicles and materials cannot be separated from the comparison of new technology and traditional technology in energy use and emissions.

So, in 1995, Argonne Laboratory in the United States conducted further studies on aluminum-intensive vehicle. As a result, it was found that the energy consumption of the recycling aluminum alloy will be evidently reduced than aluminum alloy which is directly produced with raw materials, while the result that reducing the weight of the vehicle can reduce oil consumption was founded. In 1997, Wang et al studied hybrid electric vehicles with different battery types and they found that hybrid electric vehicles reduced energy use and greenhouse gas emissions by about 40% compared to conventional steel vehicles. Argonne Laboratory studied on electric vehicle to calculate the energy use and emissions of different types of batteries in 1998, and found that because of the heavier weight of the battery, the replacement of a battery at least once during the using of vehicle, the battery need more energy use and emissions compared to other parts of the manufacturing process and compared to conventional vehicles in the process of the production of electric cars are relatively large. In 2000, MIT researchers studied the energy use and greenhouse gas emissions of medium passenger vehicles of 11 different fuels and vehicle technologies. Delucchi updated the life cycle emission model in 2003, including life cycle of fuels, vehicles, materials and infrastructure. And the whole life of the vehicle is made up of vehicle material, vehicle transportation, vehicle assembly, vehicle maintenance.

(3) Life cycle of infrastructure

More and more attention has been paid to the social and environmental impacts of the transportation system, and it has been an area of intensive research efforts. Infrastructure is an important auxiliary facility for vehicle operation, where the construction of road system is an important part of transportation infrastructure construction including road construction, road lights, traffic signal control and road signs, etc..

From an environmental point of view, it is generally believed that the impact of road construction, road maintenance and road operation on the environment is less than vehicles'. But from the perspective of life cycle of infrastructure and vehicle operation, the theory has not been clearly proven and also does not have quantitative calculation formula.

Studying on road system with life cycle analysis includes the extraction of raw materials, building materials production, road construction, road maintenance and road operation and the road scrapped demolition. The Intermodal Surface Transportation Equity Act suggested life cycle analysis should be considered in pavement design in 1991. "National Highway System (NHS) Directive Action" required all high-cost projects (more than $25 million) to undergo full life analysis. With the assistance of the Swedish national highway department, Swedish Environmental Research Institute evaluates the life cycle of the road construction, road maintenance and road operation. The use of the model in the current stage of life cycle analysis is a certain authoritative, the next section will take this model as an example. The road system includes not only the asphalt layer, concrete and stone materials, but also traffic signal control systems, road lighting facilities, traffic sign facilities, bridges and tunnels, etc. Because of the difference of geo-technical and meteorological conditions, geographical location and traffic density, the road system has its unique diversity. Therefore, it is necessary to establish a dynamic model to simulate the activities of the system under different time and conditions. The full life inventory data lists the different stages of measurement data, including energy consumption, emissions and raw material consumption and other data.

The life cycle analysis model of Sweden is currently the most authoritative one. The core problem of the model analysis is the application of pavement materials to make the life optimal, and the analysis of pavement materials includes concrete pavement, hot mix asphalt pavement, cold mix asphalt pavement. Due to the different emission factors, fuel consumption and other parameters of different types of vehicle engines, therefore, the model assumes that the vehicles on the road installed engines is conventional diesel engines, or modern low emission diesel engines. This model utilizes "functional unit" to simplify system and "functional unit" is a 1 km long and 13 m wide road. The model is used to analyze the energy consumption and emissions of pavement materials in 40 years.

11.2.2 Life Cycle of Transportation System

From the perspective of time, the whole life cycle of transportation system is the life cycle of transportation system including preliminary planning, road design, road construction, road maintenance and road demolition. Taking the road transport system as an example, this chapter analyzes the life cycle of each component of the road traffic system, and it is mainly composed of three parts: fuel, vehicle and infrastructure.

The life cycle of fuel is mainly divided into two parts: well-pump (WTP) and pump-wheel (PTW). The life cycle of WTP includes electricity and transportation emissions of two parts: the oil well to the refinery, the refinery to the gas station. And PTW is mainly concerned with the emission of vehicle fuel combustion.

The life cycle of vehicle is presented in Fig. 11-7.

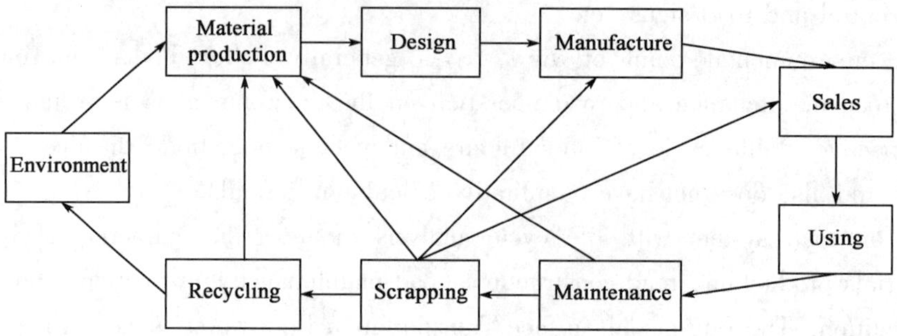

Figure 11-7 Life cycle analysis component of vehicle

Source: *Liu Ruijun*, 2009.

The life cycle of the infrastructure refers to the life cycle of the road and its ancillary facilities. Life cycle analysis of road may be divided into design, construction, management, maintenance, operation and scrapping. Some resources are consumed in design such as labors, electricity, etc., and this phase isn't considered in this chapter. In construction, it mainly takes into account the energy and emissions of energy and materials produced by the production process, fuel consumption and emissions of vehicles or ships to transport materials, fuel consumption and emissions of various vehicles and machinery in road engineering construction. In management and maintenance, applying the methods which are used in construction to this phase and the mainly considerations are fuel consumption and emissions of various maintenance vehicles and machinery. In operation, the main analysis is energy consumption and emissions of the signal lamp, lighting and other peripheral equipment. The scrap stage can be regarded as the inverse process of construction stage including demolishing, transportation, sorting, handling, recycling and reusing, materials.

The emission sources in the life cycle analysis are as follows:

· Fuel combustion. For example, fuel combustion in vehicle driving.

· Evaporation and leakage of raw materials and finished products. For example, evaporation of hydrocarbons in gasoline storage terminals.

· Ventilation and leakage of gas mixture. For example, ventilation of coal bed methane in coal mine.

· Non burning chemical reaction.

11.2.3 Fuel Cycle

Fuel cycle is an important part in life cycle analysis of transportation system, and the cycle process is as follows:

· Raw material production: mainly including energy exploitation and oil production process, for example, exploitation and production of crude oil, coal or biomass energy.

· Transportation of raw material: the process of transporting raw materials to fuel production facilities. For example, transporting crude oil from oil fields to refineries.

· Fuel production: raw materials are converted into finished product fuel or energy carrier. For example, crude oil or coal is converted to gasoline and electricity.

· Fuel transportation and storage: to transport the finished product to the end user or large service facilities. For example, gasoline will be transported for use or storage by truck to a service station, gas station, etc..

· Fuel reprocessing: high pressure pumps for liquid fuel and compression and liquefaction for gaseous fuel.

· End use: consumers use finished fuel products. For example, vehicles driving consume gasoline, diesel and other fuels.

At present, GREET model is an authoritative and international fuel cycle model. The model can be used to calculate the energy efficiency (Btu/mile) and emission rate (g/mile) of various fuel and vehicle technologies. In the GREET model, the fuel cycle is divided into three processes: production, transportation and storage of basic materials; production, transportation and storage of fuel; emissions of fuel combustion and other chemicals during vehicle operation. The energy efficiency and emission rate of three processes are calculated by the model, and calculating the total energy consumption and emissions. Then according to the change of fuel economy, the energy consumption and emissions of other alternative energy vehicles are inferred from standard gasoline or diesel vehicles. It is defined that the stage before the vehicle running is called the upper stage and the vehicle running is called the lower stage. Taking GREET 1.5 as an example to introduce energy consumption and emission of more than 30 fuels cycle in this section. And 13 feeds and 14 fuels are presented in Table 11-6.

Table 11-6 Fuel cycle in GREET 1.5

Primary energy	Fuel
Oil	Conventional gasoline
	Reformulated gasoline
	Conventional diesel
	New formula diesel
	Liquefied petroleum gas
	Residual oil generation
Natural gas	compressed natural gas
	Liquified natural gas
	Liquefied petroleum gas
	Ethanol
	dimethyl ether
	Gaseous hydrogen/concentrator
	Gaseous hydrogen/gas station
	Liquid hydrogen
	Fischer Tropsch diesel
	Electric

continued

<table>
<tr><th>Primary energy</th><th>Fuel</th></tr>
<tr><td rowspan="3">Flare gas</td><td>Ethanol</td></tr>
<tr><td>Dimethyl ether</td></tr>
<tr><td>Fischer Tropsch diesel</td></tr>
<tr><td>coal</td><td rowspan="3">Electric</td></tr>
<tr><td>uranium</td></tr>
<tr><td>Hydropower, solar and wind power</td></tr>
<tr><td>Corn: dry grinding</td><td rowspan="4">Ethanol</td></tr>
<tr><td>Corn: wet grinding</td></tr>
<tr><td>Woody biomass</td></tr>
<tr><td>Herbaceous biomass</td></tr>
<tr><td rowspan="2">Solar energy(through water electrolysis)</td><td>Gaseous hydrogen</td></tr>
<tr><td>Liquid hydrogen</td></tr>
<tr><td>Oybean</td><td>Biodiesel</td></tr>
<tr><td>Landfill gas</td><td>Ethanol</td></tr>
</table>

Source: *Wang*, 1999.

(1) Calculate the energy consumption of each stage of the upper

To calculate energy consumption and emission of fuel cycle, the GREET model calculates energy consumption (unit: Btu-British thermal units) and emission (unit: g/106 Btu). Then, the total energy consumption and emissions of the upstream stage are obtained by adding the energy use and emissions of all upstream stages.

$$\text{Energy}_{\text{in}} = \text{Energy}_{\text{out}} / \text{Efficiency} \tag{11-11}$$

where, $\text{Energy}_{\text{in}}$ means energy input at a given stage; Efficiency means unit energy output divided by energy input at a given stage including Energy supply and process fuel.

Total energy input consists of energy supply and process fuel of production processing. There are three possibilities for output process. The first possibility, all input energy supplies generate fuel by combustion such as generation process. The second, most of the input energy supplies generate fuels by chemical conversion, and the rest of the feed generate the required quality of heat or steam by burning such as the natural gas is converted to methanol, hydrogen, dimethyl ether and Fischer Tropsch diesel. The last possibility, the process of producing fuel does not contain chemical reactions such as compressed natural gas, liquefied natural gas. In this case, the production of a unit of fuel corresponds to enter a unit of energy supply, the rest of the input is a process fuel. The follow equation is used to compute the required process fuels.

$$\text{Process fuels} = 1/\text{Efficiency} - 1 \tag{11-12}$$

where, Process fuels required to generate a unit of energy at a given stage.

The total process fuel required for a given stage of production is allocated to a variety of fuels. For example, production of 106 Btu fuel requires 103 Btu process fuel, and GREET model defines the classification of fuel in 103 Btu process fuels such as diesel oil, residual oil and electricity. Because of the different emission factors of different fuel types, which basically determined the emissions, this allocation process is important for calculating emissions. The proportion of fuel required for each process in each stage can be obtained based on empirical data.

(2) Calculation on the emissions of each process of the upper stage

Based on the gas emissions per 106Btu energy consumption (g/106Btu), calculating the emissions of VOC, CO, NO_x, PM10, SO_x, CH_4, N_2O and CO_2 in a certain stage. Emissions sources include combustion emissions, non-combustion emissions, such as chemical reactions, fuel leakage and fuel evaporation.

For process combustion emissions in a given stage, the formula of emissions is as follows:

$$EM_{cm,j} = (\sum_j \sum_k EF_{i,j,k} \times EC_{j,k}) \div 1000000 \tag{11-13}$$

where, $EM_{cm,j}$ is the emission of the pollutant i in combustion; $EF_{i,j,k}$ is the emission factor of process fuels j, pollutant i and combustion technology k; $EC_{j,k}$ is the input quality in the under of process fuels j and combustion technology k.

In the stage, the formula of $EC_{j,k}$ is as follows:

$$EC_{j,k} = EC \times Share_{fuelj} \times Share_{techk,j} \tag{11-14}$$

where, in this stage, EC is the total energy consumption, seen in Eq. (11-11) and Eq. (11-12); $Share_{fuelj}$ is process fuel j accounts for the proportion of total process fuel; $Share_{techk,j}$ is process fuel j and combustion technology k accounts for the proportion of all combustion technology ($\sum_{techk,j=1}$).

For given process fuel, the proportion of each combustion technology is affected by the technical performance, cost and emission regulations. These factors are changing over time, therefore GREET model has two kinds of emission factor including current and future emission factors. The emission factors of VOC, CO, NO_x, PM10, SO_x, CH_4, N_2O and CO_2 can be obtained in U. S. Environmental Protection Agency. The emission factors of CO_2 and SO_x have their own formulas, but they are not described here.

For non-combustion emission, some emission sources as follows are considered in GREET model.

- For liquid fuels, considering evaporative emissions of VOC; fuel spill of feed fuel and fuel in transportation, storage and distribution.
- For oil fuel, considering the spark of oilfield associated gas, ventilation emission and emissions in petroleum refinery.
- For nature gas fuel, considering the leakage in transportation, the emission of CH_4 in disposing process and the emission of CO_2 in production.
- For ethanol and biodiesel, there are NO_x and N_2O emissions in nitrification and denitrification of nitrogen fertilizer needed to grow corn, soybean and biomass.
- In the cycle of coal-fired power, CH_4 emission of coal mining and processing.

(3) Energy consumption and emissions of fuel cycle in the upper

In the upper stage, fuel combustion, transportation and distribution processes generate energy consumption and emissions. In a certain upper stage, integrating upstream energy consumption and emissions, and converting energy usage to emissions. The following formula can be used to calculate:

$$EM_i = [\sum_j (EM_{cm,\,i,\,j} + EF_{up,\,i,\,j}) \times EC_j] \div 1000000 \qquad (11\text{-}15)$$

where, EM_i is the emission of the pollutant i(g/10^6 Btu); $EM_{cm,\,i,\,j}$ is the emission of pollutant i in fuel production j (g/10^6 Btu), seen in Eq. (11-13); $EF_{up,\,i,\,j}$ is the emission of pollutant i in of fuel j (g/10^6 Btu). EC_j is the consumption of fuel j, seen in Eq. (11-11) or Eq. (11-12).

(4) Total energy consumption and emissions for fuel cycle

In the third part of the section, the consumptions and emissions of each stage of the upper have been computed, but fuel loss may occur in each stage, so the energy consumption and emissions of each stage cannot be simply added.

If fuel loss does not occur, without considering the process fuel, the finally 10^6 Btu fuel will only need 10^6 Btu feed. But if fuel loss occurs, the finally 10^6 Btu fuel will need no less than 10^6 Btu feed. Therefore, energy consumption and emissions at each stage of upstream should be adjusted to meet the actual demand. So, adjusted energy consumption and emissions can be summed up for total energy consumption and emissions.

The proportion of fuel loss in many stages of upstream is close to or equal to 0, consequently, the fuel loss factor is close to or equal to 1 in most cases. However, liquid fuels and gaseous fuels exist fuel volatilization and leakage in transportation and storage. Volatilization and leakage of fuel will discharge VOC or other components in most cases.

(5) Energy consumption and emissions of vehicle operation

The unit of energy consumption and emissions in the vehicle operation phase is miles, and the final energy consumption unit is Btu/mile, the unit is g/mile. In vehicle running, energy consumption and emissions mainly include two aspects. On the one hand, it is the transportation and distribution of feed and fuel in the upstream stage. On the other hand, it is the process of vehicles running on the road in the downstream stage. And the energy consumption is calculated by the fuel economy of the vehicle.

In GREET model, the fuel economy of each vehicle type is obtained by calculating the economy of gasoline. And the fuel economy of standard gasoline vehicles can be directly obtained from prediction result of the DOE's energy information administration. And the fuel economy of the standard diesel vehicles equals the fuel economy of standard gasoline vehicles multiplied by the fuel economy improvement rate, for example, the fuel economy of conventional compression ignition diesel vehicles is 35% higher than that of gasoline vehicles. The use of alternative fuels such as spark and compression ignition, the fuel economy of the vehicle will change, so the calculation of emissions should be multiplied by the corresponding emission reduction rate. The emissions of VOC, CO, NO_x, CH_4, N_2O of standard gasoline vehicles and standard diesel vehicles can be calculated directly or indirectly by the Mobile 5B model of the Environmental Protection Agency of the United States, and the result can be applied to GREET model. PM10 emissions are calculated by Part 5 of the U. S. Environmental Protection Agency, the emission of SO_x can be obtained directly in the GREET model, and CO_2 is obtained by the method of carbon conservation. Besides, vehicle VOC emissions include exhausting, evaporation, operating loss, resting loss and refueling emissions, vehicle PM emissions include exhaust gas, tire wear and brake wear, and other emissions of pollutants exist only in the exhaust gas.

(6) Total energy consumption and emissions of fuel cycle

In the fourth part of this section, the calculation methods of energy consumption and emissions in the upstream stage are introduced and the units are Btu and g/10^6 Btu, and the energy consumption and emissions of each vehicle are introduced in the fifth part and the units are Btu/mile and g/mile. Therefore, in order to calculate the total energy consumption and emissions, it is necessary to add energy consumption and emissions at the upstream and downstream stages. In GREET model, the upstream energy consumption and emissions are converted into mile based units, namely, energy consumption and emissions per mile equal to the energy consumption and emissions per 10^6 Btu were divided by the energy consumption per mile of vehicles, then energy consumption and emissions can be summed up in the upstream and downstream stages, and the vehicle's energy consumption per mile is based on the fuel economy of the vehicle.

(7) Total urban emissions of five standard pollutants

The five standard pollutants in GREET model——VOC, CO, NO_x, PM10 and SO_x——usually cause local air pollution, consequently the location an emissions are necessary considered. According to the different discharge positions, the GREET model measures the emission of five standard pollutants with total emissions and urban emissions. Total emissions are the total amount of emissions that occur throughout the various stages of the fuel cycle and urban emissions occur only within the boundaries of a given urban area.

Depending on the location of the vehicle, emissions in the vehicle operation phase may occur inside the city or outside the city. The location of the upstream stage is determined by the location of the facility which is subject to raw material supply, the transportation cost of raw materials, and the emission standards stipulated by the city. Because of the raw materials (oil, natural gas, biomass etc.) are usually located outside the city, and the transportation cost of raw materials is much higher than the transportation cost of fuel, so the upstream stage emission sites are often located in the city outside except for fuel distribution.

In whole processes, due to emissions often occur in different time and place, when accurately calculating air quality and emissions, it is necessary to adjust according to the different time, but when the fuel production and consumption balance, the influence of this factor can be ignored.

The calibration of the parameters is not specific in this section such as the efficiency of the fuel, the proportion of the process fuel, the proportion and the emission rate of a given fuel combustion technology, etc..

The energy consumption of the fuel cycle in the GREET model is calculated as 10^6 Btu. The total energy consumption of each stage is calculated for the energy consumption and emissions of the upstream stage. The model includes a database of combustion factors generated by the combination of various process fuels and various combustion technologies, which can be used to calculate the combustion emissions in each process. Among them, the main emissions of the vehicle during the operation phase include the exhaust emissions, volatile VOC emissions, tire wear PM10, etc..

11.2.4 Vehicle Cycle

The fuel cycle in the GREET1.5 model described in the section 4 and section 5 in this chapter includes fuel cycle and vehicle operation. But in this section, the vehicle cycle described in the GREET 2.7 model includes the energy consumption and emissions of different vehicle types and vehicle materials. The vehicle cycle includes the following processes: the recovery and reuse of the vehicle material, the vehicle component production, the vehicle assembly, the vehicle operation and the vehicle scrapping. And the vehicle operation phase belongs to the fuel cycle stage and the vehicle circulation stage. At present, the model can calculate the energy consumption and emission such as the vehicle component production, battery production, liquid production and use, vehicle assembly, scrapping and recycling. But it doesn't include energy consumption and emissions of raw materials or vehicle transportation. As the location of each production process has an important impact on urban air pollution, it is necessary to do further study. Meanwhile, the model does not take into account the costs of user's vehicle and fuel, raw material supply and resource consumption, industry and government support for new technologies, consumer acceptance of new technologies and other factors, so it cannot provide comprehensive information for decision makers.

As shown in Fig. 11-8, the energy consumption and emission data of fuel cycle combustion calculated by GREET1 model are input into GREET2. The results of fuel cycle and vehicle operation are used to calculate the total energy of the vehicle cycle. When calculating the energy consumption and emissions, the vehicle cycle is divided into 4 groups: vehicle materials; batteries; liquid for vehicles; vehicle assembly, scrap and recycling. The vehicle materials include the raw materials reuse, transportation and processing, and the vehicle materials production, manufacture and processing. The battery includes the production and manufacture of battery material. Vehicle liquids include refrigerants, lubricating oil, glass-water, steering fluid, brake fluid, gearbox oil production, and scrapping. Vehicle assembly, scrapping and recovery include scrapping and recycling, vehicle assembly and paint. In Fig. 11-9, it shows the total life cycle of the fuel cycle in the upstream stage——well to pump(the blue part)——the downstream stage of the fuel cycle——the pump to well(the green part), and the vehicle cycle(the red part).

(1) Vehicle specifications

The vehicle specifications have a great influence on the vehicle performance. At the same time, the materials quantity of each type of vehicle is calculated separately. The total weight of the vehicle is mainly composed of three parts: the parts of the vehicle, the battery and all kinds of liquid. The parts of the vehicle include eight main systems: the body system, the power system, the transmission, the chassis, the electric motor, the generator, the electric controller and the fuel cell appendage. These eight systems do not necessarily exist in a certain type of vehicle such as internal combustion engine vehicles include only the body, power system, rotating device and chassis. The battery system includes a lead battery and fittings for starting. For hybrid electric vehicles and fuel cell vehicles, the power drive systems may also include NiMH batteries or lithium batteries. The liquid used in the vehicle includes the lubricating oil of the engine, the fluid in the power steering, the brake oil, the lubricating oil of the automatic transmission, the cooling fluid of the transmission system, the glass-water and the adhesive, etc.

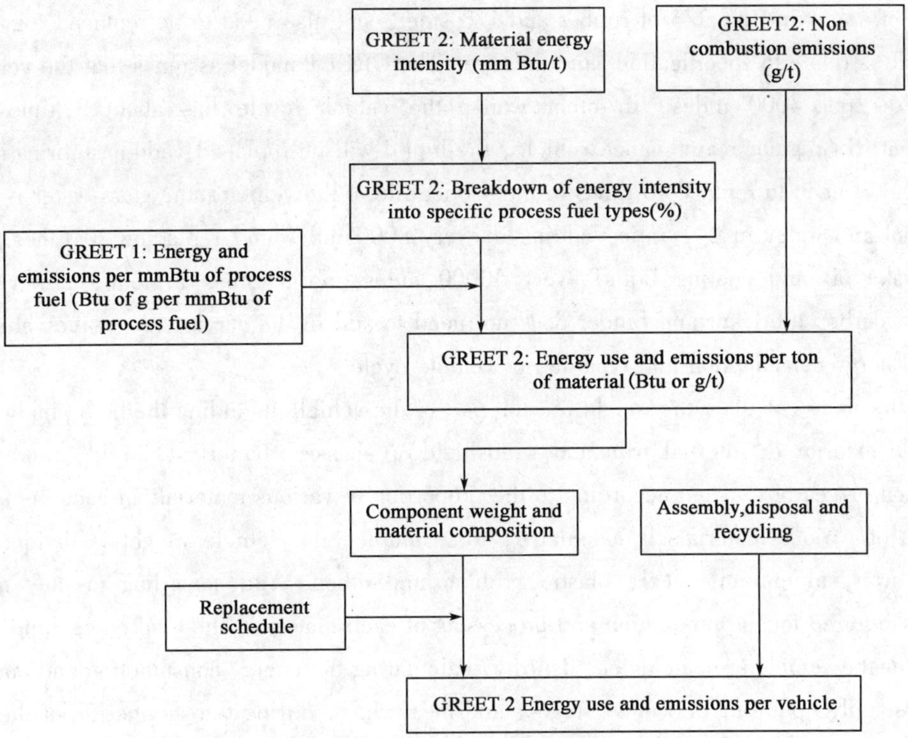

Figure11-8 Logic simulation analysis of vehicle cycle in GREET model

Source: *A. Burnham, et al.*, 2006.

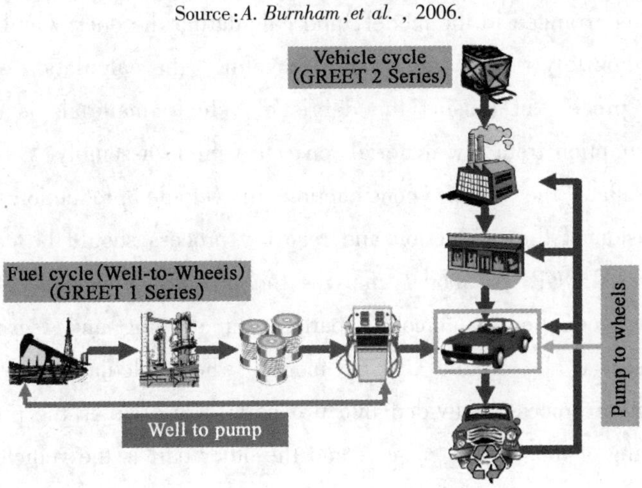

Figure 11-9 Fuel and vehicle cycle diagram

Source: *A. Burnham, et al.*, 2006.

(2) Replacement of batteries, tires and liquid in vehicles

In vehicle cycle, the batteries, tires and vehicle fluids need to be replaced according to their situation. So it is necessary to consider the energy consumption and emissions in the manufacturing, transportation, maintenance and so on. In addition to considering the different types of batteries used in different vehicle types, the frequencies of battery replacement should also be considered in the vehicle life. The replacement time is mainly related to the mileage of vehicles. GREET model uses the average life value which a passenger car battery traveling 160000 miles in VISION model. Tires are made of approximately 2/3 of rubber and 1/3 steel, and also need to be replaced regularly, the average life is relate to specifications and mileage. The GREET model assumes that the vehicle need replace tires per 4000 miles, in other word, the vehicle cycle has about 3 times in tires replacement. In regular maintenance vehicle, the liquid will be replaced: adding lubricating oil per 4000 miles, it need to replace 40 times in the service life of the vehicle; the glass-water is a mixture of methanol and water in 1∶1 ratio, adding it every 8000 miles and replacing 20 times in a life; adding brake oil and cooling liquid every 40000 miles and 3 times in total; power steering, automatic gearbox lubricant and binder does not need to add in the service life of the vehicle.

(3) Energy consumption and emission of vehicle cycle

The first is to calculate the weight of each part of the vehicle including the body (body in white, the vehicle exterior or internal trim and windshield), chassis, batteries, liquid, power system, transmission or gearbox. Then according to the proportion of various materials in each vehicle parts, the weight of various materials is calculated, for example, the vehicle weight is divided into the weight of iron, aluminum, steel, plastic, rubber and other. And according to the energy and emissions required for the production and processing of each material, the total energy and emissions required for the vehicle are calculated. Thirdly, calculating the energy consumption and emissions of vehicle assembly, painting and other stages, and meanwhile, during the service life of the vehicle, the batteries, tires and various vehicles liquid are changed periodically, and the corresponding replacement schedule is arranged in the model, and calculating the energy and emissions required to replace the material. Fourthly, for scrapping and recycling, the calculation of energy consumption and emissions in the process of reusing the debris of vehicle materials is carried out. Finally, calculate energy consumption from raw material reuse to vehicle assembly.

In order to calculate the energy consumption in vehicle production process, the energy consumption and emission of the production and recovery process should be calculated according to different types of material. GREET model analyzes the process of each vehicle material from raw material and material production, automobile parts manufacturing and recycling. Similar to the calculation of the energy cycle, in the GREET model, when calculating energy consumption and emissions, the calculation process is divided into two parts. One part is the production, processing, manufacturing, recycling of the "upper stage", and the other part is the vehicle assembly, scrapping and recycling of the "downstream stage". In the first part, the energy consumption and emissions are calculated in the production process and calculating energy consumption and emissions in each production step of each vehicle material. The types of materials include metal, glass, plastic, rubber, liquid for automobile, composition of battery and fuel cell. In the second part, in the automated vehicle assembly plant, GREET model mainly calculates energy consumption and emissions of vehicle assembly, painting and vehicle scrapping and recycling process. These work-welding, assembly and painting are mainly finished in the vehicle assembly plant, and the energy consumption and emission of welding is very low, so GREET model only takes into account the assembly and painting process. It is assumed that the energy required for each medium passenger car assembly is about 3.9×10^6 Btu, by calculating, paint industrial energy consumption is about 0.96×10^6 Btu accounted for 1/5 in total energy of the assembly plant, so it shows that the VOC emissions of the industry are quite large. The model also calculates the energy consumption and emissions of the battery assembly and inspection, because the current market is still dominated by lead-acid batteries, the assembly of each ton of lead-acid batteries requires 27.5×10^6 Btu energy. As for vehicle scrapping and recycling——it includes only the recycle of the vehicle, because the energy required for the recovery of the vehicle material and the material has been calculated in the first part, for scrapping and recycling, about 1.4×10^6 Btu energy are required per 3000 pounds of vehicle by calculating.

In this section, calculate the total energy consumption of medium passenger car production and scrapping process, fossil oil energy consumption, oil energy consumption, greenhouse gases emissions(methane, carbon dioxide, nitrogen oxide two) and pollutants emissions (VOC, CO, NO_x, PM10 and SO_x). By integrating 11.2.3 and 11.2.4, the GREET model calculates the energy consumption and emissions of three stages——fuel cycle, vehicle cycle and vehicle operation phase.

11.2.5 Life Cycle of Infrastructure

The infrastructure life cycle described in this section refers to the life cycle analysis of the road including the extraction of raw materials, the production of building materials, construction process, road maintenance, road operation, road demolition and road scrapping. The greatest difference between road construction and other manufacturing processes is construction conditions. The construction conditions are different in different locations and even in the same line.

(1) Model structure

The first stage of life cycle of road is the planning and construction phase, it mainly carries out road construction and related facilities construction including excavation and filling of road alignment, foundation reinforcement. The next stage is road operation and maintenance: the operation phase includes road maintenance, cleaning and weeding, peripheral facilities maintenance; the maintenance phase is mainly to repair the damaged road ensure the road safety, comfort. The frequency of road operation and road maintenance is affected by the factors such as road grade and traffic flow and it is also adjusted in road service.

When a newly-built road replace the old road, the original road usually is not demolished but in idle state. The road construction has the maximum emissions of NO_x, SO_2, CO_2, followed by the maintenance phase(NO_x emissions is larger), while emissions of road operation accounted for only a small part of the total emissions (Because Sweden mainly rely on water conservancy and nuclear power generation, NO_x, SO_2, CO_2 emission is low). The structure of the life cycle analysis model of the road is shown in Fig. 11-10.

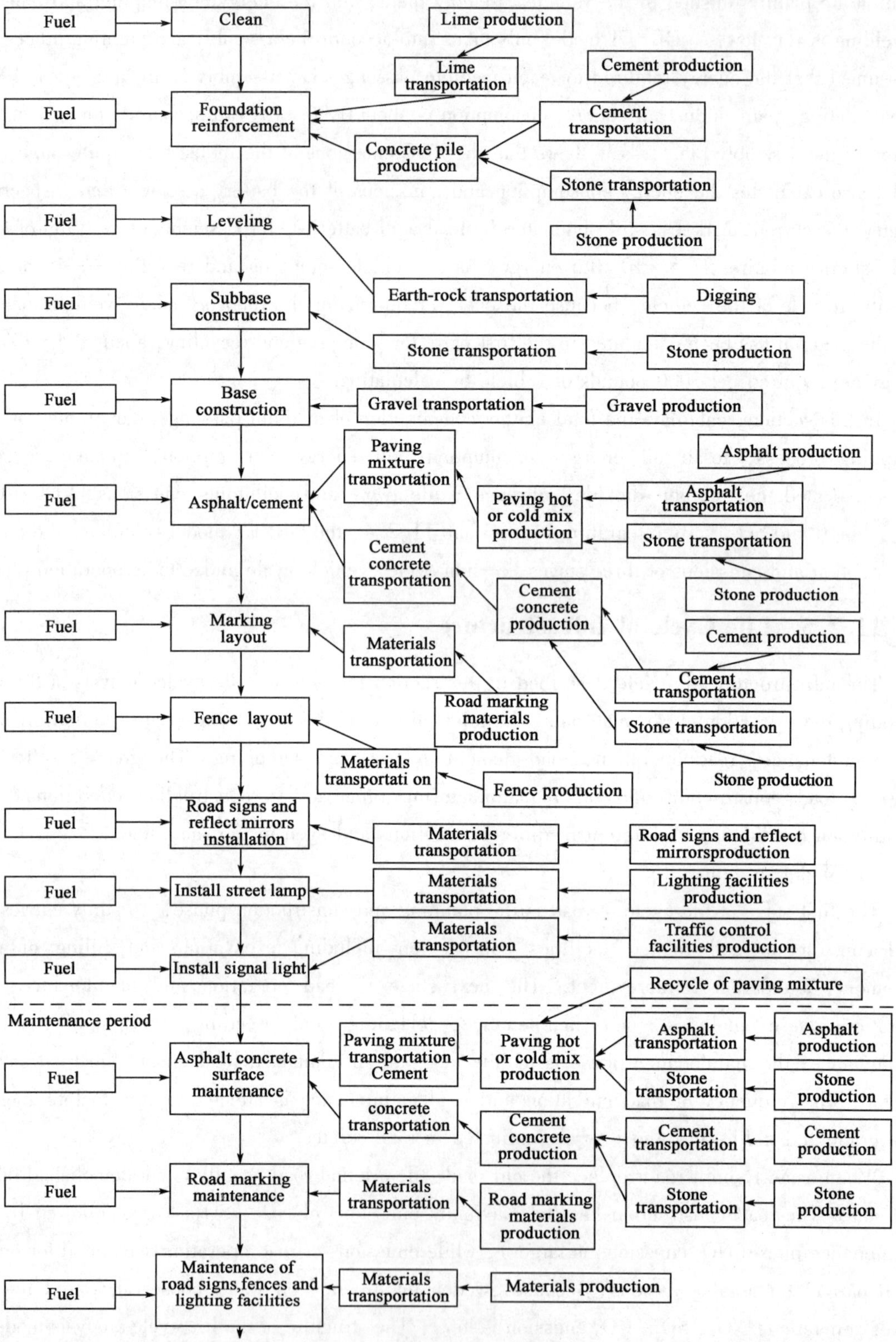
Fuel
Clean
Lime production
Lime transportation
Cement production
Fuel
Foundation reinforcement
Cement transportation
Concrete pile production
Stone transportation
Fuel
Leveling
Stone production
Fuel
Subbase construction
Earth-rock transportation
Digging
Stone transportation
Stone production
Fuel
Base construction
Gravel transportation
Gravel production
Paving mixture transportation
Asphalt production
Fuel
Asphalt/cement
Paving hot or cold mix production
Asphalt transportation
Stone transportation
Cement concrete transportation
Stone production
Cement concrete production
Fuel
Marking layout
Cement production
Materials transportation
Cement transportation
Road marking materials production
Fuel
Fence layout
Stone transportation
Materials transportati on
Fence production
Stone production
Fuel
Road signs and reflect mirrors installation
Materials transportation
Road signs and reflect mirrorsproduction
Fuel
Install street lamp
Materials transportation
Lighting facilities production
Materials transportation
Traffic control facilities production
Fuel
Install signal light
Recycle of paving mixture
Maintenance period
Asphalt concrete surface maintenance
Fuel
Paving mixture transportation Cement
Paving hot or cold mix production
Asphalt transportation
Asphalt production
Stone transportation
Stone production
concrete transportation
Cement concrete production
Cement transportation
Cement production
Fuel
Road marking maintenance
Materials transportation
Road marking materials production
Stone transportation
Stone production
Fuel
Maintenance of road signs,fences and lighting facilities
Materials transportation
Materials production

Figure 11-10

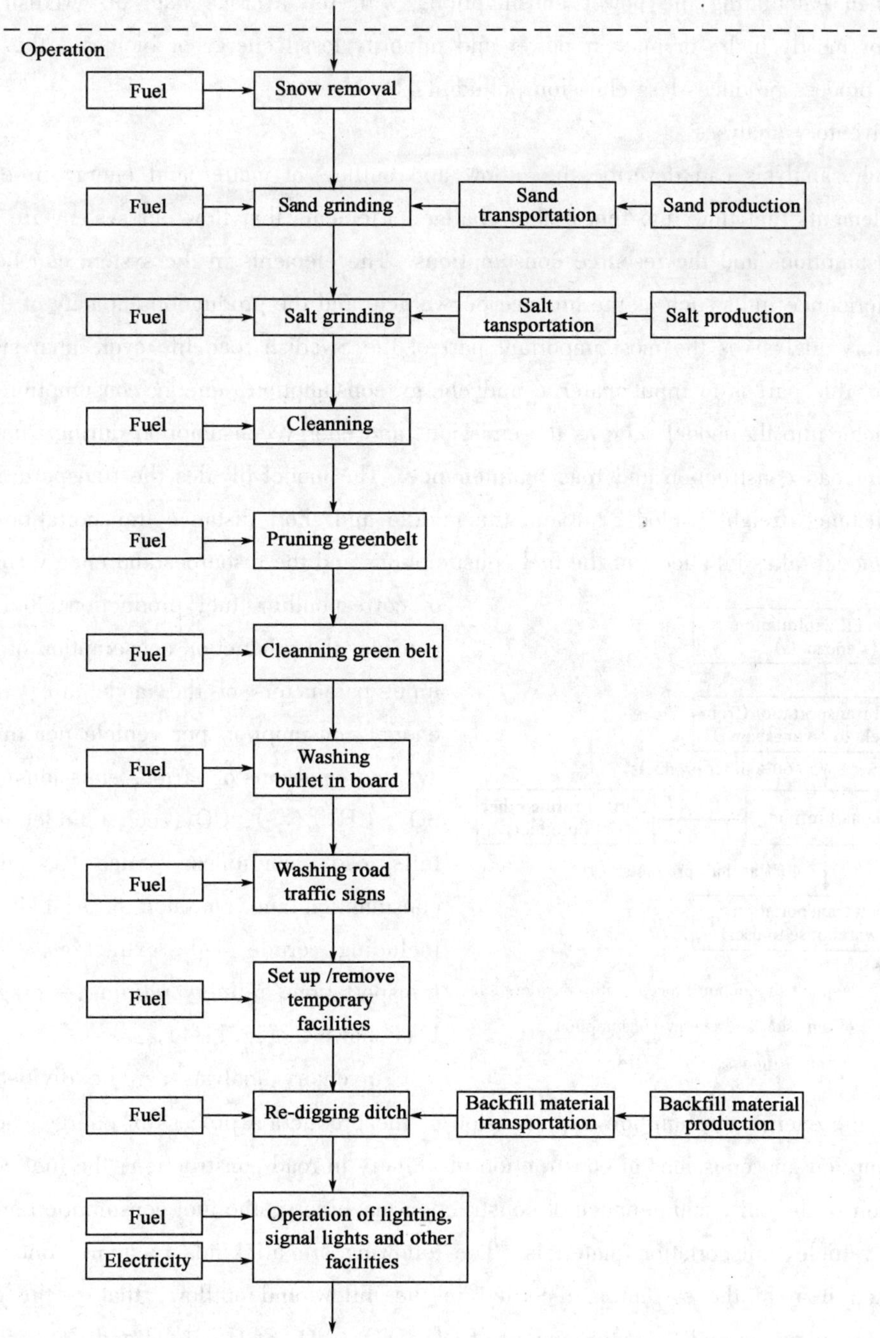

Figure 11-10 Structure of the life cycle analysis model of the road

Source: *Håkan Stripple*, 2001.

The Swedish road life cycle analysis model does not include the energy consumption and emissions generated by the machinery production. It contains only the fuel consumption by the machine and the energy consumption for the fuel production. In addition, the energy consumption and emissions of building oil refineries, cement plants and asphalt factories are not included in the model. When calculating the power consumption, with the average data of Swedish electricity generated by mostly hydro or nuclear power and minority fossil energy or biomass, thus electricity production process produces less emission pollutants.

(2) Inventory analyses

Inventory analysis can describe the inflow and outflow of matter and energy in the system. Tracking elements that flow into the system change. Elements that flow out system are emissions, energy consumptions and the resource consumptions. The elements in the system can be measured by the performance units such as the mileage per vehicle and the production capacity of the asphalt.

Inventory analysis is the most important part of the Swedish road life cycle analysis, and the main task of this part is to input material and energy consumption, energy consumption factor and emission factor into the model such as the emissions and energy consumption during trucking which happened in road construction and road maintenance. The model divides the transportation process into long distance freight loaded 32 t and the middle and short distance transportation loaded 14 tons. The model takes into account the fuel consumptions and the resources and energy consumptions of corresponding fuel production, but it doesn't consider the production consumption of truck. The input parameters of the model are: the average energy consumption per vehicle per mile and the average emissions of various emissions (CO, NO_x, SO_2, CH_4, N_2O, CO_2, etc.) under no-load and full load conditions. Such as the energy consumption and emission of asphalt production including crude oil extraction, oil tanker transportation, refinery refining, storage process. It is shown in Fig. 11-11.

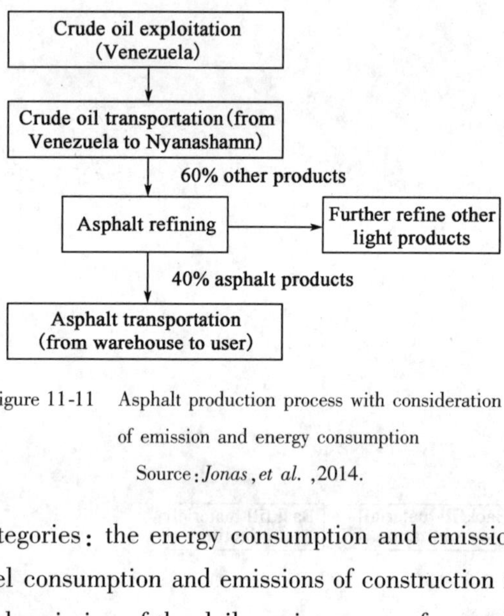

Figure 11-11 Asphalt production process with consideration of emission and energy consumption

Source: *Jonas, et al.*, 2014.

Inventory analysis can be divided into four categories: the energy consumption and emission of the production process of energy and material; fuel consumption and emissions of construction machinery in road construction; the fuel consumption and emission of the daily maintenance of construction machinery; the fuel consumption and emission of ship or vehicle transportation materials. The following are all kinds of items contained in the system, each item in the system is recorded in the inflow and outflow, that is the energy and resources consumptions and the total amount of CO, NO_x, SO_2, CH_4, N_2O and CO_2 emissions.

· The total energy consumption and emissions of energy and material production processes include:

a. Electricity production: oil, gas, coal and other resource consumption and emissions of the production process; b. asphalt production; c. hot mix asphalt production; d. cold mix asphalt production; e. crushed stone production; f. the extraction of natural gravel material; g. raw lime production; h. cement production; i. concrete production: the cement, sand, stone and water mixed with a certain proportion; j. polyethylene plastic production; k. synthetic rubber production: This material is used for concrete pavement junction; l. winter road maintenance salt production: for winter pavement antifreeze; m. aluminum: mainly used in road signs, lights, lighting and other peripheral equipment manufacturing; n. steel production: mainly used in the concrete road reinforcement and road traffic signs, lights, lighting and other peripheral equipment; o. making zinc: for hot-dip galvanized steel; p. road signs, lighting equipment, lights and other guard rails and other peripheral equipment manufacturing, installation of energy consumption, operating power consumption and so on.

· Fuel consumption and emissions of construction machinery in road construction include:

a. Logging before road construction wheel loader: mechanical fuel consumption and emissions are associate with excavation level (according to the density of excavated soil composition, and the difficulty of mining operations is divided into five level, the grade higher, the much energy consumption); b. excavator: mechanical fuel consumption and emissions are associate with excavation level; c. the automatic tilting car: mechanical fuel consumption and emissions are associate with driving conditions of construction site; d. the roller: mechanical fuel consumption and emissions related with road material and vehicle type; e. asphalt paver; f. paved asphalt emulsifier coating: mechanical fuel consumption and emissions relate with machine type and coating thickness; g. cement/lime pile reinforcement foundation: including material consumption and drilling machine fuel consumption; h. concrete pile reinforcement foundation: including material consumption and piling machine fuel consumption; i. concrete road construction in the grassroots cement stability; j. laying concrete surface layer; k. laying aggregate in concrete lane: it can be used as a deceleration zone, while preventing a large number of concrete surface water loss; l. concrete pavement joints of the seam and caulking; m. concrete and asphalt pavement grinding; n. road marking the layout; o. animal fence: includes fuel consumption for the guardrail production and installing.

· The fuel consumption and emission of the daily maintenance of construction machinery include:

a. The diesel fuel consumption for maintenance vehicles; b. in winter road maintenance, spread sand non-slip materials: including resource consumption and emissions of driving maintenance vehicles spread anti-skid sand and gravel production; c. winter road maintenance spread salt to reduce the road freezing point: the vehicle fuel consumption and emissions of spreading process; d. clear road snow; e. pruning green belt lawn; f. trimming roadside shrub; g. side ditch digging again, curing time interval generally once for 20 years; h. installing and removing snow days warning column (snow post): warning column generally established in the autumn, the following spring to remove; i. road signs cleaning: the frequency is generally twice a year; j. roadside signs post cleaning: the frequency is generally ten times a year; k. other maintenance activities.

· The fuel consumption and emission of ship or vehicle transportation materials include:

a. emissions and energy consumption during the transportation of goods vehicles; b. emissions and energy consumption during maritime transportation.

11.2.6 Optimal Scheme Comparison and Choice

Considering the alternative fuel, vehicles and infrastructure cycle process, according to the weight coefficient multiplied by the degree which various types of emissions and energy consumption have influence on the environment, the environmental load and total energy consumption of each alternative scheme are calculated. Finally the optimal scheme is selected by comparing each alternative scheme.

11.3 Game Theory

Game theory is a new modern branch of mathematics, and an important component of Operations Research. It mainly studies the equilibrium problems of rational people in the process of making decisions and behaviors.

11.3.1 Basic Theory of Game Theory

The focused issue of game theory is that, under the given information structure, how decision-makers can maximize the utility of the decision and get the balance among other decision-makers. A basic game consists of three elements of the game, that is, the decision-maker, strategies set and utility. Among them, the decision body is the participant or the player; the strategies set, the information structure, are the scope of the available strategies and actions of decision-makers; utility, that is, preference or payoff function, is the interest of decision-maker that can be quantified.

(1) Basic concepts in game theory

Players: in a game, each participant who has the right to make a decision.

Strategies set: in a game, a practical and complete action plan that can be chosen by players is called a strategy. Each person participating in the game has their own strategies set. In general, there are at least two strategies that should be included in each player's strategies set.

Payoff function: in a game, the strategies group that formed by each player in the game is called a situation. That is, the strategies group formed by n players is a situation. The set S of the whole situation can be represented by the Cartesian product of the strategies set in each player. When the situation occurs, the results of the measures will be determined. In other words, for any situation, the player i can get a payoff. Obviously, the situation is a function of S, known as the i-th player's payoff function. In this way, a vector payoff function is obtained.

Equilibrium: the state of the correlative index in a stable is called equilibrium.

(2) The concept of game theory in transportation

In the urban transport system, there is always the competition, interaction and choice between the vehicle and the vehicle, between the vehicle and the pedestrian, and between the pedestrian and the police every day. It can be said that in the process of urban transport system, the game is ubiquitous.

Using the game theory to analyze the urban traffic problem, we can have a deeper apperception and understanding of the traffic phenomenon.

Players: participants of the transport including vehicles, non-motor and pedestrians.

Strategies: when traveling, the travel mode is strategy, such as walking, riding, taking a bus and driving etc.; in the process of trip, compliance or non-compliance with traffic regulations is also the strategy. Players in different games have different strategies.

Payoffs: different travel modes have different costs and benefits. In general, travelers only consider the cost of the certain travel mode they have chosen while they never take into account the impact brought to others; in the process of trip, there will be different payoffs depending on whether it complies with traffic regulation.

Game results: different games will have different results.

11.3.2 Game Theory Case

In 2005, Chen et al. used the game theory to determine reasonable fares of the urban railway. Comparing the changing logistic relationship between the conventional public transport and the rapid railway transport due to the adjustment of fares, the Logit model and the game theory were used to build the reasonable analysis model for urban railway to analyze the phenomenon quantitatively.

(1) The relationship between urban railway revenue and fare

The revenue of urban railway system is mainly affected by passenger flow and fare: $R_r = C_r \cdot Q_r$. Use the Logit model to calculate the choosing probability of urban railway and conventional public transport:

$$P_{ijr} = \frac{\exp(-\theta C_{ijr})}{\sum_k \exp(-\theta C_{ijr})} \tag{11-16}$$

where, P_{ijr} is the sharing rate of the mode r from the traffic zone i to j; θ is coefficient; C_{ijr} is the traffic impedance of the mode r from the traffic zone i to j; C_{ijk} is the traffic impedance of the mode k from the traffic zone i to j.

The traffic impedance is:

$$C_{ijk} = \alpha_1 \cdot T_{ijk} + \alpha_2 \cdot C_k + \alpha_3 \cdot \delta_k \tag{11-17}$$

where, α_1, α_2, α_3 are the weights of each factor; T_{ijk} is the travel time of the mode k from the traffic zone i to j; C_k is the fare of the mode; δ_k is the characteristic parameters related to the mode k influenced by the comfort, punctuality, safety, and so on.

When the railway is completed and open to traffic, the travel time, convenience, comfort and other indicators will not change too much, so fare is the most influential factors on the passenger flow.

If the fares of conventional public transport remain unchanged, the relationship between revenue and fare of the urban railway system is shown in Fig. 11-12 let $\mathrm{d}R_r/\mathrm{d}C_r = 0$, then the optimal fare of railway C_r^* can be calculated.

If the fares of conventional public transport change, the relationship between revenue and fare of

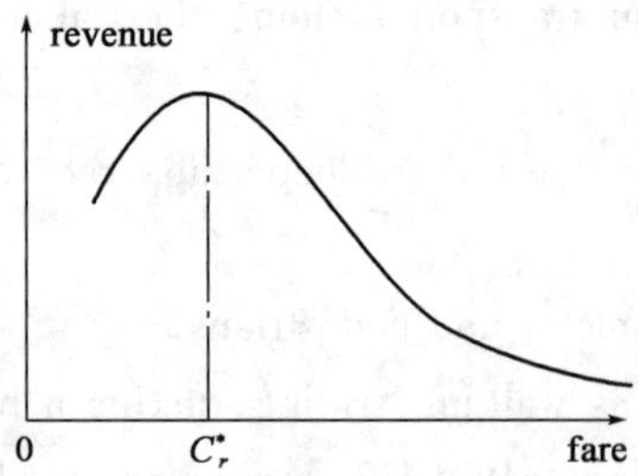

Figure 11-12 Relationship between revenue and fare of the urban railway system

Source: *Chen Kuanmin, et al.* (2005).

the urban railway system need to be examined with the change. At this point, C_r^* is no longer optimal, and the total revenue declines compared to the previous revenue. This shows that the strategy, which simple pursuit for the maximization of their own revenue without considering the action of opponents, cannot achieve the desired effect.

(2) The establishment of game model

The player are railway r and conventional public transport b, and the double matrix game model was established by the game theory:

$$G = [(r, b), (X_r, X_b), (R_r, R_b)] \tag{11-18}$$

where, X_r, X_b are the strategy sets of the player; $X_r = \{C_{1r}, C_{2r}, \cdots, C_{mr}\}$, $X_b = \{C_{1b}, C_{2b}, \cdots, C_{nb}\}$ are the possible fare strategies of railway and conventional public transport; R_r, R_b are the revenue functions of the player (ticket revenue); Agreements are shown as following:

· Decision are made only to maximize each player's own revenue.

· There is a situation (C_r^*, C_b^*), which satisfies:

$$R_r(C_r^*, C_b^*) > R_r(C_r, C_b^*) \tag{11-19}$$

$$R_b(C_r^*, C_b^*) > R_b(C_r^*, C_b) \tag{11-20}$$

If the Eq. (11-19) and Eq. (11-20) are workable at the same time, (C_r^*, C_b^*) is an equilibrium situation.

· Among many equilibrium situations, the most favorable situation strategy (C_r^{**}, C_b^{**}) is obtained to maximize the benefits of players.

In order to obtain the most favorable situation strategy (C_r^{**}, C_b^{**}), relative satisfaction of players are defined:

$$v_k^i(C_{-k}^j) = \frac{R_k(C_k^j, C_{-k}^j)}{\max\limits_{i=1,2,\cdots,m} [R_k(C_k^i, C_{-k}^j)]} \tag{11-21}$$

where, k is the player; $-k$ is the opponent of k; $R_k(C_k^j, C_{-k}^j)$ are the revenues when the player k uses the strategy C_k^i, while his opponent uses the strategy C_k^j.

The equilibrium situation (C_r^*, C_b^*) must satisfy $v_r(C_r^*, C_b^*) + v_b(C_r^*, C_b^*) = 2$. The other situations (C_{ir}, C_{jb}) satisfy $v_r(C_{ir}, C_{jb}) + v_b(C_{ir}, C_{jb}) < 2$. Therefore, as long as the equilibrium situation is found, it is easy to find the most favorable situation by comparing the revenue function to determine the reasonable fare.

11.4 Monte Carlo Simulation

The Monte Carlo method is also known as statistical simulation method, in 1940s, it was proposed by the S. M. and J. Ulam von Neumann who were the "Manhattan plan" members. The Monte Carlo method is a numerical calculation and simulation method which is based on statistical theory, through the research, analysis and experiment of the system model, the information of the real system is obtained which is characterized by simple and fast, and avoiding the mathematical derivation and calculation.

11.4.1 Principles and Procedures of Monte Carlo simulation

(1) The principles of Monte Carlo simulation

Monte Carlo method uses frequency of random events to estimate the probability in order to obtain the solution of the problem. The basic idea is to construct the probability model of the problem, and then calculate the approximate value by calculating the statistical characteristics of parameters. Monte Carlo method is a calculation method.

The basic principle of Monte Carlo simulation method is based on the law of large numbers and the central limit theorem. It assumes function and the probability density distribution of the variables have been known. The Monte Carlo method uses a random number generator to extract the values of each set of random variables directly or indirectly sampling data of function Y can be obtained by repeated independent sampling, and these data meet the characteristics of normal distribution. When the number of simulations is enough, the probability distribution of the function Y which is similar to the actual situation can be inferred, so its numerical characteristics are calculated.

(2) The steps of Monte Carlo method

· For random events, the correct description and simulation are necessary for the probability process and a probabilistic model is established. For non-random events, it needs to be converted into random events, that is, building the probability model with some parameters.

· The probability distribution function of the model is known to produce the random variables with known probability distribution. Random number is the basic tool for the realization of Monte Carlo simulation, a variety of random sampling is based on random numbers, while the uniform distribution is the most widely used probability distribution.

· Determine the random variables, and calculate random sampling data, including the minimum value, the maximum value, the expected value and the standard deviation.

· Repeat step 3 and generate the probability distribution curve of N random samples.

· Repeat the steps 3 and 4, analyze the mean, standard deviation and other statistical characteristics. The solution of the practical problem is obtained.

11.4.2 The Example of Monte Carlo

In 2010, Zhang Xiaohui simulated the reliability of the metro vehicle system by Monte Carlo method. According to the different characteristics of the vehicle equipment, a different failure distribution function was used to simulate the stochastic process of the failure of the vehicle equipment unit.

The equipment units' samples of the subway vehicle system were chosen randomly by Monte Carlo method to judge the status of equipment units. Combine it with the simulation algorithm of time sequence to obtain the timing information of the system failure.

(1) Sampling method of system state based on normal distribution

Assuming that the failure follow the normal distribution $N(\lambda, \sigma)$, the failure-free interval $[-U_j, U_j]$ is determined by the reliability or failure-free probability inherent in the equipment unit. The higher the reliability of the equipment unit is, the greater the failure-free interval. The failure of system is determined by whether the random number falls within the failure-free interval.

Assuming that the system consists of m equipment units, the vector $\boldsymbol{X}$ represents the random state of the equipment units in the system.

$$\boldsymbol{X} = (X_1, X_2, \cdots, X_j, \cdots, X_m) \tag{11-22}$$

The random state of the equipment unit j was represented by X_j judging by the normal random number x_j to obtain the random state sequence. If the equipment unit is under normal operation, the value of X_j is 1; if the equipment is under the abnormal running state, X_j value is 0:

$$X_j = \begin{cases} 0 & x_j > U_j \text{ or } x_j < -U_j \\ 1 & -U_j < x_j < U_j \end{cases} \tag{11-23}$$

(2) Sampling method of failure time based on normal distribution

Assuming that the failure lasting time of each equipment unit follows the normal distribution, a random distribution sequence of failure lasting time can be obtained by combining with the system state matrix. The average maintenance time $\varphi(ij)$ of the equipment unit j in the i-th simulation state follows the normal distribution:

$$\varphi(ij) = N(\mathrm{MTTR}_j, 1) \qquad (i = 1, 2, \cdots, n;\ j = 1, 2, \cdots, m) \tag{11-24}$$

$$\varepsilon_{ij} = \varphi(ij)(1 - X_{ij}) \qquad (i = 1, 2, \cdots, n;\ j = 1, 2, \cdots, m) \tag{11-25}$$

where, MTTR means average maintenance time(h) for equipment unit j; ε_{ij} is the maintenance time of the unit j in the i-th simulation state; X_{ij} means 0-1 random state sequence of equipment unit j.

The failure maintenance time $\delta_i(h)$ of system in the i-th simulation state, which equals the maximum value of the total failure time of each equipment unit in the same state. The vector δ is the maintenance time simulation sequence of system failure.

$$\delta_i = \max(\varepsilon_{ij}) \qquad (i = 1, 2, \cdots, n;\ j = 1, 2, \cdots, m) \tag{11-26}$$

(3) Analysis of system state

The reliability evaluation index of metro vehicle system was used to analyze the different states of each unit. Readers can refer to the original content for the details of the calculation process.

References

[1] Shen Hongyan. Theory, method and application of highway construction policy based on life cycle[D]. Shanghai: Tongji University, 2007.

[2] Wang Landao. Research on key links in improving the service quality of common highways in Guangdong Province[R]. Guangdong, Guangdong Highway Administration, 2016.

[3] Chen Qun. Research on life cycle management of expressway engineering[M]. Xiamen: Xiamen University Press, 2009.

[4] J. Wennström. Life Cycle Costing in Road Planning and Management: A Case Study on Collision-free Roads[R]. Sweden: KTH School of ABE, 2014.

[5] Brian Pallasch, Joshua Schank. Maximizing the Value of Investments Using Life Cycle Cost Analysis[R]. America: the Eno Center for Transportation and the American Society of Civil Engineers, 2014.

[6] Todd Litman. What's it worth? Economic Evaluation for Transportation Decision-Making[R]. Canada: Victoria Transport Policy Institute, 2006.

[7] Håkan Stripple. Life Cycle Assessment of Road A Pilot Study for Inventory Analysis[R]. Gothenburg, Sweden: IVL Swedish Environmental Research Institute Ltd, 2001.

[8] Liu Ruijun, Shi Liwei, Ge Yunyong, et al. Preliminary Study on Automobile Parts Design Based on Green Manufacture Technology[J]. Machinery Design and Manufacture, 2009.

[9] M. Q. Wang. GREET1.5 -Transportation Fuel-Cycle Model[R]. The United States: Argonne National Laboratory, 1999.

[10] A. Burnham, M. Wang and Y. Wu. Development and Applications of GREET 2.7-The Transportation Vehicle-Cycle Model[R]. The United States: Argonne National Laboratory, 2006.

[11] Mark A. Delucchi. A Lifecycle Emissions Model (LEM): Lifecycle Emissions from Transportation Fuels, Motor Vehicles, Transportation Modes, Electricity Use, Heating and Cooking Fuels and Materials[R]. California: Institute of Transportation Studies, 2003.

[12] Chen Kuanmin, Luo Xiaoqiang. Game Analysis of Reasonable Fares for Urban Rapid Rail Transit[J]. Journal of Chang'an University(Natural Science Edition), 2005, 25(4):52-55.

Chapter 12 Evaluation Method of Transport Decision Making

Evaluation method of transport decision making is used to evaluate objects comprehensively by mathematical models, which considers a number of interrelated and interactive evaluation indexes as a whole according to certain evaluation purposes and criteria. The overall thinking of these kinds of evaluation methods is the same, that is, to determine the evaluation object, establish the index set, determine the index weight, and calculate the evaluation level, develop mathematical models, and analyze evaluate the results.

12.1 Typical Evaluation Indexes of Transport Planning

The implementation of transport planning will have a significant impact on the transport system, such as changes in individual travel mode, changes in the surrounding environment, and the transfer of economic activities and so on. Transport system is closely linked to socio-economic and environmental systems, and it links different geographical areas. In order to improve the transport system, the transport planning needs to be evaluated from different aspects to ensure the practicability.

This section refers to the American Highway Capacity Manual HCM2000, Capacity and Service Quality Manual of Public Transport, and Urban Transportation Planning Second Edition. Summarizing the typical evaluation indexes of transport planning from seven aspects, including capacity, level of service, overall performance, ecology and environment, safety, economy, mobility and accessibility, which can be used to evaluate and compare the pros and cons of different schemes to provide the appropriate information for decision-making.

12.1.1 Capacity

Capacity is used to describe the maximum number of vehicles or pedestrian that can pass a certain point, lane or segment at a certain time. It is recommended that segment basic capacity and bus capacity should be chosen to evaluate the transport planning as shown in Table 12-1. And the capacity should be adjusted with the changes of conditions (From Table 12-2 to Table 12-4).

Table 12-1 The evaluation index of freeway segments basic capacity

The speed of free flow (km/h)	120	110	100	90
The basic capacity [pcu/(h · ln)]	2400	2350	2300	2250

Source: *HCM*2000.

Table 12-2 The evaluation index of highway segments basic capacity

Highway grade	Design speed (km/h)	The basic capacity [pcu/(h · ln)]
Class Ⅰ	100	2000
	80	1800
	60	1600
Others	80	2800
	60	2500
	≤40	2400

Data source: JTG B01—2014.

Table 12-3 Estimation of transit capacity

Dwell time (s)	Transit capacity (vehicle/h)	
	$g/c = 0.50$	$g/c = 1.00$
15	63	100
30	43	63
45	32	46
60	36	36
75	22	30
90	19	25
105	16	22
120	15	20

Note: Dwell time = the service time of the busiest door + the time of opening and closing the door; suppose the interval time of buses is 15 min, and the rate of queue is 0.25, and the deviation of residence time is 0.6.

Source: *HCM*2000.

Table 12-4 Capacity indexes of other traffic facilities

Classification	Indexes	Descriptions	Data source
Capacity	Service volume for pedestrian	Assuming the effective width of walkway is 1.5 m, the level of service for pedestrian is divided into five grades from A to E according to pedestrian volume per 15 min	HCM2000
	Bicycle path widths	The path width is 2.4 m for two lanes; the path width is 3.0 m for three lanes	HCM2000
	Bicycle capacity	Under the continuous flow, the capacity of two-way bicycle lanes is 1600 vehicles/(h · ln), and the capacity of one-way bicycle lanes is 3200 vehicles/(h · ln). Under the interrupted flow, the capacity of one-way bicycle lanes is 2000 vehicles/(h · ln)	HCM2000

Capacity is the main constraint to the development of transport system. It is essential especially in planning the strategic decision-making for mode choice of transport corridor way and indicating the dominant position of public transport.

12.1.2 Level of Service(LOS)

The level of service is the standard to describe the quality of traffic operation. The indexes, such as level of service of basic segments, delay and hindrance, are evaluated from the aspects of segment, intersection and slow traffic which could facilitate decision-makers to form intuitive understandings of the quality of transport system. The indexes are shown in the Table 12-5 to Table 12-7.

Table 12-5 Transport planning of Standard of LOS for freeway basic segments

LOS	Biggest density [pcu/(km · ln)]	The speed of free flow is 120 km/h			The speed of free flow is 110 km/h		
		Minimum speed (km/h)	Maximum v/c	Maximum service flow rate [pcu/(h · ln)]	Minimum speed (km/h)	Maximum v/c	Maximum service flow rate [pcu/(h · ln)]
A	7	120	0.34	840	110	0.33	770
B	11	120	0.55	1320	110	0.51	1210
C	16	114.6	0.77	1840	108.5	0.74	1740
D	22	99.6	0.92	2200	97.2	0.91	2135
E	28	85.7	1.00	2400	83.9	1.00	2350
F	>28 [pcu/(km · ln)]						
A	7	100	0.3	700	90	0.28	630
B	11	100	0.48	1100	90	0.44	990
C	16	100	0.7	1600	90	0.64	1440
D	22	93.8	0.9	2065	89.1	0.87	1955
E	28	82.1	1.00	2300	80.4	1.00	2250
F	>28 [pcu/(km · ln)]						

Source: *HCM*2000.

Table 12-6 Transport planning of LOS for multilane highway segments

LOS	The speed of free flow(mi/h)	Density [pcu/(mi · ln)]
A	All	0 ~ 11
B	All	11 ~ 18
C	All	18 ~ 26
D	All	26 ~ 35
E	60	35 ~ 40
	55	35 ~ 41
	50	35 ~ 43
	45	35 ~ 45
F	60	>40
	55	>41
	50	>43
	45	>45

Source: *HCM*2010.

Table 12-7 The commonly used indexes of evaluation of transport planning schemes(LOS)

	Indexes	The commonly used standard	From
LOS	Level of service for avenue	It is divided into six grades from A to F according to the average free flow speed and level of avenues, which belongs 85% of the free flow speed to LOS grade A and belongs 40% of the free flow speed to LOS grade D	HCM2000
	Level of avenue	It is divided into four grades from 1 to 4 according to the average free flow speed, which belongs 90 ~ 70km/h to grade 1, 70 ~ 55km/h to grade 2, 55 ~ 50km/h to grade 3, and 50 ~ 40km/h to grade 4	Rutherford, 1994[1]
	LOS for signalized intersection	It is divided into six grades from A to F according to the delay(seconds/person), which belongs delay ≤ 10s to grade A of LOS and delay from 30 to 40s to grade D	HCM2000
	Failure rate	It represents the rate that stops are all occupied by the buses in the stations so that buses cannot stop	HCM2000
	Hindrance	It is divided into six grades from A to F according to the obstacle rate(%), which belongs hindrance ≤ 10s to grade A of LOS and hindrance from 40 to 70s to grade D	TRB, 2000[2]
	Transit-Auto Travel Time	It is divided into six grades from A to F according to time lapse, which belongs no time lapse between transit-auto to grade A of LOS, time lapse from 31 to 45min to grade D, and time lapse ≥ 60min to grade F	TCQSM[3]

[1] Rutherford, S. 1994. Multimodal evaluation of passenger transportation. NCHRP synthesis of Highway Practice 201. Washington, D. C. : National Academy Press.

[2] Transportation Research Board. 2000. Highway capacity manual. Washington, D. C. : National Academy Press.

[3] Transportation Research Board. 2000. Transit Capacity and Quality of Service Manual 2nd Edition. Washington, D. C.

continued

	Indexes	The commonly used standard	From
LOS	LOS for coverage percentage of the transit	It is divided into six grades from A to F according to coverage percentage of the transit (%), which belongs coverage percentage of the transit ≥90% to grade A, and belongs coverage percentage of the transit ≤50% to grade F	TCQSM
	LOS for standing capacity	It is divided into six grades from A to F according to the standing area of passengers(m^2/ person), which belongs the standing area of passengers > 1.00 m^2/ person to grade A of LOS, and belongs from 0.36 to 0.5 m^2/ person to grade D and passengers feel comfortable at this time	TCQSM
	Effective walkway width	Effective walkway width = total width of the walkway-correction factor; if there only exists the physical division line, the correction factor (one sided) is 0.5 m; if there exists buildings, trees or shrubs, the correction factor is 0.7 m; and if there exists the buildings with windows, the correction factor is 1.0 m	TRB, 2000
	LOS for walking path	It is divided into six grades from A to F according to the standing space of pedestrian (m^2/ person), which belongs the standing space from 0.9 to 1.4 m^2/ person to grade D of LOS, and the walkway capacity of grade E is 82 person/(m · min)	TCQSM
	LOS for stairways	It is divided into six grades from A to F according to the standing space (m^2/person), which belongs the standing space from 0.7 to 0.9 m^2/person to grade D of LOS, and pedestrian are limited to overtake and the pause often occurs the halfway and reverse flow caused serious conflict at this time	TCQSM
	LOS for queuing and waiting area	It is divided into six grades from A to F according to the standing space (m^2/ person), which belongs the standing space from 0.3 to 0.7 m^2/ person to grade D of LOS	TCQSM
	Transit availability	It is divided into six grades from A to F according to the average headway(min), which belongs the average headway from 15 to 20 min to grade C of LOS and this is the maximum acceptable waiting time	TCQSM
	Travel time reliability	It is the probability that actual travel time is less than or equal to the expected travel time	As reported in Smith, 1999[1]

---

[1] Smith, S. 1999. Guidebook for transportation corridor studies: A process for effective decision-making. NCHRP Report 435. Washington, D.C.: National Academy Press.

continued

	Indexes	The commonly used standard	From
LOS	Transit reliability	It is the index to measure the service time and transit headways rules of buses, which effect the waiting time and arrival time of passengers	HCM2000
	Local peak transit headways	It is divided into six grades from A to F according to the average headway(min), which belongs the average headway time less than 10min to grade A, and belongs from 15 to 20 min to grade C which is the maximum acceptable time, and belongs from 21 to 30 min to grade D in which there is no attractive to passengers	TCQSM

Measuring the LOS is to quantify the users' perception reflecting the degree of comfort and acceptability of the components of transport system structurally. The indexes in the table measures LOS of different subjects to meet diverse requirements of the development which could be adapted to the different needs of decision makers.

12.1.3 Performance

In order to reflect the characteristics of total traffic volume and optimize traffic structure, indicators in Table 12-8 daily transit person trips, daily work trips by mode and percent CBD trips by transit and so on——are recommended to be calculated and compared for different schemes.

Table 12-8 Common indicators for transportation planning (Total performance)

Classification	Index	Data source
Overall performance	Daily transit person trips	Rutherford, 1994
	Daily work trips by mode	Rutherford, 1994
	Mode split for work trips	—
	Mode split for work trips to downtown	—
	Percent CBD trips by transit	SEWRPC, 1994
	Transport time reliability	Cambridge Systematics, et al., 2000
	Added cost due to congestion	Cambridge Systematics, et al., 2000
	Average weekday average trip length	Transportation system plan performance evaluation in Portland, Oregon

Note: The probability of actual travel time is less than or equal to the expected travel time.

12.1.4 Ecology and Environment

Transportation planning has an impact on the ecological environment, which is closely related to the sustainable development of society and economy and the life quality of residents. Indicators in

Table 12-9 are recommended to describe the impact of transportation planning on ecology and environment according to Rutherford, S(1994), Southeast Wisconsin Regional Planning Commission (1994) et al..

Table 12-9 Common indicators for transportation planning (Ecology and environment)

<table>
<tr><th>Classification</th><th colspan="2">Index name</th><th>Data Source</th></tr>
<tr><td rowspan="13">Ecology and environment</td><td colspan="2">Acres of prime environ land lost</td><td>SEWRPC, 1994</td></tr>
<tr><td rowspan="6">Tons of air pollution per day</td><td>Carbon monoxide (CO)</td><td>Ambient air quality standards, United States</td></tr>
<tr><td>Hydrocarbon (HC)</td><td>Ambient air quality standards, United States</td></tr>
<tr><td>Volatile organic compounds (VOC)</td><td>Ambient air quality standards, United States</td></tr>
<tr><td>Nitrogen oxide compounds $(NO)_x$</td><td>Ambient air quality standards, United States</td></tr>
<tr><td>Particulate matter $(PM)_x$</td><td>Ambient air quality standards, United States</td></tr>
<tr><td>Others</td><td>Ambient air quality standards, United States</td></tr>
<tr><td colspan="2">Impact of wildlife quantity and living environment</td><td>Rutherford, 1994</td></tr>
<tr><td colspan="2">Impact of water quality</td><td>Rutherford, 1994</td></tr>
<tr><td colspan="2">Impact of vegetation area</td><td>Rutherford, 1994</td></tr>
<tr><td colspan="2">Occupancy of soil and agriculture</td><td>Rutherford, 1994</td></tr>
<tr><td colspan="2">Occupancy of wetland</td><td>Rutherford, 1994</td></tr>
<tr><td>Influence of noise</td><td>A high degree of quiet ≤ 57dB(A); picnic areas, schools, playing field ≤67dB(A); developedregion≤72dB(A)</td><td>FHWA exterior noise abatement criteria[dB(A)]</td></tr>
</table>

Ecology and environment are the foundation of sustainable development for society and economy. On the one hand, it is inevitable that traffic development will change environment, and the purpose of transportation planning is to reduce traffic system's negative influence as possible. On the other hand, the decision makers improve ecological environment by transportation planning.

12.1.5 Safety

Indicators in Table 12-10 are recommended to evaluate the safety performance according to Kumares C. Sinha, Samuel Labi(2007) et al..

Table 12-10 Common indicators for transportation planning (Safety influence)

Classification	Index	Quarry
Security influence	Annual transit crash rates	Cambridge Systematics, et al., 1996
	Annual non-rider crash rates	Cambridge Systematics, et al., 1996
	Percent of pass miles on facilities with lowest accident exposure	SEWRPC, 1994
	Annual crash rates	Rutherford, 1994
	Number of fatal crashes	Transportation decision making
	Pavement condition	Transportation decision making

Safety is the first element of traffic design. In order to ensure the safety of life and property, safety evaluation index should be developed to reduce accident risk in transportation planning. In Table 12-10, evaluating the road safety from traffic participants can directly reflect existing risk items in panning schemes.

12.1.6 Economy

Economic factors will directly affect the implementation of transport planning programs. According to Cambridge Systematics et al. (1996), Capital District Transportation Committee etc. (2000), it is recommended to measure the impact of economic impact by defining ratio of benefit and cost(B/C), total capital cost, land use and planning and other indicators, as shown in Table 12-11.

Table 12-11 Common indicators(economic impact) **for evaluation of transportation planning**

Classification	Index name	Common standard	Source
Economic impact	Public finance	—	Cambridge Systematics et al., 1996
	Cost avoidance	—	Cambridge Systematics et al., 1996
	Economic growth rate	—	Cambridge Systematics et al., 1996
	Benefit/cost, B/C	If the B/C value is less than 1.0, the scheme would be discarded.	Evaluation matrix for MIS in Albany, New York, 2000
	Total capital cost	—	Rutherford, 1994
	Land use and planning	Whether it is consistent with regional and local planning demands	Rutherford, 1994
	Tax impacts	—	Rutherford, 1994
	Forecast of revenues from potential new sources	—	Rutherford, 1994

continued

Classification	Index name	Common standard	Source
Economic impact	Employment impact	—	Rutherford, 1994
	Value of time	Average unit value	Rutherford, 1994
	Annual incidence cost	—	Cambridge Systematics et al., 1996
	Annual operating cost	—	Rutherford, 1994
	Annual maintenance cost	—	Rutherford, 1994
	Truck transport cost per truck-mile	—	Cambridge Systematics et al., 2000
	Vehicle miles travelled (VMT)	—	Transportation system plan performance evaluation in Portland, Oregon
	Person miles travelled (PMT)	—	Transportation system plan performance evaluation in Portland, Oregon
	Projecting person-carrying capacity	—	As reported in Smith, 1999
	Average weekday VMT arterial and highway transit	—	Evaluation of transportation system plans, Southeastern Wisconsin, 1994
	Annual fuel consumed annually	—	Evaluation of transportation system plans, Southeastern Wisconsin, 1994
	Maximum passenger capacities of grade-separated rail transit	Under the condition that operation time interval is 45-70 s: the train length is 60 m, passenger capacity is 10000 people/hour/track; train length is 120 m, passenger capacity is 22000 people/hour/track; train length is 180 m, passenger capacity is 36000 people/hour/track	TRB
	Truck origin/destination patterns	To determine the lines of high-flow freight	Cambridge Systematics et al., 2000

The change of transportation system has a direct and indirect complex impact on regional economic activities. The complexity of the research object leads to the challenge of understanding the complex relationship among them and making the essential factors of the economic impact clearly. Table 12-11 lists some of the important indicators of economic impact, and provides valid information for decision makers in the comparative evaluation of alternatives.

12.1.7 Mobility and Accessibility

Mobility and accessibility is one of the key factors in determining individual lifestyle and regional development. HCM2000, TCQSM, Smith(2000), S(1999) etc.. Recommended the use of the availability of transit services, transit use, travel reliability. Indexes to measure the mobility and accessibility are as shown in Table 12-12.

Table 12-12 Common indexes for evaluation of transportation planning
(impact on mobility and accessibility)

Classification	Index name	Common standard	Source
Impact on mobility and accessibility	Availability of transit services	—	Cambridge Systematics et al., 1996
	Transit use	—	Cambridge Systematics et al., 1996
	Travel reliability	The proportion of personal travel time which is not higher than the average of 10%	TTI, 2000
	Travel rate	Travel rate = travel time (min)/section length (miles) = 60/average speed (miles/h)	TTI, 2000
	Transit accessibility	Measure the reachability of pedestrians, bicycles, motor vehicles and the statutory disabled people to the public transport system	HCM2000
	Transit reliability	The probability that actual travel time is less than or equal to the expected travel time	HCM2000
	Walk time	The time for people walking 1/4 mile to reach or leave the bus station	CTPS, 1997
	Wait time	Assuming 50% of the distance (change percentage circumstantially)	CTPS, 1997
	Transfer time	—	CTPS, 1997
	Households within 1/4 mile transit	—	Porland MEIRO, 1995
	Jobs within 1/4 mile transit	—	Porland MEIRO, 1995
	Maximum link utilization	—	As reported in Smith, 1999
	Number of users	—	As reported in Smith, 1999
	System utilization	—	As reported in Smith, 1999
	Road congestion rate	—	As reported in Smith, 1999

continued

Classification	Index name		Common standard	Source
Impact on mobility and accessibility	Congested travel		Congested road (miles) × traffic volume	TTI, 2000
	Percent roadside congested		—	Land-use scenario evaluation in Baltimore, 1995
	Regional delay		—	As reported in Smith, 1999
	Major area accessibility	Proportion of 40% of jobs	—	Evaluation of transportation system plans, Southeastern Wisconsin, 1994
		40 min of major medical center	—	
		40 min of major rec. center	—	—
		40 min of higher ed	—	—
		60 min of airport	—	

The purpose of calculating the accessibility index is to reflect the degree of difficulty in traveling and the spatial distribution of the population. During the evaluation, the accessibility of the project area is described, and the suggestions for the transport development are proposed, for improving the construction of traffic network and promoting the balanced development of transportation system.

In 1950s and early 1960s, planners usually recommended the implementation of investment scheme with the largest reward. With the development of transportation planning, people are gradually interested in the influence of traffic. The evaluation of the scheme is transformed from a single benefit and cost evaluation into a diversified evaluation including level of service, ecology and environment, and safety.

From Table 12-12, it is obviously that the countries in European and American pay more attention to the interaction between transportation and urban development, guided by the "people based" thought, and they put the public as the foundation and seek solutions in the public recognition. However, the current domestic urban transport planning is still in the stage of motor vehicle oriented development. Taking the classification of the level of service in China and the United States as an example, it can be found that there is a big difference on the evaluation scales between domestic and foreign countries. Therefore, in order to seek a series of evaluation indexes which can reflect the traffic characteristics of China, select the optimal decision based on the judgement of decision makers on the importance of evaluation criteria, it is recommended to refer to the index system and evaluation method of developed countries and regions properly.

12.2 Analytic Hierarchy Process

In the early 1970s, Analytic Hierarchy Process (AHP) was proposed by Professor T. L. Saaty, an American operational research scientist. It is a concise, practical method for systematic analysis and evaluation, which can analyze in both qualitative and quantitative ways.

The basic idea of AHP is setting up a hierarchical structure model according to the problem to describe the function of the system, and give the evaluation standard to compare each two system element in the same hierarchy (such as goal, criterion and scheme) to obtain the judgment matrix. Based on the eigenvector of the judgment matrix, the weight of the element in the hierarchy and the comprehensive weights of each hierarchy are calculated. The comprehensive evaluation value of different schemes is obtained, which provides the basis for selecting the optimal scheme.

Applying analytic hierarchy process to transport system can realize multi-index comprehensive evaluation of transport system. In addition, the contribution of different indexes to comprehensive benefit is not the same.

Using the analytic hierarchy process to carry out systematic evaluation often need the following four steps:

· List the elements of evaluation system, analyze correlation between elements, and establish the hierarchy model by structural analysis method.

· Give the evaluation standard and scale. From the elements in the top hierarchy, compare each two system element in the same hierarchy to establish a judgment matrix;

· According to the judgment matrix, the priority vector (or the eigenvector of the judgment matrix) of each element in the same hierarchy is calculated;

· Calculate the comprehensive weight of each hierarchy element, and sort the elements according to the result.

12.2.1 Establish Hierarchical Structure

Based on the clarified problem, the hierarchical structure model is established following sorting the elements in accordance with the different attributes to establish. Elements of the same hierarchy play a dominant role on the all or part of the elements of the next hierarchy, while it is subject to the elements of the previous hierarchy. Levels can be divided into three hierarchies:

· The target hierarchy. The target hierarchy contains only one element to analyze the predetermined objective or ideal result of the problem.

· The intermediate hierarchy. The intermediate hierarchy contains the intermediate steps involved to achieve the objectives, which may consist of several levels.

· The program hierarchy. The program hierarchy is the lowest level, which includes the various measures, decision schemes, and others to achieve the objectives.

12.2.2 Establish Judgment Matrix

By comparing the each two elements to obtain the judgment matrix A, a_{ij} is generally used to represent the relative importance of a_i to a_j, which is determined jointly by the experts and the decision makers. Judgment scales which represent the relative importance of a_i to a_j are usually expressed as a 1-9 scale, as shown in Table 12-13.

Table 12-13 Judgment scales and meanings of Judgment matrix

Value	The relative importance of the two elements
1	The two elements are with the same importance
3	The former is slightly important than the latter
5	The former is obviously important than the latter
7	The former is intensely important than the latter
9	The former is extremely important than the latter
2,4,6,8	The intermediate value of the above-described judgment scale

The judgment matrix can be established according to the judgment scale.

$$A = \begin{bmatrix} a_{11} & a_{12} & \cdots & a_{1n} \\ a_{21} & a_{22} & \cdots & a_{2n} \\ \cdots & \cdots & \cdots & \cdots \\ a_{n1} & a_{n2} & \cdots & a_{nn} \end{bmatrix} = (a_{ij})n \times n \tag{12-1}$$

where, $a_{ij} > 0$, $a_{ij} = 1/a_{ji}$, $a_{ii} = 1$.

12.2.3 Calculate the Priority Vector of Each Element in the Same Hierarchy

· If the judgment matrix is a $n \times n$ matrix, the n-th root of the product of the each row elements of the matrix could be calculated firstly:

$$\overline{W_i} = \sqrt[n]{M_i} \tag{12-2}$$

where, $M_i = \prod_{j=1}^{n} b_{ij}$, $(i = 1, 2, \cdots, n)$.

· Orthogonalize the above results, that is, to calculate the average of the above numbers. There is the relative weight of each element:

$$W_i = \frac{\overline{W_i}}{\sum_{k=1}^{n} \overline{W_i}} \qquad (i = 1, 2, \cdots, n) \tag{12-3}$$

where, $W_i = (W_1, W_2, \cdots, W_n)^{\mathrm{T}}$ is the requested priority(eigenvalue) vector.

12.2.4 Calculate the Comprehensive Weight of Each Hierarchy Element

The ultimate goal of AHP is to calculate the comprehensive weights to determine the relative importance of each scheme. In order to achieve the objectives, the relative weights of all the elements to the upper layer are needed to get the relative weight of all the elements to the objective (Table 12-14).

Table 12-14 The Calculation Method of the Comprehensive Weights

Scheme A	C_1	C_2	…	C_n	Comprehensive weights
	b_1	b_2	…	b_n	
A_1	a_{11}	a_{12}	…	a_{1n}	$W_1 = \sum_{j=1}^{n} b_j \cdot W_{1j}$
A_2	a_{21}	a_{22}	…	a_{2n}	$W_2 = \sum_{j=1}^{n} b_j \cdot W_{2j}$
A_3	a_{31}	a_{32}	a_{3j}	a_{3n}	$W_3 = \sum_{j=1}^{n} b_j \cdot W_{3j}$
A_n	a_{n1}	a_{n2}	…	a_{nn}	$W_4 = \sum_{j=1}^{n} b_j \cdot W_{4j}$

where, $b_j(j=1, 2, \cdots, m)$ is the relative weight of the intermediate hierarchy C to the target hierarchy D.

According to the above steps, the comprehensive weights of the scheme A to the target hierarchy D is calculated, and the priority of the scheme can be arranged according to the comprehensive weights to obtain the satisfied scheme which is the scheme with the largest weight.

AHP is a systematic, mathematical and modeling method, which requires the elements involved in the problem and unambiguous relationships between each two elements, but the amount of data required is small. Currently 1-9 scale AHP method created by Satty is widely used, but the application is limited to the system evaluation with no more than 9 objects.

12.2.5 The Case of AHP

A City is a new industrial city of iron and steel industry, however traffic congestion becomes more and more serious with the development of production, and the investment in transportation projects is urgent to expand the traffic capacity. There are three schemes: transportation demand management, intelligent transportation, transportation systems management. Arrange and prioritize the schemes using the analytic hierarchy process.

· List the transportation system elements and analyze relationships, and then establish the hierarchical structure of the system model, as shown in Fig. 12-1.

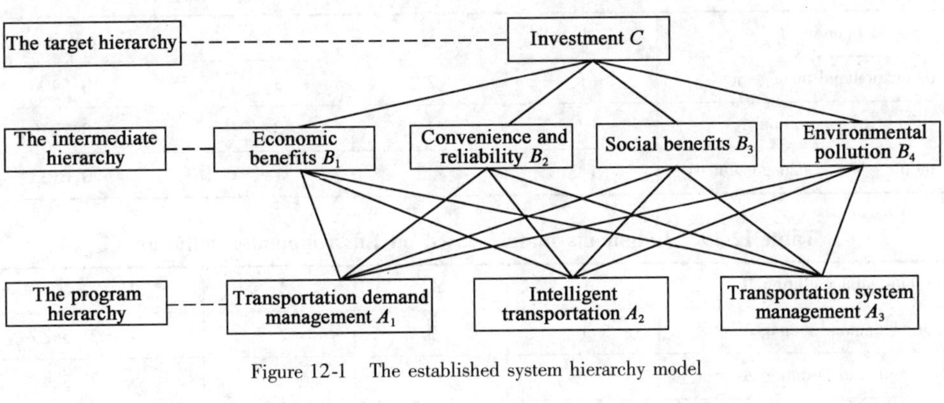

Figure 12-1 The established system hierarchy model

· Give the evaluation standard and scale, and then establish a judgment matrix (Table 12-15).

Table 12-15 The judgment matrix based on the investment (target) hierarchy

Investment C	B_1	B_2	B_3	B_4	The priority vector
Economic benefits B_1	1	3	3	4	0.4944
Convenience and reliability B_2	1/3	1	4	3	0.2854
Social benefits B_3	1/3	1/4	1	2	0.1290
Environmental pollution B_4	1/4	1/3	1/2	1	0.0912

The judgment matrix is a 4 ×4 matrix, so the 4th roots of the product of the matrix elements are calculated first:

$$\overline{W_1} = \sqrt[4]{M_1} = \sqrt[4]{1 \times 3 \times 3 \times 4} = 2.4495, \overline{W_2} = \sqrt[4]{M_2} = \sqrt[4]{(1/3) \times 1 \times 4 \times 3} = 1.4142$$

$$\overline{W_3} = \sqrt[4]{M_3} = \sqrt[4]{(1/3) \times (1/4) \times 1 \times 2} = 0.6389$$

$$\overline{W_4} = \sqrt[4]{M_4} = \sqrt[4]{(1/4) \times (1/3) \times (1/2) \times 1} = 0.4518$$

Orthogonalize the above results to get the priority vector of B_1, B_2, B_3, B_4. Then based on the intermediate hierarchy, a judgment matrix and the priority vector of the matrix is obtained for the program hierarchy. As shown in Table 12-16 to Table 12-19.

Table 12-16 Judgments matrix based on economic benefits

Economic benefits B_1	A_1	A_2	A_3	The priority vector
Transportation demand management A_1	1	1/7	1/5	0.0719
Intelligent transportation A_2	7	1	3	0.6491
Transportation systems management A_3	5	1/3	1	0.2790

Table 12-17 Judgments matrix based on Convenience and reliability

Convenience and reliability B_2	A_1	A_2	A_3	The priority vector
Transportation demand management A_1	1	5	3	0.6483
Intelligent transportation A_2	1/5	1	1/2	0.1220
Transportation systems management A_3	1/3	2	1	0.2297

Table 12-18 Judgments matrix based on Social benefits

Social benefits B_3	A_1	A_2	A_3	The priority vector
Transportation demand management A_1	1	2	3	0.5400
Intelligent transportation A_2	1/2	1	2	0.2970
Transportation systems management A_3	1/3	1/2	1	0.6133

Table 12-19 Judgments matrix based on Environmental pollution

Environmental pollution B_4	A_1	A_2	A_3	The priority vector
Transportation demand management A_1	1	3	5	0.6483
Intelligent transportation A_2	1/3	1	2	0.2297
Transportation systems management A_3	1/5	1/2	1	0.1220

· The results of the comprehensive weight of each hierarchy element are shown in the Table 12-20.

Table 12-20 The results of the comprehensive weight

Investment C	B_1	B_2	B_3	B_4	The comprehensive weight
	0.4944	0.2854	0.1290	0.0912	
A_1	0.0719	0.6483	0.5400	0.6483	0.3493
A_2	0.6491	0.1220	0.2970	0.2297	0.4150
A_3	0.2790	0.2297	0.1633	0.1220	0.2357

The comprehensive weights are calculated as following:

$$0.4944 \times 0.0719 + 0.2854 \times 0.6483 + 0.1290 \times 0.5400 + 0.0912 \times 0.6483 = 0.3493$$

$$0.4944 \times 0.6491 + 0.2854 \times 0.1220 + 0.1290 \times 0.2970 + 0.0912 \times 0.2297 = 0.4150$$

$$0.4944 \times 0.2790 + 0.2854 \times 0.2297 + 0.1290 \times 0.1633 + 0.0912 \times 0.1220 = 0.2357$$

According to the comprehensive weights, the 3 schemes are arranged as A_2, A_1, A_3 that is, choosing the scheme of the intelligent transportation.

12.3 Delphi Method

Delphi method is to put forward the letter request to experts in related fields based on the problems, and the views of experts are integrated, sorted out, and summarized. The results will be provided as an anonymous feedback to the experts and seek advice again until the views tend to focus to get more consistent and reliable views.

12.3.1 Basic Theory of Delphi

In the 1940s, the Delphi Method was put forward by Helm and Dalke and developed by TJ Gordon and Rand Corporation. In 1946, Delphi method was used by Rand Corporation for the first time, and is widely used since then.

The general process of Delphi is: Delphi prediction method is to design consultation tables according to the purposes and requirements of the forecast, and then provide selectively hire experts with the related situation and information of predictive problems. After experts answering the consultation tables according to their own judgment, the forecasters collect and sum up the opinions of the experts, and then design the second round of consultation tables to let experts compare their own judgments with others to modify their judgments. In this way, after several rounds of feedback, after the views tending to focus, the investigation is ended to aggregate the views, and sorted into a forecast report. Therefore, the forecasting step of Delphi is described by a "round". There are the implementation steps of Delphi:

Step 1: Develop an outline of the decision. The objectives should be determined firstly, such as the design of the consultation tables; besides judgment standard and scale should be identified; finally the familiarity level of decision-making should be estimated.

Step 2: Choose the experts. The selected experts generally are those who are respected or engaged in the work for several decades, which is the key to Delphi method.

Step 3: Propose forecasting and decision making. Experts are sent letters or interviewed individually to request each expert to put forward opinions and basis for decision-making and ask them to indicate whether additional information is required.

Step 4: Modify the decisions. The decision-making organizers sort out and summarize views to make it structured, and then back them to the experts to put forward new requirements.

Step 5: Determine the decision results. After several round of modification, decision-making views can be determined by the experts' final views.

Delphi method can only be used in the case that there is little historical data for the future forecast, otherwise probability estimation, fuzzy mathematics or other methods are needed in order to get a more accurate estimate. Delphi method is simple and easy to use, but the subjectivity is too strong to limit the final result, so it is often used for the medium-and long-term forecasts of less complex systems.

12.3.2 Case of Delphi

The number of existing berths in a port area is inadequate and plans to be expanded. In order to conduct a feasibility study on the project, the future traffic situation must be predicted. Four economists, three researchers, four leaders, six business managers and three user representatives were invited to forecast the maximum cargo volume, the most likely cargo volume and the minimum cargo volume. The prediction method was carried out using Delphi method. After three rounds of feedback, the results of cargo ship forecast were obtained. The three rounds of the results were shown in Table 12-21.

Table 12-21 The three rounds of the forecast of cargo volume

Panel members		The first round			The second round			The third round		
		The minimum cargo volume	The most likely cargo volume	The maximum cargo volume	The minimum cargo volume	The most likely cargo volume	The maximum cargo volume	The minimum cargo volume	The most likely cargo volume	The maximum cargo volume
Economists	A	100	240	340	100	280	320	100	300	320
	B	140	200	300	140	200	300	140	200	300
	C	200	240	280	160	200	240	200	280	300
	D	20	48	148	36	88	188	36	164	188
Researchers	A	120	220	340	140	200	280	100	200	300
	B	160	220	320	140	180	280	100	140	240
	C	40	100	220	88	140	240	80	140	240
Leaders	A	60	180	240	80	176	240	88	180	240
	B	76	88	124	88	112	136	88	112	136
	C	80	120	180	88	136	176	88	136	176
	D	64	88	124	68	100	124	112	148	248

continued

Panel members		The first round			The second round			The third round		
		The minimum cargo volume	The most likely cargo volume	The maximum cargo volume	The minimum cargo volume	The most likely cargo volume	The maximum cargo volume	The minimum cargo volume	The most likely cargo volume	The maximum cargo volume
Business managers	A	80	140	200	80	140	200	100	180	200
	B	80	140	220	80	140	220	120	200	240
	C	90	130	210	85	140	210	85	140	210
	D	85	140	230	85	130	230	85	130	200
	E	90	160	220	90	160	220	90	160	230
	F	85	150	200	85	140	210	80	150	220
User representatives	A	30	70	100	40	100	120	40	110	140
	B	220	250	300	180	220	280	160	220	260
	C	70	140	280	80	150	250	80	150	225
Total								1972	3440	4613

According to the statistical tables, appropriate calculation methods can be used to forecast the cargo volume, such as averages and median forecasts (weighted averages can also be used).

· The calculation method of average forecasts is:

The average of minimum cargo volume = 1972/20 = 99 (ship)

The average of most likely cargo ship volume = 3440/20 = 172 (ship)

The average of highest cargo volume = 4613/20 = 231 (ship)

Monthly cargo volume in the fourth year = (99 + 172 + 231)/3 = 167

· The calculation method of median forecasts is:

The median of minimum cargo volume = 95 (ship)

The median of most likely cargo volume = 155 (ship)

The median of maximum cargo volume = 223 (vessel)

The ship volume forecast: (95 + 155 + 223)/3 = 158 (ship)

12.4 Fuzzy Comprehensive Assessment (FCA)

There are a lot of fuzzy concepts such as "quite" and "very" in real life, which are difficult to describe in a precise mathematical way. There are no obvious dividing lines between these concepts, not forming the "standards" in human mind. Fuzzy mathematics experiences the process from the precise to the fuzzy, which is different with the statistical mathematics from the inevitable to the accidental.

12.4.1 Principle and Procedure of Fuzzy Comprehensive Evaluation

In 1965, Professor LA Zadeh published *fuzzy set theory* proposing "membership functions" to describe the difference in the transition marking the birth of the Fuzzy Mathematics, breaking the absolute relationship of " belongs to" or " does not belong to" in the classical set theory. Academician Guan Zhaocheng is the advocator and facilitator of fuzzy set theory in China. And Prof. Wang Peizhuang put forward a specific application method of fuzzy mathematics, namely fuzzy comprehensive evaluation method.

Fuzzy comprehensive evaluation method uses the membership degree theory of fuzzy mathematics to convert the qualitative evaluation to quantitative evaluation. Fuzzy set theory can be used to evaluate the impact of the project, especially suitable for engineering project evaluation which is difficult to quantify accurately. Firstly, determine the evaluation index sets of the evaluation objects, and then determine the weights and membership functions of indexes to obtain the fuzzy judgment matrix. The fuzzy judgment matrix and the weight vectors of the indexes are fuzzy evaluated and normalized to get the fuzzy comprehensive evaluation results of the transport system, and sort the evaluation results of the program set to find out the best plan.

The fuzzy reasoning principle and steps of fuzzy evaluation are shown as follows:

· Determine the set of evaluation elements for the system evaluation project:

$$\nu = \{\nu_i\} \qquad (i = 1, 2, \cdots, n)$$

· Determine the weight coefficient row vector for each evaluation element: $P = P_i$;

· Determine the evaluation standard and the relating value: $E = \{E_i\} \quad (i = 1, 2, \cdots, n)$;

· Calculate the fuzzy comprehensive judgment matrix of evaluation elements in system: $R = R_{ij}$;

· Weight the fuzzy comprehensive judgment matrix, and the fuzzy comprehensive evaluation results are obtained: $S_i = P \cdot R$;

· Calculate the feasibility of each evaluation project: $N_i = S_i \cdot E^{\mathrm{T}}$;

· Compare the feasibility of the projects.

12.4.2 The Case of Fuzzy Comprehensive Evaluation

A transportation department carried out a comprehensive evaluation of the received six planning projects to select the best. In order to discharge priority as the reference for decision-making, the fuzzy comprehensive evaluation is used. The method was shown as follows:

· Determine the set of evaluation elements U = {the necessity of the proposition U_1, the advancement of the technology U_2, the feasibility of the implementation U_3, the rationality of the economic U_4, social benefits U_5}. The six planning projects are recorded as: (A_1, A_2, A_3, A_4, A_5, A_6).

· Determine the weight coefficient row vector for each evaluation element: $P = (P_1, P_2, P_3, P_4, P_5) = (0.15, 0.2, 0.1, 0.25, 0.3)$;

· Determine the evaluation standard and the relating value: $E = (0.9, 0.7, 0.5, 0.3, 0.1)$;

· Calculate the fuzzy comprehensive judgment matrix by professional detection:

a. The nine experts evaluated the first planning program A_1 according to the evaluation of the project, weighted coefficient, and rating. The evaluation results were shown in Table 12-22.

Table 12-22 Evaluation results of experts on the planning program A_1

Planning program A_1	Weighted coefficient	Rating				
		0.9	0.7	0.5	0.3	0.1
U_1	0.15	0	6	3	0	0
U_2	0.20	5	3	1	0	0
U_3	0.10	0	4	4	1	0
U_4	0.25	0	7	2	0	0
U_5	0.30	4	4	1	0	0

b. Calculate the fuzzy judgment matrix: where: $\gamma_{ij} = \dfrac{d_{ij}}{\sum_{j=1}^{n} d_{ij}}$ represents normalizing the fuzzy elements r_{ij} in the matrix; d_{ij} represents the elements of the matrix $D = (d_{ij})$.

$$D = \begin{bmatrix} 0 & 6 & 3 & 0 & 0 \\ 5 & 3 & 1 & 0 & 0 \\ 0 & 4 & 4 & 1 & 0 \\ 0 & 7 & 2 & 0 & 0 \\ 4 & 4 & 1 & 0 & 0 \end{bmatrix}$$

The fuzzy judgment matrix is:

$$R_1 = \begin{bmatrix} 0.00 & 0.67 & 0.33 & 0.00 & 0.00 \\ 0.56 & 0.33 & 0.11 & 0.00 & 0.00 \\ 0.00 & 0.44 & 0.44 & 0.12 & 0.00 \\ 0.00 & 0.78 & 0.22 & 0.00 & 0.00 \\ 0.44 & 0.44 & 0.12 & 0.00 & 0.00 \end{bmatrix}, \ r_{12} = 6/9 = 0.67, \ r_{21} = 5/9 = 0.56$$

According to the requirements of normalization, the value of r_{34} and r_{53} in the matrix are changed to 0.12.

c. Weight the fuzzy comprehensive evaluation matrix, and the fuzzy comprehensive evaluation result is obtained:

$$S_1 = PR = (0.15 \quad 0.2 \quad 0.1 \quad 0.25 \quad 0.3) = \begin{bmatrix} 0.00 & 0.67 & 0.33 & 0.00 & 0.00 \\ 0.56 & 0.33 & 0.11 & 0.00 & 0.00 \\ 0.00 & 0.44 & 0.44 & 0.12 & 0.00 \\ 0.00 & 0.78 & 0.22 & 0.00 & 0.00 \\ 0.44 & 0.44 & 0.12 & 0.00 & 0.00 \end{bmatrix}$$

$$= (0.224, 0.538, 0.204, 0.012, 0.000)$$

d. Calculate the feasibility of each evaluation project: $N_i = S_i E^{\mathrm{T}}$.

$$N_1 = S_{1E}^{T} = (0.224, 0.538, 0.204, 0.012, 0.0)(0.9, 0.7, 0.5, 0.3, 0.1)^{\mathrm{T}} = 0.7$$

The feasibility of the project is 0.7. According to the above method, the feasibility of the other planning projects can be obtained in turn:

$$N_2 = 0.47, N_3 = 0.41, N_4 = 0.56, N_5 = 0.64, N_6 = 0.43$$

e. Compare the feasibility of the projects, and the order of priority of the six planning projects *is*: A_1, A_5, A_4, A_2, A_6, and A_3.

12.5 BP Neural Network

With the development of computer technology, a large number of connected parallel distributed processors are constructed from the perspective of imitating human brain intelligence, that is, artificial neural network, because pre-programmed procedures can no longer fit. Neural networks are able to automatically learn from previous data without the need for complex query and presentation processes, and the method can automatically approximate the functions that best characterize the sample data regularity and reveal non-linearity of the data. Nonlinear mapping ability and approximation function of neural network are widely used in pattern recognition, image processing, control system design, market forecast management, and communication technology.

12.5.1 The Basic Theory of Neural Networks

The earliest neurons are modeled by the American psychologist W. McCulloch and the mathematician W. Pits, who found that human brain neurons act like an on-off switch, introduced the step threshold function, and used the circuit to form a simple neural network model, that is, the BP model. The structure is shown in Fig. 12-2.

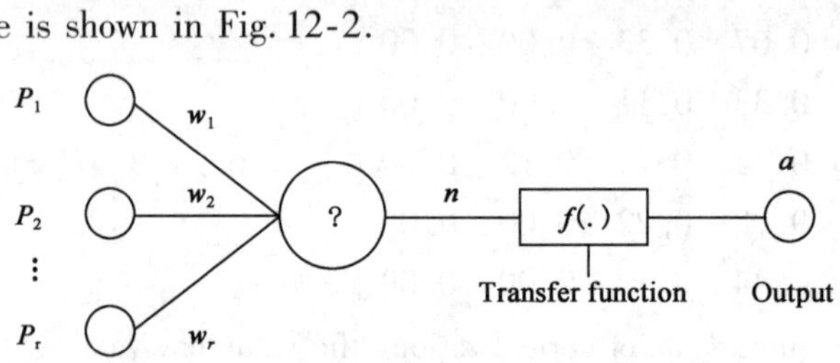

Figure 12-2 MP Neural network model

Source: *Jin Demin*, 2004.

MP neuron structure model includes:

A set of connection weights P_j whose connection strength is controlled by the weights on each connection;

The weights w_j which represents excitation when it is positive but depressing when it is negative;

The summation unit Σ which is used to calculate the weight of each input;

The nonlinear excitation function $f(.)$ acts as a nonlinear mapping and limits the neuron output range (typically [0, 1] or [−1, +1]);

The thresholds: θ_k.

The output formula of neuron k is:

$$y_k = \varphi(\sum_{j=1}^{r} w_j \cdot p_j - \theta_k) = \begin{cases} 1, & v_k \geq 0 \\ 0, & v_k < 0 \end{cases} \tag{12-4}$$

The BP evaluation principle of neural network is shown as follows. The input signal A^K outputs signal C^K on the output node through the intermediate node (implied point). By adjusting the connection strength w_{ij} between the input node and the implicit node, the connection strength between the hidden layer node and the output node, and the threshold value, the error is reduced in the gradient direction to obtain the desired output Y^K, and the network parameters (weight and threshold) corresponding to the error are determined.

Back propagation network (BP network), which is composed of MP neurons, is usually a propagation algorithm based on the error direction, and it can present as a directed graph which is composed of the nodes connected by the neuron function. The BP network consists of input layer, hidden layer, and output layer. The input of the i-th layer is connected with the output of the i-1 layer only, as shown in Fig. 12-3. It can be used in pattern recognition and function approximation reflecting the function mapping. The input in the k-1 layer of the i-th neuron is $y_i^{(k-1)}$, and the output is $y_j^{(k)}$, and then the relation between input and output is expressed as:

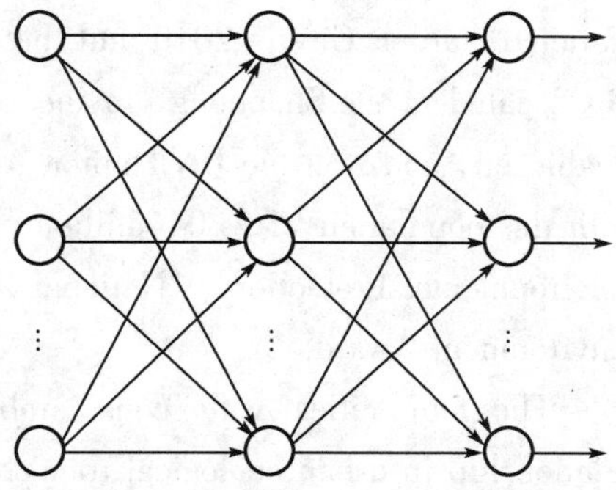

Figure 12-3 BP network

Source: *Yu Yuewu*, 2013.

$$y_j^{(k)} = f\left[\sum_{i=1}^{N_{k-1}} w_{ij}^{(k-1)} y_i^{(k-1)} - \theta_j^{(k)}\right] \tag{12-5}$$

where, $w_{ij}^{(k-1)}$ represents the connection strength from the $k-1$ layer of the i-th neuron to the k layer of the j-th neuron; N_k represents the number of neurons in the k layer; $f(-)$ represents the transfer function of the neuron.

12.5.2 Study Method

Neural network is achieved by adjusting its own parameters over time. According to the amount of information provided by the environment, learning can be divided into supervised learning, unsupervised learning, and reinforcement learning.

Supervised learning needs a set of input-output training samples (give the correct answer) to adjust the system parameters according to the difference from the known output and input; unsupervised learning adjusts parameters or structure to reveal features of the external input through the self-organization of the system according to statistical laws of data from environment; reinforcement learning outputs the evaluation but not the correct answer and improves its performance through evaluation.

The neural network has the ability to adapt. When the steady state changes, the neural network repeats learning treating every different input as a new example.

12.5.3 The Case of BP Network Used in Evaluation of Urban Ecosystems

(1) The background of the city

The levels of urban ecological transportation in Zhuhai City and cities which are similar to Zhuhai, are evaluated using the BP neural network model.

Zhuhai City is an important city located at the southern of Pearl River Estuary in Guangdong Province. It is one of the five special economic zones in China with the population of 1.56 million (2010 census statistics). Zhuhai is a new garden city titled with "romantic city"; Yuxi City is located in the middle of Yunnan Province with a population of 2.13 million. With high grain yield and good tobacco leaves, it was titled with "grain warehouse of Yunnan Province", "the hometown of tobacco". It was awarded the "Top Ten Chinese leisure livable eco-city", and named the National Garden City in 2010 and the National Sanitary City in 2011; Rizhao City is a coastal port city located in the Shandong Province, adjacent to the Yellow Sea, which was known as ecologically livable city and won the UN Habitat Award; Haikou City, the provincial capital of Hainan Province with the population of 2.04 million, was titled with "Top Ten Cities" "Model City of National Environmental Protection" "National Garden City" and other reputation, and won the China Habitat Environment Award.

The four cities with considerable scale mentioned above are with a strong competitive relationship in urban ecological transportation. In order to effectively guide the development strategy of ecological transportation, it is necessary to evaluate the urban ecological traffic conditions.

According to the index system of urban eco-traffic evaluation, the indicators of ecological traffic evaluation are collected shown in Table 12-23.

Table 12-23 Raw data of the cities

Criteria layer	Indicator level	Raw data			
		Haikou	Rizhao	Zhuhai	Yuxi
B1 the integrity of the transportation system	C1 90% travel time of resident(min)	36	37	32	33
	C2 the number of buses/ten thousand people	12	14.3	15.8	9.3
	C3 the coverage of bus stations(%)	90	91	91	87
	C4 the average of transfer(times)	1.2	1.6	1.7	1.2
	C5 the ratio of transit(%)	18.6	17.2	16.5	17.6
	C6 supply-demand ratio of parking space in CBD	0.2	0.5	0.3	0.4
	C7the mean speed of arterial streets(km/h)	28	30	30	27
	C8 the ratio of the level of service of arterial streets below D(%)	21	25	22	23
	C9 the density of urban road network(km/km)	6.5	5.2	7.5	4.6
	C10 road area per capita(%)	6.45	24.5	22.6	8.15
	C11 the connectivity of urban road network	63	60	65	63
	C12 the level of traffic management informatization(%)	82	77	81	76
	C13 the ratio of urban transport specialized personnel(%)	64	63	66	69
B2 the safety of the traffic network	C14 the ability of accident coping	82	84	86	79
	C15 The satisfaction with traffic police from the crowd	82	83	86	76
	C16 the density of police service (people/ten thousand vehicles kilometer)	—	—	—	—
	C17 the number of people to coordinate traffic safety(people)	3.77	4.5	4.1	5.4

continued

Criteria layer	Indicator level	Raw data			
		Haikou	Rizhao	Zhuhai	Yuxi
B3 the environment of the transportation system	C18 the ratio of land use for urban traffic(%)	2.86	1.5	1	0.98
	C19 the ratio of investment for traffic environment in GDP(%)	0.8	0.7	1	0.8
	C20 the replacement rate of using clean energy(%)	1.3	1.3	1.2	1.9
	C21 the coverage of urban green space(%)	37	43	42.1	40.2
	C22 the accommodation coefficient of atmospheric impact(%)	0.74	0.7	0.66	0.71
	C23 the accommodation coefficient of fuel consumption(%)	0.6	0.5	0.4	0.7
B4 the coordination of the landscape	C24 the protection rate of historic interest and natural scenery(%)	0.95	0.92	0.93	0.9
	C25 the richness of greening plant color, shape and so on as season changes	0.75	0.75	0.75	0.5
	C26 the degree of the attention to landscape	0.5	0.5	0.5	0.75
	C27 the degree of ornamental	0.75	0.75	0.5	0.5
B5 the equity of the traffic culture	C28 the protection capability of the traffic laws and regulations(%)	78	82	79	78
	C29 the progress rate of urban transportation science and technology(%)	42	47	39	42
	C30 Driving comfort(%)	75	71	68	72

(2) The specific process of urban ecosystem assessment

The data in Table 12-24 are normalized using the tramnmx function in the MATLAB. The tramnmx function normalizes the new samples when the network has been trained. The format of the call is:

$$[\mathrm{pln}] = \mathrm{tramnmx}(\mathrm{pl}, \mathrm{min}p, \mathrm{max}p)$$

where pln is the value after the normalization and pl is the new sample data value.

The normalized data are input into the trained BP neural network, and then the results are anti-normalized by postmnmx function in MATLAB. The results of four urban ecological traffic rankings are shown in Table 12-24.

Table 12-24 The output of the neural network

Cities	Yuxi	Haikou	Zhuhai	Rizhao
The output of the neural network	77.39	86.84	79.13	80.63

(3) Analysis of the evaluation

According to the evaluation results, the ecological transportations of the four cities are ranked in turn as Haikou, Rizhao, Zhuhai, Yuxi. The ecological traffic levels of Zhuhai and Rizhao are relatively close, and their disadvantages are more obvious compared to Haikou.

12.6 Barrel Theory

American management scientist Peter put forward that the amount of water that hold in the bucket depends on the shortest piece of board, rather than the longest, that is, the barrel theory or short-board effect.

12.6.1 The Principles of Barrel Theory

In 1840, Justus von Liebig, a German chemist, pointed out that the nutrients which require only trace amounts determine the crop growth, rather than the big supply nutrient, that is, minimum factor rule. In 1969, the barrel theory was proposed in *The Peter Principal* written by American management experts Laurence Peter whose core idea was that the amount of water that hold in the bucket depends on the shortest piece of board, rather than the longest, that is, the system function does not depend on the advantages but the disadvantages, so the barrel theory is also called short-board effect.

System components are often uneven, and the overall quality of the system is determined by the disadvantages of the system. Improving the most vulnerable aspects of system can affect the system operation obviously. If all aspects intercoordinate with each other to make the system more even, the system can run better to avoid the extreme situations.

12.6.2 The Case of Barrel Theory

The case of barrel theory is shown in Refs. Zhou Wei and Ma Shu hong,2003.

12.7 SWOT Analysis

SWOT (strengths, weaknesses, opportunities, threats) analyzes advantages, disadvantages, opportunities and threats of the system to combine the internal resources with the external environment.

12.7.1 Basic Theory of SWOT

Based on the analysis of internal and external competitive environment and competitive situation, SWOT analysis combines the internal strengths and weaknesses, and external opportunities and threats. They are arranged as a matrix form to analyze using the system analysis method to obtain decision-making conclusions.

SWOT can be used to analyze the development strategy of satellite cities of major cities in China, and the main reasons are shown as following.

· The essence of the development strategy of satellite cities is the pursuit of the largest social and economic benefits, which is similar to the business.

· The benign development strategy of foreign satellite cities is a sustainable development model to guide the development strategy in China. However, the distinctive features of satellite cities in China especially differences in the degree of marketization and Urbanization etc. , SWOT analysis provides an effective way to combine benign development strategy of foreign satellite cities with the practice and features of satellite cities in China.

· Internal and external factors which effect satellite cities development can be sorted out and analyzed by SWOT analysis to find the favorable factors, adverse factors and problems.

SWOT analysis starts from the established goal, and then summarizes the SWOT elements to generate different strategies and form the core strategies of the satellite cities.

SWOT analysis process can be divided into the stages shown as following.

(1) Factor Analysis of the development strategy of satellite cities in China

The external environment situation and internal conditions of satellite cities are analyzed to grasp the current and potential opportunities and challenges, and confirm advantages and disadvantages. Three parts are included:

· Determine the SWOT elements

a. Internal factors analysis. Internal factors include strengths (S) and weaknesses (W), which are positive and negative factors in the development of the system. As to the development strategy of satellite cities, internal factors refer to the land use, space environment and the city function (mainly reflecting in the function and structure of the land).

b. External factors analysis. External factors include opportunities (O) and threats (T), which are the favorable situation and unfavorable factors in the external environment. They emphasize the changes of external competitive environment and the possible impacts on the development of satellite cities, generally including political, technology, social culture, population, market and other areas.

· Weight elements

Weight the k-th factor of strengths (S) S_k, which indicates the importance of the k-th factor compared to all strengths. Meanwhile, $\sum_{k=1}^{n} S_k = 1$. The others factors weight in the same way.

· Score each factors

The evaluation score S_k' of the k-th factor of strengths (S) is given to understand the adaptability of factors, which indicates the actual utilization of the k-th factor. The scores 1-4 points represent unsuitable, under-adapted, basic adaptation and adaptation respectively. Take the score 1 for the k-th factor of strengths as an example, and the score indicates the strength should get more attention, because it has not been fully exploited. The factors are scored in the same way.

· Calculate the comprehensive evaluation value of factors

The weight of the k-th factor of strengths (S) S_k is scored S_k'. The comprehensive evaluation value S of strengths (S) are:

$$S = \sum_{k=1}^{n} S_k \cdot S'_k \tag{12-6}$$

Obviously, the maximum comprehensive evaluation value is 4.0 showing that the development makes good use of internal advantages. The other factors are shown as following:

$$W = \sum_{k=1}^{n} W_k \cdot W'_k \tag{12-7}$$

$$O = \sum_{k=1}^{n} O_k \cdot O'_k \tag{12-8}$$

$$T = \sum_{k=1}^{n} T_k \cdot T'_k \tag{12-9}$$

(2) Strategy formation based on SWOT element cross-analysis

Strategies are generated using SWOT analysis, especially the self-analysis and cross-analysis in the elements. Base on the strengths, weaknesses, opportunities and threats of the planning satellite city, self-analysis and cross-analysis are used to take the advantages of the strengths, overcome the weaknesses, seize the opportunities, and meet the challenges (Fig 12-4).

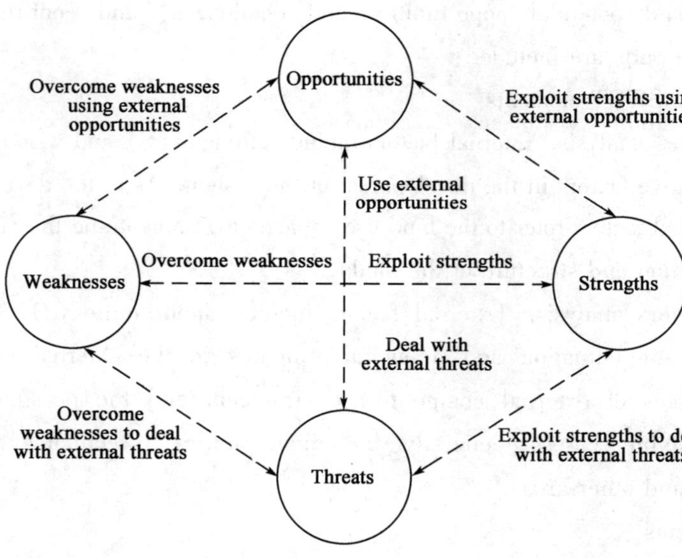

Figure 12-4 SWOT analysis

Source: *Cao Sha*, 2008.

(3) Select core strategy

Select the core strategy according to the comprehensive evaluation value of factors.

12.7.2 The Case of Tai Da Satellite City Using SWOT Analysis

(1) The development of Tai Da satellite city

Tai Da is an industrial-pilot satellite city in Tianjin province. Since 1984, the development of Tai Da has gone through more than 20 years, which can be divided into three stages. See Table 12-25 for details.

Table 12-25 The development characteristics of Tai Da during three periods

Periods		development characteristics
The first period 1985—1994	1985—1989	Single function of processing; practitioners all lived outside the area
	1990—1994	Single function of processing with a little life service function; a few practitioners lived in the area but lack of community construction; low land use intensity and landscape quality
The second period 1995—1999		Urban functions tended to diversify with the resident population increasing steadily; however, land use intensity and landscape quality are low, and urban space expansion is disorder and decentralization, and public welfare facilities are lacked
The third period since 2000		The urban function is integrated, and the life service function is diversified with resident population growing quickly; urban space accessibility improved significantly; however, the commuter population is still large due to the infancy of community construction

(2) SWOT analysis and its comprehensive evaluation value of the development of Tai Da

Three periods of the development of Tai Da showed life function become the important content of the development of satellite cities with the development of urban functions and industrial structure. The accessibility in the space, municipal infrastructure, environment protection and green level has been greatly improved. According to the formula (1), (2), (3) and (4) to calculate the comprehensive evaluation of various factors, the SWOT analysis of Tai Da is shown in Table 12-26.

Table 12-26 The comprehensive evaluation value of SWOT factors of TaiDa

SWOT factors		Weight	Evaluation value	Comprehensive evaluation value	Total
Strengths (S)	The traffic accessibility between Tianjin and Beijing has been improved	0.2	2	0.4	2.6
	It becomes the driving force to economic development of the Binhai New Area due to economic strength greatly enhanced	0.4	2	0.8	
	The advantage of location	0.2	4	0.8	
	A broad space for the development	0.2	3	0.6	
Weaknesses (W)	Low land intensity	0.3	2	0.6	1.8
	The public transport network has not been completed yet	0.3	2	0.6	
	High rate of land use of industry	0.2	1	0.2	
	The characteristics of urban landscape is not strong; the geographical and cultural connotation are lacked; and community construction is in infancy	0.2	2	0.4	

continued

SWOT factors		Weight	Evaluation value	Comprehensive evaluation value	Total
Opportunities(O)	The development and opening up of Binhai New Area have been brought into the five-year national plan-"Eleventh Five"	0.3	1	0.3	1.7
	Tianjin is in the formation stage of urban spatial pattern	0.2	2	0.4	
	The national investment in public transport had been increased	0.3	2	0.6	
	In-depth understanding of the TOD planning concept	0.2	2	0.4	
threats(T)	The large gap in the economic, social and other areas between Beijing and Tianjin	0.2	2	0.4	2.6
	The improvement of requirements to living environment	0.3	3	0.9	
	The change of the preference to enterprise location; the adjustment of industrial structure	0.3	3	0.9	
	The integrity and high efficiency of land use are required based on the sustainable development of cities	0.2	2	0.4	

(3) Formation of the strategy based on cross-analysis

The S, W, O, T factors are cross-matched to analyze the feasible strategy shown in Fig. 12-5. These strategies promote the satellite city functional self-reliance, environmental ecology and space integration.

(4) The core strategy of the development of Tai Da

Table 12-26 showed that Tai Da should adopt the SO (advantage + opportunity) and WO strategies (inferiority + opportunity). Take the WO strategies as the main to take advantage of strengths and opportunities, especially giving priority to the industries with traditional, comparative and resource advantages to strengthen their market competitiveness. Meanwhile pay attention to the overall development of regional economy.

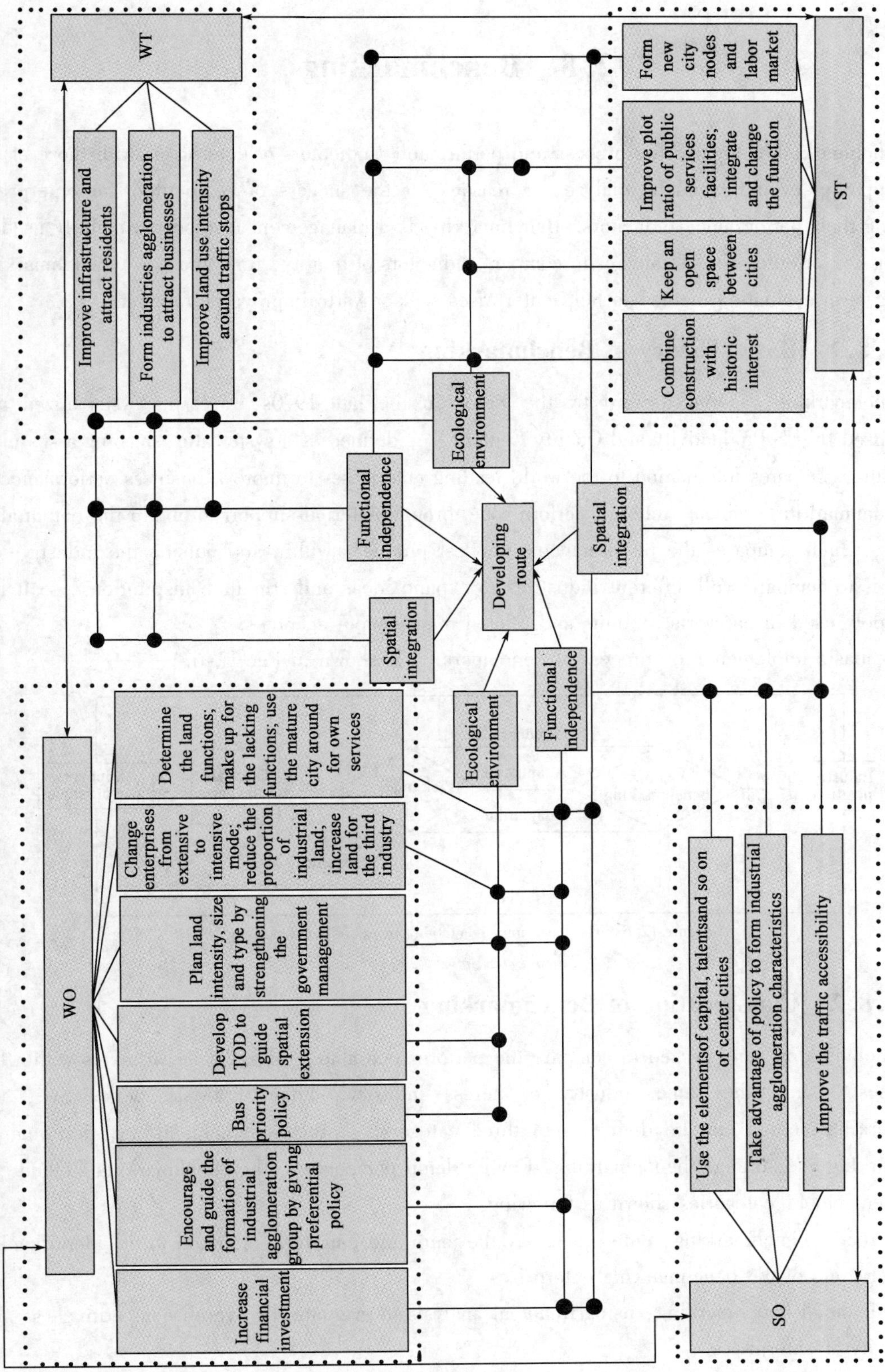

Figure 12-5 The development strategies of satellite cities in China

Soure: *Cao Sha*, 2008.

12.8 Benchmarking

Benchmarking compares the process and performance indicators of enterprises with those of the best companies or indicators to analyze the reasons for the success of competitors for enterprises improving their performance indicators. Benchmarking is a management method particularly used in the formation of enterprises strategies to compare indicators of quality, time and cost. Benchmarking is a long-term evaluation method to help enterprises seek ways to improve performance.

12.8.1 Basic Theory of Benchmarking

Benchmarking was put forward by the Xerox in the late 1970s, and was systematized and standardized by US Productivity and Quality Center. It is defined as a systematic, ongoing assessment process that compares information to the world leading enterprises to improve business performance.

Benchmarking promotes internal performance through external support to obtain the potential of industry, which compares the performance with best practices within and outside the industry. Its essence is to compare with different industries to expand ideas and stimulate inspirations, so it has been widely used in enterprises, units and related management agencies.

The basic implementation process of benchmarking is shown in Fig. 12-6.

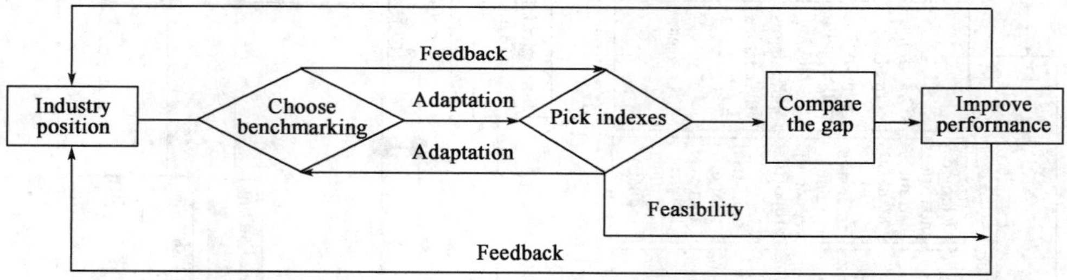

Figure 12-6 The basic implementation process of benchmarking

Source: *Liu Jingzhi*, 2006.

12.8.2 Classification of Benchmarking

Benchmarking can be used to compare the performance among different departments within the enterprises, within the same industry or across industry. From a broad perspective, the benchmarking method can be divided into three categories: process benchmarking, performance benchmarking and strategic benchmarking. From a detail perspective, the benchmarking method can be divided into 11 categories shown as following:

· Process benchmarking: enterprises pay the main and long-term attention to the identification and observation of the benchmarking enterprises.

· Financial benchmarking: using financial analysis to evaluate the overall competitiveness and productivity of enterprises.

· Benchmarking from an investor perspective: comparing within the industry to find the investment opportunities from the investor perspective.

· Benchmarking in the public sector: government departments development and innovation can be achieved to improve the quality, efficiency and effectiveness of government investment.

· Performance benchmarking: competitive positions of enterprises are analyzed by comparing products and services.

· Product benchmarking: when new products are developed or existing products are upgraded, this method is used to compare the advantages and disadvantages of these with the original products.

· Strategic benchmarking: it focuses on the competition behaviors of other enterprises.

· Functional benchmarking: it focuses on the specific aspect of the enterprises.

· Best-in-class benchmarking: it uses to compare with the industry leading enterprises or the enterprises which are the best in some aspects.

· Operational benchmarking: it uses to analyze from staffing and productivity to the office process or other aspects of business operation.

· Energy benchmarking: Buildings or enterprises compare their energy consumption data with those of competitors to evaluate the energy consumption.

In 2008, the Global Benchmarking Network conducted a comprehensive survey of benchmarking covering more than 40 countries and surveying more than 450 companies. 77% of companies used the Mission and Vision Statements and Customer Surveys, and 72% used SWOT method, and 68% used Informal Benchmarking, and 49% used Performance Benchmarking, and 39% used Best Practice Benchmarking. Performance Benchmarking, Informal Benchmarking, SWOT and Best Practice Benchmarking had relatively good prospects. The application of the benchmarking method in the transportation industry is also very extensive, such as comparing the total mileage, road network density and other indicators in China with developed countries.

12.8.3 The Case of Benchmarking

Benchmarking has a wide application in evaluation index of traffic safety, such as average accidents rates and average accidental death rates as shown in Fig. 12-7, Table 12-27 and Fig. 12-8, Table 12-28.

Table 12-27 Average traffic crashes rate in 2011—2015

City name	Population	Traffic crashes	2015	2014	2013	2012	2011
Bellevue, WA	135000	1922	14.2	13.1	13.5	13.7	14.7
Boca Raton, FL	87552	3847	43.9	44.5	44.1	47.7	50.5
Boise, ID	223670	3725	16.7	16.6	11.9	12.0	15.6
Boulder, CO	104810	3593	34.3	33.4	36.3	32.1	32.1
Broken Arrow, OK	107000	1975	18.5	18.5	17.2	16.2	15.8
Carisbad, CA	112229	2076	18.5				
Cedar Rapids, IA	129195	4463	34.5	38.5	32.0	31.4	30.7
Chesapeake, VA	233908	2685	11.5	29.6	28.3	28.1	28.1
Chula Vista, CA	257989	1330	5.2	4.4	4.2	4.6	4.6

continued

City name	Population	Traffic crashes	2015	2014	2013	2012	2011
Columbia, MO	118519	5750	48.5	44.4	35.4	34.7	35.9
Coral Springs, FL	124282	2519	20.3	21.4	21.6	33.0	32.9
Edmond, OK	89926	1516	16.9	17.3	16.8	19.2	17.1
Fort Collins, CO	158600	4412	27.8	27.2	26.4	24.7	26.3
Fremont, CA	226551	1853	8.2	7.0	7.1	7.9	7.9
Gariand, TX	234533	3429	14.6	14.0	12.9	12.7	13.9
Grand Prairie, TX	185453	3446	18.6	18.3	15.7	16.0	16.4
Henderson, NV	286273	3613	12.6	13.0	15.4	15.2	14.6
Irving, TX	228610	3553	15.5	12.5	11.3	10.4	11.0
Lakewood, CO	147220	4631	31.5	29.7	29.8	27.9	29.4
Lawrence, KS	97193	2873	29.6	32.2	28.7	31.3	30.3
Lincoin, NE	272996	8854	32.4	31.0	31.3	30.8	33.3
Naperville, IL	144108	3500	24.3	23.4	23.3	20.3	20.1
Norman, OK	119362	2431	20.4	20.5	23.3	27.4	26.7
Olathe, KS	134308	3060	22.8	20.2	20.3	20.5	1.7
Overiand Park, KS	187730	4769	25.4	23.4	23.9	24.4	25.5
Peoria, AZ	163839	2020	12.3	12.0	11.3	11.7	
Plano, TX	271140	5829	21.5	19.5	19.2	19.0	18.5
Richardson, TX	102430	1967	19.2	17.4	16.4	17.1	16.6
San Angelo, TX	98975	2774	28.0	28.7	28.3	28.2	27.0
Springfield, MO	165378	7315	44.2	45.9	48.7	50.0	51.5
Average	164962	3524	23.1	23.4	22.6	23.0	23.9

2015 average traffic crashes per 1000 citizens is 23.1

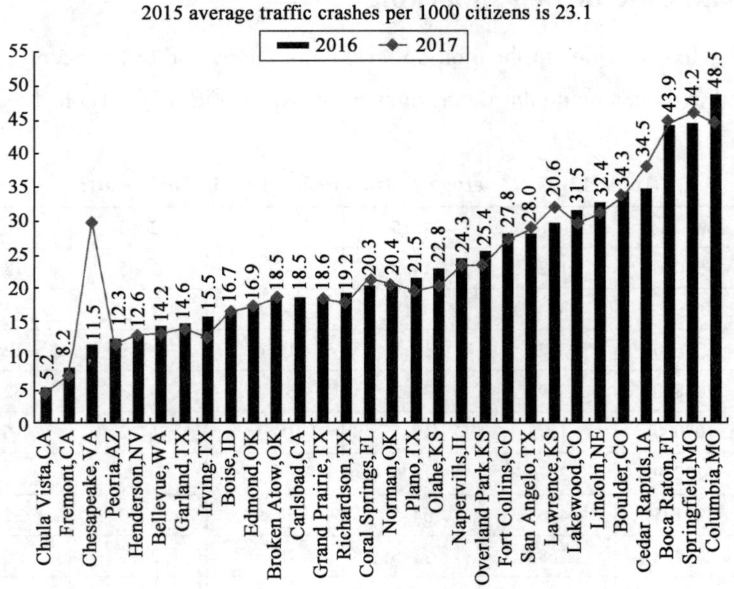

Figure 12-7 Average traffic crashes rate in 2016—2017

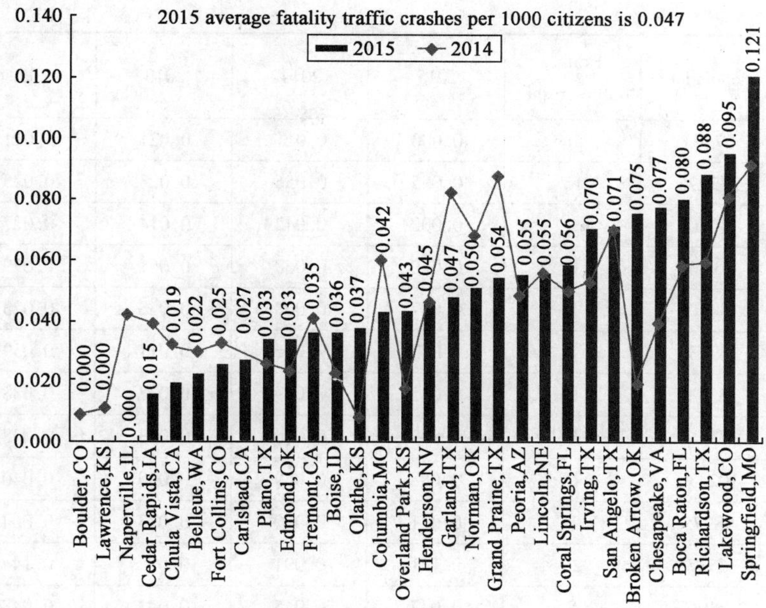

Figure 12-8 Average accidental fatality rate in 2014—2015

Table 12-28 Average Fatality Traffic Crashes rate in 2011—2015

City name	Population	Fatality traffic crashes	2015	2014	2013	2012	2011
Bellevue, WA	135000	3	0.002	0.030	0.008	0.016	0.016
Boca Raton, FL	87552	7	0.080	0.059	0.105	0.070	0.035
Boise, ID	223670	8	0.036	0.023	0.033	0.024	0.024
Boulder, CO	104810	0	0.000	0.010	0.000	0.030	0.048
Broken Arrow, OK	107000	8	0.075	0.019	0.078	0.120	0.071
Carisbad, CA	112299	3	0.027				
Cedar Rapids, IA	129195	2	0.015	0.039	0.016	0.055	0.008
Chesapeake, VA	233908	18	0.077	0.039	0.044	0.044	0.097
Chula Vista, CA	257989	5	0.019	0.031	0.020	0.032	0.033
Columbia, MO	118519	5	0.042	0.060	0.055	0.046	0.028
Coral Springs, FL	124282	7	0.056	0.050	0.072	0.041	0.050
Edmond, OK	89926	3	0.033	0.023	0.059	0.012	0.048
Fort Collins, CO	158600	4	0.025	0.032	0.020	0.021	0.028
Fremont, CA	226551	8	0.035	0.041	0.032	0.019	0.028
Gariand, TX	234533	11	0.047	0.081	0.047	0.053	0.066
Grand Prairie, TX	185453	10	0.054	0.087	0.072	0.061	0.108
Henderson, NV	286273	13	0.045	0.047	0.029	0.070	0.022
Irving, TX	228610	16	0.070	0.053	0.068	0.073	0.051
Lakewood, CO	147220	14	0.095	0.082	0.042	0.063	0.084

continued

City name	Population	Fatality traffic crashes	2015	2014	2013	2012	2011
Lawrence, KS	97193	0	0.000	0.011	0.021	0.011	0.023
Lincoin, NE	272996	15	0.055	0.056	0.023	0.023	0.027
Napervile, IL	144108	0	0.000	0.042	0.014	0.027	0.014
Norman, OK	119362	6	0.050	0.068	0.061	0.079	0.044
Oiathe, KS	134308	5	0.037	0.008	0.038	0.023	0.000
Overiand Park, KS	187730	8	0.043	0.016	0.011	0.039	0.023
Peoria, AZ	163839	9	0.055	0.049	0.037	0.038	
Plano, TX	271140	9	0.033	0.026	0.023	0.038	0.038
Richardson, TX	102430	9	0.088	0.059	0.030	0.040	0.020
San Angelo, TX	98975	7	0.071	0.070	0.073	0.064	0.043
Spingfield, MO	165378	20	0.121	0.091	0.074	0.144	0.075
Acerage	164962	8	0.047	0.045	0.041	0.048	0.050

References

[1] Wang Yongtao, Zhang Yulin. Misuse Analysis of Analytic Hierarchy Process[J]. Journal of Henan University of Technology (Social Science Edition),2006,(12):132-134.

[2] Deng Yusheng, Deng Dongfeng, Tang Min. Research on the Application of Analytic Hierarchy Process in Life Cycle Assessment[J]. Environmental Science and Technology, 2009,32(6): 169-171.

[3] Shao Chunfu. Principles of traffic planning [M]. Beijing: China Railway Publishing House, 2006.

[4] SHAO Yingying. Study on the Scope Management of Urban Transportation Hub [D]. Tianjin: Tianjin University of Technology, 2008.

[5] Jin Demin. Research on theory and integration of life-cycle risk management system for neural network engineering [D]. Tianjin: Tianjin University, 2004.

[6] Shi Ligang. Research on the ecological design of large space public buildings [D]. Harbin: Harbin Institute of Technology, 2007.

[7] Jia Ziruo. Analysis of Urban Traffic Congestion Based on Game Theory [J]. Logistics Technology, 2012,31(3):56-63.

[8] Ye Xiaoqing. Research on the Evaluation of Highway Coordination Development Based on Low Carbon and Economy[D]. Shandong: China Ocean University, 2013.

[9] Zhang Naiyu, Ruan Pingfan. Neural network and fuzzy control [M]. Beijing: Tsinghua University Press, 1998.

[10] Yue Yuewu. Research on evaluation of urban ecological transport system based on BP[D]. Nanjing: Nanjing Forestry University, 2013.

[11] Xing Tingyan, Lv Jianjun, Wu Liang. Urban environment fuzzy prediction and comprehensive evaluation information system [M]. Wuhan: China University of Geosciences Press, 2006.

[12] Liu Shuyan. Transportation System Engineering [M]. Wuhan: China Communications Press, 2006.

[13] Wikipedia. Benchmarking [EB/OL]. https://en. wikipedia. org/wiki/Benchmarking.

[14] Zhou Wei, Ma Shuhong. Research on adaptability of highway traffic and economic development based on barrel theory[J]. China Journal of Highway and Transport, 2003,16(3):77-82.

[15] Shao Zufeng. Application of game theory in road traffic management[J]. Road Transportation and Safety, 2006,6(3):8-10.

[16] Cao Sha. Research on the development strategy of China's satellite city based on big cities [D]. Xi'an: Chang'an University, 2008.

[17] Manual H C. HCM2000[M]. Washington, DC: Transportation Research Board, 2000.

[18] Manual H C. HCM2010 [M]. Washington, D. C. : Transportation Research Board, National Research Council , 2010.

[19] Rutherford G S. Multimodal evaluation of passenger transportation [M]. Transportation Research Board, 1994.

[20] Kittelson & Associates, United States. Federal Transit Administration, Transit Cooperative Research Program, et al. Transit capacity and quality of service manual[M]. Transportation Research Board, 2003.

[21] Smith S A. Guidebook for transportation corridor studies: A process for effective decision-making [M]. Washington, D. C. : National Academy Press. 1999.

[22] Southeastern Wisconsin Regional Planning Commission. A Regional Transportation System Plan for Southeastern Wisconsin, 2010[M]. The Commission, 1994.

[23] Cambridge Systematics , M. Meyer. Performance-based planning manual[M]. Washington, D. C. : National Academy Press, 2000.

[24] Council W A P. Regional Transportation Plan [J]. St. Paul, Minn. : Metropolitan Council, 1996.

[25] Bowlby, W. ,J. Higgins, J. Reagan. Noise barrier cost reduction procedure STAMINA 2. 0/ OPTIMA: User's manual [J] . Computer Aided Design , 1982.

[26] Capital District Transportation Committee. Draft expanded project proposal/major investment study, Interstate I-90 exit 8 ,Phase 2 , connector, ITS test bed[M]. Albany, NY, 2000b.

[27] Texas Transportation Institute. Urban mobility study. Keys to estimating mobility in urban areas [J]. College Station: TX,2000.

[28] Central Transportation Planning Staff. Transfer penalties in urban mode choice modeling. Travel Model Improvement Program [J]. Washington, D. C.: U. S. Department of Transportation,1997.

[29] Portland METRO. short list of technical rankings and assessment of administrative criteria [J]. Portland, OR,1995.

[30] Baltimore Metropolitan Planning Organization. Growth management and transportation: Alternative futures for the Baltimore region[J]. Baltimore, MD,1995.

[31] Kumares C. Sinha, Samuel Labi. Transportation Decision Making: principles of project evaluation and programming [M]. US:Wiley, 2007.

[32] Liu Jingzhi, Guan Zhiwei, Wei Liquan. Application of Benchmarking Method in Performance Evaluation of China's Express Delivery Industry[J]. China Storage and Transportation, 2006 (5):106-107.

[33] Rutherford, S. Multimodal evaluation of passenger transportation. NCHRP synthesis of Highway Practice 201. Washington, D. C. :National Academy Press, 1994.

[34] Transportation Research Board. Highway capacity manual. Washington, D. C. : National Academy Press, 2000.

[35] Transportation Research Board. Transit Capacity and Quality of Service Manual 2nd Edition. Washington, D. C, 2000.

[36] Smith, S. Guidebook for transportation corridor studies: A process for effective decision-making. NCHRP Report 435. Washington, D. C.: National Academy Press, 1999.

Appendix 1

Example of Travel Distribution Prediction Method

1. Unique growth factor method

【**Example A1-1**】 Determine the travel distribution matrix in the target year using three zones, O-D matrix in base year and predicted value of target year(Table A1-1).

Table A1-1 O-D matrix at present and predicted value of target year

O	*D*			Total	Predicted value
	1	2	3		
1	3	4	2	9	18
2	4	5	4	13	20
3	2	3	3	8	25
Total	9	12	9	30	63

【**Sol.**】 · The production growth factor of each zone is given by:

$$F_{O1}^{0}=\frac{O_1^{\mathrm{f}}}{O_1^{0}}=\frac{18}{9}=2.000$$

$$F_{O2}^{0}=\frac{O_2^{\mathrm{f}}}{O_2^{0}}=\frac{20}{13}=1.538$$

$$F_{O3}^{0}=\frac{O_3^{f}}{O_3^{0}}=\frac{18}{9}=3.125$$

· By multiplying production growth factor with Table A1-1, we obtain Table A1-2.

Table A1-2 O-D matrix calculated by unique growth factor method

O	*D*			Total	Target value
	1	2	3		
1	6.0	8.0	4.0	18.0	18.0
2	6.1	7.7	6.2	20.0	20.0
3	6.3	9.4	9.3	25.0	25.0
Total	18.4	25.1	19.5	63.0	63.0

So we obtain the target year O-D distribution matrix which meets the travel constraints.

2. Average growth factor method

【**Example A1-2**】 Table A1-3 shows the current O-D distribution matrix. Table A1-4 shows the productions and attractions of future year. Try to use this information to get distribution of future year by average growth factor method. Set the convergence criterion was $\varepsilon=3\%$.

Table A1-3 Current O-D distribution matrix

O	*D*			Total
	1	2	3	
1	3	4	2	9
2	4	5	4	13
3	2	3	3	8
Total	9	12	9	30

Table A1-4 Productions and attractions of target year

O	*D*			Total
	1	2	3	
1				18
2				20
3				25
Total	23	22	18	63

【**Sol.**】 By average growth factor method:

· The production growth factor F_{Oi}^{O} and attraction growth factor F_{Dj}^{O} is given by

$$F_{O1}^{0}=\frac{O_1^{f}}{O_1^{0}}=\frac{18}{9}=2.000$$

$$F_{O2}^{0}=\frac{O_2^{f}}{O_2^{0}}=\frac{20}{13}=1.538$$

$$F_{O3}^{0}=\frac{O_3^{f}}{O_3^{0}}=\frac{25}{8}=3.125$$

$$F_{D1}^0 = \frac{D_1^f}{D_1^0} = \frac{23}{9} = 2.556$$

$$F_{D2}^0 = \frac{D_2^f}{D_2^0} = \frac{22}{12} = 1.833$$

$$F_{D3}^0 = \frac{D_3^f}{D_3^0} = \frac{18}{9} = 2.000$$

- First approximation: $q_{ij}^1 = q_{ij}^0 \times (F_{Oi}^0 + F_{Dj}^0)/2$.

$$q_{11}^1 = q_{11}^0 \times (F_{O1}^0 + F_{D1}^0)/2 = 3 \times (2.000 + 2.556)/2 = 6.834$$
$$q_{12}^1 = q_{12}^0 \times (F_{O1}^0 + F_{D2}^0)/2 = 4 \times (2.000 + 1.833)/2 = 7.666$$
$$q_{13}^1 = q_{13}^0 \times (F_{O1}^0 + F_{D3}^0)/2 = 2 \times (2.000 + 2.000)/2 = 4.000$$
$$q_{21}^1 = q_{21}^0 \times (F_{O2}^0 + F_{D1}^0)/2 = 4 \times (1.538 + 2.556)/2 = 8.188$$
$$q_{22}^1 = q_{22}^0 \times (F_{O2}^0 + F_{D2}^0)/2 = 5 \times (1.538 + 1.833)/2 = 8.428$$
$$q_{23}^1 = q_{23}^0 \times (F_{O2}^0 + F_{D3}^0)/2 = 4 \times (1.538 + 2.000)/2 = 7.076$$
$$q_{31}^1 = q_{31}^0 \times (F_{O3}^0 + F_{D1}^0)/2 = 2 \times (3.125 + 2.556)/2 = 5.681$$
$$q_{32}^1 = q_{32}^0 \times (F_{O3}^0 + F_{D2}^0)/2 = 3 \times (3.125 + 1.833)/2 = 7.437$$
$$q_{33}^1 = q_{33}^0 \times (F_{O3}^0 + F_{D3}^0)/2 = 3 \times (3.125 + 2.000)/2 = 7.688$$

The results are given by Table A1-5.

Table A1-5 The first iteration of O-D matrix

O	D			Total
	1	2	3	
1	6.834	7.666	4.000	18.500
2	8.188	8.428	7.076	23.692
3	5.681	7.437	7.688	20.806
Total	20.703	23.531	18.764	62.998

- Recalculate F_{Oi}^1 and F_{Dj}^1.

$$F_{O1}^1 = \frac{O_1^f}{O_1^1} = \frac{18}{18.500} = 0.973$$

$$F_{O2}^1 = \frac{O_2^f}{O_2^1} = \frac{20}{23.692} = 0.844$$

$$F_{O3}^1 = \frac{O_3^f}{O_3^1} = \frac{25}{20.806} = 1.202$$

$$F_{D1}^1 = \frac{D_1^f}{D_1^1} = \frac{23}{20.703} = 1.111$$

$$F_{D2}^1 = \frac{D_2^f}{D_2^1} = \frac{22}{23.531} = 0.935$$

$$F_{D3}^1 = \frac{D_3^f}{D_3^1} = \frac{18}{18.764} = 0.959$$

· Convergence judgment.

We need to re-iterate the growth factor as some errors of F^1_{Oi} and F^1_{Dj} are greater than 3%.

· Second iteration.

$$q^2_{11} = q^1_{11} \times (F^1_{O1} + F^1_{D2})/2 = 3 \times (2.000 + 2.556)/2 = 6.834$$
$$q^2_{12} = q^1_{12} \times (F^1_{O1} + F^1_{D2})/2 = 4 \times (2.000 + 1.833)/2 = 7.666$$
$$q^2_{13} = q^1_{13} \times (F^1_{O1} + F^1_{D3})/2 = 2 \times (2.000 + 2.000)/2 = 4.000$$
$$q^2_{21} = q^1_{21} \times (F^1_{O2} + F^1_{D1})/2 = 4 \times (1.538 + 2.556)/2 = 8.188$$
$$q^2_{22} = q^1_{22} \times (F^1_{O2} + F^1_{D2})/2 = 5 \times (1.538 + 1.833)/2 = 8.428$$
$$q^2_{23} = q^1_{23} \times (F^1_{O2} + F^1_{D3})/2 = 4 \times (1.538 + 2.000)/2 = 7.076$$
$$q^2_{31} = q^1_{31} \times (F^1_{O3} + F^1_{D1})/2 = 2 \times (3.125 + 2.556)/2 = 5.681$$
$$q^2_{32} = q^1_{32} \times (F^1_{O3} + F^1_{D2})/2 = 3 \times (3.125 + 1.833)/2 = 7.437$$
$$q^2_{33} = q^1_{33} \times (F^1_{O3} + F^1_{D3})/2 = 3 \times (3.125 + 2.000)/2 = 7.688$$

The results are given by Table A1-6.

Table A1-6 The second iteration of O-D matrix

O	*D*			Total
	1	2	3	
1	7.117	7.317	3.864	18.298
2	8.006	7.490	6.383	21.879
3	6.569	7.950	7.229	21.748
Total	21.692	22.757	17.476	61.925

· Recalculate F^2_{Oi} and F^2_{Dj}.

$$F^2_{O1} = \frac{O^f_1}{O^2_1} = \frac{18}{18.298} = 0.984$$

$$F^2_{O2} = \frac{O^f_2}{O^2_2} = \frac{20}{21.879} = 0.914$$

$$F^2_{O3} = \frac{O^f_3}{O^2_3} = \frac{25}{21.748} = 1.150$$

$$F^2_{D1} = \frac{D^f_1}{D^2_1} = \frac{23}{21.692} = 1.060$$

$$F^2_{D2} = \frac{D^f_2}{D^2_2} = \frac{22}{22.757} = 0.967$$

$$F^2_{D3} = \frac{D^f_3}{D^2_3} = \frac{18}{17.476} = 1.030$$

· Convergence judgment.

We need to re-iterate the growth factor as some errors of F^2_{Oi} and F^2_{Dj} are greater than 3%.

· The third iteration.

$$q^3_{11} = q^2_{11} \times (F^2_{O1} + F^2_{D1})/2 = 7.274$$

$$q_{12}^{3}=q_{12}^{2}\times(F_{O1}^{2}+F_{D2}^{2})/2=7.136$$
$$q_{13}^{3}=q_{13}^{2}\times(F_{O1}^{2}+F_{D3}^{2})/2=3.890$$
$$q_{21}^{3}=q_{21}^{2}\times(F_{O2}^{2}+F_{D1}^{2})/2=7.904$$
$$q_{22}^{3}=q_{22}^{2}\times(F_{O2}^{2}+F_{D2}^{2})/2=7.044$$
$$q_{23}^{3}=q_{23}^{2}\times(F_{O2}^{2}+F_{D3}^{2})/2=6.205$$
$$q_{31}^{3}=q_{31}^{2}\times(F_{O3}^{2}+F_{D1}^{2})/2=7.258$$
$$q_{32}^{3}=q_{32}^{2}\times(F_{O3}^{2}+F_{D2}^{2})/2=8.412$$
$$q_{33}^{3}=q_{33}^{2}\times(F_{O3}^{2}+F_{D2}^{2})/2=7.878$$

The results are given by Table A1-7.

Table A1-7 The third iteration of O-D matrix

O	D			Total
	1	2	3	
1	7.274	7.136	3.890	18.300
2	7.904	7.044	6.205	21.153
3	7.258	8.412	7.878	23.548
Total	22.436	22.592	17.973	63.001

· Recalculate F_{Oi}^{3} and F_{Dj}^{3}.

$$F_{O1}^{3}=\frac{O_1^{f}}{O_1^{3}}=\frac{18}{18.300}=0.984$$

$$F_{O2}^{3}=\frac{O_2^{f}}{O_2^{3}}=\frac{20}{21.153}=0.946$$

$$F_{O3}^{3}=\frac{O_3^{f}}{O_3^{3}}=\frac{25}{23.548}=1.602$$

$$F_{D1}^{3}=\frac{D_1^{f}}{D_1^{3}}=\frac{23}{22.436}=1.025$$

$$F_{D2}^{3}=\frac{D_2^{f}}{D_2^{3}}=\frac{22}{22.592}=0.974$$

$$F_{D3}^{3}=\frac{D_3^{f}}{D_3^{3}}=\frac{18}{17.973}=1.002$$

· Convergence judgment.

We need to re-iterate the growth factor as some errors of F_{Oi}^{3} and F_{Dj}^{3} are greater than 3%.

· The fourth iteration.

$$q_{11}^{4}=q_{11}^{3}\times(F_{O1}^{3}+F_{D1}^{3})/2=7.361$$
$$q_{12}^{4}=q_{12}^{3}\times(F_{O1}^{3}+F_{D2}^{3})/2=7.036$$
$$q_{13}^{4}=q_{13}^{3}\times(F_{O1}^{3}+F_{D3}^{3})/2=3.719$$
$$q_{21}^{4}=q_{21}^{3}\times(F_{O2}^{3}+F_{D1}^{3})/2=7.852$$
$$q_{22}^{4}=q_{22}^{3}\times(F_{O2}^{3}+F_{D2}^{3})/2=6.829$$

$$q_{23}^4 = q_{23}^3 \times (F_{O2}^3 + F_{D3}^3)/2 = 5.813$$
$$q_{31}^4 = q_{31}^3 \times (F_{O3}^3 + F_{D1}^3)/2 = 7.369$$
$$q_{32}^4 = q_{32}^3 \times (F_{O3}^3 + F_{D2}^3)/2 = 8.321$$
$$q_{33}^4 = q_{33}^3 \times (F_{O3}^3 + F_{D3}^3)/2 = 8.700$$

The results are given by Table A1-8.

Table A1-8 The fourth iteration of O-D matrix

O	*D*			Total
	1	2	3	
1	7.361	7.036	3.719	18.116
2	7.852	6.829	5.813	20.494
3	7.369	8.321	8.700	24.390
Total	22.582	22.186	18.232	63.000

· Recalculate F_{Oi}^4 and F_{Dj}^4.

$$F_{O1}^4 = \frac{O_1^f}{O_1^4} = \frac{18}{18.120} = 0.993$$

$$F_{O2}^4 = \frac{O_2^f}{O_2^4} = \frac{20}{20.494} = 0.976$$

$$F_{O3}^4 = \frac{O_3^f}{O_3^4} = \frac{25}{24.390} = 1.025$$

$$F_{D1}^4 = \frac{D_1^f}{D_1^4} = \frac{23}{22.582} = 1.019$$

$$F_{D2}^4 = \frac{D_2^f}{D_2^4} = \frac{22}{22.186} = 0.991$$

$$F_{D3}^4 = \frac{D_3^f}{D_3^4} = \frac{18}{18.232} = 0.987$$

· Convergence judgment.

Since all errors of F_{Oi}^4 and F_{Dj}^4 are less than 3%, the iteration is stopped. The future distribution using average growth factor method is given by Table A1-8.

3. Detroit method

【Example A1-3】 Same with Example A1-2 by using Detroit method.

【Sol.】 · The production growth factor F_{Oi}^0 and attraction growth factor F_{Dj}^0 is given by:

$$F_{O1}^0 = \frac{O_1^f}{O_1^0} = \frac{18}{9} = 2.000$$

$$F_{O2}^0 = \frac{O_2^f}{O_2^0} = \frac{20}{13} = 1.538$$

$$F_{O3}^0 = \frac{O_3^f}{O_3^0} = \frac{25}{18} = 1.389$$

$$F_{D1}^0=\frac{D_1^f}{D_1^0}=\frac{23}{9}=2.556$$

$$F_{D2}^0=\frac{D_2^f}{D_2^0}=\frac{22}{12}=1.833$$

$$F_{D3}^0=\frac{D_3^f}{D_3^0}=\frac{18}{9}=2.000$$

· Then get the inverse of generation growth factor: $G^0=T^0/T^f$.

$$G^0=\frac{T^0}{T^f}=30/63=0.476$$

· First approximation: $q_{ij}^1=q_{ij}^0\cdot F_{Oi}^0\cdot F_{Dj}^0\cdot G^0$.

$$q_{11}^1=q_{11}^0\cdot F_{O1}^0\cdot F_{D1}^0\cdot G^0=7.300$$
$$q_{12}^1=q_{12}^0\cdot F_{O1}^0\cdot F_{D2}^0\cdot G^0=6.980$$
$$q_{13}^1=q_{13}^0\cdot F_{O1}^0\cdot F_{D3}^0\cdot G^0=3.808$$
$$q_{21}^1=q_{21}^0\cdot F_{O2}^0\cdot F_{D1}^0\cdot G^0=7.485$$
$$q_{22}^1=q_{22}^0\cdot F_{O2}^0\cdot F_{D2}^0\cdot G^0=6.710$$
$$q_{23}^1=q_{23}^0\cdot F_{O2}^0\cdot F_{D3}^0\cdot G^0=5.857$$
$$q_{31}^1=q_{31}^0\cdot F_{O3}^0\cdot F_{D1}^0\cdot G^0=7.604$$
$$q_{32}^1=q_{32}^0\cdot F_{O3}^0\cdot F_{D2}^0\cdot G^0=8.180$$
$$q_{33}^1=q_{33}^0\cdot F_{O3}^0\cdot F_{D3}^0\cdot G^0=8.925$$

The results are given by Table A1-9.

Table A1-9 The first iteration of O-D matrix

O	*D*			Total
	1	2	3	
1	7.300	6.980	3.808	18.088
2	7.485	6.710	5.857	20.052
3	7.604	8.180	8.925	24.709
Total	22.389	21.870	18.590	62.849

· Recalculate F_{Oi}^1 and F_{Dj}^1.

$$F_{O1}^1=\frac{O_1^f}{O_1^1}=\frac{18}{18.088}=0.995$$

$$F_{O2}^1=\frac{O_2^f}{O_2^1}=\frac{20}{20.052}=0.997$$

$$F_{O3}^1=\frac{O_3^f}{O_3^1}=\frac{25}{24.709}=1.012$$

$$F_{D1}^1=\frac{D_1^f}{D_1^1}=\frac{23}{22.389}=1.027$$

$$F_{D2}^1=\frac{D_2^f}{D_2^1}=\frac{22}{21.870}=1.006$$

$$F_{D3}^{1}=\frac{D_{3}^{f}}{D_{3}^{1}}=\frac{18}{18.590}=0.968$$

· Convergence judgment.

We need to re-iterate the growth factor as some errors of F_{Oi}^{1} and F_{Dj}^{1} are greater than 3%.

· Get the inverse of generation growth factor.

$$G^{1}=T^{1}/T^{f}=62.849/63=0.998$$

· The second approximation: $q_{ij}^{2}=q_{ij}^{1}\cdot F_{Oi}^{1}\cdot F_{Dj}^{1}\cdot G^{1}$.

$$q_{11}^{2}=q_{11}^{1}\cdot F_{O1}^{1}\cdot F_{D1}^{1}\cdot G^{1}=7.445$$

$$q_{12}^{2}=q_{12}^{1}\cdot F_{O1}^{1}\cdot F_{D2}^{1}\cdot G^{1}=6.973$$

$$q_{13}^{2}=q_{13}^{1}\cdot F_{O1}^{1}\cdot F_{D3}^{1}\cdot G^{1}=3.660$$

$$q_{21}^{2}=q_{21}^{1}\cdot F_{O2}^{1}\cdot F_{D1}^{1}\cdot G^{1}=7.649$$

$$q_{22}^{2}=q_{22}^{1}\cdot F_{O2}^{1}\cdot F_{D2}^{1}\cdot G^{1}=6.717$$

$$q_{23}^{2}=q_{23}^{1}\cdot F_{O2}^{1}\cdot F_{D3}^{1}\cdot G^{1}=6.641$$

$$q_{31}^{2}=q_{31}^{1}\cdot F_{O3}^{1}\cdot F_{D1}^{1}\cdot G^{1}=7.887$$

$$q_{32}^{2}=q_{32}^{1}\cdot F_{O3}^{1}\cdot F_{D2}^{1}\cdot G^{1}=8.311$$

$$q_{33}^{2}=q_{33}^{1}\cdot F_{O3}^{1}\cdot F_{D3}^{1}\cdot G^{1}=8.726$$

The results are given by Table A1-10.

Table A1-10 The second iteration of O-D matrix

O	*D*			Total
	1	2	3	
1	7.445	6.973	3.660	18.078
2	7.649	6.717	5.641	20.007
3	7.887	8.311	8.726	24.924
Total	22.981	22.001	18.027	63.008

· Recalculate F_{Oi}^{2} and F_{Dj}^{2}.

$$F_{O1}^{2}=\frac{O_{1}^{f}}{O_{1}^{2}}=\frac{18}{17.951}=1.003$$

$$F_{O2}^{2}=\frac{O_{2}^{f}}{O_{2}^{2}}=\frac{20}{20.007}=0.999$$

$$F_{O3}^{2}=\frac{O_{3}^{f}}{O_{3}^{2}}=\frac{25}{24.924}=1.003$$

$$F_{D1}^{2}=\frac{D_{1}^{f}}{D_{1}^{2}}=\frac{23}{22.981}=1.001$$

$$F_{D2}^{2}=\frac{D_{2}^{f}}{D_{2}^{2}}=\frac{22}{22.001}=0.999$$

$$F_{D3}^{2}=\frac{D_{3}^{f}}{D_{3}^{2}}=\frac{18}{18.027}=0.998$$

· Convergence judgment.

Since all errors of F_{Oi}^2 and F_{Dj}^2 are less than 3% , the iteration is stopped. The future distribution using Detroit method is given by Table 5-11.

4. Frater method

【Example A1-4】 Same with Example A1-2 by using Frater method.

【Sol.】 · The production growth factor F_{Oi}^2 and attraction growth factor F_{Dj}^2 is given by:

$$F_{O1}^0=\frac{O_1^f}{O_1^0}=\frac{18}{9}=2.000$$

$$F_{O2}^0=\frac{O_2^f}{O_2^0}=\frac{20}{13}=1.538$$

$$F_{O3}^0=\frac{O_3^f}{O_3^0}=\frac{25}{8}=3.125$$

$$F_{D1}^0=\frac{D_1^f}{D_1^0}=\frac{23}{9}=2.556$$

$$F_{D2}^0=\frac{D_2^f}{D_2^0}=\frac{22}{12}=1.833$$

$$F_{D3}^0=\frac{D_3^f}{D_3^0}=\frac{18}{9}=2.000$$

· The location faction L_i and L_j is given by:

$$L_{i1}^0=\frac{O_1^0}{\sum\limits_j q_{1j}^0\cdot F_{Dj}^0}=\frac{9}{3\times 2.556+4\times 1.833+2\times 2}=0.474$$

$$L_{i2}^0=\frac{O_2^0}{\sum\limits_j q_{2j}^0\cdot F_{Dj}^0}=\frac{13}{4\times 2.556+5\times 1.833+4\times 2}=0.474$$

$$L_{i3}^0=\frac{O_3^0}{\sum\limits_j q_{3j}^0\cdot F_{Dj}^0}=\frac{18}{2\times 2.556+3\times 1.833+3\times 2}=1.084$$

$$L_{j1}^0=\frac{D_1^0}{\sum\limits_i q_{i1}^0\cdot F_{Oi}^0}=\frac{9}{3\times 2+4\times 1.538+2\times 3.125}=0.499$$

$$L_{j2}^0=\frac{D_2^0}{\sum\limits_i q_{i2}^0\cdot F_{Oi}^0}=\frac{12}{4\times 2+5\times 1.538+3\times 3.125}=0.479$$

$$L_{j3}^0=\frac{D_3^0}{\sum\limits_i q_{i3}^0\cdot F_{Oi}^0}=\frac{9}{2\times 2+4\times 1.538+3\times 3.125}=0.461$$

· Then we obtain q_{ij}^1.

$$q_{11}^1=q_{11}^0\cdot F_{O1}^0\cdot F_{D1}^0\cdot(L_{i1}^0+L_{j1}^0)/2=7.461$$

$$q_{12}^1=q_{12}^0\cdot F_{O1}^0\cdot F_{D2}^0\cdot(L_{i1}^0+L_{j2}^0)/2=6.987$$

$$q_{13}^1=q_{13}^0\cdot F_{O1}^0\cdot F_{D3}^0\cdot(L_{i1}^0+L_{j3}^0)/2=3.740$$

$$q_{21}^1=q_{21}^0\cdot F_{O2}^0\cdot F_{D1}^0\cdot(L_{i2}^0+L_{j1}^0)/2=7.658$$

$$q_{22}^1=q_{22}^0\cdot F_{O2}^0\cdot F_{D2}^0\cdot(L_{i2}^0+L_{j2}^0)/2=6.724$$

$$q_{23}^1 = q_{23}^0 \cdot F_{O2}^0 \cdot F_{D3}^0 \cdot (L_{i2}^0 + L_{j3}^0)/2 = 5.758$$
$$q_{31}^1 = q_{31}^0 \cdot F_{O3}^0 \cdot F_{D1}^0 \cdot (L_{i3}^0 + L_{j1}^0)/2 = 12.644$$
$$q_{32}^1 = q_{32}^0 \cdot F_{O3}^0 \cdot F_{D2}^0 \cdot (L_{i3}^0 + L_{j2}^0)/2 = 13.430$$
$$q_{33}^1 = q_{33}^0 \cdot F_{O3}^0 \cdot F_{D3}^0 \cdot (L_{i3}^0 + L_{j3}^0)/2 = 14.484$$

The results are given by Table A1-11.

Table A1-11 The first iteration of O-D matrix

O	*D*			Total
	1	2	3	
1	7.461	6.987	3.740	18.188
2	7.658	6.724	5.758	20.140
3	12.644	13.430	14.484	40.558
Total	27.763	27.141	23.983	78.886

· Recalculate F_{Oi}^1 and F_{Dj}^1.

$$F_{O1}^1 = \frac{O_1^f}{O_1^1} = \frac{18}{18.188} = 0.990$$

$$F_{O2}^1 = \frac{O_2^f}{O_2^1} = \frac{20}{20.140} = 0.993$$

$$F_{O3}^1 = \frac{O_3^f}{O_3^1} = \frac{25}{40.558} = 0.616$$

$$F_{D1}^1 = \frac{D_1^f}{D_1^1} = \frac{23}{27.763} = 0.828$$

$$F_{D2}^1 = \frac{D_2^f}{D_2^1} = \frac{22}{27.141} = 0.811$$

$$F_{D3}^1 = \frac{D_3^f}{D_3^1} = \frac{18}{23.983} = 0.751$$

· Convergence judgment.

We need to re-iterate the growth factor as some errors of F_{Oi}^1 and F_{Dj}^1 are greater than 3%.

· The location faction L_i and L_j is given by:

$$L_{i1}^1 = \frac{O_1^1}{\sum_j q_{1j}^1 \cdot F_{Dj}^1} = \frac{18.188}{7.461 \times 0.828 + 6.987 \times 0.811 + 3.740 \times 0.751} = 1.242$$

$$L_{i2}^1 = \frac{O_2^1}{\sum_j q_{2j}^1 \cdot F_{Dj}^1} = \frac{20.140}{7.658 \times 0.828 + 6.724 \times 0.811 + 5.758 \times 0.751} = 1.250$$

$$L_{i3}^1 = \frac{O_3^1}{\sum_j q_{3j}^1 \cdot F_{Dj}^1} = \frac{40.558}{12.644 \times 0.828 + 13.430 \times 0.811 + 14.484 \times 0.751} = 1.258$$

$$L_{j1}^1 = \frac{O_1^1}{\sum_i q_{i1}^1 \cdot F_{Oi}^1} = \frac{27.763}{7.461 \times 0.990 + 7.658 \times 0.993 + 12.644 \times 0.616} = 1.219$$

$$L_{j2}^1 = \frac{O_2^1}{\sum_i q_{i2}^1 \cdot F_{Oi}^1} = \frac{27.141}{6.987 \times 0.990 + 6.724 \times 0.993 + 13.430 \times 0.616} = 1.241$$

$$L_{j3}^1 = \frac{O_3^1}{\sum_i q_{i3}^1 \cdot F_{Oi}^1} = \frac{23.983}{3.740 \times 0.990 + 5.758 \times 0.993 + 14.484 \times 0.616} = 1.308$$

· Then we obtain q_{ij}^2.

$$q_{11}^2 = q_{11}^1 \cdot F_{O1}^1 \cdot F_{D1}^1 \cdot (L_{i1}^1 + L_{j1}^1)/2 = 7.526$$
$$q_{12}^2 = q_{12}^1 \cdot F_{O1}^1 \cdot F_{D2}^1 \cdot (L_{i1}^1 + L_{j2}^1)/2 = 6.965$$
$$q_{13}^2 = q_{13}^1 \cdot F_{O1}^1 \cdot F_{D3}^1 \cdot (L_{i1}^1 + L_{j3}^1)/2 = 3.545$$
$$q_{21}^2 = q_{21}^1 \cdot F_{O2}^1 \cdot F_{D1}^1 \cdot (L_{i2}^1 + L_{j1}^1)/2 = 7.773$$
$$q_{12}^2 = q_{22}^1 \cdot F_{O2}^1 \cdot F_{D2}^1 \cdot (L_{i2}^1 + L_{j2}^1)/2 = 6.744$$
$$q_{13}^2 = q_{23}^1 \cdot F_{O2}^1 \cdot F_{D3}^1 \cdot (L_{i2}^1 + L_{j3}^1)/2 = 5.492$$
$$q_{31}^2 = q_{31}^1 \cdot F_{O3}^1 \cdot F_{D1}^1 \cdot (L_{i3}^1 + L_{j1}^1)/2 = 7.987$$
$$q_{32}^2 = q_{32}^1 \cdot F_{O3}^1 \cdot F_{D2}^1 \cdot (L_{i3}^1 + L_{j2}^1)/2 = 8.383$$
$$q_{33}^2 = q_{33}^1 \cdot F_{O3}^1 \cdot F_{D3}^1 \cdot (L_{i3}^1 + L_{j3}^1)/2 = 8.597$$

The results are given by Table A1-12.

Table A1-12 The second iteration of O-D matrix

O	*D*			Total
	1	2	3	
1	7.526	6.965	3.545	18.036
2	7.773	6.744	5.492	20.009
3	7.987	8.383	8.597	24.967
Total	23.286	22.092	17.634	63.012

· Recalculate F_{Oi}^2 and F_{Dj}^2.

$$F_{O1}^2 = \frac{O_1^f}{O_1^2} = \frac{18}{18.036} = 0.998$$

$$F_{O2}^2 = \frac{O_2^f}{O_2^2} = \frac{20}{20.009} = 0.999$$

$$F_{O3}^2 = \frac{O_3^f}{O_3^2} = \frac{25}{24.967} = 1.001$$

$$F_{D1}^2 = \frac{D_1^f}{D_1^2} = \frac{23}{23.286} = 0.998$$

$$F_{D2}^2 = \frac{D_2^f}{D_2^2} = \frac{22}{22.092} = 0.996$$

$$F_{D3}^2 = \frac{D_3^f}{D_3^2} = \frac{18}{17.634} = 1.021$$

· Convergence judgment.

Since all errors of F_{Oi}^2 and F_{Dj}^2 is less than 3%, the iteration is stopped. The future distribution by using Detroit method is given by Table A1-12.

5. Furness method

【Example A1-5】 same with Example A1-2 by using Furness method.

【Sol.】 · The first approximation: set all $F_{Dj} = 1$ to obtain the production growth factor which meet the constraints:

$$F_{O1} = \frac{O_1^f}{O_1} = 18/9 = 2.000$$

$$F_{O2} = \frac{O_2^f}{O_2} = 20/13 = 1.538$$

$$F_{O3} = \frac{O_3^f}{O_3} = 25/8 = 3.125$$

As this result cannot meet the convergence judgment, we update O-D matrix by multiplying the production growth factor to get the Table A1-13.

Table A1-13 The first iteration of O-D matrix

O	*D*			Total
	1	2	3	
1	6.000	8.000	4.000	18.000
2	6.152	7.690	6.152	19.994
3	6.250	9.375	9.375	25.000
Total	18.402	25.065	19.527	9.994

· Begin the second iteration based on the Table A1-13 with updating the attraction growth factor first.

$$F_{D1} = \frac{D_1^f}{D_1} = \frac{23}{18.402} = 1.250$$

$$F_{D2} = \frac{D_2^f}{D_2} = \frac{22}{25.065} = 0.878$$

$$F_{D3} = \frac{D_3^f}{D_3} = \frac{18}{19.527} = 0.922$$

And again, multiply Table A1-13 by the attraction growth factor, we obtain the new O-D matrix in Table A1-14.

Table A1-14 The second iteration of O-D matrix in middle

O	*D*			Total
	1	2	3	
1	7.500	7.024	3.688	18.212
2	7.690	6.752	5.672	20.114
3	7.813	8.231	8.644	24.688
Total	23.003	22.007	18.004	63.013

As the results cannot meet the convergence judgment, we update the production growth factor based on Table A1-14.

$$F_{O1} = \frac{O_1^f}{O_1} = \frac{18}{18.212} = 0.988$$

$$F_{O2} = \frac{O_2^f}{O_2} = \frac{20}{20.114} = 0.994$$

$$F_{O3} = \frac{O_3^f}{O_3} = \frac{25}{24.688} = 1.013$$

We multiply Table A1-14 by the attraction growth factor to obtain the new O-D matrix.

· Using Table A1-15 to obtain the attraction growth factor.

$$F_{D1} = \frac{D_1^f}{D_1} = \frac{23}{22.968} = 1.001$$

$$F_{D2} = \frac{D_2^f}{D_2} = \frac{22}{21.989} = 1.001$$

$$F_{D3} = \frac{D_3^f}{D_3} = \frac{18}{18.038} = 0.998$$

Table A1-15 The second iteration of O-D matrix

O	*D*			Total
	1	2	3	
1	7.410	6.940	3.644	17.993
2	7.644	6.711	5.638	19.993
3	7.914	8.338	8.756	25.008
Total	22.968	21.989	18.038	9.995

As the results meet the convergence judgment, we stopped iteration and obtained the distribution in the future year.

6. The double-restriction gravity model

【Example A1-6】 Table A1-16 shows distribution at present and predicted value in future year. Table A1-17 shows the travel times between the traffic zones. Try to use the gravity model to obtain distribution of future year. Set the convergence criterion was 3%.

Table A1-16 O-D matrix at present and predicted value in future year

O	*D*			Total	Predicted value
	1	2	3		
1	3	4	2	9	18
2	4	5	4	13	20
3	2	3	3	18	25
Total	9	12	9	30	63

Table A1-17 Travel time between the traffic zones

R_{ij}	1	2	3
1	2	4	4
2	4	1	2
3	4	2	2

【Sol.】 · Using trail method get the relative error is less than 3% when $\gamma = 1.4$, thus take this value as the parameter value.

$$f(R_{11}) = R_{11}^{-1.4} = 2^{-1.4} = 2.639$$

$$q_{11} = 1.462 \quad \cdots$$

We can get q_{ij} by same method.

Thus, we obtain the O-D matrix of gravity model (Table A1-18).

Table A1-18 O-D matrix of gravity model

q_{ij}	1	2	3
1	1.462	4.424	1.810
2	8.278	1.585	3.137
3	4.246	2.145	1.579

As $c' = 3.25$, $c = 3.33$, make the relative error is 2.4%, the results meet the conditions.

· Using production and attraction of future year, and time impedance matrix to calculate, then get the future year O-D matrix.

Thus we get the final results in Table A1-19.

Table A1-19 O-D matrix in future year

O	*D*			Total
	1	2	3	
1	3.220	8.129	6.651	18.000
2	13.948	1.916	4.136	20.000
3	15.069	5.462	4.469	25.000
Total	32.237	15.507	15.256	63.000

Appendix 2

Four-stage Model with CUBE

1. CUBE modeling

The core of transportation modeling is the equilibrium theory of traffic economy and travel supply and demand. Travel supply includes transport infrastructure such as roads, bridges, rails, trains, taxis, and airports. And travel demand derives from demand of activities, such as freight transport and services. Traffic economy is mainly reflected on transportation costs including expected trip time, distance, fee and other related expenses. Costs often increase with the growth of demand, and demand decreases accompanied by reduced costs.

Therefore, the overall process of four stage modeling is: the travel demand is estimated based on socioeconomic and demographic parameters (production and attraction); the demand is also assigned to traffic zones based on travel costs. After that, different travel modes are separated by modeling; second, the trips by modes (trip distribution) are obtained by multiplying the daily interval parameter and then is assigned to a particular road networks; finally, the updated cost is fed back to the trip distribution to be updated iteratively. Fig. A2-1 shows the overall process.

The first thing is to create APP file before using the CUBE to build the four stage model. Open the CUBE soft and Click File > New > Application, then input the information of

Fig. A2-2 and click OK to save it. (Note: In this instance, the code for each module has been shown in Appendix 2)

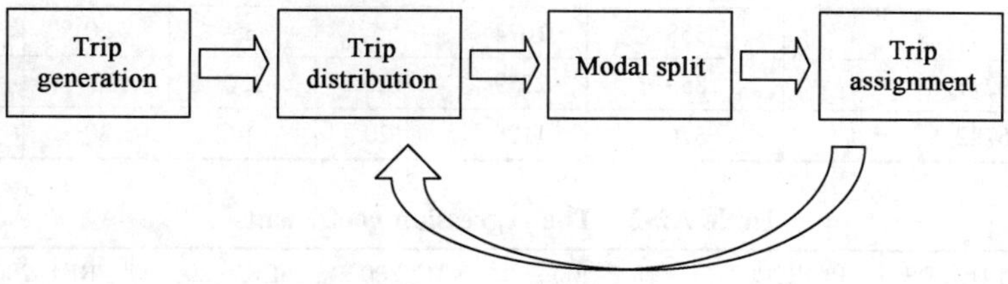

Figure A2-1 The overall process of four stage modeling

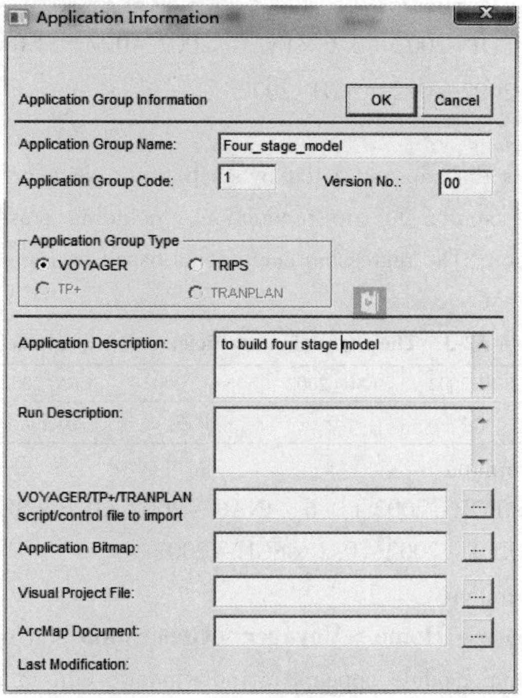

Figure A2-2 Create APP

1.1 Trip generation

Trip production and trip attraction forecast the total number of trips generated and attracted by each zone among the study area. The commonly used methods are cross classification, regression analysis and discrete selection.

(1) Trip production

The regression analysis is to build the regression model based on the different attribute data, and the parameters of the model are estimated by EXCEL or SPSS. Then this model is applied to the forecasting of trip generation. In this instance, the attribute data of each zone is stored in "zones. dbf". The attribute data of each zone is shown in Table A2-1, and the regression coefficients are shown in Table A2-2.

Table A2-1 The attribute data of each zone

ZONE	NAME	AREA	DISTRICT	HOUSEHOLDS	POP_2002	EMP_2002	INAG_2002	SERV_2002	RET_2002	SCH_2002
1	Zone 1	2650901.6	1	581	1743	60	20	40	0	1500
2	Zone 2	880892.12	1	358	1074	55	35	20	0	0
3	Zone 3	1590276.8	1	853	2559	720	300	320	100	1200
4	Zone 4	1356782.6	1	376	1128	120	40	80	0	0

Table A2-2 The regression coefficients

Var	HOUSEHOLDS	POP_2002	EMP_2002	INAG_2002	SERV_2002	RET_2002	SCH_2002
Coe	0	0.3	0	0.6	0.7	45	0.2

So, the trip production formula is:

$$P = 0.3 \times POP\_2002 + 0.6 \times INAG\_2002 + 0.7 \times SERV\_2002 + 45 \times RET\_2002 + 0.2 \times SCH\_2002$$

(2) Trip attraction

Trip attraction forecasts the trips attracted by each traffic zone or specific use of land. The methods for forecasting are similar to trip production, including cross classification, regression analysis and discrete selection. The regression coefficients based on regression analysis are shown in Table A2-3.

Table A2-3 The regression coefficients of trip attraction

Var	HOUSEHOLDS	POP_2002	EMP_2002	INAG_2002	SERV_2002	RET_2002	SCH_2002
Coe	0	1.8	0	0.6	0.6	45	0.1

So the trip attraction formula is:

$$A = 1.8 \times POP - 2002 + 0.6 \times INAG - 2002 + 0.6 \times SERV - 2002 + 45 \times RET - 2002 + 0.1 \times SCH - 2002$$

(3) Call and edit Generation

After creating APP, choose **Home > Voyager > Generation** and select the default template. When the Generation program module appears in the window, edit input and output files. Table A2-4 shows the files and introductions.

Table A2-4 The input and output files of GENERATION in trip generation

	Step	Description
Input	Create script file automatically(.s)	Script file for editing
	Load zone file (zones. dbf)	Record the attribute data(instant documents attached to books)
Output	Create run log file(*.prn)	Storage the run log
	Create PA file (Zonal PAData 1)	Storage forecasting yields P and A values for each zone

In this instance, the files' input use "Link to…". Taking loading the "zones. DBF" as an example, right-click "**Zonal Data 1**" of enter the file box and select "**Link to...**" > "**Link to File...**", appear the file selection box, select zone. DBF, and click open. The file input finished.

This method can also create a new input file with the same steps, just select the input file box and enter the file name and type. If nonexistent, it will automatically create the file. The all output files of the program need to create with the same as the new input file, not repeat them. So the input and output of the complete Generation application in this instance is shown in Fig. A2-3. (Note: Right-click "GENERATION", check Hide unused file for Program, making the program more concise)

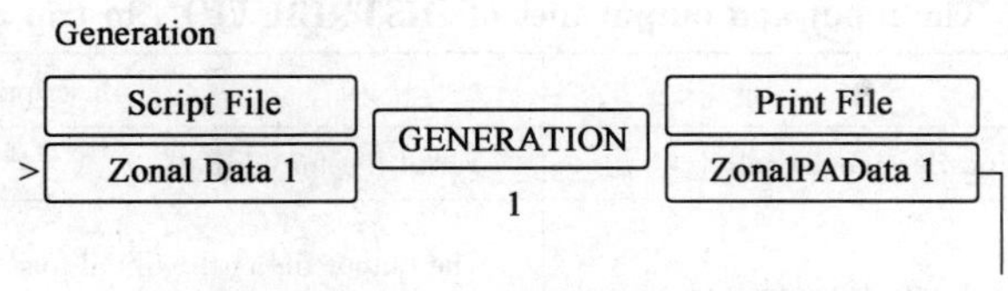

Figure A2-3 The input and output files of GENERATION in trip generation

(4) Run Generation and show the results

Double-click the operation command "**GENERATION**", run and obtain the trip production and attraction results. Different balance mode will get a different output. The output matrix file under different balance mode are shown in Table A2-5.

Table A2-5 Comparison of different balance mode

Mode	A2P			P2A			NHB		
Result	TAZ	PRODUCTION	ATTRACTION	TAZ	PRODUCTION	ATTRACTION	TAZ	PRODUCTION	ATTRACTION
	1	863	1477	1	1942	3323	1	1477	1477
	2	357	874	2	804	1966	2	874	874
	3	5912	4265	3	13303	9598	3	4265	4265
	4	418	934	4	942	2102	4	934	934
	合计值	7550	7550	合计值	16991	16989	合计值	7550	7550

1.2 Trip distribution

The trip distribution forecasts the total amount (unit: person/day) that will be assigned to each zone.

(1) Calculate the initial impedance of the road network

The initial impedance matrix consists of the minimal trip time under the free flow road network. Call "**HIGHWAY**" to calculate the initial impedance.

The input and output files of **HIGHWAY** are shown in Table A2-6 and Fig. A2-4.

Table A2-6 The input and output files of HIGHWAY in initial impedance

	Step	Description
Input	Create script file automatically(.s)	Script file for editing
	Load network file (network. net)	Input the network file (instance documents attached to books)
Output	Create run log file(*. prn)	Storage the run log
	Create impedance matrix (*. mat)	Storage the initial value

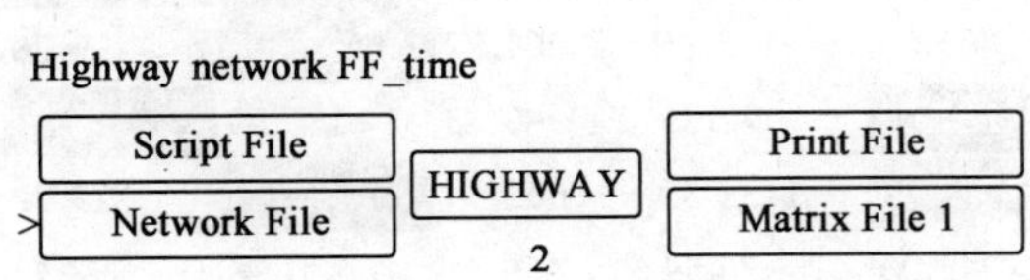

Figure A2-4 The input and output files of HIGHWAY in initial impedance

(2) Calculate the trip distribution

Trip distribution can be completed by "**DISTRIBUTION**" application module. Call "**DISTRIBUTION**" and select default template. Table A2-7 and Fig. A2-5 show the input and output files of "**DISTRIBUTION**".

Table A2-7 The input and output files of DISTRIBUTION in trip distribution

	Step	Description
Input	Create script file automatically(* . s)	Script file for editing
	Load initial road impedance matrix(* . mat)	The output file of the initial road impedance calculation phase. Directly load the local file, but also link to output file
	Load PA file(* . dbf)	The output file of the trip generation phase. Directly load the local file, but also link to output file
Output	Create run log file(* . prn)	Storage the run log
	Create PA distribution matrix(* . mat)	Storage the PA distribution value

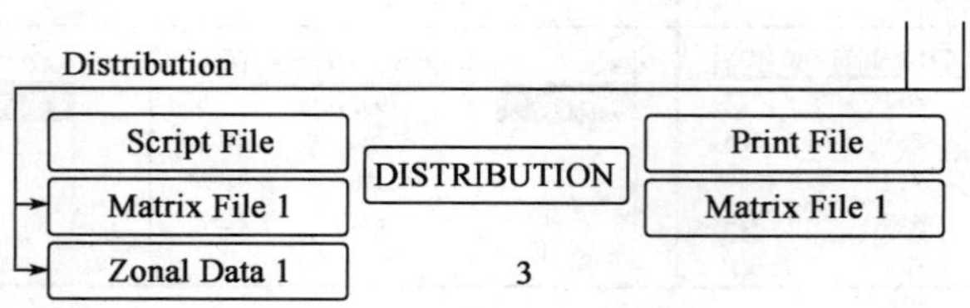

Figure A2-5 The input and output files of DISTRIBUTION in trip distribution

In **DISTRIBUTION**, the file input is different from the previous, where it is needed to use the output file of previous module. Of course, it still can use the "Link to . . . " to connect to the output file, but this method is slightly cumbersome. In CUBE, it provides a simple link method: right-click the required output file, hold and drag it to enter the file box, after releasing the mouse, there will appear a connection line, which means the completion of the file input. The input and output of the complete "**DISTRIBUTION**" application module in this instance is shown in Fig. A2-5.

Double-click the run command "**DISTRIBUTION**", after running successfully, open the output matrix file and the trip distribution matrix is shown Fig. A2-6.

*1 total

	Sum	1	2	3	4
	7550.00	1477.00	874.00	4265.00	934.00
1	863.00	177.75	106.97	479.04	99.24
2	357.00	72.36	49.78	186.59	48.27
3	5912.00	1151.35	662.94	3368.39	729.32
4	418.00	75.54	54.31	230.98	57.17

Figure A2-6 The trip distribution matrix

1.3 Modal split

Modal split estimates the proportion or quantity of a particular mode of transportation system in the travel distribution. According to the different objects, the travel modes can be divided into public transportation and private transportation. According to the different analysis objects, the method is divided into two categories: aggregate model and disaggregate model. In CUBE, MATRIX will be used for modal split.

(1) Call and edit MATRIX

The completely input and output files of MATRIX are shown in Table A2-8 and Fig. A2-7.

Table A2-8 Input and output files of MATRIX in modal split

	Step	Description
Input	Create script file automatically(.s)	Script file for editing
	Load PA distribution matrix (*.mat)	The matrix output file of Distribution phase will be as matrix file 1's input file
	Load initial road impedance matrix(*.mat)	Initial road impedance matrix is the Matrix File 2's input file
	Load public impedance matrix (Pub_FF_time. mat)	Instant document attached to books-Pub_FF_time. mat-is the matrix file 3's input file
Output	Create run log file(*.prn)	Storage the run log
	Create PA trip distribution matrix of each mode(*.mat)	Storage

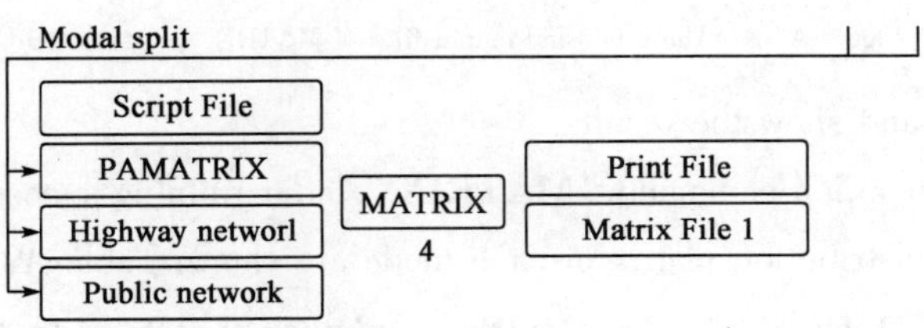

Figure A2-7 The input and output files of MATRIX in modal split

(2) Run MATRIX and show the results

Double click the operation command "**MATRIX**", after running successfully, open the output matrix file and the trip distribution matrix of each mode is shown Table A2-9.

Table A2-9 The PA trip distribution of each mode

Travelmode	AUTO	PT
PA matrix	(see AUTO matrix below)	(see PT matrix below)

AUTO (tabs: ✓ *1 AUTO, 2 PT, 3 TOTAL)

	Sum	1	2	3	4
	7379.91	1460.73	865.63	4185.44	868.11
1	797.68	177.75	99.56	431.77	88.60
2	330.20	67.56	49.78	169.23	43.63
3	5853.07	1143.64	662.33	3368.39	678.71
4	398.96	71.78	53.96	216.05	57.17

PT (tabs: 1 AUTO, ✓ *2 PT, 3 TOTAL)

	Sum	1	2	3	4
	170.10	16.27	8.38	79.56	65.89
1	65.32	0.00	7.41	47.27	10.64
2	26.80	4.80	0.00	17.36	4.64
3	58.94	7.71	0.62	0.00	50.61
4	19.04	3.76	0.35	14.93	0.00

1.4 PA matrix to OD matrix

In the first three stages of the travel demand forecasting, it is calculated based on traffic zone of production and attraction, taking person as a unit. However, in the stage of trip assignment, it is calculated and analyzed with the starting point and the end point of trip, taking vehicle as a unit. Therefore, before the trip assignment, it is necessary to convert the PA matrix to OD matrix. And the person's trip matrix into the car matrix according to a certain carrier rate, CUBE can use the "**MATRIX**" application to achieve this purpose.

(1) Call and edit MATRIX

Call the "**MATRIX**" application and select the default template. The steps for editing the input and output files are shown in the Table A2-10 and Fig. A2-8.

Table A2-10 The input and output files of MATRIX in PA to OD

	Step	Description
Input	Create Script file automatically (*.s)	Script file for editing
	Load PA distribution matrix of each mode (.*mat)	The output file of modal split
Output	Create run log file(*.prn)	Storage the run log
	Create OD trip distribution matrix of each mode(*.mat)	Storage

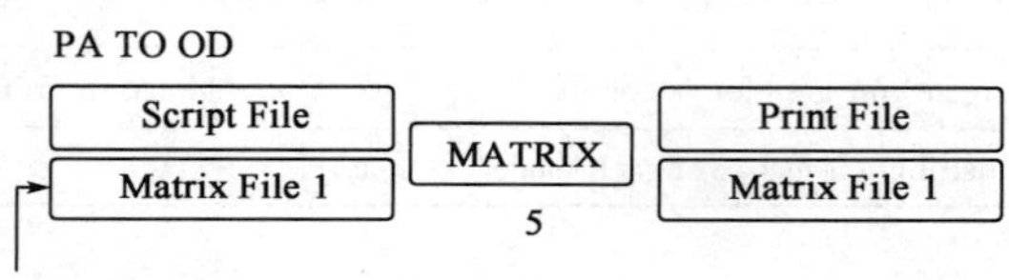

Figure A2-8 The input and output files of MATRIX in PA to OD

(2) Run MATRIX and show the results

Double-click the operation command "**MATRIX**", after running successfully, open the output matrix file and the trip distribution matrix of each mode are shown Table A2-11.

Table A2-11 The OD trip distribution of each mode

Travel mode	AUTO	PT
PA matrix	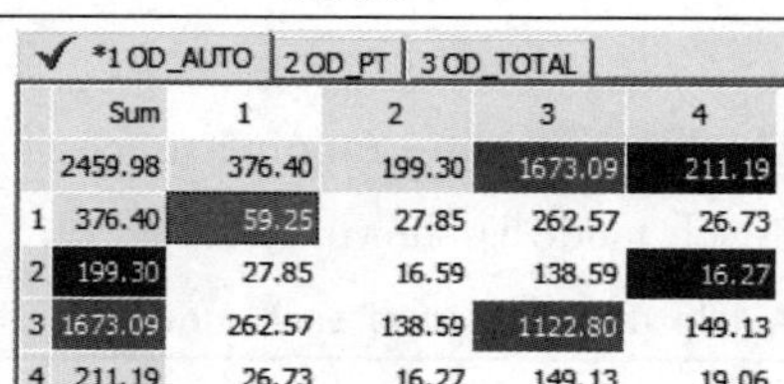	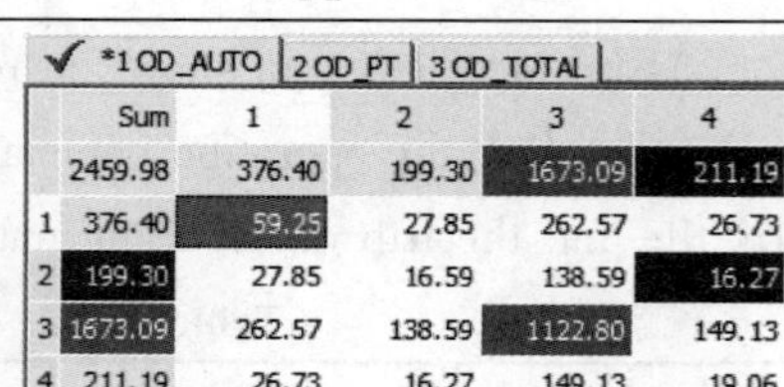

AUTO (tabs: ✓ *1 OD_AUTO | 2 OD_PT | 3 OD_TOTAL):

	Sum	1	2	3	4
	2459.98	376.40	199.30	1673.09	211.19
1	376.40	59.25	27.85	262.57	26.73
2	199.30	27.85	16.59	138.59	16.27
3	1673.09	262.57	138.59	1122.80	149.13
4	211.19	26.73	16.27	149.13	19.06

PT (tabs: ✓ *1 OD_AUTO | 2 OD_PT | 3 OD_TOTAL):

	Sum	1	2	3	4
	2459.98	376.40	199.30	1673.09	211.19
1	376.40	59.25	27.85	262.57	26.73
2	199.30	27.85	16.59	138.59	16.27
3	1673.09	262.57	138.59	1122.80	149.13
4	211.19	26.73	16.27	149.13	19.06

1.5 Trip assignment

The trip assignment is to assign the forecasted O-D matrix of the future year to the road network and obtain the traffic volume on the network. Trip assignment is a key step in urban travel demand forecasting, which provides data support for the evaluation of future planning. CUBE calls the "**HIGHWAY**" application for trip assignment.

(1) Call and edit HIGHWAY

Call the "**HIGHWAY**" application and select the default template. The procedure for editing the input and output files is shown in the Table A2-12.

Table A2-12 The input and output files of HIGHWAY in trip assignment

Index	Step	Description
Input	Create Script file Automatically(* . s)	Script edit file
	Load the OD matrix (* . mat)	PA to OD's output matrix file as input file
	Load network file(network. net)	Road network file
Output	Create a new run log file(* . prn)	Store running log
	Create new road network file (* . net)	Assign trips to network

The completed Highway application is shown in Fig. A2-9.

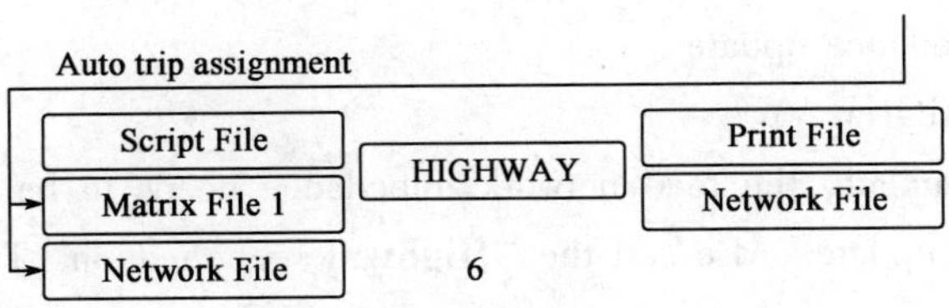

Figure A2-9 The input and output files of HIGHWAY in trip assignment

(2) Run HIGHWAY and show the results

Double-click the run command "**HIGHWAY**", open the output network file after the end of the operation. At this point there is no label on the road network file, you can mark the traffic flow and set the bandwidth guided by the following instructions.

①Mark traffic volume

Select "**Post All**" in the marked section under the "**Home**" menu of the menu bar, select "**v_1**" for the tag and choose OK.

②Set bandwidth

In the menu bar to perform "**Analysis > Bandwidth**", set the variable select "**v_1**", select OK(Fig. A2-10). The trip distribution results after the setup are shown in Fig. A2-11.

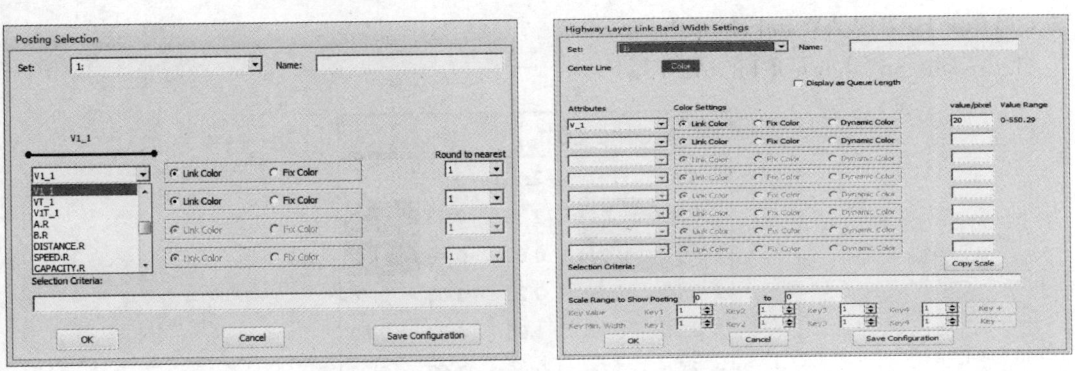

Figure A2-10 Traffic volume and bandwidth settings

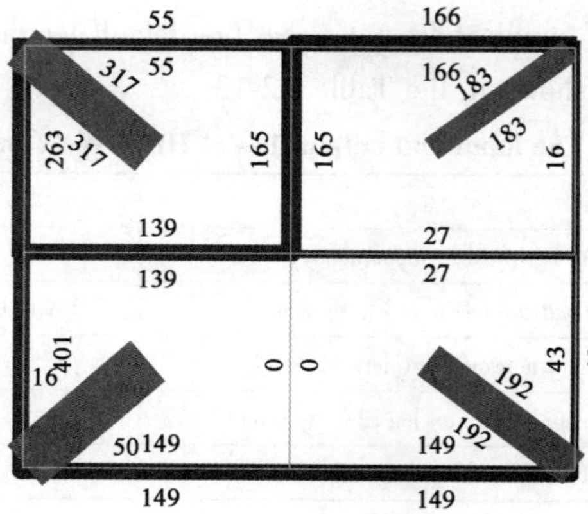

Figure A2-11 Traffic assignment results

1.6 Highway impedance update

(1) Call and edit HIGHWAY

After the trip assignment, the road network impedance needs to be updated to facilitate the subsequent iteration and update. Also call the "**Highway**" application. The input and output files are shown in Table A2-13.

Table A2-13 The input and output files of Highway in the highway impedance update

Input	Create script file(* . s)
	Connect the road network after the trip assignment(* . net)
Output	Create log file(* . prn)
	Create network impedance matrix file(* . mat)

The Highway program after editing is shown in Fig. A2-12.

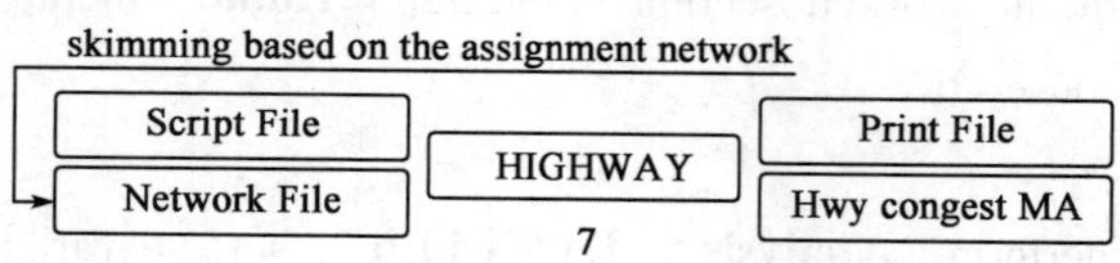

Figure A2-12 The input and output files of Highway in highway impedance update

(2) Run HIGHWAY and show the results

The results are shown if Fig. A2-13.

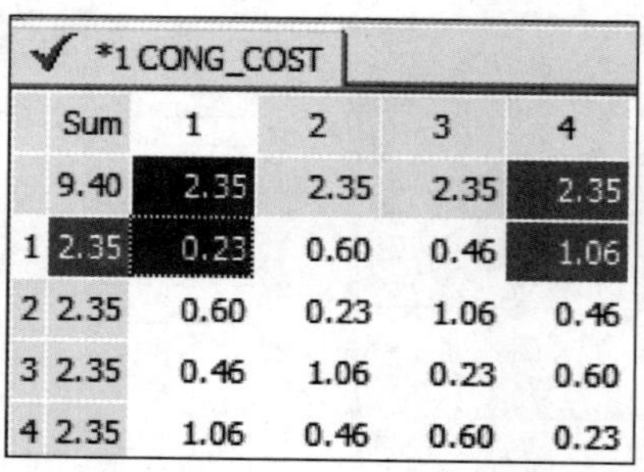
*1 CONG_COST

	Sum	1	2	3	4
	9.40	2.35	2.35	2.35	2.35
1	2.35	0.23	0.60	0.46	1.06
2	2.35	0.60	0.23	1.06	0.46
3	2.35	0.46	1.06	0.23	0.60
4	2.35	1.06	0.46	0.60	0.23

Figure A2-13 Network impedance update matrix

1.7 Iterative loop

(1) Set up loop control

In this section, the entire four-stage iteration will be cycled to achieve the convergence criteria or number of iterations. In this instance, the fix maximum number of iterations is set. Select the **LOOP** command from the **HOME** tab, set up the loop control, fill in the Fig. A2-14, and click OK.

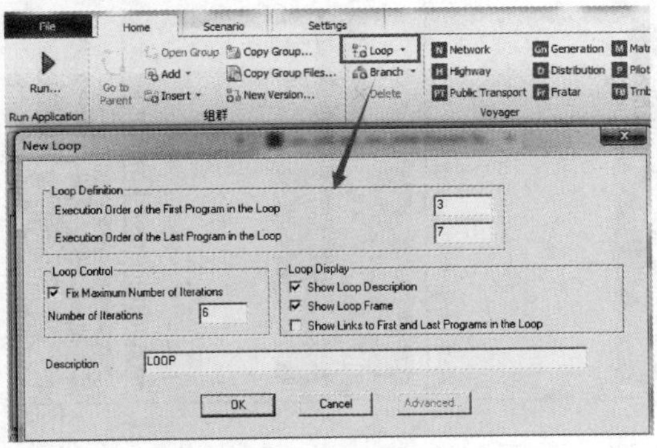

Figure A2-14 Setting up loop control

(2) Loop input and output

Click the matrix output file under Highway network FF_time (run order 2), press and drag mouse to the loop control box, and then let it go (Fig. A2-15).

Press and hold the Loop controller output box, drag and drop mouse to Distribution (run order 4) and Modal split (run order 5) Highway matrix on the input matrix to let it go, select "**OK**" in the pop-up Application Manager window.

Click the output matrix file on the "skimming based on assignment network" to drag mouse to the second input box in the loop control box to create a complete loop control for the Highway network (Fig. A2-16).

Click "**RUN**" under the "**HOME**" tab, select Run Application now from Task Monitor, click "OK" there will be a complete four-stage loop (Fig. A2-17).

2. The general syntax of CUBE

CPS (CUBE Process Script) **the basic syntax (1)**

basic syntax:

COMMAND keyword = value

COMMAND are always listed separately, followed by one or more spaces

KEYWORD always followed by | = | to be assigned

Example: REPORT FILEO = Y

Some keywords will have subscripts

Example: PATHLOAD MW [1] = PATHTRACE (TIME)

Some keywords will automatically move a command

Example: TRIPSIJ [1] = MI. 1. 1

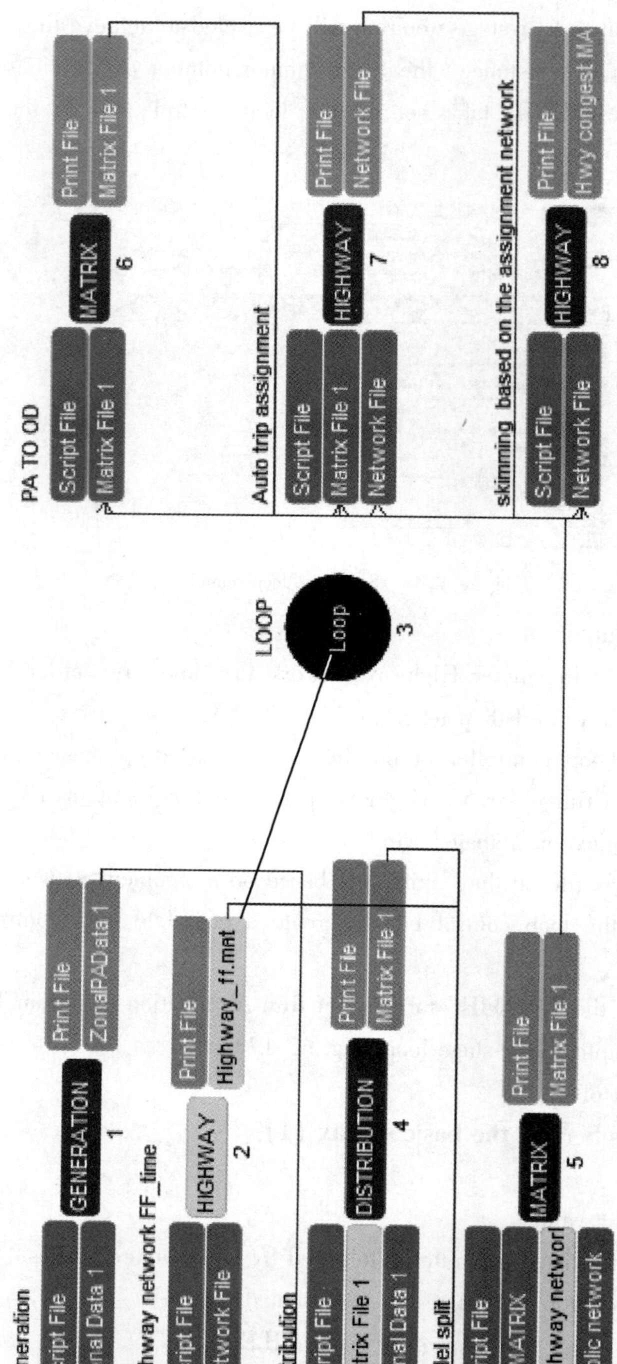

Figure A2-15 Cycle control

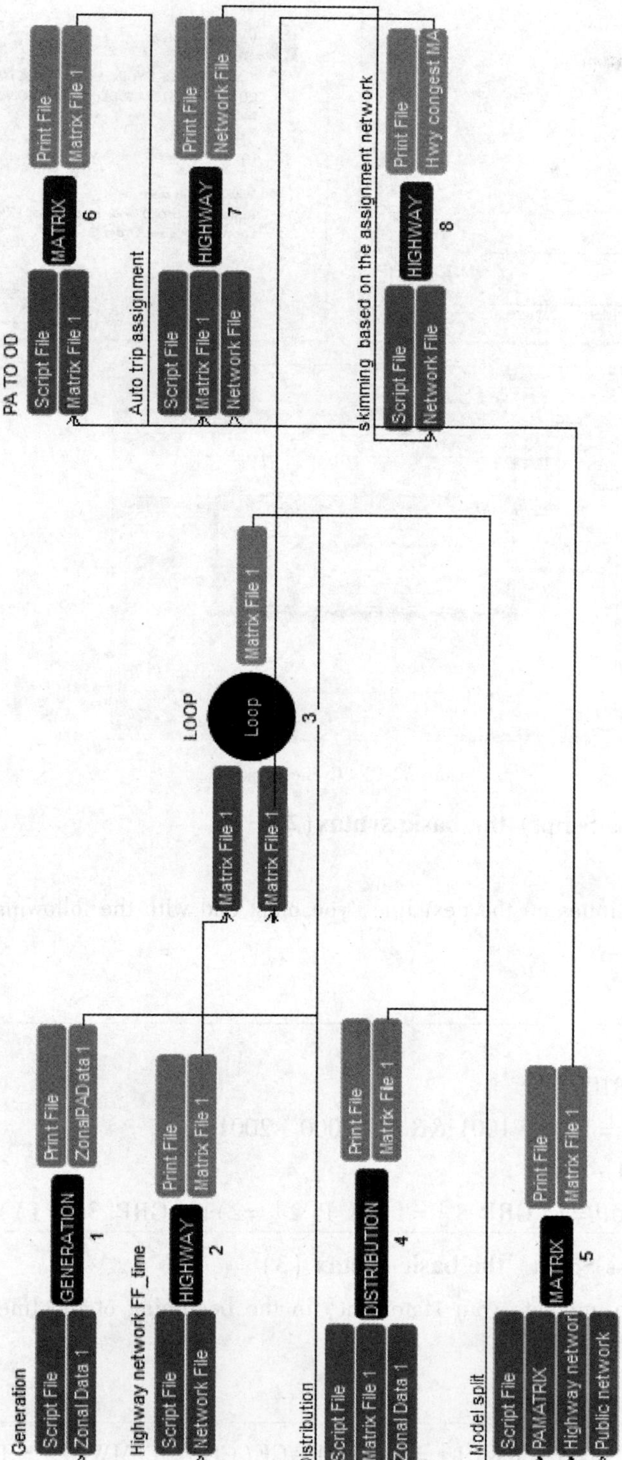

Figure A2-16 The final effect of the recycling process

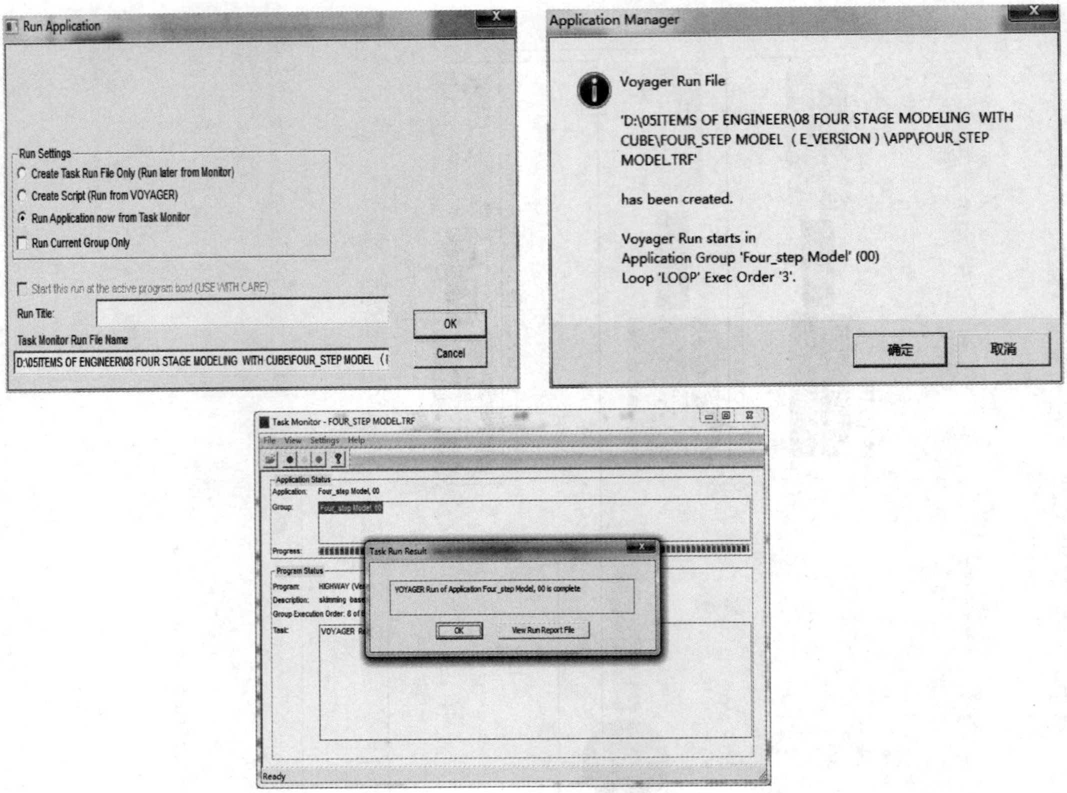

Figure A2-17 Cyclic iterations

CPS (CUBE Process Script) **the basic syntax(2)**

CPS continues:

If the statement continues on the next line, you must end with the following operator:

+ − * / , = | &

E. g:

```
PATH = COST,
MW[3] = MI. 1. TRIPS,
SELECTLINK = (L = 1000 - 1001 && L = 2000 - 2001),
SELECTGROUP = 1 - 3,5,
SELECTLINKGROUP = ((GRP[1] = 1 && P[2] = 2) || (GRP[3] = 1))
```

CPS (CUBE Process Script) **the basic syntax (3)**

As far as possible to annotate your statement, in the beginning of the line or use the ";" to start writing text.

E. g:

```
PATH = TIME, PENI = 1, MW[1] = PATHTRACE(COST), MW[2] = TIMECOST
;MW[1] and MW[2] could be different because penalties are used
;in the path. If MW[1] = PATHTRACE(TIME), they would be the same.
```

You can use / * ··· * / to comment the entire sentence as a comment.

Examples of script statements

```
RUN   PGM = NETWORK
FILEI  NETI = MY2000. ALT. NET
FILEO  NETO = TOTVOL. ALT. NET
COMP  TOTVOL =   V1_1 * 1 +        ; Passenger Vehicles
                 V2_1 * 1.2 +      ; Small Trucks
                 V3_1 * 2.5        ; Big Trucks
ENDRUN
```

Examples of expressions

◆Speed = Distance / Time

◆Address = Street + ',' + City + ',' + State + ' ' + ZipCode

Note: The user must be aware of the logic and rationality of the operation, such as the divisor is not zero.

Mathematical expressions are written in traditional formulas and follow traditional computational priorities

+, −, *, /, ^

Examples of built-in math functions are shown in Table A2-14.

Table A2-14 Examples of build-in math functions

ABS(x)	Absolute value
CmpNumRetNum(V1,OP,V2,R1,R2)	Use the operator OP to compare V1 and V2, and return R1 if true, otherwise R2 is returned
EXP(x)	e^x
INT(x)	Returns the integer and truncates the fraction
LN(x)	Seek natural logarithm
LOG(x)	Seeking commonly used logarithmic
MAX(x,y,...)	Find the maximum value
MIN(x,y,...)	Find the minimum value
POW(x,y)	x^y
ROUND(x)	Returns an integer and rounds the fraction
SQRT(x)	$\sqrt{x}$
RAND()	Returns a random floating point number between 0 and 1
RANDOM(n)	Returns a random integer between 0 − (X − 1)

Examples of built-in character functions are shown in Table A2-15.

Table A2-15 Examples of build-in character functions

FORMAT(x,w,d,str)	The number x is converted to a string. Width w, decimal places d
TRIM(str)	Delete trailing spaces
LTRIM(str)	Delete leading spaces

continued

FORMAT(x,w,d,str)	The number x is converted to a string. Width w, decimal places d
DUPSTR(str,n)	Copy the character n times
STR(v,w,d)	Variable v converted to a string, w character length, decimal places d
SUBSTR(str,b,n)	Extract the substring
STRPOS(str,str2)	Returns the position of the substring
STRLEN(str)	Character length
STRUPPER(str)	Put the string in uppercase
STRLOWER(str)	Lower the string

Examples of logical expressions are shown in Table A2-16.

Table A2-16 Examples of logical expressions

A = B	A equal B.
A = B	A equal B.
A ! = B	A not equal B.
A> = B	A is greater than, or equal to, B.
A< = B	A is less than, or equal to, B.
A > B	A is greater than B.
A < B	A is less than B.
A < > B	A is not equal to B.
& or &&	Logic AND
| or ||	Logic Or

E. g:

◆If (i = 1 – 10,20,30 & j = 100 – 200,301,310)

◆If (area > 3 | (CapClass * 50 * Lanes) < 3000)

Special examples of matrix functions are shown in Table A2-17.

Table A2-17 Special examples of matrix functions

ROWSUM ()	Row sums
ROWCNT ()	the number of none zero values
ROWMIN ()	Row minimum
ROWMAX ()	Row maximum
ROWAVE ()	Row average
ROWFIX ()	Convert to integer values
ROWFAC ()	Row factor
ROWADD()	Matrix merging
ROWMPY()	Matrix multiplication
ROWDIV()	Matrix division
MATVAL()	Random values from the matrix
ARRAYSUM()	Returns the sum of the column values

3. CUBE Four-stage model complete code

3.1 Generation

```
RUN PGM = GENERATION PRNFILE = " ......"
FILEO PAO[1]  = "......",
FORM =6.0,LIST = z P[1] A[1] DBF = t, NAMES = TAZ,PRODUCTION,ATTRACTION
                                    ; Set the
                                    ;output format
FILEI ZDATI[1]  = "......"
PARAMETERS ZONES =4                 ; Set the total number of traffic zones
PROCESS PHASE = ILOOP               ; Used to perform cell cycle, calculate production and
                                    ; attraction

P[1]  =(0.3 * pop_2002  +  0.6 * inag_2002  +
        0.7 * serv_2002  +  45 * ret_2002   +         ; Travel production calculation
                                                      ; formula
        0.2 * sch_2002)

A[1]  =(1.8 * pop_2002    +  0.6 * inag_2002   +
         0.6 * serv_2002   +  45 * ret_2002     +      ; Travel attraction calculation
                                                       ;formula
         0.1 * sch_2002)

ENDPROCESS

PROCESS PHASE = ADJUST                    ; Used to adjust or balance the final trip
                                          ;generation and attraction
BALANCE    A2P =1                         ;Select the balance adjustment method
ENDPROCESS
ENDRUN
```

3.2 Calculate the initial impedance matrix of the road network

```
RUN PGM = HIGHWAY PRNFILE = "...... "
FILEO MATO[1]  = "......",
MO =1, NAME = COST                                          ; Set the output matrix format
FILEI NETI  = "......"

PROCESS PHASE = ILOOP
PATHLOAD PATH = TIME,MW[1] = PATHTRACE(TIME)      ; Calculate the shortest time
COMP MW[1][I] = ROWMIN(1) *0.5
```

```
ENDPROCESS

ENDRUN
```

3.3 Distribution

```
RUN PGM = DISTRIBUTION PRNFILE = "...... "
FILEO MATO[1] = "......",
MO = 1,NAME = total
FILEI ZDATI[1] = "......"
FILEI MATI[1] = "......"
SETPA P[1] = zi.1.Production A[1] = zi.1.Attraction   ; Set the PA value
maxiters = 99,                                ; Set the maximum number of cycles
maxRMSE = 5                                   ; Set the maximum variance
LOOKUP NAME = FF,                             ; Define the friction factor tab. name
LOOKUP[1] = 1, RESULT = 2,
INTERPOLATE = Y,
R = 0.01 1200  ',                             ; Define friction factor data
    '1    1000  ',
    '5     500  ',
    '7     200  ',
    '10    100  ',
    '25     50  ',
    '50      5  '
GRAVITY PURPOSE = 1, LOS = mi.1.cost FFACTORS = ff   ; Application of gravity model
ENDRUN
```

3.4 Modal split

```
RUN PGM = MATRIX PRNFILE = "...... "
FILEO MATO[1] = "......",
MO = 1 - 3 NAME = auto,pt,total             ; Matrix file format definition
FILEI MATI[3] = "......"                    ; Bus initial cost matrix
FILEI MATI[2] = "......"                    ; Road network initial cost matrix
FILEI MATI[1] = "......"                    ; Traffic distribution matrix
CHOICE, alternatives = car, pt, demand = mi.1.1, costs = mi.2.1, mi.3.1,
                                              ; Enter the
                                              ;binary logit Calculate the instruction
      odemand = 21,31, startmw = 60, split = total, 0.2, car, pt
MW[1] = mw[21]
MW[2] = mw[31]
```

```
MW[3] = mw[21] + mw[31]

ENDRUN
```

3.5 PA to OD

```
RUN PGM = MATRIX PRNFILE = "…… "
FILEO MATO[1] = "……",
MO = 1 - 3 NAME = OD_auto, OD_pt, OD_total
FILEI MATI[1] = "……"

mw[1] = 0.5 * mi.1.auto + 0.5 * mi.1.auto.T          ; PA to OD calculation formula
mw[2] = 0.5 * mi.1.pt + 0.5 * mi.1.pt.T
mw[3] = 0.5 * mi.1.total + 0.5 * mi.1.total.T
mw[1] = mw[1]/3
mw[2] = mw[2]
ENDRUN
```

3.6 Trip assignment

```
RUN PGM = HIGHWAY PRNFILE = "…… "
FILEO NETO = "……"
FILEI NETI = "……"
FILEI MATI[1] = "……"
PARAMETERS COMBINE = EQUI, GAP = 0.005, MAXITERS = 99
                                                    ; Cycle parameter setting
PROCESS PHASE = LINKREAD
CAPACITY = LI.CAPACITY * 1.0
IF (li.linktype = 1)  LINKCLASS = 1
ENDPROCESS
PROCESS PHASE = ILOOP
PATHLOAD PATH = time,                        ; Search the path and assign traffic
      VOL[1] = MI.1.1
COMP MW[1][I] = rowmin(1) * 0.5             ; Estimate intrazonal time
ENDPROCESS
PROCESS PHASE = ADJUST

function {
tc[1] = t0 * (1.0 + 0.15 * ((v/c)^8))         ;BPR function
      }
ENDPROCESS
```

```
ENDRUN
```

3.7 Update impedance of road network

```
RUN PGM = HIGHWAY PRNFILE = "······················································"
FILEO MATO[1] = "······························································",
MO = 1,NAME = COST
FILEI NETI = "······································································"

PROCESS PHASE = LINKREAD
    DISTANCE = LI. DISTANCE
    SPEED = LI. CSPD_1
    T0 = Distance/Speed * 60
    T1 = T0
    C = LI. CAPACITY * 1.0
ENDPROCESS

PROCESS PHASE = ILOOP
PATHLOAD PATH = LI. TIME_1, ;TIME is automatically set equal to T1
  MW[99] = PATHTRACE(LI. TIME_1),              ; SKIM on the road (second step)
MW[100] = PATHTRACE(DIST)
MW[1] = MW[99]
  MW[2] = MW[100]
  JLOOP
    IF(I = J)
      MW[1] = ROWMIN(99)/2
      MW[2] = ROWMIN(100)/2
    ENDIF
  ENDJLOOP
  MW[3] = MW[2] * 10 + MW[1] * 30
ENDPROCESS
ENDRUN
```